The Cambridge Handbook of Community Empowerment

Power and empowerment are critical topics for social change. This handbook maps out ways that people can collectively engage with, influence, and change systems that affect their lives, particularly the systems that maintain inequality and oppression. It includes in-depth examinations of a variety of approaches to building and exercising community power in local organizations, institutions, and settings. Each chapter examines a particular approach, critically engaging with contemporary research on how and when collective action can be most effective at producing change within communities and societal systems. By examining a range of approaches in diverse contexts, this book provides new insights for scholars, practitioners, and engaged resident-leaders aiming to be more precise, strategic, and innovative in their efforts to build and sustain community power. It is the ideal resource for those working with community groups to build more just and equitable systems.

BRIAN D. CHRISTENS is Professor of Human and Organizational Development at Vanderbilt University, USA, where he directs the PhD program in Community Research and Action. His research is focused on how different organizational approaches to collective action – and different interorganizational network dynamics – can lead to changes in systems that benefit communities. His research also seeks to understand sociopolitical development processes among participants in these types of change efforts. He is the author of *Community Power and Empowerment* (Oxford University Press, 2019).

Cambridge Handbooks in Psychology

The Cambridge Handbook of Community Empowerment

Edited by

Brian D. Christens
Vanderbilt University

CAMBRIDGE
UNIVERSITY PRESS

CAMBRIDGE
UNIVERSITY PRESS

Shaftesbury Road, Cambridge CB2 8EA, United Kingdom

One Liberty Plaza, 20th Floor, New York, NY 10006, USA

477 Williamstown Road, Port Melbourne, VIC 3207, Australia

314–321, 3rd Floor, Plot 3, Splendor Forum, Jasola District Centre, New Delhi – 110025, India

103 Penang Road, #05-06/07, Visioncrest Commercial, Singapore 238467

Cambridge University Press is part of Cambridge University Press & Assessment, a department of the University of Cambridge.

We share the University's mission to contribute to society through the pursuit of education, learning and research at the highest international levels of excellence.

www.cambridge.org
Information on this title: www.cambridge.org/9781009153737

DOI: 10.1017/9781009153720

© Cambridge University Press & Assessment 2024

First published 2024

A catalogue record for this publication is available from the British Library

A Cataloging-in-Publication data record for this book is available from the Library of Congress

ISBN 978-1-009-15373-7 Hardback
ISBN 978-1-009-15374-4 Paperback

Contents

Figures

Tables

Contributors

JOHANNA REED ADAMS
University of Missouri

RAMA P. AGUNG-IGUSTI
University of Western Australia

NICOLE E. ALLEN
Vanderbilt University

KAYLA M. ANDERSON
Vanderbilt University

ASTRAEA AUGSBERGER
Boston University

BIANCA J. BALDRIDGE
Harvard University

PARISSA JAHROMI BALLARD
Wake Forest University

ANA BESS MOYER BELL
2nd Act

LAUREN M. BIGGER
Emory University

MELANIE BRAZZELL
Johns Hopkins University and University of California–Santa Barbara

KYMBERLY L. BYRD
ResultsLab

BRIAN D. CHRISTENS
Vanderbilt University

MARY ELIZABETH COLLINS
Boston University

JESSICA J. COLLURA
The Ohio State University

JERUSHA CONNER
Villanova University

MOISÉS G. CONTRERAS
Harvard University

DANIEL G. COOPER
Metropolitan Planning Council, Chicago

KIMALEE DICKERSON
University of North Carolina at Chapel Hill

VIRGINIA DOWNING
University of Wisconsin–Madison

ADRIENNE M. DUKE
Auburn University

ALBERT W. DZUR
Bowling Green State University

KEVIN ESCUDERO
Brown University

ANISE GOLD-WATTS
KPMG International

CARL D. GREER
University of Wisconsin–Madison

KRISTA A. HAAPANEN
Vanderbilt University

CAROLYN M. HENDRIKS
Australian National University

EMILY A. HENNESSY
Harvard University

MING HU
Macau University of Science and Technology

ROSHANI J. JAYAWARDANA
Victoria University

MEAGAN R. JOSEPH
Impact Prevention

SAMUEL P. KEAST
Victoria University

MICHELLE C. KEGLER
Emory University

BEN KIRSHNER
University of Colorado Boulder

MARIAH KORNBLUH
University of Oregon

SAM LAPOINT
Massachusetts General Hospital

YULONG LIAN
Nanjing University

WILSON MAJEE
University of Missouri

ROBERT A. MARX
San José State University

SARAH HULTINE MASSENGALE
University of Missouri Extension

SUVARNA V. MENON
Northern Illinois University

JOAN S. M. MEYERS
California Polytechnic State University, San Luis Obispo

KATHRYN Y. MORGAN
Sewanee: The University of the South

MICHAEL D. O'BRIEN
Boston College

LOREN PEABODY
University of Wisconsin–Madison

AGATA Z. PIETRZAK
University of South Florida

SANJAY PINTO
Cornell University and the Roosevelt Institute

V. PAUL POTEAT
Boston College

OLGA PRUSHINSKAYA
Democracy at Work Institute

AMY F. QUAYLE
Victoria University

HOLLY RAFFLE
Ohio University

CLAIRE RIPPEL
University of Missouri–St. Louis

SHANNON T. SANCHEZ-YOUNGMAN
University of New Mexico

LAURA HANSON SCHLACHTER
AmeriCorps Office of Research and Evaluation

CHRISTOPHER C. SONN
Victoria University

PAUL W. SPEER
Vanderbilt University

MOLLIE F. STEVENS
Impact Prevention

TAFADZWA TIVARINGE
The Spencer Foundation

NINA WALLERSTEIN
University of New Mexico

XIAOYUN WANG
Renmin University of China

RASHEDA L. WEAVER
Iona College

MEGAN K. YANG
Boston College

Building Community Power

An Introduction

Brian D. Christens

Introduction

This book is about ways that people can collectively engage with and influence the systems that affect their lives, particularly to change systems that create or maintain inequality and oppression. The collective capacity to do this can be referred to as *social* or *community power*. The group-level processes that develop these types of power and capacity can be described as *community empowerment* processes. These processes are often rooted in local neighborhoods, schools, and nonprofit and voluntary organizations. Their influence and impacts, however, can radiate well beyond their localities. Community empowerment processes can produce needed changes in societal and community systems (e.g., changes that bring about more equitable policies or practices) while simultaneously creating contexts that are beneficial for participants (e.g., settings that foster social connectedness and skill development).

Despite this great potential and many notable accomplishments, however, these processes are inherently challenging. Cultivating settings within and/or across organizations that create collectivities capable of sustained action is no easy task. Nor is contesting the interests of entrenched defenders of status quo systems. It should not be surprising that these efforts frequently fall short of achieving their ambitious goals of making policies and systems more egalitarian and restorative.

Understanding why some efforts can build, exercise, and sustain community power while others struggle to do so requires learning about distinct approaches, how these approaches operate across different contexts, and the unique strengths of challenges of different approaches. Community empowerment processes differ in many ways. Some of these differences are readily apparent and others are subtle. In some cases, we may still lack the basic vocabulary needed to make important distinctions.

Through deep examinations of numerous approaches in different contexts, the chapters in this book provide insights into what community empowerment approaches have in common and what is specific to only some. Each chapter offers a current view of interdisciplinary social research on a particular approach to building and exercising community power. The chapter authors have learned about these approaches from a variety of forms of experience, often including direct participation and systematic inquiry (many of the authors conduct work at the research–practice interface). Each chapter provides recommendations on how the beneficial effects of the approach they are describing can be reinforced and how challenges and limitations can be navigated and mitigated. In some cases, the chapter authors also provide insights into how certain approaches can lead into, build upon, and complement each other. The overarching goal of this book is enhancing understanding so that these approaches can be pursued more strategically and studied more rigorously, to greater cumulative effect.

This introductory chapter begins by discussing a definition of empowerment that underpins the contributions in this book. The term has now been so widely used that it is necessary to be painstakingly precise about its intended meaning. The way this term is used in this book differs from what it may connote based on usage across different discourses.

After establishing a definition, I describe some of the orienting perspectives for this book. First, the book takes a holistic or "ecological" view of empowerment processes, meaning that community-level and organizational dynamics are understood to be inextricably linked to participatory behaviors and psychological dynamics. Second, within this broader ecology, this book is centered on organizational approaches, since these are what determine how micro- and macro-level dynamics in empowerment processes interface with each other. Third, despite this emphasis on organizational approaches, each chapter also examines what is understood about how learning and human development take place within the organizational settings comprised by the approach they are describing. Fourth, many chapters explicitly reference a multidimensional view of community power, with situational, institutional, and systemic dimensions. I outline each of these dimensions and how understanding them can be valuable for understanding and power dynamics. Fifth, I briefly describe an integrated understanding of this multidimensional view of community power and an ecological orientation to empowerment.

Building from this conceptual backdrop, I then describe the structure and contents of this book, which is organized into six parts, grouping chapters into categories of approaches: (1) organizing and activism, (2) participatory governance, (3) civil society and coalitions, (4) enterprise, (5) participatory and community arts, and (6) education and engaged research. This is followed by a discussion of the book's scope, a description of the common elements of each chapter, and, finally, some thoughts on different ways that readers can engage with and make use of this book.

What Does Community Empowerment Mean?

When it entered the lexicon around fifty years ago, the term "empowerment" was associated with struggles for equal rights and social justice. As it has proliferated in various discourses, however, it has suffered from terminological confusion and crises of meaning. In a sense, the term has been coopted. Here I discuss five interrelated issues with current uses of the term: (1) broad and varied definitions, (2) individualism, (3) depoliticization, (4) confusion about roles, and (5) collaboration and conflict.[1] Examining these issues helps to clarify the meaning of the term as it is used in this book.

Broad and Varied Definitions

Definitions and implied meanings of the term "empowerment" have varied within the academic literature, but popular uses of the term have been even broader and more diverse. In advertisements, for example, the term can often be taken to mean something akin to self-confidence, self-help, or self-actualization. Those deploying the term in human services and programs often mix aspects of the term's meaning in various scholarly traditions with assumptions that pervade more popular uses (such as in marketing). In a review of the uses of the term in health promotion programs, for instance, Woodall et al. (2012) conclude that "the term [empowerment] has been used with reckless abandon, with many health promotion projects and interventions (seemingly regardless of their function) aiming to 'empower' the populations they are working with" (p. 743).

This broader colloquial usage is at odds with the orientations of the contributors to this book in many ways. A definition that succinctly locates our perspectives is that empowerment describes *processes through which people and groups take action to gain greater control over their lives and environments*. This definition is rooted in theories of empowerment developed in community psychology and related applied disciplines (Gutiérrez, 1990; Maton, 2008; Rappaport, 1981, 1987).

Individualism

This definition of empowerment involves actions by *people* and *groups*, but in many invocations of "empowerment" there is little or no discussion of groups or collective actions. Processes by which groups build and exercise social or community power clearly have psychological aspects to them.[2] Yet it is crucial to differentiate any discussion of psychological processes from the individualist orientation that is implicit in many uses of the term "empowerment." In foundational work on the concept of psychological empowerment, for instance, Zimmerman (1990) argued that it must be clearly distinguished

---

1 These issues are described in greater detail in chapter 3 of *Community Power and Empowerment* (Christens, 2019), which examines the historical underpinnings and evolution of the term "empowerment" in theory and in common usage.
2 Liberation and oppression are both psychopolitical (Prilleltensky, 2008).

from "individual empowerment." Instead, psychological empowerment was theorized as one aspect of what takes place within group process and contexts of collective action. The holistic understanding of empowerment – with inextricable psychological, organizational, and community processes occurring simultaneously – is reflected in the contributions to this book.

Depoliticization

Many invocations of empowerment – especially those that are overly focused on individuals to the detriment of groups and collective action – are not coherently or realistically linked to changes in community power relations. In this book, chapters describe how power is being built and exercised by and within organizations and collectivities and how these can challenge elite interests and create changes in systems. All approaches described in these chapters have at least the possibility (and in many cases the express purpose) of enacting and/or working toward forms of democratic egalitarianism and liberation from oppression. The value orientation of many of the approaches described in this book is similar to what Wright (2016) described as the three core values of social emancipation: (1) *equality/fairness*, or the goal of equal access to the conditions people need to flourish; (2) *democracy/freedom*, or the goal of equal access to the means to meaningfully participate in decision-making relevant to people's lives; and (3) *community/solidarity*, or the goal that cooperation is not motivated solely by instrumental self-interest, but also by concern for others and/or moral obligation.

Confusion about Roles

In many uses of the term "empowerment," it is implied or overtly claimed that it is something that can be done *to* someone or given to them (i.e., Person/Group A *empowered* Person/Group B). This notion is plainly at odds with the description of empowerment as processes by which people and groups take action to alter systems and power relations. Instead, empowerment processes unfold as groups endeavor to develop their own capacities and take actions to alter systems and conditions. These processes can of course be helped along in various ways by people or organizations who are not the primary actors in the effort (e.g., funders, practitioners, policymakers, adult allies of youth activists, etc.), but it is important not to conflate this with "empowering" people and groups. In some instances, during the review and revision processes, I encouraged contributors to this book to reconsider phrasing that might lead to confusion around the roles of various entities and actors. The perspective throughout this book is therefore that empowerment processes are led and carried out by those directly involved (e.g., members, residents, students), while others may help to maintain or cocreate structures and settings that are conducive to those processes and provide support in various ways.

Collaboration and Conflict

A fifth issue that has contributed to confusion around what empowerment means revolves around the extent to which these processes are understood as more collaborative or more conflictual, and whether the collaboration or conflict is taking place within groups or between groups. Some who have adopted the term "empowerment" to describe educational or prevention-focused programs, for instance, may preclude the possibility of conflict-based approaches and emphasize collaborative efforts. This constrains possibilities for altering power relations. At the other end of the spectrum, some discussions of empowerment have emphasized the need for conflict and struggle to transform the status quo. These have sometimes prompted critiques from a feminist perspective (e.g., Riger, 1993; Stall & Stoecker, 1998) that conflict is being pursued to the detriment of collaborative processes. The chapters in this book analyze approaches with a range of guiding orientations for how they navigate and decide when to prioritize collaborative or conflictual processes, both within their groups and with other community actors and organizations. The reality is that there is often a complex interplay between collaboration and conflict, so community empowerment processes must be understood to include both. In fact, a key determinant of the effectiveness of these efforts involves discernment about when conflict will be necessary and when collaborative approaches will suffice.

Orienting Perspectives for This Book

Ecological View of Empowerment Processes

In contrast to notions of "individual empowerment" discussed earlier, empowerment theory has developed with the clear intent of understanding and promoting collective action processes. Rappaport (1987), for instance, described empowerment processes from an ecological perspective, emphasizing the interdependence of people and groups. Influenced by this same perspective, Zimmerman (2000) outlined empowerment processes and outcomes at the psychological, organization, and community levels of analysis. Although empirical studies have often focused primarily on only one of these ecological (micro-, meso-, and macro-systemic) levels of analysis or another, many scholars have been clear that dynamics at each level are dependent on the others. This holistic conception of empowerment – what Simon (1994) called its "dual focus" (p. 15) on people and their environments – is part of the enduring appeal of empowerment theory.

At the macro-systemic end of the spectrum, empowerment processes involve the pursuit of systemic changes to improve community conditions and the shifts in power relations necessary to achieve these changes (e.g., Conner & Zaino, 2014; Freudenberg & Tsui, 2014; Speer et al., 2020). Viewed through the lens of political theory, these processes can build capacities that enable democratic governance and institutions to succeed (Hendriks et al., 2020). At the micro-systemic end of the spectrum, psychological empowerment processes involve greater levels of community participation, gains in understanding of how social and political power operates within change processes, and increases in participants' perceived control in the sociopolitical domain (Ballard et al., 2021; Choi et al., 2021). These micro-level and macro-level dynamics are mediated through organizational structures and dynamics (Rothman et al., 2019).

Emphasis on Organizational Approaches

Organizations and the participatory settings that they foster are the meso-level structures where psychological (micro-level) and community (macro-level) processes interconnect. Organizations and settings are thus the lynchpins for building and exercising community power (Han, 2016; Krauss et al., 2020). Empowering community settings are those that develop capacity to address social issues, in part through cultivating the skills and leadership capacities of those who are participating (Aber et al., 2010; Maton, 2008). Settings like these exist within a variety of types of organizations, including voluntary associations, interorganizational alliances, and social movement organizations.

Empowering community settings tend to have some features in common regardless of their context or the particular approach that they are taking. For instance, *opportunity role structure* is a feature of organizational settings that has been defined as "the amount, accessibility, and arrangement of formal positions or roles within an organization that provides opportunities for members to take control of group tasks and build their skills and competencies" (Peterson & Zimmerman, 2004, p. 135). Opportunity role structure appears to be one distinguishing feature of a wide variety of types of empowering community settings (Krauss et al., 2020; Maton & Salem, 1995; Powell & Peterson, 2014). Other features may vary according to particular contexts and goals. For instance, some settings orient their activities more toward mutual support/aid, while others are more focused on achieving systemic and structural changes, yet settings at both ends of this spectrum may foster empowerment processes (Chetkovich & Kunreuther, 2006; Wilke & Speer, 2011).

Researchers have sought to understand these distinctions across various types of settings, including which features of settings are *ecological commonalities* (features like opportunity role structure that tend to be the same across many setting types) and which are *ecological specificities* (those that more likely vary based on context; Maton & Salem, 1995; Peterson & Speer, 2000). In addition, some setting features may be especially important for or differentially experienced by certain subgroups or categories of participants (Peterson & Hughey, 2002). Individual participants, moreover, typically experience a variety of types of organizational settings, and there may be benefits for both participants and organizations to particular sequences of participatory behaviors or group-level regularities and dynamics. Although much remains unknown about the features that make civic associations and social movement organizations effective (Andrews et al., 2010), it is clear that a variety of settings and types of organizations are needed, and collaborative relationships between organizations are also key (Akiva & Robinson, 2022; Shumate & Cooper, 2022).

Attention to Learning and Human Development

The primary goal of building community power is to change systems, not the people who are affected by them. Nevertheless, involvement in community change processes often has a profound influence on people: on their relationships, their worldviews, their skills, the actions they choose to take, and their conceptions of themselves and their capabilities. As mentioned earlier, this interrelated set of developmental processes can be described as psychological empowerment. These processes are also sometimes described as civic and/or sociopolitical development (Fernández & Watts, 2023; Flanagan & Christens, 2011), especially in studies of younger people. These various frameworks for understanding how people learn and develop as they take part in social action have some broad commonalities and some notable differences in terms of their relative emphases (see Christens et al., 2016).

Sociopolitical development theory, for instance, has been deeply influenced by Freire's (1973) work on conscientization and has therefore emphasized learning and cognitive development, especially through the study of critical consciousness (Rapa & Godfrey, 2023). Critical reflection – people's ability to understand and critique their sociopolitical contexts – is the component of critical consciousness that has received the most attention in research, with a number of studies finding associations with positive developmental indicators, particularly among marginalized youth (Heberle et al., 2020). This is in part because it has been theorized as a precursor to actions intended to help bring about systemic changes (Watts et al., 2011). Scholars of critical consciousness have recently called for increased attention to actions and behaviors due to the recognition that behaviors and cognitive development have a bidirectional influence (Diemer et al., 2021).

Civic development, meanwhile, has had a stronger relative emphasis on the actions that people are taking as they engage with civic life. Research has examined the various forms that civic engagement can take in different sociopolitical contexts, in different phases of life, among people and groups with varied identities, and toward different ends and values (Sherrod et al., 2010). The conceptualization of engagement in this body of literature has tended to be broader than the notion of "critical action" that comprises the behavioral component of critical consciousness. Meanwhile, research on psychological empowerment has emphasized perceptions of agency in the sociopolitical domain, which has often been operationalized as one's perception that they are capable of playing important roles in bringing about changes in the systems that affect their lives (Peterson et al., 2011). Research on psychological empowerment processes has been particularly attentive to settings and contexts (e.g., Rutledge, 2023), to relational development processes (Langhout et al., 2014; Russell et al., 2009), and to participants' learning about how power operates in social change processes (Lardier et al., 2021; Speer et al., 2019).

Scholarship using each of these frameworks for understanding learning and development in civic/sociopolitical action is influencing those using the other frameworks, and work is continually advancing within and across them. For instance, a recent edited volume is dedicated entirely to advancing understandings of the settings and contexts that foster critical consciousness (Godfrey & Rapa, 2023). The organizational approaches that are described in this handbook depend on the types of experiential learning and leadership development processes that are captured by these psychological constructs, but again, if these processes are occurring apart from collective efforts to exert influence, change systems, and/or alter power relations, then empowerment processes are not really taking place. What is occurring might be better described instead as training or consciousness raising.

Multidimensional View of Community Power

Those who are engaged in empowerment processes are seeking to bring about changes to existing systems that are manifestations of entrenched power imbalances. They therefore frequently find themselves involved in contention with elites and other defenders of status quo power relations. Those who wield power often exercise it in multiple ways, ranging from the overt and direct, to more subtle and even hidden ways. To change unjust systems, community groups must also build and exercise power in multifaceted ways. One useful lens for understanding and describing community power dynamics is built on a three-dimensional concept of power first proposed by Lukes (2005).[3] These three dimensions of power can be labeled (1) the situational dimension, (2) the institutional dimension, and (3) the systemic dimension (Alford & Friedland, 1985). This framework has been adopted in some studies of empowerment processes (e.g., Evans & Fernandez-Burgos, 2023; Speer, 2008) and is taken up by many of the contributors to this handbook.

Situational

Community organizer Saul Alinsky (1971) argued that power can be derived from two primary sources: organized money and organized people. The overt

---

3 This multidimensional view of power is illustrated in Gaventa's (1980) study of an Appalachian mining town.

conflicts that emerge between competing interests in public life (often with more organized money on one side and more organized people on the other) can be understood as the situational dimension of power. Think of standoffs between management and labor unions, environmental groups opposing the construction of a new highway, or local political factions lining up on different sides of a proposed municipal policy or backing different candidates for elected offices. Which side prevails? What sorts of negotiations take place? Are concessions made by one side or the other? Building and exercising power in the situational dimension includes all of the strategic moves to try to "win" in debates over the issues that have emerged into public contestation. For groups whose main source of power is people rather than money, the fundamental practices of community organizing are indispensable (Han et al., 2021).

Institutional

One thing that this situational view leaves out is that many problems and issues never emerge into overt public contention, and power relations often determine which ones do. The institutional dimension of power refers to efforts of people and groups to prevent some things from emerging into open debate and/or cause others to. These agenda-setting efforts often take place out of public view. One example is attempting to control how information is shared or conveyed (e.g., owning journalistic outlets or seeking to shape how they cover the news). Another example is attempts to influence who is included or excluded in forums where information is exchanged or decisions are made (e.g., getting allies onto boards or other decision-making bodies). The exercise of power's institutional dimension can even involve efforts to distract from one issue by raising controversies about another. Because many of the ways that power dynamics manifest in the institutional dimension have to do with what does *not* take place, at least in full public view, this dimension of power is less easily observed and understood than dynamics that are playing out in the situational dimension, but it is crucial for understanding what emerges there.

Systemic

The systemic dimension refers to how power shapes people's perceptions of community issues, about the range of possible alternatives, and the desirability and plausibility of those alternatives. This ideological dimension of power is the most fundamental – it is determinative of what takes place in the other two dimensions. Yet it is also the least easily observed dimension of power, since it shapes conceptions of rationality (Flyvbjerg, 2002) and what is considered "natural." Understanding the systemic dimension of power can help to explain apparent contradictions that manifest across the other two dimensions, such as when people express support for systems or policies that are clearly harmful to them. Elites are operating in the systemic dimension of power when they, for instance, seek to naturalize status quo arrangements and stoke fears about possible alternatives. Reciprocally, community organizing groups are operating in the systemic dimension of power when they deliberately resist and complicate these types of dominant narratives and craft new narratives and ways of understanding the world (Haapanen et al., 2023; Oyakawa, 2015).

Integrated Understanding of Community Power and Empowerment

An ecological model for understanding empowerment processes – with inter-related psychological, organizational, and community processes occurring simultaneously – can be understood as operating across all three of the dimensions of power described in the previous section. Table 0.1 (an adaptation of table 6.3 in Christens, 2019, p. 146) briefly summarizes some of the dynamics and processes taking place at the intersections of each of these ecological levels of empowerment and dimensions of community power.

In the situational dimension, for instance, self-perceptions of sociopolitical control are developed by participants in collective actions, which can also establish community leadership and enhance residents' sense of collective efficacy. Organizational structures are necessary to catalyze and sustain these types of activities. Those that provide participatory niches and social support that can generate a sense of connectedness (or a "sense of community") among participants are especially vital.

In the institutional dimension, participants are developing skills, including those required for bringing other residents into community action processes and encouraging their development as grassroots leaders. At a community level, this builds capacity to identify and assess problems, to develop strategies for addressing them, and to mobilize organizations and networks to influence key institutional decision-making processes. This depends on organizations and networks that can engage in organizational learning and strategize about how to influence and alter power relations.

Finally, in the systemic dimension, participants in empowerment processes engage in critical reflection that builds greater understanding of how power operates. This understanding is fostered through, for instance, collective efforts to disrupt dominant narratives and shape new public narratives (Ganz, 2011). Again, these psychological and collective capacities are developed in organizational settings with structures and dynamics that can foster critical reflection and strategy for altering public perceptions.

This model and its theoretical underpinnings are explored in greater depth in *Community Power and Empowerment* (Christens, 2019). That book, however, has only one detailed case description: in chapter 6 (pp. 144–151) I described the work of the Philadelphia Student Union (PSU) – a long-standing youth organizing initiative in the US – according to this multidimensional and multilevel model of power and empowerment. I chose this case

Table 0.1 *Ecological model of community power and empowerment.*

	Psychological	Organizational	Community
Situational	• Community and organizational participation • Perceived sociopolitical control	↔	• Organizational viability and leadership • Social support, sense of community in organizations • Opportunity role structure	↔	• Broad participation and collective action • Collective efficacy • Community-based leadership
Institutional	• Relational dynamics: developing leaders, facilitating, collaborating, mobilizing, bridging	↔	• Co-empowered subgroups and subgroup linkages • Organizational learning and systems thinking • Networks and coalitions, systems alignment	↔	• Mobilization structures/networks • Issue/problem assessment capacity • Power mapping, institutional alignment
Systemic	• Understanding of the source, nature, and instruments of social power • Critical reflection	↔	• Group-based belief system • Critical analysis of power • Strategy for systemic transformations and shaping public understanding	↔	• Social/collective analysis of root causes of community issues • Critical awareness and resistance to hegemony • Shifting public narratives and frames

primarily because of research by Jerusha Conner, Sonia Rosen, and their collaborators, which has examined the PSU's practices and impacts from a variety of vantage points (Conner, 2011; Conner & Rosen, 2015; Conner et al., 2013; Rosen & Conner, 2021), demonstrating concrete examples of nearly every facet and level of the model. This handbook, in turn, begins with a chapter on youth organizing by Jerusha Conner, and then goes on to explore a number of other approaches to building and exercising community power.

Structure and Contents of this Book

The chapters in this book are organized into six parts. The parts represent themes or common threads between chapters. They are not mutually exclusive categories. In fact, in many cases, the approaches grouped into one part of the book are taking place because of, in concert with, or in hopes of producing the types of efforts described in other chapters in other parts of the book. It could easily be argued that some chapters belong in different parts of the book than where they are. Clustering the chapters into these thematic parts, however, invites comparisons among approaches that share some key commonalities.

Part I Organizing and Activism

Community organizing is a process through which residents come together and build power to investigate and take sustained collective action on systemic issues that negatively affect their daily lives. Often termed "grassroots" community organizing, these processes are clearly aligned with the concept of empowerment as described so far in this chapter.[4] The field of community organizing has grown such that there are now perennial organizing initiatives in nearly every US metropolitan area (Braxton et al., 2013; Wood & Warren, 2002), and similar types of initiatives are taking place in many other countries (e.g., Harcourt, 2003; Menon & Allen, 2021; Mihaylov, 2021; Tivaringe & Kirshner, 2021). Many initiatives are built by organizing within and across other local institutions (e.g., faith-based institutions, community centers, neighborhood associations). Many initiatives are focused on changing multiple systems (e.g., housing, education, safety). Some prioritize leadership by specific populations and groups, such as immigrants (Escudero, 2020) or younger people (Conner, 2020; Ginwright, 2009; Kirshner, 2015). Approaches and models differ in many ways across this diverse field of practice, but commonalities across nearly all community organizing efforts

---

4 Accordingly, studies of community organizing have been influential in the development of empowerment theory (e.g., Speer & Hughey, 1995).

include their intent to develop broad-based grassroots leadership while simultaneously addressing issues of common concern.

"Organizing" and "activism" are terms that are sometimes used interchangeably. Community organizers, however, often sharply contrast their approaches to social change with those of activists (Swarts, 2011). Activism can connote more individualized, expressive, and/or episodic forms of social action. Yet activism is a crucial component of broader social movements, which often have many different avenues for participation and roles that participants can play (e.g., Isaac et al., 2020). The chapters in Part I examine these two interrelated phenomena – organizing and activism – across different issues and contexts, including youth organizing in the US (Chapter 1 by Conner) and South Africa (Chapter 2 by Tivaringe and Kirshner), organizing around domestic violence in India (Chapter 3 by Menon and Allen), congregation-based community organizing (Chapter 4 by Speer), immigrant organizing and activism (Chapter 5 by Escudero), and online racial justice advocacy in the US (Chapter 6 by Brazzell). Each of these chapters synthesizes insights from specific struggles for social justice, enabling an understanding of the sometimes-subtle differences in strategies employed by organizers and activists across different contexts and focal issues.

Part II Participatory Governance

Organizing and activism primarily seek to influence democratic decision-making from outside of formal governance processes. In contrast, the chapters in the Part II examine efforts to open up formal governance processes to deeper forms of participation and deliberative processes. Representative democracies around the world now hold periodic elections for leaders of executive, legislative, and sometimes judicial branch offices. Residents are asked to select from among candidates whose policy platforms may represent only slight variations from the status quo but whose appeals nevertheless often stimulate negative partisanship (Bankert, 2024). Voting in these sorts of elections is a relatively passive form of participation in democratic governance and shared decision-making. Many residents therefore channel their efforts into other forms of involvement in nongovernmental civil society, such as those described in other parts of this book.

Government and civil society reciprocally influence each other, however, and organized efforts by residents can open new spaces for participatory governance. For example, institutional reforms such as participatory budgeting have been undertaken as concessions to pressure from organized groups in some polities. In other cases, democratically minded public officials have sought to open governance processes to more civic engagement and deliberation, such as in participatory urban planning processes. And in some other cases still, resident-led groups have directly taken up problem-solving roles that have traditionally been handled by public sector entities, at times upending policy frameworks in the process (Hendriks & Dzur, 2021).

Collectively, these types of efforts have been termed *empowered participatory governance* (EPG) by Fung and Wright (2003), who identified common features of EPG across different case examples. All of the instances they studied involved residents deliberatively developing potential solutions to specific, concrete problems. Deliberative decision-making processes varied, as did the extent to which once-centralized authorities or responsibilities were delegated to or claimed by the more grassroots participatory processes. The chapters in Part II of this book reveal both the great potential of EPG processes and the real tensions and practical issues that efforts of this sort must navigate if they are to approach their democratic ideals. Chapter 7 (by Dzur and Hendriks) describes *citizens governance spaces*, which in many cases operate within the interface between resident-led civil society and governance. The other three chapters describe promising models for participatory governance that are simple in concept but complex in practice: participatory budgeting (Chapter 8 by Peabody), participatory urban planning (Chapter 9 by Cooper), and youth policy advocacy in municipal governance (Chapter 10 by Augsberger and Collins). Again, each chapter provides valuable insights for those seeking to implement each one of these approaches, and the collection enables comparisons across the approaches, including how different efforts have approached the design of deliberative processes and institutional reforms.

Part III Civil Society and Coalitions

"Nonprofit" is a term that tends to call to mind the provision of charitable services and/or people exercising their right to form voluntary associations. Particularly in more industrialized countries, however, the nonprofit sector has become so large and diverse that entire lines of scholarship are dedicated to mapping its constantly expanding and evolving contours (e.g., Salamon, 2010). Some of this proliferation of the nonprofit organizational form is due to competitive outsourcing of services that were once performed by governments. In fact, in the US, nonprofits – rather than government agencies – are now the providers of most government-funded services (Lecy & Van Slyke, 2013). Other sources of growth in the nonprofit sector include foundations acting as tax shelters for the wealthy and political advocacy organizations funded to protect their corporate interests. Organizations that challenge elite interests in pursuit of social justice of course do persist as a subset of the nonprofit sector (Domhoff, 2009), though they sometimes struggle to operate as truly community-driven efforts within the confines of a sector dominated by the priorities, assumptions, and perspectives of philanthropists (Eikenberry, 2009; INCITE! Women of Color Against Violence, 2009).

Observers and practitioners alike have long noted that a common obstacle to achieving community-level improvements is a lack of communication, coordination, and collaboration across the diverse array of organizations that relate to each issue or system (e.g., safety, food security, educational equity). This has inspired efforts to build leadership and collaborative capacity among organizations to enable them to act collectively to achieve and sustain progress on systemic changes. Community leadership development (Chapter 11 by Majee, Massengale, Rippel, and Adams) is one approach to this. Rooted in the philosophy and infrastructure of US land-grant universities, this approach seeks to develop and guide diverse resident-leaders as they seek to address complex local issues. Chapter 12 (by Kegler and Bigger) describes community coalitions, a very common formalized structure for local systems changes. Coalitions aim to facilitate leadership development and interorganizational collaboration. Yet coalitions have been critiqued for primarily engaging professionals working to address issues rather than those who are most directly affected by their focal issues.[5] Chapter 13 (by Collura, Raffle, Joseph, and Stevens) describes efforts to infuse coalition structures with younger leaders, who are often among those excluded from these types of settings.

Finally, Chapters 14 (by Anderson and Christens) and 15 (by Hu, Wang, and Lian) describe neighborhood associations – a long-standing hyperlocal approach to civil society development. Neighborhood associations can act both as independent vehicles for local empowerment processes and as building blocks for citywide change efforts. They can also act, however, to defend the interests of wealthier property owners, reinforcing disparities within and across neighborhoods. Relationships between governmental entities and neighborhood associations are complex; how associations navigate these relationships is a key determinant of their effectiveness as influential yet independent grassroots entities. This is perhaps most true in countries like China where, as Hu, Wang, and Lian describe in Chapter 15, the national authorities are directly involved in local neighborhood governance.

Part IV Enterprise

Most of the approaches described in this book (and in research on empowerment processes more generally) focus on building power to change resource distribution through social and political processes rather than through economic processes. For some activists and organizers, avoiding direct entanglement in economic processes is at least partly ideological. They may prefer to distance their work as much as possible from capitalist enterprise and the many problems that it generates and exacerbates (poverty, worker exploitation, environmental destruction, etc.). Others may simply be overwhelmed by the scale and complexity of the globalized economy and lack strategies for involvement in this arena that can also help to accomplish

---

5 Some coalitions are prioritizing broader engagement with residents rather than working primarily with organizational leaders (Kegler et al., 2019).

emancipatory agendas (Christens & Collura, 2012). Whatever the reasons, the aggregate effect can be to cede the marketplace, the sites of production and consumption, and all of their associated economic power to unquestioned capitalist control.

Establishing more democratic and egalitarian ways of participating in economic activities can have a range of beneficial effects, including the potential to improve the working conditions and economic well-being of employees and to generate collective resources for public goods and/or to support other types of empowerment processes (e.g., community organizing initiatives or social movement organizations). Efforts of this sort can also develop capacity and creativity, pushing participants to conceive of and experiment with various attempts to organize economic activities in more democratic and egalitarian ways (Hahnel & Wright, 2014). Worker-owned cooperatives are a compelling model for empowerment-oriented enterprises, yet operating them within globalizing capitalist economies brings about a range of challenges and tensions (Meyers, 2022). There is also currently a great deal of enthusiasm for social enterprise and social entrepreneurship and the potential contributions of these approaches to community development (Weaver, 2022). There are also concerns that these approaches can reposition businesses and wealthy elites as those best equipped to solve social problems, obscuring their roles in creating and perpetuating these very problems (McGoey, 2016). The chapters in Part IV examine these two approaches – worker cooperatives (Chapter 16 by Meyers, Pinto, Schlachter, and Prushinskaya) and employment social enterprises (Chapter 17 by Byrd and Weaver) – providing rich insights into the possibilities and challenges of operating enterprises in ways that are consistent with an empowerment orientation.

Part V Participatory and Community Arts

Discussions of empowerment approaches and strategies can tend to emphasize instrumental objectives (i.e., which policies or systemic changes they may influence and how) to the detriment of more expressive elements of these processes. People who participate in group-based efforts to bring about change, however, are often driven to do so by the particularities of their experiences of inequities and oppressive systems. These experiences often involve pain and fear, but there are also often intertwined narratives of hope and joy (Rappaport, 2000). Sharing personal stories with others who are involved in systems change efforts can be elemental to sociopolitical development processes for participants, simultaneously shaping personal and collective narratives focused on justice and the urgent need for collective action (Ganz, 2011; Gupta, 2021).

Art and creative expression can provide especially potent demonstrations of personal experiences and perspectives. Of course, part of their value is independent of the roles they can play in facilitating collective action and social change. Creating a beautiful object or performance is in some sense an end in itself. But arts and other creative endeavors that take place as part of empowerment processes can also help to forge connectedness, draw attention to social issues, resist dominant narratives, and shape perceptions and imagination around more just potential futures. In other words, it is possible for arts to contribute to shifts in all three of the dimensions of power (situational, institutional, and systemic) discussed earlier. In fact, they are perhaps best suited to operating in power's systemic dimensions. This potential for arts to play crucial roles in empowerment processes is exemplified in the two chapters in Part V of this book: Hennessy, Gold-Watts, Pietrzak, Lapoint, and Bell discuss participatory arts for vulnerable populations (Chapter 18), and Sonn, Agung-Igusti, Jayawardana, Quayle, and Keast describe community arts, decoloniality, and epistemic justice (Chapter 19).

Part VI Education and Engaged Research

All approaches described in this book provide opportunities for learning through experience within different community change processes. The set of approaches described in Part VI either take place within or through institutions devoted to formal education or they center the educational experiences of their participants – who are often young people. Some approaches seek to broaden the opportunities for civic learning and engagement that exist within schools. These approaches are broadly aligned with what Dewey (1902) described as schools functioning as social centers. He argued that a school should not be a space in which young people are segregated from society to be instructed in preparation for adult responsibilities (e.g., participation in democratic processes), instead advocating that a school should be "a thoroughly socialized affair in contact at all points with the flow of community life" (p. 75). This type of civically engaged education would not only benefit the students enrolled at the school but could also provide "a continuous education for all classes of whatever age" (p. 83).

Action civics, described in Chapter 20 (by Morgan and Ballard), is one approach that is specifically influenced by Dewey and other advocates for progressive democratic education. Working with teachers (and sometimes with other adults who volunteer and/or represent partner organizations), students engage in research, action, and reflection on local community issues that directly concern them, learning about civic decision-making and power dynamics in the process. Youth participatory action research (YPAR) is another approach that can support civic learning during efforts to bring about change in school and community settings. Although it is often undertaken in out-of-school-time settings, Chapter 22 (by Dickerson, Kornbluh, and Duke) makes the case that YPAR can be particularly valuable when conducted within schools.

School-based gender–sexuality alliances (GSAs) provide social support and opportunities for learning and community-building among LGBTQ+ youth and their allies. They also often function as vehicles for collective action against the discrimination and injustices that these young people face in their schools and community environments. Chapter 21 (by Poteat, Marx, O'Brien, and Yang) describes power and empowerment processes in school-based GSAs, synthesizing the growing body of research on organizational and setting-level features of GSAs that are associated with their effectiveness in meeting their goals. Community-based educational spaces (CBESs) can also provide complementary resources and opportunities for learning and positive youth development, including civic or sociopolitical development (Akiva & Robinson, 2022; Baldridge, 2019). Chapter 23 (by Contreras, Downing, Greer, and Baldridge) examines the history and potential for CBESs to contribute to transformative community-level changes. Finally, scholars – including many of the authors of chapters in this book – are engaging with community empowerment processes through research. Community-engaged and participatory research approaches are increasingly common as elements of efforts to produce more equitable systems and communities (e.g., Ortiz et al., 2020; Stoecker & Falcón, 2022). Chapter 24 (by Haapanen, Wallerstein, and Sanchez-Youngman) examines this array of approaches from the perspective of power and empowerment, drawing attention to the sometimes-subtle differences in the ways that community groups and researchers can partner in the pursuit of shared goals.

Thoughts on the Scope and Coverage of this Book

Part of the appeal of a handbook-scale edited volume is its ability to incorporate a broader scope than is possible in many other formats for published scholarship. The range of approaches that are described by the chapters in this book deliver on that potential in many ways. Determining the specifics of the book's scope and contents, however, was challenging and in some ways frustrating. The breadth of the approaches that are included here makes the inevitable omissions and over/under-emphases more conspicuous than they might be in a more constrained curated collection (e.g., a journal special issue). Having struggled with these questions of scope and coverage while editing this handbook, it occurred to me that it could be useful to give readers a sense of some ways that I view the finished collection mapped onto the broader terrain of possibilities, including where it succeeds and falls short of comprehensive coverage from my perspective. I will comment here on three dimensions of coverage: geographic, topical, and disciplinary.

In terms of geographic coverage, the US is overrepresented. I live in the US, and my awareness of organizational approaches to power-building is primarily based in North American contexts. This handbook does, however, attempt to take a global perspective in several respects. First, there are chapters on approaches (and by authors) in a variety of places around the world. In addition to the US, authors and/or case descriptions are from Australia, Brazil, China, India, South Africa, and Spain. Although this array certainly does not approach global coverage, it does provide insights into efforts taking place on six continents. Moreover, while corresponding with authors regarding their chapters, I encouraged all, regardless of location, to take a global perspective whenever possible. For instance, if a chapter is especially focused on a type of empowering community setting, strategy, or model in a particular country or part of the world, I asked authors to compare the history and prevalence of this type of approach in their focal country with others (to the extent that this was known). If an approach is specific to only certain places, I asked authors to explain (or at least to reflect on) why that might be. Most chapters consequently provide international comparisons, even while they are focused primarily on a particular locality.

In addition to editorial provincialism, the overrepresentation of North America also reflects an unevenness in the geographic distribution of scholars and scholarship on community empowerment processes. I encountered some of the reasons for this imbalance directly while inviting contributions to this handbook. In several cases, I invited authors working outside of the US or Europe to contribute chapters, but despite their interest in doing so, they were unable to. In one case, would-be chapter authors were understandably concerned that writing affirmatively about resistance movements in their country would make them a target of government repression. In another case, authors who agreed to contribute a chapter were hindered by economic conditions in their country and related demands placed on them in their university contexts. It stands to reason that many of the places where action-oriented scholarship on empowerment processes could be most useful are some of the same places where it faces the greatest obstacles.

In terms of topical coverage, I sought to invite contributions on as many major varieties of community-driven and/or participatory action to change systems as possible. But, of course, complete coverage is unachievable, even within the North American context which received the most attention. There are many other types of empowering community settings that are not discussed. For example, mutual help organizations have been the focus of some highly influential studies of empowerment processes in community psychology (e.g., Luke et al., 1991). In addition, several of the most important and influential approaches were not included. Labor unions, for example, are crucial institutions for building and exercising power. Many of the types of organizations that are covered in this volume have worked with labor unions (e.g., the worker cooperatives described by Meyers and colleagues in Chapter 16 and the student organizing movements described Tivaringe and Kirshner in Chapter 2). A chapter on labor union revitalization was planned (from authors in a country where, like in many other places, unions have declined), but this was the chapter mentioned earlier that could not be completed because of competing demands in universities due to resource scarcity. In addition to long-standing and influential approaches such as labor organizing, there are newer approaches that are not featured, such as restorative approaches (e.g., restorative justice and justice reinvestment; Lugalia-Hollon & Cooper, 2018; Winn, 2021). Although they are not the focus of entire chapters, however, emerging approaches are sometimes described in chapters on related approaches. For instance, restorative approaches are described in Chapters 1, 7, and 19.

The book does achieve a wide array of perspectives from different applied social science disciplines. As the contributor biographies describe, contributors have backgrounds in social work, urban planning, political science, sociology, psychology, public health, community development, education, public affairs, nonprofit management, and theater. Theory, applied research, and practice related to empowerment processes have taken place within and at the intersections between some of these fields and have been influenced by some others. Still others are relatively new to the conversation, or at least to the ways of discussing the phenomena outlined earlier in this introductory chapter. In some cases, certain disciplines are understandably most attentive to certain aligned approaches (e.g., developmental psychologists and other scholars of human development tending to study approaches and settings that prioritize youth engagement). The goal for this volume has been to establish enough commonality across contributions that these different disciplinary perspectives could be in conversation without impeding the sharing of discipline-specific concepts, frameworks, approaches to empirical study, and so on. The next section describes some of the ways I sought to achieve this balance from the initial invitation through editorial review and revisions to chapters.

What the Chapters Contain

Introductions

Each chapter author (and/or team of authors) was invited to contribute based on their expertise on a different approach to community empowerment. I provided all potential contributors with a sample chapter outline containing suggestions for how they might structure their chapter drafts.[6] I suggested that each contribution begin with an introduction to the approach that the chapter describes, including a brief history and purpose of the approach, a description

---

6 I also provided most authors with a sample chapter draft (often Chapter 1 on youth organizing by Conner and/or Chapter 20 by Morgan and Ballard) so that they could see an example of how another contributor chose to organize their content. If other chapter drafts were ready to be shared and had special relevance to a contributor or team of contributors, I sometimes shared additional chapter drafts.

of how this sort of effort tends to be initiated, a description of its organizational structure(s), the prevalence of the setting type or approach (with international comparison data whenever possible), and the growth trajectory of this approach – in terms of numbers and types of organizations/settings and participants. There is wide variation in terms of how much of this information is known for the different approaches featured in this book, so each chapter varies accordingly in the level of detail that can currently be provided.

Case Descriptions

Following this introductory information, I asked contributors to consider including a succinct description of an exemplary effort that could ground readers in the concrete details of an instantiation of each approach. These are not intended as full-fledged case studies (although they often draw from case studies published elsewhere) but rather as more succinct case descriptions of specific efforts that can illustrate the potential of each approach to achieve impacts on systems and community conditions while facilitating learning and skill development among participants. These case examples are sometimes drawn from chapter authors' own research and/or practice experience. Others are case examples that authors understand vicariously through published research and other forms of coverage. Authors were asked to describe the features of the effort that enable the kinds of impacts that make it notable. However, instead of only showcasing the achievements of exemplary efforts, I also encouraged authors to discuss the challenges and complexities that these groups are navigating. Table 0.2 lists the exemplar case descriptions that appear in each of the chapters.

These case descriptions concretize the different approaches and enliven the more general discussion in other sections of each chapter. Some contributors chose to describe more than one example case. Often these multiple cases were strategically selected to showcase important dimensions of variance within the types of efforts that the chapter describes. For instance, in Chapter 17, on employment social enterprises, Byrd and Weaver chose to describe United Teen Equality Center for the noteworthy scope of its work within a single city and the Center for Economic Opportunities for the notable scale of its work across thirty cities in eleven states. Chapter 21, on GSAs, is the only chapter that does not include a case description. The chapter authors grappled with how to select a case example to include since there are multiple dimensions of variance among GSAs (and even within GSAs from year to year), including the types of activities that they prioritize and, for example, the relative emphasis on support or advocacy. This variation is often reflective of adaptability in response to members' interests and needs. The authors were concerned that providing a case example might inadvertently convey that a certain emphasis or set of activities represents a "best" type of GSA. They therefore instead sought to describe a range of GSAs and their activities more

Table 0.2 *Case descriptions in this book.*

Chapter title	Author(s)	Case description (location)
Part I: Organizing and Activism		
1: Youth Organizing	Conner	Asian/Pacific Islander Youth Promoting Advocacy and Leadership (CA, USA)
2: Youth Activism in Postapartheid South Africa	Tivaringe and Kirshner	Equal Education and the Fallists Movements (South Africa)
3: Domestic Violence and Community Organizing in India	Menon and Allen	"Shakti" (pseudonym; India)
4: Congregation-Based Community Organizing	Speer	PICO California (USA)
5: Immigrant Organizing and Activism	Escudero	Immigrant Youth Activism and the Federal DREAM Act (USA)
6: Online Racial Justice Advocacy	Brazzell	Color of Change (USA)
Part II: Participatory Governance		
7: Citizens' Governance Spaces	Dzur and Hendriks	Som Energia (Spain)
8: Participatory Budgeting	Peabody	Porto Alegre (Brazil); New York City (USA)
9: Participatory Urban Planning	Cooper	We Will Chicago (USA)
10: Youth Policy Advocacy in Municipal Governance	Augsberger and Collins	Boston Mayor's Youth Council (MA, USA)
Part III: Civil Society and Coalitions		
11: Community Leadership Development	Majee, Massengale, Rippel, and Adams	Neighborhood Leadership Academy and the Experience in Community Enterprise and Leadership (EXCEL) Program (MO, USA)
12: Community Coalitions and Empowerment	Kegler and Bigger	California Healthy Cities and Communities (CA, USA)
13: Youth-infused Community Coalitions	Collura, Raffle, Joseph, and Stevens	River Hills Prevention Coalition (southeastern OH, USA)
14: Neighborhood Associations and Community Change	Anderson and Christens	Neighborhood Revitalization Program (MN, USA)
15: State-Led Community (Dis)empowerment in China	Hu, Wang, and Lian	Zung Neighborhood (Yangzhou, China)

Table 0.2 (*cont.*)

Chapter title	Author(s)	Case description (location)
Part IV: Enterprise		
16: A New Generation of Worker Cooperatives	Meyers, Pinto, Schlachter, and Prushinskaya	Golden Steps (NY, USA); Cooperative Home Care Associates (NY, USA)
17: Employment Social Enterprises	Byrd and Weaver	Center for Economic Opportunities (USA); United Teen Equality Center (MA, USA)
Part V: Participatory and Community Arts		
18: Participatory Arts for Vulnerable Populations	Hennessy, Gold-Watts, Pietrzak, Lapoint, and Bell	2nd Act (New England, New York City, and Cleveland, OH, USA)
19: Community Arts, Decoloniality, and Epistemic Justice	Sonn, Agung-Igusti, Jayawardana, Quayle, and Keast	Next In Colour (Melbourne, Australia); Brimbank LIVE (Brimbank, Australia)
Part VI: Education and Engaged Research		
20: Action Civics	Morgan and Ballard	Generation Citizen (USA); Design Your Neighborhood (TN, USA)
21: Gender–Sexuality Alliances	Poteat, Marx, O'Brien, and Yang	Chapter does not include a case description
22: Youth Participatory Action Research in School Settings	Dickerson, Kornbluh, and Duke	Leadership Class (USA); School Club (USA); After-School Program (USA)
23: Community-Based Education	Contreras, Downing, Greer, and Baldridge	Urban Underground (WI, USA)
24: Community-Engaged Research	Haapanen, Wallerstein, and Sanchez-Youngman	Policy Action for Environmental Justice (southern CA, USA); Youth Engagement and Action through Art (NM, USA)

succinctly throughout the chapter. The thoughtful selection (and thoughtful nonselection) of cases – and the chapter authors' insightful descriptions of them – provides a rich set of exemplars that can vividly clarify and ground some of the more conceptual discussions within each chapter.

Research on Power and Empowerment Processes

Each chapter addresses the approach that it is describing from the perspective of how it builds and exercises community power. As discussed earlier, contributors have a variety of disciplinary and professional backgrounds, and the terminology that they use to describe these dynamics sometimes differs as a result. In rounds of editorial feedback to chapter authors, I did not seek to have contributors coalesce around particular theoretical perspectives, terminologies, or frameworks (such as the ones presented earlier in this introductory chapter), but I did seek to cultivate sufficient substantive and conceptual commonalities so that cross-disciplinary points of connection could be more readily detectable. The sample chapter outline that I provided to chapter authors suggested that they address power dynamics (1) at the community level (e.g., efforts to change local policies and practices), (2) at the level of psychology (e.g., learning, grassroots leadership development), and (3) within and across organizational settings. The following are the prompts that I provided to authors for each of these "levels":

Community Power

- What kinds of community changes (e.g., policy changes, environmental changes) do these types of groups/initiatives tend to pursue? How do they pursue them?
- How do they build and exercise social power and/or change power relationships?
- How often are their efforts to change systems effective?
- Is there evidence that they can help change power relationships/community power structures?
- Are there ripple effects as these groups build networks and coalitions or participate in movements?

Psychological Empowerment Processes

- Has research examined psychological changes (e.g., socioemotional development, relationship development, behavioral changes) among participants as a result of their involvement?
- What do participants learn? How do they develop as leaders in these settings?
- Are there typical patterns or trajectories of participation or leadership?
- What sorts of relationships are built?
- Do patterns differ for any subgroups of participants?

Features of Settings, Processes, and Organizations

- Which features of these settings can facilitate building and exercising social power? Features might include the structure of participatory roles available to participants, the frequency or types of meetings, group dynamics, social norms, or leadership dynamics.
- Do some features inhibit empowerment processes or lead to differential outcomes?
- Are some roles, meeting types, or dynamics especially impactful?
- Which features differentiate the most impactful of these types of settings/processes from those that have less impact?
- What is known about the influence of broader contextual factors on how these settings work?

I encouraged contributors to consider these prompts and then to structure their chapters in ways that suited the available evidence. What is known about how empowerment processes take place varies considerably across the different approaches examined in the book. Through rounds of editorial feedback, I encouraged contributors to present not only the potential benefits of the approach they described in their chapter, but also the challenges, limitations, trade-offs, ambiguities, tensions, and so on.

Applications and Future Research

At the conclusion of each chapter, I suggested that contributors reflect on key takeaways for ongoing research and action. Many of the approaches explored in this book have rarely had the kind of focused attention that these chapters provide, especially from the vantage point of community power and empowerment. Scrutiny from this perspective yields implications for practitioners and community leaders and the constituencies that they seek to engage and mobilize. There are often also broader recommendations for policymakers, funders, or other stakeholders. Finally, viewing each of these approaches and the available empirical evidence on how they build and exercise community power enables contributors to identify gaps and priorities for future research.

Ways This Book Can Be Used

Most who are engaged with community-driven and/or community-engaged systems change efforts will not have had direct experience with the full array of approaches described here. This book enables a broader understanding of a variety of different approaches, clarifies some of their key similarities and differences, and suggests ways that they might inform, influence, or complement each other. This broad view can lead to greater dexterity and strategic decision-making within scholarship and practice related to each of these approaches. It can also stimulate more holistic thinking about how these different approaches can establish greater connectivity and perhaps come closer to achieving some of their shared goals as a result.

The book also provides opportunities to deeply examine the current state of research on approaches of particular relevance or interest. Each chapter curates the most pertinent research and offers recommendations for how the effects of the approach they are describing can be amplified and how to navigate challenges and limitations. There is thus the possibility of using individual chapters to achieve greater depth of knowledge on discrete approaches and of examining chapters on other approaches for greater breadth. In the concluding chapter, I pick back up with this point and highlight some examples of both kinds of insights. I will meet you back there after you have had the chance to dig into the compelling material presented in these chapters.

References

Aber, M. S., Maton, K. I., & Seidman, E. (Eds.). (2010). *Empowering settings and voices for social change*. Oxford University Press.

Akiva, T., & Robinson, K. H. (2022). *It takes an ecosystem: Understanding the people, places, and possibilities of learning and development across settings*. Information Age Publishing.

Alford, R., & Friedland, R. (1985). *The powers of theory: Capitalism, the state, and democracy*. Cambridge University Press.

Alinsky, S. D. (1971). *Rules for radicals: A pragmatic primer for realistic radicals*. Vintage.

Andrews, K. T., Ganz, M., Baggetta, M., Han, H., & Lim, C. (2010). Leadership, membership, and voice: Civic associations that work. *American Journal of Sociology, 115*(4), 1191–1242.

Baldridge, B. (2019). *Reclaiming community: Race and the uncertain future of youth work*. Stanford University Press.

Ballard, P. J., Muscatell, K. A., Hoyt, L. T., Flores, A. J., & Mendes, W. B. (2021). An experimental laboratory examination of the psychological and physiological effects of civic empowerment: A novel methodological approach. *Nonprofit and Voluntary Sector Quarterly, 50*(1), 118–142.

Bankert, A. (2024). *When politics becomes personal: The effect of partisan identity on anti-democratic behavior*. Cambridge University Press.

Braxton, E., Buford, W., & Marasigan, L. (2013). *2013 National Field Scan*. The Funders' Collaborative for Youth Organizing. https://fcyo.org/resources/2013-national-youth-organizing-field-scan-the-state-of-the-field-of-youth-organizing

Chetkovich, C., & Kunreuther, F. (2006). *From the ground up: Grassroots organizations making social change*. ILR/Cornell University Press.

Choi, S. K., Bauermeister, J., Muessig, K., Ennett, S., Boynton, M. H., & Hightow-Weidman, L. (2021). A multidimensional model of sexual empowerment among young Black men who have sex with men: A latent profile analysis. *AIDS and Behavior, 25*, 679–688.

Christens, B. D. (2019). *Community power and empowerment*. Oxford University Press.

Christens, B. D., & Collura, J. J. (2012). Local community organizers and activists encountering globalization: An exploratory study of their perceptions and adaptations. *Journal of Social Issues, 68*(3), 592–611.

Christens, B. D., Winn, L. T., & Duke, A. M. (2016). Empowerment and critical consciousness: A conceptual cross-fertilization. *Adolescent Research Review, 1*(1), 15–27.

Conner, J. O. (2011). Youth organizers as young adults: Their commitments and contributions. *Journal of Research on Adolescence, 21*(4), 923–942.

Conner, J. O. (2020). *The new student activists: The rise of neo-activism on college campuses*. Johns Hopkins University Press.

Conner, J. O., & Rosen, S. M. (2015). Zombies, truants, and flash mobs: How youth organizers respond to and shape youth policy. *National Society for the Study of Education, 114*(1), 203–220.

Conner, J. O., & Zaino, K. (2014). Orchestrating effective change: How youth organizing influences education policy. *American Journal of Education, 120*(2), 173–203.

Conner, J. O., Zaino, K., & Scarola, E. (2013). Very powerful voices: The influence of youth organizing on educational policy in Philadelphia. *Educational Policy*, *27*(3), 560–588.

Dewey, J. (1902). The school as social center. *The Elementary School Teacher*, *3*(2), 73–86.

Diemer, M. A., Pinedo, A., Bañales, J., Mathews, C. J., Frisby, M. B., Harris, E. M., & McAlister, S. (2021). Recentering action in critical consciousness. *Child Development Perspectives*, *15*(1), 12–17.

Domhoff, G. W. (2009). The power elite and their challengers: The role of nonprofits in American social conflict. *American Behavioral Scientist*, *52*(7), 955–973.

Eikenberry, A. M. (2009). Refusing the market: A democratic discourse for voluntary and nonprofit organizations. *Nonprofit and Voluntary Sector Quarterly*, *38*(4), 582–596.

Escudero, K. (2020). *Organizing while undocumented: Immigrant youth's political activism under the law*. New York University Press.

Evans, S. D., & Fernandez-Burgos, M. (2023). From empowerment to community power in participatory budgeting. *American Behavioral Scientist*, *67*(4), 578–592.

Fernández, J. S., & Watts, R. J. (2023). Sociopolitical development as emotional work: How young organizers engage emotions to support community organizing for transformative racial justice. *Journal of Adolescent Research*, *38*(4), 697–725.

Flanagan, C. A., & Christens, B. D. (2011). Youth civic development: Historical context and emerging issues. *New Directions for Child and Adolescent Development*, *134*, 1–9.

Flyvbjerg, B. (2002). Bringing power to planning research: One researcher's praxis story. *Journal of Planning Education and Research*, *21*(4), 353–366.

Freire, P. (1973). *Education for critical consciousness*. Bloomsbury Publishing.

Freudenberg, N., & Tsui, E. (2014). Evidence, power, and policy change in community-based participatory research. *American Journal of Public Health*, *104*(1), 11–14.

Fung, A. & Wright, E. O. (2003). *Deepening democracy: Institutional innovations in empowered participatory governance*. Verso.

Ganz, M. (2011). Public narrative, collective action, and power. In S. Odugbemi & T. Lee (Eds.), *Accountability through public opinion: From inertia to public action* (pp. 273–289). World Bank Publications.

Gaventa, J. (1980). *Power and powerlessness: Quiescence and rebellion in an Appalachian valley*. University of Illinois Press.

Ginwright, S. A. (2009). *Black youth rising: Activism and radical healing in urban America*. Teachers College Press.

Godfrey, E. B., & Rapa, L. J. (Eds.). (2023). *Developing critical consciousness in youth: Contexts and settings*. Cambridge University Press.

Gupta, J. (2021). Resistance, race, and subjectivity in congregation-based community organizing. *Journal of Community Psychology*, *49*(8), 3141–3161.

Gutiérrez, L. M. (1990). Working with women of color: An empowerment perspective. *Social Work*, *35*(2), 149–153.

Haapanen, K. A., Christens, B. D., Freeman, H. E., Speer, P. W., & Crowell-Williamson, G. (2023). Stories of self, us, and now: Narrative power for health equity in grassroots community organizing. *Frontiers in Public Health*, *11*, 1144123.

Hahnel, R., & Wright, E. O. (2014). *Alternatives to capitalism: Proposals for a democratic economy*. New Left Project.

Han, H. (2016). The organizational roots of political activism: Field experiments on creating a relational context. *American Political Science Review*, *110*(2), 296–307.

Han, H., McKenna, E., & Oyakawa, M. (2021). *Prisms of the people: Power and organizing in twenty-first-century America*. University of Chicago Press.

Harcourt, W. (2003). The impact of transnational discourses on local community organizing. *Development*, *46*(1), 74–79.

Heberle, A. E., Rapa, L. J., & Farago, F. (2020). Critical consciousness in children and adolescents: A systematic review, critical assessment, and recommendations for future research. *Psychological Bulletin*, *146*(6), 525–551.

Hendriks, C. M., & Dzur, A. W. (2021). Citizens' governance spaces: Democratic action through disruptive collective problem-solving. *Political Studies*, *70*(3), 680–700.

Hendriks, C. M., Ercan, S. A., & Boswell, J. (2020). *Mending democracy: Democratic repair in disconnected times*. Oxford University Press.

INCITE! Women of Color Against Violence (Ed.). (2009). *The revolution will not be funded: Beyond the non-profit industrial complex*. South End Press.

Isaac, L. W., Coley, J. S., Cornfield, D. B., & Dickerson, D. C. (2020). Pathways to modes of movement participation: Micromobilization in the Nashville Civil Rights Movement. *Social Forces*, *99*(1), 255–280.

Kegler, M. C., Wolff, T., Christens, B. D., Butterfoss, F. D., Francisco, V. T., & Orleans, T. (2019). Strengthening our collaborative approaches for advancing equity and justice. *Health Education & Behavior*, *46*(Suppl. 1), 5S–8S.

Kirshner, B. (2015). *Youth activism in an era of education inequality*. New York University Press.

Krauss, S. E., Zeldin, S., Abdullah, H., Ortega, A., Ali, Z., Ismail, I. A., & Ariffin, Z. (2020). Malaysian youth associations as places for empowerment and engagement. *Children and Youth Services Review*, *112*, 104939.

Langhout, R. D., Collins, C., & Ellison, E. R. (2014). Examining relational empowerment for elementary school students in a yPAR program. *American Journal of Community Psychology*, *53*(3–4), 369–381.

Lardier, D. T., Opara, I., Garcia-Reid, P., & Reid, R. J. (2021). The mediating role of ethnic identity and social justice orientation between community civic participation, psychological sense of community, and dimensions of psychological empowerment among adolescents of color. *The Urban Review*, *53*, 403–423.

Lecy, J. D., & Van Slyke, D. M. (2013). Nonprofit sector growth and density: Testing theories of government support. *Journal of Public Administration Research and Theory*, *23*(1), 189–214.

Lugalia-Hollon, R., & Cooper, D. (2018). *The war on neighborhoods: Policing, prison, and punishment in a divided city*. Beacon Press.

Luke, D. A., Rappaport, J., & Seidman, E. (1991). Setting phenotypes in a mutual help organization: Expanding behavior setting theory. *American Journal of Community Psychology*, *19*(1), 147–167.

Lukes, S. (2005). *Power: A radical view* (2nd ed.). Palgrave Macmillan. (Original work published 1974).

Maton, K. I. (2008). Empowering community settings: Agents of individual development, community betterment, and positive social change. *American Journal of Community Psychology, 41*, 4–21.

Maton, K. I., & Salem, D. A. (1995). Organizational characteristics of empowering community settings: A multiple case study approach. *American Journal of Community Psychology, 23*(5), 631–656.

McGoey, L. (2016). *No such thing as a free gift: The Gates Foundation and the price of philanthropy*. Verso.

Menon, S. V., & Allen, N. E. (2021). Community organizing and counter narratives in the response to domestic violence in India. *American Journal of Community Psychology, 67*(1–2), 184–194.

Meyers, J. S. M. (2022). *Working democracies: Managing inequality in worker cooperatives*. ILR/Cornell University Press.

Mihaylov, N. L. (2021). Speaking power to power: Grassroots democracy in the anti-fracking movement in Bulgaria. *Journal of Community Psychology, 49*(8), 3054–3078.

Ortiz, K., Nash, J., Shea, L., Oetzel, J., Garoutte, J., Sanchez-Youngman, S., & Wallerstein, N. (2020). Partnerships, processes, and outcomes: A health equity-focused scoping meta-review of community-engaged scholarship. *Annual Review of Public Health, 41*(1), 177–199.

Oyakawa, M. (2015). "Turning private pain into public action": The cultivation of identity narratives by a faith-based community organization. *Qualitative Sociology, 38*(4), 395–415.

Peterson, N. A., & Hughey, J. (2002). Tailoring organizational characteristics for empowerment: Accommodating individual economic resources. *Journal of Community Practice, 10*(3), 41–59.

Peterson, N. A., & Speer, P. W. (2000). Linking organizational characteristics to psychological empowerment: Contextual issues in empowerment theory. *Administration in Social Work, 24*(4), 39–58.

Peterson, N. A., & Zimmerman, M. A. (2004). Beyond the individual: Toward a nomological network of organizational empowerment. *American Journal of Community Psychology, 34*(1/2), 129–145.

Peterson, N. A., Peterson, C. H., Agre, L., Christens, B. D., & Morton, C. M. (2011). Measuring youth empowerment: Validation of a sociopolitical control scale for youth in an urban community context. *Journal of Community Psychology, 39*(5), 592–605.

Powell, K. G., & Peterson, N. A. (2014). Pathways to effectiveness in substance abuse prevention: Empowering organizational characteristics of community-based coalitions. *Human Service Organizations: Management, Leadership & Governance, 38*(5), 471–486.

Prilleltensky, I. (2008). The role of power in wellness, oppression, and liberation: The promise of psychopolitical validity. *Journal of Community Psychology, 36*(2), 116–136.

Rapa, L. J., & Godfrey, E. B. (Eds.). (2023). *Critical consciousness: Expanding theory and measurement*. Cambridge University Press.

Rappaport, J. (1981). In praise of paradox: A social policy of empowerment over prevention. *American Journal of Community Psychology, 9*(1), 1–25.

Rappaport, J. (1987). Terms of empowerment/exemplars of prevention: Toward a theory for community psychology. *American Journal of Community Psychology, 15*(2), 121–148.

Rappaport, J. (2000). Community narratives. Tales of terror and joy. *American Journal of Community Psychology, 28*(1), 1–24.

Riger, S. (1993). What's wrong with empowerment. *American Journal of Community Psychology, 21*(3), 279–292.

Rosen, S. M., & Conner, J. (2021). Negotiating power: How youth organizers recast the debate about school reform. *Journal of Community Psychology, 49*(8), 3017–3032.

Rothman, L., De Vijlder, F., Schalk, R., & Van Regenmortel, M. (2019). A systematic review on organizational empowerment. *International Journal of Organizational Analysis, 27*(5), 1336–1361.

Russell, S. T., Muraco, A., Subramaniam, A., & Laub, C. (2009). Youth empowerment and high school gay–straight alliances. *Journal of Youth and Adolescence, 38*(7), 891–903.

Rutledge, J. D. (2023). Exploring the role of empowerment in Black women's HIV and AIDS activism in the United States: An integrative literature review. *American Journal of Community Psychology, 71*(3–4), 491–506.

Salamon, L. M. (2010). Putting the civil society sector on the economic map of the world. *Annals of Public and Cooperative Economics, 81*(2), 167–210.

Sherrod, L., Torney-Purta, J., & Flanagan, C. A. (Eds.). (2010). *Handbook of research on civic engagement in youth*. Wiley.

Shumate, M., & Cooper, K. R. (2022). *Networks for social impact*. Oxford University Press.

Simon, B. L. (1994). *The empowerment tradition in American social work*. Columbia University Press.

Speer, P. W. (2008). Social power and forms of change: Implications for psychopolitical validity. *Journal of Community Psychology, 36*(2), 199–213.

Speer, P. W., & Hughey, J. (1995). Community organizing: An ecological route to empowerment and power. *American Journal of Community Psychology, 23*(5), 729–748.

Speer, P. W., Gupta, J., & Haapanen, K. (2020). *Developing community power for health equity: A landscape analysis of current research and theory*. Robert Wood Johnson Foundation.

Speer, P. W., Peterson, N. A., Christens, B. D., & Reid, R. J. (2019). Youth cognitive empowerment: Development and evaluation of an instrument. *American Journal of Community Psychology, 64*(3–4), 528–540.

Stall, S., & Stoecker, R. (1998). Community organizing or organizing community? Gender and the crafts of empowerment. *Gender & Society, 12*(6), 729–756.

Stoecker, R., & Falcón, A. (Eds.). (2022). *Handbook on participatory action research and community development*. Edward Elgar.

Swarts, H. (2011). Drawing new symbolic boundaries over old social boundaries: Forging social movement unity in congregation-based community organizing. *Sociological Perspectives, 54*(3), 453–477.

Tivaringe, T., & Kirshner, B. (2021). Learning to claim power in a contentious public sphere: A study of youth movement formation in South Africa. *Journal of the Learning Sciences, 30*(1), 125–150.

Watts, R. J., Diemer, M. A., & Voight, A. M. (2011). Critical consciousness: Current status and future directions. *New Directions for Child and Adolescent Development, 134*, 43–57.

Weaver, R. L. (2022). *Social entrepreneurship: A practical introduction.* Routledge.

Wilke, L. A., & Speer, P. W. (2011). The mediating influence of organizational characteristics in the relationship between organizational type and relational power: An extension of psychological empowerment research. *Journal of Community Psychology, 39*(8), 972–986.

Winn, M. T. (2021). *Justice on both sides: Transforming education through restorative justice.* Harvard Education Press.

Wood, R. L., & Warren, M. R. (2002). A different face of faith-based politics: Social capital and community organizing in the public arena. *International Journal of Sociology and Social Policy. 22*(9–10), 6–54.

Woodall, J. R., Warwick-Booth, L., & Cross, R. (2012). Has empowerment lost its power? *Health Education Research, 27*(4), 742–745.

Wright, E. O. (2013). Transforming capitalism through real utopias. *American Sociological Review, 78*(1), 1–25.

Wright, E. O. (2016). Real utopias and the dilemmas of institutional transformation. *Justice, Power, and Resistance, Foundation Volume*(September), 33–52.

Zimmerman, M. A. (1990). Taking aim on empowerment research: On the distinction between individual and psychological conceptions. *American Journal of Community Psychology, 18*(1), 169–177.

Zimmerman, M. A. (2000). Empowerment theory: Psychological, organizational and community levels of analysis. In J. Rappaport & E. Seidman (Eds.), *Handbook of community psychology* (pp. 43–63). Kluwer Academic/Plenum Publishers.

PART I

Organizing and Activism

1 Youth Organizing

Jerusha Conner

Introduction

Throughout US history, youth have played instrumental roles in driving social change. From the American Revolutionary War (Werner, 2009) to the abolition, suffrage, and labor rights struggles of the nineteenth and early twentieth centuries (Light, 2015), the social movements of the 1950s and 1960s (McAdam, 1988), and the intersectional campaigns for racial, economic, and climate justice of today, youth have long been on the frontlines of progressive, liberatory social projects. Historically, much of this engagement has been momentum-based, catalyzed by pivotal moments that inspired young people to join causes or movements; however, during the 1990s, a new structure-based model for engaging and supporting youth change agents emerged: youth organizing.

Many of the nonprofit organizations that pioneered this new model of youth organizing formed in response to the dominant discourse and policies of the era, which framed low-income youth of color as dangerous populations in need of tight surveillance and social control. The cover story in a 1995 issue of *The Weekly Standard* warned of "The Coming of Super-predators," and the term quickly caught on in mainstream media and political rhetoric, facilitating the passage of harsh social policies targeting purportedly dangerous youth (Kwon, 2013). Examples of such policies included gang injunctions, policies that increased criminal penalties for youth who committed felonies and allowed those aged fourteen or older to be tried and convicted as adults, and the federal 1994 Gun-Free Schools Act, which ushered in a new era of zero-tolerance gun policies in schools.

Drawing from the new field of youth development, which instead emphasized youth's assets and their potential to contribute to society, the youth organizing groups of the 1990s focused specifically on engaging low-income youth of color, aged thirteen to eighteen, and building their collective capacity to counteract the damaging policy perspectives of the day. From its inception, youth organizing has therefore integrated programming focused on promoting young people's healthy holistic development through the work of community organizing for local change.

Programmatic Features

Three core programmatic elements distinguished these early youth organizing groups: developmental supports, political education, and organizing work. Although I describe each in turn below, it is important to note that these core elements are typically pursued in tandem and work to complement and extend one another.

Developmental supports aim to build youth's skills and competencies. Sometimes these supports took the form of workshops, healing circles, or retreats; other times they were instantiated as in-house academic tutoring, college or career counseling, or mentoring structures. Crafted to be responsive to youth's needs, interests, and intersectional identities, they aimed to meet youth where they were and honor their aspirations. With its grounding in youth development principles, this strength-based approach ran counter to efforts that intended to "fix" "at-risk" youth or prevent them from becoming or developing problems. In addition to cultivating youth's assets, these supports became a way to retain group members.

Political education occurred in workshops or meetings structured to elicit the expertise that youth hold, rooted in their lived experience, while stimulating their development of critical consciousness or their understanding of the ways in which vectors of power, privilege, and oppression operate in society to reproduce inequality and naturalize violence against the most marginalized. Both pedagogically and on a curricular basis, the political education models used in youth organizing programs often drew inspiration from the popular educational techniques that Paulo Freire developed while working to organize illiterate farmworkers in Brazil (Christens & Kirshner, 2011; Conner, 2014; Freire, 1973; Kwon, 2013; Nguyen & Quinn, 2018; Su, 2009).

Finally, organizing strategies involve building a base of people and supporting them to: develop bonds of trust as they discern shared concerns and arrive at consensus about the problems most impacting them and their communities; collectively imagine solutions to those problems; identify decision-makers who could enact those solutions; and, finally, employ a range of tactics intended to pressure these decision-makers to accede to their demands. These tactics may include meetings with policymakers, public testimony, media strategy, and various forms of direct action. As this work is sustained over time, community organizing holds the potential not only to effectuate changes in practice and policy, as groups' demands are met, but also to build the collective power of their members and shift institutional or social power dynamics. An oft-cited definition of youth organizing speaks to this range of intended outcomes: youth organizing is "a youth development and social justice strategy that trains young people in community organizing and advocacy and assists them in employing these skills to alter power relations and create meaningful institutional change in their communities" (Listen, Inc., 2003, p. 9). As one of the earliest funders in the field, Robert Ross, has noted, youth organizing delivers a triple bottom line, driving change at three levels: youth, issue, and community (Shah et al., 2018).

Trends in Participation and Focus

Since the 1990s, youth organizing groups have proliferated. In its 2021 field scan, the Funders' Collaborative on Youth Organizing (FCYO) identified 312 youth organizing groups in the US (Valladares et al., 2021). This number represents a more than twofold increase over the previous field scan in 2013, which identified 111 such groups. Concentrated in California but present throughout the country, the groups represented in the 2021 field scan take different forms, focus on different institutions or issue areas, and use different approaches. Slightly more than a third do not have a full-time organizer on staff. While some youth organizing groups are youth-led and youth-run, a growing share (70 percent) is intergenerational, involving youth–adult partnerships and joint work.

Despite this variation, the three core elements discussed previously (developmental supports, political education, and organizing work) remain central. More than 80 percent of the groups surveyed include political education and leadership development activities in their programming, and all groups were pursuing organizing campaigns to change policies, institutions, or systems. As was the case in previous field scans, education reform remains the most common issue area, possibly because education continues to be a universal experience for youth. Education is followed by local issues, such as transportation or city services, and health. Most groups develop a "focus and expertise on a set of primary issues" (Valladares et al., 2021, p. 26) but engage in other issue areas through partnerships with other groups. The most frequently cited "shared issues" were criminal justice, employment, gender/LGBTQ+ rights, and immigrant rights.

Marginalized youth continue to constitute the core leadership of youth organizing groups. Seventy-five percent of the groups surveyed reported significant representation of Latinx or Hispanic youth within their leadership ranks, with 73 percent reporting the same for LGBTQ+ youth and 70 percent for Black or African American youth. More than half of youth organizing groups active in 2020 (53 percent) included high rates of immigrant and refugee youth leaders.

As hinted at previously in the findings about shared issues, an important trend in the field has been the growth in partnership and coalitional work, especially at the national level. An early account of youth organizing identified participation in alliances and networks as a hallmark of this model, distinguishing it from traditional youth leadership or civic engagement programming, but most of these alliances were formed in local communities or across a single state (Listen, Inc., 2003). By 2013, 77 percent of youth organizing groups reported involvement in networks or coalitions, and 82 percent of them reported involvement at the national level. As the number of youth organizing groups has grown, so too has the share involved in networks and alliances, and now 98 percent of youth organizing groups report such activity. The founding of FCYO in 2000 marked a significant development in this regard, because it created platforms and opportunities for groups to convene, learn from and alongside one another, and form alliances.

The Alliance for Education Justice (AEJ) offers an example. An alliance of twenty-six youth organizing groups, AEJ seeks "to end the war on youth in our schools" (AEJ, n.d.) and to promote a vision of education as liberatory and transformative. The AEJ has authored research reports and toolkits, sent policy proposals to Congress, led trainings in the school-to-prison pipeline, and held days of action, such as that of April 15, 2010, to demand more federal funding for schools (Warren & Kupscznk, 2016). In 2017, AEJ launched its National Campaign for Police Free Schools. Based in abolitionist principles, this long-standing campaign featured a week of action in 2020, headlined by teach-ins, rallies, caravans, and appeals to school boards in cities including New York, Philadelphia, Las Vegas, and Oakland, among others.

An example of an episodic rather than sustained alliance is the collective of youth organizing groups and coalitions that together issued a joint demand letter to President Biden during the final weeks of his 2020 presidential campaign. Authors included such groups as United We Dream, Sunrise Movement, March For Our Lives, Student Action, and the Alliance for Youth Action. The letter outlined a series of policy and personnel demands addressing a wide range of issues, from climate change, gun violence prevention, and immigration to health care, education, and foreign policy. Through coalitions like this, youth organizing groups build their capacity not only to transcend the issue-based or geographic silos that focus their work but also to multiply their collective power.

Until relatively recently, organizing groups with a national presence tended to engage young adults, aged seventeen to twenty-five or eighteen to thirty, while local community-based youth organizing groups focused on middle and high school student populations (Braxton, 2016). These trends were disrupted with the rise of March For Our Lives in 2018 and the Sunrise Movement in 2017, two youth-led groups respectively focused on passing comprehensive gun reform and on the Green New Deal. Both groups engage youth aged twelve to thirty. Additionally, although both draw heavily on the strategies of base building, direct action, and political mobilization, they initially were less attentive to local community issues and youth development principles than traditional youth organizing groups. In yet another departure for the field, they are largely fueled by White middle-class and upper-middle-class youth. Recognizing the limitations of this representation, these two groups have worked to advance a sophisticated intersectional analysis of the root causes and disproportionate effects of gun violence and climate change, respectively. They center social justice in their messaging, programming, and direct actions, and they strive to uplift the leadership of youth of color.

As more youth have become politicized by the horrific mass shooting at Marjory Stoneman Douglas High School or by the escalating climate crisis and find inspiration in the activism of youth like X González and Greta Thunberg, the youth organizing landscape is shifting. Nonetheless, it is important to be clear that not all youth-led organizations exemplify youth organizing, and the terms "organizer" and "activist" are not synonymous. The essential features of youth organizing are that it engages the most marginalized, promotes holistic development, creates meaningful change, and develops a leadership pipeline (Valladares et al., 2020). Organizing, therefore, is a specific model, situated under the broader umbrella category of "activism." Furthermore, while activism is not beholden to any one political ideology, youth organizing groups tend to embrace a radical, justice-oriented social analysis to orient the development of young people's critical consciousness, so these political commitments also distinguish youth organizing from youth activism writ large.

An Example: Asian/Pacific Islander Youth Promoting Advocacy and Leadership

Founded in 1998 in Oakland, California, Asian/Pacific Islander Youth Promoting Advocacy and Leadership (AYPAL) is a youth organizing group that exemplifies these essential features (engaging the most marginalized, promoting holistic development, creating meaningful change, and developing a leadership pipeline). AYPAL draws together young people, aged fourteen to eighteen, from Cambodian, Chinese, Filipino, Korean, Laotian, Mien, Samoan, Tongan, and Vietnamese immigrant and refugee communities. Most are from low-income backgrounds and attend the city's public schools (Kwon, 2013). The mission of AYPAL is to promote social justice, youth community involvement, and youth leadership (Kwon, 2013). On its website, AYPAL boasts that it has supported more than 500 Youth Leaders and engaged over 5,000 young people in grassroots campaigns since its founding (AYPAL, 2021). Moreover, the organization has become a key site for Asian/Pacific Islander (API) youth from diverse backgrounds to come together to critically examine and collectively change the negative conditions that impact their lives, such as everyday anti-Asian racism, the criminalization of API youth, and the gentrification of their neighborhoods.

AYPAL uses a range of programming to attract API youth, build their collective leadership, and involve them in political advocacy and critical action. AYPAL's approach to political education follows Freirean principles of popular education, in which facilitators draw knowledge from participants with the aim of building their critical consciousness, inspiring action, and achieving liberation. Youth interns, who receive modest stipends, plan and lead free workshops twice a week for their peers on topics such as "the elements of hip-hop" and gentrification (Kwon, 2013, p. 24). AYPAL's programming activities also include team-building workshops as a means of fostering strong, supportive relationships within the organization. Leadership development occurs through culturally responsive skill-building, organizing campaigns, and collaborative work within and beyond the group. In fact, coalitions have been central to AYPAL since it began as a collective, drawn from six different nonprofits in Oakland (Kwon, 2013). In addition to collaborating with other organizers, such as labor groups, for direct actions, AYPAL has formed partnerships with public agencies and organizations, including the Oakland Unified School District and the statewide Campaign for Quality Education Coalition. Finally, through its Cultural Arts Activism programming, AYPAL celebrates and leverages the creativity of youth changemakers. At a winter Fresh Off the Block (FOB) Youth Art Show and a spring May Arts Festival, youth showcase cultural and artistic products, ranging from fashion to guerrilla theater, that challenge stereotypes and myths about the API community, celebrate traditions, and advance campaign efforts.

Throughout its twenty-six-year history, AYPAL has orchestrated many effective campaigns. Working in coalition with more than twenty local organizations over a two-year period between 2001 and 2003, AYPAL was able to block the planned expansion of a juvenile hall on the outskirts of Oakland (Kwon, 2013). Setting their sights on a federal policy that was adversely impacting the lives of families in the refugee community, AYPAL launched a campaign in 2002 to pressure their congresswoman to sponsor legislation to repeal the Illegal Immigration Reform and Immigrant Responsibility Act (IIRIRA), a bill that facilitated the deportation of refugees who had been previously convicted of a crime, even if they had served their time. Although the congresswoman never met directly with AYPAL, instead assigning her aide to represent her in scheduled meetings with them and sending them video messages of support, she did finally cosponsor a bill in 2004 to repeal IIRIRA (Kwon, 2013).

Other AYPAL campaigns have focused on education, including demanding policies to require an ethnic studies curriculum, the unlocking of bathrooms during passing periods, the dissemination of written grading policies, and the end of police harassment of students in schools (Nygreen et al., 2006). In 2019, AYPAL helped to pass and implement a resolution to disaggregate school and district-wide data by students' ethnicities. Part of the resolution mandated the introduction of new categories on district enrollment forms, such as Tongan and Mien, which had not been previously acknowledged. AYPAL argued persuasively that collecting and then disaggregating data would allow school leaders to better understand the needs of unique populations of students, support them, and convey the message to them that they are seen and belong. Their resolution passed unanimously (Lee, 2019). Over the last two decades, AYPAL has achieved many notable successes while building a strong base of

API young people who are passionate about effecting meaningful changes in Oakland schools and the community.

Power and Empowerment Processes

The goal of building power features prominently in many of the mission statements of youth organizing groups. Indeed, helping youth to learn to exercise their collective power to effect change is a priority of youth organizing. In what follows, I review the research relevant to psychological empowerment and community power. Then, I identify the setting features that facilitate their development.

Psychological Empowerment

The bulk of the research on youth organizing focuses on the gains that accrue to participants as a result of their involvement. Framed in terms of psychological empowerment, these gains can be grouped into affective, behavioral, cognitive, and relational domains (Christens, 2019). Because some of this work examines psychological empowerment outcomes in large samples of youth organizers, representing a range of different groups (Flores, 2020; Rogers & Terriquez, 2016; Watts et al., 2018), it may partially obscure the specific contexts and campaigns in which these outcomes were forged. Nonetheless, the literature does generally accord with Christens's (2019) perspective that psychological empowerment is inextricably bound up in community and organizational empowerment processes. As youth work to change their communities, they change themselves, and these changes are indicative of empowerment processes.

Affective

Because youth organizing requires participants to confront and closely examine systems of oppression and injustice in order to change them, healing justice work has become a core part of many organizing groups (Ginwright, 2010). Health and well-being outcomes have therefore received a good amount of attention in the youth organizing literature (Ginwright, 2015; Ortega-Williams et al., 2020; Rosen et al., 2018). For youth from marginalized communities, healing from oppression and trauma is a predicate to healthy development and psychological empowerment.

Recent large-scale quantitative studies have confirmed what smaller, qualitative case studies of youth organizing groups have long suggested: Youth organizing supports the development of valuable emotional competencies, including emotional regulation and self-management or the ability to calibrate emotional responses, take positive risks, and persist through setbacks (Flores,

2020; Watts et al., 2018). In her study of nearly 1,400 youth organizers, Terriquez (2017) found that 84 percent of respondents credited youth organizing with helping them learn to take better care of their emotional well-being.

Research is also clear that youth organizing helps members develop strong feelings of political efficacy (Delgado & Staples, 2008; Kirshner, 2015; Lewis-Charp et al., 2003; Nicholas & Eastmann-Mueller, 2020; Shah, 2011) or belief in their capacity to contribute to collective change efforts (Gambone et al., 2006; Ginwright & Cammarota, 2006; Kirshner, 2015; Moya, 2017). These developmental outcomes are strong signifiers of psychological empowerment. In her study comparing youth organizers to a matched set of peers in more traditional youth development programs, Flores (2020) found that youth organizers developed a significantly greater sense of "contribution" than their peers. Defined as a "young person's ability to make a difference" (Flores, 2020, p. 22), contribution can be compared to notions of sociopolitical control, which entails not only feelings of policy control but also a sense of leadership competence (Zimmerman & Zahniser, 1991). Numerous studies demonstrate that youth develop leadership skills through their involvement in organizing (Christens & Dolan, 2011; Constanza-Chock et al., 2016; Lewis-Charp et al., 2003; Ortega-Williams et al., 2020). Indeed, creating a generation of leaders poised to transform society is part of the underlying theory of change espoused by many youth organizing groups.

Behavioral

Youth organizing has been theorized as an opportunity structure that catalyzes sociopolitical development (Christens & Kirshner, 2011). A key indicator of such development is critical sociopolitical action, or efforts to bring about more just and equitable communities and institutions (Watts & Flanagan, 2007). Researchers have found that as they engage in organizing, youth form strong commitments to taking action (Gambone et al., 2006; Ginwright & Cammarota, 2006; Kirshner, 2015; Moya, 2017; Rogers et al., 2012; Shah, 2011), reflecting the behavioral dimension of psychological empowerment. Studies of youth organizing alumni have revealed that these commitments persist after many years, translating into professional choices as well as civic and political engagement in adulthood (Conner, 2011; Mira, 2013; Nicholas et al., 2019). Compared to a general population, youth organizing alumni were significantly more likely to belong to a political or community-based organization, to have assumed a leadership role in these organizations, to volunteer, to have worked on an issue affecting their community, to have engaged in a protest or rally, and to have registered to vote (Rogers & Terriquez, 2013). Consistent with the notion of a leadership pipeline, these behavioral channels of psychological empowerment feed into ever-larger flows of community power.

Cognitive

If critical sociopolitical action is one hallmark of sociopolitical development, critical consciousness, or a robust understanding of the way social, political, and economic institutions sustain inequality and injustice, is another. A large body of work has demonstrated how youth organizers develop a critical orientation, critical awareness, or critical consciousness through organizing (Christens & Dolan, 2011; Conner, 2014; Curnow et al., 2019; Gambone et al., 2006; Moya, 2017; Nicholas & Eastmann-Mueller, 2020; Quinn & Nguyen, 2017; Watts & Flanagan, 2007). Christens et al. (2016) have explicated the conceptual linkages between critical consciousness and psychological empowerment.

Civic knowledge and skills represent another set of learning outcomes that have been well documented by scholars of youth organizing. Civic knowledge includes an understanding of formal politics and schemas for social change (Rogers et al., 2012), while civic skills encompass research skills (e.g., the ability to gather, analyze, and report data), systems-thinking and social analysis skills, public speaking skills, and strategic planning skills (Christens & Dolan, 2011; Delgado & Staples, 2008; Kirshner, 2015; Terriquez et al., 2020). Cultivated in the context of collective political action campaigns, these enhanced skills and understandings reflect the cognitive dimension of psychological empowerment.

Relational

Because relational organizing – member recruitment, relationship-building, mentoring new leaders – is integral to the core work of community organizing, it is not surprising that psychological empowerment processes in youth organizing would involve a relational component. Through organizing, youth develop strong horizontal peer-to-peer relationships (Terriquez et al., 2020) as well as the ability to collaborate productively with other communities (Quinn & Nguyen, 2017). Constanza-Chock et al. (2016) find that through engagement in media-making, youth organizers forge "lasting bonds, intergenerational connections, and community ties" (p. 7). Other work has shown how youth organizers strengthen their social networks and social capital through this work (Baker-Doyle, 2016; Rosen et al., 2018; Yee, 2016). These findings are particularly noteworthy in light of research that shows that youth enter organizing contexts with lower levels of initial social capital than matched peers in other youth development programs (Flores, 2020). As they build relationships within and across youth organizing groups, youth organizers deepen their interpersonal skills, including empathy, listening skills, and the ability to bridge differences (Christens & Dolan, 2011; Flores, 2020; Lewis-Charp et al., 2003; Warren et al., 2008), becoming more empowered change agents and leaders in the process.

Community Power

Theorists have proposed different approaches to conceptualize and empirically measure power at the local or community level. One of the most useful comes from Christens (2019), who, drawing on Lukes (1974), identifies three different dimensions of community power: situational, institutional, and systemic. The situational dimension directs attention to who wins and who loses in public contests over issues. The institutional dimension focuses on which issues are brought to the fore in public debate and which are not. The systemic dimension, meanwhile, concerns how ideology and public opinion are shaped. Mapping findings from the extant literature on youth organizing to this framework helps illuminate the variety of ways in which youth organizers have built community power over the last three decades, during a time of entrenched neoliberalism and ongoing state violence against Black and Brown youth. Although less research on youth organizing has focused on community power than on psychological empowerment processes and outcomes, evidence exists to suggest that youth organizing can build civic capacity to press for and achieve justice-oriented change at the local level.

Situational

An important indicator of the situational dimension of community power is broad participation, both in youth organizing groups and in the collective actions they organize. Mass mobilizations of youth have occurred sporadically over the past three decades and have become particularly visible since 2018, as youth have taken to the streets to demand gun violence prevention, climate action, and racial justice. Certainly, not all of the young people who participated in the youth-led movements of 2018–2020 were members of youth organizing groups, but youth organizing groups were well poised to organize and leverage these collective actions for policy change.

For example, after the killing of George Floyd sparked national protests for police accountability and abolition, several school districts across the country moved to sever their ties with police departments. In many of the places where these changes occurred, youth organizers had been laying the groundwork for years, educating district leaders and the general public about the mechanics and effects of the school-to-prison pipeline, pressing for change, and proposing alternative investments, such as #counselorsnotcops (Warren, 2021). Although the situational dimension of community power draws attention to visible "wins," such as severed police contracts, it obscures the time it takes for groups to mount and sustain pressure campaigns on decision-makers as well as the vigilance required after changes are announced to ensure adequate follow-through. Nonetheless, documenting the wins is a critical step in demonstrating the community power that youth organizing groups have amassed.

In their analysis of the victories reported by youth organizing groups between 2010 and 2012, Braxton et al. (2013) found that wins spanned education justice, immigrant rights, environmental justice, food justice, and health domains. Slightly more than half (57 percent) of the victories were scored at the community level, while 21 percent occurred at the state level, and one victory was reported at the federal level: Deferred Action for Childhood Arrivals (DACA), which immigrant rights organizers had been working towards, in the form of the Dream Act, since 2000.

Across studies of youth organizing, three kinds of wins have emerged as salient: positive wins, negative wins, and putative or symbolic wins. Although a particular campaign may culminate in all three types of win, the distinctions are useful for empirical purposes.

Positive wins are those that introduce a new idea or involve a new allocation of public funds to areas youth organizers have identified as worthy of investment. Examples include winning the implementation of translational and interpretation services in all Human Service agencies in Rhode Island, the opening of an affordable fresh fruit and vegetable market in Brooklyn, NY, and new curricular mandates, such as a required course in "racial and social justice," which youth organizers were able to secure in one California school district (Braxton et al., 2013). Commitments from city or district leaders to fund new programs for youth is another example of the type of positive wins youth organizers have been able to achieve (Christens & Dolan, 2011; Warren & Mapp, 2011). For instance, youth organizers in Long Beach, Los Angeles, Boston, and Philadelphia were able to secure significant funding for the implementation of Wellness Centers, Health Resource Centers, or Student Success Centers in their high schools (Braxton et al., 2013; Conner et al., 2013).

Negative wins occur when groups successfully block an unwanted policy proposal from passing or repeal or substantially rewrite harmful existing legislation. Negative wins can be seen in youth organizers' successful thwarting of efforts to privatize or permanently shutter schools (Braxton et al., 2013; Conner et al., 2013), expand juvenile hall (Kwon, 2013), cut public vouchers that provide free transportation to and from school (Moore, 2011), and gentrify their neighborhoods (Abad, 2021; Delgado & Staples, 2008). In Illinois, youth organizers led and won a campaign to shut down a series of coal plants across the state (Braxton et al., 2013). Campaigns to dismantle the school-to-prison pipeline have also resulted in significant victories, including revoked zero-tolerance policies and rewritten student codes of conduct (Fernandez et al., 2016; Warren, 2018).

A policy change is not the only form of win that youth organizers can attain during publicly visible contests over issues. Youth organizers achieve putative or symbolic wins when they successfully discredit a policymaker or expose the flawed logic in a policymaker's proposal. Through public testimony or confrontations with policymakers, youth can begin to erode or chip away at the political power that officials hold (Rosen & Conner, 2021). The youth's power in these moments represents both the situational and systemic dimensions of power, as they not only win the moment of the contest (situational) but also shape public understanding and interpretation of the issue (systemic). When youth organizers from Youth vs Apocalypse confronted Senator Dianne Feinstein in her office about the Green New Deal, Feinstein's response, steeped in adultism, was to dismiss the youth by saying, "I know what I'm doing," implying that they did not, and instructing one of them to run for senate herself so "you can do it your way." The Senator observed that she had recently been reelected by a plurality of voters and that the young people in her office were not among those who had voted for her (because they were too young to do so). During the nearly fifteen-minute interaction, Feinstein moved between dismissing the youth, patronizing them, and attempting to conciliate them by offering one an internship. The viral video of the contest, which has been viewed more than 15.5 million times, represents a symbolic victory for the youth organizers in that their moral power prevailed over Feinstein's entrenched political power, even stimulating a parody sketch of the Senator on *Saturday Night Live*. The video ignited what Sunrise Movement organizers, drawing on the work of Saul Alinsky, call "a moment of the whirlwind" (Engler & Engler, 2016, p. 54), when new attention is driven to a cause and hearts and minds in the broader public shift.

Institutional

The institutional dimension of youth organizers' power can be seen in how they help shape the agenda or highlight issues of concern. Youth organizers use three main approaches to agenda-setting: creating a moment of conflict that compels a response; working cooperatively with policymakers on specific proposals; and participating in conversations with decision-makers before the agenda is fully determined.

Youth organizers use public testimony or direct action, in concert with media strategy, to elevate issues for public debate that might otherwise go unnoticed by adult decision-makers. Often by drawing public attention to the problems they face, youth organizers force the hands of decision-makers, who may appear negligent or callous if they fail to respond in a timely fashion. Oakes and Rogers (2006) recount how youth organizers with Californians for Justice planned an event at a district headquarters, to which they invited the media. At the event, they unveiled photos they had taken of dirty and inoperable school bathrooms, lacking in paper towels, soap, toilet paper, and, in some cases, functional stall doors. The district responded swiftly by increasing custodial staff, passing policies that required daily restroom checks to ensure restrooms were clean and fully stocked, and inviting the health department to perform random inspections. Youth organizers' powerful, often emotional testimony about matters ranging from school overcrowding, outdated or insufficient textbooks, and mold or vermin in classrooms to hazardous waste sites and displacement due to gentrification have the potential to attract media attention and public outcry, building pressure on policymakers to remedy the problems youth have exposed (Abad, 2021; Gallay et al., 2016).

While youth organizers know how to strike an adversarial posture when agitating for change, they also know how to work cooperatively with decision-makers to advance shared priorities (Su, 2009). In Chicago, during the summer of 2020, a group of youth organizers, united under the hashtag #CopsOutCPS, worked with members of the City Council to draft a #FreePoliceSchools ordinance (Garcia, 2020). Similarly, AYPAL's data dis-aggregation campaign involved working closely with a school board member who authorized their resolution.

In addition to working directly with adult allies or champions who possess institutional or political power, youth organizing groups may help shape the agenda by meeting with policymakers to express their concerns and share ideas. Fifty-seven percent of youth organizing groups in 2020 reported that they regularly scheduled meetings with policymakers as part of their cam-paigns (Valladares et al., 2021). Becoming known and establishing a reputa-tion as engaged stakeholders can lead to invitations to collaborate on initiatives. For example, in Denver, scholars found that Padres y Jovénes Unidos' successful campaign to redesign a once-struggling school helped youth and adult allies "have an organized voice in educational decisions while district officials invite them to participate in creating and implementing pol-icies, like the district's new restorative justice discipline code" (Warren & Mapp, 2011, p. 262). More recently, over one month before President Biden announced his first series of executive actions related to the "gun violence public health epidemic," the White House invited fourteen youth organizers from groups such as GoodKids MadCity, Youth Over Guns, and March For Our Lives to a virtual discussion on community violence prevention. The readout of the meeting reported that "participants shared their perspectives around the intersectionality of gun violence, how to craft successful community-based violence interventions, and the importance of survivor-led and victim-centered policymaking in the community violence prevention space" (The White House, 2021). The fact that these groups were given a seat at the table is a testament to the organizational power they have built and evidence of the institutional dimension of their community power.

Systemic

The systemic dimension of community power is the most difficult to document empirically, as it can be hard to tie changes in public opinion directly to youth organizing groups' efforts; however, the prevalence of the counternarrating or *testimonio* strategy in youth organizing suggests that these groups often work to "flip the script" and disrupt mainstream understandings of them, the policies that affect them, and the institutions that shape their lives (Conner & Rosen, 2016). At a national level, youth organizers in the immigrant rights struggle have been particularly adept at reframing undocumented youth from illegal immigrants or aliens to DREAMERs, innocents with limitless potential (Terriquez, 2015). Negron-Gonzalez (2016) argues that through acts of civil disobedience immigrant youth organizers have further leveraged the DREAMER frame to shape the national debate on belonging, deservingness, and "illegality," laying the groundwork for the Obama administration to pass DACA. At the community level, youth organizers have likewise advanced alternative frames to challenge prevailing ideology. For example, to counter a media narrative that characterized Black youth as violent, rampaging thugs, the Philadelphia Student Union staged an action in a public square in a wealthy area of the city, in which they arranged themselves in a tight, organized formation and recited a call-and-response chant that drew attention to their identities as leaders, thinkers, innovators, organizers, artists, and as a youth movement (Conner & Rosen, 2015). Their action was designed to shift public perceptions of Black youth.

In addition to shaping public perceptions of them, youth organizers work to change prevailing policy narratives. For example, Sinclair-Lewis and Rodriguez (2021) identify various frames used by youth organizers with the Black Swan Academy (BSA) in Washington, DC, as they attempted to influence public interpretations of the policy changes needed following the murder of George Floyd. In their public-facing political education work and their pressure campaigns on elected officials, they cast the police as a racist institution, called for funds to be invested in youth's needs, and put forward reimagined conceptions of safety. Because of the effectiveness of these frames, Sinclair-Lewis and Rodriguez (2021) argue, the media, elected officials, and other community leaders credited BSA with achieving small-scale policy wins, including the DC State Board of Education passing a resolution for police-free schools, the DC Council voting to change who controls the hiring of police officers in schools, and the creation of a DC Police Reform Commission. The systemic and situational dimensions of their community power, therefore, interacted to bolster one another.

Setting Features That Facilitate Empowerment Processes

There is little doubt that the three core programmatic features identified at the outset of this chapter – developmental supports, political education, and organizing work – redound to the psychological empowerment and community power outcomes described previously. Developmental supports (e.g., healing circles) scaffold affective and relational empowerment outcomes, while political education enhances cognitive empowerment outcomes, particularly the development of critical consciousness and critical thinking skills. Meanwhile, organizing work is instrumental to developing civic knowledge and skills as well as lasting changes in civic commitments and behaviors. Organizing campaigns likewise foster community power, as meetings with policymakers, direct actions, media strategy, and public testimony can help shape the agenda, influence public opinion, and catalyze policy change.

Most of the research on psychological empowerment has focused on the impacts of internal program meetings, workshops, and in-house programming, while most of the work on community power has concentrated on the effects of engaging in visible public actions; however, in effective youth organizing models, these internal and external setting types are inextricably linked. Therefore, isolating the effect of participation in actions relative to planning meetings or listening sessions is impractical. Nonetheless, because organizing groups may emphasize different elements, with some foregrounding internal healing justice work and others focusing more heavily on policy advocacy, future research could examine the differential impacts of these varied approaches.

In addition to the three core programmatic elements or setting types, researchers have identified other signature characteristics of youth organizing that facilitate empowerment processes. Again, the bulk of this research and theorizing focuses on setting features that inure to the benefit of the youth members. Researchers have found that youth organizing offers a potent site for learning because it enables young people to address problems that are directly *relevant* to their lives (Conner, 2014; Rogers et al., 2012; Watts et al., 2018). As they engage with these problems, youth organizers participate in an *experiential learning cycle*, which entails stages of research and preparation, analysis, authentic action or performance, and reflection (Christens & Dolan, 2011; Watts et al., 2018). The *critical orientation* of this cycle and the learning environment in general, with its explicit attention to internal as well as external dynamics of power and privilege, has also often been cited as influential in shaping youth organizers' experiences and outcomes (Nguyen & Quinn, 2018; Rogers et al., 2012; Su, 2009). Finally, scholars have highlighted the unique opportunities that youth organizing groups present for *accelerated, collectivist leadership* (Govan et al., 2015; Rosen, 2019; Rosen & Conner, 2016; Watts et al., 2018) and *authentic, caring relationships* with both adults and other youth (Christens & Kirshner, 2011; Warren & Mapp, 2011; Watts et al., 2018) as distinctive setting features integral to youth organizing groups' success in attracting and retaining members. Researchers have also studied the power-sharing norms and social practices that contribute to a supportive organizational culture, in which all members' contributions are valued and affirmed (Nicholas & Eastmann-Mueller, 2020; Rosen, 2016). Additionally, they have examined how this deep cultural work shapes values, collective identity, and a sense of shared fate among organizational members (Warren & Mapp, 2011).

Because community power cannot exist without psychological empowerment, and vice versa, it seems reasonable to assume that the same setting features discussed previously contribute to community power; however, comparatively little research has examined the mechanics of community empowerment processes in youth organizing and the features of the groups that have proven most adept at setting the agenda, achieving policy victories, and (re)shaping public opinion. From anecdotal evidence, we know that youth organizing groups do not need to be long-standing to earn a seat at the policy table; they do not need to be intergenerational or have adult staff to stage powerful direct actions that create "moments of the whirlwind"; and they do not need to be large in size to score critical policy wins. As discussed subsequently, more research is needed to identify the cross-cutting features of youth organizing groups that are associated with generating and sustaining community power.

Relatedly, more attention could be paid to the broader contextual features that shape how these groups operate. The challenges youth face in contesting neoliberalism have been well elucidated (Conner & Rosen, 2016; Kennelly, 2011; Kwon, 2013), as have the challenges of philanthropic dependency amid funding vicissitudes (Braxton et al., 2013). Case studies of youth organizing campaigns have revealed the opportunities and constraints that arise in a specific community at a specific moment in time to facilitate or stymie a campaign's success. Nonetheless, more comparative and longitudinal research is needed to illuminate how the broader sociopolitical environment, through both its institutions and its prevailing ideology, creates enabling or constraining conditions for youth organizing. Such research could trace the evolution of various youth organizing ecosystems over time as they impact the political will and capacity of a community to take youth's concerns seriously.

Application

The research reviewed in the previous sections raises implications for youth activists, funders, and youth organizing groups.

Generation Z has been heralded for its unusually high levels of critical social attunement and political engagement. Some research has linked this generation's unprecedented voter turnout levels in the US in 2018 and 2020 to the surge in youth activism since 2018 (CIRCLE, 2021). While the March For Our Lives marches in 2018, the climate strikes that preceded the UN General Assembly in 2019, and the racial justice protests in the summer of 2020 were among the largest youth mobilizations in history, the narrative of the surge in youth activism elides the work that youth organizing groups have been doing for decades, often in these same issue areas.

As more young people turn to activism, create nonprofit organizations (i.e., 501(c)(3)s), and/or adopt the term "organizer," there are a few lessons to be gleaned from the youth organizing groups that have been engaged in these struggles for many years. The most sacrosanct of the first principles of youth organizing is that the leadership of youth with marginalized identities matters.

Youth organizing rests on the premise that those most directly impacted must take the lead in naming the problems, designing the solutions, and mounting collective action to demand change. This is not to say that there is no role for White, middle-class and upper-middle-class youth in the struggle; solidarity across groups with different social identities is critical. However, before attempting to launch a new activist-oriented nonprofit organization, aspiring youth activists might want to survey the local youth organizing landscape, identify those groups that have already been working in this space, particularly in their local community, and lift up or take cues from their leadership, adopting for themselves roles as allies or accomplices.

Similarly, funders should prioritize investing in groups that center the leadership of low-income youth of color, LGBTQ+ youth, and immigrant or refugee youth, while recognizing that these groups might not always have the internal capacity to generate competitive proposals. Writing a grant proposal or funders' report is not always the best use of organizers' time. In the past few years, funding for youth activism, advocacy, and electoral work has significantly increased, but these resources have not always reached the groups that are led by youth most impacted by racism and poverty. A lack of access to funding has caused some attrition in the youth organizing field. Furthermore, the funding that does reach youth organizing groups does not always provide them with runways long enough to step back from the frantic pace of organizing to engage in deep visioning or strategic planning work. Funders interested in building the transformative leadership of youth subjugated by oppression must recognize that the work of psychological and community empowerment takes time as well as sufficient resources.

Finally, organizers must be prepared to confront numerous tensions as they undertake this work. The dynamic interplay between psychological and community empowerment means that youth organizing groups must be attentive to balancing both processes. Some of the youth activist groups that have recently burst onto the scene have been so determined to build social power and achieve policy change that they have been slower to develop robust developmental supports and political education programming. Focusing solely on mobilizing the base and policy advocacy, to the exclusion of youth development, healing, and consciousness raising, may lead to a cycle of burnout, atrophying membership, and failed or flawed policy recommendations that are not grounded in a deep critical social analysis. Although in theory "youth leadership development and community development through youth organizing [are] two sides of the same coin," real tensions between the two imperatives can play out in practice (Christens & Dolan, 2011, p. 542). Therefore, it is critical, as Christens and Dolan (2011) note, to enact "cycles of organizing and leadership development" (p. 542) in ways that do not privilege one goal above the other but rather understand both processes as interdependent and equally deserving of investments of time, energy, and material resources (Warren & Mapp, 2011).

As they seek to build durable power, youth organizers must be prepared to address an array of additional challenges. One constant threat is adultism, which can manifest as a "double-edged sword" by which youth are discounted either as the pawns of adults and crisis actors or as idealistic dilettantes who do not fully understand the complexities of institutional change (Conner, 2016). Relatedly, the role and responsibilities of adults in youth-led groups can sometimes give rise to tension or controversy, especially when there is disagreement about how to proceed with a campaign. How to support older youth as they age through and eventually out of youth-led organizations presents yet another difficulty, as pathways to other intergenerational or adult organizing groups may not be well articulated. Furthermore, staff can be strained as they try to organize *and* meet the complex needs of youth living in under-resourced communities beset by a host of structural problems. In many cases, staff become the main points of contact for youth experiencing homelessness, food insecurity, abuse, threats of deportation, or generational trauma. For these reasons, leadership development for staff has been identified as a pressing need in the field (Valladares et al., 2021).

Future Research

At least four productive avenues for future research emerge from this review. First, as the field has grown and the population of youth organizers has further diversified in age, geographic region, gender, and along other identity markers, it becomes possible to explore questions about whether all youth benefit equally from organizing or whether youth with certain identities are more likely to benefit than others. Although case studies have elucidated the transformational impact of organizing on distinct groups of youth organizers, such as LGBTQ+, undocumented, and immigrant and refugee youth, variance in empowerment outcomes has yet to be examined, especially in large-scale survey data.

The field would likewise benefit from empirical evidence that examines the shared setting features that distinguish groups that have been particularly effective in building and sustaining community power across issues areas and geographic contexts. How do different youth organizing approaches and group features, like their size or structure, relate to the scope and scale of the victories they achieve situationally, institutionally, and systemically? Because much of the literature to date has focused on building the field and providing evidence of the effectiveness of youth organizing, less attention has been paid to questions of why some groups fold, why some groups gain traction while others do not, and how groups manage internal conflicts and even crises of leadership. In order to draw more robust implications for practice, it is important to begin surfacing the lessons from negative cases and comparing the design elements of groups that are more and less successful in building a base, carrying out campaigns, and accomplishing the individual, institutional, and systemic changes they seek.

Third, the rise in alliances and coalitions, especially at the national level, presents a rich opportunity to study how learning happens within these networks and shapes the development of community power. How does collaboration with groups from different states or communities influence local organizing work and community empowerment processes? How do groups borrow from and build on one another's efforts? Under what conditions do coalitions of groups with various levels of community power collectively achieve broader social power?

Finally, more research is needed on youth organizing in non-Western (Tivaringe & Kirshner, 2021) and nondemocratic contexts. By examining youth organizing in geopolitical settings other than Canada and the US, researchers will build a broader, but more contextually attuned understanding of the processes, challenges, and transformative possibilities of youth organizing. What factors facilitate and impede youth organizing in various political economies, and what role does civil society play in supporting youth organizing? How have social media and digital organizing contributed to transnational movements, and how have these movements been enacted by local organizers on the ground in different communities around the world? These and related questions offer promising lines for future inquiry.

A popular chant at youth-led protests asserts, "Ain't no power like the power of youth, cuz the power of youth don't quit." Over the last two and half decades, the youth organizing field appears to have borne out this prophetic vision. Their power is demonstrable, worthy of further empirical study, and as needed now as ever to address the pressing social issues of our day.

References

Abad, M. (2021). *Movement vulnerability and the quotidian dimensions of youth organizing*. Paper delivered at the annual meeting of the American Educational Research Association.

AEJ. (n.d.). *Alliance for Educational Justice* [Facebook page]. www.facebook.com/4EdJustice/

AYPAL. (2021, April 14). *Power to the youth*. www.aypal.org/

Baker-Doyle, K. (2016). Studying sociopolitical development through social network theory. In J. Conner & S. Rosen (Eds.), *Contemporary youth activism: Advancing social justice in the United States* (pp. 163–184). Praeger.

Braxton, E. (2016). Youth leadership for social justice: Past and present. In J. Conner & S. Rosen (Eds.), *Contemporary youth activism: Advancing social justice in the United States* (pp. 25–38). Praeger.

Braxton, E., Buford, W., & Marasigan, L. (2013). *National field scan*. Funders' Collaborative on Youth Organizing.

Christens, B. D. (2019). *Community power and empowerment*. Oxford University Press.

Christens, B. D., & Dolan, T. (2011). Interweaving youth development, community development, and social change through youth organizing. *Youth & Society*, *43*, 528–548.

Christens, B. D., & Kirshner, B. (2011). Taking stock of youth organizing: An interdisciplinary perspective. *New Directions for Child and Adolescent Development*, 134, 27–41.

Christens, B. D., Winn, L. T., & Duke, A. M. (2016). Empowerment and critical consciousness: A conceptual cross-fertilization. *Adolescent Research Review*, *1*(1), 15–27.

CIRCLE. (2021). *Youth activism and community change*. CIRCLE. https://circle.tufts.edu/our-research/youth-activism-and-community-change

Conner, J. (2011). Youth organizers as young adults: Their commitments and contributions. *Journal of Research on Adolescence*, *21*(4), 923–942.

Conner, J. (2014). Lessons that last: Former youth organizers' reflections on what and how they learned. *Journal of the Learning Sciences*, *23*, 447–484.

Conner, J. (2016). Pawns or power players? The grounds on which adults dismiss or defend youth organizers. *Journal of Youth Studies*, *19*(3), 403–420.

Conner, J., & Rosen, S. M. (2015). Zombies, truants, and flash mobs: How youth organizers respond to and shape youth policy. In J. Conner, R. Ebby-Rosin, & A. S. Brown (Eds.), *Student voice in American educational policy* (pp. 203–220). Teachers College Record.

Conner, J., & Rosen, S. M. (Eds.). (2016). *Contemporary youth activism: Advancing social justice in the United States*. Praeger.

Conner, J., Zaino, K., & Scarola, E. (2013). "Very powerful voices": The influence of youth organizing on educational policy. *Educational Policy*, *27*, 561–588.

Constanza-Chock, S., Schweidler, C., Basilio, T., McDermott, M., Lo, P., & Ortenbuger, M. (2016). Media in action: A field scan of media & youth organizing in the United States. *Journal of Digital and Media Literacy*, *4*(1–2).

Curnow, J., Davis, A., & Asher, L. (2019). Politicization in process: Developing articles, political concepts, practices, epistemologies, and identities through activist engagement. *American Educational Research Journal*, *56*(3), 716–752.

Delgado, M., & Staples, L. (2008). *Youth-led community organizing: Theory and action*. Oxford University Press.

Engler, M., & Engler, P. (2016). *This is an uprising: How nonviolent revolt is shaping the twenty-first century*. Bold Type Books.

Fernandez, J., Kirshner, B., & Lewis, D. (2016). Strategies for systemic change: Youth community organizing to disrupt the school-to-prison nexus. In J. Conner & S. Rosen (Eds.), *Contemporary youth activism: Advancing social justice in the United States* (pp. 93–112). Praeger.

Flores, K. S. (2020). *Transforming positive youth development: A case for youth organizing*. Funders' Collaborative on Youth Organizing.

Freire, P. (1973). *Education for critical consciousness*. Continuum.

Gallay, E., Lupinacci, J., Sarmiento, C., Flanagan, C., & Lowenstein, E. (2016). Youth environmental stewardship and activism for the environmental commons. In J. Conner & S. M. Rosen (Eds.), *Contemporary youth activism* (pp. 113–132). Praeger.

Gambone, M., Yu, H., Lewis-Charp, H., Sipe, C., & Lacoe, J. (2006). Youth organizing, identity-support, and youth development agencies as avenues for involvement. *Journal of Community Practice, 14*(1), 235–253.

Garcia, K. (2020). *Chicago youth activists for #CopsOutCPS provide answers to questions about police free schools*. The Tribe. https://thetriibe.com/2020/07/chicago-youth-activists-for-cops-out-cps-provide-answers-to-questions-about-police-free-schools/

Ginwright, S. (2010). *Black youth rising: Activism and healing in urban America*. Teachers College Press.

Ginwright, S. (2015). *Hope and healing in urban education: How urban activists and teachers are reclaiming matters of the heart*. Routledge.

Ginwright, S., & Cammarota, J. (2006). Introduction. In S. Ginwright, P. Noguera, & J. Cammarota (Eds.), *Beyond resistance: Youth activism and community change* (pp. xii–xxii). Routledge.

Govan, R. H., Fernandez, J. S., Lewis, D. G., & Kirshner, B. (2015). International perspectives on youth leadership development through community organizing. *New Directions for Student Leadership, 2015*(148), 87–99.

Kennelly, J. (2011). *Citizen youth: Culture, activism, and agency in a neoliberal era*. Palgrave McMillan.

Kirshner, B. (2015). *Youth activism in an era of education inequity*. New York University Press.

Kwon, S. A. (2013). *Uncivil youth: Race, activism, and affirmative governmentality*. Duke University Press.

Lee, J. F. (2019). *We passed and implemented a historic data resolution* [Video]. Vimeo. https://vimeo.com/313232421

Lewis-Charp, H., Yu, H., Soukamneuth, S., & Lacoe, J. (2003). *Extending the reach of youth development through civic activism: Outcomes of the youth leadership development initiative*. Social Policy Research Associates.

Light, J. (2015). Putting our conversation in context: Youth, old media and political participation 1800–1971. In D. Allen & J. Light (Eds.), *From voice to influence: Understanding citizenship in the digital age* (pp. 19–33). University of Chicago Press.

Listen, Inc. (2003). *An emerging model for working with youth* (Occasional Papers Series on Youth Organizing No. 1). Funders' Collaborative on Youth Organizing.

Lukes, S. (1974). *Power: A radical view*. Macmillan.

McAdam, D. (1988). *Freedom summer*. Oxford University Press.

Mira, M. (2013). Pushing the boundaries: What youth organizers at Boston's Hyde Square Task Force have to teach us about civic engagement. *Democracy and Education, 21*, 1–13.

Moore, J. (2011). No transportation, no education! *Voices in Urban Education, 30*, 5–12.

Moya, J. (2017). Examining how youth take on critical civic identities in classrooms and youth organizing spaces. *Critical Questions in Education, 8*(4), 457–475.

Negron-Gonzalez, G. (2016). Unlawful entry: Civil disobedience and the undocumented youth movement. In J. Conner & S. Rosen (Eds.), *Contemporary youth activism: Advancing social justice in the United States* (pp. 271–288). Praeger.

Nicholas, C., & Eastmann-Mueller, H. (2020). Supporting critical social analysis: Empowerment processes in youth organizing. *Urban Review*, *52*, 708–729.

Nicholas, C., Eastmann-Mueller, H., & Barbich, N. (2019). Empowering change agents: Youth organizing groups as sites for sociopolitical development. *American Journal of Community Psychology*, *63*, 46–60.

Nguyen, C., & Quinn, R. (2018) "We share similar struggles": How a Vietnamese immigrant youth organizing program shapes participants' critical consciousness of interracial tension, *Race Ethnicity and Education*, *21*(5), 626–642.

Nygreen, K., Kwon, S., & Sánchez, P. (2006). Urban youth building community: Social change and participatory research in schools, homes, and community-based organizations. *Journal of Community Practice*, *14*(1–2), 107–123.

Oakes, J., & Rogers, J. (with Lipton, M.). (2006). *Learning power: Organizing for education and justice*. Teachers College Press.

Ortega-Williams, A., Wernick, L., DeBower, J., & Braithwaite, B. (2020). Finding relief in action: The intersection of youth-led community organizing and mental health in Brooklyn, New York City. *Youth & Society*, *52*(4), 618–638.

Quinn, R., & Nguyen, C. (2017). Immigrant youth organizing as civic preparation. *American Educational Research Journal*, *54*(5), 972–1005.

Rogers, J., & Terriquez, V. (2013). *Learning to lead: The impact of youth organizing and the educational and civic trajectories of low-income youth*. Institute for Democracy, Education, and Access.

Rogers, J., & Terriquez, V. (2016). "It shaped who I am as a person": Youth organizing and the educational and civic trajectories of low-income youth. In J. Conner & S. Rosen (Eds.), *Contemporary youth activism: Advancing social justice in the United States* (pp. 141–161). Praeger.

Rogers, J., Mediratta, K., & Shah, S. (2012). Building power, learning democracy: Youth organizing as a site of civic development. *Review of Research in Education*, *36*, 43–66.

Rosen, M., Gennari, A., & Mandic, C. (2018). *Youth-led organizing: A strategy for healing and child welfare systems change*. Foster Youth in Action.

Rosen, S. (2016). Identity performance and collectivist leadership in the Philadelphia Student Union. *International Journal of Leadership in Education: Theory and Practice*, *19*(2), 224–240.

Rosen, S. (2019). So much of my very soul: How youth organizers' identity projects pave agentive pathways for civic engagement *American Educational Research Journal*, *56*(1), 237–243.

Rosen, S., & Conner, J. (2016). Conceptualizing youth activists' leadership: A multidimensional framework. In J. Conner & S. Rosen (Eds.), *Contemporary youth activism: Advancing social justice in the United States* (pp. 59–78). Praeger.

Rosen, S., & Conner, J. (2021). Negotiating power: How youth organizers recast the debate about school reform. *Journal of Community Psychology*, *49*(8), 3017–3032.

Shah, S. (2011). *Building transformative youth leadership: Data on the impacts of youth organizing*. Funders' Collaborative on Youth Organizing.

Shah, S., Buford, W., & Braxton, E. (2018). *Transforming youth and communities: New findings on the impact of youth organizing*. Funders' Collaborative on Youth Organizing.

Sinclair-Lewis, K., & Rodriguez, S. (2021). *"Love us, don't harm us!" Youth organizing for racial justice and police-free schools in Washington DC*. Paper delivered at the annual meeting of the American Educational Research Association.

Su, C. (2009). *Streetwise for booksmarts: Grassroots organizing and education reform in the Bronx*. Cornell University Press.

Terriquez, V. (2015). Training young activists: Grassroots organizing and youths' civic and political trajectories. *Sociological Perspectives, 58*(2), 223–242.

Terriquez, V. (2017). *Building healthy communities through youth leadership*. USC Program for Environmental and Regional Equity.

Terriquez, V., Villegas, R., Villalobos, R, & Xu, J. (2020). The political socialization of Latinx youth in a conservative political context. *Journal of Applied Developmental Psychology, 70*, 101188.

The White House (2021, February 18). *Readout of the White House's meeting with young community violence prevention advocates*. The White House. www.whitehouse.gov/briefing-room/statements-releases/2021/02/18/readout-of-the-white-houses-meeting-with-young-community-violence-prevention-advocates/?emci=080d7f9e-4075-eb11-9889-00155d43c992&emdi=0b0d7f9e-4075-eb11-9889-00155d43c992&ceid=1549635

Tivaringe, T., & Kirshner, B. (2021). Learning to claim power in a contentious public sphere: A study of youth movement formation in South Africa. *Journal of the Learning Sciences, 30*, 125–150.

Valladares, S., Valladares, M. R., Garcia, M., Baca, K., Kirshner, B., Terriquez, V., Sanchez, J., & Kroehle, K. (2021). *2020 Field Scan*. Funders' Collaborative on Youth Organizing.

Warren, M. (2018). *"Lift us up, don't push us out!" Voices from the frontlines of the education justice movement*. Beacon.

Warren, M. (2021). Remarks delivered at the business meeting of the Grassroots Youth and Community Organizing special interest group of the American Educational Research Association.

Warren, M. & Kupscznk, L. (2016). The emergence of a youth justice movement in the United States. In J. Conner & S. Rosen (Eds.), *Contemporary youth activism: Advancing social justice in the United States* (pp. 39–58). Praeger.

Warren, M., Mapp, K., & The Community Organizing and School Reform Project. (2011). *A match on dry grass: Community organizing as a catalyst for school reform*. Oxford University Press.

Warren, M., Mira, M., & Nikundiwe, T. (2008). Youth organizing: From youth development to school reform. *New Directions for Youth Development, 117*, 27–42.

Watts, R., & Flanagan, C. (2007). Pushing the envelope on youth civic engagement: A developmental and liberation psychology perspective. *Journal of Community Psychology, 35*, 1–14.

Watts, R., Kirshner, B., Govan, R., & Fernandez, J. (2018, August 11). *Powerful youth, powerful communities: An international study of youth organizing*. research2action.net. www.research2action.net/wp-content/uploads/2019/03/

2018-Powerful-Youth-Powerful-Communities-Final-Research-Report-4dist .pdf

Werner, E. (2009). *In pursuit of liberty: Coming of age in the American Revolution.* Potomac Books.

Yee, M. (2016). "We have the power to make change": The struggle of Asian immigrant youth against school violence. In J. Conner & S. Rosen (Eds.), *Contemporary youth activism: Advancing social justice in the United States* (pp. 289–310). Praeger.

Zimmerman, M., & Zahniser, J. (1991). Refinements of sphere-specific measures of perceived control: Development of a sociopolitical control scale. *Journal of Community Psychology, 19*(2), 189–204.

2 Youth Activism in Postapartheid South Africa

Tafadzwa Tivaringe and Ben Kirshner

Introduction

Confronted with dwindling opportunities to access higher education, South African students took to the streets and staged massive protests that led to the national shutdown of higher education institutions in 2015–2016. Popularly known as the #FeesMustFall movement, the protests highlighted the plight that many students faced in accessing higher education and catalyzed the adoption of a nationwide "Fee-Free" policy, which enabled students from low-income households to access tertiary education (Bosch, 2017; Ndlovu, 2017a; Tivaringe, 2019). Political action led by South Africa's youth is not new. South Africa's struggle against injustice has seen various cohorts of youth emerge as key agents of social change since the early parts of the twentieth century. Until the #FeesMustFall movement, however, scholars characterized post-1994 youth as disengaged from politics and less committed to democratic values than prior generations (e.g., Deegan, 2002; Mattes, 2012; Posel, 2013).

The marked contrast between representations of postapartheid youth and their actions during the #FeesMustFall protests point to a gap in prevailing knowledge about contemporary youth political action in South Africa. How did a cohort that is "disengaged" and "not committed to democracy" (Bosch, 2017; Deegan, 2002; Ndlovu, 2017a) end up organizing a powerful national movement that led to a swift policy change? In this chapter, we seek to address this gap by examining the ways in which youth have been and continue to be active political agents within South African communities. We argue that, while electoral returns and survey evidence may suggest disengagement from political action, youth continue to exercise collective agency and enact social change in several arenas. To this end, we begin by mapping historical shifts in youth activism in South Africa and offer two noteworthy cases of contemporary youth organizing for social change. Thereafter, we review studies of contemporary youth activism in South Africa to identify psychological empowerment processes and discuss the features of these settings that support youth agency and political engagement and the evidence of shifts in community power. In conclusion, we consider implications for youth movements and scholarship about youth activism.

Shifting Modes of Youth Activism

During the protracted struggle against apartheid that led to the historic shifts in governing power in the early 1990s, youth activism in South Africa tended to manifest within the contexts of and alongside organized mass liberation movements, such as the African National Congress (ANC), the Pan-African Congress, and the Black Consciousness Movement (Taylor, 1997). Within national liberation movements, youth chapters emerged in the early 1940s as a way to tap into young people's energy and facilitate organizational renewal through providing a pipeline of future leaders. It is not surprising, therefore, that notable leaders of the ANC, such as Oliver Tambo and Nelson Mandela, were erstwhile figureheads in the movement's youth chapter, the African National Congress Youth League (ANCYL; Posel, 2013). By the 1960s, students at Black (African, Colored, and Indian) tertiary institutions established Student Representative Councils and religion-based structures that had ties to but were partly autonomous from national liberation movements. These organizing groups quickly morphed into national structures, like the University Christian Movement and the South Africa Student Organization, which drew on Black consciousness philosophy to mobilize youth to challenge the White supremacy architecture that characterized the apartheid regime (Taylor, 1997).

At the end of apartheid and the election of Nelson Mandela in 1994, mass liberation movements transformed into political parties tasked with the governing of the postapartheid democratic state. This shift was accompanied by a corresponding shift in priorities, political terrain, and forms of political participation (Dawson & Sinwell, 2012). In the absence of the apartheid state, mass community support for the parties was no longer automatic or guaranteed. Even more, because national liberation was linked to overcoming conditions of structural poverty born out of disenfranchisement by the apartheid architecture, the masses expected the political parties to transform their material conditions (Taylor, 1997). Within this political terrain, in which erstwhile liberation movements had transitioned into nascent political parties that needed to compete for the mandate to govern, youth party chapters (locally known as youth wings) became elevated as the primary mode of youth activism. Indeed, youth chapters became a viable option to monitor the "parental authority" of liberation heroes and presented a lucrative pathway to attaining the gains of freedom (Posel, 2013, p. 63). Inversely, during this time immediately following the ANC's assumption of power, alternative spaces for political activism became less attractive and community-led forms of youth political participation dwindled (Everatt, 2002; Posel, 2013).

By the early 2000s, however, a new kind of community-based youth organizing began to surface. Spurred on by frustrations about the lack of transformation in the material conditions of a majority non-White population and the ineffectiveness of youth wing chapters in checking the power of political elites, young people began to step outside the structure of party politics and focus on what we call *issue-based activism*. Within this phenomenon of grassroots, issue-based activism, we highlight two cases: Equal Education's Minimum Norms and Standards campaign and the Fallists movements. We focus on these cases because of their major impacts on public awareness and government policy and because they attracted and engaged large numbers of young people. We do not think of these campaigns as "representative"; they are in fact unique for their size and political impact relative to other expressions of youth activism and civic engagement in contemporary South Africa. We choose these two because they embodied two distinct approaches to issue-based activism within the South African context.

Case Examples

The Evolution of a Social Movement Organization: The Case of Equal Education

Equal Education (EE) was formed in 2008 by students at the University of Cape Town who were dissatisfied with the lack of transformation in South Africa's education system. In consultation with established activists, educators, and community members, these youth sought to (1) highlight how inequities in the education system disproportionately affected students in low-income neighborhoods locally known as *townships* and rural areas and (2) use research and activism to advance equality in and improve the quality of the country's education system (Brockman, 2016; Tivaringe, 2018). This social change agenda is currently advanced by approximately 7,000 activists – mostly composed of Black high school and post-high school youth – who lead a movement of learners, parents, and teachers. To date, EE has waged many youth-led campaigns that have catalyzed notable shifts toward advancing equity in the country's school system, thereby offering an illustrative model for how contemporary youth cohorts are exercising political agency and shaping community conditions.

We were part of a research team that conducted an ethnographic study of EE between 2014 and 2017 (Watts et al., 2018). Data from this project point to the salience of three key features of EE's organizing model in catalyzing youth action and enhancing young people's capacity to shape South Africa's policy agenda. First, EE's current organizational structure is characterized by a democratically elected National Council that enables members to shape the movement's agenda to a degree that would not be possible within a typical nonprofit setting (Kirshner et al., 2021). Adopted in 2012, this organizational structure shifted strategy and leadership accountability from the purview of staff to a vote by members. Consequently, young high school scholars from various EE youth chapters across the country have the necessary institutional infrastructure to learn, debate, and shape the movement's mission to advance equity in the country's education system. Given that one of EE's campaigns,

Minimum Norms and Standards, was recently adopted as a national policy after extensive organizing, it is clear that the movement's organizational structure enables young people to not only identify problems within their schools but also become architects of policy solutions to endemic inequities (Tivaringe & Kirshner, 2021).

Second, EE's organizing model is simultaneously youth-centric and intergenerational (Tivaringe & Kirshner, 2021). As some scholars have pointed out (e.g., Bosch, 2017; Everatt, 2002; Mattes, 2012; Ndlovu, 2017a), youth political participation has been diminishing in recent years, especially due to charges that youth lack the struggle credentials necessary to make meaningful political contributions. For this reason, advancing social change within this context necessitates a complex balance between asserting young people's role as agents of change and honoring the role of older generations in fighting unjust systems. After all, the older generations fought gallantly to end the apartheid system. Within this context, EE has managed to mobilize youth and adults as comrades-in-arms by, among other things, adopting an explicitly intergenerational mantra ("Every Generation Has Its Struggle"), instituting various recurring political education events (e.g., teach-ins and lectures) where youth and adults learn about and from each other, and embracing a distributed conception of expertise that recognizes the inherent value that each generation brings to the fight against educational injustice. Furthermore, because such mobilization efforts center young people, EE's organizing model is (re)configuring the country's political landscape by positioning young people as capable and legitimate political agents.

The third and last key feature of EE's organizing model is its nonpartisan commitment to (re)establishing ties between young people and various established political stakeholders, such as churches, trade unions, and other civic groups. As discussed earlier, the period immediately following the end of apartheid was characterized by a growing move toward party political engagement via youth chapters and a corresponding retreat of other community-led forms of participation. Suffice to say, these trends led to a relative decline in the number of young people participating in politics (Bosch, 2017; Mattes, 2012; Ndlovu, 2017a). Against this backdrop, EE's approach adopts an explicitly nonpartisan agenda that frames educational injustice as a community issue that requires multistakeholder solutions. During our data collection period, we witnessed numerous events in which EE brought together leaders from churches, trade unions, and other civic groups to learn with and from its youth members. While youth reported multiple developmental and political benefits that emerged from such engagements, we were particularly struck by the way in which ties with established political stakeholders were instrumental during campaigns. We observed that EE's national campaigns were successful in large part because they tapped into a wide array of community voices. Protests associated with such campaigns tended to feature prominent trade unionists and other civic leaders, teachers and education leaders, and elders representing various community institutions like churches and *stokvels* (informal financial savings clubs). Such extensive participation was instrumental in casting light on educational injustice and lent credence to the legitimacy and role of youth as agents of political change in contemporary South Africa (Kirshner et al., 2021; Tivaringe & Kirshner, 2021).

Decentralized Youth Activism: The Case of the Fallists Movements

Youth organizing in postapartheid South Africa has also been characterized by the emergence of new forms of decentralized issue-based student activism seeking to engender transformation in the country's higher education system. Unlike the case of EE, which relates to youth who are members of a registered civic group, this kind of activism is typified by open participation in a fluid and collective social change agenda shaped by university students. Notable examples were #RhodesMustFall (which sought to remove colonial symbols on university campuses, such as British imperialist Cecil John Rhodes' statue), #PatriachyMustFall (which sought to end patriarchy as a social structure), and #FeesMustFall (which sought to remove financial barriers to accessing higher education). As research on these movements shows, they are unified by a shared contemporary decolonial agenda that emerged and intensified between 2015 and 2017 (Bosch, 2017; Griffiths, 2019; Ndlovu, 2017a; Nyamnjoh, 2016). In the sections that follow, we refer collectively to these "#_MustFall" actions as Fallists movements and identify three key features of this mode of organizing (Luescher, 2016; Ramaru, 2017).

One key defining feature of Fallists movements is that they feature a decentralized organizational structure. As accounts by both scholars and activists show, the direction of these movements tended to be collectively shaped by participating university students rather than an established central decision-making body (Bosch, 2017; Griffiths, 2019; Xaba, 2017). In their description of the features of #RhodesMustFall, for example, Ndelu et al. (2017) note that because the movement manifested across all twenty-six of South Africa's diverse university campuses, organizing across these locales "meant a much more decentralized structure, with each campus' members providing direction to its protests in specific and singular ways" (p. 2). Indeed, similar patterns were evident in #FeesMustFall. As Strong (2018) observes, "the range of political actions that make up #FeesMustFall have taken on different ideological and organizational distinctions within and across campuses" (p. 275). These accounts depict Fallists movements as typified by multiple nodes with a broad spectrum of demands that, at times, were misaligned (Bosch, 2017; Ndelu et al., 2017; Ndlovu, 2017b; Samanga, 2016; Strong, 2018). The decentralized character of these Fallists movements is also captured by how they self-identified. For instance, the University of Cape Town (UCT) chapter of #RhodeMustFall described its mission as "an independent collective of students, workers and staff who have come together to end institutionalized racism and patriarchy at UCT" (UCT RMF, n.d.). Despite being decentralized, power hierarchies and designated leadership did emerge. There is research that shows that some individuals, such as Kanyisa Ntombini, Nompendulo Mkatshwa, and Chulani Maxwele, became prominent in shaping the direction of the movement (Hodes, 2017; Pillay, 2016; Xaba, 2017). Nevertheless, we are arguing that the direction of these movements was shaped collectively through persuasion and contestation in ways unlike a structure that features a central decision-making body.

Second, Fallists movements were typified by a fluid social change agenda characterized by an iterative goal-setting process. Whereas participation in civic groups typically entails working within a set social change agenda that is defined by the organization's founding goals and sometimes funder priorities, Fallists movements generally involved (re)creating goals in response to input from the collective. This meant that specific goals around advancing decolonization were correspondingly contested and dynamic. As Luescher (2016, p. 22) notes, shifts in social change goals within the #RhodesMustFall movement led to "mushrooming" of "derivative" movements, such as #BlackStudentsMovement, #PatriarchyMustFall, #ReformPukke, #TheTransCollective, and #TuksUprising. Similarly, Ndelu et al. (2017) observe that "contested space within #RhodesMustFall at UCT" led to the formation of groups like #TheTransCollective and #PatriarchyMustFall that centered Black feminist, queer, and trans approaches to decolonization. This approach democratized goal-setting and surfaced intersectional forms of organizing to unprecedented degrees. Writing on the difference between Fallists movements and their historical antecedents, Ndelu et al. (2017, p. 3) note that "they [Fallists] have, unlike earlier student struggles, brought to the fore a clear and powerful feminist challenge to the cisheteronormative patriarchy – in broader society as well as within the student movements." As we reflect on such successes, we believe that the dynamic goal-setting process that characterized Fallists movements catalyzed previously marginalized sections of youth to political action because it facilitated an intersectional social change agenda that was inclusive, reflective, and learning-oriented (Ndlovu, 2017b; Xaba, 2017).

A third feature of Fallists movements was that they were characterized by savvy use of the Internet, particularly social media, as an organizing space. Although university grounds were incubating spaces – and therefore played a significant place-based role in the identity of these movements – the Internet was a key tool for organizing and movement-building (Hodes, 2017; Luescher et al., 2017). The "truly innovative dimension" of the Fallists movements, Luescher (2016, p. 23) writes, "is the extent to which student activists and sympathizers took to social media and the internet." Even more, in her analysis of Twitter (now known as X) engagements linked to the #RhodesMustFall movement, Bosch (2017) notes that

> Twitter certainly created a space for the voicing of black pain in ways that we do not see in any other medium or social space, mediated or otherwise. Listening is evidenced by the fact that users often acknowledged others'

arguments, or modified their own positions, in relation to the posts of others and their online conversations with those users. In this instance, there was certainly a plurality of voices and opinions, the kind of racial and political diversity that is seldom seen in other offline spaces.   (p. 229)

Twitter and other online forums were not only spaces for discussion and debate but also functioned as tools for organizing events and mass action. Major protest marches, such as the Walk to Parliament in Cape Town and the Walk to the Union Buildings (the official seat of the South African government, which also houses the Presidential offices in Pretoria), brought out large masses of people; these were publicized almost entirely on social media. Such mass events were critical to drawing public attention to the movement and, in the case of #FeesMustFall, creating public pressure on the government to respond to demands. Also, opportunities to connect with campus chapters and local organizers were facilitated by widespread use of social media to publicize events and chapter activities.

Both as a space for education and as a tool to mobilize students, the Internet catalyzed youth political action. Indeed, in a context in which declining youth participation in politics was linked to a mainstream media that is disconnected and "irrelevant to the lives of young people" (Ndlovu, 2017a, p. 29), Internet-based mediums such as Facebook and Twitter revitalized youth political engagement and enabled young people to shape the public sphere and political discourse to a degree that had been infeasible in the years leading up to the Fallists movements.

Summary

Equal Education's campaign for Minimum Norms and Standards and the Fallists movements demonstrate two highly impactful mobilizations of contemporary South African youth. They illustrate the passion, persistence, and power that young people have brought to social and political life in the past decade. In the next section, we step back from these two cases to review a broader literature on youth empowerment in South Africa, addressing psychological processes, setting-level processes, and shifts in community power. Throughout, we continue to draw on evidence from EE and Fallists movements while also drawing on studies of other expressions of youth empowerment and activism.

Review of Research

Psychological Empowerment Processes

Research on psychological empowerment processes among youth activists in South Africa shows a mix of findings that are not reducible to a single story. On the one hand, there is a good deal of survey research, much of it with national samples, that suggests disenchantment with the government and skepticism about the promise of democracy (Bosch, 2013). Mattes (2012), for example, concluded from nationally representative survey research that young people (called the Born Frees because they were born after 1994) were less committed to democracy than prior generations. He attributes this disenchantment in large part to, "frustrating encounters with the political process, victimization by corrupt officials, and enduring levels of unemployment and poverty" (p. 151). Similarly, Bosch (2013) administered a survey in 2012 in four of South Africa's largest provinces and found that youth (ages fifteen to thirty) "are generally disinterested in and mistrustful of political institutions, political parties; and that there are low levels of trust in the legal system, the police and the parliament" (p. 125).

Although there is ample evidence of disenchantment with formal processes of governance, there is also an emerging literature on the psychological dimensions of issue-based youth activism. Scholars have studied activism in several contexts, including nongovernmental organizations (NGOs), universities, informal settlements, and the Internet. These vary in their levels of intentionality as learning environments, the issues motivating youth participation, and the evidence of psychological empowerment. Given the small number of studies and varying methods across them, we do not make broad claims about "outcomes" of activism but instead organize our review in terms of distinct settings and the kinds of experiences reported in the literature.

Youth NGOs as Settings for Agency, Leadership, and Community Connectedness

Nongovernmental organizations are designed environments that typically rely on philanthropic or donor funding and are motivated by specific goals and ideological assumptions about youth development and civic engagement. Buire and Staeheli (2017), for example, conducted a fascinating study of the ecosystem of civic NGOs, including interviews with over forty NGO leaders, observations of NGO meetings, and participatory research projects with six youth organizations, which arrived at two broad conclusions. First, they found some evidence consistent with the critique that NGOs operate more as instruments of a neoliberal capitalist state than as inculcators of grassroots democracy. Echoing analyses of the "nonprofit industrial complex" in the US (Kwon, 2013) and youth development discourses internationally (Sukarieh & Tannock, 2014), the authors write that the pedagogies of citizenship in civic NGOs prioritize individualism, entrepreneurialism, and personal empowerment rather than political analysis and collective action.

At the same time, although the curricula and programming were geared toward more individualist and apolitical leadership development, in practice, young people often reappropriated these experiences and skills toward political ends. Buire and Staeheli (2017) found that many young people who participated in civic NGOs were also active in more disruptive or radical politics, notably the

#RhodesMustFall and #FeesMustFall mobilizations, even if the actions were "at odds with the messaging of their organizations" (p. 186)

> Indeed, the tools that are taught – tools such as the use of media, of fun and humor, of seemingly small acts, in addition to research skills and communication – may enable activists to become more effective in radical action; at the very least, they have been successful in helping some activists draw attention to their demands.   (p. 187)

The transformative possibilities of civic NGOs can also be observed in the learning experiences of youth in EE, which started as an NGO but transformed into a social movement organization with elected leadership and membership chapters across the country. In their study of EE, Watts et al. (2018) reported youth leadership and civic engagement outcomes in three areas: "critical thinking and analysis," such as understanding the historical roots of contemporary struggles; "community leadership and action," such as how to engage in organized social justice campaigns; and "social and emotional learning," including the ability to manage one's emotions while working with others. This combination of general leadership skills with specific experiences of activism and voice, including civil disobedience and public marches, offers an illustration of the powerful combination of general youth development skills with more critical political analysis (see also Govan et al., 2015).

University Student Movements as Sites of Decolonial Praxis

Much of the research about Fallists activism has focused on the formation of the movements and the political impacts they had on university campuses and higher education policy. Here we synthesize the kinds of psychological outcomes that researchers observed or documented among young people in these movements. One of the few studies designed specifically to assess these psychological outcomes was carried out by Wawrzynski and Naik (2021), who surveyed 1,238 students at a predominately Black comprehensive university in South Africa's Eastern Cape, which was host to intensive protests on its campus from 2014 to 2017. The survey, administered in 2017, examined demographic factors associated with participation and perceived social, emotional, and civic "noncognitive" outcomes associated with participation. Students who identified as Black were the most likely to be active politically relative to other racial and ethnic identity groups. Students who participated in political activism organizations, community engagement activities, or both reported significantly higher civic and social and emotional learning outcomes. A key finding was also that those who lived on campus were far more likely to be active – and to experience the associated psychological benefits – than those commuting to school.

Other research about empowerment processes in the Fallists movements has focused on psychological outcomes connected to their decolonial agenda.

Several scholars, for example, analyzed evidence of critical consciousness and related forms of decolonial praxis that emerged in the university protests (Canham, 2018; Luescher et al., 2017; Mahale & Matete, 2022). Canham argues that young people from poor and working-class backgrounds who attended university were bound to organize and resist oppression because of the combination of their life experiences and exposure to critical perspectives and frameworks at university. Mahali and Matete focused specifically on the experiences of "black womxn" in the Fallists movements. In their analysis of weblog posts, radio interviews, newspaper articles, videos, social media posts, and news clips, they identify tensions that emerged when some male Fallists leaders expressed an antifeminist and exclusionary stance toward women. In contrast to historic movements that deprioritized issues of gender and sexuality, they argue that this campus-based activism differed in its insistence by many on an intersectional approach that centered queer and transgender Black women: "black womxn are saying 'no more!' at full volume. No longer will they support black patriarchs who do not acknowledge their struggles" (Mahale & Matete, 2022, p. 142).

Student activism on campuses between 2015 and 2017 also energized conversations and articulations about the meaning of Black consciousness and racial identity. Stuurman (2018) carried out and studied dialogues to understand how Black students at Nelson Mandela University thought about contemporary student activism in relation to race and transformation. Stuurman argues that student activism on campus "should be viewed within the context of the larger black freedom struggles taking place in South Africa" (p. 6) and argues that students were fundamentally calling for greater representation in decision-making and greater control of the circumstances that affect their lives, including the production of knowledge in universities. Stuurman argues that the dialogues represented calls for greater solidarity and group consciousness among Black students.

In summary, the documentation of student participation in the Fallists movements suggests that student participation was linked to a host of critical psychological processes that advanced a decolonial and liberatory agenda. Spaces for dialogue, discussion, and disagreement spurred greater awareness of intersectional identities and critical consciousness. Furthermore, the concerted organizing efforts in these movements suggest that these psychological processes also facilitated collective resistance to inequity. Although we do not make strong empirical claims about psychological outcomes given the lack of systematic psychological research, we nonetheless see evidence that new forms of political consciousness were fundamental to student organizing on campuses.

Psychological Empowerment in Local Militant Protests

Studies have also documented youth participation in localized, sometimes violent protests in informal settlements, typically focused on grievances related to corruption and failures of local governance to provide basic services (Banjo, 2013; Dawson, 2014; Lodge & Mottiar, 2016). How these activities are described is contested. Popular media and elected officials often refer to young people as hooligans or thugs who are being manipulated by community leaders to take violent action, such as fighting with police or destroying property (Canham, 2018). In contrast, scholars frame this more as grassroots "street corner" activism based on material grievances that speaks to young people's desire for rights, dignity, and representation. Canham (2018, p. 23) cites a young person who was quoted in a sociological study by Von Holdt et al. (2021):

> It is an insult to my intelligence for people to think we are marching because someone has bought us liquor. We are not mindless. People, especially you who are educated, think we are marching because we are bored. We are dealing with real issues here. Like today we don't have electricity. We have not had water for a whole week.

Canham argues that community psychology has not accurately theorized this protest activity, particularly the complex mix of rational material grievance and affective rage, which he argues is fundamentally part of a broader decolonial project.

Similar themes were reported by Dawson (2014), who completed an ethnographic study of youth who participated in the 2011 protests in Zandspruit informal settlement motivated by frustrations with local government corruption and failures to deliver basic services. The author argues that two key constructs help explain the motivations and experiences of youth protesters: the politics of waiting and envy. Waiting refers to the experience of being old enough to set out on one's own but unable to achieve key milestones of employment or housing due to structural barriers in the economy. At the collective level, this notion of waiting "accounts for the impatience and discontent owing to the mismatch between the expectations placed on the state and the absent, inadequate and uneven delivery of services and houses" (p. 869). Young people in these spaces, often working under the leadership of older community members, used public spaces to congregate, discuss grievances, and track events. Youth argued that their only way to get heard or seen was through violence or striking:

> If we just sit, this problem is not going to be fixed. We have to fight until we get what we want . . . nowadays, people cannot just listen by talking, you have to fight until they get an understanding, this is the only way.   (p. 877)

Dawson concludes that young people acquired a sense of agency and political consciousness through protests, even if this emerging awareness was not tightly coupled with a broader political movement or ideological frame.

Psychological Empowerment on the Internet

A growing arena of scholarship globally focuses on the Internet as a setting for politicization and activism (Ito et al., 2015; Jenkins et al., 2016; Middaugh &

Kirshner, 2014; Mutsvairo, 2016). Regarding the South African context, research on Internet-mediated activism takes two forms. One, discussed in the case study of the Fallists movements discussed earlier, pertains to the role of the Internet as a vehicle for organizing in-person actions and protests. Luescher et al. (2017), for example, call this an "internet-age networked student movement" (p. 231). Platforms such as Facebook and Twitter enabled students to learn from each other, find connections across physical distances, and experience the sense of purpose that is associated with social movements (Bosch, 2017). Twitter was a tool not merely for coordinating mass actions but also for influencing mainstream media narratives and educating followers, particularly in terms of challenging dominant narratives about the colonial past and producing new ones, or what Bosch calls "a collective project of resistance to normative memory production" (Bosch, 2017, p. 222). Luescher et al. (2017) hasten to conclude, however, that the relationship between place-based, face-to-face actions and virtual community-building and organizing was a dynamic, mutually dependent one deserving of further research to conceptualize this interdependence.

There is a second type of research about psychological empowerment on the Internet that is less evidently connected to place-based organizing or political action. Bosch's (2013) study of Facebook use among South African youth argues that the platform provided a space for "subactivism" (p. 121) at the margins of the public sphere. Specifically, her study analyzed data from ten focus groups with Cape Town youth and a national survey of 956 youth. Bosch's findings are consistent with other studies showing low levels of trust in police, parliament, and the legal system. At the same time, she reports plentiful evidence of identity-based activism, particularly around marginalized sexual identities, and she argues that this experience of finding, creating, and sustaining communities is a form of empowerment and agency that is "an important dimension of citizenship and democracy" (p. 128).

Features of Settings That Foster Youth Empowerment

Understanding youth activism in South Africa calls for historicized, situated, and decolonial perspectives. In addition to historical awareness of the prominent roles played by Black youth in bringing down the apartheid system in the late twentieth century, there are also important historical gradations between 1994 and 2021 that call for attention, including the emergence of social media in the 2000s and the mass Fallists movements starting in 2015.

We organized our review of empowerment processes in terms of differences among varied contexts for youth engagement and activism, from the pedagogies of citizenship advanced in civic-oriented NGOs to the militant protests found among unemployed youth in townships and informal settlements. Each setting offered slightly different aims, ideologies, and opportunity structures. Civic NGOs are guided by an overt curriculum, often influenced by international philanthropy, which emphasizes skills and virtues such as leadership, entrepreneurialism, social and emotional competence, and community participation. As presented by Buire and Staeheli (2017), these settings, although shifting civic action from the political sphere to the sphere of personal development and interpersonal teamwork, cultivate skills and competencies that some young people repurpose in creative and political ways.

University-based movements to decolonize higher education and make education accessible for all, on the other hand, were characterized by their decentralized character, their appeal to masses across the country, and their more radical character – anchored in critiques of White supremacy, patriarchy, and capitalism. That said, we do not want to overstate the difference between the two. This is because while the Fallists movements demonstrated more spontaneity and emergent qualities, they also were anchored in learning and development for participants. Discussions and debates, sometimes taking place over Twitter, challenged young people of all backgrounds to understand South Africa's colonial past, the persistence of White Eurocentric hegemony in universities, and the significance of intersectional identity as a basis for organizing and transformation.

The studies of youth participation in protest movements in poor communities, often lacking stable housing and basic services, suggest a different "setting" for activism. Here, young people's experience of unemployment and lack of access to higher education, in tandem with grievances against local party officials, provided an urgent material basis for protest. Studies of youth experiences, often drawing on ethnographic methods for which informal conversation and trust were key, report that demonstrations, which were sometimes violent, represented a last resort for young people excluded from political decision-making and facing insurmountable obstacles to stable employment. These were contexts in which young people demonstrated collective organizing and agency to change their material conditions. It remains to be seen whether local formations such as these take on the qualities of social movements guided by ideology and broad political goals or remain limited to more local and disparate foci.

Finally, the Internet and related social media platforms offer their own distinct setting for youth civic engagement and activism. Theorizing the Internet as a setting deserves its own chapter, if not a whole book, as illustrated by the rapidly growing literature on this topic (Bosch, 2013, 2017; Hussen, 2018; Kangere et al., 2017; Zuckerman, 2014). Our review suggests multiple ways in which the Internet functioned as a setting for organizing and activism. Facebook groups and platforms where affinity groups come together to exchange ideas offer opportunities for identity, agency, and belonging that may be especially critical for those experiencing isolation or marginalization in their everyday physical lives (Ito et al., 2013). These are spaces where young people can challenge heteronormativity and assert intersectional identities, themselves being forms of activism in the cultural realm (Bosch, 2013).

For activist formations with aspirations to change policy or build movements, the Internet functions very differently. Equal Education, as discussed earlier, was primarily a face-to-face organizing group that formed chapters in multiple South African provinces. Members there used social media to amplify messages and draw attention to their educational justice campaigns. For the Fallists movements, because of their more decentralized character and focus on decolonial praxis, the Internet played a more central role both for organizing emergent mass demonstrations and engaging in debates about the direction and principles of the struggle. This diversity of functions provided by the Internet, whether in isolation from the physical world or as a vehicle for action in it, suggests that it has so pervaded everyday life that it cannot be thought of as a homogeneous setting, but instead it is as variegated as social life itself.

Although these contexts shape different pathways of civic engagement, there is also a common underlying thread that explains much of the activism by Black youth in the postapartheid period: disenchantment and frustration with the government's uneven and slow delivery on promises of the antiapartheid struggle. Similar to research about marginalized youth in the US, activism is in part fueled by the contradiction between the promise of education and economic mobility and the lived realities of inequity and structural racism (Kirshner, 2015). This contradiction is deepened by a second one giving rise to decolonial praxis. Many young people argue that although the seat of government shifted in 1994, South Africa's most powerful institutions – higher education among them – have not been liberated from their origins in White supremacist rule. This interest in decolonization is not limited to educated elites; Canham (2018) argues, "The wave of sometimes violent protests raging through South Africa has brought decolonization into the common lexicon and consciousness of ordinary people" (p. 320).

Shifts in Community Power

Until now, we have reviewed the evidence of psychological empowerment processes and the features of the settings associated with them. What about the impacts of youth activism on shifts in power relations and societal change? How might we understand the impacts of youth activism if we shift the unit of analysis from individual activists and their proximal settings to broader changes in power relations?

Conceptualizing community power is thorny and can go in many directions depending on one's theoretical framework. For the purposes of this summary, we draw on a theory of community power that differentiates between *situational*, *institutional*, and *normative* power (Christens, 2019; Healey, 2015, Lukes, 1974). Summarized briefly, *situational* power, also called the first face of power, refers to a group's power to organize people for direct political action. This kind of power determines who wins and loses in visible public conflicts, often over specific kinds of policy demands made to local governments.

Institutional power, also called the second face of power, represents the power to set the agenda for what kinds of policies will be discussed or ignored. Less visible than situational power, institutional power happens behind the scenes as groups develop alliances and coalitions that give them greater influence over decision-making agendas. Unlike situational power, institutional power is more enduring and far-reaching.

The third face of power refers to *normative* power, or the power to shape common sense. This power to shape what is "normal" and taken for granted as true – the ideological terrain – is arguably the most influential type of power. An example might be the contest over whether education, health care, or the environment are public goods or private commodities. The first and second faces of power are almost superfluous if people's common sense tells them they do not have rights to quality education or affordable health care. How organizers frame issues, including moral narratives about rights and justice and attributions about causes and solutions, creates new normative contexts for ordinary people to make demands on government.

Situational Power

Christens (2019) articulates a relationship between psychological, institutional, and community dimensions of empowerment in correspondence to the three faces of power. Specifically, psychological processes associated with situational power tend to develop into three main forms of community empowerment: broad participation, collective efficacy, and leadership and social power. The challenge, though, is that empirical research that documents how psychological processes are interrelated with community empowerment remains scant, partly because these causal connections are difficult to capture. Yet, as we reflect on the youth organizing evidence from South Africa, we see promising evidence that can illuminate the connections between psychological experiences of situational power and broader community shifts.

We observed the strongest evidence of these connections during our ethnographic research with EE, in which we followed cohorts of youth across a three-year period (Watts et al., 2018). Our interview data are replete with stories of youth who joined the movement seeking a space to "just hang out" as peripheral participants but soon became full participants who were at the forefront of (1) canvassing community support for the movement's numerous campaigns, (2) organizing protests aimed at challenging injustice at their schools, and (3) leading marches that led to the adoption of a national policy meant to improve the infrastructure of the country's school system. Because we employed a longitudinal design, we were afforded a unique opportunity to map individual psychological development born out of organizing efforts onto corresponding observations about shifts in community power. Equal Education youth reported how, for example, encounters with provincial and national government officials during protests emboldened their belief in their own capacity as political actors. Simultaneously, these instances of youth-led direct political action also reconfigured public imagination of the role of youth in postapartheid South Africa. Youth could no longer be merely perceived as "Born Frees" who lacked legitimate credentials to shape the policy agenda. Instead, by winning public policy battles with government officials, they were solidifying their status as capable political actors and pushing back against sociocultural structures that had long constrained their agency as social actors.

The small but growing body of research on Fallists movements in South Africa also corroborates the link between individual psychological development and shifts in community power. As researchers note, Fallists movements started as localized protests that sought to shift specific aspects of campus life. Yet, given that participation in these organizing efforts involved intentionally seeking deeper knowledge about addressing injustices in robust ways, the students developed deeper awareness of inequities and the connections between seemingly localized struggles. Indeed, this heightened awareness facilitated a transition from campus-specific frames (e.g., Open Stellenbosch) toward more collective framing (e.g., #FeesMustFall, #PatriachyMustFall), which enabled broader participation and collective action. For us, the trajectory of these developments (i.e., the progression from psychological development within disparate campuses to national collective action) attests to one important route through which situational power can facilitate broader community shifts.

Institutional Power

Regarding institutional power, Christens (2019) posits that psychological processes linked to institutional power tend to be associated with three main forms of community empowerment: mobilization structures/networks, problem assessment capacity, and power mapping/institutional alignment. Here, too, data from youth organizing in South Africa are illuminating. When EE youth realized that the lack of basic infrastructure in their schools was a common phenomenon that typified schooling in low-income and rural areas, they reconfigured their organizing strategy to match the nationwide scale of the challenge. This shift required them to move beyond school-based models of enacting change, such as confronting the principal, to stepping into the public sphere and developing alliances necessary to exert greater influence over shaping the country's policy agenda. During this period, we observed how EE youth pursued extensive coalition-building efforts that involved facilitating, collaborating, mobilizing, and bridging ties with multiple policy stakeholders, such as teacher unions, community leaders, taxi unions, and other NGOs. Importantly, because alliance-building within this context involved managing differences between stakeholders with dissimilar primary interests, EE youth developed relationship-building skills that enhanced their political power. In turn, exercising adroit leadership that tapped into the legitimacy of established social institutions like unions, churches, and civic society groups enabled the movement to make school infrastructure a key part of the country's policy agenda. Indeed, these broad mobilizing networks were integral in compelling the government to ultimately adopt EE's infrastructure campaign, Minimum Norms and Standards, into a national policy.

Comparable evidence on the association between institutional power and the ecology of empowerment can also be found in research on the Fallists movements. Organizing that happened at twenty-six separate university campuses had to step outside of campus-specific frames to grow into a formidable and coherent organizing movement that ultimately unified multiple stakeholders, including university faculty and staff, unions, community leaders, and civic groups. Like the EE case, such a transition entailed power mapping and extensive strategic coalition-building efforts that involved facilitating, collaborating, mobilizing, and bridging ties with multiple policy stakeholders across different institutions. Ultimately, these broad networks were integral in catapulting transformation, particularly in higher education, to become the country's foremost policy agenda.

Normative Power

Contemporary youth activism in South Africa has arguably had its greatest impact in the terrain of worldviews and ideologies, particularly in the Fallists movements. Here we can draw a connection between the kinds of psychological empowerment reported by activists and shifts in the broader ideological terrain. Although challenging to document systematically, articles and reporting about #RhodesMustFall and #FeesMustFall show how a generation of students became galvanized around an agenda to decolonize the university and make it more accessible for all. Efforts to denaturalize university policies and practices rooted in European colonialism, from its statues to its curriculums, challenged what people took to be normal or common sense. Reports describe students being galvanized by new frameworks for making sense of their social identities and asserting their right to belong at the university. This decolonial praxis followed many directions, not just as a critique of Eurocentrism or the persistence of colonial mindsets, but also in terms of new conceptions of gender and sexual identity.

These movements, in tandem with examples from the service-delivery protests and EE's campaigns for education infrastructure, suggest a shift in *normative power* related to the legitimacy of the Born Free generation as a political force. Whereas media narratives about youth in the late stages of apartheid and the immediate decade after the ANC's assumption of power tended to dismiss youth as apolitical and nihilistic, an upsurge in youth activism since 2010 has challenged normative assumptions about who has the legitimate right to lead and govern South Africa. Equal Education's motto, "Every Generation Has Its Struggle," captured that effort to frame youth activism as a movement that continued the moral authority of the antiapartheid movement even if its issues were uniquely contemporary (Kirshner et al., 2021).

Implications

This review of contemporary youth activism contains several lessons that apply not just to actors in South Africa but also to activists and scholars worldwide. We organize our reflections in terms of two categories: youth movements and scholars.

Lessons for Activist Movements

In reviewing studies about the Fallists movements, it is clear that, despite being highly decentralized and not situated in a particular organization or NGO, they reflected a strong dedication to learning and education. In addition to the mass demonstrations that received the greatest media attention, actions in the Fallists movements included teach-ins, workshops, and debates (Mahali & Matete, 2022). There was a great deal of learning and consciousness-raising within protest spaces. Social media, using hashtags such as #RhodesMustFall, #FeesMustFall, and #PatriarchyMustFall, was also host to educational threads and arguments about South Africa's history and present (Bosch, 2017). Young people engaged in passionate exchanges of ideas – sometimes leading to internal tensions and disagreements – about the nature of the decolonial project.

This effort to make space for learning and study can also be seen in the work of EE, as described earlier. Youth groups, which met face to face throughout different parts of the country, were guided by a curriculum that emphasized a mix of skill development, political analysis, and historical understanding. Youth "equalizers" learned about the history of antiapartheid struggle and drew connections between that past and their contemporary struggle for equal education (Tivaringe & Kirshner, 2021).

These two examples suggest a commitment to learning and study that may be of interest to youth organizers globally. Both cases show the ways in which a strong generational consciousness among the young was anchored in an appreciation for the long struggles of prior generations. This historical awareness may have helped youth activists forge alliances with members of older generations and carve out a space for their own contemporary struggle credentials.

This commitment to historical understanding was accompanied, at least in the case of the Fallists movements, with intensive deliberations about what it would mean to decolonize the university. Not surprisingly, there was no single narrative about the decolonial project that emerged in this movement, which may itself represent a productive lesson for other movements. Marginalized groups shaped the direction of the movements in ways that were collaborative and democratic. We do not mean to romanticize or paper over real conflicts and tensions that happened among the movements' actors, but openness and disagreement can be seen as signs of healthy and participatory democratic processes.

The strong intergenerational character of both forms of youth organizing, we believe, holds promise for a positive sum approach to enacting social change. Too often, agonistic relations between young people and adults, such as when adults tokenize youth or exclude them from decision-making tables, stand in the way of an effective social change agenda (Warren & Kirshner, 2022). Additionally, some models of organizing – especially from the US – have tended to assume a static generational divide between youth and adults that undermines the potential of youth-led intergenerational organizing (Tivaringe & Kirshner, 2021). Sukarieh and Tannock (2014) write, for example, that limiting activism to an age-based identity can undermine ties to other constituencies, such as organized labor or environmentalists, and weaken movement infrastructure, such as if experienced activists are regularly aging out of their status as youth. Yet, what we see in both cases discussed earlier is that youth decided that to effect transformation in the education system required building and managing coalitions with key stakeholders in politics, such as teacher unions, university staff, civic leaders, and other community organizing groups. Of course, establishing such alliances came with its own challenges. On balance, however, it is undeniable that the impacts of these organizing efforts were elevated precisely because they were intergenerational.

Implications for Future Research

Just as young people in South Africa in the 1970s and 1980s focused international attention on human rights struggles, recent movement-building by contemporary youth suggests that South African youth are, yet again, at the vanguard of global youth struggles, indicating the need for research attention from scholars in South Africa and around the world. We can put to rest narrative of young people as disengaged from and apathetic about civil society. True, many youth may be disenchanted with partisan electoral politics, but their restlessness for change and desire for access to education and employment fuel varied forms of issue-based engagement. Studies of the forms that these take in South Africa suggest several implications for scholars around the world.

The patient movement-building of EE, for example, offers a compelling model of organizational transformation, as this group transformed from its origins as an NGO into a geographically disparate movement governed by leadership elected by members, including leaders who were once members themselves. As we have called for in a recent publication (Tivaringe & Kirshner, 2021), the EE case bears important lessons for research on youth activism because of the way EE shifted from a bounded learning environment to a contested public sphere. Whereas studies about youth civic engagement often stay internal to the settings that cultivate such forms of engagement, we need more work that looks at what happens when young people step out into an agonistic public sphere where assumptions of benevolence toward youth do not hold.

During an era of renewed attention to decolonial agendas throughout the world, student activism to transform and decolonize the universities in South Africa also suggests important agendas for research. What is the relationship, for example, between activism focused on symbols (e.g., tearing down statues of Cecil Rhodes) and activism focused on policy change (e.g., eliminating student fees)? The apparently symbiotic or interdependent relationship between this combination in the Fallists movements – of psychological consciousness-raising on the one hand and tangible policy goals on the other – raises long-standing questions about their causal relationship in social change. Under what conditions do spaces for asserting identity and challenging cultural narratives lead to political projects? Moreover, as suggested by the expansion of #FeesMustFall to an agenda that included rights for campus workers, how can student movements escape campus politics to adopt broader agendas alongside labor rights and women's rights?

These questions, taken up in productive ways by South African scholars although by no means exhausted, call for comparative international research as well. After all, it is not just in South Africa that young people are showing disenchantment with conventional party politics and instead choosing grass-roots issue-based activism to express their interests and build solidarities (Jenkins et al., 2016; Strong, 2018; Sukarieh & Tannock, 2014; Warren & Kirshner, 2022). At the same time, the division between issue-based activism and conventional politics is not a clean one. Although they may not be running parties or electoral campaigns, the youth movements in South Africa had clear policy aims that put them directly into conversations with the government and how it should be held accountable to its citizens. In some places, this distinction is breaking down as organizing groups run candidates for office and think in creative ways about what it means to build political power. More research is needed on the intersections between the kinds of issue-based engagement that young people are demonstrating and how these might translate in creative ways into influence on and participation in formal governance.

We are in a moment of upswing in assertions of voice and power by young generations around the world on issues from climate change to education to human rights. One can see in places such as Chile, Brazil, and South Africa evidence of student movements that ally with labor and environmental movements to assert power and exert influence on the political system (Salinas & Fraser, 2012; Tarlau, 2019). There is also a compelling critique that certain forms of NGO-mediated and donor-funded activism advance a neoliberal political agenda, such as when calls for youth agency and empowerment either do not question or actively endorse the shrinking public sector and privatization of public goods (Sukarieh & Tannock, 2014). Comparative international research that attends to the differences among geopolitical contexts and illuminates how young organizers open up space for ingenuity and radical leadership will be valuable as the need for human rights, environmental justice, and participatory democracy grows ever more urgent.

References

Ahmed, A. K. (2020). #RhodesMustFall: How a decolonial student movement in the global south inspired epistemic disobedience at the University of Oxford. *African Studies Review, 63*(2), 281–303.

Banjo, N. J. (2013). Youth and service delivery violence in Mpumalanga, South Africa. *Journal of Public Administration, 48*(2), 251–266.

Bosch, T. (2013). Youth, Facebook, and politics in South Africa. *Journal of African Media Studies, 5*(2), 119–130.

Bosch, T. (2017). Twitter activism and youth in South Africa: The case of #RhodesMustFall, *Information, Communication & Society, 20*(2), 221–232.

Brockman, B. (2016). Every generation has its struggle: A brief history of Equal Education (2008–2015). In A. Heffernan & N. Nieftagodien (Eds.), *Students must rise: Youth struggle in South Africa before and beyond Soweto '76* (pp. 168–179). NYU Press.

Buire, C., & Staeheli, L. A. (2017). Contesting the "active" in active citizenship: Youth activism in Cape Town, South Africa. *Space and Polity, 21*(2), 173–190.

Canham, H. (2018). Theorising community rage for decolonial action. *South African Journal of Psychology. 48*(3), 319–330.

Chigudu, S. (2020). Rhodes Must Fall in Oxford: A critical testimony. *Critical African Studies, 12*(3), 302–312.

Christens, B. D. (2019). *Community power and empowerment*. Oxford University Press.

Dawson, H. (2014). Youth politics: Waiting and envy in a South African informal settlement. *Journal of Southern African Studies, 40*(4), 861–882.

Dawson, M. C., & Sinwell, L. (Eds.). (2012). *Contesting transformation: Popular resistance in twenty-first-century South Africa*. Pluto Press.

Deegan, H. (2002). A critical examination of the democratic transition in South Africa: The question of public participation. *Commonwealth and Comparative Politics, 40*(1), 43–60.

Everatt, D. (2002). Marginalisation re-created? Youth in South Africa 1990–2000 and beyond. In B. Trudell, K. King, S. McGrath, & P. Nugent (Eds.), *Africa's young majority*. Centre for African Studies: University of Edinburgh.

Govan, R. H., Fernández, J. S., Lewis, D. G., & Kirshner, B. (2015). International perspectives on youth leadership development through community organizing. *New Directions for Student Leadership*, *148*, 87–99.

Griffiths, D. (2019). #FeesMustFall and the decolonised university in South Africa: Tensions and opportunities in a globalising world. *International Journal of Educational Research*, *94*, 143–149.

Healey, R. (2015). *Organizing for governing power*. Grassroots Policy Project. https:// grassrootspowerproject.org/analysis/organizing-for-governing-power/

Hodes, R. (2017). Questioning "Fees Must Fall." *African Affairs*, *116*(462), 140–150.

Hussen, T. S. (2018). Social media and feminist activism: #RapeMustFall, #NakedProtest and #RUReferenceList movements in South Africa. In T. Shefer, J. Hearn, K. Ratele, & F. Boonzaier (Eds.), *Engaging youth in activism, research and pedagogical praxis: transnational and intersectional perspectives on gender, sex, and race* (pp. 199–214). Routledge.

Ito, M., Gutiérrez, K., Livingstone, S., Penuel, B., Rhodes, J., Salen, K., Schor, J., Sefton-Green, J., & Watkins, S. C. (2013). *Connected learning: An agenda for research and design*. Digital Media and Learning Research Hub.

Ito, M., Soep, E., Kligler-Vilenchik, N., Shresthova, S., Gamber-Thompson, L., & Zimmerman, A. (2015). Learning connected civics: Narratives, practices, infrastructures. *Curriculum Inquiry*, *45*(1), 10–29.

Jenkins, H., Shresthova, S., Gamber-Thompson, L., Kligler-Vilenchik, N., & Zimmerman, A. (2016). *By any media necessary*. NYU Press.

Kangere, M., Kemitare, J., & Michau, L. (2017). Hashtag activism: Popularizing feminist analysis of violence against women in the Horn, East and Southern Africa. *Feminist Media Studies*, *17*(5), 899–902.

Kirshner, B. (2015). *Youth activism in an era of education inequality*. NYU Press.

Kirshner, B., Tivaringe, T., & Fernández, J. S. (2021). "This was 1976 reinvented": The role of framing in the development of a South African youth movement. *Journal of Community Psychology*, *49*(8), 3033–3053.

Kwon, S. A. (2013). *Uncivil youth: Race, activism, and affirmative governmentality*. Duke University Press.

Lodge, T., & Mottiar, S. (2016). Protest in South Africa: Motives and meanings. *Democratization*, *23*(5), 819–837.

Luescher, T. M. (2016). Frantz Fanon and the #MustFall movements in South Africa. *International Higher Education*, (85), 22–24.

Luescher, T. M., Loader, L., & Mugume, T. (2017). #FeesMustFall: An Internet-age student movement in South Africa and the case of the University of the Free State. *Politikon*, *44*(2), 231–245.

Lukes, S. (1974). *Power: A radical view*. Palgrave Macmillan.

Mahali, A., & Matete, N. (2022). #MbokodoLeadUs: The gendered politics of black womxn leading campus-based activism in South Africa's recent university student movements. *Journal of Contemporary African Studies*, *40*(1), 132–146.

Mamdani, M. (1995). *Citizen and subject: Contemporary Africa and the legacy of late colonialism*. Princeton University Press.

Mattes, R. (2012). The "Born Frees": The prospects for generational change in post-apartheid South Africa. *Australian Journal of Political Science*, *47*(1), 133–153.

Middaugh, E., & Kirshner, B. (Eds.). (2014). *#youthaction: Becoming political in the digital age*. Information Age Press.

Mutsvairo, B. (Ed.). (2016). *Digital activism in the social media era: Critical reflections on emerging trends in Sub-Saharan Africa*. Palgrave Macmillan.

Naidoo, L. (2016). Contemporary student politics in South Africa: The rise of the black-led student movements of #RhodesMustFall and #FeesMustFall in 2015. In A. Heffernan & N. Nieftagodien (Eds.), *Students must rise: Youth struggle in South Africa before and beyond Soweto '76* (pp. 180–190). NYU Press.

Ndelu, S., Dlakavu, S., & Boswell, B. (2017). Womxn's and nonbinary activists' contribution to the RhodesMustFall and FeesMustFall student movements: 2015 and 2016. *Agenda, 31*(3–4), 1–4.

Ndlovu, M. W. (2017a). *#FeesMustFall and youth mobilisation in South Africa: Reform or revolution?*. Routledge.

Ndlovu, M. W. (2017b). Fees Must Fall: A nuanced observation of the University of Cape Town, 2015–2016. *Agenda, 31*(3–4), 127–137.

Nyamnjoh, B. (2016). *#RhodesMustFall: Nibbling at resilient colonialism in South Africa*. African Books Collective.

Pillay, S. R. (2016). Silence is violence: (Critical) psychology in an era of Rhodes Must Fall and Fees Must Fall. *South African Journal of Psychology, 46*(2), 155–159.

Posel, D. (2013). The ANC Youth League and the politicization of race. *Thesis Eleven, 115*(1), 58–76.

Ramaru, K. (2017). Feminist reflections on the Rhodes Must Fall movement. *Feminist Africa, 22*, 89–96.

Salinas, D., & Fraser, P. (2012). Educational policy and contentious politics: The 2011 Chilean student movement. *Berkeley Review of Education, 3*(1), 17–47.

Samanga, R. (2016). *#FeesMustFall: Where do we go from here?* OkayAfrica. www .okayafrica.com/fees-must-fall-movement-south-africa-op-ed/

Seekings, J. (1996). The "lost generation": South Africa's "youth problem" in the early-1990s. *Transformation: Critical Perspectives on South Africa, 29*, 103–125.

Seekings, J., & Nattrass, N. (2008). *Class, race, and inequality in South Africa*. Yale University Press.

Strong, K. (2018). Do African lives matter to Black Lives Matter? Youth uprisings and the borders of solidarity. *Urban Education, 53*(2), 265–285.

Stuurman, S. (2018). Student activism in a time of crisis in South Africa: The quest for "black power." *South African Journal of Education, 38*(4), 1–8.

Sukarieh, M., & Tannock, S. (2014). *Youth rising? The politics of youth in the global economy*. Routledge.

Tarlau, R. (2019). *Occupying schools, occupying land: How the Landless Workers Movement transformed Brazilian education*. Oxford University Press.

Taylor, V. (1997). The trajectory of national liberation and social movements: The South African experience. *Community Development Journal, 32*(3), 252–265.

Tivaringe, T. (2018). Youth-led change in South Africa's education system. In C. Del Felice & O. P. Onyeigwe (Eds.), *Youth in Africa, agents of change* (pp. 55–64). Casa África.

Tivaringe, T. (2019). The social unemployment gap in South Africa: Limits of enabling socio-economic redress through expanding access to higher education. *Education Policy Analysis Archives, 27*(155) 1–31.

Tivaringe, T., & Kirshner, B. (2021). Learning to claim power in a contentious public sphere: A study of youth movement formation in South Africa. *Journal of the Learning Sciences, 30*, 125–150.

UCT RMF (n.d.). *RhodesMustFall mission statement* [Facebook page]. https://m.facebook.com/p/Rhodes-Must-Fall-South-Africa-100069747536114/

Valladares, S., Kirshner, B., & Trejo, B. (2020). *Power memo*. Research Hub for Youth Organizing, University of Colorado Boulder.

Von Holdt, K., Langa, M., Molapo, S., Ngubeni, K., Dlamini, J., & Kirsten, A. (2011). *The smoke that calls: Insurgent citizenship, collective violence and the struggle for a place in the new South Africa*. Centre for the Study of Violence and Reconciliation and Society, Work and Development Institute, University of the Witwatersrand.

Warren, S., & Kirshner, B. (Eds.). (2022, January 20). *Youth activism through a global lens* [Special issue]. The Forge: Organizing Strategy and Practice. https://forgeorganizing.org/article/democracy-moves-youth-activism-through-global-lens

Watts, R., Kirshner, B., Govan, R., & Fernandez, J. (2018). *Powerful Youth, Powerful Communities: An international study of youth organizing*. Powerful Youth, Powerful Communities. www.research2action.net

Wawrzynski, M. R., & Naik, S. (2021). Exploring outcomes from student activism in South Africa. *Journal of College Student Development, 62*(3), 327–344.

Xaba, W. (2017). Challenging Fanon: A Black radical feminist perspective on violence and the Fees Must Fall movement. *Agenda, 31*(3–4), 96–104.

Zuckerman, E. (2014). New media, new civics? *Policy & Internet, 6*(2), 151–168.

3 Domestic Violence and Community Organizing in India

Suvarna V. Menon and Nicole E. Allen

Introduction

Domestic Violence in India

Domestic violence is a pervasive social issue in India, although given low rates of disclosure to formal agencies (International Institute for Population Sciences, 2007), true prevalence rates are hard to ascertain. Estimates from the National Family Health Survey 2015–16 (NFHS-4; International Institute for Population Sciences, 2017) suggest a lifetime prevalence of spousal violence of 31.1 percent, while other national estimates describe lifetime prevalence rates varying from 18 to 70 percent (e.g., International Institute for Population Sciences, 2007; Krishnan, 2005; Yoshikawa et al., 2012). Studies also suggest that the vast majority of cases of violence remain undisclosed. For example, the NFHS-3 (International Institute for Population Sciences, 2007) found that only a third of domestic violence survivors disclosed the violence to formal agencies.

Data from the World Health Organization comparing prevalence rates of domestic violence in India to other countries suggest that women in Southeast Asia are at higher risk for lifetime domestic violence than women from Europe or the US (World Health Organization, 2013). Further, while domestic violence is a global issue, there are distinct cultural expressions of this phenomenon in India. For example, violence is perpetrated not just by one's spouse, but also by in-laws (Kaur & Garg, 2010; Krishnan et al., 2012). One study found that 40 percent of women sampled from a postnatal ward described their mothers-in-law as the instigators of violence against them (Muthal-Rathore et al., 2002). Similarly, dowry-based harassment is a significant contributor to domestic violence perpetrated against women (Jeyaseelan et al., 2007), with research showing that mothers-in-law who had themselves experienced dowry demands were five times more likely to harass their daughters-in-law over dowries (Jeyaseelan et al., 2015). Kalokhe et al. (2015) argue for a culturally tailored definition of domestic violence for India based on their finding that domestic violence in India was characterized by control over women's reproductive decision-making, mobility, social networks, finances, and access to food, widespread acceptance of sexual abuse, presence of witnesses, psychological abuse for infertility, dowries, and having daughters, and perpetration of domestic violence by husbands and in-laws.

Domestic violence in India is perpetuated within a hierarchical social system (defined by one's class, caste, and gender) and fueled by deeply patriarchal norms (Menon & Allen, 2018; Visaria, 2000). Prevalence estimates also vary based on rural versus urban locations in India (International Institute for Population Sciences, 2017). For example, dowry demand has been found to be significantly higher in rural areas (23 percent) as compared to urban slum areas (18 percent; Jeyaseelan et al., 2015). This study also found that illiteracy and lower socioeconomic status were associated with higher risk for dowry demands, with illiterate husbands from lower socioeconomic backgrounds being 1.3 times more likely to demand dowries compared to literate husbands from moderate to high socioeconomic backgrounds, and with mothers-in-law with lower socioeconomic backgrounds who had experienced dowry demands themselves being 14 times more likely to demand dowries as compared with those with moderate or high socioeconomic backgrounds and who had not experienced any dowry demands. Overall, studies have shown that risk for domestic violence is associated with lower socioeconomic status, poverty, lower educational achievement, and lower caste (Babu & Kar, 2009; Raj et al., 2018). Therefore, an intersectionality of gender, class, and caste can put women at different levels of risk for domestic violence.

Community beliefs and norms that support domestic violence are likely to negatively impact women's help-seeking efforts, leaving them with fewer avenues for support. Various studies have found high levels of normative acceptance of domestic violence in India (Garcia-Moreno et al., 2005), which has been associated with higher risk for perpetration of domestic violence (e.g., Kalokhe et al., 2018). Thus, intervening to interrupt and prevent domestic violence requires not only support for survivors and efforts to facilitate their empowerment, but also shifts in the community norms and community response to such violence.

Domestic Violence Response in India

The response to domestic violence in India has been implemented in two radically different and frequently opposing contexts: the first is the formal or institutional response, which includes systems like the police, law enforcement, and judicial system, and the second is the nongovernmental and grassroots response to domestic violence, which includes efforts by community-based agencies to support survivors of violence and promote social change in the response to gender-based violence (Menon & Allen, 2018).

Suneetha and Nagaraj (2006) describe three critical phases in the understanding of the domestic violence discourse in India, arguing that these were moments of crucial significance that informed a historical understanding of the conceptual shifts around domestic violence. The authors describe the first phase as the "dowry" phase during the 1970s, being characterized by concerns about dowry-related violence. Next was the "domestic violence" phase of the 1990s, which acknowledged other forms of violence and power tactics within the marital relationship. The final stage in the late 1990s was when domestic violence began to be characterized as a development or empowerment-related issue. According to the authors, this paradigm shift has facilitated the work of nongovernmental organizations (NGOs) in strengthening the institutional response to domestic violence and has called for the inclusion of informal sources of support in intervention, along with an explicit emphasis on the empowerment of survivors as a programmatic goal.

Formal coordinating councils, which have been formed to address domestic violence in some countries such as the US (Allen, 2006), do not exist in the Indian context. Recent efforts to change systems in response to domestic violence in India, however, suggest that various agencies are attempting to work collaboratively to address this social issue (Ahmed-Ghosh, 2004; Daruwalla et al., 2019a). For example, significant efforts are being made to increase collaboration between systems like law enforcement and grassroots organizations or research institutes as a way to improve services for women and increase sensitivity in services (e.g., Dave, 2013). Our previous research on the formal systems response to gender-based in India suggests that NGOs are at the heart of the institutional change process, providing leverage to further systems change work within the institutional response to gender-based violence (Menon & Allen, 2018).

A recent study focused on an informal settlement community found that an acknowledgment of a greater incidence of domestic violence among friends and family was associated with higher rates of domestic violence perpetration (Kalokhe et al., 2018), possibly due to a normalization of violence. Based on their findings, the authors argue for interventions that challenge community norms on domestic violence and that work with communities to help them expand their definition of behaviors constituting domestic violence. In line with this and fueled by NGO- and civil society-led efforts, in contrast to earlier responses to domestic violence that focused on strengthening formal systems, recent interventions have emphasized primary prevention through community activism and community mobilization (Daruwalla et al., 2019a). Such comprehensive interventions, which include individual service provision, along with primary prevention through community engagement and mobilization, have been recommended in other larger-scale reviews. For example, reviews by Ellsberg et al. (2015, 2018) on effective community-based interventions for gender-based violence in low- and middle-income countries have found that multisectoral programs that engage with multiple stakeholders and work to challenge normalization of violence, along with addressing risk factors for violence, appeared to be the most successful in transforming social norms. Similarly, Semahegn et al.'s (2019) review on interventions for preventing domestic violence in low- and lower-middle-income countries recommends that prevention should focus on cultural gender-norm transformation, engagement of stakeholders, empowerment of women, capacity-building, engaging men and other influential people (e.g., in-laws and neighbors), and integrating services across sectors.

Community mobilization-based interventions similar to the one described later in this chapter have been implemented in various low- and middle-income countries to combat domestic violence (e.g., Bradley et al., 2011; Gupta et al., 2013; Pronyk et al., 2006). For example, interventions focusing on building community power in response to domestic violence have also been implemented in countries like Uganda, Nicaragua, and Tanzania (Abramsky et al., 2014; Grabe et al., 2014; Wagman et al., 2015) and in India (Bradley et al., 2011; Daruwalla et al., 2019b). Such approaches acknowledge the cultural norms that promote gender-based violence (Biswas, 2017) and attempt to combat normalization of violence through community mobilization focused on generating awareness, creating zero tolerance for violence, facilitating empowerment of women to seek support, and providing participation and leadership opportunities to community members, positioning them as agents of change (e.g., Daruwalla et al., 2019b; Menon & Allen, 2020, 2021a). Multilevel interventions like these have the potential to be transformative by not just addressing the needs of survivors (e.g., through crisis counseling and advocacy) but also engaging in social change efforts that change the milieu in which violence occurs (e.g., through community mobilization and building community power).

Next, we describe an exemplary effort by a grassroots agency to engage in community mobilization and facilitate empowerment of survivors and community members in response to domestic violence in rural communities in the Delhi National Capital Region (NCR), India. The case example draws on data collected by the authors in 2017 as part of a larger study (see Menon & Allen, 2020, 2021a, 2021b). The findings discussed in this chapter are based on data drawing on semistructured interviews with survivors, agency staff members, and community members, participant observation over a period of two months, and archival data from the grassroots agency described in the next section (e.g., case files, newsletters, annual reports).

An Exemplar: "Shakti" NGO Response to Domestic Violence

Founded in 1983, "Shakti" (the name has been changed) is an NGO located in New Delhi, India, that aims at creating a violence-free and gender-just society. The agency's primary mechanisms of action are through capacity-building, advocacy, and social action. Shakti explicitly states women's empowerment as being one of their central goals. Shakti adopts a bottom-up approach in empowering women and encourages their participation as stakeholders in processes of change. Shakti's work on domestic violence is focused

Figure 3.1 *Shakti's multilevel approach.*

at three levels (see Figure 3.1): first, at the individual or survivor level, the organization runs domestic violence centers for survivors experiencing violence, where they can receive services and advocacy free of cost; second, at the formal systems level, they engage in collaborative efforts with formal systems (e.g., police, legal agencies, government) to improve the formal response to domestic violence; and third, at the community level, they engage in extensive grassroots programming in targeted low-income, rural, shantytown communities in the Delhi NCR region, focused on building capacity and community power to respond to domestic violence. Shakti worked with five target communities around Delhi, which included five low-income informal neighborhood settlements. Such informal settlements are widely prevalent all across India and are characterized by overcrowding, lack of access to adequate resources (e.g., water and sanitation), unsafe or inadequate building structures, high poverty, and unemployment or employment through the informal sector (United Nations-Habitat, 2004).

Agency staff members include office-based staff members who are responsible for overseeing projects, conducting stakeholder trainings and advocacy work, and counselors, who are mostly recruited from target communities and trained to provide counseling and mediation services to survivors. Counselors also engage in community-based engagement work to promote community-building efforts.

Survivor Services

The domestic violence centers run by Shakti provide counseling and mediation services with family members and/or the perpetrator(s), advocacy services (including assistance with community resources; e.g., legal options), and vocational skills training. The centers accept walk-in clients, telephone referrals, and online referrals from individuals and formal agencies. The agency initially ran five centers throughout Delhi, but only two were active during the time of data collection due to funding constraints. Archival data indicated that 651 cases of domestic violence had been registered with Shakti since 2015. Of these, 272 (41.8 percent) cases resulted in reconciliation and 242 (37.2 percent) cases were provided with legal services. Additionally, Shakti facilitates local community meetings and women's support groups aimed at generating awareness about women's legal rights and providing emotional support to survivors of violence.

Systems Advocacy and Coordinated Care

Shakti engages in systems-level advocacy and facilitates collaborations with stakeholders. They routinely conduct gender sensitization trainings with police, paramedics, and corporate organizations. Additionally, they conduct interface meetings involving important stakeholders where key issues related to the response to gender-based violence are presented and concerns are discussed and addressed in a public forum.

Community-Building

Finally, Shakti engages in community mobilization and community-building efforts through regular local community meetings aimed at generating awareness about domestic violence and women's legal rights. Archival data indicated that Shakti had conducted meetings with 24,364 women and 15,340 men. They facilitate the creation of women's support groups that are aimed at providing emotional support to survivors of violence. Through their engagement with the agency, women, their partners, and community members have the opportunity to become part of Women's Leadership Groups, Men's Leadership Groups, or Youth Leadership Groups. These local community leadership and action groups encourage participants to take on roles as community leaders and changemakers. Members conduct regular meetings to discuss community problems and address the problem of gender-based violence in their community through awareness-raising exercises and workshops. As a part of their community-based efforts, staff members also conduct door-to-door surveys in target communities that aim to document abuse and raise awareness among households about domestic violence and about Shakti and its services.

Women Served by Shakti

Survivors engaged with Shakti are predominantly from underprivileged backgrounds and, based on our data, most did not have an education beyond eighth grade. Women interviewed for our study reported experiencing violence that included physical abuse ("My husband used to hit me and beat me. One time my daughter was at eight months during my pregnancy and he hit me in the stomach"), sexual abuse ("Even if I don't like to or don't want to, he would still pressurize me to do sex. Sometimes he would force me. I used to feel like I am being mentally tortured"), emotional abuse and control ("His mother started talking badly to me, wouldn't let me phone my parents – she had locked the phone. When I tried go, she would block my way and not let me near the phone. They didn't let me talk to anyone – not allowing me to go out of the house, not allowing me to go to my parents – it was like I was imprisoned by them"), severe neglect of their physical and emotional needs ("My mother-in-law said surgeries are not a big thing. Do all the housework, wash all of the clothes. There was just one or two rotis [bread] that she gave – one in the day and one in the evening"), and dowry-related violence ("My mother-in-law said that until you bring home a motorcycle, my son will keep harassing you like this").

Most women reported experiencing harassment from their husbands as well as their in-laws. Women reported varying levels of support from informal supports like family. While some women reported receiving support from parents ("My mom and dad did not want me to go back to them"), others reported that even though their parents felt bad about their situation and they were able to confide in them, they expected the daughter to remain with the husband/in-laws ("They told me little fights do happen I should just tolerate it"). While some women accepted this as part of the culture they lived in, other women reported resentment about the lack of support ("If they cared, wouldn't they think, I won't send my daughter over there? Why did they send me there?").

Survivors reported many cultural forces that prevented them from disclosing the violence. This included an acceptance and normalization of violence ("My mom said 'look child you have to bear some things, this is the fate of women, these things happen in all marriages, you have to bear it – it's okay'"), the importance of honor ("My in-laws would say 'how long will you keep her there [with parents] – people will laugh at you, your neighbors will ask questions and gossip, so there will be a loss of face for you,'" "The humiliation and loss of face is only mine – they have no such loss of face"), the role of gender ("Here [with in-laws] I am a woman, so I should be kept pressured," "Girls are not considered humans at all"), and the cultural importance of marriage ("My father used to say, she's a girl – she may be unhappy but girls are best in their in-laws house – she should stay there," "The parents feel that she's married now, she has to stay there").

The agency's centers are physically located in the same local community, and staff members emphasize a relational approach in their work with community members. This appeared to facilitate the creation of support and trust rather than a focus on hierarchy between the agency and the broader community. This nonhierarchical relationship was seen in counseling sessions as well as during community meetings, where staff members appeared to know community members and their families well. Importantly, staff members expressed an appreciation for the complexity of community needs, with an acknowledgment that community members were the experts and would take the lead in terms of implementing interventions ("The people going in the field are told to have larger ears and smaller mouths that listen more, and talk less"). A staff member described how this facilitates openness in the community toward their programs:

> I think people are extremely open. Most of us who go to the field have been taught, have learned and believe that we know nothing about the field as compared to the person living there. So all the projects are extremely flexible.

Most counselors working for Shakti have been identified from the same communities and subsequently trained, which staff members described as beneficial because "it's not somebody like myself going from [site A] to [site B] and trying to train. The core team is who lives there. So people know that you understand what is the situation, because you are living in that situation."

Psychological Empowerment Processes

The concept of psychological empowerment has received a lot of attention within community psychology and has consequently been defined in different ways (e.g., Cattaneo & Goodman, 2014; Maton, 2008; Rappaport, 1987). For example, Rappaport (1987) defines it as "the mechanism by which people, organizations, and communities gain mastery over their lives" (p. 122). A decade later, Zimmerman (1995, 2000) proposed a multilevel and multidimensional framework of psychological empowerment that involves three components: an emotional or intrapersonal component, referring to self-perceptions of one's competence in achieving goals in the sociopolitical domain; a cognitive or interactional component, referring to the skills and critical understanding necessary for exerting sociopolitical influence; and a behavioral component, referring to the actions taken by the individual to achieve their goals. Similarly, Cattaneo and Goodman (2014) define empowerment as "an iterative process in which a person who lacks power sets a personally meaningful goal oriented toward increasing power, takes action toward that goal, and observes and reflects on the impact of this action, drawing on his or her evolving self-efficacy, knowledge, and competence related to the goal" (p. 647). This conceptualization involves both intrapersonal and social components such that individuals build personal resources and take action by drawing on community resources.

Shakti's work and its empowerment agenda appear to facilitate empowerment processes for community members or bystanders, which may consequently promote engagement in social or community action related to domestic violence and for survivors of violence, who may be more likely to take action against their perpetrators, be self-reliant, be able to access resources, or achieve the goals that they set for themselves (Cattaneo & Goodman, 2014).

Psychological Empowerment of Survivors

As victims of chronic control and coercion, domestic violence survivors often experience a loss of agency (Stark, 2007), making empowerment one of the central goals of the response to domestic violence (Cattaneo & Goodman, 2014; Goodman & Epstein, 2008; Kasturiranjan, 2008), which is often conceptualized as a proximal outcome that may lead to other distal outcomes like safety (Cattaneo & Goodman, 2014). Survivor-centered models that emphasize empowerment of survivors have been adopted by grassroots and advocacy agencies in the US and involve an emphasis on choice, voice, and strengths-based approaches (e.g., Davies & Lyon, 2014; Sullivan & Bybee, 1999). Studies with survivors in the US show that a sense of control during the help-seeking process is associated with greater satisfaction with formal systems (Cattaneo & Goodman, 2010), greater help-seeking and disclosure of abuse (Hotaling & Buzawa, 2003), and better mental health (Cattaneo & Goodman, 2010).

Cattaneo and Chapman (2010) propose that an empowerment approach includes identifying personally meaningful goals, thinking about possible avenues to achieving these goals, and selecting the option that is best suited to the individual survivor. This is often one of the most central steps of a survivor-driven program that recognizes women's unique circumstances and needs (e.g., Sullivan & Bybee, 1999). For Shakti, an important part of staff members' work with women involves providing them with knowledge, skills, and resources that allow them to make independent choices for their well-being (see Figure 3.2; Menon & Allen, 2021b). This is especially important in the target communities where women are most often illiterate, lack appropriate knowledge about laws and legal recourses available to them, are often isolated from sources of support, and face extensive family pressure against disclosing violence. Shakti's approach emphasizes rights-based language with a focus on educating women about domestic violence laws and their rights (Menon & Allen, 2021b). Thus, for most survivors, this means beginning at the first stage of understanding and labeling behaviors as domestic violence as opposed to normalizing them, which then prompts help-seeking (Menon & Allen, 2021b).

For survivors who wish to pursue legal options, counselors spend various sessions engaging in extensive legal advocacy, providing information about what the process would involve, and preparing families for how to proceed (Menon & Allen, 2021b). Case files indicated that women were given information about different options like reconciliation through mediation or legal avenues during the first couple of meetings and were subsequently connected

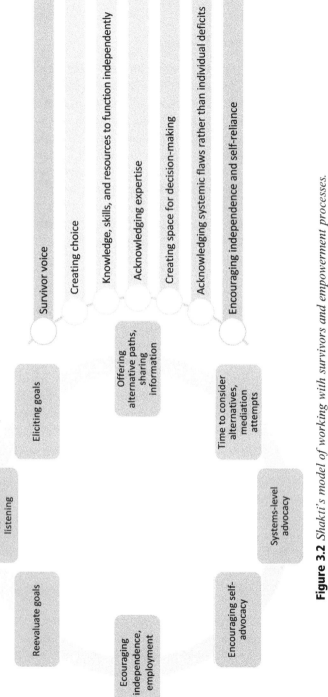

Figure 3.2 *Shakti's model of working with survivors and empowerment processes.*

to resources in the community depending on their needs (Menon & Allen, 2021b). If women preferred to reconcile with their partners, counselors included the partner or in-laws in mediation and counseling sessions, followed by routine follow-ups and home visits to check on long-term safety and prevent recidivism. For individuals seeking legal recourse, counselors initially assisted women by going to meet lawyers, accompanying them to the court, and advocating on their behalf. Over time, they encouraged survivors to take the lead and engage in self-advocacy, such that survivors felt confident going to court on their own. Women saw this as helpful for modeling self-advocacy and giving them confidence in approaching formal systems. One survivor stated (see Menon & Allen, 2021b):

> The nervousness and tension of going to court and seeing things I had never seen before, I felt more comfortable when Didi [elder sister, referring to counselor] would go with me. Now I do not feel as nervous seeing the lawyer, as before. I feel more confident, and I feel like I can go by myself.

Women also talked about how this access to knowledge about resources in the community, and about their own rights, leads to a sense of confidence in them, along with a willingness to take action ("When you find out that you have these rights, your confidence increases because you find out that you can complain about the injustice against you").

Cattaneo and Chapman (2010) include the process of reflecting on one's progress as part of the impact of the empowerment process. At Shakti, staff members emphasized the cyclical nature of their work with survivors and the need to reevaluate survivor goals at each stage. Once any immediate crisis had been dealt with, staff members often brought up the importance of self-reliance and employment with women in order to assist them with vocational training and financial independence, thus reducing a potential barrier to leaving an abusive situation. For example, one survivor described how staff members arranged employment and training for her in her area of interest (as a beautician), stating that she now felt confident and was planning to open her own salon (see Menon & Allen, 2021b).

A wide range of empowerment-related outcomes were reported by both survivors and staff members at Shakti. These outcomes varied depending on the goals that women approached the agency with. Consistent with their goals, many women reported continuing their relationship and experiencing an improved and positive home environment following their engagement with the agency. Others reported successfully separating from their abusive husbands or in-laws and reported receiving regular spousal support to support their children or themselves. Many women had sought and were successfully pursuing employment opportunities, being financially independent regardless of whether they were living with their partners ("I have my own money now. He can't keep my kids hungry. In my house, I can carry my own expenses. I get courage from that") or living independently ("It's been one year since my case closed, and now I am making my own money, and raising my kids by myself"). Many survivors used rights-based language to describe how they felt confident that they could assert their rights, disclose the violence, and seek help in the future. Notably, all women who were interviewed reported seeing positive changes in themselves, referring to these changes in varied terms like "confidence," "courage," and "determination."

Psychological Empowerment of Community Members

Shakti also aims to facilitate empowerment processes among community members to take collective action through community organizing. Maton et al. (2011) argue that empowerment is central to efforts directed at bringing about meaningful social change related to marginalized individuals. Community organizing has been described as a process through which community members take collective action regarding social issues of mutual concern (Christens et al., 2021). It has been found to promote sociopolitical development, psychological empowerment, and civic engagement (Speer et al., 2021). This can be a particularly important path to combat deeply entrenched cultural norms against disclosing domestic violence in India (Menon & Allen, 2018). Community organizing can take different forms, but it typically involves the elements of assessment and relationship development, participatory research, action or mobilization, and evaluation and reflection (Christens & Speer, 2015). A widely used model of community organizing follows Alinsky's (1971) model of marginalized individuals working together to identify common problems and engaging in collective action focused on social change and exercising political power (Christens, 2019).

Shakti's work in the community appeared to facilitate empowerment processes among community members who had the opportunity to be community leaders or be associated with the agency as "permanent members" (see Menon & Allen, 2020). These members were able to take on leadership roles that enabled them to facilitate social change in their communities, provide support to survivors, and facilitate community discussions on social issues like gender equity and domestic violence (Menon & Allen, 2020). For example, a survivor reflected on her decision to be a part of a Women's Leadership Group, stating, "With what I have been through, when any sisters or daughters come to me, I can't bear their unhappiness. Since I have got help from here [Shakti], I also try to help them ... I bring them here." Similarly, a community member described feeling confident in intervening in cases of domestic violence: "I feel like I have some power too. Like if I see violence is happening somewhere, then at least I can explain to them that they can come here ... I know that I am connected to 'Shakti'" (see Menon & Allen, 2021a). Community leaders reported feeling empowered to provide support and resources to survivors of violence who approach them for help, given their association with Shakti and the knowledge they had gained through this association.

Community leaders also described initiating conversations with neighbors and friends about gender-based issues and attempting to educate others in the community. They described how Shakti's community engagement led to efforts by the community to engage in organizing and community-building even in the absence of Shakti's active involvement. For example, one youth member noted:

> The biggest thing I believe is when the women ended up having their own meeting and they would tell other women about the legal act for domestic violence, and it helped other women. So that was a big achievement for our society, because no one talked about it before.

Participants described these community-led efforts as playing a role in supporting and facilitating women's empowerment processes. Community members expressed support for women disclosing abuse and seeking help and described a growing willingness to disclose abuse in their community since Shakti's involvement. One male youth member contrasted this with a preoccupation with keeping the family intact and described how intervention from community members assisted a survivor in seeking help by encouraging her to call the police in response to ongoing violence at home. Thus, these networks of community leaders and change agents promote a culture of supporting disclosing abuse and providing support to survivors of violence.

Community Power and Empowerment

Grassroots organizations that focus on increasing community members' engagement with social issues and promoting citizen participation are ideal sites for studying how these agencies can build community power. These settings can also be understood as a community resource that allows people to share stories and provide opportunities for personal growth and community participation (Trickett, 2011). Community empowerment has been defined in various ways in the literature. Christens (2019) proposes a framework for community empowerment aligned with three dimensions of community power: situational, institutional, and systemic. Per this framework, situational power is associated with aspects of community empowerment like participation, collective action, leadership, and collective efficacy. Institutional power is associated with networks of empowering organizations, problem assessments, and power mapping. Finally, systemic power is associated with collective analysis of community problems and the shaping of public narratives that provide for recasting or reframing these narratives (Christens, 2019). Aiyer et al. (2015) define community empowerment as involving three components: the intracommunity component, which involves relationships among neighborhood residents, trust in the community, collective efficacy, and social cohesion; the interactional component, which includes interactions

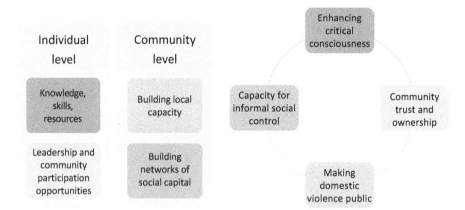

Figure 3.3 *Empowerment processes at the individual and community level and mechanisms of community empowerment.*

that promote social capital and social control; and, finally, the behavioral component, which includes collaborations between residents and community agencies that lead to collective actions to improve community or neighborhood conditions. Shakti's model of building community empowerment and power aligns closely with these models (see Figure 3.3).

At the community level, Shakti's community-based actions facilitate capacity-building within the community and appear to increase social capital among community members (see Menon & Allen, 2020). Interviews, observations, and archival data highlighted the emphasis that the agency placed on creating catalysts of change in the community to expand the resources available to survivors of violence. Thus, the agency focuses on community-building and training activities that facilitate the role of community leaders and position them as agents of change in the community (Menon & Allen, 2020). These community leaders also become useful resources for survivors in need of help. Agency staff members described a belief in deinstitutionalizing social change, with a focus on creating capacity and facilitating empowerment processes among community members to be agents of social change.

Through a long history of engagement with the community, Shakti is also able to facilitate community members' social capital by promoting the creation of networks of interpersonal relationships among community members and with the agency (Menon & Allen, 2020). For example, the boys in the youth group described how their work had recently been publicized in a television interview that got them recognition among peers in their community who were not previously associated with the agency and subsequently expressed interest in being involved with them. A staff member described how women's engagement with the agency and positive survivor outcomes facilitate help-seeking among other women who also approach the agency through the survivor, stating, "They become prepared to fight not just what happened to them but they also come for the injustice happening against their daughters." These mechanisms align with Christens' (2019) situational power domain of community empowerment and with Aiyer et al.'s (2015) conceptualization of intracommunity and interactional components of community empowerment.

Shakti's emphasis on building capacity within communities also promotes the community's capacity for informal social control and intervention (Menon & Allen, 2020), mapping onto Aiyer et al.'s (2015) behavioral component of community empowerment. Thus, rather than institutionalizing the response to domestic violence, which comes with its own barriers, Shakti's work facilitates informal community-based interventions. For example, community leaders described taking on the role of providing support to survivors when the counselors are not present or being able to intervene in cases of violence in their community, with an emphasis on discussing problems openly and providing women with the support they needed rather than silencing violence behind closed doors. Female members who joined the local leadership groups reflected on how they were able to help other women in the community, emphasizing the role of neighbors and relatives in intervening and in supporting survivors.

Community members appeared to believe that their community had improved in its ability to combat crime or violence. Participants made statements like, "Women at least know more about their rights. The men here, too, have stopped indulging in their vices as much. They have started to go away from that," and, "Yeah, we do not need the police as much. We don't see police that often here."

At the systems level (see Figure 3.4), Shakti's long history of advocacy and promoting systems change through activities like trainings, interface meetings, and institutional advocacy appears to be associated with processes like the creation of interagency networks and an increase in community trust in formal systems. The agency's reputation and its efforts at engaging with different agencies appears to have helped with the creation of a large interagency network, which facilitates referrals of cases to the agency and assists staff members in providing targeted referrals to survivors who come to them. This network of providers includes doctors, nurses, police officers, lawyers, and government officials. The agency's work has also led to various policy-building efforts through various advisory committees that staff members are actively a part of. These mechanisms map onto Christens' (2019) institutional power dimension of community power. For example, one staff member noted:

> The whole networking and creating relationships with the different stakeholders really helps. So when there's a survivor of domestic violence, she knows that she can go to this lawyer. And a lot of these lawyers and police officers – because we've had very long-standing relationships many of them – offer free counseling. Because we have long-term contacts with the police, we know which police station is available at which time, which women constables will be responsive, so we can contact them accordingly.

Shakti's facilitation of interface meetings, which are conducted with various formal agencies and stakeholders, similar to a townhall meeting, are conducted in a public domain. This allows community members to discuss their problems with stakeholders in an open and transparent manner, facilitating community trust in formal systems and promoting system accountability.

Mechanisms Facilitating Community Empowerment

Various mechanisms could be identified as facilitating the building and exercising of community power (see Figure 3.3). These are described below (see also Menon & Allen, 2020).

Knowledge, Skills, and Resources

Shakti's community-building activities like community meetings appear to increase community members' knowledge, skills, and resources (Menon & Allen, 2020). Archival data from the agency provided various examples of the kinds of knowledge that were imparted to community members, like the difference between marital rape and acquaintance or stranger rape, emotional abuse as a form of domestic violence, and other gender-based issues. Specifically, with respect to domestic violence, archival data indicate that the agency informs community members about what constitutes domestic violence, emphasizing domains beyond physical violence and describing the prevalence and normalization of emotional violence, dowry-related violence, and marital rape. They also discuss issues of power and control and financial control.

Community-based participants and survivors were able to reflect on the different ways in which the agency had facilitated their personal growth and development through the acquisition of new knowledge, awareness of social issues, and skills as a result of their engagement with the agency. One male youth member stated that while formal education focused solely on the skewed gender ratio in India, the agency was able to provide them with a more nuanced understanding of gender-based issues and domestic violence. One of the older community members, who was also a *panchayat* (local governing group) leader in the community, reflected on how he learned about domestic violence as well, despite being a community leader for over twenty years, stating, "I used to think it was just meddling in other people's problems." Women in the community also described how the agency's work had facilitated knowledge about women's rights and legal protections and stated that this knowledge prevents women from feeling "trapped."

Opportunities for Community Participation and Leadership

Shakti also provides community members with ample opportunities for community participation and leadership (Menon & Allen, 2020), facilitating their

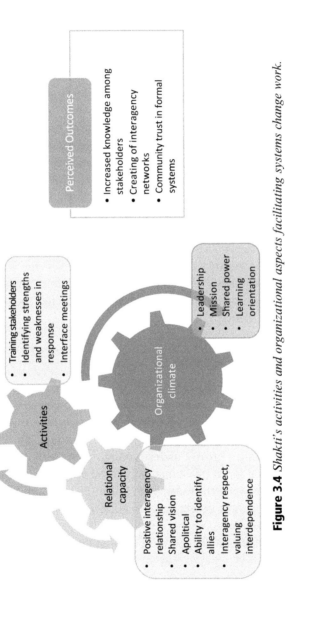

Figure 3.4 *Shakti's activities and organizational aspects facilitating systems change work.*

situational power (Christens, 2019). Participants' narratives reflected that their community participation was also associated with a sense of community responsibility ("People just think of themselves, it is also important to think of the community … our community should change, so we have to do something").

Notably, in one of the community meetings conducted during the study period, the male youth members described how they continued conducting their own meetings even after the agency lost funding to support their meetings. They described continuing multiple community-building and awareness exercises in the neighborhood on themes like promoting education for girls and doing street plays on various social issues like domestic violence. One youth member described his growing interest in social issues as a result of his engagement with the agency and how it fueled his desire to initiate meetings in the neighboring informal settlement community following the success of meetings in his own community. He stated that discussions in these meetings cover a wide range of topics, with issues ranging from community problems and community problem-solving (like installing septic tanks) to harassment of women in the community. Thus, by providing community members with opportunities to associate with the agency and take on roles as community leaders, Shakti is able to facilitate opportunities for leadership, personal growth, development, and skill-building that cover social and community problems more broadly rather than being restricted to social action related to domestic violence.

Increased Critical Consciousness

Shakti's community-engaged work also appears to be associated with an increase in community members' critical consciousness, defined as the process by which marginalized or oppressed people learn to critically analyze their social conditions and act to change them (Watts et al., 2011). Participants described gaining a greater understanding of gender issues, domestic violence, and harassment faced by women and of the importance of supporting women and their empowerment (Menon & Allen, 2020). Community members also described being more conscious about divisions of labor within the household, and female members corroborated seeing changes in their partners or siblings as a result of their participation in community meetings.

Community Trust and Ownership

Shakti's community engagement appeared to facilitate a sense of community trust in the agency and promote social cohesion among community members. Interviews and observations also suggested that there was a sense of community ownership in the agency and its work among members. Community members appeared to view themselves as being part of the agency. Similarly, community members who had taken on leadership roles appeared to take the initiative to convince other community members about the mission and work of the agency. Participants described how the community gradually developed trust in the agency, stating that initial distrust and wariness regarding the agency's work was followed by confidence in the agency after multiple women were assisted through their association with Shakti. It is important to note that this research was undertaken more than seven years after the agency's community-building efforts were first initiated. Thus, many of the positive outcomes described in this chapter are likely to be the result of sustained community involvement and trust built over multiple years within the community. Further, our data are also biased by the self-selective nature of our sample. Thus, these findings cannot be generalized to all members of the community (see Menon & Allen, 2020 for a detailed discussion).

Application and Future Research

Social change efforts have often been criticized for overemphasizing either the individual or the systems level (Christens, 2010) without attending to the other. In contrast, approaches such as those described in this chapter that acknowledge the interdependence of individuals and communities and therefore prioritize community engagement and action appear to be crucial for social change efforts. The exemplar described in this chapter is only one such example of an intervention designed to address domestic violence, and it is a part of a growing group of community-based intervention and prevention programming in developing countries.

While research documenting the efficacy of multilevel, community-based interventions for domestic violence appears to be in its early stages, the extant research seems to be equivocal in terms of the effectiveness of such interventions, with studies demonstrating varied levels of success depending on the program. A number of studies have documented reduced levels of violence following such interventions (e.g., Abramsky et al., 2014; Doyle et al., 2018; Wagman, 2015) in other countries. For example, Wagman et al. (2015) found a reduced prevalence of domestic violence following a community mobilization intervention in Uganda.

Similar interventions have been documented in India with some degree of success (Chakraborty et al., 2020; Daruwalla et al., 2019b; Krishnan et al., 2012; Nair et al., 2020). For example, the Society for Nutrition, Education and Health Action (SNEHA), based in Mumbai, follows a similar approach to the one described in this chapter, with an emphasis on ensuring survivors' access to protection and justice, empowering women to assert their rights, and mobilizing communities to fight against domestic violence (Daruwalla et al., 2019a). The agency works on building community power through participatory efforts and opportunities for local leadership that focus on awareness-building and action to support survivors, enhance the capacities of individuals, and promote community networks (Daruwalla et al., 2019a). Studies have demonstrated that the agency's efforts have been associated with a growing trend of cases being reported to the counseling center, with community referrals being the largest contributor to referred cases (Daruwalla et al., 2015). Another study in rural Jharkhand (Nair et al., 2020) examined the effects of community mobilization through participatory learning and action meetings, with results suggesting that these efforts were associated with more women condemning domestic violence as unacceptable, fewer incidents of violence, and more willingness to disclose violence and seek help. In another study, More et al. (2017) found positive effects on the health of women and children and a lower prevalence of domestic violence in the intervention group in a cluster randomized controlled trial of a community-based intervention.

Daruwalla et al. (2019a) have proposed a theory of change for interventions such as these designed to promote community mobilization and social change in the response to domestic violence. According to this theory, community mobilization aims toward primary prevention through increasing awareness and secondary prevention through identification of survivors and connecting them with resources and support. Thus, community members help respond to domestic violence by supporting survivors and helping them make effective choices on the one hand and by increasing community awareness of domestic violence as a social issue on the other.

In contrast to the studies reviewed earlier, some studies involving randomized controlled trials have failed to find a significant effect for similar interventions in India (e.g., Chatterji et al., 2020; Holden et al., 2016; Jejeebhoy & Santhya, 2018) and Nepal (e.g., Clark et al., 2020). Some reasons that have been proposed to explain the lack of significant effects include deeply entrenched patriarchy and gender inequality, low social cohesion, and lack of time to effectively implement the interventions and track progress (e.g., Chatterji et al., 2020; Clark et al., 2020). Researchers have also attempted to identify some of the challenges involved in doing such community-engaged work. For example, Daruwalla et al. (2015) describe challenges like encountering a pervasive patriarchal structure, which assumes the survivor's choices and rights as secondary to that of her family, thus resulting in reduced agency and choice for the survivor. This meant that intervention needed to involve the survivor's family in order to educate them and convince them to support her or allow her basic freedom and rights. The authors also described ethical dilemmas involved in balancing the need to get the community involved in addressing gender-based violence and survivors' rights to privacy and self-determination. In another context in India, Jejeebhoy and Santhya (2018) describe some of the challenges involved in the implementation of similar approaches, like lack of leadership skills among the people delivering the intervention, differences in literacy levels, difficulties engaging and involving participants from the target communities, high rates of dropping out, and difficulty maintaining fidelity to the program. Further, many programs such as the one described in this chapter depend on funding from international agencies and donors, who are often in a position to define what agency activities get prioritized. For example, funding agencies often favor economic empowerment programs rather than social empowerment programs, given that the former provide faster results (Chaudhuri & Morash, 2019). Thus, for agencies involved in such transformative work, a big challenge in doing community-engaged work that requires a long-term commitment and prolonged engagement is that the goals and priorities of the agency's work may shift depending on funding decisions, adversely impacting the target communities.

Community mobilization and organizing efforts like those described by Shakti's model, along with individual-level work with survivors, appear to play an important role in fueling counternarratives that indicated shifting norms around domestic violence and the response to violence (see Menon & Allen, 2021a). By directly combating a culture of silencing of the violence experienced by women in the community, models such as these appear to play an important role in bringing issues of domestic violence to the public social domain and facilitating community norms that support disclosure of violence and provide support to survivors. Further, fostering the narrative of domestic violence as a social rather than a private issue serves to emphasize capacity for social control as a way to promote social change in the response to domestic violence. This is particularly important in the Indian cultural context, in which domestic violence is seen as a private issue and silencing of the violence is the norm (Menon & Allen, 2018). Thus, by taking an approach to community organizing that makes problems public and builds networks of relationships among community members, such grassroots efforts can help to empower communities to enact social change. Approaches focused on community action and change such as these have potential for success, particularly in close-knit or densely populated communities (Gram et al., 2019), where informal social norms can exert a powerful influence on behavior (Daruwalla et al., 2019a). Such an approach is also supported by the social disorganization theory perspective, which suggests that community mobilization efforts and social cohesion can promote communities' ability to regulate neighborhood crime (Sampson, 1997) and that capacity for informal social control is associated with reduced domestic violence (Browning, 2002). Shakti's openness to and facilitation of mediation and reconciliation efforts with the partner or in-laws also appear to work in their favor by allowing entry into what is otherwise a "private" sphere of the relationship, with a recognition in the community that Shakti's focus is not to break up the family but to follow the survivor's lead. Such models highlight how grassroots community-based interventions have the potential to facilitate changes at the individual and community level, which in turn can help to facilitate social change in the response to domestic violence. The effectiveness of such models can be enhanced by including partnerships from local community members and tailoring interventions to the specific cultural and social contexts of the target community.

Future studies adopting a longitudinal design could examine the impacts of enhancing the capacity for social control on domestic violence disclosures and crime rates in these communities. In addition to highlighting critical mechanisms of change that appear to be at play in the agency's work with the community and survivors of violence, the findings described in this chapter highlight key ways in which this community-based approach is distinct from dominant approaches in the US, like the emphasis on deinstitutionalizing the response to domestic violence, inculcating capacity for informal social control, creating networks of informal and formal supports for women, and its joint emphasis on individual-, systems-, and community-level change.

References

Abramsky, T., Devries, K., Kiss, L., Nakuti, J., Kyegombe, N., Starmann, E., ... Watts, C. (2014). Findings from the SASA! Study: A cluster randomized controlled trial to assess the impact of a community mobilization intervention to prevent violence against women and reduce HIV risk in Kampala, Uganda. *BMC Medicine, 12*(1), 1–17.

Ahmed-Ghosh, H. (2004). Chattels of society: Domestic violence in India. *Violence Against Women, 10*(1), 94–118.

Aiyer, S. M., Zimmerman, M. A., Morrel-Samuels, S., & Reischl, T. M. (2015). From broken windows to busy streets: A community empowerment perspective. *Health Education and Behavior, 42*, 137–147.

Alinsky, S. D. (1971). *Rules for radicals: A pragmatic primer for realistic radicals.* Vintage.

Allen, N. E. (2006). An examination of the effectiveness of domestic violence coordinating councils. *Violence Against Women, 12*(1), 46–67.

Babu, B. V., & Kar, S. K. (2009). Domestic violence against women in eastern India: A population-based study on prevalence and related issues. *BMC Public Health, 9*(1), 1–15.

Biswas, C. S. (2017). Spousal violence against working women in India. *Journal of Family Violence, 32*(1), 55–67.

Bradley, J. E., Bhattacharjee, P., Ramesh, B. M., Girish, M., & Das, A. K. (2011). Evaluation of Stepping Stones as a tool for changing knowledge, attitudes and behaviours associated with gender, relationships and HIV risk in Karnataka, India. *BMC Public Health, 11*(1), 1–11.

Browning, C. R. (2002). The span of collective efficacy: Extending social disorganization theory to partner violence. *Journal of Marriage and Family, 64*, 833–850.

Cattaneo, L. B., & Chapman, A. R. (2010). The process of empowerment: A model for use in research and practice. *American Psychologist, 65*(7), 646.

Cattaneo, L. B., & Goodman, L. A. (2010). Through the lens of therapeutic jurisprudence. *Journal of Interpersonal Violence, 25*(3), 481–502.

Cattaneo, L. B., & Goodman, L. A. (2014). What is empowerment anyway? A model for domestic violence practice, research, and evaluation. *Psychology of Violence, 5*(1), 84–94.

Chakraborty, P., Osrin, D., & Daruwalla, N. (2020). "We learn how to become good men": Working with male allies to prevent violence against women and girls in urban informal settlements in Mumbai, India. *Men and Masculinities, 23* (3–4), 749–771.

Chatterji, S., Stern, E., Dunkle, K., & Heise, L. (2020). Community activism as a strategy to reduce intimate partner violence (IPV) in rural Rwanda: Results of a community randomised trial. *Journal of Global Health, 10*(1), 1–17.

Chaudhuri, S., & Morash, M. (2019). Analyzing the importance of funding for gender focused empowerment programs. *Advances in Gender Research, 27*, 167–181.

Christens, B. D. (2010). Public relationship building in grassroots community organizing: Relational intervention for individual and systems change. *Journal of Community Psychology, 38*(7), 886–900.

Christens, B. D. (2019). *Community power and empowerment.* Oxford University Press.

Christens, B. D., & Speer, P. W. (2015). Community organizing: Practice, research, and policy implications. *Social Issues and Policy Review, 9*(1), 193–222.

Christens, B. D., Gupta, J., & Speer, P. W. (2021). Community organizing: Studying the development and exercise of grassroots power. *Journal of Community Psychology, 49*(8), 3001–3016.

Clark, C. J., Shrestha, B., Ferguson, G., Shrestha, P. N., Calvert, C., Gupta, J., … Oakes, J. M. (2020). Impact of the Change Starts at Home Trial on women's experience of intimate partner violence in Nepal. *SSM – Population Health, 10*, 100530.

Daruwalla, N., Jaswal, S., Fernandes, P., Pinto, P., Hate, K., Ambavkar, G., … Osrin, D. (2019a). A theory of change for community interventions to prevent domestic violence against women and girls in Mumbai, India. *Wellcome Open Research, 4*, 54.

Daruwalla, N., Machchhar, U., Pantvaidya, S., D'Souza, V., Gram, L., Copas, A., & Osrin, D. (2019b). Community interventions to prevent violence against women and girls in informal settlements in Mumbai: The SNEHA-TARA pragmatic cluster randomised controlled trial. *Trials, 20*(1), 1–12.

Daruwalla, N., Pinto, P., Ambavkar, G., Kakad, B., Wadia, P., & Pantvaidya, S. (2015). Increased reporting of cases of gender based violence: A retrospective review of a prevention programme in Dharavi, Mumbai. *Women Health Open Journal, 1*(2), 22–30.

Dave, A. (2013). Strategic alliance, a way forward for violence against women: A case for the Special Cells, India. *Violence Against Women, 19*(10), 1203–1223.

Davies, J., & Lyon, E. (2014). *Domestic violence advocacy: Complex lives/difficult choices.* Sage.

Doyle, K., Levtov, R. G., Barker, G., Bastian, G. G., Bingenheimer, J. B., Kazimbaya, S., Nzabonimpa, A., Pulerwitz, J., Sayinzoga, F., Sharma, V., & Shattuck, D. (2018). Gender-transformative Bandebereho couples' intervention to promote male engagement in reproductive and maternal health and violence prevention in Rwanda: Findings from a randomized controlled trial. *PLoS ONE, 13*(4), e0192756.

Ellsberg, M., Arango, D. J., Morton, M., Gennari, F., Kiplesund, S., Contreras, M., & Watts, C. (2015). Prevention of violence against women and girls: What does the evidence say? *The Lancet, 385*(9977), 1555–1566.

Ellsberg, M., Ullman, C., Blackwell, A., Hill, A., & Contreras, M. (2018). What works to prevent adolescent intimate partner and sexual violence? A global review of best practices. In D. A. Wolfe and J. Temple (Eds.), *Adolescent dating violence: Theory, research, and prevention* (pp. 381–414). Academic Press.

García-Moreno, C., Jansen, H. A., Ellsberg, M., Heise, L., & Watts, C. (2005). *WHO multi-country study on women's health and domestic violence against women.* World Health Organization.

Goodman, L., & Epstein, D. (2008). *Listening to battered women: A survivor centered approach to advocacy, mental health, and justice.* American Psychological Association.

Grabe, S., Dutt, A., & Dworkin, S. L. (2014). Women's community mobilization and well-being: Local resistance to gendered social inequities in Nicaragua and Tanzania. *Journal of Community Psychology, 42*(4), 379–397.

Gram, L., Fitchett, A., Ashraf, A., Daruwalla, N., & Osrin, D. (2019). Promoting women's and children's health through community groups in low-income and middle-income countries: A mixed-methods systematic review of mechanisms, enablers and barriers. *BMJ Global Health, 4*(6), e001972.

Gram, L., Kanougiya, S., Daruwalla, N., & Osrin, D. (2020). Measuring the psychological drivers of participation in collective action to address violence against women in Mumbai, India. *Wellcome Open Research, 5*, 22.

Gupta, J., Falb, K. L., Lehmann, H., Kpebo, D., Xuan, Z., Hossain, M., . . . Annan, J. (2013). Gender norms and economic empowerment intervention to reduce intimate partner violence against women in rural Côte d'Ivoire: A randomized controlled pilot study. *BMC International Health and Human Rights, 13*(1), 1–12.

Holden, J., Humphreys, M., Husain, S., Khan, S., & Lindsey, S. (2016, August 1). *Evaluation of the Madhya Pradesh safe cities initiative 2013–2016.* DFID India. www.sddirect.org.uk/resource/evaluation-madhya-pradesh-safe-cities-initiative

Hotaling, G. T., & Buzawa, E. S. (2003). *Forgoing criminal justice assistance: The non-reporting of new incidents of abuse in a court sample of domestic violence victims.* Department of Criminal Justice, University of Massachusetts.

International Institute of Population Sciences. (2017). *National Family Health Survey (NFHS-4), 2015–16.* International Institute of Population Sciences.

International Institute for Population Sciences. (2007). *National Family Health Survey (NFHS-3), 2005–06: India: volume I.* International Institute of Population Sciences.

Jarrett, R. L., Sullivan, P., & Watkins, N. (2005). Developing youth social capital in extracurricular programs. *Journal of Research on Adolescence, 33*, 41–55.

Jejeebhoy, S. J., & Santhya, K. G. (2018). Preventing violence against women and girls in Bihar: Challenges for implementation and evaluation. *Reproductive Health Matters, 26*(52), 92–108.

Jeyaseelan, V., Kumar, S., Jeyaseelan, L., Shankar, V., Yadav, B. K., & Bangdiwala, S. I. (2015). Dowry demand and harassment: Prevalence and risk factors in India. *Journal of Biosocial Science, 47*(6), 727–745.

Jeyaseelan, L., Kumar, S., Neelakantan, N., Peedicayil, A., Pillai, R., & Duvvury, N. (2007). Physical spousal violence against women in India: some risk factors. *Journal of Biosocial Science, 39*(5), 657–670.

Kalokhe, A. S., Iyer, S. R., Kolhe, A. R., Dhayarkar, S., Paranjape, A., Del Rio, C., . . . Sahay, S. (2018). Correlates of domestic violence experience among recently-married women residing in slums in Pune, India. *PLoS ONE, 13*(4), e0195152.

Kalokhe, A. S., Potdar, R. R., Stephenson, R., Dunkle, K. L., Paranjape, A., Del Rio, C., & Sahay, S. (2015). How well does the World Health Organization definition of domestic violence work for India? *PLoS ONE, 10*(3), e0120909.

Kasturiranjan, A. (2008). Empowerment and programs designed to address domestic violence. *Violence Against Women, 14*(12), 1465–1475.

Kaur, R., & Garg, S. (2010). Domestic violence against women: A qualitative study in a rural community. *Asia Pacific Journal of Public Health, 22*(2), 242–251.

Krishnan, S. (2005). Do structural inequalities contribute to marital violence? Ethnographic evidence from rural South India. *Violence Against Women, 11*, 759–775.

Krishnan, S., Subbiah, K., Khanum, S., Chandra, P. S., & Padian, N. S. (2012). An intergenerational women's empowerment intervention to mitigate domestic violence: Results of a pilot study in Bengaluru, India. *Violence Against Women, 18*(3), 346–370.

Maton, K. I. (2008). Empowering community settings: Agents of individual development, community betterment, and positive social change. *American Journal of Community Psychology, 41*(1–2), 4–21.

Maton, K. I., Seidman, E., & Aber, M. S. (2011). Empowering settings and voices for social change: an introduction. In M. S. Aber, K. I. Maton, & E. Seidman (Eds.), *Empowering settings and voices for social change* (pp. 1–11). Oxford University Press.

Menon, S. V., & Allen, N. E. (2018). The formal systems response to violence against women in India: A cultural lens. *American Journal of Community Psychology, 62*(1–2), 51–61.

Menon, S. V., & Allen, N. E. (2020). Community organizing and transformative change in the response to domestic violence in India. *American Journal of Community Psychology, 66*(1–2), 106–118.

Menon, S. V., & Allen, N. E. (2021a). Community organizing and counter narratives in the response to domestic violence in India. *American Journal of Community Psychology, 67*(1–2), 184–194.

Menon, S. V., & Allen, N. E. (2021b). Empowering practices with domestic violence survivors in India. *Violence Against Women, 28*(3–4), 1008–1032.

More, N. S., Das, S., Bapat, U., Alcock, G., Manjrekar, S., Kamble, V., . . . Osrin, D. (2017). Community resource centres to improve the health of women and children in informal settlements in Mumbai: A cluster-randomised, controlled trial. *The Lancet Global Health, 5*(3), e335–e349.

Muthal-Rathore, A., Tripathi, R., & Arora, R. (2002). Domestic violence against pregnant women interviewed at a hospital in New Delhi. *International Journal of Gynaecology and Obstetrics, 76*, 83–85.

Nair, N., Daruwalla, N., Osrin, D., Rath, S., Gagrai, S., Sahu, R., . . . Prost, A. (2020). Community mobilisation to prevent violence against women and girls in eastern India through participatory learning and action with women's groups facilitated by accredited social health activists: A before-and-after pilot study. *BMC International Health and Human Rights, 20*(1), 1–12.

Ohmer, M. L. (2007). Citizen participation in neighborhood organizations and its relationship to volunteers' self- and collective efficacy and sense of community. *Social Work Research, 31*, 109–120.

Perkins, D. D., Hughey, J., & Speer, P. W. (2002). Community psychology perspectives on social capital theory and community development practice. *Community Development, 33*(1), 33–52.

Pronyk, P. M., Hargreaves, J. R., Kim, J. C., Morison, L. A., Phetla, G., Watts, C., . . . Porter, J. D. (2006). Effect of a structural intervention for the prevention of intimate-partner violence and HIV in rural South Africa: A cluster randomised trial. *The Lancet, 368*(9551), 1973–1983.

Putnam, R. (1995). Bowling alone: America's declining social capital. In L. Crothers & C. Lockhard (Eds.), *Culture and politics: A reader* (pp. 223–234). Palgrave Macmillan.

Raj, A., Silverman, J. G., Klugman, J., Saggurti, N., Donta, B., & Shakya, H. B. (2018). Longitudinal analysis of the impact of economic empowerment on risk for intimate partner violence among married women in rural Maharashtra, India. *Social Science & Medicine, 196*, 197–203.

Rappaport, J. (1987). Terms of empowerment/exemplars of prevention: Toward a theory for community psychology. *American Journal of Community Psychology, 15*(2), 121–148.

Sampson, R. J., Raudenbush, S. W., & Earls, F. (1997). Neighborhoods and violent crime: A multilevel study of collective efficacy. *Science, 277*, 918–924.

Semahegn, A., Torpey, K., Manu, A., Assefa, N., Tesfaye, G., & Ankomah, A. (2019). Are interventions focused on gender-norms effective in preventing domestic violence against women in low and lower-middle income countries? A systematic review and meta-analysis. *Reproductive Health, 16*(1), 1–31.

Speer, P. W., & Hughey, J. (1995). Community organizing: An ecological route to empowerment and power. *American Journal of Community Psychology, 23*(5), 729–748.

Speer, P. W., Christens, B. D., & Peterson, N. A. (2021). Participation in community organizing: Cross-sectional and longitudinal analyses of impacts on socio-political development. *Journal of Community Psychology, 49*(8), 3194–3214.

Speer, P. W., Peterson, N. A., Zippay, A., & Christens, B. D. (2010). Participation in congregation- based organizing: Mixed-method study of civic engagement. In M. Roberts-DeGennaro & S. J. Fogel (Eds.), *Using evidence to inform practice for community and organizational change* (pp. 200–217). Lyceum.

Stark, E. (2007). *Coercive control: How men entrap women in personal life* (1st ed.). Oxford University Press.

Sullivan, C. M., & Bybee, D. (1999). Reducing violence using community-based advocacy for women with abusive partners. *Journal of Consulting and Clinical Psychology, 67*, 43–53.

Suneetha, A., & Nagaraj, V. (2006). A difficult match: Women's actions and legal institutions in the face of domestic violence. *Economic and Political Weekly, 41*(41), 4355–4362.

Trickett, E. (2011). Settings and empowerment. In M. S. Aber, K. I. Maton, & E. Seidman (Eds.), *Empowering settings and voices for social change* (pp. 94–106). Oxford University Press.

United Nations-Habitat. (2004). The challenge of slums: Global report on human settlements 2003. *Management of Environmental Quality: An International Journal, 15*(3), 337–338.

Visaria, L. (2000). Violence against women: A field study. *Economic and Political Weekly, 35*(20), 1742–1751.

Wagman, J. A., Gray, R. H., Campbell, J. C., Thoma, M., Ndyanabo, A., Ssekasanvu, J., . . . Brahmbhatt, H. (2015). Effectiveness of an integrated intimate partner violence and HIV prevention intervention in Rakai, Uganda: Analysis of an intervention in an existing cluster randomised cohort. *The Lancet Global Health, 3*(1), e23–e33.

Watts, R. J., Diemer, M. A., & Voight, A. M. (2011). Critical consciousness: Current status and future directions. *New Directions for Child and Adolescent Development, 134*, 43–57.

Welzel, C., Inglehart, R., & Deutsch, F. (2005). Social capital, voluntary associations and collective action: Which aspects of social capital have the greatest "civic" payoff? *Journal of Civil Society, 1*(2), 121–146.

World Health Organization. (2013). *Global and regional estimates of violence against women: Prevalence and health effects of intimate partner violence and non-partner sexual violence.* World Health Organization.

Yoshikawa, K., Agrawal, N. R., Poudel, K. C., & Jimba, M. (2012). A lifetime experience of violence and adverse reproductive outcomes: Findings from population surveys in India. *Bioscience Trends, 6*(3), 115–121.

Zimmerman, M. A. (1995). Psychological empowerment: Issues and illustrations. *American Journal of Community Psychology, 23*, 581–600.

Zimmerman, M. A. (2000). Empowerment theory: Psychological, organizational, and community levels of analysis. In J. Rappaport & E. Seidman (Eds.), *Handbook of community psychology* (pp. 430–463). Plenum Press.

4 Congregation-Based Community Organizing

Paul W. Speer

Introduction

Congregation-based community organizing (CBCO) represents an approach to building collective power capable of affecting change by engaging local faith institutions as primary constituents in community organizing efforts. Congregation-based community organizing initiatives seek to draw from across diverse faiths and denominations. Further, they do not exclusively engage faith institutions but also may include schools, neighborhoods, and labor and other institutional bases as constituent members. Faith-based institutions are nevertheless the overwhelming base of CBCO initiatives. Accordingly, these organizing efforts are anchored in the values, symbols, and traditions emanating from diverse faith traditions.

Distinctions and Definitions

It is important to acknowledge at the outset the frequent confusion around what exactly constitutes community organizing. Many individuals self-identify as community organizers, yet their activities are quite diverse. For example, individual community activists attend many protests, marches, and other activities in support of people and causes within their community, and it is not uncommon for such individuals to be labeled or to self-identify as community organizers. Similarly, staff members of nonprofit organizations whose primary focus is community outreach and recruitment of community residents to participate in social service programs or to mobilize residents or service recipients to endorse predetermined positions on specific community concerns are sometimes titled "community organizers." Both of these examples can be contrasted with specific staff roles in organizational structures explicitly existing to practice community organizing. These organizational structures (i.e., community organizing groups) are explicitly designed to build social power sufficient to enable some form of collective to have an influence in local decision-making. Within such community organizing efforts, "community organizers" are staff whose work roles include a broad range of functions, but the primary focus is on developing leadership skills and capacities among local residents and cultivating collective power.

This confusion is not limited to how we understand individual roles, such as the role of a staff community organizer. There also exists a puzzling diversity of descriptions and labels across groups said to be engaged in community organizing. There are important differences in activities, methods, and philosophies among organizations describing their work as community organizing. For example, some groups execute initiatives determined by a national office in a predominantly "top-down" manner, whereas other groups build participation and determine efforts locally through participant input in a predominantly "bottom-up" approach. Adding to the confusion, many community organizing groups emphasize distinctions between their specific philosophies, practices, or models from other community organizing groups, leading to an escalation in terminology that seeks to distinguish particular organizing efforts from various others.[1] It may be helpful to consider the family resemblance concept as articulated by Wittgenstein (2009) in relation to the broad range of activities labeled "community organizing." The family resemblance notion holds that rather than a clear set of essential properties defining a construct, some phenomena are best defined by a set of similarities across dimensions of a phenomena – sufficient overlap across dimensions then constitutes what is classified as the phenomena.

This notion of overlap across key dimensions is used by Wood and Warren (2002) to identify the following six distinguishing characteristics of CBCO groups.

Faith-Based

The CBCO approach is grounded in the moral values and traditions that stem from religious faith, to varying degrees and often quite powerfully.

Broad-Based

Though anchored in faith organizations, CBCO initiatives are ecumenical or interfaith, pulling from a diverse group of congregations, synagogues, temples, and mosques. Additionally, CBCO initiatives attract many schools, unions, or other community-based institutions like neighborhood associations. Broad-based organizations intentionally recruit member institutions that are both secular and religious.

Locally Constituted

CBCO initiatives organize in areas that range from large neighborhoods to entire cities. Although linked within national and regional networks, the emphasis is on local grassroots organizing.

---

1 Common labels used to distinguish distinct forms of community organizing include "neighborhood," "electoral," "power-based," "transformative," "constituency," "youth," "faith-based," "labor," "democratic," "pressure group," "congregational," "identity-based," "civic," "women-centered," "community-building," "Marxist," "participatory," "school-based," "progressive," and "social-action" (Speer & Han, 2018).

Multi-Issue

The CBCO approach is focused on grassroots organizing. This means that local congregations and secular groups determine their own priorities among a variety of pressing issues facing their communities. This translates into CBCO initiatives working on a range of issues (i.e., affordable housing, access to credit, educational issues) rather than becoming groups that work on single issues, like a housing group or an environmental group.

Professionally Staffed

Although CBCO groups are composed almost entirely of volunteers, they all hire professional organizers to recruit and train local leaders to work within their own organizations and networks. Professional staff work to develop local leaders and to train residents to identify issues of concern, to analyze factors contributing to problems, and to build and exercise social power to improve communities.

Political, but Nonpartisan

CBCO initiatives are active in the public arena, and their actions are often criticized by conservative faith groups as aligning with more progressive causes. Nevertheless, CBCO is firmly nonpartisan.

These six characteristics are helpful in identifying broad parameters that CBCO initiatives have in common, but they are evolving and may be somewhat less representative characteristics than they once were. For example, the emphasis on local constitution is a less representative characterization when over half of the groups are working at state and national levels. There are, however, additional features of CBCO initiatives beyond these broad characteristics that are important to understand. To address what it is about CBCO that makes it an important area of study in relation to power and empowerment, this chapter first describes the historical emergence of CBCO. Next, several key dimensions of CBCO practice are examined. Additionally, there is a description of how the congregational or faith dimension is manifest in community organizing practice. Implications for power and empowerment are then discussed.

Emergence and Development of Congregation-Based Community Organizing

As noted, there has been a proliferation of terms used to describe particular models or approaches to community organizing. Even within what is commonly called CBCO, the terms "values-based," "institutional-based," and "faith-based" are often applied to CBCO practices (Christens et al., 2008).

The *values* label takes the focus off faith explicitly, as none of these efforts seek to recruit people to a faith or denomination, and a values emphasis elevates commonalities across diverse faith perspectives. Congregation-based community organizing builds on constituencies within faith organizations seeking to put faith values into action in local communities. Characterizing the values linking groups in this organizing approach elevates the principles and essential qualities of love, justice, and community that undergird many faith traditions as well as many secular institutions. Application of the *institutional* label to CBCO efforts emphasizes the engagement of one constituency among many (i.e., neighborhoods, labor, or schools). An institutional label acknowledges that constituents are drawn from faith organizations among local civic infrastructures, thus de-emphasizing the practices, traditions, or epistemologies of faith organizations in favor of the constituent base that the organizing draws from. Finally, the terms *faith-based* and *congregation-based* organizing are often used synonymously.

Wood and Fulton (2015) argue that although most CBCO initiatives retain a predominance of faith organizations as members, increasing diversity among CBCO institutional members (e.g., schools, civic groups, labor unions), declining membership within faith organizations themselves, and several institutional crises within faith organizations (sexual abuse, Dokecki, 2004; gay marriage, O'Donovan, 2008) make "congregation-based community organizing" a less accurate descriptor than it once was. They argue that "faith-based community organizing" is a more appropriate term because the engagement of religious meaning and symbols within CBCO practice remains central to this practice, even as the constituent composition draws a smaller proportion from faith groups. In contrast to the perspective offered by Wood and Fulton (2015), this chapter adheres to the CBCO moniker because the long-term decline of membership and participation in faith groups and institutional crises within religious organizations make the "faith" feature of this organizing process both practically and symbolically less potent. Additionally, there is substantial variability across groups in the centrality and extent to which religious meaning and symbols are employed in organizing practices. This is not to deny the importance of faith in these practices, but the term "congregation," often associated with faith groups, may better capture collective practices. "Congregation" is a term often applied to faith groups, but its meaning relates to the act of assembly or coming together – thus capturing the increasing inclusivity among CBCO efforts. Although the term "congregation" rather than "faith" is used in this chapter, the use of faith traditions and symbols is critical to CBCO practice and will be described in more detail later.

History of Congregation-Based Community Organizing

Congregation-based community organizing is first and foremost about organizing, and the history of CBCO is intertwined with the history of community organizing. Many point to Saul Alinsky as the originator of modern community organizing (Hart, 2001; Horwitt, 1989; Wood, 2002). Alinsky is critically important to community organizing, but he is better understood as a synthesizer, popularizer, and promoter of organizing rather than an originator. When thinking about the history of community organizing, some go as far back as scriptural examples of organizing describing how David's strategic use of existing resources prevailed over the institutionalized capacities of Goliath (Ganz, 2010). Still, Alinsky was unquestionably the catalyst for popularizing community organizing in mid-twentieth-century America. In 1939, he developed Back of the Yards, a community organization in the back of the Chicago stockyards. Alinsky went on to write two books that brought attention to community organizing, as well as developing the Industrial Areas Foundation (IAF) as a training and support network for community organizing across the country. Critically, Alinsky worked with faith communities and appreciated the importance of faith organizations in the composition of community life, although it was many years after his death that the IAF moved from a neighborhood-based constituency to a CBCO model of practice. Many refer to the "Alinsky model" and the principles and strategies he describes in his books and put into practice as a community organizer. To attribute the principles and strategies in his books solely to Alinsky is a misreading of history, however. Alinsky did a great service to advancing these principles and understandings of organizing and in developing training institutes and networks of community organizations in the US, but it is important to note that he promoted and disseminated many existing organizing principles and strategies rather than inventing them himself.

For example, Alinsky learned much about labor organizing practices from John L. Lewis, the head of the Congress of Industrial Organizations (CIO; Horwitt, 1989). Furthermore, the organizing principles Alinsky describes in his books emerged from the passing of wisdom across untold generations of people and oppressed communities where understanding about power and methods for fighting exploitation and suffering had been derived through effort, persistence, and creativity emerging from those pursuing social justice against large odds – both in the US and across the globe (Slate, 2012). As an example, about the time Alinsky went to graduate school at the University of Chicago, Owen Whitfield, a Black pastor from Mississippi, and Claude Williams, a White pastor from Tennessee, were acting on their faith in response to the exploitation they saw among their parishioners and communities by combining labor organizing and the faith practices of their evangelical congregations. They ultimately developed an organization called the People's Institute of Applied Religion (Gellman & Roll, 2011) that was very much akin to what Alinsky developed as the IAF. Whitfield and Williams built multiracial efforts that drew on evangelical symbols and practices but focused on how faith could bring justice here on Earth rather than in the by-and-by. They merged faith with labor organizing so that members were not just seeking higher wages but an end to deeper injustices – specifically Jim Crow and segregation (Gellman & Roll, 2011).

Another example is the work of Ella Baker, an extraordinary community organizer who was central to the National Association for the Advancement of Colored People (NAACP; in the 1940s–1950s), to the Southern Christian Leadership Conference (SCLC) headed by Dr. Martin Luther King, Jr. (in the 1950s), and to the Student Nonviolent Coordinating Committee (SNCC; in the 1960s). Baker embraced a secular worldview but worked closely with people of faith throughout the south, anchoring her organizing approach to practices drawn from her experiences accompanying her mother to activities of the National (Black Baptist) Women's Convention as a young girl (Ransby, 2003) – practices that elevated listening, humility, proximity, pragmatism, and fearlessness. Similarly, Kelley (1990) described organizing efforts in the 1930s and 1940s by Black members of the Alabama Communist Party who blended their faith traditions with a radical political tradition to advance economic justice, racial equity, and civil rights.

The point is that Alinsky was, indeed, central to popularizing and advancing an understanding and awareness of community organizing – and he was clear about the importance of faith communities in organizing practices. However, the practices and principles Alinsky described in his books distilled and articulated organizing wisdom and practice drawn from generations of organizers rather than an approach developed solely on his own, as is often implied by descriptions of "the Alinsky model." Alinsky did contribute organizing insights himself, but his brilliance is perhaps best understood through his ability to synthesize existing knowledge and to systematize organizing practice in the service of bolstering the development of power and community change.

Alinsky launched the IAF in 1940 as a training institute that worked with neighborhood groups in cities throughout the US. The organizing efforts he was involved in had a reputation for achieving important impacts for the people and communities involved, but after achieving their immediate goals the groups often collapsed soon after. Following Alinsky's death in the early 1970s, IAF projects struggled to sustain active organizations. In hindsight, organizing efforts, as with all aspects of society, were caught up in the social, political, and economic shifts that had been evolving for some time. Postwar deindustrialization had accrued for decades by this point, and globalizing processes were weakening labor organizing and industrial employment (Christens & Speer, 2015; Speer & Han, 2018). Urban disinvestment, suburbanization, and decline of social capital dramatically weakened urban institutions, which contributed to the decline of participation in civic life, including in local community organizing.

In the early 1980s, the IAF made a strategic shift by concentrating on faith groups rather than geographic or neighborhood constituencies, as faith groups were one of the few viable local institutions in lower-income urban contexts (Warren & Wood, 2001). This shift was soon adopted by several other national community organizing networks, namely PICO (now Faith in Action), Gamaliel, and the Direct Action and Research Training (DART) Center (Hart, 2001). As noted, religious groups have always been a part of organizing, movements, and other social change efforts (Ganz, 2010; Morris, 1984; Payne, 1995). Among groups exclusively focused on community organizing, this shift from neighborhood organizing to a focused and explicit operation anchored in faith organizations had not previously taken place.

The Texas IAF pioneered a multifaith, multiracial model for organizing that built sustainable political power and mounted successful campaigns for improvements in neighborhood infrastructure, schools, and affordable housing (Warren, 2001). While the shift to congregations was in part a response to deindustrialization and the mobility of populations, this change also represented a strategy to take traditional organizing into the cultural realm and tap into theological symbols, financial stability, and relatively robust networks anchored in faith communities (Osterman, 2002; Warren, 2001; Wood, 2002). This change, from a neighborhood to a primarily congregational constituency, profoundly altered the course of contemporary community organizing, making CBCO worthy of close study.

The Growth of Congregation-Based Community Organizing

The focus of this chapter is on CBCO in the US context, but CBCO exists in many international contexts, though not as pervasively as in the US. Congregation-based community organizing has been practiced in Britain for some time (Warren, 2009; Wood, 2003), but efforts exist elsewhere, most notably Africa, South America, and the Caribbean (Faith in Action, 2023; Olarinmoye, 2012). The principles and practices of CBCO support its generalizability to multiple contexts based on what Fligstein and McAdam (2012) term "the existential function of the social," or the universal need for humans to form relationships and community with others to enable collective action and meaning-making. Beyond prioritizing these fundamental human needs for community and meaning, CBCO practices are emergent, bottom-up, participant-led processes, thus allowing their application in a way that conforms to diverse cultures and traditions. This context-dependent structure of CBCO practices makes the approach less prone to forms of neocolonialism so pervasive in international development settings (Langan, 2018). Finally, the deep historical roots of CBCO described earlier in the chapter focus on the US context, but that orientation should be tempered with an understanding that traditional organizing practices are not exclusive to the US. For example, the civil rights movement in the US and the South Asian freedom struggles in the early twentieth century were deeply intertwined, with practices and strategies passed bidirectionally between these efforts (Slate, 2012). Although the focus of this chapter is on the US context, the "existential function of the social" reflects the universal historical struggle by humans, across both time and space, to challenge exploitation and injustice, making CBCO broadly applicable to contexts across the globe.

In a report detailing the landscape of congregation-based organizing within the US in 1999, Wood and Warren (2002) describe CBCO as "one of the broadest based initiatives in the American public sphere" (p. 7). They note that much of the popularity of CBCO stems from the fact that religious organizations have tended to be relatively stable institutions, even in distressed neighborhoods. Importantly, congregation models of organizing demonstrate that religious institutions can still be sources of progressive advocacy. There are strong relationships between many religious groups and right-wing politics, namely religious evangelicals and political conservatives. This connection became a political force with the election of Ronald Reagan (Steensland & Wright, 2014) and has continued to grow through the election of Donald Trump – a connection that is prevalent in the public mind (Margolis, 2020). The manifestation of this connection is pervasive – for example, the engagement of many conservative Christians and faith groups to support access to firearms (Vegter & Kelley, 2020). Critically, CBCO is an example of people and organizations explicitly acting from a faith perspective who run counter to this well-known alignment with conservative and reactionary political positions.

In a follow-up to their 1999 study, Wood et al. (2012) explored the landscape of CBCO eleven years later, examining changes in the field over the previous decade. They found that CBCO activity had expanded in the US, with more organizing groups but fewer organizational memberships composed of faith congregations (faith groups dropping from 88 to 80 percent over the period studied). In 1999 there were thirty-three states where at least some CBCO was active, and by 2011 that number had grown to thirty-nine states. Another trend they reported is that CBCO efforts had expanded in geographic scale over that time period. Although CBCO is anchored in communities and cities, they found that half of the CBCO initiatives engaged in organizing sought to affect change at state levels, and they reported some efforts working at national scales. Beyond issues of scale, over this time frame CBCO groups also deepened the work they were doing on issues of racism and ethnic marginalization, an arena that has, historically, been less explicitly addressed by CBCO initiatives. Finally, as to the substantive issues organizing groups were found to be invested in, there were six issues that over half of all organizing efforts in 2011 reported working on: poverty (70 percent of all groups surveyed), education (66 percent), health care (57 percent), immigration (54 percent), housing (53 percent), and criminal justice (53 percent).[2]

---

2 As noted by Wood and Warren (2002), CBCO initiatives are multi-issue organizations, so percentages add up well beyond 100 percent.

The Impact of Congregation-Based Community Organizing

Since the 1980s, when several community organizing groups turned to congregation-based models, there has been remarkable success from this approach. This success is a key reason why a focus on CBCO is critical for studies of community empowerment. There are far too many efforts to describe, but as an example, the first "living wage" ordinance in the US was developed by the CBCO group Baltimoreans United in Leadership Development (BUILD) in Baltimore, MD, an affiliate of the IAF organizing network (Brooks, 2007; Martin, 2006). This initiative required city employees as well as contracted employees to receive a wage that would sustain a family of four above the poverty line. Since that time, living wage ordinances have been developed in many cities throughout the US and globally. As another example, Nehemiah Housing was an initiative that redeveloped abandoned housing in east New York and made high-quality, affordable housing available for low-income and working-class families. Over 4,500 Nehemiah homes were built in east New York, and most residents then occupying this new affordable housing had incomes less than 50 percent of the median income (Phipps et al., 1994). Furthermore, the initiative is reported to improve neighborhoods overall (Deslippe, 2019), as well as to produce spillover effects that were shown to elevate property values of the blighted neighborhoods in close proximity to the Nehemiah homes (Ellen, 2001).

As an example of community impact with a bit more detail, ISAIAH, a CBCO in Minnesota, started working on transportation issues in 2002 based on concerns of residents that emerged from relational conversations with organization members and community residents. Over the next few years, leaders of the ISAIAH organization conducted substantial research and learned about a long-proposed light rail line between Minneapolis and St. Paul, as well as about regional transit systems and their relationships with jobs, health, and community well-being. By 2005, ISAIAH was actively supporting the long-proposed light rail line, but the state's governor vetoed funding for the transit system three times over a two-year period, claiming that resources were too limited to fund this system. ISAIAH leaders developed a theologically oriented articulation of their perspective based on hope, values, and abundance. They pressured state legislators to support the transit bill, and when the governor vetoed it for a fourth time, the legislature overrode that veto (Speer et al., 2014).

Soon after passage of the bill, planning authorities removed three stops along the rail line – the three stops with the highest percentage of non-White populations in proximity to them. Planning officials justified this action based on a federal regulation called the "cost effectiveness index," claiming that those stops would undermine the project's economic feasibility (Blackwell et al., 2012). ISAIAH responded by engaging organizations capable of evaluating the economic, health, and other impacts of the proposal and expanding their outreach to community residents, seeking broader input and engagement. Through the ongoing outreach and research conducted by ISAIAH during over 100 meetings ranging from 10 to 3,500 participants and the analyses of economic and health impacts by experts in those fields, ISAIAH leaders learned that retaining those three stops would not undermine the system's economic feasibility, but removing those stops would be detrimental to the health and economic well-being of the region. ISAIAH then pressured the US Secretary of Transportation to alter federal policy regarding the cost effectiveness index and to expand such assessments to include health and social considerations along with economic ones. The Secretary modified that regulation by following ISAIAH's more expansive guidelines, and local officials reinstated the three stops. The Central Corridor rail line between Minneapolis and St. Paul was completed in 2014. These brief examples across issues of income, housing, and transportation provide some sense of CBCO impacts, but there are many examples across the CBCO field.

It is important to note that explicit community organizing efforts not using congregation models have also achieved great successes. For example, the community organization Association of Community Organizations for Reform Now (ACORN) pressured H&R Block, the largest commercial tax preparer in the US, to cease their exploitative price gouging of lower-income households through "refund anticipation loans" (RALs) – short-term loans pushed on clients for expected tax refunds based on H&R Block's tax preparation work. To get a sense of the value of this exploitative mechanism for H&R Block, they issued 3 million such loans in 1999, which grew to 4.5 million loans by 2001. In 2001, they generated $133 million in revenue from these RALs, which yielded $68 million in profits for H&R Block – a 50 percent rate of profit (Berube et al., 2002). ACORN chapters in cities throughout the country brought attention and pressure to how H&R Block was extracting massive profits from some of the lowest-income American households just as tax season was starting in January. H&R Block agreed to meet with ACORN leaders within days, where they negotiated an agreement in which H&R Block would provide educational materials and transparent information about the cost of RALs and they agreed to cease the administrative fees charged for RALs – a reduction of $200 million in fees annually to H&R Block (Fisher et al., 2007), among other concessions.

Although reporting and public awareness are limited, these examples demonstrate that community organizing efforts can be impactful. Impactful work is not limited to CBCO by any means, but CBCO has demonstrated a remarkable track record of participation and success relative to other approaches (Han et al., 2021; Warren, 1998; Wood, 2002). Although all of these cases are truncated, the ISAIAH example demonstrates several features of CBCO. First, it demonstrates power through the sustained engagement of volunteer leaders over many years. Second, leader reflections about how to act in the face of the governor's vetoes shows how faith traditions informed the actions of the group and the narrative developed about hope and abundance. Third, it demonstrates a systemic analysis of community issues that shuns simplistic understandings for fuller analyses of the interdependence of different systems. The scope of CBCO successes makes it an important phenomenon to consider in relation to community empowerment.

Features of Congregation-Based Community Organizing Drawn from Traditional Organizing

Beyond the six dimensions used by Warren and Wood (2001) to define CBCO initiatives, there are important features and practices within CBCO that are important to describe. First, it is a practice connected to the values drawn from the faith traditions of those participating. Importantly, faith organizations also represent an ideological perspective that runs counter to the dominant market-based ideology in American society. The anticommunist fervor through the postwar period (Sugrue, 1995) and the rise of neoliberal ideology since the mid-1970s (Evans & Sewell, 2013) have both been used to suppress critique of systemic analyses and reinforce ideologies attributing human suffering to individual flaws (Pyysiäinen et al., 2017). Organizing efforts have often been undermined by insinuating communist infiltration and other nefarious plots (Gellman & Roll, 2011; Ransby, 2003), but such labeling is less effective when targeted at people explicitly affiliated with faith organizations and their public declarations connecting scriptural references to the community policies they are demanding.

Community organizing practices and approaches used in CBCO align with a rich tradition of organizing in labor unions, social movements, and similar change efforts (Delgado, 1986; Fisher, 1994; McAlevey, 2016; Payne, 1995; Ransby, 2003; Warren, 2001; Wood, 2002). These traditional practices can be distinguished from the proliferation and broad usage of terms related to organizing, as previously described in relation to definitions of "community organizer" and "community organizing." In addition to the characteristics of CBCO noted previously (broad-based, multi-issue, political but nonpartisan, etc.), there are features of traditional community organizing practice that are common to all CBCO initiatives. These traditional approaches, in combination with how cultural aspects of faith organizations are absorbed within CBCO, are critical to CBCO's success (Day, 2012).

Relationship Development

Relational models of community organizing invest in building deep, meaningful, and sustained connections between people (Whitman, 2018; Wood, 2002). At community scales, relational organizing develops connections between organizations (Neal & Christens, 2014; Speer et al., 2014). Relational organizing invests deeply in people by cultivating leadership skills (Medellin et al.,

2021; Speer et al., 2021) and in fostering robust collectivities by investing in organizational development efforts (McCarthy & Walker, 2004). Relationships are key because they are fundamental for developing collective power. As voluntary structures, strong relationships produce shared understanding, accountability, and commitment among participants and represent the central source through which CBCO initiatives hold power. Relationships, and the trust that flows from relationships, allow CBCO to sustain activities over time and thus wield organizational power.

This relational emphasis can be contrasted with mobilizing strategies that characterize most social movement efforts. In mobilizing, issues, tactics, and planning are predetermined, and individuals who are politically aligned with the identified issue are recruited to participate in support of the mobilizing effort (Haug, 2013; Johnson et al., 2000). Although mobilizing is an activity at one stage of the community organizing process, CBCO participants invest heavily in identifying the issues of concern based on their lived experiences, in meeting with knowledgeable institutions and actors to research causes of the issue, and in analytic and tactical choices to improve or resolve the issue through the exercise of collective power (Medellin et al., 2021; Speer & Hughey, 1995).

The major method for developing relationships in CBCO involves "one-on-ones": conversations between organizational leaders or community organizers and community residents in which the leader or organizer listens to the experience of residents (Christens, 2010; Robinson & Hanna, 1994; Schutz & Sandy, 2011). One-on-ones require leaders and organizers to listen to others, and listening requires sensitivity to the perceptions, beliefs, and challenges experienced by individuals (Whitman, 2018). Beyond listening, developing relationships with others requires candid dialogue. Having candid dialogue is a challenge, particularly when this dialogue occurs across race, gender, class, sexual orientation, or other characteristics that divide people and communities (Speer & Christens, 2015), but skills in listening and understanding the experience of others are the basis for building relationship with others and are central practices in CBCO.

Self-Interest and Challenge

While listening is a part of the relational approach to organizing that is central to CBCO practice, there are deeper elements of listening in the one-on-one process that are critical. One-on-ones represent an ongoing practice of many, many dyadic interactions rather than singular events. As leaders and organizers meet with community members over time, they listen for the self-interest of the individual they are meeting with.

Self-interest is often equated with "selfishness," but in the CBCO worldview self-interest is not a self-centered or myopic orientation of one over others in the community. In organizing, self-interest is discerned by listening to the stories, experiences, and priorities that individuals share in conversation (Oyakawa, 2015; Speer & Christens, 2015). Within this sharing, people communicate what they value – caring for an elderly parent, or a child's struggles in school, or a neighbor's victimization from crime. Within such stories, self-interest is discerned through the emotion expressed, which captures the care, the pain, and the anger people feel. Listening for and understanding the self-interest within the stories people share are critical because the values reflected in what people care about drive their anger – and these are the emotions people will act on.

The concept of self-interest is tied to what is described as public versus private relationships (Alinsky, 1971; Schutz & Sandy, 2011). Private relationships are viewed as those anchored in love, as between family members or close friends. In private relationships we may get angry with one another, but we are loyal and forgiving, and we can count on those relationships even when we do wrong (albeit with consequences). In contrast, public relationships are based on accountability and respect, and they are freely chosen. Organizing seeks to develop public relationships (Chambers, 2003). Recognizing that public relationships are freely chosen means they cannot be taken for granted in the way that private relationships are. In this context, public relationships will only be maintained if they are built on respect and accountability. Developing organizational cultures that understand self-interest and public relationships offers the potential for people to come together and build something collectively that is greater than themselves – to build power (Gupta, 2021), but developing a culture of accountability and respect takes a great deal of effort (Fulkerson, 2012).

Another aspect of developing strong public relationships is that, as in any relationship, there will be times of disagreement, disengagement, and conflict (Schutz & Sandy, 2011). Congregation-based community organizing draws upon traditional organizing perspectives in this arena too. Leaders and organizers work to develop skills in challenging others and, at times, agitating others as part of the listening process (Medellin et al., 2021). The ability to challenge someone – someone you are listening to and, over the longer term, someone you are building a relationship with – is a critical competency in organizing. Challenges may center around an analysis, assumption, perception, or belief. The purpose of challenging is to advance an understanding of the causes of the issues confronted by an individual or group and to deepen reflections on individual and collective values. The capacity for leaders and organizers to challenge or agitate comes in proportion to the strength of relationship they have with an individual (Speer & Christens, 2015). Within CBCO cultures, the notion of challenge or agitation does not equate to a severe interaction but may manifest as a direct question posed in a thoughtful way or asking why an individual acted as they did in a particular circumstance. Application of concepts like self-interest, public relationships, accountability, and challenge are fundamental to traditional organizing models and they are a part of all CBCO practice.

The Organizing Process

Congregation-based community organizing, drawing from traditional organizing approaches, goes through several stages of activity as part of the normal organizing process. There are many variants to labels describing this process, and there can be additional stages identified, but at a basic level we may describe the traditional stages of the organizing process as: assessing community issues and priorities, researching the causes and consequences of identified community priorities, taking action to address the community issue, and evaluating and reflecting on the lessons and impacts of change efforts (Speer et al., 1995).

It is important to note that the mechanisms of relationship development, self-interest, and agitation or challenge are practices that cut across all stages of organizing activity. There are also many other practices and organizing terms tied to traditional organizing that are part of the CBCO process such as cutting an issue (Alinsky, 1971; Schutz & Sandy, 2011), public targets (Rusch & Swarts, 2015), research actions (Christens & Speer, 2011), house meetings (Day, 2012), and many others. For CBCO, however, key stages of the organizing process are assessment, research, action, and reflection (Speer et al., 1995).

In assessment stages of the organizing process, many one-on-ones are conducted to understand the lived experience of residents and participants of the CBCO. Assessment is not about taking a survey or tallying up the most prevalent issues but about understanding what experiences and struggles people are dealing with and listening for connections between issues that may appear unrelated. In the assessment phase, community leaders and organizers listen for issues that have strong emotion and anger in relation to them. As dominant community concerns surface, leaders and organizers do one-on-ones with individuals they have spoken with previously to share what they have learned and test understandings and potential paths forward for the CBCO.

Once the assessment process has discerned specific concerns shared across many residents within the community, a process of research is undertaken to better understand the causes of and potential solutions for the identified issue. The CBCO research process seeks to understand the systemic roots of the identified issue. Because the assessment process will have identified the issue based on the breadth of common experience across the community, the source of the problem is likely to be systemic rather than individualized (Christens et al., 2007). In the research process, CBCO groups seek to engage a broad range of actors with knowledge about the specific issue. This often includes professionals, academics, public officials, and the like, and the number of research meetings typically ranges between ten and fifty, depending on the scope of the issue. The research process not only achieves greater understanding of community systems and the specific issue but is also a stage during

Figure 4.1 *A public congregation-based community organizing meeting taking action to pressure for policy change.*

which CBCO participants develop skills in public speaking, civic understanding, and community analysis. Lastly, the research process is a mechanism for CBCO groups to build relationships at the organizational level with other groups and institutions across the community.

Once a CBCO has conducted an analysis of the causal factors contributing to the issue, the group identifies organizations and institutions within the community with authority to redress the issue. Groups then meet with the identified authority, present their analysis, and request that this authority remedy the issue (see Figure 4.1). At this stage, the organization or institution with the authority to impact the issue often balks at implementing changes. Though not articulated directly, this resistance is the product of other powerful actors who benefit from particular arrangements – the same arrangements that are the sources of the negative community impacts that the CBCO is addressing. Though organizations or institutions with authority are often sympathetic to the CBCO, they are in a bind because acting to resolve this issue would anger powerful interests. If the identified organization or institution with the authority to resolve the issue declines to act, the CBCO then holds public events or "actions," where the CBCO exercises collective power to pressure the targeted organization to execute the changes that the CBCO is seeking to make. At this public action stage, it is critical that CBCOs have obtained a clear analysis of how much power they can wield and have the ability to do so, as well as of how much power existing interests have to maintain the status quo. The success or failure of the CBCO process in affecting community change depends on this analysis of power and the capacity to exercise the CBCOs collective power.

The final stage in the organizing process is an evaluation and reflection stage. Evaluation occurs within the CBCO process with each activity in the organizing process, but in this final stage groups work to take stock of what has been learned and how the CBCO has developed through this arc of activity on the specific issue addressed. This evaluation examines how the CBCO, as a collective entity, has performed: Has the group expanded participation of residents? Has the group formed relationships with organizational and institutional actors? What has the group learned about power dynamics in the broader community? Congregation-based community organizing also asks questions about how the faith of participants informed the process: In what ways was your faith tested while working on this community issue? How has your faith changed through this process? What kinds of questions have the organizing provoked for you or the congregation to which you belong? Answers to these questions then help strengthen the CBCO as it moves back into the assessment stage with another issue in the future.

Although these stages represent traditional community organizing practices, CBCO is a blend of both traditional organizing practices and congregational or faith-based cultural features. In their combination, CBCO represents an impactful formula for community change (Fulkerson, 2012; Wood, 2002).

Manifestation of Faith as a Central Feature of Congregation-Based Community Organizing

Through their associations with religious institutions, CBCOs have expanded their cultural repertoire beyond these traditional organizing practices. As an example, CBCO organizers often discuss charity as an essential but over-represented component of congregational activity. The charity focus can be contrasted with justice, which, while strongly rooted in religious teaching, is often ignored relative to charity work by religious groups. Organizers and CBCO leaders have become adept at connecting the organizing process to justice-oriented traditions within various denominations and faiths. Adaptations of organizing that incorporate religious, social, and moral teachings have proven powerful in sustaining involvement in collective action (Jacobsen, 2001; Wood, 1999).

Several scholars explicitly focus on how religious traditions are drawn upon to enrich CBCO practice. Warren (2001) goes so far as to say that religion and politics have been fused into a "theology of organizing." It is important to describe several religious traditions that have been actively incorporated in CBCO. One tradition is represented in Catholic social teachings, which address the need for a moral economy that is concerned with the poor and vulnerable in society (Hart, 2001; Warren, 2001; Wood, 2002). This tradition elevates ethical principles from Catholic teachings and papal encyclicals as guidelines for action, thus challenging the laity to consider their actions in relation to their faith rather than acquiescing to market forces as standards for guiding society. Second are African American Christian social action traditions (Hart, 2001; Warren, 2001; Wood, 2002). These traditions are described as highly biblical, drawing upon scriptural resources that emphasize love, justice, liberation, hope, and redemptive suffering. Central to this tradition are explicit connections between the social and spiritual meanings of these scriptural resources. A third tradition central to the connection of faith to community organizing is liberation theology (Hart, 2001; Wood, 2002). This work, identified most closely with Gustavo Gutierrez and also drawing on Catholic social teachings, promotes practices and activities within small-group communities in which groups consider the challenges of lived experience and inform action with theological reflection. Liberation theology promotes exercising faith in everyday living rather than reserving faith-related thoughts and actions for religious services. A fourth religious tradition intertwined with community organizing is that of the social gospels as expressed in American Protestantism (Hart, 2001; Warren, 2001). This tradition addresses the ethics of Christian life in the face of capitalism and modern economic life. The emphasis within American Protestant traditions is on modifying pervasive market logics with a view of life that prioritizes gospel teachings and an embrace of human solidarity rather than competitive individualism. Finally, a fifth tradition is Christian realism (Hart, 2001). This tradition maintains a rather pessimistic view of human nature. In confronting that negative view of human nature, the Christian realist tradition holds that Christians are compelled to bring their faith into the world. In their view, faith requires confronting evil in the world, and this translates into acting in the world of politics.

These theological traditions are interwoven into the philosophy and practice of CBCO, but these traditions are rarely explicitly stated (Hart, 2001; Jacobsen, 2001; Wood, 2002). Rather than direct declarations about how theology is expressed in CBCO practice, various denominational and faith participants are free to express their theologies as they understand them, with an appreciation of the diverse faith groups that are also a part of CBCO groups, revealing a pluralist approach to how theologies are expressed in CBCO.

This diversity is important and is supported through a lack of fixed rules or behavioral requirements for membership within CBCO. Although membership is open, organizing processes within CBCO adhere to a disciplined set of practices. The use of Socratic methods helps sustain the balance of openness and discipline that serves to support an organizational culture that tolerates difference while holding groups together regarding the broader goals for community change. Wood (2002) describes CBCO culture as "less a unified whole than a rope with many fibers." The customs, rituals, and languages that have formed around CBCO practices have been enriched by the faith dimension in CBCO, which has helped develop bonds that support holding these organizations together despite their diversity.

Cultural Shift

Overall, the way religious traditions are interwoven into the practice of CBCO speaks to an important understanding of this congregational approach to organizing – the deep engagement of cultural elements of faith as important supports for both the internal development of organizations as well as the efficacy and impact that these organizing groups have on the broader communities in which they are embedded (Swarts, 2011; Warren, 2001; Wood, 2002). One manifestation of these faith traditions is what Hart (2001) terms "modes of discourse" in CBCO. He describes how modes of discourse vary across different organizing groups, whether progressive or conservative, secular or faith-driven, geographic or institutional. These "modes" refer more to how ideas and feelings are expressed as opposed to what is expressed. Broadly, some organizational cultures shape member expressions about thoughts and feelings in a rational, detached way, whereas other cultures support more emotive, expressive, and transcendent forms of expression. Hart finds that progressive groups are overwhelmingly rational and detached, while conservative group tend toward the expressive. In his research, Hart (2001) finds the nature of internal discourse and the cultural practices of CBCO to merge these two modes of discourse. Congregation-based community organizing culture supports emotive and transcendent expressions while also adhering to the facts and evidence of the community issues they are confronting. His observation is that this blending helps explain what is unique as well as what is effective about CBCO, and it also points to how a high tolerance for diversity and variability across the individuals and groups is maintained within CBCO.

For example, Rusch and Swarts (2015) describe how a tension was navigated in one California CBCO. Members drawn largely from Latino Catholic congregations were opposed to a California ballot initiative seeking to block access to health and education for undocumented youth. In contrast, a number of participants from White, working-class, Protestant denominations in the same CBCO were in support of the initiative. To address these differences, members were expressive in discussing their perspectives, and the group researched details of the initiative, met with policy analysts about expected impacts of the proposal on local communities, and discussed religious teachings to inform options for how to proceed. In this case, group members came to a consensus to oppose the ballot initiative, and they even went further, urging county officials to refuse to implement this initiative (Proposition 187) if it were to pass at the state level. County officials passed this resolution, pledging to resist this initiative at the urging of the CBCO, and the CBCO actively campaigned against the statewide initiative. This county was only one of eight counties statewide (out of a total of fifty-eight counties) that had a majority of residents oppose this initiative.

The details about how consensus was negotiated in this example are not known, but Hart's (2001) focus on *constrained* versus *expansive* expressions in organizing groups speaks to a quality within groups that supports a particular organizational culture. Groups with a constrained culture tend to be more instrumental and outcome-focused; they are often procedural and limit dialogue to just the issue they are working on (the environment, schools, etc.) while avoiding articulations about how one feels or what an issue means to someone. In contrast, expansive communication styles within organizing groups articulate more emotive and expressive sentiments among members. Organizational cultures characterized as expansive encourage members to voice personal interpretations and deeply held values when sharing with a group. Hart emphasizes that CBCO efforts tend to take progressive stances on community issues, but the way they engage members in discourse embraces passions and transcendent language to produce a richer cultural context and more effective organizing.

These features of religious traditions capture what has been central to congregation-based organizing: greater attention to and an explicit focus on cultural elements of community organizing practice (Delehanty & Oyakawa, 2018; Fulkerson, 2012; Gupta, 2021; Hart, 2001; Levad, 2019; Osterman, 2006). Some emphasize that CBCO has been successful by incorporating cultural dynamics within CBCO processes that draw upon and actively engage the cultural symbols of faith traditions (Wood, 2002). Others emphasize cultural practices within CBCO groups that support member expressions and reflections on faith in relation to community issues (Hart, 2001). Others still focus on the deeper values driving individual participants, as well as the values driving the powerful community actors that organizing groups encounter in their social change efforts (Christens & Speer, 2015; Jacobsen, 2001). For example, Gupta (2021) describes how faith reflections have been explicitly engaged to address race and racism through the CBCO process. The combination of faith communities as an important constituency, the embrace of the central values within congregations of many faiths, explicit attention being given to cultural elements within faith traditions that support organizing processes, and the adherence to time-honored practices of community organizing have yielded an efficacy to and increased the impact of the practice of CBCO, making CBCO critical for studies of community power.

An Example and Interpretation of Congregation-Based Community Organizing

This case example is excerpted from a talk by Dr. Jose Carrasco (an organizer, trainer, and organizing consultant) entitled "Beyond the Good Samaritan," presented to the School of Social Work at Rutgers University (Carrasco,

2000). When the text uses the first person, it is from the perspective of Carrasco, the organizer.

Context of a Family

Ruben and Betty had been married for eighteen years. Born in Mexico, Ruben was a naturalized citizen, while Betty was born and raised in east Los Angeles. The couple had three children, the oldest a sixteen-year-old high school student named Johnny. Like others in poor and working communities, Ruben was aware of the organizing effort but had questions regarding it as well as the church's participation. He lacked trust in community organizations. Moreover, he felt that the only people these organizations ever did anything for were lazy welfare recipients who did not want to work.

For Ruben, attending church had become a waste of time. He felt he and his family were up to their necks in problems and struggling to survive; *"en pura cagada"* (in crap), as he put it. He seldom attended or participated in church or school activities anymore, except on special occasions directly involving the children. He readily complained about the bad public schools that produced young illiterate "thugs" for gangs participating in daily violence around neighborhood parks, drive-by shootings, drugs, break-ins, and other social afflictions. Moreover, he was concerned that they might be losing their son, Johnny, to gangs, and he feared that his older daughter would eventually take the same path. Given money and opportunity, Ruben would have moved his family elsewhere a long time ago, like so many others he had watched depart the community. In short, he was skeptical about both his neighborhood and his family's future. Meanwhile, Betty, whose family was from the neighborhood, was a frequent churchgoer and did volunteer work at the school. Although she was as aware and concerned about all the problems they were facing, Betty saw the neighborhood as home. The barrio provided her and the children with social and spiritual connections. However, like her husband, she could only complain about the problems they faced. Neither had ever been involved in any form of community activity.

Initiation of the Organizing Process

My first contact with Ruben was through a nun who taught at the parish school that two of his children attended. Following several calls and much resistance on his part, I was able to visit Ruben at his home, where I noticed a group of youth loitering about the street nearby. As I entered the home, his teenage son was going out to join the group of young people.

During our conversation, Ruben was courteous but showed little interest, and he quickly informed me that his intent was only to listen. So, I provided my credentials and pointed out that the pastor and sisters at his parish were also involved. I proceeded to inquire about his concerns; his response was that "everything is fine." When asked if he ever felt concern about his children leaving the house or whether the groups of young people standing around the streets had ever been a problem, his response was the same: "No problems." At this point, Ruben let me know his views regarding community groups, his lack of confidence in the church, and how doubtful he was as to any remedy. He finished by politely informing me that he and his wife were too busy to become involved and that they were thinking about moving from the area. During all this time, I could see Betty in the kitchen seemingly going about her business but making sure she could hear the details of our conversation. Recalling the young people outside, the disarray of the neighborhood, and his son leaving the house, I decided to risk the possibility that Ruben's love of family was still greater than his pride. Rather than accept the thought that this intelligent, caring, and perplexed individual did not care enough about his home and family to act on their behalf given the opportunity, I decided to challenge him. At worst, he would ask me to leave.

Moreover, with luck, his wife might be ready to intervene with some thoughts of her own. As I stood to leave, I stoically suggested to Ruben that it was probably for the best that his schedule was too busy for any involvement, especially since the group of young people hanging around the corner outside probably had plenty of time to give his son. As I proceeded toward the door, the wife suddenly entered the room asking if there was a way to contact me if they wished to talk again.

I received a call from Ruben two days later; we met at a McDonald's near his home. This time he shared his anger about the neighborhood and his sense of helplessness about his family; in particular, he expressed fear of losing his son to gangs and the difficulty it was causing for the family, including difficulties between him and his wife. Then, as if embarrassed by his confession, Ruben said, "So, now that I've told you all these things, what are you and your committee of ministers going to do about it? Are you going to be like everyone else and promise to solve all the problems then forget about it?"

Implication for Congregation-Based Community Organizing

This brief excerpt from Carrasco's presentation captures some important themes about the CBCO process and what makes this process important for community empowerment scholarship. First, it starts from a bottom-up approach – an organizer visiting a barrio family based on the suggestion of a parish nun. This initial contact was not a "cold call" – contacting someone with no connection – but captures a relationship that may be understood as a "weak tie" between the faith community (the nun in this instance) and a household with an inactive member of the congregation. Second, the organizer's interactions were invested in understanding Ruben and Betty and their family; it was not about recruiting this family to engage on a predetermined issue or in getting this family to attend a meeting or program activity. This

focus demonstrates how CBCO practices adhere to many traditional organizing approaches that are centered on people and relationships rather than issues
and outcomes (Alinsky, 1971; Payne, 1995; Ransby, 2003). The issues
addressed and the tangible community outcomes achieved are critically
important to CBCO, but they are thought to flow from prioritizing people
and relationships in what Rappaport might call a paradox (Rappaport, 1981).
Third, yet closely related to centering relationships in the CBCO process, this
case shows how the organizer accepted this family for who they were as
opposed to what social scientists term "selection processes" (Christens et al.,
2011). The organizer started with members of a faith community but was not
seeking individuals with particular attributes for recruitment, such as those
concerned about particular issues (e.g., youth, crime, environment), those with
particular political orientations (e.g., libertarian, conservative, socialist, liberal), or those with particular demographic characteristics (e.g., sexual identity, age, race, income) – the interest was in Ruben and Betty and their lived
experience. Most critical about the focus on this couple was the organizer
investing time to visit with the husband, Ruben, despite needing to make
several calls and experiencing resistance from him. Critical to effective
CBCO practice was the organizer's acceptance of Ruben's perceptions – not
for the substance of his perceptions (i.e., the initial characterizations that
everything in the neighborhood was "fine," his feeling that community organizations just helped "lazy welfare recipients," and [after opening up about how
he really felt] his feeling that "the committee of ministers" should address his
problems), but that these responses reflected Ruben's perceptions and experiences, and they needed to be heard and respected for what they were.

The Resolution

Carrasco in this case goes on to explain that his response to Ruben's question
'What are you doing to do about it?' was, "You're asking the right question,
Ruben, but the wrong person. The question is not what am I or some
committee going to do about it; but rather, what are you going to do about
it? I will make one pledge: You will not have to do it alone." Over a period of
months and years, Ruben and Betty became active with others in the organizing process who were experiencing the same worries about their families and
the same feelings of hopelessness to address their concerns about neighborhood deterioration, crime, and limited opportunities for their children. Ruben
visited friends and neighbors and participated in much of the research activity
around the organization's work on crime and the need for youth programs.
During a meeting with the Area Police Commander, Ruben assumed a
leadership role by bringing others and providing personal testimony during
the meeting. Most important for Ruben and Betty was that, after the public
meeting with the Police Commander, participants in the organizing effort
convened to briefly evaluate the meeting. Suddenly, Ruben's son came up to

his father, put his arm around him, and said, "I didn't know you could do things like this!" Ruben and Betty remained active in their parish organization, while their son and older daughter helped to form a youth organizing group that participated in youth issues with the broader organization. The organizing effort went on to make significant improvements for neighborhood youth, but it also provided space for this family to turn their isolation into deeper connections with others and an understanding of how to have agency as individuals and as a community.

Implications for Community Empowerment

While CBCO has produced important successes and community impacts, there are also challenges to this approach. Due to the bottom-up nature of the CBCO process, it is by nature slow, and issues can change quickly when new crises befall a community (Speer & Christens, 2013). Because of the urgency of so many social problems, the slowness of the CBCO process often renders it unacceptable to community residents. The field as a whole is confronting challenges from neoliberalism, globalization, and economic restructuring (Christens & Speer, 2015; Speer & Christens, 2015), from crises within religious organizations and the decline of participation in faith communities (Dokecki, 2004; Franck & Iannaccone, 2014; O'Donovan, 2008), and from the scale of social control moving away from local institutions to national and global actors (Christens & Speer, 2015; Speer & Christens, 2013).

These are serious challenges for achieving community empowerment, but CBCO has proven to be remarkably effective at community empowerment and social change despite these challenges. Congregation-based community organizing is important for understanding processes of community empowerment because this approach has demonstrated success in terms of community-level impacts (Deslippe, 2019; Speer & Christens, 2012; Speer et al., 2003, 2014; Warren, 2001; Wood, 2002).

One implication for scholars of community empowerment is that the principles and traditional practices of relational community organizing can be tailored to the contexts and cultures of different institutional settings to achieve impacts for the broader community. In the same way that relational community organizing was brought to congregations of faith communities, organizing has the potential to be applied to other community institutions and contexts, such as education, health care, service agencies, or labor organizations.

Generalized to the community level, community empowerment can be understood as an expression of the following: multisector relational development, institutional linkages across sectors, and collective attention to common community issues (Speer & Hughey, 1995). Multisector relational development implies the application of relational community organizing practices to diverse community institutional constituencies. This would require sophisticated community organizers, or what Fligstein and McAdam (2012) term "institutional entrepreneurs," to apply relational organizing practices in an innovative way that is sensitive to the cultural frames and logics of acting within particular institutions. Just as CBCO did with religious congregations, sectors and constituencies within the community can engage similar organizing processes to build organizational power.

Second, the community empowerment process also unfolds through linkages between organizations and institutions within a community. To develop community empowerment, not just organizational empowerment, which is what CBCO represents, CBCO could be dramatically enhanced if there were other powerful organization- and institution-level entities to collaborate with – hence the need for multisector (as opposed to just religious congregation) development. Such collaborations exist to some extent now for CBCO initiatives, but often the only other institutional actors with sufficient power to affect change are corporate actors, whose interests run counter to CBCO initiatives. Organizational and institutional interests never align perfectly, but if there were greater breadth of powerful actors, developing and exercising these linkages would represent community empowerment. Examples of organizational linkages at community scales to impact community-level outcomes exist (Cooper & Christens, 2019; Safford, 2009), but more effort in studying the development of these linkages is needed.

Finally, collective attention to common community issues represents the capacity of powerful organizations to direct a community's attention to particular topics of concern. Major public debates within communities are often about investments in real estate developments, sports stadiums, or similar proposals that are in the interests of powerful corporate actors. In contrast, when topics like schools or housing are elevated to public debate, the focus is less often on investments in these areas than on the problems with these areas. Greater community empowerment will require relational power across many constituencies, linkages between these organizational actors, and the ability to focus collective attention on issues that matter for residents of the community. Developing these capacities within communities offers great potential for the exercise of power and community change.

Empowerment outcomes at the community scale require many empowered organizations and collaborations across those organizations within a community. Ideally, communities with such infrastructures provide contexts and opportunities for their citizens to engage in shaping community life. Although building empowered communities is a long-term process, there are successful models of this work (Safford, 2009; Whyte & Whyte, 1988).

The descriptions of CBCO provided here offer interesting possibilities for approaches to cultivate community empowerment. Relational organizing practices within religious congregations will not translate directly to other organizations and institutions. The way in which organizers attended to meaning and culture within congregations is key to the potential for translating the principles of relational organizing to other community settings and contexts.

References

Alinsky, S. D. (1971). *Rules for radicals: A pragmatic primer for realistic radicals.* Vintage Books.

Berube, A., Kim, A., Forman, B., & Burns, M. (2002). *The price of paying taxes: How tax preparation and refund loan fees erode the benefits of EITC.* Brookings Institution.

Blackwell, A. G., Thompson, M., Freudenberg, N., Ayers J., Schrantz, D., & Minkler, M. (2012) Using community organizing and community building to impact on policy. In M. Minkler (Ed.), *Community organizing and community building for health and welfare* (3rd ed.) (pp. 371–385). Rutgers University Press.

Brooks, F. (2007). The living wage movement: Potential implications for the working poor. *Families in Society, 88*(3), 437–442.

Carrasco, J. (2000, April 24). *Beyond the Good Samaritan* [Invited Talk]. Rutgers School of Social Work.

Chambers, E. T. (2003). *Roots for radicals: Organizing for power, action, and justice.* Continuum.

Christens, B. D. (2010). Public relationship building in grassroots community organizing: Relational intervention for individual and systems change. *Journal of Community Psychology, 38*(7), 886–900.

Christens, B. D., & Speer, P. W. (2011). Contextual influences on participation in community organizing: A multilevel longitudinal study. *American Journal of Community Psychology, 47*(3–4), 253–263.

Christens, B. D., & Speer, P. W. (2015). Community organizing: Practice, research, and policy implications. *Social Issues and Policy Review, 9*(1), 193–222.

Christens, B. D., Hanlin, C. E., & Speer, P. W. (2007). Getting the social organism thinking: Strategy for systems change. *American Journal of Community Psychology, 39*(3–4), 229–238.

Christens, B. D., Jones, D. L., & Speer, P. W. (2008). Power, conflict, and spirituality: A qualitative study of faith-based community organizing. *Forum: Qualitative Social Research, 9*(1), 21.

Christens, B. D., Peterson, N. A., & Speer, P. W. (2011). Community participation and psychological empowerment: Testing reciprocal causality using a cross-lagged panel design and latent constructs. *Health Education & Behavior, 38*(4), 339–347.

Cooper, D. G., & Christens, B. D. (2019). Justice system reform for health equity: A mixed methods examination of collaborating for equity and justice principles in a grassroots organizing coalition. *Health Education & Behavior, 46*(Suppl. 1), 62S–70S.

Day, K. (2012). Introduction to the special issue on faith-based organizing in the USA. *International Journal of Public Theology, 6*(4), 383–397.

Delehanty, J., & Oyakawa, M. (2018). Building a collective moral imaginary: Personalist culture and social performance in faith-based community organizing. *American Journal of Cultural Sociology, 6*(2), 266–295.

Delgado, G. (1986). *Organizing the movement: The roots and growth of ACORN.* Temple University Press.

Deslippe, D. (2019). "As in a civics text come to life": The East Brooklyn Congregations' Nehemiah housing plan and "citizens power" in the 1980s. *Journal of Urban History, 45*(5), 1030–1049.

Dokecki, P. R. (2004). *The clergy sexual abuse crisis: Reform and renewal in the Catholic community.* Georgetown University Press.

Ellen, I. G., Schill, M. H., Susin, S., & Schwartz, A. E. (2001). Building homes, reviving neighborhoods: Spillovers from subsidized construction of owner-occupied housing in New York City. *Journal of Housing Research, 12*(2), 185–216.

Evans, P., & Sewell, W. H. (2013). The neoliberal era: Ideology, policy, and social effects. In P. A. Hall & M. Lamont (Eds.), *Social resilience in the neoliberal era* (pp. 35–68). Cambridge University Press.

Faith in Action. (2023, May 18). *Where we work.* Faith in Action. https://faithinactioninternational.org/where-we-work/

Fisher, R. (1994). *Let the people decide: Neighborhood organizing in America.* Twayne Publishers.

Fisher, R., Brooks, F., & Russell, D. (2007). "Don't be a blockhead": ACORN, protest tactics, and refund anticipation loans. *Urban Affairs Review, 42*(4), 553–582.

Fligstein, N., & McAdam, D. (2012). *A theory of fields.* Oxford University Press.

Franck, R., & Iannaccone, L. R. (2014). Religious decline in the 20th century West: Testing alternative explanations. *Public Choice, 159,* 385–414.

Fulkerson, M. M. (2012). Receiving from the other: Theology and grass-roots organizing. *International Journal of Public Theology, 6*(4), 421–434.

Ganz, M. (2010). *Why David sometimes wins: Leadership, organization, and strategy in the California farm worker movement.* Oxford University Press.

Gellman, E. S., & Roll, J. (2011). *The gospel of the working class: Labor's southern prophets in New Deal America.* University of Illinois Press.

Gupta, J. (2021). Resistance, race, and subjectivity in congregation-based community organizing. *Journal of Community Psychology, 49*(8), 3141–3161.

Han, H., McKenna, E., & Oyakawa, M. (2021). *Prisms of the people: Power and organizing in twenty-first century America.* University of Chicago Press.

Hart, S. (2001). *Cultural dilemmas of progressive politics: Styles of engagement among grassroots activists.* University of Chicago Press.

Haug, C. (2013). Organizing spaces: Meeting arenas as a social movement infrastructure between organization, network, and institution. *Organization Studies, 34*(5–6), 705–732.

Horwitt, S. D. (1989). *Let them call me rebel: Saul Alinsky his life and times.* Vintage Books.

Jacobsen, D. A. (2001). *Doing justice: Congregations and community organizing.* Fortress Press.

Johnson, K., Noe, T., Collins, D., Strader, T., & Bucholtz, G. (2000). Mobilizing church communities to prevent alcohol and other drug abuse: A model strategy and its evaluation. *Journal of Community Practice, 7*(2), 1–27.

Kelley, R. D. G. (1990). *Hammer and hoe: Alabama communists during the great depression*. University of North Carolina Press.

Langan, M. (2018). *Neo-colonialism and the poverty of "development" in Africa*. Palgrave Macmillan.

Levad, A. (2019). Repairing the breach: Faith-based community organizing to dismantle mass incarceration. *Religions, 10*(1), 42.

Margolis, M. F. (2020). Who wants to make America great again? Understanding evangelical support for Donald Trump. *Politics and Religion, 13*(1), 89–118.

Martin, I. (2006). Do living wage policies diffuse? *Urban Affairs Review, 41*(5), 710–719.

McAlevey, J. F. (2016). *No shortcuts: Organizing for power in the new gilded age*. Oxford University Press.

McCarthy, J. D., & Walker, E. T. (2004). Alternative organizational repertoires of poor people's social movement organizations. *Nonprofit and Voluntary Sector Quarterly, 33*(3), 97s–119s.

Medellin, P. J., Speer, P. W., Christens, B. D., & Gupta, J. (2021). Transformation to leadership: Learning about self, the community, the organization, and the system. *Journal of Community Psychology, 49*(8), 3122–3140.

Morris, A. D. (1984). *The origins of the civil rights movement: Black communities organizing for change*. The Free Press.

Neal, J. W., & Christens, B. D. (2014). Linking the levels: Network and relational perspectives for community psychology. *American Journal of Community Psychology, 53*(3–4), 314–323.

O'Donovan, O. (2008). *Church in crisis: The gay controversy and the Anglican communion*. Cascade Books.

Olarinmoye, O. O. (2012). Faith-based organizations and development: Prospects and constraints. *Transformation: An International Journal of Holistic Mission Studies, 29*(1), 1–14.

Osterman, P. (2002). *Gathering power: The future of progressive politics in America*. Beacon Press Books.

Osterman, P. (2006). Overcoming oligarchy: Culture and agency in social movement organizations. *Administrative Science Quarterly, 51*, 622–649.

Oyakawa, M. (2015). "Turning private pain into public action": The cultivation of identity narratives by a faith-based community organization. *Qualitative Sociology, 38*(4), 395–415.

Payne, C. M. (1995). *I've got the light of freedom: The organizing tradition and the Mississippi freedom struggle*. University of California Press.

Phipps, A. A., Heintz, K., & Franke, M. (1994). *Evaluation of the Nehemiah Housing opportunity program*. US Department of Housing and Urban Development, Office of Policy Development and Research.

Pyysiäinen, J., Halpin, D., & Guilfoyle, A. (2017). Neoliberal governance and "responsibilization" of agents: Reassessing the mechanisms of responsibility-shift in neoliberal discursive environments. *Distinktion: Journal of Social Theory, 18*(2), 215–235.

Ransby, B. (2003). *Ella Baker & the Black Freedom Movement: A radical democratic vision*. University of North Carolina Press.

Rappaport, J. (1981). In praise of paradox: A social policy of empowerment over prevention. *American Journal of Community Psychology, 9*(1), 1–25.

Robinson, B., & Hanna, M. G. (1994). Lessons for academics from grassroots community organizing: A case study – The Industrial Areas Foundation. *Journal of Community Practice, 1*(4), 63–94.

Rusch, L., & Swarts, H. (2015). Practices of engagement: Comparing and integrating deliberation and organizing. *Journal of Community Practice, 23*(1), 5–26.

Safford, S. (2009). *Why the garden club couldn't save Youngstown: The transformation of the rust belt.* Harvard University Press.

Schutz, A., & Sandy, M. G. (2011). *Collective action for social change: An introduction to community organizing.* Palgrave Macmillan.

Slate, N. (2012). *Colored cosmopolitanism: The shared struggle for freedom in the United States and India.* Harvard University Press.

Speer, P. W., & Christens, B. D. (2012). Local community organizing and change: Altering policy in the housing and community development system in Kansas City. *Journal of Community & Applied Social Psychology, 22*(5), 414–427.

Speer, P. W., & Christens, B. D. (2013). An approach to scholarly impact through strategic engagement in community-based research. *Journal of Social Issues, 69*(4), 734–753.

Speer, P. W., & Christens, B. D. (2015). Community organizing. In V. C. Scott & S. M. Wolfe (Eds.), *Community psychology: Foundations for practice* (pp. 220–236). Sage.

Speer, P. W., & Han, H. (2018). Re-engaging social relationships and collective dimensions of organizing to revive democratic practice. *Journal of Social and Political Psychology, 6*(2), 745–758.

Speer, P. W., & Hughey, J. (1995). Community organizing: An ecological route to empowerment and power. *American Journal of Community Psychology, 23* (5), 729–748.

Speer, P. W., Christens, B. D., & Peterson, N. A. (2021). Participation in community organizing: Cross-sectional and longitudinal analyses of impacts on sociopolitical development. *Journal of Community Psychology, 49*(8), 3194–3214.

Speer, P. W., Hughey, J., Gensheimer, L. K., & Adams-Leavitt, W. (1995). Organizing for power: A comparative case-study. *Journal of Community Psychology, 23* (1), 57–73.

Speer, P. W., Ontkush, M., Schmitt, B., Raman, P., Jackson, C., Rengert, K. M., & Peterson, N. A. (2003). The intentional exercise of power: Community organizing in Camden, New Jersey. *Journal of Community & Applied Social Psychology, 13*(5), 399–408.

Speer, P. W., Tesdahl, E. A., & Ayers, J. F. (2014). Community organizing practices in a globalizing era: Building power for health equity at the community level. *Journal of Health Psychology, 19*(1), 159–169.

Steensland, B., & Wright, E. L. (2014). American evangelicals and conservative politics: Past, present, and future. *Sociology Compass, 8*(6), 705–717.

Sugrue, T. J. (1995). Reassessing the history of postwar America. *Prospects, 20,* 493–509.

Swarts, H. (2011). Drawing new symbolic boundaries over old social boundaries: Forging social movement unity in congregation-based community organizing. *Sociological Perspectives, 54*(3), 453–477.

Vegter, A., & Kelley, M. (2020). The Protestant ethic and the spirit of gun ownership. *Journal for the Scientific Study of Religion, 59*(3), 526–540.

Warren, M. R. (1998). Community building and political power – A community organizing approach to democratic renewal. *American Behavioral Scientist, 42*(1), 78–92.

Warren, M. R. (2001). *Dry bones rattling: Community building to revitalize American democracy.* Princeton University Press.

Warren, M. R. (2009). Community organizing in Britain: The political engagement of faith-based social capital. *City & Community, 8*(2), 99–127.

Warren, M. R., & Wood, R. L. (2001, October 30). *Faith-based community organizing: The state of the field.* Interfaith Funders. https://crcc.usc.edu/report/faith-based-community-organizing-the-state-of-the-field/

Whitman, G. (2018). *Stand up!: How to get involved, speak out, and win in a world on fire.* Berrett-Koehler Publishers.

Whyte, W. F., & Whyte, K. K. (1988). *Making Mondragon: The growth and dynamics of the worker cooperative complex.* Cornell University Press.

Wittgenstein, L. (2009). *Philosophical investigations.* John Wiley & Sons.

Wood, R. L. (1999). Religious culture and political action. *Sociological Theory, 17*(3), 307–332.

Wood, R. L. (2002). *Faith in action: Religion, race, and democratic organizing in America.* University of Chicago Press.

Wood, R. L. (2003, October 29). *Renewing congregations: The contribution of faith-based community organizing.* Interfaith Funders. https://crcc.usc.edu/report/renewing-congregations-the-contribution-of-faith-based-community-organizing/

Wood, R. L., & Fulton, B. R. (2015). *A shared future: Faith-based organizing for racial equity and ethnical democracy.* University of Chicago Press.

Wood, R. L., & Warren, M. R. (2002). A different face of faith-based politics: Social capital and community organizing in the public arena. *International Journal of Sociology and Social Policy, 22*(9–10), 6–54.

Wood, R. L., Fulton, B. R., & Partridge, K. (2012, October 29). *Building bridges, building power: Developments in institution-based community organizing.* Interfaith Funders. https://crcc.usc.edu/report/building-bridges-building-power-developments-in-institution-based-community-organizing/

5 Immigrant Organizing and Activism

Kevin Escudero

Introduction

Immigrant organizing and activism in the US emerged from both the formal and informal political participation of immigrants since the country's founding in the late eighteenth century.[1] Central to this history is the role of race and its far-reaching effects on the development of US immigration policy (Ong Hing, 2003). Beginning in the mid-nineteenth century, immigrants arriving to the US increasingly hailed not only from western Europe but also from Asia and Latin America, a trend that has continued to the present day. Racist nativist fears regarding immigrants from Asia resulted in the first racially based immigration ban: the Chinese Exclusion Act, which was in place from 1882 to 1943 (Perez Huber et al., 2008). The Act resulted in the emergence of Chinese immigrants as constituting the nation's first undocumented immigrant population (Lee, 2004). A key development that further accelerated this demographic shift in the composition of the US immigrant population was the passage of the Immigration and Nationality Act of 1965. The Act abolished the national origins quota system of visa allocation based on the USA's 1890 Census, which favored western European immigrants (who later became racially coded as White) and instead implemented an annual 20,000-visa cap per Eastern Hemisphere country alongside a seven-category preference system (Ngai, 2014). While seemingly more egalitarian in its treatment of potential migrants, the Act's imposition of a 120,000 non-country specific cap on Western Hemisphere migration did not account for historical migration flows (Ngai, 2014). In fact, the Act resulted in the first-of-its-kind implementation of quotas for Latin American immigrants, including Mexican nationals, who, as a result of their participation in the US guest worker program (the Bracero Program) during the 1940s–1960s, had developed a circular pattern of

---

1 It is important to recognize the settler colonial roots of the US as a nation founded on the attempted erasure and replacement of Indigenous peoples throughout Turtle Island. Characterizations of the US as a "nation of immigrants" in which "we are all immigrants to this land" is thus a false narrative, and one that only works to further perpetuate the invisibility of Indigenous peoples. Indigenous people across Turtle Island today persist, and they continue to maintain and to perpetuate their linguistic, cultural, and political systems in the face of ongoing practices of US settler colonialism (Dunbar-Ortiz, 2021).

entering the US periodically for work and then returning to their families back in Mexico (Loza, 2016; Massey et al., 2003). Mexican immigrants were seen by the federal government as suitable workers but not as future US citizens (Gutiérrez, 1995; Ngai, 2014). Set against a broader history of migration between the US and Mexico throughout the borderlands region (a significant portion of which previously constituted part of the Mexican state), the Act's passage resulted in a rise of Mexican undocumented immigration by individuals who, upon returning to Mexico to rejoin their families as they had done seasonally for years, found themselves unable to secure visas to return to the US (Ngai, 2014). Nevertheless, these individuals' previous employers under the Bracero Program continued to recruit workers directly, even preferring to do so given the formal terms of the government's guest worker program (Ngai, 2014).

During the post-1965 period, there was an unanticipated increase in the number of immigrants arriving from Asia to the US, facilitated by their use of the newly developed family-based migration category as part of the Act's preference system (Ancheta, 2006). As such, immigrants admitted in this manner were not subject to the 20,000-visa quota per country, allowing for an exponential increase in Asian migration utilizing this route of entry (Ancheta, 2006). In the 1960s, 1970s, and 1980s, US interventionist foreign policy in Latin America and Asia aimed at curtailing the expansion of communism globally resulted in the arrival of large numbers of refugees from Central America and Southeast Asia. These refugees were often disbursed across the country and settled in working-class neighborhoods alongside other racial/ethnic minority communities (Tang, 2015). More recently, during what has come to be known as the post-9/11 era, the US refugee population shifted to consist of greater numbers of individuals from Central Asia, South Asia, and the Middle East (Maira, 2009). As this brief overview has demonstrated, the racial composition of the nation, especially in terms of the US immigrant population, has been shaped largely by racially informed policies at the federal level.

Upon arrival to the US, many (soon-to-be) White and non-White immigrants secured employment in agriculture and factories, while others opted to open their own businesses. People of color, including immigrants of color, were often excluded from formal labor organizing spaces created to advocate for workplace rights. And when organized labor spaces did become open to non-White workers, workers of color expressed skepticism about joining these organizations, and rightfully so. As historian Robin D. G. Kelly (1999) explains:

> While Black, Latino, and Asian-American working people devised workplace strategies to protect themselves and their families, very few people of color could be found in labor unions before the CIO's [Congress of Industrial Organizations] rise in 1935. Part of their reluctance to support trade unions had to do with organized labor's rather mixed record on racial equality ..... European workers came to see themselves as white ... [and] the vast majority of exploited white laborers rejected the Black freedom struggle, and sided

with wealthy Whites. Similarly, in California, anti-Chinese sentiment galvanized the multi-ethnic "white" working class and forged a dynamic union movement on the West Coast.   (p. 46)

At the same time, workers of color created their own organizing spaces, spaces that in some instances included members of multiple racial groups (Almaguer, 2008). Yet even community of color labor organizing spaces were not immune from perpetuating xenophobic sentiments, resulting in the exclusion of immigrant workers from these spaces. A prominent example of this was the United Farm Workers union, made up of Mexican and Filipino farm workers, which viewed immigrant workers, especially undocumented workers, as a threat owing to their potential role as strikebreakers for organizers looking to secure increased wages and benefits (Bardacke, 2013; Gutiérrez, 1991).

Moreover, when employing the term "immigrant," it is important to distinguish between the multiple groups of individuals who fall into this category. In addition to the lenses of race and ethnicity, immigration scholars have often discussed the experiences of immigrants in terms of an individual's generational status and their legal status in the US. Generational status refers to the nexus of nativity (whether a person is US born or foreign born) as well as the age and life stage during which they immigrated (e.g., pre-, during, or post-adolescence). According to sociologist Rubén Rumbaut (2004), the first generation refers to individuals "born and socialized in another country who immigrate as adults," while the second generation "refers to the U.S.-born children and U.S.-socialized children of foreign-born parents" (p. 1165). There is also another group of individuals who are often referred to as "members of the 1.5 generation." As Rumbaut (2012) explains, members of the 1.5 generation "immigrate as children ... and are largely socialized in the host country" (p. 1). Immigrant legal status refers to whether an individual is documented or undocumented in the US. For individuals who are documented, they can have a variety of legal statuses, including holding a nonimmigrant visa or immigrant visa, having legal permanent residency, being a naturalized US citizen, or being a refugee. The term "refugee" refers to an individual who has been displaced to a third country and is seeking resettlement in another country, often due to war, civil unrest, and/or persecution (though this is not a full list of the reasons why someone might become a refugee). As compared to immigrants, refugees are granted temporary legal status upon arrival in the third country and often an abbreviated pathway to citizenship. Some individuals who claim refugee status (or asylum if they have already entered the country in which they are seeking to be resettled and are applying for resettlement from within that country) have their claims denied and thus are not afforded the unique legal protections of being recognized as refugees. Refugees are immigrants, though immigrants with specific legal protections, while immigrants must generally meet a certain set of criteria to be considered refugees.

An Example: Undocumented Immigrant Youth Activism and the Federal DREAM Act

Today, one of the immigrant groups that has become highly visible in the US news for its participation in political organizing activism is "the DREAMers." Named after the proposed, though yet to be passed, federal bill first introduced in 2001 – the Development, Relief, and Education for Alien Minors (DREAM) Act – this group of activists consists of individuals who are members of the 1.5 generation and who hail primarily from Latin America and Asia (though some individuals are from African and European nations as well).[2] If passed, the DREAM Act would provide two pathways for undocumented immigrant youth to access US citizenship. These pathways are completing two years of US military service or two years of higher education at a US college/university (National Immigration Law Center, 2011). To qualify for the bill, individuals must have also entered the US before age sixteen and be under thirty-five (or thirty-two in some iterations of the bill) (National Immigration Law Center, 2011). At the time of writing, the closest the bill came to becoming law was in 2010, when it passed in the House of Representatives but was five votes short of passing in the Senate (CNN Wire Staff, 2010).

As the DREAMer narrative frequently goes, during adolescence undocumented immigrant youth are socialized in ways that are very similar to their second-generation US-born peers. It is not until undocumented immigrant youth seek to obtain a driver's license or to apply for college (when they are required to provide a social security number) that they learn of their undocumented status. With the guidance of nonprofit legal and immigrant rights organizations, the DREAMer narrative was developed in a manner that rendered undocumented immigrant youth as "American," high achieving, and not guilty of "breaking the law" (Nicholls, 2013). Elaborating on the construction of this narrative largely as a response to common critiques of undocumented immigration levied by anti-immigrant activists, social movement scholar Walter Nicholls (2013) explains:

> By countering stereotypes, the themes cleanse the youths of the three main stigmas attributed to undocumented immigrants. [According to this new narrative], the undocumented youths are normal Americans (and not irreducibly foreign), the best and the brightest (and not free-riding welfare cheats or terrorizing gang members), and bear no fault of their own for their immigration status (and not truly "illegal"). (p. 53)

---

2 It is important to note that while the term "DREAMer" originated with the introduction of the federal DREAM Act, in the years since its initial introduction in 2001 and subsequent reintroductions certain states have passed their own "DREAM Act" legislation. These state-level bills, however, are not able to provide undocumented immigrant youth with a pathway to US citizenship. Instead, they many times entail access to in-state tuition rates when attending public colleges and universities and, in some instances, access to state financial aid.

Figure 5.1 *Mock DREAM Act graduation ceremony at the Civic Center in San Francisco, CA, during the summer of 2012. San Francisco Bay Area undocumented immigrant youth participate in a mock graduation ceremony wearing their caps and gowns symbolizing their potential contributions to the US as prospective citizens if the federal DREAM Act were to be passed. Professor Angela Davis served as the event's keynote speaker. Photo by Kevin Escudero.*

This is not to say, however, that undocumented immigrant youth activists were oblivious to the contradictions (and limitations) of such a narrative, or that they did not work to challenge (and complicate) it (Abrego & Negrón-Gonzales, 2020; Chauvin & Garcés-Mascareñas, 2014; Escudero, 2017; Nicholls, 2013, p. 58). Certain groups of activists critiqued how the bill's two pathways for accessing US citizenship reinscribed and reaffirmed notions of worthiness and deservingness often present in US immigration laws (Negrón-Gonzales et al., 2015). In the process, these movement participants argued that the bill did not recognize the full humanity of immigrant community members and instead divided community members along lines of "worthiness" and ability to "contribute" to the US, which often fell along generational boundaries (Jaffe, 2007; Pallares, 2014). This in turn impacted the differences in claims-making behaviors between first- and 1.5-generation undocumented immigrants (Abrego, 2011; Gleeson, 2010). Additionally, while the DREAM Act would provide a pathway to US citizenship for immigrant youth, their parents would have no access to adjusting their legal status. Some individuals who entered the US as youth and spent their adolescence there also would most likely end up aging out of eligibility for the DREAM Act due to the bill's age provisions. Though efforts to pass the bill at the federal level have been ongoing since 2001, at the time of writing this chapter (twenty or so years later) it had still not been passed.

Undocumented immigrant youth, including the cohort of "DREAMers" as they came to be known in the US, are not a monolithic group of individuals (Escudero, 2020; Terriquez, 2015). Rather, as recent scholarship has shown, undocumented immigrant youth hail from multiple parts of the globe, and their experiences are often the result of the nexus of their racial/ethnic identity

Figure 5.2 *Civil disobedience action by undocumented immigrant activists in front of the Hilton Hotel in Chicago, IL, during the spring of 2013. These undocumented youth used PVC pipes to connect themselves to one another while laying atop a banner that reads "400,000 Not 1 More Deportation." Activists protested the Obama administration's record number of deportations (over 400,000 individuals) and the administration's differential treatment of undocumented youth in comparison to their parents and other older community members. Photo by Kevin Escudero.*

and immigrant legal status (Enriquez, 2019; García, 2017; Patler, 2014). In fact, Tereza Lee, an undocumented Korean immigrant who was born in Brazil and grew up in Chicago, was the individual whose experience helped motivate the authoring and introduction of the DREAM Act in 2001 (Kelly, 2018; Levere, 2020). Another Asian undocumented organizer who was active in the undocumented immigrant youth movement, Tam Ngoc Tran, was born in Germany to Vietnamese refugee parents and raised in Southern California. Sharing her testimony on May 18, 2007, before the House Judiciary Committee's Subcommittee on Immigration, Citizenship, Refugees, Border Security, and International Law, Tran elaborated on the feeling of being stuck that her undocumented immigrant status placed on her. Despite being considered closer to members of the second generation born in the US because of having also spent her adolescence in the country, as Tran explains, she was unable to "grow up" and to move out of being treated as a child due to the limitations of her legal status, a situation that suspended her and her peers in a perpetual state of limbo. As she shared:

> This is my first time in Washington, DC, and the privilege of being able to speak today truly exemplifies the liminal state I always feel like I'm in. I am lucky because I do have a government ID that allowed me to board the plane here to share my story and give voice to thousands of other undocumented

students who cannot. But I know that when I return home tonight, I'll become marginalized once again .... Without the D.R.E.A.M. Act, I have no prospect of overcoming my state of immigration limbo; I'll forever be a perpetual foreigner in a country where I've always considered myself an American.

Tran's powerful testimony demonstrates the limitations of undocumented immigrant status on her daily life and the lives of others like her (Asian and otherwise) while also countering the lack of perceived agency that someone who is undocumented might have, as demonstrated by her ability to travel to the nation's capital and share her testimony before a House Judiciary Subcommittee. Tran and Lee are examples of the highly powerful and inspirational leadership of undocumented immigrant women at the forefront of the national movement for immigration reform. Activists like Lee and Tran built national networks, both those tied to national and regional immigrant rights organizations and more grassroots-oriented ones, to advance their cause, which remains ongoing today.

Like previous moments of immigrant rights organizing, which were largely shaped by the landscape of local politics, undocumented immigrant youth's political activism has similarly been tied to these local-level dynamics. This is perhaps even more relevant to their efforts given that subfederal entities – states, counties, and cities – possess a certain amount of leeway in terms of the support that they can provide for immigrants, in particular undocumented immigrants, as well as the enforcement mechanisms that they choose to employ (Gulasekaram & Ramakrishnan, 2015; Rodríguez, 2008). Nevertheless, given the fear that many undocumented community members have faced (and continue to face) stemming from the various political agendas of leaders at the federal and subfederal levels over the past several decades, one of the undocumented immigrant youth movement's primary mechanisms for building community has been through the use of social media and other related online platforms (Zimmerman, 2016). As Zimmerman (2016) explains, activists' use of such platforms led to their utilization of the strategy of coming out as undocumented through the development of what she calls "transmedia testimonios" (p. 1892). These testimonios assisted activists in "contest[ing] the power of the law, which sustains itself through the silencing of migrants who live in the shadows. By revealing their undocumented status in narrative form, [these] youth undermine[d] the forms of silence that [have kept] them in a state of perpetual fear" (p. 1892). Though dispersed across the country and unable to obtain driver's licenses to travel freely across the country prior to 2012, these online networks assisted undocumented immigrant youth in mobilizing a national social movement, one that resulted in several important political wins for immigrant youth and other members of the undocumented immigrant community.[3] While the movement initially formed to

---

3 In June 2012, President Obama, due to the pressure levied by undocumented immigrant organizers and their allies, announced the Deferred Action for Childhood Arrivals (DACA) program. The program provided qualifying undocumented immigrant youth with a two-year stay of

advocate for the passage of the federal DREAM Act, a bill that would have provided a pathway to US citizenship for qualifying undocumented immigrant youth, the movement's efforts have since broadened. Recognizing the limitations of full membership, in this case US citizenship, for members of other marginalized communities in the US, particularly for US citizen communities of color, some organizers have begun utilizing an abolitionist agenda to advocate for an end to deportations (and immigrant incarceration) (Cardenas, 2018; Gomberg-Muñoz, 2012; Unzueta Carrasco & Seif, 2014).

Power and Empowerment Processes

Scholarship on immigrant communities' cultivation of power has had to balance between immigrants' participation in the formal political arena and grassroots immigrant rights activism. Literature by political scientists has often highlighted immigrants' political behavior and their potential promise as future voters. Sociologists, historians, and some political scientists have focused on exploring the relationship between structural systems of oppression (e.g., US immigration laws, continued suspension in a state of "migrant illegality," and racism), migrants' everyday lives, and their responses to counteracting such systems. In this chapter, I bring together multiple social science literatures on immigrant organizing and activism to explain how these literatures contribute to furthering our understanding of immigrant political activism in the US through themes of building community power and processes of psychological empowerment.

Community Power

Naturalization has served as the primary pathway for immigrants to acquire US citizenship and, in turn, take advantage of the full array of avenues for political participation that the US has to offer. As researchers at the Migration Policy Institute (a nonpartisan research and policy-based organization dedicated to the study of immigration globally) explain: Naturalization consists of a two-way agreement between immigrants and their new country of citizenship regarding their membership and participation in the nation state (Sanchez & Batalova, 2021).[4] One of the responsibilities that these newly pronounced

deportation, a social security number, and a work permit. DACA recipients were also eligible to apply for "advanced parole" to leave the US for a predetermined period of time (usually for educational or humanitarian reasons) and to reenter the country afterwards. While in 2017 President Trump ended the program, his actions were challenged in federal court and the program was reinstated, though litigation remains ongoing. Momentum to enact the DACA program was largely due to the desire for a quick resolution to the situation facing a growing number of undocumented immigrant youth in the US given the federal government's inability to pass the federal DREAM Act during 2001–2010 and the near passage of the bill in 2010.

4 For additional information about the Migration Policy Institute and its mission, see www .migrationpolicy.org/about/about-migration-policy-institute. To read more of the Institute's

citizens are expected to take part in is voting (at the federal and subfederal levels) and civic engagement. Yet, given the emphasis placed on naturalization as a pathway to political participation, some political theorists have argued that an unbundling of rights from citizenship would help ensure the equitable treatment of large numbers of noncitizens residing in a given country, particularly during the many years they reside in a nation prior to naturalization (Song, 2009). Moreover, scholarship on the naturalization process for immigrants in the US has called for a closer examination of which immigrant groups are able to naturalize and under what circumstances this occurs (Aptekar, 2015; Bloemraad, 2006). Access to naturalization is often contingent upon the resources offered by the local government and community-based organizations to support immigrants in navigating the naturalization bureaucracy and paying the fees associated with doing so (Bloemraad, 2006). Some immigration scholars have also raised the important question of whether these newer cohorts of immigrants in the US are being viewed similarly to previous cohorts of largely White immigrants who were seen as "Americans in waiting" rather than perpetual foreigners expellable from the nation at any time (Motomura, 2007, as cited in Coutin, 2011). Yet, as scholars writing on this topic have noted, questions remain regarding what changes the future may hold for political parties to engage immigrants as naturalized immigrants and the children of immigrants constitute a greater proportion of the voting population in the US.[5]

Prior to naturalization, immigrants (including those individuals with limited and/or no access to naturalization) have been (and continue to be) active in political organizing and activism. Citing a report entitled "Lessons Learned About Civic Participation among Immigrants," anthropologist Catherine B. Brettell notes how its authors found "that restricting the focus of attention on voter registration and citizenship (in its legal sense) can be limiting ... [and] that restricting the definition of civic participation to political activity diminishes the importance of involvement in more local issues and activities ..."[6] Activities associated with such participation

research on immigrant community members' experiences with naturalization (in the US and globally) and with regard to their civic engagement in their new home countries, see www.migrationpolicy.org/topics/citizenship-civic-engagement.

5 Related literature on this topic includes Hochschild et al. (2013), McCann and Jones-Correa (2020), Ramakrishnan and Bloemraad (2008), and Wong et al. (2011).

6 This can be partially explained by the fact that many central provisions of the US Constitution apply to all individuals in the US regardless of their immigrant legal status (Romero, 2005). This has been despite the fact that, as anthropologist and legal studies scholar Susan Coutin (2011) writes, "[t]he rights of resident noncitizens have emerged as one of the most polarizing issues in the United States in the latter half of the past decade" (p. 290). In fact, efforts to curtail some of the rights that noncitizens held reached an apex "in 1996 [when] a series of immigration and related reforms eroded key protections that legal permanent residents had enjoyed, making the distinction between citizens and noncitizens, regardless of immigration status of the latter, more salient than before" (p. 296). In the midst of an increasingly hostile climate in terms of attitudes toward immigrants at the federal and subfederal levels over the past several decades, immigrants' political participation in the US has taken a variety of forms and remained steadfast.

include "passive activities such as following politics in the news, or active behaviors such as ... protests ...; membership in community-based organizations; petitioning government, participation in school-based parental organizations; contributing time or money to candidates or political organizations; or, in rare cases, assuming organizational leadership roles or running for political office" (DeSipio, 2012, p. 176). According to Brettell, and as discussed by political scientist Louis DeSipio (2012), important areas to focus on when seeking to understand immigrant civic and political engagement are community-based and grassroots organizations, religious institutions, and transnational networks with their previous home nations. In analyzing data on the impacts of all three of these organizational types on immigrant political mobilization, DeSipio (2012), as cited in Brettell, finds that immigrants are only slightly less likely than members of the US-born population to participate in civic organizations (p. 7). DeSipio (2012), as cited in Brettell, also makes the case that it might be that these organizations need to learn how to better recruit and effectively engage members of the immigrant community rather than there being a lack of interest on the part of immigrant community members to join such organizations (p. 8). Looking at the case of Chinese and Mexican immigrants' participation in labor organizations, workers' centers, advocacy and social service organizations, ethnic voluntary associations, and religious institutions, political scientist Janelle Wong found similar trends (Wong, 2006).

In the same vein, researchers have begun to examine the relationship between federal laws and policies (e.g., US immigration and citizenship laws) and grassroots activism, a process that occurs at the "meso-level" of the US immigrant rights movement and has often been facilitated by nonprofit and community-based organizations. In *The Immigrant Rights Movement: The Battle Over National Citizenship*, Walter Nicholls (2019) discusses how immigrant rights activists intentionally and strategically worked to scale their efforts from the grassroots level to a national organizational/policy level. Nicholls explains:

> [T]he process of moving from local battles to a national social movement ... is by no means straight-forward. It entail[ed] building a countrywide infrastructure, creating relations and influence with federal government officials, and constructing a compelling voice that resonates with the norms and moral sensibilities of nationals. [This book] suggests that the movement's growing prominence ... was made possible by the accumulation of economic, political, and cultural capital. (p. 26)

Combined, these three forms of capital help facilitate the codification of immigrant political power as part of an infrastructure that endures over time as different individuals participate in the movement and various community concerns emerge (p. 28). The formalization of immigrant political power in this manner, however, Nicholls notes, also raised the risk of reproducing the status quo investment in national citizenship rather than transforming the inequalities created by citizenship (and noncitizenship) more broadly (p. 29). An organizational approach to advancing immigrant rights also raises the concern of power imbalances between directly impacted community members and organizations' professional staff members, as well as funders' roles in shaping the agenda of various immigrant rights organizations (pp. 32–34). Similarly, calling for a greater engagement of immigration scholarship with the literature on organizations, sociologists Irene Bloemraad, Ali Chaudhary, and Shannon Gleeson (2022) add:

> We argue that while international migration (IM) scholars have developed a rich scholarship on migration and integration processes, analytical attention to [immigrant organizations] has been rare … [W]e suggest that scholars interested in studying [immigrant organizations] should focus on inequities stemming from immigrants' community-level vulnerabilities, including noncitizenship and the stigmatization of groups deemed as potential threats (i.e., outsiders) due to nativity, religion, national origin, language, ethno-racial background, and other ascriptive markers of otherness.   (p. 320)

While there is not sufficient space in this chapter to fully explore the myriad immigrant rights organizations involved in the movement across the country and the related networks that they have developed, a prime example of this research is Els de Graauw's *Making Immigrant Rights Real: Nonprofits and the Politics of Integration in San Francisco*. Focusing on immigrant-serving organizations in San Francisco, organizations whose membership is constituted by a broad cross-section of immigrant community members, political scientist Els de Graauw (2016) found that organizations frequently served a mediating role between grassroots political mobilizations and elected officials who, at the local level, implemented federal laws and policies.

Moreover, a growing body of scholarship has emphasized immigrants' quest for access to US citizenship rights through routes other than naturalization. What has come to be known colloquially as "the US immigrant rights movement" is centered around securing access to US citizenship *and* preventing the deportations of immigrant community members. Immigrant organizers, including members of the undocumented immigrant community, have utilized a broad set of tactics for advancing their fight for a pathway to US citizenship, including phone banking, lobbying their local and federal legislators, suing the federal government, launching regional migrant caravans to raise awareness about their cause, and taking part in acts of civil disobedience (Escudero & Pallares, 2021; Kuang, 2016; Patler & Gonzales, 2015; Solórzano, 2022).

A galvanizing moment for immigrants and their allies in the movement took place in 2006 with a set of national marches protesting a proposed federal bill, H.R. 4437. If passed, H.R. 4437 would have reclassified being an undocumented immigrant in the US from a civil to a criminal infraction and penalized anyone who assisted an undocumented individual (including US citizen family members of undocumented immigrants). Newspaper and television media across the country chronicled the widespread support for members of the US immigrant community, who came out in historic numbers, especially in large urban centers such as Los Angeles and Chicago (Pallares & Flores-González, 2010; Voss & Bloemraad, 2011). Voss and Bloemraad (2011) employ a social movement studies approach to understand how the marches emerged, why there was such a large turnout, and what impact the marches had on future prospects for immigrant political mobilization in the US. Political scientist Chris Zepeda-Millán's book *Latino Mass Mobilization: Immigration, Racialization, and Activism* asks related questions focusing on the role of fear and stigma of immigrant community members in serving as a catalyst for participation in social movement activism (Zepeda-Millán, 2017). Irene Bloemraad and Kim Voss' recent special issue of the *Journal of Ethnic and Migration Studies* more than ten years after the formative 2006 immigrant rights marches asked scholars of immigrant political mobilization to pause and reflect on whether the marches were part of a unique political moment or were tied to a longer history of immigrant rights organizing that came together when the community was under such great duress.

Despite appeals for inclusion in the nation state, immigrant rights activists have also increasingly engaged in critical discussions on what it means to seek citizenship in a settler colonial nation state. In developing a theory of border imperialism that brings together the process of "illegalization" of undocumented immigrants and the settler colonial nation state's continued violence toward the region's Indigenous peoples, scholar activist Harsha Walia brings our attention to the macro-level forces at play in such a process. Walia (2013) explains:

> Border imperialism encapsulates four overlapping and concurrent structurings: first, the mass displacement of impoverished and colonized communities resulting from asymmetrical relations of global power, and the simultaneous securitization of the border against those migrants whom capitalism and empire have displaced; second, the criminalization of migration with severe punishment and discipline of those deemed "alien" or "illegal"; third, the entrenchment of a racialized hierarchy by arbitrating who legitimately constitutes the nation-state; and fourth, the state-mediated exploitation of migrant labor, akin to conditions of slavery and servitude, by capitalist interests. (p. 4)

As part of this framework, Walia's conceptualization of colonialism draws our attention to the ways that settler nation state borders disrupt and enact violence upon the lives of Indigenous communities who hold a different, nonextractive and noncapitalist relationship to land and have done so for generations. A recent example of these principles in action was the protest of then President Trump's restrictions on arrivals (immigrant and nonimmigrant) from certain Muslim-majority nations, which came to colloquially known as the "Muslim Ban" (Yalamarty, 2020).[7] The chant "No Ban on Stolen Lands"

---

7 For further discussion of growing calls for Indigenous and immigrant solidarity, particularly as a result of an increasingly critical analysis of the meaning of calls for membership in a settler

called into question the settler nation state government's authority to impose such an immigration ban in light of its ongoing violence against the land's Indigenous peoples. By working to recenter the perspectives of Turtle Island's (North America's) Indigenous peoples in the development and regulation of US immigration policy, activists found an effective way to bring together Indigenous activists' efforts to challenge and curtail the power of the colonial nation state (which at the time was seeking to construct an oil pipeline through the lands of the Standing Rock Sioux Tribe) and the state's effort to prevent the arrival of migrants from certain Muslim-majority nations.

Psychological Empowerment Processes

Given that a central focus of immigrants' participation in civic engagement and political organizing has been shaped by their status as noncitizens as well as the US immigrant rights movement's focus on securing a pathway to citizenship for all immigrant community members, it is not surprising that immigrant legal status has a profound impact on immigrants' mental health and well-being. Migrants' liminal legal status – as partially documented or undocumented – and the precarity that follows can be understood through the frameworks of what scholars have termed "migrant illegality" and legal violence.[8] Taken together, these two concepts can assist in providing a window onto the ways that immigrants experience the law but also seek to contest its delegitimizing effects in their everyday lives. For those with a tenuous immigrant legal status, being rendered "illegal" and thus deportable is a part of the spectrum that migrants seek to avoid, resulting in a cycle of fear, stress, and anxiety with regard to one's immigrant legal status.

Discussing the experiences of Mexican undocumented immigrants in the US (the largest undocumented population in the country), anthropologist Nicholas DeGenova (2004) defines "migrant illegality" as follows:

> "Illegality" is lived through a palpable sense of deportability – the possibility of being removed from the space of the US nation-state. The legal production of "illegality" provides an apparatus for sustaining Mexican migrants' vulnerability and tractability – as workers – whose labor-power, inasmuch as it is deportable, becomes an eminently disposable commodity.   (p. 161)

By suspending immigrants in an ongoing state of precarity and vulnerability through the production of "migrant illegality," migrants are not only made vulnerable but treated by the state as disposable. Recently, scholars have

---

colonial nation state, see the New York University Asian Pacific American Center's event entitled "No Ban on Stolen Lands: A #NODAPL Teach-in for Standing Rock & Muslim/Immigrant/Refugee Bans." A recording of the event can be found here: https://apa.nyu.edu/no-bans-on-stolen-lands/.

8 For an in-depth discussion of liminal legality as a theoretical framework and its impacts on immigrants' everyday lives, particularly the case of immigrants from El Salvador and Guatemala, see Menjívar (2006).

sought to adapt DeGenova's framework of migrant illegality across a variety of geographic, social, and racial/ethnic community contexts (Menjívar & Kanstroom, 2014). In describing the type of violence that regimes of migrant illegality enact in migrants' everyday lives, sociologists Cecilia Menjívar and Leisy Abrego (2012) put forth the framework of legal violence. According to the authors, legal violence "captures the suffering that results from and is made possible through the implementation of the body of laws that delimit and shape individuals' lives on a routine basis" (p. 1387). A rich and growing segment of social psychological research has built on these findings, demonstrating the deleterious effects of immigrant legal status, particularly undocumented immigrant status, on an individual's lived experience and others in their community (Ellis, 2021; Gonzales et al., 2018; Suárez-Orozco et al., 2011).

Immigrant rights activists have increasingly sought to address the root causes of the fear, stress, and stigma that immigrant community members experience and their cumulative effects in their lives. In the case of undocumented immigrant youth, much of this work has focused on the college/university context, getting colleges/universities to develop the necessary infrastructure to fully support these members of the campus community. This was a result of activists frequently being forced to disclose their status with faculty, staff, and administrators as a means of educating them about their situations and the unique challenges they face (Abrego, 2006; Enriquez, 2011; Muñoz, 2015; Patler, 2018). These efforts have been highly successful in the establishment of undocumented student resource centers, many of which include counseling and psychological support services for undocumented students at their campus (Cisneros et al., 2022). At the University of California, Berkeley, for instance, as part of a campus Innovation Grant for Equity, Inclusion, and Diversity, the campus' Center for Race and Gender and its Latinx Research Center (formerly the Center for Latino Policy Research) carried out a campus-wide inquiry into ways that the university could better support undocumented immigrant students. Paired with the university's development and launch of the Haas Undocumented Community Resource Center (the result of student advocacy, student–administrative partnerships, and funding from Elise Haas), the university has become a leader nationally in providing holistic support structures for undocumented undergraduate and graduate students.[9]

Outside the college/university context, undocumented youth organizers have infiltrated federal immigrant detention centers to expose the injustices being done at those facilities, and they have partnered with allies to demand the closure of these centers. Some of these efforts are chronicled in the PBS film *The Infiltrators*, based on the experiences of two undocumented

---

9 Findings from the Center for Race and Gender and the Latinx Research Center project and a follow-up project conducted in 2019 can be found here: www.crg.berkeley.edu/research/undocumented-students-research-initiative/.

immigrant youth who infiltrated a detention facility in Florida in 2012. Launched by the same undocumented youth organization that infiltrated the Broward Detention Center in 2012, the National Immigrant Youth Alliance, three undocumented youth residing in the US traveled to Mexico and joined six individuals residing in Mexico who had formerly lived in the US as undocumented immigrants. Together, they marched to the Nogales border crossing and demanded entry into the US, where they then planned to apply for asylum. Known colloquially as the "Dream 9," these nine activists were allowed to enter the US but immediately upon entry were brought to the Eloy Detention Center, where they were held for two weeks. After spending two weeks in detention, where they began to organize with fellow undocumented immigrants, members of the Dream 9 were released and allowed to fight their cases while residing in the country. Many of the Dream 9 participants did several media appearances and sought to report to members of the public the injustices that they witnessed and experienced while at the detention center. Taking together the activities of undocumented immigrant youth organizing to improve the climate at the colleges/universities that they attend and infiltrating immigrant detention centers to dismantle them "from the inside out," these youth have very proactively sought to address the structural mechanisms that perpetuate the fear, stigma, and anxiety that come with being a partially documented or undocumented individual in the US today.

Application and Future Research

In this section, I begin by highlighting four implications of research on immigrant organizing and activism for political leaders. I then outline and discuss two recommendations for social scientists researching these and related topics.

Recommendations for Political Leaders

Below are four recommendations for ways that data collected about immigrant community members can be utilized by political leaders in a more nuanced manner to ensure that these leaders are able to represent all members of the communities that they serve. This will also assist in accounting for the full effects of the immigrant population on the future of the US federal and subfederal political landscape.

First, while a great deal of scholarship has highlighted the fact that immigrants who have not yet become US citizens are unable to take part in the formal political arena (i.e., voting), it is important for political leaders to keep in mind that immigrants, as noted earlier, can be (and have historically been seen as) "Americans in waiting." This means that despite the inequalities in the naturalization process, these immigrants will most likely at some point in the future have the option to become US citizens (and thus become future voters). According to the Pew Research Center, in 2017 there were an estimated 45.7 million foreign-born individuals residing in the US (Budiman et al., 2020). Some 20.7 million individuals (45 percent of the overall US foreign-born population) were naturalized US citizens (Budiman et al., 2020). And 12.3 million individuals (27 percent of the overall US foreign-born population) were legal permanent residents and thus individuals with a clear pathway to naturalization once they meet the requirements to do so, requirements that include taking a civics exam and completing an interview with an immigration officer (Budiman et al., 2020).[10]

Second, it is necessary for policymakers to keep in mind that, even prior to becoming US citizens, immigrants are part of US citizen families and communities. While 10.5 million individuals (23 percent of the US foreign-born population) are undocumented and as a result have limited pathways to naturalization, this figure includes Deferred Action for Childhood Arrivals (DACA) recipients, individuals in the process of being sponsored for citizenship by a family member, and individuals married to US citizens (Budiman et al., 2020). These are not the only ties, however, that noncitizens have to US citizens. Previous research by the Pew Research Center found that, in 2010, 46 percent of undocumented immigrants were parents of US citizen children (Pew Research Center, 2013). This has resulted in a growing number of US citizen children being raised by undocumented immigrant parents (Yoshikawa, 2011). Lawmakers must thus keep in mind that policies affecting the lives of immigrants, including undocumented immigrants who might have a tenuous pathway to accessing US citizenship, can also have a direct impact on the lives of US citizens.

Third, given the numbers of noncitizens in the US, both documented and undocumented, and the limited agency that they have in determining the laws that ultimately impact the lives of all individuals residing in the country, political leaders might consider increasing support for the creation of political leadership positions that do not require one to be a US citizen.[11] This could also entail reclassifying elected positions that currently require US citizenship status if it is not critical to one's ability to carry out the role. This would assist in preparing noncitizen community members to become civically and politically active once they do naturalize.

---

10 For more information about the US naturalization process, please see the US Citizenship and Immigration Services website: www.uscis.gov/citizenship/learn-about-citizenship/10-steps-to-naturalization.

11 It is important to note that some municipalities have begun to allow noncitizens to vote in local elections, and additional research on the effects of these laws would be helpful for advancing scholarship in this area (Kini, 2005; Vasilogambros, 2021). Given that noncitizen voting rights are more common in European countries, comparisons might also be drawn with the practices in those nations (Groenendijk, 2008).

Fourth, the US immigrant community is heterogeneous and includes a broad range of political opinions and viewpoints. Scholarship on the voting behaviors of Asian American and Latinx immigrants, the two largest immigrant communities in the country today, has shown an interesting but also somewhat divergent set of dilemmas. Asian Americans as a whole have been shown to lean democratic overall, while younger generations tend to be slightly more democratic leaning than their parents' generation (Wong & Shah, 2021). At the same time, as was seen in the lead up to the 2016 and 2020 presidential elections, there is a growing number of conservative voters of color, even within the Latinx community. As recent studies have shown, these developments were in part due to a decades-long courting of the "Hispanic vote" by Republican Party officials (Cadava, 2021). Thus, while progressive Latinx voters and community organizers are often spotlighted in the media, conservative voters in the Latinx community (or Hispanic community) are often overlooked. A question that further research might address is: Will subsequent generations of Asian American and Latinx voters follow these same trends, and if so, what implications will this have for how political leaders might court future immigrant voters?

Recommendations for Social Science Researchers

Social science research on immigrant organizing and activism has been instrumental in shedding light on the macro-level (policy) and micro-level (community/grassroots) experiences of immigrant community members. This section provides two recommendations regarding the ways that the collected data can continue to provide a holistic and accurate representation of the US immigrant community.

First, at the beginning of this chapter I briefly mentioned the experiences of refugee communities alongside those of other members of the US immigrant population. Yet, there is an important legal distinction between immigrant and refugee individuals under international and US legal systems. Recent scholarship, such as political scientist Rebecca Hamlin's *Crossing: How We Label and React to People on the Move*, has underscored the need to complicate the migrant/refugee binary, one that often reproduces false notions of deservingness and worthiness already present in the law (Hamlin, 2021). Similarly, the emergence of a field of critical refugee studies has worked to center refugee community members' lived experiences while also contextualizing these experiences within the legal and political forces at play (Espiritu, 2014). I therefore agree with David Scott FitzGerald and Rawan Arar (2018), who argue "that the sociology of international migration and refugee studies can mutually enrich one another and push theorization in both directions" (p. 388). In future scholarship, I would urge social and political science researchers to consider ways that they might examine the experiences of immigrant and refugee organizing relationally to reveal the similarities and differences in activists' approaches to leveraging power and fighting for increased rights.

Second, social scientists who study immigration, in particular demographers, have long noted the difficulty of collecting data about members of the undocumented immigrant community. Recently, increasingly innovative ways have been developed to account for the experiences of this population in large-scale datasets (Capps et al., 2018, 2020). Another approach to gathering more accurate data about members of this community might be to train local community members, activists, and staff members of community-based organizations in quantitative data collection and data analysis. This might be accomplished through the development of a free summer research institute with an applied focus. Such an approach would empower these leaders and staff members to more fully engage with research about their community and to propose (and carry out) their own research projects in which they dictate the type of data collected, their use, and their dissemination. An alternative approach could be to pair researchers with community leaders to collaborate on the development of a research project that will meet both the researchers' and community members' needs while building on their preexisting skill sets.

References

Abrego, L. (2006). "I can't go to college because i don't have papers": Incorporation patterns of Latino undocumented youth. *Latino Studies, 4*, 212–231.

Abrego, L. (2011). Legal consciousness of undocumented Latinos: Fear and stigma as barriers to claims-making for first- and 1.5-generation immigrants. *Law and Society Review, 45*(2), 337–369.

Abrego, L., & Negrón-Gonzales, G. (2020). *We are not dreamers: Undocumented scholars theorize undocumented life in the United States.* Duke University Press.

Almaguer, T. (2008). *Racial fault lines: The historical origins of White supremacy in California.* University of California Press.

Ancheta, A. (2006). *Race, rights, and the Asian American experience.* Rutgers University Press.

Aptekar, S. (2015). *The road to citizenship: What naturalization means for immigrants and the United States.* Rutgers University Press.

Bardacke, F. (2013). The UFW and the undocumented. *International Labor and Working-Class History, 83*, 162–169.

Brettell, C. B. (n.d.). *From civic to political engagement: the role of associations and organizations.* American Academy of Arts & Sciences. www.amacad.org/publication/political-and-civic-engagement-immigrants/section/5

Bloemraad, I. (2006). *Becoming a citizen: Incorporating immigrants and refugees in the United States and Canada.* University of California Press.

Bloemraad, I., & Voss, K. (2020). Movement or moment? Lessons from the pro-immigrant movement in the United States and contemporary challenges. *Journal of Ethnic and Migration Studies, 46*(4), 683–704.

Bloemraad, I., Chaudhary, A. R., & Gleeson, S. (2022). Immigrant organizations. *Annual Review of Sociology*, *48*, 319–341.

Budiman, A. (2020, August 20). *Key findings about U.S. immigrants*. Pew Research Center. www.pewresearch.org/fact-tank/2020/08/20/key-findings-about-u-s-immigrants/

Budiman, A., Tamir, C., Mora, L., & Noe-Bustamante, L. (2020, August 20). *Facts on U.S. immigrants, 2018: Statistical portrait of foreign-born population in the United States*. Pew Research Center. www.pewresearch.org/hispanic/2020/08/20/facts-on-u-s-immigrants/

Cadava, G. (2021). *The Hispanic Republican: The shaping of an American political identity, from Nixon to Trump*. Harper Collins.

Calavita, K. (1989). The contradictions of immigration lawmaking: The Immigration Reform and Control Act of 1986. *Law and Policy*, *11*(1), 17–47.

Capps, R., Bachmeier, J. D., & Van Hook, J. (2018). Estimating the characteristics of unauthorized immigrants using US Census data: Combined sample multiple imputation. *Annals of the American Academy of Political and Social Science*, *677*(1), 165–179.

Capps, R., Gelatt, J., Ruiz Soto, A. G., & Van Hook, J. (2020, December). *Unauthorized immigrants in the United States: Stable numbers, changing origins*. Migration Policy Institute. www.migrationpolicy.org/research/unauthorized-immigrants-united-states-stable-numbers-changing-origins

Cardenas, C. (2018, August 9). *5 young activists on what abolishing ICE actually means*. Remezcla. https://remezcla.com/lists/culture/abolish-ice-activists/

Chauvin, S., & Garcés-Mascareñas, B. (2014). Becoming less illegal: Deservingness frames and undocumented immigrant incorporation. *Sociology Compass*, *8*(4), 422–432.

Cisneros, J., Valdivia, D., Reyna Rivarola, A. R., & Russell, F. (2022). "I'm here to fight along with you": Undocumented student resource centers creating possibilities. *Journal of Diversity in Higher Education*, *15*(5), 607–616.

CNN Wire Staff. (2010, December 18). *Procedural vote on DREAM Act fails in Senate*. CNN Politics. www.cnn.com/2010/POLITICS/12/18/congress.dream.act/index.html

Coutin, S. (2011). The rights of noncitizens in the United States. *Annual Review of Law and Social Sciences*, *7*, 289–308.

de Graauw, E. (2016). *Making immigrant rights real: Nonprofits and the politics of integration in San Francisco*. Cornell University Press.

DeGenova, N. (2004). The legal production of Mexican/migrant "illegality." *Latino Studies*, *2*, 160–185.

DeSipio, L. (2012). Immigrant participation. In M. R. Rosenblum & D. J. Tichenor (Eds.), *Oxford handbook of the politics of international migration* (pp. 171–189). Oxford University Press.

Dunbar-Ortiz, R. (2021). *Not "a nation of immigrants": Settler colonialism, White supremacy, and a history of erasure and exclusion*. Beacon Press.

Ellis, B. (2021). The psychology of migrant "illegality": A general theory. *Law and Social Inquiry*, *46*(4), 1236–1271.

Enriquez, L. (2011). "Because we feel the pressure and we feel the support": Examining the educational success of undocumented immigrant Latina/o students. *Harvard Educational Review*, *81*(3), 476–499.

Enriquez, L. (2019). Border hopping Mexicans, law-abiding Asians, and racialized illegality: Analyzing undocumented college students' experiences through a relational lens. In N. Molina, D. Martinez HoSang, & R. A. Gutiérrez (Eds.), *Relational formations of race: Theory, method, and practice* (pp. 257–277). University of California Press.

Escudero, K. (2017, March 21). *Immigration reform 2.0: Going beyond the "good" vs. "bad" immigrant framework*. LatinoUSA. www.latinousa.org/2017/03/21/immigration-reform-2-0-going-beyond-good-vs-bad-immigrant-framework-opinion/

Escudero, K. (2020). *Organizing while undocumented: Immigrant youth's political activism under the law*. New York University Press.

Escudero, K., & Pallares, A. (2021). Civil disobedience as strategic resistance in the US immigrant rights movement. *Antipode, 53*(2), 422–444.

Espiritu, Y. L. (2014). *Body counts: The Vietnam War and militarized refuge(es)*. University of California Press.

FitzGerald, D. S., & Arar, R. (2018). The sociology of refugee migration. *Annual Review of Sociology, 44*, 387–406.

García, S. J. (2017). Racializing "illegality": An intersectional approach to understanding how Mexican-origin women navigate an anti-immigrant climate. *Sociology of Race and Ethnicity, 3*(4), 474–490.

Gleeson, S. (2010). Labor rights for all? The role of undocumented immigrant status for worker claims making. *Law and Social Inquiry, 35*(3), 561–602.

Gomberg-Muñoz, R. (2012). Inequality in a "postracial era." *DuBois Review, 9*(2), 339–353.

Gonzales, R. G., Ellis, B. D., Rendón-García, S. A., & Brant, K. (2018). (Un) authorized transitions: Illegality, DACA, and the life course. *Research in Human Development, 15*(3–4), 345–359.

Groenendijk, K. (2008). *Local voting rights for non-nationals in Europe: What we know and what we need to learn*. Migration Policy Institute. www.migrationpolicy.org/sites/default/files/publications/Groenendijk-final%5B1%5D.pdf

Gulasekaram, P., & Ramakrishnan, K. (2015). *The new immigration federalism*. Cambridge University Press.

Gutiérrez, D. (1991). *Sin fronteras?*: Chicanos, Mexican Americans, and the emergence of the contemporary Mexican immigration debate, 1968–1978. *Journal of American Ethnic History, 10*(4), 5–37.

Gutiérrez, D. (1995). *Walls and mirrors: Mexican Americans, Mexican immigrants, and the politics of ethnicity*. University of California Press.

Hamlin, R. (2021). *Crossing: How we label and react to people on the move*. Stanford University Press.

Hochschild, J., Chattopadhyay, J., Gay, C., & Jones-Correa, M. (2013). *Outsiders no more?: Models of immigrant incorporation*. Oxford University Press.

Jaffe, S. (2007, October 17). *Our parents are the original dreamers: how to fight for a clean DREAM Act*. Truthout. https://truthout.org/articles/our-parents-are-the-original-dreamers-how-to-fight-for-a-clean-dream-act/

Kelley, R. D. G. (1999). Building bridges: The challenge of organized labor in California communities of color. *New Labor Forum, 5*, 42–58.

Kelly, M. L. (2018, June 20). *The original DREAMer recalls "all pervasive" fear as an undocumented child*. NPR All Things Considered. www.npr.org/2018/

06/20/622002025/the-original-dreamer-recalls-all-pervasive-fear-as-an-undocu
mented-child

Kini, T. (2005). Sharing the vote: Noncitizen voting rights in local school board elections. *California Law Review*, *93*(1), 271–321.

Kuang, J. (2016, May 25). *Activist sues immigration agencies over denial of deferred deportation renewal*. Chicago Tribune. www.chicagotribune.com/news/break ing/ct-immigrant-activist-daca-lawsuit-met-20160525-story.html

Lee, E. (2004). *At America's gates: Chinese immigration during the exclusion era, 1882–1943*. University of North Carolina Press.

Levere, J. L. (2020, May 12). *From piano to dreamer: The inspiring story of Tereza Lee*. New York Public Radio. www.wqxr.org/story/piano-dreamer-tereza-lee/

Loza, M. (2016). *Defiant Braceros: How migrant workers fought for racial, sexual, and political freedom*. University of North Carolina Press.

Maira, S. M. (2009). *Missing: youth, citizenship, and empire after 9/11*. Duke University Press.

Massey, D. S., Durand, J., & Malone, N. J. (2003). *Beyond smoke and mirrors: Mexican immigration in an era of economic integration*. Russell Sage Foundation.

McCann, J. A., & Jones-Correa, M. (2020). *Holding fast: Resilience and civic engagement among Latino immigrants*. Russell Sage Foundation.

Menjívar, C. (2006). Liminal legality: Salvadoran and Guatemalan immigrants' lives in the United States. *American Journal of Sociology*, *111*(4), 999–1037.

Menjívar, C., & Abrego, L. (2012). Legal violence: Immigration law and the lives of Central American immigrants. *American Journal of Sociology*, *117*(5), 1380–1421.

Menjívar, C., & Kanstroom, D. (Eds.). (2014). *Constructing immigrant "illegality": Critiques, experiences, and responses*. Cambridge University Press.

Motomura, H. (2007). *Americans in waiting: The lost story of immigration and citizenship in the United States*. Oxford University Press.

Muñoz, S. M. (2015). *Identity, social activism, and the pursuit of higher education*. Peter Lang.

National Immigration Law Center. (2011, May). *DREAM Act: A summary*. National Immigration Law Center. www.nilc.org/issues/immigration-reform-and-executive-actions/dreamact/dreamsummary/

Negrón-Gonzales, G., Abrego, L. J., & Coll, K. (2015). Introduction: Immigrant Latina/o youth and illegality: Challenging the politics of deservingness. *Association of Mexican-American Educators Journal (AMAE)*, *9*(3), 7–10.

Ngai, M. (2014). *Impossible subjects: Illegal aliens and the making of modern America*. Princeton University Press.

Nicholls, W. (2013). *The DREAMers: How the undocumented youth movement transformed the immigrant rights debate*. Stanford University Press.

Nicholls, W. (2019). *The immigrant rights movement: The battle over national citizenship*. Stanford University Press.

Ong Hing, B. (2003). *Defining America through immigration policy*. Temple University Press.

Pallares, A. (2014). *Family activism: Immigrant struggles and the politics of noncitizenship*. Rutgers University Press.

Pallares, A., & Flores-González, N. (2010). *Marcha! Latino Chicago and the immigrant rights movement*. University of Illinois Press.

Patler, C. (2014). Racialized illegality: The convergence of race and legal status among Black, Latino, and Asian-American undocumented young adults. In V. Carty, R., Luévano, & T. Woldemikael (Eds.), *Scholars and Southern California immigrants in dialogue: New conversations in public sociology* (pp. 93–114). Lexington Press.

Patler, C. (2018). To reveal of conceal: How diverse undocumented youth navigate legal status disclosure. *Sociological Perspectives, 61*(6), 857–873.

Patler, C., & Gonzales, R. G. (2015). Framing citizenship: Media coverage of anti-deportation cases led by undocumented immigrant youth organizations. *Journal of Ethnic and Migration Studies, 41*(9), 1453–1474.

Perez Huber, L., Benavides Lopez, C., Malagon, M., Velez, V., & Solorzano, D. G. (2008). Getting beyond the 'symptom,' acknowledging the 'disease': Theorizing racist nativism. *Contemporary Justice Review, 11*(1), 39–51.

Pew Research Center. (2013, January 29). *A nation of immigrants*. Pew Research Center. www.pewresearch.org/hispanic/2013/01/29/a-nation-of-immigrants/

Ramakrishnan, S. K., & Bloemraad, I. (Eds.). (2008). *Civic hopes and political realities: Immigrants, community organizations, and political engagement*. Russell Sage Foundation.

Rodríguez, C. M. (2008). The significance of the local in immigration regulation. *Michigan Law Review, 106*, 567–642.

Romero, V. (2005). *Alienated: Immigrant rights, the constitution, and equality in America*. New York University Press.

Rumbaut, R. (2004). Ages, life stages, and generational cohorts: Decomposing the immigrant first and second generations in the United States. *International Migration Review, 38*(3), 1160–1205.

Rumbaut, R. (2012). Generation 1.5, educational experiences of. In J. A. Banks (Ed.), *Encyclopedia of diversity in education*. SAGE Publications.

Sanchez, M. G., & Batalova, J. (2021, November 10). Naturalized Citizens in the United States. Migration Policy Institute. www.migrationpolicy.org/article/naturalization-trends-united-states

Solórzano, R. R. (2022). *Notes from the Trail of Dreams*: The KKK, face-offs, and radical risk-taking *movidas*. *Latino Studies, 20*, 4–27.

Song, S. (2009). Democracy and noncitizen voting rights. *Citizenship Studies, 13*(6), 607–620.

Suárez-Orozco, C., Yoshikawa, H., Teranishi, R. T., & Suárez-Orozco, M. M. (2011). Growing up in the shadows: The developmental implications of unauthorized status. *Harvard Educational Review, 81*(3), 438–472.

Tang, E. (2015). *Unsettled: Cambodian refugees in the NYC hyperghetto*. Temple University Press.

Terriquez, V. (2015). Intersectional mobilization, social movement spillover, and queer youth leadership in the immigrant rights movement. *Social Problems, 62*(3), 343–362.

Tran, T. (2007, May 18). *Testimony of Tam Tran: House Judiciary Committee's Subcommittee on Immigration, Citizenship, Refugees, Border Security, and*

International Law. National Immigration Law Center. www.nilc.org/wp-content/uploads/2015/11/tam-tran-2007-05-18.pdf

Unzueta Carrasco, T., & Seif, H. (2014). Disrupting the dream: undocumented youth reframe citizenship and deportability through anti-deportation activism. *Latino Studies, 12*(2), 279–299.

Vasilogambros, M. (2021, July 1). *Noncitizens are slowly gaining voting rights*. Stateline. https://stateline.org/2021/07/01/noncitizens-are-slowly-gaining-voting-rights/

Voss, K., & Bloemraad, I. (Eds.). (2011). *Rallying for immigrant rights: the fight for inclusion in 21st century America*. University of California Press.

Walia, H. (2013). *Undoing border imperialism*. AK Press.

Wong, J. (2006). *Democracy's promise: Immigrants and American civic institutions*. University of Michigan Press.

Wong, J., & Shah, S. (2021). Convergence across difference: Understanding the political ties that bind with the 2016 National Asian American Survey. *RSF: The Russell Sage Foundation Journal of the Social Sciences, 7*(2), 70–92.

Wong, J., Ramakrishnan, S. K., Lee, T., & Junn, J. (2011). *Asian American political participation: Emerging constituencies and their political identities*. Russell Sage Foundation.

Yalamarty, H. (2020). Lessons from "no ban on stolen land." *Studies in Social Justice, 14*(2), 474–485.

Yoshikawa, H. (2011). *Immigrants raising citizens: Undocumented parents and their young children*. Russell Sage Foundation.

Zepeda-Millán, C. (2017). *Latino mass mobilization: immigration, racialization, and activism*. Cambridge University Press.

Zimmerman, A. (2016). Transmedia testimonio: Examining undocumented youth's political activism in the digital age. *International Journal of Communication, 10*, 1886–1906.

6 Online Racial Justice Advocacy

Melanie Brazzell

Introduction

From Civil Rights to Black Lives Matter

Just as White supremacy is embedded in the genocidal founding of the US, so too have communities of color and their allies always mounted resistance to racism and advocacy for racial justice. One of the most influential struggles for racial justice in the twentieth century was the civil rights movement.[1] The more reformist wing of the movement employed a "master frame" (Snow & Benford, 1992) of "equal rights" that was so resonant it became a template for other racial justice movements in the US and globally, as well as movements around feminist, LGBTQ+, and disability issues. In contrast, the more militant wing of the Black freedom struggle, embodied by the Black Panthers, was organized around concepts like Black power, self-determination, and anti-imperialism. This wing also went on to inspire the Chicano movement and the American Indian movement, as its alternative frame about community or people power "diffused" (Givan et al., 2010) to other marginalized racial groups.

The rise of identity-based organizing in the 1960s and this wide variety of new movements has been captured under the umbrella term "the New Left" (Mills, 1960). The New Left moved away from a traditional leftist, socialist, or labor politics unified primarily by questions of class, now overshadowed by the betrayals of Stalin and the Soviet Union. This new model of organizing mobilized people around various other axes of oppression, some connected to identity (race and ethnicity, sexuality, gender, disability) and others to specific issue areas (the environment, war/the military/nuclear weapons, apartheid in South Africa or Palestine). For some, this led to a fragmentation of separate issue areas that competed with one another for resources and attention.

For others, these axes were understood as connected or intersectional. For example, despite the labor movement's discrimination against Black people,

---

1 The civil rights movement has also been highly influential on social movement research. When used as a case study, the movement has fueled key theoretical developments like political process theory, though the whiteness of these analyses has also been called into question (Bracey, 2016).

many generations of US Black radicals like W. E. B. DuBois, Ella Baker, Pauli Murray, George Jackson, and Angela Davis integrated resistance to capitalism into their resistance to racism, using an analysis later formulated by Cedric Robinson as "racial capitalism" (Robinson, 2005). For many Black activists and intellectuals, these interconnections were also transnational, since the experience of the transatlantic slave trade had scattered the Black diaspora across the world. Black activists in the Global North connected their struggles with those of Black liberationists in the Global South, including the anti-colonial struggles in present-day Congo and Ghana, as well as antiapartheid campaigns in South Africa (Munro, 2017).

Decolonization efforts in the Global South and racial justice movements in the US both peaked in the 1960s, before losing momentum and facing back-lash in the decades following. While hard-won civil rights in the US were formally protected, structural racism in housing, employment, education, the criminal legal system, finance, health, and the media persisted in more indirect and informal ways. These were upheld by policy platforms like Nixon's war on crime, Reagan-era neoliberal economics, Clinton's welfare reform, and the rise of mass incarceration, which disproportionately targets Black and Latino people. As racism has taken on new forms and faces, resistance has also adapted.

Contemporary US racial justice advocacy is a vast field, tackling issues that range from mass incarceration to immigration reform, gentrification, environmental justice, and health care access in a time of pandemic. This chapter uses case studies from a small swathe of that sector and puts them into a broader context through dialogue with the literature on social movements and Black Studies. The chapter draws on my collaborative research with the racial justice organization Color Of Change (COC), as well as my ongoing research and practice with the movement for transformative justice alternatives to prison and policing for gendered violence. As such, this chapter focuses on a specific area of racial justice organizing against the carceral state (which includes policing, prisons, migrant detention centers, locked psychiatric centers, and other sites of punishment).

I look specifically at the last decade of organizing in the US for Black Lives Matter, which peaked in two waves of momentum, both in response to police murders of Black men. The first "cycle of contention" (Tarrow, 1998) began after the murder of Michael Brown in Ferguson, MO, in the summer of 2014; the second began after the suffocation of George Floyd in Minneapolis, MN, in the summer of 2020. Mobilizations under the banner of Black Lives Matter in the subsequent months drew out millions of people, making them the largest documented protests in US history (Buchanan et al., 2020). Each time police murdered yet another Black person, new protest waves formed or intensified in specific cities, as protestors showed up with renewed energy to #SayHerName or #SayHisName. The movement used Opal Tometi, Alicia Garza, and Patrice Khan-Cullors' phrase "Black Lives Matter" as its collective action frame, shifting from the "rights frame" of the civil rights era to a broader frame about the worth of Black life. This countered the hegemonic narrative that criminalizes Black people and treats their lives as disposable.

This frame has been remarkably resonant on a global scale, mobilizing millions of people outside the US to protests and actions. The year 2020 saw Black Lives Matter actions on every continent, including Antarctica. My research on transnational transformative justice with activists and scholars in Europe, North America, and Australia suggests that US abolitionist politics continue to be a reference point and guiding light for movements in other nation state contexts (Brazzell & Meiners, 2022).

In the decades between the storied civil rights movement and the Black Lives Matter movement, whose history is still being written, women and queer people of color have played a decisive role. Though women served as key leaders in the civil rights movement, particularly as mid-level leaders who bridged between formal organizations and informal community structures (Robnett, 2000), they were often marginalized. Martin Luther King's charismatic individual leadership is remembered more than Ella Baker's out-of-the-spotlight approach to developing a "leaderful" movement (Ransby, 2003). Gender concerns were seen as a distraction or as "dirty laundry." Yet when women of color sought to address these concerns about sexism in a different venue; in the nascent feminist movement that bloomed after the civil rights movement's peak, they often found it dominated by White women unwilling to address issues of race.

In response, women and queer people of color at the crossroads of racism, sexism, and more, like Audre Lorde, June Jordan, Marsha P. Johnson, the Combahee River Collective, and bell hooks, claimed their own spaces and voices for writing, consciousness-raising, and organizing. They articulated the ways that gender and race, as well as age, ability, sexuality, capitalism, and other vectors of oppression, intersected with one another. This approach was later popularized in academia by Kimberlé Crenshaw (1991) as "intersectionality." This work was continued in the early 2000s by transformative justice organizing against both state and gendered violence by groups like INCITE! Women, Gender Non-Conforming, and Trans People of Color Against Violence.

The most recent Black Lives Matter wave of organizing continues this legacy through Black queer feminist leadership and ideology by the likes of Charlene Carruthers, adrienne maree brown, Alexis Pauline Gumbs, and many others. Black male victims of police brutality have often been in the foreground, but frames like #SayHerName and #BlackTransLivesMatter surface the stories of Black women and trans victims of police violence. Black Youth Project 100 (BYP100) represents an organizational embodiment of this submerged legacy. The membership-based organization was founded in 2013 in connection with a convening organized by queer Black elder

Dr. Cathy Cohen. BYP100 organizes youth aged eighteen to thirty-five and has chapters in ten cities as well as national campaigns. The organization is explicit about its use of a "Black, queer, feminist lens … centered on ending systems of anti-Blackness and emphasizing the urgency of protecting folks living on the margins of the margins, including women, girls, femmes, and the gamut of LGBTQ folk" (Black Youth Project 100, 2022a, p. 100). Two of the six planks in the organization's "Agenda to Build Black Futures" focus explicitly on marginalized genders: "Value the Worth of Women's Work" and "Support Trans* Wealth and Health" (Black Youth Project 100, 2022b).

While Black women and queer people reclaim these marginalized, intersectional legacies of antiracism, others working on racial justice have broken with more mainstream legacies of reformism and respectability politics. Tef Poe, an organizer and rapper in Michael Brown's hometown of Ferguson, MO, told the old guard: "This ain't your daddy's civil rights movement," a phrase that he later included as a refrain in his music. He is referring in part to tactical differences among generations of Black freedom struggle. The contemporary movement has used more militant tactics, including property destruction, in comparison to the disciplined nonviolence of civil rights groups like the Student Nonviolent Coordinating Committee and King's Southern Christian Leadership Conference.

Technological Evolutions Shaping Antiracist Organizing

The racial justice movement has evolved because of intertwined transformations in both ideology (e.g., intersectionality) and in the material and technological bases for mass mobilization. Theda Skocpol's work sheds light on the rise of New Left-style identity and issue-based organizing in the 1960s through her diagnosis of a broader shift in voluntary civic organizations in the US "from membership to management" over the last century (Skocpol, 2003). Whereas cross-class federations like the Fraternal Order of Eagles had previously built a constituency of dues-paying members in the early twentieth century, technological shifts like direct mail and mass media allowed organizations to reach the public more directly in the 1950s and 1960s.

These changes allowed organizations to shift from reliance on a dues-paying membership and seek money and recruits more widely – a potentially democratizing change. The nimbleness of this new approach unencumbered organizations from the complexity of formal membership structures for decision-making. Yet, Skocpol argues, this has "diminished democracy." Why? It has also made civic organizations more dependent on contributions from wealthy individuals, foundations, or the government, shaping their approaches to attract resources from the few at the top rather than the many at the bottom. This has led many organizations to rely heavily on a professionalized staff with little participation from or accountability to the constituencies they claim to represent or advocate for. People are seen more as individual consumers than active participants in an organization. Organizers and scholars of color have also critiqued this phenomenon and its unique impacts on antiracist, queer, and feminist organizations. For example, INCITE! Women, Gender Non-Conforming, and Trans People of Color Against Violence coined the term "nonprofit industrial complex" to describe the influence of neoliberal capitalism on the form and function of nonprofit organizations (INCITE!, 2007).

The rise of the Internet and social media has only lowered transaction costs for organizations, allowing them to scale up and reach more and more people cheaply. While the era of mass media provided a scarcity of information through just a few curated TV programs and stations, the era of social media floods us with a nearly unmanageable surplus. Rather than professional journalists gatekeeping the news, citizen journalists can report from their own perspectives. While mass media's concentration into a few big channels created a centralized chokepoint for data, social media's decentralization allows information to move more freely. While this democratizes the field and allows marginalized groups to become creators of their own stories, it also creates problems with credibility, disinformation, and "fake news." Gatekeeping still shapes what people see and interact with online, but rather than the editorial discretion of a news company in the mass media era, it is now in the hands of the algorithms of the platforms one uses. This can create echo chambers where one person's feed may feature videos of the Black Lives Matter uprisings while another's only highlights TikTok challenges or cat videos. The techno-utopianism that characterized the early Internet years of the 1990s overlooked the fact that technology is designed and used by people embedded in structural inequities of race, gender, class, ability, and more. They go on to embed those inequities in the technologies they make and use (see, e.g., Benjamin, 2019).

The forms of activism that these new technologies have enabled are also ambivalent, giving activists and advocates new "technological affordances" that also come at a price. Some have critiqued online activism as low-stakes, hobby "slacktivism" (Morozov, 2012). Just as Gil Scott-Heron once sung that the "revolution will not be televised" ("The revolution will not go better with Coke/The revolution will not fight the germs that cause bad breath"; Scott-Heron, 1971), some also claimed that the revolution "will not be tweeted" (Gladwell, 2010). And yet, in the case of the Arab Spring in 2012 in Tunisia, Egypt, and elsewhere in the Middle East/North Africa region, it was. As Zeynep Tufekci illustrates in her book *Twitter and Tear Gas: The Power and Fragility of Networked Protest* (2017), Facebook, Twitter (now known as X), and other social networks were crucial for connecting millions of participants who unexpectedly escalated protest to a fever pitch and toppled authoritarian regimes in Egypt and Tunisia. In the US, these platforms also enabled the spontaneous occupation of Wall Street, which sparked a nationwide Occupy movement that advocated for economic justice for the 99 percent, the working-class majority of the country. This new netroots approach (a portmanteau of "Internet" and "grassroots") also heralded the power of mailing lists like MoveOn to rally people around the country to quickly respond to political challenges through petitions and emails to their representatives (Karpf, 2012). The netroots also made space for a horizontal, self-organized Black feminist blogosphere exemplified by the Crunk Feminist Collective and for Black Twitter as a digital counter-public to the White mainstream of social media networks (Jackson et al., 2020).

Momentum Community, a movement training institute and incubator that has launched organizations like Sunrise and IfNotNow, distinguishes between "mass protest" and "structure-based organizing" traditions in its analysis of social movement history (Momentum, 2022). Social networks are particularly good at enabling the kinds of activism that belongs to the "mass protest" tradition: direct actions by regular people. These spread virally in what Momentum calls "whirlwind moments" and attract new participants exponentially, creating a sense of crisis and possibility that can shift public opinion rapidly. This approach most often uses a strategy of mobilizing: focusing transactionally on maximizing the quantity of participants (Han, 2014). But this scale often comes at the expense of building the capacity of individuals and the organization to grow and/or persist.

The "structure-based tradition," in contrast, organizes a pregiven, usually geographically rooted community structure (like a workplace, neighborhood, religious institution, or school). Rooted in the labor movement and Saul Alinsky's "community organizing" model (Alinsky, 1971), this approach uses intensive relationship-building and leadership development to build a resilient organization that often pushes for change incrementally over a longer period of time. This approach most often uses a strategy of organizing, now sometimes referred to as "relational organizing," which focuses on quality as well as quantity, transforming participants by building their leadership skills and ability to organize others (Han, 2014).

Tufekci's findings about digital activism in the early 2010s confirm Momentum's theory: Mass protest movements like the Arab Spring could mobilize millions more people than earlier, pre-Internet movements, but they were unable to forge these loose ties into strong organizations that could weather political shifts and implement long-lasting change. When technology substitutes for organizational structure, "organizing without organizations" (Shirky, 2008) runs into problems: People often lack the capacity to navigate conflict, make decisions, and build consensus (Tufekci, 2017). And when technology substitutes for organizational culture, activists often replicate the culture of the social media platforms they are using, typically suffused with racism, transphobia, disinformation, and polarization.

The two waves of contention that make up the last decade of the Black Lives Matter movement each started as mass protests enabled by technological developments. They were triggered by images of Black death made possible by phone video-recording technology and spread from city to city through social networks. While these mobilizations have been spontaneous, they have also been networked to existing organizations and have spawned the formation of new ones. These organizations grapple with how to build long-term power after the protests simmer down and frontline activists burn out. The case example threaded throughout this chapter offers an example of how one organization, COC, has tried to hybridize both the scale of the protest tradition and the depth of the structure-based tradition. It has used its formid-able digital power to achieve widespread antiracist mobilization while build-ing deep relationships through online-to-offline organizing.

Case Example: Color Of Change

Color Of Change describes itself as the largest online Black civil rights organization in the country. Color Of Change's wide range of campaigns on a number of racial justice issues and its organizing both online and offline make it a useful exemplar of the diversity of antiracist advocacy in the US today. Founded in 2005 by James Rucker and Van Jones, COC was initially intended to leverage email list models such as MoveOn to spur mobilization among Black Internet users. Ten years later, COC had 1.01 million subscribers in 2015. By the end of 2021, that number had risen to 6.1 million as a result of the organization's success at scale.

Color Of Change aims for "real world change that Black people can feel" and centers the cultivation of Black joy. In service of this goal, COC has a multi-issue theory of change that ranges from economic to media to electoral justice. Color Of Change has led successful campaigns against anti-Black racism on the part of corporations, politicians, and media. In collaboration with its partners, COC has successfully pressured tech companies like Twitter to ban Donald Trump and Facebook to address its hate content policies. The organization has made waves in the culture industry by convincing RCA Records to drop R. Kelly for his abuse of Black women and in sports by pressuring the US Olympic and Paralympic Community to stop censuring political self-expression like raised fists and bended knees by Black athletes. Later in this chapter, I focus in particular on COC's work to reform the criminal justice system by electing progressive district attorneys and prosecutors.

Color Of Change has a similarly expansive organizational structure, which, together with its membership, has grown massively since the Black Lives Matter uprisings of 2020. This provides a "big tent" for the Black community and allies, with many campaigns serving as entry points for members. A transition from online to offline organizing has allowed COC to balance this scale with greater depth – for instance, through long-term membership structures like squads that focus on transformative relationship-building. I explore this "big tent" in greater detail later in the chapter.

Color Of Change uses culture as the building block of its political home for Black people and their allies, focusing on storytelling, aesthetics, and values. Color Of Change took the "3 Bs" framework from religious communities of believing, becoming, and belonging (Smidt et al., 2009) and turned it on its head by putting "belonging" first in the sequence (a trend that many in the contemporary church are also now doing). Belonging or feeling at home should be the first emotional-aesthetic experience Black people have in a COC space, whether online or offline. Identity, not ideology, is the force aligning members and staff across a massive and complex organization.

Power and Empowerment in Racial Justice Advocacy

In the following sections, I use the literature on community power, empowerment, organizational theory, civic engagement, and social movements to make sense of racial justice advocacy. I look specifically at recent Black Lives Matter mobilizations through three lenses: the macro or structural level, the meso or organizational level, and the micro or individual level.

A macro lens looks at community power, or the power organized groups of people are able to build and leverage for political and cultural change in various institutions (media, education, public health, and government policy) at various levels (the community, city, state, and federal levels). I use Lukes' model of three dimensions of power (2005), as elaborated by Christens (2019), to unpack recent Black Lives Matter successes regarding criminal legal system reform. I examine these outcomes at three levels: the situational (the first face), the institutional (the second face), and the systemic (the third face).

Then I turn to a micro lens by looking at individual psychological empowerment processes within groups organizing for racial justice for Black people. Black queer feminist approaches like healing justice and transformative justice have brought embodiment, emotions, healing, and spirituality into racial justice organizing paradigms. This has brought "empowerment" back to its collective and radical roots and integrated marginalized elements beyond the masculinist focus on control and self-determination into an understanding of empowerment. I use Zimmerman's (1995) approach by looking at three components of psychological empowerment: the emotional (in this case, expressions of Black joy), the cognitive (through political education), and the behavioral (in forms of care and community-building focused on Black women).

Lastly, I look at the meso-level organizational settings that bridge psychological empowerment and capacity-building at an individual level with external, macro-level outcomes like policy changes and culture shifts. I draw on Han, McKenna, and Oyakawa's concept of the "prism" (2021) to explain how organizations transform individual "inputs" like people and resources (micro-level) into organized constituencies (meso-level), refracting their power outwardly in the public sphere for political change (macro-level). I coin the term "Black prism" to describe organizations that build the power of Black constituents, and I explore the design elements that can build an effective Black prism. One of them is the creation of a social or political home. I draw on research projects led by Sonia Sarkar (Sarkar et al., 2021) and Katrina Gamble (2021) to understand racial justice organizations as social or political homes. I return to the case of COC to discuss the organizational design choice it has made to hybridize both scale and depth, mobilizing and organizing, in order to build this political home for Black people.

Community Power

Defining and measuring a community's power are vexing issues for social scientists. Lukes' well-known "three faces of power" model describes three levels at which domination occurs: through outright wins (the most obvious), through agenda-setting and gatekeeping, and through the ideological formation of beliefs and desires. This model has been updated by Christens (2019) to look not only at coercive or top-down "power over" but also at horizontal, interdependent "power with," the kind of power that many social movements want to build. He offers a conceptual model for three levels at which activists and advocates contest for power: the situational, the institutional, and the systemic. These are arenas where racial justice advocates have the opportunity to dismantle "power over" and build "power with" others.

Situational

The situational level describes wins or losses, answering the question: "Who wins the game?" This first face of power is the most visible form of power. In the Black Lives Matter protest cycles, the most visible expression of power was sheer turnout to demonstrations. An estimated 15–26 million people participated in the most recent round of Black Lives Matter contention in the summer of 2020 (Buchanan et al., 2020). According to US Census data, these figures constitute roughly 4.5–7.8 percent of the US population (US Census Bureau, 2021), making it the largest documented US protest movement in history.

These protests rippled out internationally, resonating with local struggles like the #EndSARS movement in Nigeria that calls for the disbanding of a notoriously abusive police unit called the Special Anti-Robbery Squad. In Australia, activists used the banner of Black Lives Matter to express outrage about the deaths of Aboriginal people in police custody. In Mexico, activists drew connections between police murders in the US and in their own country, particularly of migrants like Victoria Esperanza Salazar, a refugee from El Salvador murdered by four police officers in Tulum in 2021. "There is a George Floyd in every country," shared South African journalist Lynsey Chutel (quoted in Westerman et al., 2020). The network of local chapters that grew out of the first Black Lives Matter protest cycle calls itself the "Black Lives Matter Global Network" to capture this global scope.

Another way of measuring the first face of power for the Black Lives Matter movement's goal of police accountability is to look at rates of prosecution and conviction for police shootings. An estimated 1,000 people are fatally shot by police in the US each year, and the rate for Black people is more than twice that of Whites (Tate et al., 2022). Yet the charge and conviction rates for police murders are extremely low, with only forty-two officers convicted of murder or manslaughter between 2005 and 2020 (Thomson-DeVeaux, 2020). Black Lives Matter protestors pressured prosecutors and district attorneys to charge police in several high-profile police murders, some of which resulted in convictions. Several of these recent successful cases were in Minnesota, where the second wave of Black Lives Matter uprisings began. Derek Chauvin, whose murder of George Floyd in Minneapolis in 2020 triggered those uprisings, was convicted of three charges of murder and manslaughter for Floyd's death and sentenced to 22.5 years in prison. In addition, the three police officer bystanders who did not intervene as Chauvin kneeled on Floyd's neck for nearly ten minutes were sentenced to between 2.5 and 3.5 years in prison in a federal civil rights trial. Police officer Kim Potter was also convicted in early 2022 in Minnesota for murdering Daunte Wright during a traffic stop, despite her claims that she meant to use her taser and not her gun.

Another expression of the first face of power is direct action, a form of protest in which people leverage their own power to accomplish their goals rather than pressuring others (corporate, government, or other actors) to do so. The civil rights movement's sit-ins and freedom rides directly desegregated lunch counters in the Jim Crow South and faced violent backlash as a result. Similarly, Black Lives Matter protestors also made direct interventions in their local aesthetic and epistemic landscapes by toppling a number of monuments honoring Confederate or colonial figures, removing visual reminders of White supremacy. According to the Southern Poverty Law Center, 169 Confederate symbols were removed in 2020, ninety-four of them monuments. In comparison, only fifty-eight monuments were removed between 2015 and 2019 (Southern Poverty Law Center, 2021), suggesting that the Black Lives Matter movement accelerated the rate of removal of racist monuments and memorials. These publicly visible forms of contention serve as expressions of the first face of power.

Institutional

Beyond the first face of power, how have racial justice activists burst through White supremacist gatekeeping and altered the political agenda? This second face of power is about not who wins the game but who sets the rules. By directly confronting local, state, and federal policy regarding policing, activists began to change the rules of the game by attacking upstream factors that enable police violence.

Organizers won a number of criminal justice reforms: Six cities won bans on police use of chemical or military-grade weapons, four cities achieved bans on police use of facial recognition technology, and twenty-five cities removed police and "resource officers" from their schools (Interrupting Criminalization, 2020, p. 15). The #8CantWait campaign by an organization called Campaign Zero has focused on use of force policies, which determine when a police officer can use force against a civilian. Research indicates that police officers are more likely to use force when the officer and civilian are of different races or genders, particularly White officers and Black civilians (Wright & Headley, 2020). The campaign advocates for eight reforms to restrict use of force, including a requirement to de-escalate and a ban on chokeholds like the one that killed George Floyd. According to the organization, nineteen states have enacted at least one of these policies since June 2020 (Campaign Zero, 2022).

In the struggle to increase accountability for so-called killer cops, racial justice organizations have also taken aim at qualified immunity, or laws that protect police and other public officials from being sued by individuals when their constitutional rights are violated. These efforts have been less successful. Thirty-five state bills launched in the eighteen months after George Floyd's murder failed in the face of opposition by police and police unions; only Colorado was successful at ending the practice (Kindy, 2021).

However, the more radical, abolitionist wing of the movement has focused on defunding rather than reforming police departments. This is part of a larger policy program aimed at cutting off resources for what they perceive as systems of death (like police, prisons, borders, the military, etc.) and resourcing life-giving systems like health care, education, jobs, and housing. This framework has been called "invest–divest" by the Movement for Black Lives network and "defund and refund" by the Bay Area's Anti-Police Terror Project. How successful has the movement been in achieving this second face of power? Interrupting Criminalization, a project led by abolitionists Mariame Kaba and Andrea Ritchie, reports that organizers in twenty cities in 2020 succeeded in removing $840 million from police budgets and got at least $160 million invested into community programs (Interrupting Criminalization, 2020, p. 15). Time will tell how enduring these budgetary changes prove to be, and progress can be tracked at the Social Movement Support Lab's Defund Data project (defunddata.org).

Another upstream win was organizers' focus on participatory budgeting to enable greater participation by community members in the creation of their local budgets for police as well as education and other community programs. For example, Seattle City Council cut $30 million from its police budget and agreed to a participatory budgeting process whereby community members decide how best to reallocate these funds for programs that better provide safety. This is a "policy feedback loop" (Hertel-Fernandez, 2020) in which a policy change has immediate impacts as well as long-term impacts that enable what policies can be made in the future.

In addition, antiracist organizations have become increasingly involved in electoral politics in order to field and support candidates who back their agenda. This is another way of changing the rules of the game – by changing who is making the rules. Color Of Change, for example, talked with local partners across the country to discuss a new electoral approach in the movement's ecosystem and organized donors to invest in identifying and running candidates willing to transform the criminal justice system. Color Of Change has engaged in forty district attorney races since 2016, achieving twenty-nine successful wins by endorsed candidates.

Another step in changing the rules of the game is to change who can vote for candidates. Coalitions of antiracist organizations are currently, as of 2023, pushing for voting rights legislation to protect the votes of marginalized citizens, including people of color. States that exclude formerly incarcerated people with felony charges from voting, such as Florida and Virginia, have seen big pushes to re-enfranchise those citizens (though both steps toward voter restoration have since been overturned by Republican lawmakers, governors, and/or courts).

Systemic

The third and most elusive face of power is represented by the forces of ideology and public opinion that shape the beliefs and desires that people bring to "the game." Movement activists largely shift this face of power by creating new "public narratives" (Ganz, 2009), or what social movement scholars call "collective action frames," which tell a political story from a new or different perspective.

The Black Lives Matter movement inherited a civil rights movement "rights"-based frame but opted to shift to a less legal and more affective frame about human life and dignity through the phrase #BlackLivesMatter. In the first cycle of Black Lives Matter contention, starting in 2014, may advocates and activists faced counter-frames of #AllLivesMatter and #BlueLivesMatter (a reference to police lives as "blue").

The turn to emotion, spirituality, and humanity inherent in a focus on Black life is characteristic of the queer feminist leadership of the movement. They brought intersectional frames that draw on what BYP100 calls the "Black Queer Feminist (and Trans) Lens." Hashtags like #BlackTransLivesMatter and #SayHerName (Crenshaw & Ritchie, 2015) surface the perspectives of Black queer people and Black women, whose stories were too often submerged by the dominant tellings and retellings of the civil rights movement.

Another major frame shift was the rise of the abolition frame. In the 1990s, an organization called Critical Resistance was formed. It hosted several large conferences where antiprison and prison reform activists of all stripes converged to name and fight mass incarceration. The organization began using the term "abolition" to point out continuities between prison and slavery and resistance to both (Critical Resistance 10 Publications Collective, 2008). In so doing, they constructed an intergenerational arc of abolition and reframed the present as the heroic inheritance of a centuries-old struggle. This idea is captured in part by the "Black radical tradition" (Robinson, 2005) informing Black resistance internationally and across time. Despite this long arc, abolition was a newer and more provocative idea for mainstream antiracist activists, and so frame crystallization took longer. While Critical Resistance's work has always focused on what it calls the "prison–industrial complex" (a set of interests that funnel marginalized people from the police to courts to prison cells), abolition was still associated with prisons. It took some time for this frame to diffuse to the police as well. (In contrast, frames about abolishing prison have been less popular, and prison in general has been less of a focus of attention in the most recent Black Lives Matter uprisings.)

The "defund the police" frame emerged as a loose cousin to the abolition frame. It is a more concrete and measurable goal, but its relationship to abolition as an ideological end goal is vague. By framing around something pragmatic, "defund the police" has been able to unite activists across a broad spectrum. Abolitionists find it a pragmatic "nonreformist reform" (Critical Resistance, n.d.; Gorz, 1967) that brings them one step closer to their ultimate aims, while reformers, who are more agnostic about those aims, have also been able to adopt this frame for its pragmatism.

While new frames and narratives undergird struggles for situational and institutional power, the third face of power often shows itself best in the cultural outcomes of movements, which are so difficult to measure. Thus, these new frames have seeded new imaginations of a world without racism, prisons, or police, often captured in science fiction, visual arts, and other forms of cultural organizing. In theory, narrative and culture shifts should have downstream effects on the second and first faces of power. While new media technologies have allowed racial justice narratives to reach people more quickly and directly, these technologies have reflected and exacerbated US racial segregations, keeping communities in political and racial echo chambers of like-minded people.

Psychological Empowerment Processes

While community power offers a macro lens on social change, psychological empowerment allows us to focus microscopically on individual-level transformation. As a term, "empowerment" was employed by Black radicals to describe economic and social self-determination. Empowerment was a measure of one's control over the conditions in which one lived, and achieving it required collective organizing – for instance, in the form of an organization or a party (like the Black Panther Party). As the term entered academia and social service professions, "empowerment" lost its political roots and came to be associated more with individual feelings than collective processes. "Empowerment" has been coopted into neoliberal managerial vocabularies that do not genuinely shift power relations but only change the feelings of those living inside them: managers "empowering" their employees, social workers "empowering" clients, or corporations "empowering" consumers. Empowerment here is less about power than improved performance or quality of life.

Public health has begun to rebuild the connection between power and mental health. Researchers have documented how structural racism creates stress for people of color that negatively impacts their physical and mental health (Bailey et al., 2017). Public health organizations are starting to come around to an understanding that police harassment and violence are also significant health hazards for racialized groups, with the American Association of Public Health going so far as to call for community-based alternatives for safety in a policy statement (2018).

Black women's organizing has often emphasized the holistic relationship between macro-level power and micro-level empowerment. For example, Julia Sudbury's (1998) concept of "the politics of transformation" draws on her study of Black women's organizations and combines external social change with the internal transformations of consciousness-raising. In this section, I explore how Black racial justice organizers practice psychological empowerment. Zimmerman (1995) describes three core components of psychological empowerment: emotional, cognitive, and behavioral. In the following, I look at the role of Black joy, political education, and care and community-building for Black women to explore these components in contemporary Black antiracism organizing.

Each of these is shaped by the contributions of Black queer feminist movements for healing justice and transformative justice. The healing justice framework was first articulated by the Kindred Southern Healing Justice Collective (a network of healers and health practitioners in the southeast US) in 2006. It connects individual trauma with the social and intergenerational traumas of oppression, and it links individual healing and collective justice. The healing justice framework diagnoses disparities in health access and outcomes as the result of a privatized and individualized health model coupled with the state's abandonment, pathologizing, or criminalization of poor and racialized populations who need healing from trauma. Healing justice looks to ancestral practices, connections to land and plants, and cultural memory for more communal understandings of health and healing. Transformative justice, developed by queer people and women of color at the intersections of antiracist and feminist movements, aims to address interpersonal violence (particularly gendered and sexualized violence) without using state violence (like police or prisons). Transformative justice has encouraged organizations and individual activists to build their capacities for navigating accountability, conflict, support, and harm outside of a punitive approach. BYP100, for instance, has convened a "Healing and Safety Council" with representatives from its national staff and local chapters, as well as a paid coordinator for the council (Green et al., 2018). This "holistic human resources team" works to transform organizational and wider movement culture "to seed Black liberation organizational work that is radically caring, deeply accountable, and wondrously inclusive" (Green et al., 2018, p. 916).

These approaches have brought embodiment, emotions, healing, and spirituality into racial justice movements previously dominated by masculinist paradigms of independence rather than interdependence, with a focus primarily on tactics, impacts, and outcomes rather than organizational culture and community wellness. These frameworks also return "empowerment" to its collective and radical origins because healing and transformative justice explicitly link micro-level and macro-level transformation.

Emotional: Black Joy

Technological advances have put decent-quality video cameras in many peoples' pockets, allowing the recording of law enforcement violence and the circulation of these videos on social media to reach a wider audience. While documentation of state violence against Black people has been crucial in some efforts to hold public officials accountable, it has also subjected Black people to constant retraumatization through repeated depictions of Black suffering. Black bodies, particularly Black women and trans bodies, appear both hypervisible (surveilled and tracked) and invisible (their pain does not register to White ears and audiences) in this visual culture.

Black activists and scholars have expressed different "racialized emotions" (Green et al., 2018) in response to this ongoing exposure to Black death. Against the stereotype of the "angry Black woman" used to silence Black women's justified rage, Audre Lorde spoke of "the uses of anger" (2007), bell hooks spoke of "killing rage" (1996), and Brittney Cooper spoke of the "superpower of eloquent rage" (2018). But joy is another racialized emotion that has become popular for countering images of Black death with images of Black flourishing. Hashtags like #BlackGirlMagic and #BlackBoyJoy focus on joyful Black children in order to reclaim the innocence that the government and the media often deny Black children.

This visual culture of resistance is also Afro-futurist, nurturing imaginations of a future in which Black life is sacred rather than disposable. Black Lives Matter has been accompanied by a rise in Black science fiction and Afro-futurism that insists that "there are black people in the future" (There Are

Black People in the Future, n.d.). This signals the deep crises of the present like ecological catastrophe and fascist politics and a desire for radically transformed futures. This is exemplified in the poetic novels and collages of Alexis Pauline Gumbs and adrienne maree brown's claiming of a new generation of sci-fi writers of color as "Octavia's Brood" (in reference to author Octavia Butler). In "Black Joy in the Time of Ferguson," professor and spoken word poet Dr. Javon Johnson writes about the connections between Black joy and radical imagination: "... made somewhat whole again through black joy – that is, the black love, laughter, hugs, and smiles that for a moment offer us glimpses of radical democracy, freedom, and utopia" (Johnson, 2015, p. 181).

Color Of Change has dared to claim Black joy itself as a metric of power. As an organization, COC aims to approach Black people holistically rather than transactionally. What unites COC's varied online and offline campaigns is the all-encompassing theory of change to improve Black people's lives by positively impacting their everyday experiences: when they encounter police, when they go to work, or when they turn on the TV or log on to Twitter. This comprehensive vision cannot be met by instrumental and transactional metrics of power, which tend to focus on quantitative measures such as the number of people mobilized to knock doors or send texts or voter turnout at the polls. The proper metric for the Black political power COC wants to build is something daring and evasive of easy quantification: Black joy.

Color Of Change cultivates Black joy through large events like Black Women's Brunches, Black Men's Cookouts, "Black Joy Drive-In" movie screenings during the COVID-19 pandemic, and a Juneteenth "Dinner in Black." These draw on the Black church, family cookouts, and Black fraternities and sororities as models that feel more like home than a meeting. As COC was forced back into online space during the pandemic, organizers have ensured that there is still joy at online events through dancing, music, and food, whether it is a dine-and-dial event with food delivery to participants' doors or a textathon combined with a Halloween costume party.

Cognitive: Political Education

From the civil rights freedom schools to today's abolitionist study groups, political education has often been a central element to antiracist organizing. The mainstream education that people receive formally in schools and informally from the media is often told from a perspective that privileges White norms. Antiracist struggles playing out within the field of education include teachers unions pushing to diversify their workforce and students fighting to add Ethnic Studies to their curricula. On the other side of the political spectrum, there has also been an organized parental backlash against perceived bias in teaching and curricular materials labeled as "critical race theory."

While struggling for equity within the education system, some organizations also cultivate their own spaces for political education outside this sector. Many draw on Paulo Freire's idea of popular education as articulated in *Pedagogy of the Oppressed* (2014). Through his work in the mid-twentieth century teaching peasants to read in Brazil and Chile, Freire developed a model of critical pedagogy that breaks down power relations by situating teachers and students as equals in a democratic classroom. It also challenges participants to examine the ways they have internalized their oppression, carrying it out even when their oppressors are nowhere to be found. Undoing this internalization requires a process Freire called *conscientização*, or developing a critical consciousness of social and political injustice and acting against it. The goal of *conscientização* is the exercise of agency in the service of what Freire saw as our vocation: becoming more human.

In her study of racial justice activists in Chicago, Dr. Jordie Davies finds that political education functions as a "mobilizing mechanism" (2021, p. 48) that serves as the link moving people from political alienation to political participation. Education transforms experiences of alienation (which may be caused by one's marginal identity, by the experience of institutional failure, or by choosing solidarity with marginalized people) into action. Davies understands political education broadly: "individual or group study, formal or informal education, one on one conversations, events and actions" (Davies, 2021, p. 124). She recounts a story from the Chicago Alliance, which used weekly tabling with educational materials to build community support for a Civilian Police Accountability Council. Their presence was so regular that neighbors started to expect them.

Political education can bring people into an organization, but many organizations also see education as part of their task. Chaniqua D. Simpson, Avery Walter, and Kim Ebert's study of BYP100 describes how the organization uses political education to promote an ideology that they refer to as the "Black Queer Feminist (and Trans) Lens" (BQFL; 2021). The organization uses political education to locate this ideology within a longer intergenerational timeline that they refer to as the "Black radical tradition." The organization maintains close relationships with movement elders like Dr. Cathy Cohen, Dr. Barbara Smith, and Dr. Barbara Ransby. As a formal membership organization, the entry of new members is an opportunity to share this ideology at orientations, political education meetings, workshops, and general body meetings. Newcomers are socialized into this lens through readings from Black feminists like bell hooks, the Combahee River Collective, and former BYP100 Director Charlene Carruthers. This ultimately builds the political subjectivities of BYP100 members and enables them to bring this critical consciousness back to their friends and family.

In the Black racial justice ecosystem, political education appears to be both a mechanism to funnel people from alienation into political action and a way to socialize them into the norms of an organization. This education provides new stories, concepts, and frames that offer an epistemic break with White supremacy. The theoretical frameworks offered by political education programs like BYP100's BQFL connect individual empowerment ("free your mind") with the larger macro-level power that the organization is trying to build (e.g., a world without police).

Behavioral: Centering Black Women in Care and Community-Building

Black feminists have long challenged the gendered separations between public and private life, between electoral politics and everyday politics with a lower-case "p," and valorized kitchen-table emotional and care labor as the invisible backbone of Black political power. Black women have long performed the undervalued work of building familial and political homes. In the civil rights movement, Belinda Robnett (2000) found that Black women were mid-level leaders who provided vital links between organizations and communities, although their leadership was not acknowledged in the public narrative of the movement. Contemporary organizations like the Me Too movement, the Marsha P. Johnson Institute, the Black Women's Blueprint, and the African American Policy Forum's #SayHerName campaign, and BYP100's "She Safe, We Safe" campaign put Black women front and center in their organizing.

Color Of Change's events have also centered mutual aid and Black women's care, such as personal protective equipment (PPE) delivery during the COVID-19 pandemic and Serve Our Sisters events, where participants assemble care packages for women returning from incarceration. One of COC's most popular events, which has drawn over 30,000 Black women in twenty-five different cities, are its Black Women's Brunches. At the start of these events, women enter lavish hotel ballrooms to find name tags, "Black Girl Magic" buttons, and a pastel flower backdrop where they can pose for photos. They find their seats at large tables, often with women they do not yet know. Their host starts with an ice-breaker to stir up discussion ("What's your favorite movie? What's the best girl group of all time? Where's the best chicken in the city?"). Notably for a political organization, there is no specific policy issue on the agenda. No one stands at the podium to give a speech or presentation. Instead, the women attendees are the guests of honor. This open format gives Black women room to talk about their vision for their communities.

"We don't want or need these new people's first introduction to Color of Change being that they need to work," said the Black Women's Brunch originator Jade Magnus Ogunnaike. "We want regular working-class Black women to come, sit, enjoy themselves, have a good time, and just have a luxurious experience." Magnus Ogunnaike described her litmus test for the design of events and activities like the brunches thus: "Could my mother do this? Could a single, working mother do this? What would it take to get her out the door and to this event?" Thoughtful details like free parking, childcare, and a delicious breakfast help facilitate these mornings of care and community-building. These events also end with an invitation to the next get-together, seeding COC's most recent strategic priority: local squads that can serve as vehicles for long-term, in-person organizing.

When Magnus Ogunnaike designed the Black Women's Brunches, she drew inspiration from the United Order of Tents, a secret society of Black women founded in 1867 whose most committed members, many of them elderly, are referred to as Queens (and sometimes wear tiaras):

> When I was creating Black Women's Brunch, I was drawing on traditions of different things that I'd been a part of since I was a little kid. The Black church, for one. My mom's Black women's bible study . . . or cookouts. These are the things that are sort of intrinsic to our culture, Black American culture, and easily replicable.

Color Of Change's events for Black women are examples of behaviors or practices that an organization can cultivate for their members' empowerment. These also create a vessel for the realization of the other emotional and cognitive aspects of psychological empowerment, such as Black joy and political education. As these examples show, organizational settings often (though not necessarily) serve as vehicles for these forms of psychological empowerment.

Organizational Setting

What mediates between the macro-level power outcomes and micro-level psychological empowerment are the meso-level mobilizing structures in which both occur. Mobilizing structures are "collective vehicles, informal as well as formal, through which people mobilize and engage in collective action" (McAdam et al., 1996, p. 3). These structures include both explicitly political organizations as well as preexisting institutions and informal networks from which an organization can recruit not just individuals but entire networks (known to social movement scholars as "block recruitment"). For example, in the civil rights movement, the Southern Christian Leadership Conference could draw on the Black church and the Student Nonviolent Coordinating Committee on students in university settings (Morris, 1981, 1986).

Earlier, I discussed protest-based and structure-based organizing traditions, as defined by Momentum. Protest-based organizing sits on one side of the spectrum with generally flexible but weak organizational structures (e.g., a loose sense of leadership and decision-making) and structure-based organizing sits on the other side with strong but rigid organizational structures (e.g., they are often hierarchical). Social movement scholars and practitioners have argued over the appropriate role for organizations in harnessing activist energy (Piven & Cloward, 1979) and the merits of different organizational structures. Here, I choose to focus on organizations as one vehicle within a diverse ecology of mobilizing structures. I have mentioned COC and BYP100, but other key organizations within the post-Black Lives Matter racial justice advocacy ecosystem include the Movement for Black Lives network. Formed in 2014 to "debate and co-create a shared movement wide strategy," the network now consists of over fifty organizations that issued a wide-ranging policy platform called the "Vision for Black Lives" (Movement for Black Lives, 2022).

Hahrie Han, Elizabeth McKenna, and Michelle Oyakawa's (2021) work indicates that the relationship between individual activists and power outcomes is not a simple one. More people and more resources do not immediately translate to more power. They argue that organizations serve rather as "prisms" that refract a constituency's resources (white light) into external political power (colored light). The internal design of the prism determines its capacity to translate people power into political power.

In this section, I look at the elements of a "Black prism," or a prism that can build and refract Black political power. I draw on the work of Katrina Gamble (2021) and Sonia Sarkar et al. (2021) on political and social homes to talk about the features of an organizational setting that make constituents feel "at home." In building out the "Black prism," one question for internal organizational design is the choice of scale or depth. Mobilizing strategies are associated with scale; these tend to be shallow but wide-reaching and make good use of online social networks for tapping into people's weak ties. Depth is achieved through the building of strong ties through organizing. This requires a deep investment in member transformation and leadership for the long term, which cannot scale as quickly with existing tools. In Han's comparative study of mobilizing and organizing strategies (2014), she found that the strongest organizations combined both. In the following, I return to our case study, COC, to explore how COC tries to hybridize both approaches to achieve success.

Political and Social Homes

There is a long tradition of Black people creating counter-publics and separate, Black-centered and Black-affirming spaces for themselves in the face of exclusion. Just as Black people have been redlined and gentrified out of physical homes, they have also been redlined and gentrified out of political spaces. A recent Sojourner Strategies report by Katrina L. Gamble, entitled "The Power of Building a Political Home: Black Civic Engagement and Movement Organizing," lists some of the highest-ranking characteristics Black respondents said they seek in a Black political home. Such a home should include all Black people, deeply engage with community members, promote unity, be joyful, and have the ability to influence elected officials and those in power.

Sonia Sarkar and colleagues have studied social homes regarding thirteen movement organizations, many of them with multiracial constituencies and engaged in multi-issue work that includes racial justice, two of which were specifically Black-focused organizations (COC and Organization for Black Struggle). They find that "organizations frequently invest in four common elements that they believe will support individual and collective member transformation as well as enhance recruitment and retention: a. addressing whole-person needs via culture, community-building, and care; b. internal accountability and decision-making; c. political education; and d. enabling smaller 'sub-homes' within the home" (Sarkar et al., 2021, p. 3).

Gamble's and Sarkar's findings bridge the elements discussed in this chapter related to community power (ability to influence those in power so as to shape community conditions) and psychological empowerment (a range of emotional, cognitive, and behavioral empowerment practices). This suggests that the political/social home is the bridge where these layers of power can holistically coexist and bolster one another within a mutually beneficial ecology.

Scale: Color Of Change's Big Tent

What is the organizational design of COC's political home? Color Of Change is a broad tent. Ideologically, this suits COC's goal of representing all Black people in the US, a constituency whose beliefs are very diverse. A wide variety of campaigns and targets, as well as the opportunity for squads to organize their own petitions, enables this ideological openness. Organizationally, the big tent has a lot of doors that offer multiple points of access for new members. Participation is understood as part of a matrix of engagement (see Figure 6.1) rather than a ladder. Each side of the matrix – digital, action, communications, and field – represents one set of doors into the organization. For instance, someone may first engage with COC through the organization's Instagram account (the "communications" side), then sign a petition (the "action" side). From there, they might receive and forward COC emails (the "digital" side) and eventually attend a squad meeting (the offline "field" side).

Inside the big tent, staff face the added challenge of tracking the organization's subscribers as they move through its many doors. This is daunting, particularly since COC membership has recently seen a massive increase of 115 percent after the 2020 Black Lives Matter uprisings, with a current estimated total of 6.1 million subscribers. How does COC manage this scale without stretching the tent too thin? Color Of Change's technological expertise guides its approach to building offline avenues to membership, as its leadership has made significant investments in the organization's data infrastructure. This has helped COC to overcome the challenges of a voter file that chronically undercounts Black voters and inadequate data tools for tracking COC's complex matrix of engagement. An expanded team of thirteen data staff is using member data to help understand the character of specific lanes

Figure 6.1 *Color Of Change's matrix of member engagement.*

into the big tent, how members move to and between those lanes, and which pathways into the organization prove to be "the stickiest."

Despite these difficulties, the matrix provides an egalitarian approach that does not force a fixed template of leadership onto members. As Senior Organizing Director Shannon Talbert explained: "We don't weight any action as higher than another. For some people, money may be more accessible; they don't have as much time to give. Or for some people, time may be more accessible and they have more time to give." This allows COC to be responsive to people's needs (particularly those of Black women facing multiple forms of marginalization), recognize the diversity of people coming in and what they have to offer, and assume that they will weave between online and offline engagement in ebbs and flows of activity. While the matrix might appear looser than a ladder of engagement, COC believes that it can potentially allow longer-term engagement for marginalized constituencies by preventing burnout.

What knits together this matrix is, again, culture – the "ultimate form of decentralized command and control," according to Maine People's Alliance Codirector Ben Chin. Color Of Change's digital-native expertise in communications and brand-building has created resonant aesthetics and messaging for a Black audience rather than a one-size-fits-all audience. This brand and aesthetic move agilely across online and offline spaces, just as members move between different "sides" of the matrix.

Depth: Color Of Change's Squads for Relational Organizing

While COC has built out organizational structures to scaffold the massive scale it has established, leaders like former Vice President Arisha Hatch also pivoted intentionally toward hybridizing this scale with depth. One experiment to this end has been to build a specific pathway in the big tent for relational organizing aimed at long-term, transformational outcomes through local squads. While this pathway currently organizes only a slice of COC's overall membership, the volunteers within these squads take on much greater leadership and participation roles than other members.

The doorway to squad membership is COC's "Black joy" events, such as a Juneteenth "Dinner in Black" or socially distanced "Black Joy Drive-In" movie screening during the COVID-19 pandemic. Staff create a template and predesigned program for the events then recruit members to a host committee to execute the events. Members are encouraged to develop their leadership and organizing skills by recreating the events for family and friends using COC's toolkit and guided support from COC's organizing staff. This model is based on COC's leadership development approach, where members are encouraged to talk about community issues, share knowledge with their networks, bring more people into subsequent actions, and leverage people power to win campaigns.

After their first taste of a COC event, staff organizers follow up with members through one-on-one conversations. They plug these into one of the organization's nineteen local squads, which organized over 8,000 members as of 2020. Monthly squad meetings draw in anywhere from fifteen to forty-five members on average and serve relational goals by spotlighting new members' stories.

Squad meetings also serve strategic goals by plugging people into local, state, and federal election campaigns. In district attorney races in which COC squads participated in the three election cycles of 2016, 2018, and 2020, my research indicates that successful district attorney races in this period were often (with the exception of the Midwest) clustered around cities with squads (Brazzell & Sarkar, 2022). This suggests that this relational membership structure has been crucial to successfully implementing COC's electoral strategy around criminal justice reform.

In the off-cycle outside election seasons, squad activities turn to accountability, holding elected officials to their campaign promises. Since this membership infrastructure is still relatively new and had only gone through one electoral cycle by 2020, organizers are learning that this accountability work requires more strategic capacity on the part of members than electoral work does. This has led COC to experiment with how to level up its leadership development through national programs such as its Storytelling Academy and a member website with an interactive political education component.

Looking forward, the organization is considering ways to support squad members in building their strategic capacity to run their own local campaigns. Leadership has discussed a member-led fundraising structure to resource squad projects, a national convention for setting squad priorities (a vision postponed by the COVID-19 pandemic), or a national member-led governance structure for all of the squads.

The organizational "Black prism" that COC is building aims to create a "big tent" political home that can welcome the diversity of the Black community and its multiracial allies. This Black prism balances scale (through wide-reaching digital mobilization for short-term goals like elections) with depth (through face-to-face squad organizing aimed at long-term power-building) in the hopes of building a resilient prism that can magnify Black joy and political power.

Applications and Future Research

This chapter offers social movement practitioners, researchers, and funders a macro-level overview of the history, strategy, and major accomplishments of racial justice activism against police, prisons, and the carceral state, particularly as related to the Black Lives Matter movement. It also describes the individual, micro-level practices inspired by a healing justice and transformative justice approach that can facilitate psychological empowerment processes among movement participants, like Black joy, political education, and community-building activities centered on Black women. And lastly, it tracks how a meso-level organizational "Black prism" such as COC can effectively mediate between these two levels. These findings are US-specific, and their usefulness in other contexts where social movements are less beholden to the nonprofit–industrial complex or whose movement organizational infrastructure looks different is limited.

I am particularly interested in the additional pathways for research at the organizational meso-level. One persistent problem is that funders and organizations often use metrics for power that privilege scale and mobilizing approaches, calculating power in terms of numbers of doors knocked or signatures on a petition gathered by volunteer canvassers. But how can we develop measurements for the outcomes of relational organizing that which are long rather than short term, collective rather than individual, and transformational rather than instrumental? For example, how do we measure lives changed by political education and its downstream consequences for the rest of a person's life? How do we measure a goal as ambitious and embodied as Black joy? A recent research collaboration between data team staff at COC and researchers at the Democracy and Power Innovation Fund have set themselves to that very task (McKinney Gray et al., 2022).

In addition to offering organizations ways to measure both scale and depth, we also need qualitative insights into how organizations build both scale and depth, and how they calibrate the right balance of the two at different moments in their trajectory. For example, what organizational design features can provide cohesion across the vast scale of a large organization's staff and members while balancing the need for staff and member autonomy? In-depth case studies and process tracing can illuminate some of these processes. These questions apply far beyond the racial justice ecosystem, but that ecosystem of organizations may have unique learnings to offer.

Lastly, we need research that examines what happens inside an organizational prism to translate individual, micro-level actions into collective power and macro-level change. Research can expand on Gamble and Sarkar's social and political home findings to better understand the mechanisms through which organizations promote individuals' sense of belonging and how this differs for different constituencies and identities (queer, disabled, etc.). Research can also explore the practices that best promote a healthy organizational culture at various organizational sizes, from a small, local, grassroots groups to a national "big tent" like COC.

References

Alinsky, S. (1971). *Rules for radicals: A pragmatic primer for realistic radicals*. Random House.

American Public Health Association. (2018, November 13). *Addressing law enforcement violence as a public health issue (policy no. 201811)*. American Public Health Association. www.apha.org/policies-and-advocacy/public-health-policy-statements/policy-database/2019/01/29/law-enforcement-violence

Bailey, Z. D., Krieger, N., Agénor, M., Graves, J., Linos, N., & Bassett, M. T. (2017). Structural racism and health inequities in the USA: Evidence and interventions. *The Lancet, 389*(10077), 1453–1463.

Benjamin, R. (2019). *Captivating technology: Race, carceral technoscience, and liberatory imagination in everyday life*. Duke University Press.

Black Youth Project 100. (2022a). *About Black Youth Project 100*. Black Youth Project 100. www.byp100.org/about

Black Youth Project 100. (2022b). *Agenda to Build Black Futures*. Black Youth Project 100. www.agendatobuildblackfutures.com/view-agenda

Bonilla-Silva, E. (2019). Feeling race: Theorizing the racial economy of emotions. *American Sociological Review, 84*(1), 25.

Bracey, G. E. (2016). Black movements need Black theorizing: Exposing implicit whiteness in political process theory. *Sociological Focus, 49*(1), 11–27.

Brazzell, M., & Meiners, E. R. (2022). Transnational transformative justice: An opening roundtable. In A. Bierria, B. Lober, & J. Caruthers (Eds.), *Abolition feminisms: Organizing, survival, and transformative practice* (pp. 263–292). Haymarket Books.

Brazzell, M., & Sarkar, S. (2022, February 5). *Black joy as power: A case study of national organizing strategy*. P3 Lab, Johns Hopkins University. https:// d3n8a8pro7vhmx.cloudfront.net/hahrie/pages/1200/attachments/original/164 4441182/Deep_Dive_Color_of_Change_02_05_2022.pdf?1644441182

Buchanan, L., Bui, Q., & Patel, J. K. (2020, July 3). *Black Lives Matter may be the largest movement in U.S. history*. The New York Times. www.nytimes.com/ interactive/2020/07/03/us/george-floyd-protests-crowd-size.html

Campaign Zero. (2022). *8 Can't Wait*. Campaign Zero. https://8cantwait.org

Christens, B. D. (2019). *Community power and empowerment*. Oxford University Press.

Cooper, B. (2018). *Eloquent rage: A Black feminist discovers her superpower*. St. Martin's Publishing Group.

Crenshaw, K. (1991). Mapping the margins: Intersectionality, identity politics, and violence against women of color. *Stanford Law Review, 43*(6), 1241.

Crenshaw, K. W., & Ritchie, A. J. (2015). *Say her name: Resisting police brutality against Black women*. African American Policy Forum, Center for Intersectionality and Social Policy Studies. www.aapf.org/_files/ugd/62e126_ 9223ee35c2694ac3bd3f2171504ca3f7.pdf

Critical Resistance. (n.d.). *Reformist reforms vs. abolitionist steps in policing*. Critical Resistance. https://static1.squarespace.com/static/59ead8f9692ebee25b72f17f/ t/5b65cd58758d46d34254f22c/1533398363539/CR_NoCops_reform_vs_aboli tion_CRside.pdf

Critical Resistance 10 Publications Collective. (2008). *Abolition now!: Ten years of strategy and struggle against the prison industrial complex*. AK Press.

Davies, E. (2021). *From adherents to activists: The process of social movement mobilization* [Dissertation]. University of Chicago.

Freire, P. (2014). *Pedagogy of the oppressed* (30th anniversary ed.). Bloomsbury Publishing USA.

Gamble, K. L. (2021). *The power of building a political home: Black civic engagement and movement organizing*. Sojourn Strategies. www.sojournstrategies.com/ powerofbuildingapoliticalhome

Ganz, M. (2009). What *is public narrative: self, us & now (public narrative worksheet)*. Digital Access to Scholarship at Harvard. https://dash.harvard.edu/bitstream/handle/1/30760283/Public-Narrative-Worksheet-Fall-2013-.pdf

Givan, R. K., Roberts, K. M., & Soule, S. A. (2010). *The diffusion of social movements: Actors, mechanisms, and political effects*. Cambridge University Press.

Gladwell, M. (2010, October 4). *Small change: Why the revolution will not be tweeted*. The New Yorker. www.newyorker.com/magazine/2010/10/04/small-change-malcolm-gladwell

Gorz, A. (1967). *Strategy for labor: A radical proposal*. Beacon Press.

Green, K. M., Taylor, J. N., Williams, P. I., & Roberts, C. (2018). #BlackHealingMatters in the time of #BlackLivesMatter. *Biography*, *41*(4), 909–941.

Han, H. (2014). *How organizations develop activists: Civic associations and leadership in the 21st century*. Oxford University Press.

Han, H., McKenna, E., & Oyakawa, M. (2021). *Prisms of the people: Power & organizing in twenty-first-century America*. University of Chicago Press.

Hertel-Fernandez, A. (2020). *How policymakers can craft measures that endure and build political power*. The Roosevelt Institute.

hooks, b. (1996). *Killing rage: Ending racism*. Macmillan.

INCITE!. (2007). *The revolution will not be funded: Beyond the non-profit industrial complex*. South End Press.

Interrupting Criminalization. (2020). *The demand is still #DefundPolice*. Interrupting Criminalization. www.interruptingcriminalization.com/defundpolice-update

Jackson, S. J., Bailey, M., & Welles, B. F. (2020). *#HashtagActivism: Networks of race and gender justice*. MIT Press.

Johnson, J. (2015). Black joy in the time of Ferguson. *QED: A Journal in GLBTQ Worldmaking*, *2*(2), 177–183.

Karpf, D. (2012). *The MoveOn effect: The unexpected transformation of American political advocacy*. Oxford University Press.

Kindy, K. (2021, October 7). *Dozens of states have tried to end qualified immunity. Police officers and unions helped beat nearly every bill*. The Washington Post. www.washingtonpost.com/politics/qualified-immunity-police-lobbying-state-legislatures/2021/10/06/60e546bc-0cdf-11ec-aea1-42a8138f132a_story.html

Lorde, A. (2007). *Sister outsider: Essays and speeches*. Crossing Press.

Lukes, S. (2005). *Power: A radical view* (2nd ed.). Palgrave Macmillan.

McAdam, D. (1982). *Political process and the development of Black insurgency, 1930–1970*. University of Chicago Press.

McAdam, D. (1990). *Freedom summer*. Oxford University Press.

McAdam, D., McCarthy, J. D., & Zald, M. N. (1996). *Comparative perspectives on social movements: Political opportunities, mobilizing structures, and cultural framings*. Cambridge University Press.

McKinney Gray, M., Harris, J., & Fekade, M. (2022). *Collective Black joy events catalyze strong emotional sentiment and deepen organizational involvement* [Working paper]. Color Of Change–Democracy and Power Innovation Fund partnership.

Mills, C. W. (1960). Letter to the New Left. *New Left Review*, *5*, 18–23.

Momentum. (2022). *Momentum resources*. Momentum Community. www.momentumcom munity.org/resources

Morozov, E. (2012). *The net delusion: The dark side of Internet freedom*. PublicAffairs.

Morris, A. (1981). Black southern student sit-in movement: An analysis of internal organization. *American Sociological Review, 46*(6), 744–767.

Morris, A. D. (1986). *The origins of the civil rights movement*. Simon and Schuster.

Movement for Black Lives. (2022). *Movement for Black Lives*. https://m4bl.org

Munro, J. (2017). *The anticolonial front: The African American freedom struggle and global decolonisation, 1945–1960*. Cambridge University Press.

Oparah, J. C., & Sudbury, J. (1998). *Other kinds of dreams: Black women's organisa- tions and the politics of transformation*. Psychology Press.

Piven, F. F., & Cloward, R. A. (1979). *Poor people's movements: Why they succeed, how they fail*. Vintage Books.

Ransby, B. (2003). *Ella Baker and the Black freedom movement: A radical democratic vision*. University of North Carolina Press.

Robinson, C. J. (2005). *Black Marxism: The making of the Black radical tradition*. University of North Carolina Press.

Robnett, B. (2000). *How long? How long?: African American women in the struggle for civil rights*. Oxford University Press.

Sarkar, S., Booth-Tobin, J., & Schutt, R. (2021, December 15). *Social homes as sources of power for health equity*. P3 Lab, Johns Hopkins University. https:// d3n8a8pro7vhmx.cloudfront.net/hahrie/pages/1200/attachments/original/ 1639681721/Social_Homes_Final_Draft.pdf?1639681721

Scott-Heron, G. (1971). *The revolution will not be televised* [Record]. Flying Dutchman Records.

Shirky, C. (2008). *Here comes everybody: The power of organizing without organiza- tions*. Penguin.

Simpson, C. D., Walter, A., & Ebert, K. (2021). "Brainwashing for the right reasons with the right message": Ideology and political subjectivity in Black organiz- ing. *Mobilization: An International Quarterly, 26*(4), 401–420.

Skocpol, T. (2003). *Diminished democracy: From membership to management in American civic life*. University of Oklahoma Press.

Smidt, C. E., Kellstedt, L. A., & Guth, J. L. (2009). The role of religion in American politics: Explanatory theories and associated analytical and measurement issues. In J. L. Guth (Ed.) *The Oxford handbook of religion and American politics* (pp. 3–42). Oxford University Press.

Snow, D. A., & Benford, R. D. (1992). Master frames and cycles of protest. In A. D. Morris & C. M. Mueller (Eds.), *Frontiers in social movement theory* (pp. 133–155). Yale University Press.

Southern Poverty Law Center. (2021, February 23). *SPLC reports over 160 Confederate symbols removed in 2020*. Southern Poverty Law Center. www.splcenter.org/presscenter/splc-reports-over-160-confederate-symbols- removed-2020

Sudbury, J. (1998). *Other kinds of dreams: Black women's organisations and the politics of transformation*. Routledge.

Tarrow, S. (1998). *Power in movement: Social movements and contentious politics* (2nd ed.). Cambridge University Press.

Tate, J., Jenkins, J., Rich, S., Myuskens, J., & Fox, J. (2022, March 24). *Fatal force: Police shootings database*. The Washington Post. www.washingtonpost.com/graphics/investigations/police-shootings-database/

There Are Black People in the Future (n.d.). *About*. There Are Black People in the Future. www.thereareblackpeopleinthefuture.com/about

Thomson-DeVeaux, A. (2020, June 4). *Why it's so rare for police officers to face legal consequences.* FiveThirtyEight. https://fivethirtyeight.com/features/why-its-still-so-rare-for-police-officers-to-face-legal-consequences-for-misconduct/

Tufekci, Z. (2017). *Twitter and tear gas: The power and fragility of networked protest*. Yale University Press.

US Census Bureau. (2021). *US Census Bureau QuickFacts*. US Census Bureau. www.census.gov/quickfacts/US

Westerman, A., Benk, R., & Greene, D. (2020, December 30). *In 2020, protests spread across the globe with a similar message: Black Lives Matter*. National Public Radio. www.npr.org/2020/12/30/950053607/in-2020-protests-spread-across-the-globe-with-a-similar-message-black-lives-matt

Wright, J. E., & Headley, A. M. (2020). Police use of force interactions: Is race relevant or gender germane? *The American Review of Public Administration, 50*(8), 851–864.

Zimmerman, M. A. (1995). Psychological empowerment: Issues and illustrations. *American Journal of Community Psychology, 23*(5), 581–599.

PART II

Participatory Governance

7 Citizens' Governance Spaces

Albert W. Dzur and Carolyn M. Hendriks

Introduction

Today local communities around the world are self-organizing to fill various governance and market voids – for example, by undertaking renewable energy projects or delivering support, justice, and care services for marginalized populations. In this chapter we label these kinds of grassroots efforts "citizens' governance spaces" (CGS) – an umbrella term that captures practically focused initiatives, projects, and groups that are led by citizens working together to address a specific collective problem. While diverse communities have long developed their own solutions to collective problems (Mitlin, 2008; Ostrom, 1996), the past two decades have seen an increase in CGS across diverse sectors and countries due to a mix of economic, technical, political, and social forces (Denters, 2016; Mitlin, 2008; Smith & Stirling, 2018; Soares da Silva et al., 2018). The governance potential of citizen-led efforts such as civic enterprises and social innovation projects are also increasingly attracting the attention of global institutions and governments around the world (e.g., OECD/European Union, 2017; World Bank, 2018).[1] When the COVID-19 pandemic took hold in 2020, CGS gained popular attention around the world with the rise of local community efforts and mutual aid groups (e.g., Chevée, 2022). The recovery phase out of the COVID-19 pandemic also witnessed citizens stepping up to address the governance voids created in fiscally uncertain times.

In this chapter we situate CGS alongside related concepts in the social sciences, including public participation, community organizing, and social movements.[2] To capture the distinct form of citizen engagement engendered in CGS, we inductively draw from diverse empirical examples to lay out four key defining characteristics of these spaces. Then, we briefly examine the opportunities and risks that CGS present to contemporary societies and their challenges for conventional state institutions and civil society. Overall we shed

---

1 In some countries, CGS have been actively promoted in policy discourses – for example, under the ideas of "do-democracy" in the Netherlands (Denters, 2016) or "Big Society" in England (Aiken & Taylor, 2019).
2 This chapter adapts and expands on Hendriks and Dzur (2022).

light on a domain of civil society that has not been clearly identified, and we generate conceptual resources for further research and practical innovation.

Making Conceptual Sense of Citizens' Governance Spaces

In the early 2000s a group of Baltimore residents began meeting to figure out how their newly established community conference center would use restorative justice practices. They wanted to work with the local community by offering alternative ways to defuse interpersonal strife, ensure neighborhood safety, and reduce future harms (Abramson & Beck, 2010). Ten years later across the Atlantic a group of citizens in northeast Catalonia were putting together plans to create Som Energia – a community cooperative to produce affordable renewable energy for households in their region (Riutort Isern, 2015). Around the same time in Brisbane, two citizens who had formed Orange Sky Australia (OSA) – an organization providing mobile clothes-washing services for homeless people – were training thousands of community volunteers on how to engage in nonthreatening conversations with people living on the street.

From the outside these citizen-led initiatives might appear to be modern-day examples of the kind of community organizing or charity work that common-purpose citizens' groups have done throughout the ages. Yet when one takes a closer look at how these initiatives emerge and what they do, what comes into view is a particular mode of citizen engagement that deserves fuller scholarly attention.[3] In contrast to the participatory forums used in community consultation and deliberative engagement (Nabatchi et al., 2012), citizens are not being asked by governments, corporations, or nongovernmental organizations (NGOs) to provide advice or help make decisions. Instead they are self-organizing and leading collective problem-solving activities. In contrast to the strategies used in protest and social movement activism to oppose, support, inform, and steer policymakers (Gaventa, 2006), citizens in these bottom-up initiatives are getting on with the practical business of addressing complex issues themselves, often in highly experimental and effective ways. For example, today Baltimore Community Conferencing is diverting felony and misdemeanor cases from the juvenile courts, with judges inquiring into how they can adopt more restorative justice programs (Dzur, 2013). Today Som Energia is defying Spain's oligopolist energy sector by producing, developing, and supplying small-scale affordable electricity from renewable sources to almost 80,000 members nationwide (Pellicer-Sifres et al., 2018;

---

3 Consistent with other scholars of democratic governance, such as Fung (2006, p. 74), the term "citizen" here is not restricted to "individuals who possess the legal status of formal citizenship but rather individuals who possess the political standing to exercise voice or give consent over public decisions that oblige or affect them."

Riutort Isern, 2015).[4] Orange Sky Australia has grown into a nationwide volunteer organization, with thirty-one vans offering free laundry and shower services in locations across the continent – including in remote Indigenous communities (OSA, 2020).[5]

As we detail further later in this chapter, the social sciences have yet to capture the novel governance work undertaken in spaces as varied as the Baltimore Community Conferencing Center, the Catalonian renewable energy cooperative, and the Brisbane mobile laundry. Such spaces fall awkwardly between the "messy categories" of community organizing, civic action, social movements, and volunteering (see Aiken & Taylor, 2019). Recent surveys on contemporary modes of political participation tend to subsume these spaces under expressive public actions (e.g., Theocharis & Van Deth, 2018) or view them as part of "prepolitical" or "latent" political participation (e.g., Amnå & Ekman, 2014). Social movement studies also fall short on fully capturing citizens' motivations and the governance work they perform. In contrast to the practical protest activities of "prefigurative politics" (Yates, 2015), participants in CGS are typically not driven by a central utopian vision. The notion of "free spaces" conveys the autonomous, expressive, contentious aspects of citizen-led governance efforts (see Polletta & Kretschmer, 2013), but it is usually linked to social movements and is too capacious for describing the purpose-driven governance work being done (Polletta, 1999).

Looking more broadly at the diverse scholarship on third-sector organizations, public policy, development, planning, and volunteering, citizen-led initiatives sail under many flags.[6]

Problematically, most common labels – such as "social innovation" and "social enterprise" – are too broad to differentiate between whether the governance effort is led by citizens, states, or market actors. Even the term "coproduction" today captures a range of state-based or mixed programs, with citizen-led efforts being labelled under the largely forgotten subcategory of "community coproduction."

Key Characteristics of Citizens' Governance Spaces

In order to better capture the distinct experimental and substantive practical action enacted by these citizen-led problem-solving initiatives, we turn now to further develop the concept of CGS. Central to this concept is a "spatial" metaphor carrying different meanings. First and foremost, CGS are spaces of

---

4 From www.somenergia.coop (accessed May 18, 2022).   5 See also Chapter 17.
6 Some of these include civic enterprises (Wagenaar et al., 2015), social enterprises (Laville et al., 2015), social innovation (Moulaert et al., 2013), community-based initiatives (Edelenbos et al., 2021), community self-organization (Denters, 2016; Edelenbos et al., 2018), grassroots organizations (Mitlin, 2008), cooperatives (Borzaga et al., 2016a, 2016b), community coproduction (Bovaird & Loeffler, 2012), mutual aid or self-help groups (Chevée, 2021), and prefigurative movements (Beckwith et al., 2016); see also Chapter 16.

action where citizens come together to solve a collective issue; for example, a project, an organization, or a physical or virtual space such as a community garden, a café, or a Facebook page. But CGS can also provide alternative arenas within a given policy domain by offering novel, even disruptive framings and solutions to public problems. Some CGS are platforms of outreach, where the citizens driving the initiative seek to engage forgotten, hidden, or marginalized publics by providing a vital service (e.g., washing, justice, food, or care) or by offering opportunities for support and connection.

In sum, "CGS" is an umbrella term to describe diverse grassroots initiatives that are (1) led and driven by citizens who (2) undertake practical governance work to address a collective issue in (3) experimental and disruptive ways by (4) engaging inclusively with affected publics and working congruously with relevant state, market, and civil society organizations. We turn now to elaborate on these four key, defining characteristics of CGS.

CGS Characteristic 1: Led and Driven by Citizens

Typically a group of citizens form a group, project, or organization to undertake a practical initiative.[7] These spaces emerge from within civil society and are wholly independent (at least initially) from state or market support. Most CGS begin as small-scale local initiatives; over time some die out, while others can grow into national programs or connect with regional or transnational networks to share knowledge and experiences. Research on civic enterprises, cooperatives, and social innovations points to important contextual conditions under which citizens instigate a CGS (see Evers & von Essen, 2019). A group of citizens might initiate a project or group because they believe traditional state organizations have withdrawn or failed to address a complex, persistent, or emergent public problem (Edelenbos et al., 2021). Many CGS form to address problems faced by voiceless or highly marginalized groups, such as refugees, the homeless, drug users, or victims of violence and crime. Orange Sky Australia began in 2014 when two twenty-year-old men decided to retrofit a simple van with two washing machines, a dryer, and water tanks and then traveled around Brisbane offering free laundry facilities to those living on the street. Orange Sky Australia has snowballed into a nationwide organization with around 1,800 volunteers supporting homeless people by meeting some of life's basic needs: clean clothes and conversation (OSA, 2020). Rather than get people to sign petitions for governments to do more, OSA engages citizens in practical actions to directly assist homeless people. The underlying motivation is that if the state cannot provide basic human

---

7 Sometimes these grassroots groups may self-label as a "movement," "self-help group," "community organization," "cooperative," or "civic enterprise," creating some conceptual confusion. Not all organizations that carry such labels engage in the kind of citizen-led governance work that we focus on in this chapter. We use the term "CGS" to delineate those that do.

services such as shelter and hygiene, then organized citizens can assist by washing clothes.

In some contexts, the state may be absent or weak, so there is no other alternative than for citizens to step in (Mitlin, 2008). The Indonesian citizens' group Savy Amira was founded in 1997 by three women in Surabaya to remedy the lack of counseling and legal support for victims of gender-based violence (GBV). There were no services for GBV victims, so three local women self-organized by meeting weekly. After six months of preliminary discussions, the Savy Amira Women's Crisis Centre (WCC) was formally founded and started providing legal and psychological counseling services for victims of GBV through a twenty-four-hour hotline out of a makeshift office in a member's house. Today Savy Amira provides services across Surabaya and East Java including trainings on GBV prevention (Savy Amira, 2019b).

Citizens may also be motivated because they can no longer bear witnessing the human costs of ineffective or counterproductive policies and channel their frustration into practical experiments that seek to address the issue at hand. Citizen-led restorative justice programs, for example, have emerged around the world to address both crime and criminal justice responses to crime (Blad, 1996; Dzur, 2019; Zinsstag & Vanfaechem, 2012). In the case of the Baltimore Community Conferencing Center a group of citizens were motivated to help people handle situations where police did nothing to stop teenagers from vandalizing cars and would have made a harmful situation worse by giving young people criminal records that make them less employable (Abramson & Beck, 2010; Abramson & Moore, 2001).

Market failure can also drive citizens. Consider, for example, community-based Internet service networks, such as the RT/RW-Net in Indonesia. In the late 1990s to early 2000s, Internet services in Indonesia had scant coverage, with access limited along disparities of income, education, and geography (Suyatno, 2007). National legislation in 1999 only permitted licensed operators to build telecommunications infrastructure and transmit radio waves, which included frequencies associated with wireless Internet connection. Few Internet service providers could afford to enter the market, pushing up the price of Internet access and blocking such access. In response, some citizens took matters into their own hands by forming collectives to pool resources to build their own community networks (Suyatno, 2007). Many adopted a low-tech network called "RT/RW-Net," originally developed in 1996 by university students using walkie-talkies to share Internet connections across campus (Purbo, 2016). Small, neighborhood-based groups self-organized to form their own RT/RW networks, providing local residents with affordable Internet services. Succumbing to popular pressure, the government legalized the scofflaw network.

Citizens' governance spaces can also emerge to address holes not adequately filled by conventional civil society organizations. Serenity Café, for example, is a CGS that emerged to address substance use and recovery in Edinburgh, Scotland (Campbell et al., 2011). The café offers a physical space and governance opportunities for marginalized substance users in recovery who are not well served by existing state and NGO services. State agencies often employ know-it-all professionals and, even when working in concert with NGOs, offer only patchwork support. Moreover, family and neighborhood dynamics in civil society can push recovering substance users back to the margins where the temptations to use again are strong. The café's organizers have self-consciously crafted a new kind of entity that provides recovery support, addressing deficits in state and NGO approaches and altering patterns of interaction in the surrounding civil society (Campbell et al., 2011).

Thus far the contextual drivers of CGS have been related to perceived voids in state, market, or civil society institutions. But many CGS also emerge in contexts where there is an abundance of governance infrastructure – as in the energy and food production systems – but where people deem the dominant approach inefficient or conducive to undesirable outcomes such as carbon emissions, food waste/insecurity, or inequality. In these contexts citizens self-organize to provide a particular public good or service via an alternative governance pathway.[8] Thousands of community energy projects have emerged worldwide over the past two decades in which citizens have formed groups to produce, store, distribute, and sell renewable electricity from local solar or wind infrastructure (see Bauwens et al., 2016; Smith & Stirling, 2018). Many of these projects are driven by rising popular frustration with the failure of large energy companies and state regulators to provide affordable renewable energy, as was the case in the Catalonian Som Energia cooperative (Pellicer-Sifres et al., 2018).

In sum, CGS emerge from civil society linked to but also separate from personal, work, and formal political spheres of action. Typical of civil associations, participants in these spaces freely take up their tasks, without thinking of them as familial responsibilities, jobs, or strict duties (Warren, 2001). While initiated and led in the first instance by citizens, over time these spaces interface with relevant state, market, and civil society institutions – a theme we revisit further later in the chapter.

CGS Characteristic 2: Practical Collective Problem-Solving

Citizens in CGS do functional public work, providing public goods and services such as shelter, care, food, energy, or social welfare (Borzaga et al., 2016a, 2016b; Denters, 2016; Wagenaar et al., 2015). To participate in a CGS involves engaging in the heavy lifting of public policy: Citizens define what the problem is, form feasible plans, implement solutions, and make evaluations

---

8 Such pathways are typically more substantial governance experiments than the demonstration activities or "prefigurative politics" of social movements (see Yates, 2015).

and refinements. Their focus on undertaking practical activities that "make a difference" by achieving substantive outcomes differentiates CGS from the lobbying and protest work of many advocacy groups and social movements. Claim-making is not a central motivating force of CGS, although some "expert citizens" in these spaces may be drawn into various representational roles to share the practical knowledge they attain about what interventions work. For example, though they interact with state officials, citizens working in a community justice center are better described as "making justice" or "contributing to social order" rather than making claims on officials to do their work better.

The capacity of everyday citizens to come together to contribute to and solve collective problems is well recognized (e.g., de Souza Briggs, 2008). But what is distinct about CGS is that the governance effort is self-driven. This aspect has been referred to as "everyday making" and "public work" (Bang, 2005; Boyte, 2004), yet we think "governance" more precisely identifies the way citizens in CGS take on collective problem-solving tasks without being invited and, indeed, under conditions where citizen action may have been actively discouraged by conventional civil society and government actors. Moreover, they are self-authorizing their problem-solving work in fields of action that are typically dominated by professionals, specialists, and officials. Over time these spaces can become productive, reflective zones of civic agency that can, in fact, disrupt local community assumptions, resist social movement framings, and challenge formal state positions (Borzaga, 2016a).

CGS Characteristic 3: Innovative, Experimental, and Disruptive Interventions

Citizens in CGS do not know the answers in advance. They are almost always tackling highly complex problems with unknown solutions and fluid governance pathways and find that they must revise and adjust both strategies and objectives as they go along. The open-ended nature of their objectives and fluidity of their work set CGS apart from many of Ostrom's (1990, 1996) classic cases of community coproduction where the citizens self-organized to generate orderly, efficient, and effective solutions to discrete policy problems known in advance, such as providing access to clean water, reducing overfishing, and improving sanitation.[9] In contrast, the citizens in CGS are wrestling

9 Ostrom's work (1990, 1996) has influenced our framing of the distinct ways in which CGS operate. She showed how grassroots collective action can emerge, without market inducements or state coercion, to handle major matters, like scarce resource management, by working together to develop rules and enforcement systems. Citizens' governance spaces and Ostrom's community coproduction therefore share a common DNA. Where her research centered on efforts to solve discrete policy problems, the contours of which are largely accepted by the actors even though they may disagree on the strategies to be used to obtain a solution, our focus is on how CGS often alter the nature of the goods and services aimed for (e.g., producing "restorative" justice and "renewable" energy). With CGS, just what is to be coproduced is part of the fluid, experimental, and inclusive work process.

with chronic collective problems that are not well understood in advance of citizen action. Typically citizens in these spaces proceed into the unknown; they experiment as they go, learn about possibilities along the way, and sometimes upend established policy concepts and objectives. Through their experimental work, citizens push boundaries and expose problems or inefficiencies in existing structures, community norms, and formal rules.

CGS Characteristic 4: Engaging Collectively

Citizens' governance spaces work experimentally on public problems in a collective fashion: They draw on the skills, knowledge, and entrepreneurship among their members, participants, and broader community. While the mode of engagement and degree of power-sharing vary between organizations, empirical research suggests that many CGS are committed to working in inclusive, participatory, and empowering ways (Edelenbos et al., 2021; Pestoff & Hulgård, 2016). Diverse studies show that it is commonplace for CGS to create internal democratic governance structures to ensure that participants or members have opportunities to shape the collective decisions of the initiative (Borzaga et al., 2016a; Pestoff, 2018). Externally, many CGS reach out and engage with relevant affected publics to mobilize support or to attract members (e.g., via community events, forums, conferences); they may also hold reflective workshops, train volunteers, or convene online discussions.[10] In some instances this community engagement work can be relatively unstructured. Take, for example, the outreach work of the homeless laundry service organization OSA. While the primary goal of OSA is to offer homeless people free services to clean their clothes or have a shower, it also seeks to build community connections through conversations:

> In the one hour time it takes to wash and dry someone's clothes there is absolutely nothing to do but sit down on one of our 6 orange chairs and have a positive and genuine conversation between our everyday volunteers and everyday friends on the street.   (OSA 2016, p. 5)

Orange chair conversations form connections and open up possibilities for social change, encouraging people on the streets to become volunteers themselves, work within the organization, and learn new skills (OSA, 2020).

In many CGS, internal and external engagement activities are intricately linked. For example, the citizens who founded the renewable cooperative Som Energia were committed to addressing rising energy poverty in Spain (Riutort Isern, 2015). They adopted a cooperative organizational model, providing multiple opportunities for member engagement in local and central decisions (see Pellicer-Sifres et al., 2018; Riutort Isern, 2015). Members are encouraged

---

10 See various articles in special editions of *International Review of Sociology*, volume 26, issues 1 and 2.

Figure 7.1 *Orange Sky Australia laundry.*

to participate in local groups of between five and twenty people that meet regularly all over Spain to discuss and debate issues (Pellicer-Sifres et al., 2018, p. 104). Decisions on major strategic issues are taken through a voting procedure of the annual General Assembly, which is composed of all members – who own and operate the cooperative. In-depth qualitative research on Som Energia's member experiences has shown that the group's participatory opportunities have developed members' skills such as "the capacity to deliberate, express their own voice, respect other points of view and learn from conflict" (Pellicer-Sifres et al., 2018, p. 107). This study also found that participation facilitated a broader awareness among members of the social and political context of energy policy in Spain, raising second-order issues such as social justice, power imbalances, and citizen agency. This broader governance awareness has empowered many Som Energia members to take action in their local area – for example, to address rising energy poverty in Spain by engaging in workshops with social workers, running training sessions on how to reduce energy bills, and proposing projects for local authorities (Pellicer-Sifres et al., 2018, p. 107).

Such participatory opportunities represent a more structured approach to citizen engagement than would be found in local community organizing initiatives, which typically rely on noninstitutional arrangements such as social and community networks (Kretzmann & McKnight, 1993). Yet the procedures used in CGS are also more fluid and less rules-based than structured participatory and deliberative forums (Nabatchi et al., 2012). In many CGS, those driving the initiative adopt simple participatory processes – such as local committee structures, conversations, or community conferences – that act as scaffolding upon which citizens can make necessary procedural adjustments to suit particular contexts. This flexible approach empowers citizens to organize participatory processes on their own terms, without having to rely on participatory experts. Procedures can also be easily replicated by citizens elsewhere in other contexts and locations.

Opportunities of Citizens' Governance Spaces

Having identified the broad characteristics of CGS, in this section we consider the potential opportunities that these spaces offer, while in the sections to follow we discuss their risks and challenges for traditional state institutions and civil society.

Enabling Civic Agency

Unlike modes such as voting and consumer choice, which give contemporary citizens only a "feeling of political agency" (Ci, 2006), citizens in CGS experience a practical and tangible form of political agency that is centered around collective problem-solving and "doing." In CGS, citizens are not waiting for technocrats, governments, the market, or professionalized civil society groups to invite or mobilize them. Instead, they are stepping up, meeting challenges, being smart, and taking practical steps to address collective problems that are too big for individuals to handle on their own. By acting in constructive ways, they reveal citizen competencies often overlooked by those accustomed to mobilizing "the public" to protest, deliberate, or vote.

Rethinking and Reframing

In CGS, citizens are engaging in politics in an open and experimental way. In the absence of prescribed recipes or agendas, they are able to rethink and reframe policy problems, and sometimes in the process they offer new conceptual tools, norms, and practices. The capacity of citizens to reframe policy debates and disrupt policy expertise through practical interventions has been identified in sectors as varied as urban renewal (Wagenaar, 2007), community-based substance recovery groups (Beckwith et al., 2016; Campbell et al., 2011), elder care (Wagenaar, 2019), and grassroots innovation (Smith & Stirling, 2018).

The rethinking and reframing that citizens do in CGS can have broader follow-on effects in policy systems, often in highly dynamic and creative ways. For example, in his study of bottom-up citizens' initiatives seeking to reverse neighborhood decline, Wagenaar (2007, p. 36) found that local knowledge from the citizens started to "flow through the system, combining and recombining with the professional knowledge of politicians, administrators, professionals, and other social actors ... often forcing public officials to rethink long-held assumptions about the way things are done in the city."

Gaining Experiential Knowledge and Practical Reasoning

Citizens' governance spaces are conducive to the exercise, growth, and transmission of experiential knowledge and practical reason. Knowledge emerges through citizens' practical and participatory activities as they try to solve a collective problem rather than via a strategic attempt to develop activist counterexpertise. As citizens work together, make mistakes, confront hurdles, and interact with those they are trying to assist or serve, they accumulate extensive experiential knowledge of what techniques and practices work and what do not. Some harness ground-level knowledge and provide insights that could not be generated otherwise.

Citizens' governance spaces often encourage citizens, users, and practitioners to interact by sharing stories and experiences. This mixing of perspectives would not typically occur in more structured participatory spaces, where distinctions are often made between citizens, experts, and policymakers (Nabatchi et al., 2012). Yet CGS show how laypeople can work constructively with the experts and professionals favored by the state – and how new forms of social reason and epistemic reciprocity can develop such that lay citizens and experts learn together about the costs and consequences of policy choices.

The situated knowledge that citizens generate in CGS enables them to adapt their problem-solving abilities to the tasks at hand and can also inform long-term policy solutions, especially if it is recognized by and uploaded to policy institutions. Consider, for example, the extensive experiential knowledge accumulated in the Savy Amira WCC after twenty years of assisting women to recover from GBV. Today volunteers at Savy Amira are regularly called upon as valued experiential experts by local and provincial governments seeking inputs on how to set up state-based GBV programs (e.g., Savy Amira, 2019a).

Many CGS develop rich situated knowledge of just how dysfunctional or unjust current governance arrangements are. This has been the case for many community-led energy initiatives worldwide; in the process of overcoming various challenges to fund, build, and service renewable energy projects, they have developed critical knowledge of the failings and injustices of incumbent energy systems and the need for governance reforms (Smith & Stirling, 2018).

Citizens' governance spaces are also typically ensconced in policy networks that span regional and national boundaries. Like many restorative justice initiatives, Baltimore Community Conferencing made use of practical knowledge drawn in from similar efforts abroad, tapping restorative justice practitioners from New Zealand and Australia. While conducive to informal networking, these connections do not add up to any sort of social movement.

Enacting Inclusion, Advocacy, and Representation

Citizens' governance spaces are not just citizen-led, they are also open to currently and formerly marginalized citizens taking on productive roles.[11]

---

11 Citizens' governance space founders and routine participants may differ in their greater access to resources in comparison to members of marginalized groups. Differences such as these do not appear to be as significant as between, say, those that stand between state agents or long-time social movement activists and members of marginalized groups.

Many initiatives involve addressing complex problems (such as homelessness, law-breaking, domestic violence, mental health, and addiction) that affect the dispossessed and marginalized (e.g., Abramson & Moore, 2001; Borzaga, 2016a, 2016b; Campbell et al., 2011; Wagenaar et al., 2015). They include the poor, the elderly, the young, the formerly addicted, as well as those even further on the margins.

The citizens leading these initiatives often reach out to these marginalized citizens, actively promoting equality and power-sharing. They recognize people's interest in becoming more civically active – through peer-to-peer work, for example – once they get their lives stabilized. And if citizens have been given opportunities to be involved in the "formulation of their own means and the ends" (von Jacobi et al., 2017, p. 267), they are better placed to provide solutions to similarly marginalized others. The small group of citizens that founded the Serenity Café, for example, recognized that former drug and alcohol users were not natural "joiners" of community groups, especially given their history, social alienation, and suspicion of leaders (Campbell et al., 2011, p. 140). Ex-users and their recovery are not promising topics for social movement advocacy; very few people openly carry the identity of an ex-user into the public sphere. So their approach to engagement has focused on creating a social and supportive environment – via the café – where former users could connect and be empowered to help those vulnerable to drug abuse, such as youth (Campbell et al., 2011, p. 142).

While CGS are not in the explicit business of making representative claims, like an advocacy organization might, over time they can be drawn into policy realms where they are asked to provide experiential advocacy, drawing on their practical knowledge regarding the perspectives and experiences of the citizens they work with or seek to assist. Through their practical attempts to address collective problems, CGS render hidden experiences and perspectives (e.g., of battered women, substance users, the elderly) more visible to decision-makers. Citizens in these spaces are not claiming to be the "voice of the community," but their practical and experiential knowledge enables them to reflectively challenge stereotypes and uninformed community standpoints, as the Serenity Café example illustrates.

Possible Risks of Citizens' Governance Spaces

Though empirical studies indicate a number of distinct contributions of CGS, much is still unknown about how well they solve social problems or connect citizens to one another. Scholars have raised five such concerns.

Reproduction of Existing Inequalities in Civic Capacity

Collective action rooted in civil society may favor individuals with more discretionary time and resources to contribute to CGS. Scholars note that conventional community groups are often highly exclusive and unrepresentative of the broader public (Schlozman et al., 2012; Skocpol, 2003). Some have raised this concern in relation to civic enterprises where the worry is that they are "for the most part founded by middle-class citizens in middle-class neighbourhoods" (Wagenaar & van der Heijden, 2015, p. 132). One risk here is that CGS become forms of exclusive governance for the privileged. Another risk is that those CGS operating by and for the marginalized may be numerous yet still be outmatched by those more powerful CGS organized by the wealthy.

State Off-Loading onto Citizens and Markets (DIY Democracy)

A second major risk is that CGS may contribute to a form of DIY democracy that legitimates state withdrawal from social welfare commitments. A battered women's shelter funded and staffed by a local CGS may do good work while also providing cover for state agencies to cut funding for similar state-led programs. "While the rhetoric continues to be one of 'empowerment,' 'participation,' 'localism' and 'democratic renewal,'" note Aiken and Taylor (2019, pp. 22, 24), "the reality is often one of shifting responsibility for services to citizens and employees in pursuit of efficiency savings and, ultimately, a shrinking state." Rather than "engaging with the state," CGS are "taking over the libraries and parks that used to be run by the state." Marginalized people and those with fewer resources should not have to rely on CGS to "have the same claim on service quality and provision as other members of society have" (Taylor, 2011, p. 217).

Accountability and Regulation

A third major risk is a side effect of the ways CGS operate with relative autonomy from state and market actors. Groups bypassing administrative, legal, and accountability processes may be able to be more experimental in their approaches to social problems, but this can lead to disparate outcomes. A CGS operating a community justice center in one neighborhood may handle vandalism cases differently than a CGS in a similar neighborhood some distance away if neither organization is held to common oversight standards (Tiarks, 2019). Relatedly, in this case state justice agencies are the court of last resort to which parties dissatisfied with CGS decision-making turn, raising questions about the efficacy and desirability of CGS problem-solving in the absence of state backstops.

Ineffective and Piecemeal Governance (Small Potatoes)

A fourth risk is the potentially limited impact of CGS activity. Some critics point out that too often CGS work only offers temporary, small-bore solutions while failing to address the larger public policy issues (Eliasoph, 2013).

Citizens' governances spaces contribute "small potatoes" like community gardens and food banks that feed thousands rather than the food policy that could feed millions. Other scholars worry that CGS can myopically focus on the narrow range of problems that interest them but neglect important non-salient issues (Bovaird & Loeffler, 2012). Some have pointed out that while CGS might demonstrate alternative ways of doing things, they are not well suited to public goods that require resources to be pooled (Hendriks, 2019). A broader concern is that many micro-community projects are not only inefficient but can actually undermine the functioning and capacity of pooled infrastructure; consider, for example, how decentralized community energy initiatives can cause coordination, planning, and regulatory challenges for centralized electricity networks (CEER, 2019; Terzon, 2021).

Depoliticization of Deep Underlying Structural Issues

A fifth hazard is that CGS perpetuate a pragmatic approach to politics that fails to equip citizens for addressing deep structural issues that impact local problems. As we have shown, CGS are not activist spaces in the conventional sense; they do not typically make claims to new rights or challenge the state to protect existing rights (Aiken & Taylor, 2019). The risk here is that in working on social problems in a depoliticized way CGS fail to socialize citizens into standing up for their rights and challenge social, political, and economic institutions to work for the broad public rather than the well-resourced few. Even while benefiting "their participants and communities," CGS may "reconcile, rather than contest, the inequities produced by markets and states" when they bridge to these sectors (Barraket & Archer, 2010, p. 26).

Sustaining and Building Empowerment

Like most community organizing efforts, CGS can struggle to maintain momentum over time.

Citizens leading this kind of problem-solving governance work require considerable time, resources, and energy, and sustaining these efforts over years can be challenging. Many CGS begin with a burst of passionate citizens keen to commit energy, but they slowly die due to leadership issues or a failure to attract new participants. Some, however, do grow over time and attract more and more citizens into their governance work. As CGS grow, they can become more bureaucratized and disconnected from the citizens they are seeking to empower and engage.

One CGS that has managed to successfully navigate considerable growth in members while sustaining its commitment to citizen empowerment is Som Energia, the Spanish energy cooperative that originated in 2010 as a small local Catalonian initiative. Over a ten-year period Som Energia grew into a nationwide cooperative that produces and supplies electricity from small-scale renewable sources, such as solar and biogas, serving contracts to over 135,000 homes and businesses across Spain. Today Som Energia is both a successful business and also a cooperative with members.[12]

As discussed earlier, active participation of Som Energia members is encouraged at the local level through specific local groups. This decentralized approach via local participation not only builds and maintains the cooperative but also serves to attract new members and provides an avenue for its advocacy work for policy reform and social change.

Alongside escalating membership numbers and the growth of its commercial services, Som Energia has worked hard to sustain its local approach to empowering members. It has done this by strengthening connections between its members, the decentralized local groups, its governing body (the Governing Council), and a technical team at the center. For example, in May 2017, the General Assembly was held at group's headquarters in Girona while simultaneously also being held in twenty other cities all connected by videoconferencing. In total, over 300 members participated. Online opportunities expanded even further in 2020/2021 during the COVID-19 pandemic.

Som Energia's empowerment model also engages its members in reflective and strategic planning discussions. For example, in 2016 the cooperative embarked on a ten-month strategic reflection process with its members to collectively determine "the internal organizational model that will help us achieve the goals we set."[13] Crucially important here was a discussion about how the organization should optimally balance its internal empowerment/ participatory work with its commercial and advocacy work. What emerged from this process was a strong sense that members value not just the environmental and advocacy work of Som Energia but its participatory model[14]:

> The project's vision stands out as the achievement, the channeling of participation at the territorial level, and the spaces for participation, learning and growth .... A lot of emphasis is placed on the democratic spirit of the cooperative, thus emphasizing the horizontality and empowerment of the people.

12 Collectively, the members own and operate the Som Energia cooperative. To become a member and user of the cooperative, citizens pay 100 euros. Decisions on major strategic issues are taken through a voting procedure of the General Assembly, which is composed of all members. Each member has one vote regardless of their financial contribution. More day-to-day operational issues are overseen by a steering committee (or Governing Council) composed of six volunteer members, with the support of a larger technical team (see Riutort Isern, 2015).

13 Blog post: "Start of the participatory process of organizational and strategic reflection of the cooperative." https://blog.somenergia.coop/som-energia/proceso-participativo-reflexion-estra tegica-organizativa/2016/10/inicio-del-proceso-participativo-de-reflexion-organizativa-y-estra tegica-de-la-cooperativa/.

14 "Synthesis of the workshop of the School of September 2016 'Begin process of strategic and organizational reflection.'" https://docs.google.com/document/d/1aBKyh2Z16mWeIe7un80 4LYqomLQ6rwshQ2D_CPmGgj4/edit.

Figure 7.2 *Som Energia.*

Implications for Traditional State Institutions and Civil Society

In practice, CGS emerge and develop alongside traditional state and civil society institutions. How this broader institutional and civic context shapes, and is in turn shaped by, CGS appears to vary considerably (see Edelenbos et al., 2021). Some CGS begin as small action-oriented groups, but over the course of their "life cycle" they can professionalize and step into conventional policy advocacy roles. Sometimes these more political efforts to change the broader system can attract the attention of decision-makers, especially if they are timed in a window of "policy reform." In other instances, the informal, bottom-up, and relational ways in which citizens engage in CGS can render their civic work invisible to governments and formal civil society organizations (Eversole, 2011).

Notwithstanding this diversity, in this section we reflect on three broad implications that CGS present to conventional state and civil society institutions.

First, CGS can *reconfigure established state–civil society relations.* As shown by various examples cited in this chapter, CGS emerge in response to failures or limitations of conventional state institutions and civil society organizations (e.g., energy infrastructure, courts and police, food distribution agencies and NGOs) to address public problems. Consequently, CGS often have boundaries with and objections to particular aspects of the system – such as the courts, police departments, or large corporations. Yet under the right circumstances, many CGS might choose to carve out a congruent governance pathway that is not in direct opposition to state officials, agencies, and departments and may in fact be in collaboration or coordination with them. Some CGS wish to work with more powerful and resourced entities only on the terms established by citizens. Consider, for example, the way OSA has formed partnerships with a range of government departments, religious groups, charity organizations, private donors, and corporations (OSA, 2020). The organization is not anti-government, nor is it coopted by government and other elites. Instead it is willing to work with state or nonstate collaborators who support its mission, and this networked approach has enabled OSA to have significant reach and impact (OSA, 2020).

Citizens' governance spaces encourage conventional policy actors in government and civil society to rethink how they work together. Empirical research finds that citizens in CGS tend to work nimbly and flexibly across boundaries between sectors, institutions, and types of actors (e.g., citizens, clients, experts, professionals, policymakers, and politicians; see Edelenbos et al., 2021; Hendriks et al., 2020). In doing so they break down silos and span institutional boundaries.

Second, CGS can be *highly disruptive to existing governance protocols and regimes*. For example, when the idea for the citizen-led Serenity Café emerged in around 2009, its emphasis on abstinence as a recovery pathway sat at odds with the then Scottish government's policy focus to treat substance addiction mostly via short-term detox programs.[15] As the citizens who developed the café explain:

> We have been directly and indirectly steered away from using the term [abstinence] by potential funders, and yet not using the word to describe the recovery of the people using the Serenity Café would seem to be selling them short, because their abstinence is what they take pride in and what they perceive as keeping them alive.   (Campbell et al., 2011, p. 156)

Citizens' governances spaces can also cause governance disruptions by working in unconventional ways with marginalized groups or the broader community. Consider the disruptive way that various consumer and health cooperatives operate in Japan's competitive service provider market for elder care. Member-run cooperatives have expanded conventional notions of elderly health care in Japan by offering a range of diverse services well beyond standard home care, including programs for welfare support, mutual aid, cleaning services, food delivery, as well as recreation and social activities (Kurimoto & Kumakura, 2016). In other cases (e.g., in citizen-led needle exchanges), citizens are prepared to break rules and go against conventions to offer a problem-solving response regardless of the legal consequences (Lupick, 2018). In communities accustomed to looking away from bodies nodding off in alleyways, for which overdose deaths are not a high policy priority, norm-bending CGS operating experimental needle exchanges can be a matter of life and death.

Third, CGS can *generate tensions and opportunities for conventional civil society organizations*. Most CGS work in informal, relational, and embedded ways with communities to solve problems, unencumbered by the kinds of

---

15 While the café supports harm reduction approaches such as maintenance prescribing, it was established to demonstrate that social and community support for "abstinence" can be an effective part of supporting former users in their drug and alcohol recovery. The café's emphasis on abstinence is considered provocative for local drug treatment practitioners (see Campbell et al., 2011).

regulatory and administrative structures that can constrain formal civil society organizations. However, the informal and ephemeral nature of CGS can complicate and even undermine the work of established civil society organizations (e.g., their frontline services or policy advocacy). Consider some of the safety and liability issues that were exposed during COVID-19 pandemic, in which local neighborhood initiatives self-organized to support vulnerable residents, but their actions paradoxically posed health and safety risks to volunteers in established charity organizations as well as to those in need (e.g., Mahanty & Phillipps, 2020).

Some civil society organizations are exploring ways of working productively with CGS, particularly in contexts where volunteering via membership-based associations is in decline or where informal community initiatives are becoming more visible (Einolf et al., 2016; Steen & Brandsen, 2020). For example, Red Cross Australia has recently commissioned research on "everyday humanitarianism" after Australia's 2019–2020 catastrophic bushfires, during which many people "bypassed charitable organisations and organised their own hyper-local, agile humanitarian responses to the crisis using the knowledge, skills and resources they had to hand" (Wilson, 2020, p. 6). Red Cross Australia is using this research to find ways to practically support these "hyper-local" community efforts so that it can better harness their innovation and collective power.

Conclusion

Citizens' governance spaces manifest diverse opportunities and risks for contemporary society. On the one hand, they provide small-scale governance solutions to some of the most chronic and difficult issues that governments face, such as crime and punishment, renewable energy and environmental degradation, wellness, and addiction. They provide spaces of action where citizens rethink and reframe issues and generate innovative, experimental, and disruptive solutions that may attract the attention of relevant state, market, and civil society actors. Yet on the other hand, CGS can potentially reproduce inequalities, coopt civil society, behave unaccountably, or push the governance of essential public goods onto under-resourced or unrepresentative citizens. A broader worry is that CGS can distract citizens by keeping them busy reconciling gaps in the market or state when they should be contesting underlying structural causes of policy problems.

How well CGS can deliver societal benefits while minimizing attendant risks is the major question for future study and practical innovation in this area. Scholars and practitioners will need to more closely examine how CGS operate: the extent to which they are inclusive and participatory, how they evolve and sustain participation over time, and how the citizens involved effectively negotiate with state, market, and civil society power. Exploring the dynamics of how CGS interact with their external policy and political contexts is also important to understanding how CGS shape and are shaped by their broader institutional context. In exploring such questions it is crucial to consider the form, function, and democratic social implications of CGS marked by traditional or conservative goals, such as CGS that organize and run women's prenatal health clinics to advance antiabortion policy, CGS self-organizing to provide private security for only their property, or armed CGS that patrol borders to dissuade illegal immigration.

As the diverse examples in this chapter reveal, citizens adopt a variety of innovative approaches to govern complex policy issues on their own terms – to reduce crime, to support opioid users, to produce food, or to generate affordable renewable energy. In these grassroots policy efforts citizens are experimenting in concert with other mainstream actors, but sometimes they are also challenging and disrupting state agencies and traditional civil society associations. Overall, success for CGS is not about being completely absorbed by or autonomous from the system; hybridity and liminality seem essential to their identity, as does a commitment to impact (Wagenaar & van der Heijden, 2015, p. 132). Many citizens involved in CGS would find them less appealing if they were more formal or part of a state agency or traditional civil association. How CGS can effectively build bridges to conventional state and civil society actors without losing their distinct advantages is the subject of our ongoing research. We are also exploring practical ways that state and long-standing civil society organizations might better coordinate, support, and share resources with CGS. As CGS navigate complex relationships with both state and nonstate entities, we contend that they are generating practical lessons for governance and civil society that could provide essential guidance for reformers in the coming decade.

References

Abramson, L., & Beck, E. (2010). Using conflict to build community: Community conferencing. In E. Beck, N. P. Kropf, & P. B. Leonard (Eds.), *Social work and restorative justice: Skills for dialogue, peacemaking, and reconciliation* (pp. 149–174). Oxford University Press.

Abramson, L., & Moore, D. B. (2001). Transforming conflict in the inner city: Community conferencing in Baltimore. *Contemporary Justice Review, 4*(3/4), 321–340.

Aiken, M., & Taylor, M. (2019). Civic action and volunteering: The changing space for popular engagement in England. *Voluntas: International Journal of Voluntary & Nonprofit Organizations, 30*(1), 15–28.

Amnå, E., & Ekman, J. (2014). Standby citizens: Diverse faces of political passivity. *European Political Science Review, 6*(2), 261–281.

Bakker, J., Denters, B., Vrielink, M. O., & Klok, P.-J. (2012). Citizens' initiatives: How local governments fill their facilitative role. *Local Government Studies, 38*(4), 395–414.

Bang, H. (2005). Among everyday makers and expert citizens. In J. Newman (Ed.), *Remaking governance: Peoples, politics and the public sphere* (pp. 159–178). Policy Press.

Barraket, J., & Archer, V. (2010). Social inclusion through community enterprise? Examining the available evidence. *Third Sector Review, 16*(1), 13–28.

Bauwens, T., Gotchev, B., & Holstenkamp, L. (2016). What drives the development of community energy in Europe? The case of wind power cooperatives. *Energy Research & Social Science, 13*, 136–147.

Beckwith, M., Bliuc, A.-M., & Best, D. (2016). What the recovery movement tells us about prefigurative politics. *Journal of Social and Political Psychology, 4*(1), 238–251.

Blad, J. R. (1996). Neighborhood-centred conflict mediation: The San Francisco example. *European Journal on Criminal Policy and Research, 4*(1), 90–107.

Borzaga, C., Fazzi, L., & Galera, G. (2016a). Social enterprise as a bottom-up dynamic: Part 1. The reaction of civil society to unmet social needs in Italy, Sweden and Japan. *International Review of Sociology, 26*(1), 1–18.

Borzaga, C., Fazzi, L., & Galera, G. (2016b). Social enterprise as a bottom-up dynamic: Part 2. The reaction of civil society to unmet social needs in England, Scotland, Ireland, France and Romania. *International Review of Sociology, 26*(2), 201–204.

Bovaird, T., & Loeffler, E. (2012). From engagement to co-production: The contribution of users and communities to outcomes and public value. *Voluntas: International Journal of Voluntary & Nonprofit Organizations, 23*(4), 1119–1138.

Boyte, H. C. (2004). *Everyday politics: Reconnecting citizens and public life.* University of Pennsylvania Press.

Campbell, R., Duffy, K., Gaughan, M., & Mochrie, M. (2011). Serenity café – On the road to recovery capital. *Journal of Groups in Addiction & Recovery, 6*(1/2), 132–163.

CEER. (2019, June 25). *Regulatory aspects of self-consumption and energy communities.* CEER Report C18-CRM9_DS7-05-03. Council of European Energy Regulators. www.ceer.eu/documents/104400/-/-/8ee38e61-a802-bd6f-db27-4fb61aa6eb6a

Chevée, A. (2022). Mutual aid in north London during the Covid-19 pandemic. *Social Movement Studies, 21*(4), 413–419.

Ci, J. (2006). Political agency in liberal democracy. *Journal of Political Philosophy, 14* (2), 144–162.

de Souza Briggs, X. (2008). *Democracy as problem solving: Civic capacity in communities across the globe.* MIT Press.

Denters, B. (2016). Community self-organization: Potentials and pitfalls. In J. Edelenbos & I. V. Meerkerk (Eds.), *Critical reflections on interactive governance: Self-organization and participation in public governance* (pp. 230–253). Edward Elgar Publishing.

Dzur, A. W. (2013, December 13). *Trench democracy in criminal justice: An interview with Lauren Abramson.* Boston Review. www.bostonreview.net/articles/trench-democracy-in-criminal-justice-an-interview-with-lauren-abramson/

Dzur, A. W. (2019). *Democracy inside: Participatory innovation in unlikely places.* Oxford University Press.

Edelenbos, J., Molenveld A., & van Meerkerk I. (2021). *Civic engagement, community-based initiatives and governance capacity: An international perspective*. Routledge.

Edelenbos, J., van Meerkerk, I., & Schenk, T. (2018). The evolution of community self-organization in interaction with government institutions: Cross-case insights from three countries. *The American Review of Public Administration, 48*(1), 52–66.

Einolf, C. J., Prouteau, L., Nezhina, T., & Ibrayeva, A. R. (2016). Informal, unorganized volunteering. In D. H. Smith, R. A. Stebbins, & J. Grotz (Eds.), *The Palgrave handbook of volunteering, civic participation, and nonprofit associations* (pp. 223–241). Palgrave Macmillan.

Eliasoph, N. (2013). *The politics of volunteering*. Polity.

Evers, A., & von Essen, J. (2019). Volunteering and civic action: Boundaries blurring, boundaries redrawn. *Voluntas: International Journal of Voluntary & Nonprofit Organizations, 30*(1), 1–14.

Eversole, R. (2011). Community agency and community engagement: Re-theorising participation in governance. *Journal of Public Policy, 31*(1), 51–72.

Fung, A. (2006). Varieties of participation in complex governance. *Public Administration Review, 66*, 66–75.

Gaventa, J. (2006). Finding the spaces for change: A power analysis. *IDS Bulletin, 37*(6), 23–33.

Hendriks, C. M., & Dzur, A. W. (2022). Citizens' governance spaces: Democratic action through disruptive collective problem-solving. *Political Studies, 70*(3), 680–700.

Hendriks, C. M., Ercan, S. A., & Boswell, J. (2020). *Mending democracy: Democratic repair in disconnected times*. Oxford University Press.

Hendriks, F. (2019). Democratic innovation beyond deliberative reflection: The plebiscitary rebound and the advent of action-oriented democracy. *Democratization, 26*(3), 444–464.

Kretzmann, J., & McKnight, J. (1993). *Building communities from the inside out*. ACTA Publications.

Kurimoto, A., & Kumakura, Y. (2016). Emergence and evolution of co-operatives for elderly care in Japan. *International Review of Sociology, 26*(1), 48–68.

Laville, J. L., Young, D. R., & Eynaud, P. (Eds.). (2015). *Civil society, the third sector and social enterprise: Governance and democracy*. Routledge.

Lupick, T. (2018). *Fighting for space: How a group of drug users transformed one city's struggle with addiction*. Arsenal Pulp Press.

Mahanty, S., & Phillipps, N. (2020, March 25). *The community-led movement creating hope in the time of coronavirus*. The Conversation. https://theconversation.com/the-community-led-movement-creating-hope-in-the-time-of-coronavirus-134391

Mitlin, D. (2008). With and beyond the state – Co-production as a route to political influence, power and transformation for grassroots organization. *Environment & Urbanization, 20*(2), 339–360.

Moulaert, F., MacCallum, D., Mehmood, A., & Hamdouch, A. (Eds.). (2013). *The international handbook on social innovation*. Edward Elgar.

Nabatchi, T., Gastil, J., Weiksner G. M., & Leighnenger, M. (Eds.). (2012). *Democracy in motion: Evaluating the practice and impact of deliberative civic engagement*. Oxford University Press.

OECD/European Union. (2017). *Boosting social enterprise development: Good practice compendium*. OECD Publishing.

OSA. (2016). *Orange Sky Australia annual report 2015–2016*. Orange Sky Australia. https://adobeindd.com/view/publications/b9183de9-b84b-48a5-b384-b7fa92b7 cdae/1/publication-web-resources/pdf/OSL_AnnualReport2016_A4_CMYK_ PRESS_NOFINANCIALS.pdf

OSA. (2020). *Orange Sky Australia annual report 2019–2020*. Orange Sky Australia. https://orangesky.org.au/wp-content/uploads/2020/12/201202_Annual_ Report_FINAL_with_Financial_Report.pdf

Ostrom, E. (1990). *Governing the commons: The evolution of institutions for collective action*. Cambridge University Press

Ostrom, E. (1996). Crossing the great divide: Coproduction, synergy, and development. *World Development, 24*(6), 1073–1087.

Pellicer-Sifres, V., Belda-Miquel, S., Cuesta-Fernández, I., & Boni, A. (2018). Learning, transformative action, and grassroots innovation: Insights from the Spanish energy cooperative Som Energia. *Energy Research and Social Science, 42*, 100–111.

Pestoff, V. (2018). *Co-production and public service management: Citizenship, governance and public services management*. Routledge.

Pestoff, V., & Hulgård, L. (2016). Participatory governance in social enterprise. *Voluntas: International Journal of Voluntary & Nonprofit Organizations, 27*(4), 1742–1759.

Polletta, F. (1999). "Free spaces" in collective action. *Theory and Society, 28*(1), 1–38.

Polletta, F., & Kretschmer, K. (2013). Free spaces. In *The Wiley-Blackwell encyclopedia of social and political movements* (pp. 477–480). Wiley.

Purbo, O. W. (2016). *Sejarah internet Indonesia: Pembebasan frekuensi 2.4ghz*. OnnoWiki. http://onnocenter.or.id/wiki/index.php/Sejarah_Internet_Indonesia: Pembebasan_Frekuensi_2.4Ghz

Riutort Isern, S. (2015). The Som Energia cooperative in Spain. *Planning theory & practice, 16*(4), 569–572.

Savy Amira. (2019a, April 15). *Sabtu, (13/4/2019) telah dilaksanakan Workshop 6 pembahasan rancangan Peraturan Gubernur Provinsi Jawa Timur tentang SOP Shelter dan tersusunya SOP Rumah Aman bagi perempuan korban kekerasan di Provinsi Jawa Timur, yang memasukkan penanganan kasus bagi kornam kekerasan seksual* [Status update]. Facebook. www.facebook.com/ savyamira.sahabatperempuan/posts/2875880952421908

Savy Amira. (2019b). *Profil*. Savy Amira Women's Crisis Centre. www.savyamirawcc .com/tentang-kami/profil/

Schlozman, K. L., Verba, S., & Brady, H. E. (2012). *The unheavenly chorus: Unequal political voice and the broken promise of American democracy*. Princeton University Press.

Skocpol, T. (2003). *Diminished democracy: From membership to management in American civic life*. University of Oklahoma Press.

Smith. A., & Ely, A. (2015). Green transformations from below? The politics of grassroots innovation. In I. Scoones, M. Leach, & P. Newell (Eds.), *The politics of green transformations* (pp. 102–118). Routledge.

Smith, A., & Stirling, A. (2018). Innovation, sustainability and democracy: An analysis of grassroots contributions. *Journal of Self-Governance and Management Economics*, *6*(1), 64–97.

Soares da Silva, D., Horlings, L., & Figueiredo, E. (2018). Citizen initiatives in the post-welfare state. *Social Sciences*, *7*(12), 252.

Steen, T., & Brandsen, T. (2020). Coproduction during and after the COVID-19 pandemic: Will it last? *Public Administration Review*, *80*(5), 851–855.

Suyatno. (2007). RT-RW Net and e-democracy in Indonesia. *Journal Global dan Strategis*, *1*(2), 108–119.

Taylor, M. (2011). *Public policy in the community* (2nd ed.). Palgrave Macmillan.

Terzon, E. (2021, May 24). *Yackandandah's community battery may not be "big" but experts say it's enough to "petrify" energy providers*. Australian Broadcasting Corporation. www.abc.net.au/news/2021-05-24/community-battery-yackandandah-ausgrid-electricity-shakeup/100159460

Theocharis, Y., & Van Deth, J. W. (2018). The continuous expansion of citizen participation: A new taxonomy. *European Political Science Review*, *10*(1), 139–163.

Tiarks, E. (2019). Restorative justice, consistency and proportionality: Examining the trade-off. *Criminal Justice Ethics*, *38*(2), 103–122.

von Jacobi, N., Nicholls, A., & Chiappero-Martinetti, E. (2017). Theorizing social innovation to address marginalization. *Journal of Social Entrepreneurship*, *8*(3), 265–270.

Wagenaar, H. (2007). Governance, complexity, and democratic participation: How citizens and public officials harness the complexities of neighborhood decline. *The American Review of Public Administration 37*(1), 17–50.

Wagenaar, H. (2019). Making sense of civic enterprise. Social innovation, participatory democracy and the administrative state. *Partecipazione e conflito*, *12*(2), 297–324.

Wagenaar, H., & van der Heijden, J. (2015). The promise of democracy? Civic enterprise, localism and the transformation of democratic capitalism. In S. Davoudi & A. Madanipour (Eds.), *Reconsidering localism* (pp. 126–146). Taylor & Francis.

Wagenaar, H., Healey, P., Laino, G., Vigar, G., Riutort Isern, S., Honeck, T., Beunderman, J., & van der Heijden, J. (2015). The transformative potential of civic enterprise. *Planning Theory & Practice*, *16*(4), 557–585.

Warren, M. E. (2001). *Democracy and association*. Princeton University Press.

Wilson, S. (2020). *Everyday humanitarianism during the 2019/2020 Australian bushfire crisis*. A research project commissioned by Australian Red Cross. https://doi.org/10.4225/50/58225b8340e9a

World Bank. (2018, March). *Reaching the last mile: Social enterprise business models for inclusive development*. World Bank. http://hdl.handle.net/10986/29544

Yates, L. (2015). Rethinking prefiguration: Alternatives, micropolitics and goals in social movements. *Social Movement Studies*, *14*(1), 1–21.

Zinsstag, E., & Vanfaechem, I. (Eds.). (2012). *Conferencing and restorative justice: International practices and perspectives*. Oxford University Press.

8 Participatory Budgeting

Loren Peabody

Introduction

Participatory budgeting (PB) is a democratic process that provides a space for citizens to take part in deciding how part of a public budget is spent through a mix of deliberation, representation, and voting on budget priorities. Of all of the experiments in building institutions that embody what Fung and Wright (2003) call *empowered participatory governance*, PB stands out as the most widely practiced and the most intensively researched.

First developed in the Brazilian city of Porto Alegre between 1989 and 1991 as a strategy by the Worker's Party to deliver progressive social change through a local government still dominated by clientelistic parties, *orçamento participativo* provided an avenue for communities that were traditionally marginalized from the city's halls of power to drive the process of deciding how to invest municipal resources. As a result, city spending was significantly reoriented to the needs of the poor (Marquetti, 2000). Moreover, civil society experienced an outgrowth of activism, especially in parts of the city with a history of underdeveloped civic organization (Baiocchi, 2005). This transformation captivated the imagination of activists interested in deepening democracy around the world, especially those who gathered in Porto Alegre for the World Social Forum in the early 2000s.

Before long the idea was taken up by the World Bank, USAID, and the European Union – institutions with markedly different ideological affinities than World Social Forum participants – as PB was also seen as an efficient means to improve governance and accountability (Wampler et al., 2017). Global diffusion ensued, and by 2019 PB had spread to an estimated 11,000 cases around the world using a broad definition of the process (Dias et al., 2019).

Participatory budgeting processes vary considerably in the rules that govern them and the size of budgets they command (Cabannes, 2015). In the original "Porto Alegre model," each of the city's sixteen districts holds assemblies where ordinary residents are chosen by their peers to serve as delegates in the district's Budget Forum. While open to anybody, the assemblies tend to see higher attendance by members of neighborhood associations and other local organizations. Delegates meet regularly to deliberate on budget priorities and specific project ideas, working with city staff to learn technical details about the options. They then choose councilors to reconcile the various priorities put forward and finalize the citywide budget at the PB Council before sending it to the city council for ratification.

European and North American PB processes tend to have a more stream-lined structure in comparison. Like the Porto Alegre model, participants deliberate in decentralized fora over how to invest a dedicated portion of the capital expenditure budget (i.e., the budget excluding the city's operating and payroll expenses). On the other hand, there tends to be a predetermined distribution of resources between the districts of the municipality rather than this distribution itself falling within the scope of the deliberative process. Participatory budgeting in these regions usually has a somewhat downscaled role for budget delegates. Rather than actually selecting specific projects and priorities, delegates are tasked with winnowing down and fleshing out project ideas provided by the public. With the technical assistance of city staff, delegates develop them into feasible proposals that are then chosen through a process of district-wide voting open to all residents of the jurisdiction.

This chapter will proceed by first reviewing the goals that are potentially advanced by PB in the view of its supporters. Next it will describe some of PB's participation trends, how it diffused internationally, varieties in its insti-tutional model, and some of the main outcomes that have been identified. Clearly, it would be beyond the scope of the chapter to cover how PB has been practiced around the world and review all of the research that this breadth of application has provoked; readers interested in PB's global reach may turn to Dias (2018) or Dias et al. (2019) for the most geographically comprehensive work on offer. The focus here will be on the cases of Porto Alegre and New York City. Porto Alegre is both where PB was originally innovated and was one of the most successful cases in terms of PB's documented impacts on the empowerment of marginalized groups, on the organization of civil society more generally, on the redistribution of municipal spending, and on improve-ments in urban governance. Porto Alegre was the model for PB that was taken up by over 170 Brazilian cities in the 1990s and early 2000s, some of which replicated many of these positive outcomes. New York City, on the other hand, represents one of the largest-scale examples of PB as it was later taken up in the Global North. Though larger in scale than most, its design shares much in common with PB as it is currently practiced in North America and Europe, as well as many processes elsewhere that were established with support from large international organizations.

After highlighting how PB worked in Porto Alegre during the 1990s and in New York City in recent years, this chapter will turn to research on the degree to which PB tends to alter the community power structure after it is adopted. The first set of issues are evoked by what Nylen (2002) has called the *empower-ment thesis*: that participating in democratic innovations like PB encourages engagement in other forms of political activity among the disempowered or otherwise disengaged, thereby producing a more active civil society. The chapter then examines research on the precursors to such activity at the individual level, namely the potential effects of PB on psychological empowerment, often referred to as PB's impact as a *school of democracy* (Fung & Wright, 2003, p. 32). The conclusion will summarize the features of PB processes identified as having potential for building community power, suggest a few avenues for further research on PB, and reflect on the contemporary importance of expanding and strengthening participatory democratic experiments like PB.

Goals of Participatory Budgeting

Warnings that democracy is in crisis in the US have proliferated in recent years. From long-standing issues like countermajoritarian institutions to mounting concerns about the influence of money in politics, the disenfranchisement of voters, the polarization of parties and of the polity, and the breakdown of democratic norms, the reform of democratic institutions has moved to the center of the political agenda. Such attention is symbolized, for example, by the introduction of the For the People Act on the first day of both the 116th and 117th terms of the US House of Representatives. The growing democracy reform movement overwhelmingly emphasizes revitalizing representative institutions. Although few would deny the importance of, for instance, securing voting rights, strengthening campaign finance and ethics rules, or banning partisan gerrymandering, supporters of participatory and deliberative democracy argue that it is also crucial to create new channels for ordinary people to play direct roles in formulating the policies that affect their communities (Dryzek et al., 2019).

Wright and Fung (2003) devote particular attention to direct citizen participation to counteract the presumption of its infeasibility at scale. They propose an abstract model of new forms of public engagement termed *empowered participatory governance*: governing institutions that are participatory because they involve ordinary people in decision-making processes and empowered because the process meaningfully shapes subsequent policies and decisions (p. 5). Outcomes of the processes vary in their degree of legal bindingness, from provisional to final (Johnson & Gastil, 2015). Nevertheless, to count as *empowered* participatory governance – or as Johnson and Gastil's (2015) closely related model of *empowered deliberation* – it would have to have an actual impact on policy that is beyond advisory. New England town hall meetings are familiar to the American imagination, but they involve relatively small numbers of people in the deliberation of highly local issues; many recent cases of empowered participatory governance operate on larger scales over a broader scope of issues. Noteworthy examples apart from PB include: the

1996 People's Planning Campaign in Kerala, India (Isaac & Heller, 2003); Chicago's Local School Councils in place since 1998 (Fung, 2003); the 2010 Icelandic National Forum constitutional assembly (Landemore, 2015); the 2010 and 2020 California Citizen's Redistricting Commission (Kogan & McGhee, 2012); the 2012–2014 Irish Constitutional Convention and subsequent Citizens' Assembly on same-sex marriage and abortion (Kasdan, 2019); Decide Madrid's online participatory planning platform initiated in 2015 (Kasdan, 2019); and Community-Driven Planning and Development in Chicago's 35 Ward launched in 2015 (Democracy Beyond Elections, 2021). Many others are documented at participedia.net, a crowd-sourced platform on democratic innovations and public participation.

Theorists of empowered participatory governance have distilled three core goals that advocates of PB expect such experiments to advance: equity, civic participation, and effectiveness (Fung & Wright, 2003, p. 25). The first of these is equity. In its original Porto Alegre incarnation, leftist reformers wanted to redirect municipal spending to privilege poor and working-class communities. Engaging participatory assemblies to develop the city budget became a method to accomplish this "inversion of priorities" in a way that would garner legitimacy and rebut accusations of dealing in "clientelism of the left" (Baiocchi et al., 2011, p. 54). Observers were impressed by the equity in process that was achieved by including the participation of traditionally marginalized populations and the equity in outcomes brought about by implementing budgets that targeted less affluent parts of the city and prioritized issues of critical importance to the poor, such as health. Many social movements (e.g., Movement for Black Lives, 2022) have similarly argued that the best way to make public institutions more just is to place them under the control of the communities most impacted by their injustices through mechanisms like PB.

Cynics about the voluntary sphere, like Bourdieu (1993), might suggest that these participatory democratic institutions simply reproduce the hierarchies that exist in the broader social world, such as the status conferred by perceived expertise or various forms of capital. On the other hand, optimists like Habermas (1996) argue that despite the social and economic pressures, equal and open communication in civil society is possible and may generate a public consensus that legitimates representative democracy. Baiocchi et al. (2011) argue that both outcomes are theoretically possible but find empirical evidence that some robustly designed PB processes do tend to encourage public-mindedness among participants (pp. 22, 104). As Fung and Wright (2003) put it, "[s]ince the idea of fairness is infused in the practice of reasonable discussion, truly deliberative decision-making should tend toward more equitable outcomes than those regulated by power, status, money, or numbers" (p. 26).

A second goal beyond promoting fair decisions through an equitable process is that including popular participation in budgeting decisions may change the civic practices of participants and their communities. At the individual level, the hope is that **PB** acts as a school of democracy. Participatory fora provide new channels for citizens to get involved in public decisions, incentives to take part in collective action (as their individual effort is more likely to make a measurable difference), and opportunities to exercise voice that are lacking in traditional forms of political engagement like voting or participating in social movements (Fung & Wright, 2003, p. 27). Participants – especially those more deeply involved as delegates – may acquire knowledge about policies that affect their community, become familiar with how local politics works, develop capacities to deliberate and to persuade, come to value collective action or democratic engagement, and so on. At the aggregate level, this dynamic can foster community empowerment, mobilize supporters of reformist political parties, and contribute to a more active and dense civil society.

Civic participation has been linked to a variety of beneficial outcomes from diverse quarters, ranging from the social capital literature (e.g., Putnam, 1995) to critics interested in transcending capitalism (e.g., Wright, 2010). For Wright (2010), transcending capitalism is about organizing economic activity through *social power* – or "the capacity to mobilize people for voluntary collective action of various sorts" (p. 113) – in contrast to power based on control over economic assets or the levers of state power. "This is the equivalent," he has written, "to arguing for the radical democratization of both state and economy, and this in turn requires an associationally rich civil society" (p. 145).

Finally, features of **PB** may make for a particularly effective means to advance collective ends. Individuals personally situated close to the conditions that a policy is intended to address tend to possess unique knowledge of which even experts on the broader issue may be unaware. In a deliberative process, participants who would be directly affected by the decision are able to offer useful information about the problem and to consider alternative solutions. All of this additional debate provides heightened accountability for the governing administration, and the fact that it is accomplished through a relatively formal process fosters greater transparency (Gonçalves, 2014; Wampler & Touchton, 2019). Ultimately, governments may earn greater legitimacy, which can manifest itself in behaviors among the public like better tax compliance (Touchton et al., 2021). Although this kind of good governance may be the goal that makes **PB** attractive to international organizations like the World Bank, it is also the case that "sheer effectiveness is an important component of social justice" (Fung & Wright, 2003, p. 25). Effectiveness may have synergistic effects with the first two goals. For instance, according to Baiocchi (2003, p. 65), Porto Alegre mayor Tarso Genro made the case that PB contributed to the reelection of several Workers' Party administrations and generated public support for raising land-use taxes that provided more resources for their larger redistributive project.

Trends in Participation, Diffusion, Variations, and Outcomes

Since traditional forms of civic engagement – from voting and contributing to campaigns to submitting public comment and serving on boards and commissions – tend to overrepresent citizens who are already relatively privileged, supporters of PB hope that the prospect of delegating meaningful control over significant resources to community members will elicit more participation among residents of disadvantaged social positions (Pape & Lim, 2019, pp. 862–863). Moreover, this involvement should take place both at the low-commitment stages of the process (e.g., voting on budget proposals or attending an assembly) *and* those that require a more intensive contribution (e.g., serving as a budget delegate).

Survey data collected from participants in several PB processes have found that residents of disadvantaged social positions tend to be overrepresented as participants. For example, in the Porto Alegre 2000 cycle, among all those engaged, the percentage of women present was slightly higher than the citywide average; the percentage of low-income participants was almost triple the citywide average; the percentage of Black participants was almost double the citywide average; and the percentage of participants with lower formal educational attainment was almost four times the citywide average (Baiocchi, 2005, p. 15). Even among the more intensively engaged delegates and councilors, these social categories tended to be overrepresented. Avritzer (2009) found that while women both attended and spoke publicly in Porto Alegre's assemblies at slightly higher rates than men, lower-income residents were present in high numbers but were less likely to speak publicly (p. 90).

The most extensive research on participation in North American PB surveyed voters from six processes during the 2014–2015 cycles (Public Agenda, 2016). The study found that that many social groups that are often marginalized from traditional electoral politics were overrepresented within the PB process (see "Research on Community Power" section).

As PB spread to other social and political contexts outside Porto Alegre and took on different institutional varieties, it has at times been possible to replicate aspects of Porto Alegre's success on smaller scales, although unevenly so. First it diffused through a bottom-up process to other Brazilian cities with Workers' Party administrations during the 1990s. Eventually competing parties instituted PB as well. By 1997 there were 103 processes, and there were 170 by 2004, about half in cities with mayors from the Workers' Party (Avritzer, 2009, p. 93).

Next, as major international organizations endorsed PB, it also began to diffuse through top-down processes. For instance, Peru and the Dominican Republic have national programs that mandate a version of PB on the local level (Wampler et al., 2017, p. 58). This kind of national legislation explains the rapid take off in numbers of processes in some countries – for example, Peru had 2,089 processes in 2019 (McNulty, 2018, p. 114). According to Dias et al. (2019), Latin America had about 3,060 cases in 2019. They find that in 2018 Europe had more PB processes than other continents at around 4,580 processes. Asia had approximately 2,780 cases, although almost all of these were in Japan, Indonesia, South Korea, and Russia. Africa had roughly 950 processes, though most were in Madagascar, Cameroon, Angola, and Senegal. North America got a late start, with PB only arriving in Chicago in 2009 and New York City in 2012. As of 2019 there were 145 cases the US, eighteen in Mexico, and fifteen in Canada.

Although PB programs for municipal budgets or districts of the city are by far the most common, there are other varieties. It has been practiced at higher levels of government: at the provincial level in the Brazilian state of Rio Grande do Sul (Goldfrank & Schneider, 2006) and at the national level in Portugal (Dias, 2018). As these more centralized processes (and those of larger cities) encounter challenges in aggregating participation, experiments with more streamlined procedures have been conducted. For instance, the Portuguese nationwide processes dispense with budget delegates such that administration staff do the work of developing project ideas submitted by the public into feasible proposals and present them for public vote. Other processes lean more heavily on online engagement in place of in-person meetings. A danger with these strategies, however, is that participation becomes thinner and skewed toward more privileged residents – a finding of the Community Development Project (2015) study of PBNYC (see also Saad, 2020).

Another variation is *thematic PB*: processes that are designed to specifically address one particular domain of policy. Although thematic assemblies were added to the Porto Alegre model in 1994, this design did not receive a great deal of attention internationally until 2019 when some activists and policy-makers began to call for climate-themed PB processes (or "green PB"). In a climate-themed PB process, residents would submit ideas for projects that contribute to global warming mitigation and resilience in their locality. During the proposal development phase, delegates would work with scientific experts to score the proposals on their environmental impact. The 2019 pro-posal for a Green New Deal by Representative Alexandria Ocasio-Cortez and Senator Ed Markey (HR 109 and SR 59, 116th Congress) called for "demo-cratic and participatory processes that are inclusive of and led by frontline and vulnerable communities and workers to plan, implement, and administer the Green New Deal mobilization at the local level" (para. 4). In addition to the equity rationale highlighted by the congressmembers, the NAACP has offered the effectiveness argument that PB may be "particularly beneficial for climate resilience planning because of the local knowledge it requires and the co-benefits of climate change projects" (NAACP, 2019, p. 215). In 2020, Lisbon, Portugal, launched the first green PB process. As of 2021, Portland Metro was planning a similar green PB program, as well as processes that engage young people and that engage homeless residents.

One type of PB in which the US is leading the world in adoption trends is school PB. While a just few municipal governments have youth-targeted PB (such as Boston and Seattle), data from the Participatory Budgeting Project (2021) indicate that, in 2020, 165 schools had PB programs. After a successful pilot at Bioscience High School in Phoenix, Arizona, in 2013–2014, school PB gradually spread to other schools in the area with the assistance of nonprofit organizations and researchers at Arizona State University, reaching thirty-four programs in the metro area by 2020. The other major locus of school PB is New York City, where an initiative from the mayor's office planned to bring PB to every public high school in the city (of which there are 520). However, after briefly implementing PB in 132 schools, this program was scaled back to one that schools could opt in to. In addition to potentially meeting some of the same goals as conventional PB, school and youth PB may be particularly well suited for strengthening psychological empowerment among participants. However, such programs are at an early stage and are likely limited by the scale of the projects that are feasible given that the budgets are often quite small, with about $2,000–$5,000 per school per year being typical.

The literature on PB has identified key factors that explain the degree to which PB programs tend to make meaningful headway toward their goals, such as the prior degree of organization of civil society (Baiocchi, 2005; Wampler & Avritzer, 2004), the strength of political will (Avritzer, 2009), and the institutional design of the process (Baiocchi et al., 2011; Wampler & Touchton, 2019). A fourth rather obvious factor is simply that PB projects vary tremendously in how adequately they are funded (Cabannes, 2015). Allegretti and Copello (2018) note that in the early 2000s, larger budgets ranged to as much as $200–400 per resident per year – often in the context of the Global South, where prices tend to be lower and where there are more "low-hanging fruit" investments that make a major impact on urban life at a modest cost. Currently in the US, even high-profile PB programs like those of New York City or Chicago only allocate between approximately $5 and $25 per resident in the district per year. When Porto Alegre PB in its 1990s heyday allocated between $30 million and $120 million, or about $20–$80 per resident per year (Goldfrank & Landes, 2018, p. 169), a typical larger project might be building a new school in a disadvantaged neighborhood (Baiocchi, 2005, p. 14). In contrast, for New York City PB, a sizable school-based project might be funding bathroom renovations in one building. This difference in the stakes of PB is not lost on local residents. Goldfrank and Landes (2018) note a positive correlation between budget size and volume of participation (a finding that can be replicated using data from the Participatory Budgeting Project).

The sheer number and diversity of successful PB processes show that public budgets do not represent an arcane technical matter to be resolved by experts and career politicians. This success bolsters the idea that participatory institutions have established "proof of concept." They are viable enough to justify expanding democratic control over more of society's resources and creating more avenues for ordinary community members to directly contribute to collective decision-making. Still, it has yet to be shown that PB as it is typically practiced internationally can have the transformative effects on community power and psychological empowerment that were observed in Porto Alegre in the 1990s. Baiocchi and Ganuza (2014) have even warned that PB has lost its "empowerment dimension" (p. 36) as it has spread around the world as a governance tool that is divorced from being part of a larger project of social transformation.

Porto Alegre

Porto Alegre, a city of about 1.5 million residents centered in a metropolitan area of 4.5 million, serves as the capital of Brazil's southernmost state, Rio Grande do Sul. Although it is one of the most economically developed parts of the country, urban infrastructure and services did not keep up with the breakneck pace of urbanization that took place since the 1950s. Self-constructed informal settlements proliferated on the urban periphery, exposing stark contrasts with the affluent city center. Inequality in wealth and income extended to inequality in access to public goods provided by the municipality. For example, while 99 percent of the roads in the center of the city were paved in 1990, only between 12 and 65 percent were surfaced in the periphery (Avritzer, 2009, p. 88).

When the Workers' Party (Partido dos Trabalhadores, or PT) candidate Olívio Dutra won Porto Alegre's 1988 mayoral election without gaining a majority of seats in the city's legislature, the administration faced the prospect of needing to compromise its radical agenda and trade favors with rival parties to make any headway. At the same time, social movements and neighborhood associations had a uniquely strong presence in much of the city and, after redemocratization in the mid-1980s, expanded their demands from improved city services to greater participation in public decisions. The umbrella organization for the neighborhood associations, the União de Associações de Moradores de Porto Alegre (UAMPA), put forward the idea of participating in the budgetary process after becoming dissatisfied with the engagement schemes of the previous, left-populist administration (Avritzer, 2009). However, the first cycle of the PT's PB process in 1989 proved frustrating due to a lack of transparency and organization, making it unclear how spending proposals solicited from the public were translated into the final allocation of funds (Baiocchi, 2005).

With an economic crisis and additional disputes creating a generalized crisis in public support, in 1990 the PT doubled down on the PB strategy by further institutionalizing it and by opening more avenues for individual citizens to take part with the support of city staff rather than relying on civil society organizations to run the process (Baiocchi, 2005, pp. 37–39). The PB Council was launched with the authority to divide resources between the city's districts, to reconcile the priorities from each Budget Forum in a final citywide budget, to monitor implementation, and to refine the rules of the process. Although the city council retained the ultimate legal authority to approve the budget, the legitimacy garnered by the PB process meant that it was accepted every year without changes. And despite lacking a majority in the city council, in 1991 the PT administration succeeded in passing an increase in land-use taxes that would secure a stream of revenue to fund PB projects. Partido dos Trabalhadores candidates would go on to win mayoral elections in 1992, 1996, and 2000.

Although the precise workings of the Porto Alegre model shifted over the course of the decade (see Marquetti, 2000 for details), the broad contours of the process are as follows: The annual cycle begins "festively" with plenary meetings ("*rodadas*") in the Budget Forum of each district (Baiocchi, 2005, p. 74). Here, the mayor or their staff are present to field questions from residents in an accounting of the previous cycle. More importantly, the assembly selects forty to sixty budget delegates to represent the district. Neighborhood assemblies and other civil society groups in attendance get slots on the Forum in proportion to the number of their members present (with diminishing returns), and these groups have their own informal process for selecting volunteers to fill these positions. In the next stage, delegates meet in the districts weekly or biweekly to deliberate on the neighborhood's budget priorities and specific project ideas and work with city staff to learn technical details about the options. Sometimes this involves negotiating and forming alliances between neighborhoods. In 1994, five thematic assemblies were also introduced to represent specific budgetary issues rather than parts of the city.

Around July, a second large Budget Forum meeting is held, in which the delegates vote on budget priorities and specific projects for the district before choosing two councilors to represent the region at the Budget Council. The PB Council's forty-four members are made up of two from each of the sixteen districts, two from each of the five thematic assemblies, one from UAMPA, and one from the public employees union. The PB Council then meets twice a week for several months, working with city planners to divide the budget into general spending priorities, to apportion investment among the districts, and to select specific projects to fund. They remain in close contact with their local Budget Forum (which can recall them at any point) as they finalize the city-wide budget to present to the legislature for approval.

Participatory budgeting also takes place in the context of an ecosystem of independent civil society organizations: Neighborhood associations take part in district assemblies and put forward delegates, popular councils are assemblies of activists that sprouted or grew in conjunction with the rise of PB, and the UAMPA represents the interests of the neighborhood associations across the city.

As the PB process became more routinized and residents began to see projects successfully implemented in their neighborhoods, public participation grew to impressive levels. In 1990, 976 people took part; in 1992, this figure increased to 7,610; and by 2000, 26,807 residents were involved (Avritzer, 2009, p. 93). At about 2 percent of the city's population, this participation rate was typical of the more successful cases of PB in Brazil in the 1990s – although at the upper end of the distribution, the smaller city of Gravataí saw up to 10.5 percent of its residents participate (Baiocchi et al., 2011, p. 105). According to Marquetti (2000), this demonstrates a popular legitimacy that is all the more impressive given Brazilians' typical distrust of government institutions, fostered by a preponderance of corrupt or incompetent administrations at every level of government.

The institutionalization of PB in Porto Alegre was central to a period of dramatic improvements in governance. For Marquetti (2000), the city's innovation of PB led to a break with traditions of clientelism and dramatically increased responsiveness, accountability, and transparency:

> Community associations choose their priorities based on objective criteria. Having chosen, they have mechanisms to ensure that their wishes are carried out ... Community leaders accustomed to a client/patron relationship with city councilors either changed their ways or were replaced by a new leadership. City councilors and would-be candidates now have to confront a more demanding, informed and politicized populace. [Participatory budgeting] has also led to unprecedented transparency in the formation, allocation and implementation of the municipal budget. The permanent evaluation of governmental performance allows for poor execution to be detected and problems to be corrected.   (p. 74)

Marquetti provides a comprehensive tabulation of how this improved governance affected the lives of residents in the poorer neighborhoods, which received between four and sixteen times more municipal spending per capita than the wealthier districts of the city (as cited in Avritzer, 2009, p. 105). From 1989 to 1996, roughly 96,000 housing units were connected to the water system and 130,000 to the sewage system; the rates of garbage collection, street lighting, and road paving expansion all increased markedly; between 1988 and 1998, enrollment in municipal schools increased by 240 percent and services from the municipal hospital increased by 50 percent; and there were significant investments in social housing (Marquetti, 2000).

Despite all these accomplishments, PB in Porto Alegre is currently a shadow of its former self. Whereas in 1994 PB commanded 74.6 percent of investment expenditures and 16 percent of the total municipal budget, by 2016 PB allocations had fallen to 5.4 percent of the city's investments and just 0.6 percent of the total budget – allocations that are so austere that these resources committed to PB can be considered "almost symbolic" (Nuñez, 2018, p. 521). The process was even suspended without provoking protest in 2017 due to the lack of funds to invest. Brazil's prolonged economic crisis after 2015 certainly did not help in this regard. Nevertheless, PB was also born at a time of even more severe economic tumult, so such constraints hardly provide a sufficient explanation.

Nuñez (2018) has provided a comprehensive account of the decline of the world's most well-known participatory democratic process that highlights the loss of political will and flaws internal to PB's institutional design. After sixteen years of uninterrupted PT administrations, in 2004 the PT mayoral candidate lost to a coalition of twelve different parties. Despite running on a platform of maintaining PB, the new administration gradually eroded its capacities by transferring its coordination from the mayor's office to a new ministry, by cutting the investment budget and moving more investment decisions outside of the PB process, and by allowing the project completion rate to fall from over 80 percent to under 20 percent (Nuñez, 2018, p. 532). According to Nuñez, weaknesses of PB's institutional design include inadequate mechanisms for addressing uncompleted projects, reliance on the administration to share budgetary information, consolidating the two plenary meetings of the Budget Forums into one, and insufficient attention being given to educating and building the capacities of participants. Perhaps most integral to the Porto Alegre model is the problem of embedding representative mechanisms within the participatory process. Nuñez argues that members of the PB Council began to act more like traditional politicians – especially after being allowed to be reelected indefinitely in 2008. The principle of the self-regulation of the participatory process may be highly democratic, but allowing rules to be decided by participants themselves may also advance the interests of those who make the rules.

New York City

Participatory budgeting first came to the US when activist-researchers who had attended the 2005 World Social Forum in Porto Alegre formed an organization called the Participatory Budgeting Project in 2009 and convinced Alderman Joe Moore of Chicago's 49th Ward to adopt the model for allocating the $1.3 million of "menu money" that the city's alders dispense on capital projects in their ward. Two years later the group, along with another organization, Community Voices Heard, brought the alderman to New York City to press council members to adopt PB in their districts for similar pots of discretionary capital funds. They succeeded in convincing four councilmembers to launch PB – three progressive Democrats as well as one Republican, which was seen as important to avoid the optics of partisanship that had eventually undermined many Brazilian PB programs closely associated with the PT.

The 2011 launch of PBNYC resonated with the sentiment expressed that fall during the Occupy Wall Street protests that democratic institutions were dominated by economic elites and lacked responsiveness to the "99 percent." The early cycles proved successful, largely due to the hard work of these organizations in facilitating the process. Additional councilmembers adopted the practice in their districts: twenty-four by 2015 and thirty-three by 2019. A ballot initiative approved overwhelmingly in 2018 revised the City Charter

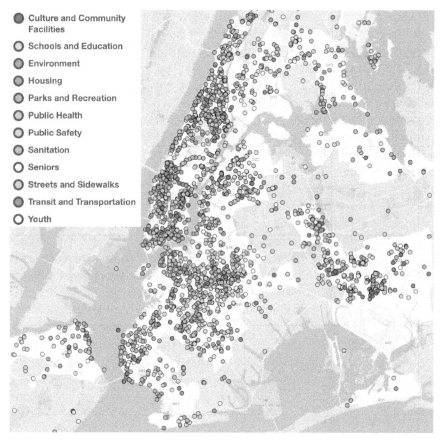

Figure 8.1 *Map of PBNYC project idea submissions for 2021. (note: although it is not possible to distinguish the types of projects in this display, the map conveys the variety of types of projects and their broad geographic distribution across the city)*
Source: *http://ideas.pbnyc.org.*

and established the Civic Engagement Commission tasked with establishing a citywide process. The commission called on the mayor to allocate at least $500 million to the new program –which would have made it the world's largest PB budget –but plans were put on hold due to the coronavirus pandemic.

The design of the PBNYC process is very typical of PB in the US and Canada. The model works through a five-stage annual cycle. First, a steering committee designs the process, usually involving city officials. Second, an outreach campaign solicits project ideas from the community through public meetings and online tools (for a map of PBNYC idea submissions and a list of project types, see Figure 8.1). Third, volunteer budget delegates get to work winnowing these project ideas and developing the feasible ones into fleshed-out proposals with the technical assistance of city staff. Fourth, district residents vote for their priorities from a list of options worked out by the delegates. Finally, the city government funds and implements the winning projects.

According to data from the Participatory Budgeting Project (2021), in 2019, the thirty-two PBNYC processes allocated nearly $39 million and engaged over 118,000 voters. Districts ranged from turning out 1,011 to 8,566 voters and averaged 3,701; as percentages of district population, this ranges from 0.63 to 5.37 percent and averages 2.33 percent. Voter turnout on this scale is comparable to that of successful Brazilian processes like Porto Alegre, which had a participation rate of around 2 percent of the city population during its heyday. However, it should be borne in mind that in Porto Alegre "participation" meant, at minimum, showing up to an in-person assembly, which is a more intensive commitment than simply casting a vote.

Effects on governance and redistribution have been less visible for PB processes in New York City or elsewhere in the US than for their Brazilian counterparts. Goldfrank and Landes (2018) argue that these limited impacts result from three factors. First, PB has been implemented by individual cities and districts rather than being sponsored by a major political party with the capacity to support its implementation on a large scale. Second, PB processes are usually designed to operate at the district level with predetermined budgets, blocking the possibility of allocating more funds to lower-income districts, as was practiced in Porto Alegre. Finally, the scale of the PB budgets in the US has simply been too small on a per-person basis to have discernable effects on societal well-being and represent too small a portion of the municipal budget to have marked impacts on local governance. Whereas prior to 2004 Porto Alegre's PB budget commanded between $30 million and $120 million, or approximately $20–$80 per resident per year (Goldfrank & Landes, 2018, p. 169), districts participating in PBNYC spent about $8 per resident in 2019 (Participatory Budgeting Project, 2021). With the city's total budget at $89 billion and capital budget at $11.2 billion, PBNYC represents 0.044 percent of overall expenditure or 0.35 percent of capital spending.

Research on Community Power

What impacts has PB had on community power? Research has found that such impacts vary considerably (Touchton et al., 2023). In many but not all Brazilian cities that adopted PB in the 1990s, the very fact that meaningful redistribution and changes in urban governance took place suggests that substantial shifts in the city's power relationships had occurred, as they would hardly have been possible otherwise. More direct indicators of community empowerment can be found in many cases in transformations of the organization and activity level of civil society following the adoption of PB. This section will turn to those impacts on civil society, namely what Nylen (2002) calls the *empowerment thesis* – or, in more neutral language, what Johnson et al. (2023) refer to as the *participation thesis* – that when individuals participate in democratic innovations like PB they become more likely to engage in other forms of political activity, resulting in a more active civil society. First, of course, PB processes need to succeed in engaging social groups that are often excluded from influencing government decisions.

The Community Development Project (2015) at the Urban Justice Center performed evaluations of PBNYC for the first four cycles that collected survey data from participants, and from which it was generally found that marginalized social groups engaged at relatively high rates. Women were overrepresented in nearly all cases, lower-income individuals were overrepresented or represented proportionally to the locality in most cases, and Black residents were overrepresented in most cases. Latinx participants and individuals with lower levels of formal educational attainment, however, were somewhat underrepresented. For instance, in the fourth cycle, 63 percent of PBNYC voters were women, 57 percent identified as people of color (in comparison to 66 percent of the total population and 47 percent of local election voters in these districts), 44 percent earned less than $50,000 per year (on par with their composition of 45 percent of the total population), and 28 percent were born outside of the US (versus 38 percent of the total population) (Community Development Project, 2015). PBNYC is open to youth, people who lack citizenship or legal immigration status, and people convicted of a felony; the researchers found that nearly a quarter of PBNYC participants faced such barriers to voting in local elections. They also found evidence regarding the effectiveness of outreach efforts. Among participants who heard about PB through a community group, door-knocking, or at a school, 75 percent identified as people of color; among those who heard about PB online, from social media, or from a councilmember, 72 percent were White.

The extensive efforts made by PBNYC organizers to engage immigrant communities were met with generally positive – though uneven – results. While Hayduk et al. (2017) found that foreign-born PB voters were overrepresented in some districts, they also identified significant barriers. Along with work, family commitments, and the lack of a sense of security among undocumented community members, language proved to be a rather intractable constraint: Participants who spoke a primary language other than English were heavily underrepresented in all districts – even in those districts where foreign-born population participation is high.

It is important for democratic innovations to engage equitably not just at the lower-commitment stages of engagement – like voting – but also at the more intensive stages – like serving as a budget delegate. Su (2017) drew on in-depth surveys with delegates and found a certain discourse of "feasibility" and "reasonableness" regarding project ideas that operated by virtue of the design of the process and was reiterated by the city staff providing technical assistance. Though notions of a "good project" may have been determined by appropriately neutral criteria, they end up privileging those who are familiar with policy jargon and often disadvantage those who are not. This process works in racialized ways, resulting at times in the "managed participation, rather than truly meaningful empowerment" of marginalized groups (Su, 2017, p. 140).

Similar dynamics sometimes appear in other North American PB processes. Pape and Lim (2019) found in a study of PB Chicago that although residents of lower socioeconomic status were highly underrepresented as voters in the process, they tended to be slightly overrepresented in the more deeply committed role as delegates. Nevertheless, such participation did not necessarily lead to further empowerment because of the exclusive focus on capital works projects, which may have inspired less interest among many low-income residents and residents of color than program funds would have (Pape & Lim, 2019, p. 876).

Finding evidence that engagement with North American PB spills over into other forms of political and civic participation has been thorny for several reasons: There are fewer processes in the region to study comparatively, operating as they do on a smaller scale means that the magnitude of their effects may be relatively subtle, and they inherently encounter the methodological challenges of estimating the effects of an experience that people self-select into. As an important exception, Johnson et al. (2023) offer perhaps the only study to date that investigates the effect of participating in PB in the US on a subsequent political activity: voting in regular elections. The authors report, "[c]omparing PB voters to similar individuals that we would expect to have participated in PB if they had the chance, we find that engaging with PB increased individuals' predicted probability of voting by 8.4 percentage points on average" (Johnson et al., 2023, p. 5). These effects were stronger for a number of groups that are often underrepresented: people under thirty years of age, people from neighborhoods with lower incomes or formal educational attainment, and African Americans.

Evidence for the empowerment thesis has been more compelling among a subset of Brazilian PB processes. Not surprisingly, considerable research has focused on the notable case of Porto Alegre. After an early round of single-case studies, researchers began to use comparative analysis and large-N quantitative studies to detect these kinds of effects for other Brazilian cities – though the impacts have been uneven and complex.

As previously mentioned, PB in Porto Alegre became famous internationally for its ability to elicit the participation of marginalized groups: Poor and working-class residents of the urban periphery were regularly overrepresented as participants (Abers, 1998). Although districts where civil society was already more highly organized saw higher participation during the early cycles, areas of the city with weaker associative traditions eventually began to engage more heavily and, after a few years, had higher rates of participation (Avritzer, 2009, p. 92). At an individual level, about a fifth of participants reported having no prior affiliation in civil society (Baiocchi, 2005, pp. 14–15). Nylen (2002), on the other hand, found a slightly different situation with respect to budget delegates in the cases of Belo Horizonte and Betim. Most

PB budget delegates may have become more civically active after becoming involved in PB, but usually they already had some degree of engagement. Participatory experiments, Nylen (2002) has written, "may be more efficacious in sustaining and developing existing nonelite political activism than in empowering disengaged or alienated citizens" (p. 135).

The empowerment thesis gains even greater traction for Brazilian cities when considering impacts on the growth of civil society organizations. Baiocchi (2003) has argued that PB "itself has helped spark growth in civil society, serving as sort of an incubator to new organizations" (p. 43). Abers (1998, p. 529) has found that after five or six years many new civic groups had sprouted in districts that previously had little civic activity. Baiocchi (2003) studied activism in one district where it was particularly underdeveloped and noted that the number of neighborhood associations grew from four in 1998 to twenty-eight in 2001. Touchton and Wampler (2014) replicated the finding that adopting PB boosted the density of civil society organizations with a large-N study using a dataset of all Brazilian municipalities consisting of greater than 100,000 residents.

Baiocchi et al. (2011) extended this research question to other Brazilian cities using quasi-experimental comparative methods. By comparing four cities where the PT narrowly won mayoral elections and subsequently implemented PB to four comparable cities where the PT narrowly lost and no PB program was launched, the authors attempted to minimize the potential for the relationship between PB implementation and outcomes in civil society to be confounded by an unobserved variable, such as some political factor that both prompts cities to initiate social change and to adopt PB. All four of the cities that adopted PB "experienced a shift in the form of engagement from traditional forms of discretionary and personalized engagement to more participatory and institutionalized modes, albeit with varying degree of success" (Baiocchi et al., 2011, p. 107). They explained this divergence with the argument that "PB reforms do open up spaces for civil society, but that impact is contingent on the preexisting state of civil society ... [in particular] the capacity for autonomous organizing" (Baiocchi et al., 2011, p. 107). Cities with weak associational traditions saw their newly formed organizations remain dependent on the state-sponsored participatory process, while those cities with a stronger history of activism saw their local organizations develop further without such a loss of autonomy.

Other works have echoed the finding that successful PB cases produced not only a quantitative growth in civil society but also a qualitative shift in the nature of activism. Baiocchi (2005) found that the institutionalized nature of engagement with PB prompted civil society organizations to grow in membership and activity level but decline in contentiousness and the frequency of protest actions (pp. 25–26). Wampler's (2012) survey of over 800 PB delegates in large Brazilian cities concluded that civil society organizations used PB to engage in direct negotiations with other organizations and to form solidaristic alliances that then carried over into action in other institutional contexts outside of PB. Wampler (2012) argues that this dynamic "helps to undercut traditional clientelistic practices while also empowering citizens and enhancing the quality of democracy" (p. 341).

These findings on the potential of PB to build community power are based on Brazil's most successful cases. However, under Workers' Party administrations in the 1990s, there was substantial variation in outcomes. For example, Wampler (2008) characterizes the PB programs in Santo André and São Paulo as "co-opted participatory democracy" because PB was used less to transform policymaking processes than to legitimate the government's own priorities with the token participation of its more active supporters. Blumenau and Rio Claro constituted "emasculated participatory democracy" because the administrations did not invest adequate resources in PB and civil society organizations did not demand meaningful participatory reforms (pp. 72–75).

Although localities with weaker associational lives can experience increases in civil society activity (e.g., Baiocchi, 2005, p. 57), it is generally accepted that more active and dense networks of voluntary associations support more successful PB processes (e.g., Avritzer, 2009). Moreover, the nature of civil society activity matters: Wampler (2008) stresses the influence of their use of contentious activity (e.g., protests), while Baiocchi et al. (2011) emphasize their autonomy from the state. In settings that lack autonomous civil society organizations, participatory institutions may engage marginalized populations, but they are likely to remain dependent on affirmative state support; where PB engages communities with a history of associationalism, a "mobilized democracy" may emerge in which organizations determine their own goals and engage the state through institutionalized demand-making (Baiocchi et al., 2011, p. 137).

Research on Psychological Empowerment

Although classic critiques of direct democracy suggest that ordinary citizens lack the proclivity or capability to take active roles in public decision-making, proponents of participatory democracy contend that these qualities are variable. Engaging with well-designed democratic experiments can be a transformative experience for people. Thus, in addition to impacts on the community power structure discussed previously, early research on PB in Brazilian cities also examined psychological changes among the individuals who participated. Researchers asked whether PB works as a school of democracy that builds participants' "deliberative capacities and dispositions" (Wright & Fung, 2003, p. 32). Whereas this question of psychological empowerment has been less central to later research on PB in North American cities, it is the primary theme of emerging work on school-based and youth-targeted PB.

Reviewing the survey literature, Wampler et al. (2017) write, "[a] variety of case studies assert that PB participants feel empowered, support democracy, view the government as more effective, and better understand budget and government processes after participating in PB" (p. 23). Wampler's (2007) survey asked Brazilian PB delegates about the level of authority that they believe delegates exercise and whose support is most needed to realize their budgetary goals. Responses to the authority questions indicate that participants did in fact "feel that they are being empowered to make decisions" (p. 73). Responses emphasizing the need to garner the support of other delegates or civil society actors rather than political officials imply that participants "engage in intra- and inter-group negotiations during PB's negotiation phase and then group pressure politics to encourage the government to fulfill their commitment to PB" (p. 74).

Ethnographic work has been able to document changes in participants' capacities and dispositions in more detail. Baiocchi (2005) found that participants in Porto Alegre deepened their knowledge of municipal administration and budgeting while developing skills involved in debating and mobilizing resources (p. 43). Abers (1998) similarly documented learning processes within Porto Alegre's PB, from how to facilitate a meeting to how to deliberate productively and congenially. Perhaps more profound was an attitudinal transformation. People who initially took part in the process to advocate for the particular concerns of their neighborhood began to support district-wide goals over time. "Through participation," Abers concluded, "people began not only to feel solidarity for others but also began to see their own interests more broadly" (1998, p. 528).

Participatory budgeting programs practiced within schools are currently proliferating rapidly in the US as a means to cultivate civic education experientially by engaging students with real issues in their community (Bartlett & Schugurensky, 2021; see also Chapter 20). Although the literature on school PB is at an incipient stage, the work that has been done is focused squarely on psychological empowerment. This is also true for research on youth PB programs, which are far less common (youth PB programs are processes that exclusively engage young people and are administered outside of schools). For instance, Augsberger et al.'s (2019) study of Boston's Youth Lead the Change explicitly aligned with Zimmerman's (1995) psychological empowerment framework. Based on interviews, focus groups, and observations, the authors highlight opportunities for and constraints to empowerment in youth PB designs, with the promising finding that participants reported "feeling in charge of the process, understanding and allocating resources, and influencing positive community change" (p. 462) (see also Chapter 10).

School PB is an especially promising context in which to study the effects of PB on psychological empowerment because it represents a smaller-scale environment for social interaction that is arguably far more meaningful for students than city government is for adults. Young people lack nearly any opportunity for civic engagement, so what happens when they are given a chance to take part in decisions over investments on their campus? Cohen et al. (2015) examined the first school PB process in the US at Bioscience High School in Phoenix, Arizona, during the 2013–2014 academic year through interviews and a pre–post survey that included twenty indicators of student knowledge, attitudes, skills, and practices. Bartlett and Schugurensky (2021) expanded this instrument to forty indicators in a study of two Arizona school PB processes designed to be inclusive of youth with disabilities. They concluded that students who participated "reported experiencing a greater sense of belonging and collaboration, an increase in psychological empowerment, and better relationships with their teachers and peers" (p. 65). With school PB growing rapidly in the US (at over 150 processes as of 2021), there is an opportunity for larger-scale studies using comparative methods. Coordinating research with the rollout of new PB programs in multiple schools could even take advantage of experimental methods to provide more rigorous evidence than has so far been obtained.

Conclusion: Strengthening Participatory Democracy

Over the past three decades, experimentation with PB has shown that the institutional design has the potential to help catalyze processes of community empowerment and contribute to a range of positive social and governance outcomes. At the same time, results have been uneven. Cases in which PB has played an integral role in moving toward empowered participatory governance are vastly outnumbered by cases that are, at best, small-scale novelties in urban infrastructure planning or, at worst, avenues of ineffectual participation that distract from more meaningful forms of collective mobilization. This reinforces Baiocchi and Ganuza's (2014) contention that while most iterations of PB that spread internationally have generally fostered "open, transparent, and egalitarian communication" (p. 43), at the same time most have abandoned the "empowerment dimension" that links citizen participation to substantial state resources and to an important range of policies through an institutionalized process.

For the cases in which PB has played a prominent role in community empowerment, how does the process work? Abers (1998) has identified mechanisms internal to the functioning of PB in Porto Alegre. The prospect of power over budgeting provides incentives for residents to participate, while PB's institutionalized procedures and accompanying outreach efforts reduce the costs of individual participation. Once drawn in, the experience of deliberation and cooperative action fosters civic skills, builds ties of trust and reciprocity, and enlarges worldviews to consider the needs of other neighborhoods and the implications for distributional justice. After investment projects that prioritize the needs of the marginalized are successfully implemented, a demonstration effect encourages more people to take part.

In addition to this internal process, successful PB programs can take on interactive dynamics with external political transformations. Support for PB by the Workers' Party helped build its reputation for being a different kind of political party than its more clientelistic competitors. In Porto Alegre in particular, PB was central to the popularity of the Workers' Party mayoral administrations, and it built public support for policies like raising taxes that furthered these administrations' redistributive agenda (Baiocchi, 2003, p. 65). More generally, Touchton et al. (2021) have found that the launch of PB programs in Brazil led to significantly higher levels of tax compliance in comparison to similar cities without PB, suggesting that PB had strengthened the legitimacy of the local state where it was implemented.

Thus, the most successful PB programs have been part of larger progressive political transformations. If the latter cannot be easily willed into existence, how can PB be qualitatively strengthened? Wampler and Hartz-Karp (2012) caution that there is no simple list of "best practices," and Cabannes (2015) argues that there is no "blueprint" that can perfect PB. Nevertheless, Wampler et al. (2017, p. 16) highlight key factors within government that are associated with successful PB outcomes, such as support from elected officials that act as PB champions, the presence of adequate state capacity, and the use of internal rules that promote inclusive and robust participation. More broadly, Baiocchi and Ganuza (2014) argue that rather than advocating for PB as a value-neutral end in itself, reclaiming PB's transformative potential entails connecting PB to other movements for social justice for deepening democratic control over the state and for reimagining cities. Most plainly, essentially all PB scholars agree that the process is stronger when it controls major public resources rather than small pots of discretionary money for urban infrastructure.

Although the literature on PB has developed substantially, there remain fertile agendas for further research. More robust data on the impacts of PB would strengthen the case for expanding it, but the proliferation of PB processes that lack the commitment of political energy and public resources makes it difficult to document such effects. Still, Wampler et al. (2017, pp. 49–50) suggest three areas that researchers should continue to pursue: explaining variation in implementation and outcomes within and between countries; surveying citizens' attitudes toward PB, particularly with pre–post research designs and through tracking participants who drop out; and comparing the merits of rules and decision-making processes between PB programs. To this list can be added the need to study novel variations of PB, such as school PB and themed PB.

Participatory budgeting responds to the following challenge: Does addressing the major obstacles to justice of our day – heightening economic inequality, the persistence of racial oppression, worsening ecological destruction, the need to invest in inclusive, sustainable cities, and so on – require broad public participation, or can they be addressed adequately through processes of representative democratic institutions and technocratic governance? In other words, could the right representatives and administrators sustain progress across these issue areas in the absence of an active and organized populace pressing for reform? To the extent that contemporary challenges require decision-making processes that are enriched by the input of those people who are closest to their impacts, these issues will likely be made more tractable by participatory democratic processes like PB. To the extent that such transformations challenge entrenched interests, they will surely require the countervailing force of active mobilization of broad swathes of the public – which, if the empowerment thesis is correct, can be helped along through empowered participatory governance.

Even if the PB programs currently operating appear too modest to address these issues, their institutional design does contain promise when it can be matched to a broader political project and scaled up. Engaging substantially more people to participate in policymaking may be essential to making reforms effective and politically sustainable, even if revitalizing the institutions of representative democracy is also necessary. Again, Porto Alegre's case is illustrative: The Workers' Party lacked a majority in the city council but found that delegating power to citizens in a democratic process lent legitimacy to progressive priorities while building community power in the process. In other words, PB strengthened the social basis for redistribution. In this way, PB is hardly a panacea, but it can be a key part of an ecology of institutions that democratize the state and economy. The demonstrated viability of PB strengthens the case for expanding democratic control over more resources and creating more spaces for community members to directly shape policymaking.

References

Abers, R. (1998). From clientelism to cooperation: Local government, participatory policy, and civic organizing in Porto Alegre, Brazil. *Politics & Society, 26*(4), 511–537.

Allegretti, G., & Copello, K. (2018). Winding around money issues. What's new in PB and which windows of opportunity are being opened? In N. Dias (Ed.), *Hope for democracy: 50 years of participatory budgeting worldwide* (pp. 35–53). Oficina.

Augsberger, A., Gecker, W., & Collins, M. E. (2019). "We make a direct impact on people's lives": Youth empowerment in the context of a youth-led Participatory Budgeting Project. *Journal of Community Psychology, 47*(3), 462–476.

Avritzer, L. (2009). *Democracy and the public space in Latin America*. Princeton University Press.

Baiocchi, G. (2003). Participation, activism, and politics: The Porto Alegre experiment. In A. Fung & E. O. Wright (Eds.), *Deepening democracy: Institutional innovations in empowered participatory governance* (pp. 45–76). Verso.

Baiocchi, G. (2005). *Militants and citizens*. Stanford University Press.

Baiocchi, G., & Ganuza, E. (2014). Participatory budgeting as if emancipation mattered. *Politics & Society*, *42*(1), 29–50.

Baiocchi, G., Heller, P., & Silva, M. K. (2011). *Bootstrapping democracy: Transforming local governance and civil society in Brazil*. Stanford University Press.

Bartlett, T., & Schugurensky, D. (2021). Reinventing Freire in the 21st century: Citizenship education, student voice and school participatory budgeting. *Current Issues in Comparative Education*, *23*(2), 55–79.

Bourdieu, P. (1993). *Language and symbolic power*. Harvard University Press.

Cabannes, Y. (2015). No blueprint for participatory budgeting: The challenge of diversity. In Y. Cabannes & C. Delgado (Eds.), *Another city is possible! Alternatives to the city as commodity: Participatory budgeting* (pp. 29–40). Charles Leopold Mayer Foundation.

Cohen, M., Schugurensky, D., & Wiek, A. (2015). Citizenship education through participatory budgeting: The case of Bioscience High School in Phoenix, Arizona. *Curriculum and Teaching*, *30*(2), 5–26.

Community Development Project. (2015). *A people's budget: A research and evaluation report on participatory budgeting in New York City*. Community Development Project. https://cdp.urbanjustice.org/sites/default/files/pbreport.pdf

Democracy Beyond Elections. (2021). *Case study: Community-driven zoning and development in Chicago's 35th Ward*. Democracy Beyond Elections. www.democracybeyondelections.org/portfolio/community-driven-zoning-and-development-in-chicagos-35th-ward/

Dias, N. (2018). *Hope for democracy: 50 years of participatory budgeting worldwide*. Oficina.

Dias, N., Enríquez, S., & Júlio, S. (2019). *Participatory budgeting world atlas*. Oficina.

Dryzek, J. S., Bächtiger, A., Chambers, S., Cohen, J., Druckman, J. N., Felicetti, A., ... Warren, M. E. (2019). The crisis of democracy and the science of deliberation. *Science*, *363*(6432), 1144–1146.

Fung, A. (2003). Deliberative democracy, Chicago style: Grass-roots governance in policing and public education. In A. Fung & E. O. Wright (Eds.), *Deepening democracy: Institutional innovations in empowered participatory governance* (pp. 111–143). Verso.

Fung, A., & Wright, E. O. (2003). Thinking about empowered participatory governance. In A. Fung & E. O. Wright (Eds.), *Deepening democracy: Institutional innovations in empowered participatory governance* (pp. 3–42). Verso.

Goldfrank, B., & Landes, K. (2018). Participatory budgeting in Canada and the United States. In N. Dias (Ed.), *Hope for democracy: 50 years of participatory budgeting worldwide* (pp. 161–176). Oficina.

Goldfrank, B., & Schneider, A. (2006). Competitive institution building: The PT and participatory budgeting in Rio Grande do Sul. *Latin American Politics and Society*, *48*(03), 1–31.

Gonçalves, S. (2014). The effects of participatory budgeting on municipal expenditures and infant mortality in Brazil. *World Development*, *53*, 94–110.

Gordon, V., Osgood, J., & Boden, D. (2016). Participatory budgeting in the United States. In N. Dias (Ed.), *Participatory budgeting in the United States* (pp. 161–176). Routledge.

Habermas, J. (1996). *Between facts and norms: Contributions to a discourse theory of law and democracy*. MIT Press.

Hayduk, R., Hackett, K., & Folla, D. T. (2017). Immigrant engagement in participatory budgeting in New York City. *New Political Science, 39*(1), 76–94.

Isaac, T. M. T., & Heller, P. (2003). Democracy and development: Decentralized planning in Kerala. In A. Fung & E. O. Wright (Eds.), *Deepening democracy: Institutional innovations in empowered participatory governance* (pp. 77–110). Verso.

Johnson, C., & Gastil, J. (2015). Variations of institutional design for empowered deliberation. *Journal of Deliberative Democracy, 11*(1), 2.

Johnson, C., Carlson, H. J., & Reynolds, S. (2023). Testing the participation hypothesis: Evidence from participatory budgeting. *Political Behavior, 45*, 3–32.

Kasdan, A. (2019). *Case studies on expanding democracy beyond elections*. Democracy Beyond Elections. www.democracybeyondelections.org/portfolio/democracy-beyond-elections-case-studies/

Kogan, V., & McGhee, E. (2012). Redistricting California: An evaluation of the Citizens Commission final plans. *California Journal of Politics and Policy, 4* (1), 1–22.

Landemore, H. (2015). Inclusive constitution-making: The Icelandic experiment. *Journal of Political Philosophy, 23*(2), 166–191.

Marquetti, A. (2000). Participatory budgeting in Porto Alegre. *Indicator SA, 17*(4), 71–77.

McNulty, S. (2018). Mandating PB: Evaluating fifteen years of Peru's national participatory budgeting law. In N. Dias (Ed.), *Hope for democracy: 50 years of participatory budgeting worldwide* (pp. 147–160). Oficina.

Movement for Black Lives. (2022). *Participatory budgeting at the local, state & federal level*. Movement for Black Lives. https://m4bl.org/wp-content/uploads/2020/05/ParticipatoryBudgeting-OnePager.pdf

NAACP. (2019). *Our communities, our power: Advancing resistance and resilience in climate change adaptation*. NAACP.

Nuñez, T. (2018). Porto Alegre, from a role model to a crisis. In N. Dias (Ed.), *Hope for democracy: 50 years of participatory budgeting worldwide* (pp. 517–535). Oficina.

Nylen, W. R. (2002). Testing the empowerment thesis: The participatory budget in Belo Horizonte and Betim, Brazil. *Comparative Politics, 34*(2), 127.

Pape, M., & Lim, C. (2019). Beyond the "usual suspects"? Reimagining democracy with participatory budgeting in Chicago. *Sociological Forum, 34*(4), 861–882.

Participatory Budgeting Project. (2021). *Where is PB happening?* Participatory Budgeting Project. www.participatorybudgeting.org/case-studies

Public Agenda. (2016, October 5). *Public spending, by the people: Participatory budgeting in the United States and Canada in 2014–15*. Public Agenda. https://publicagenda.org/resource/public-spending-by-the-people-participatory-budgeting-in-the-united-states-and-canada-in-2014-15/

Putnam, R. D. (1995). Bowling alone: America's declining social capital. *Journal of Democracy, 6*(1), 65–78.

Saad, R. (2020). *Internet voting and the equity of participatory budgeting outcomes: A study of New York City's Participatory Budgeting Initiative*. The Graduate

Center, City University of New York. https://academicworks.cuny.edu/gc_etds/3810

Su, C. (2017). Beyond inclusion: Critical race theory and participatory budgeting. *New Political Science*, *39*(1), 126–142.

Touchton, M., & Wampler, B. (2014). Improving social well-being through new democratic institutions. *Comparative Political Studies*, *47*(10), 1442–1469.

Touchton, M., McNulty, S., & Wampler, B. (2023). Participatory budgeting and community development: A global perspective. *American Behavioral Scientist*, *67*(4), 520–536.

Touchton, M., Wampler, B., & Peixoto, T. (2021). Of democratic governance and revenue: Participatory institutions and tax generation in Brazil. *Governance*, *34*(4), 1193–1212.

Wampler, B. (2007). Can participatory institutions promote pluralism? Mobilizing low-income citizens in Brazil. *Studies in Comparative International Development*, *41*(4), 57–78.

Wampler, B. (2008). When does participatory democracy deepen the quality of democracy? Lessons from Brazil. *Comparative Politics*, *41*(1), 61–81.

Wampler, B. (2012). Entering the state: Civil society activism and participatory governance in Brazil. *Political Studies*, *60*(2), 341–362.

Wampler, B., & Avritzer, L. (2004). Participatory publics: Civil society and new institutions in democratic Brazil. *Comparative Politics*, *36*(3), 291.

Wampler, B., & Hartz-Karp, J. (2012). Participatory budgeting: Diffusion and outcomes across the world. *Journal of Deliberative Democracy*, *8*(2), 13.

Wampler, B., & Touchton, M. (2019). Designing institutions to improve well-being: Participation, deliberation and institutionalisation. *European Journal of Political Research*, *58*, 915–937.

Wampler, B., McNulty, S., & Touchton, M. (2017, October 13). *Participatory budgeting: Spreading across the globe*. Open Government Partnership. www.opengovpartnership.org/stories/participatory-budgeting-spreading-across-the-globe/

Wright, E. O. (2010). *Envisioning real utopias*. Verso.

Zimmerman, M. A. (1995). Psychological empowerment: Issues and illustrations. *American Journal of Community Psychology*, *23*(5), 581–599.

9 Participatory Urban Planning

Daniel G. Cooper

Introduction

In many of the world's cities, urban planning efforts attempt to guide the future growth and development of the built environment, offering a variable range of opportunities for citizen participation. Although there are many types of plans, from comprehensive plans for large metropolitan areas all the way down to small areas and neighborhoods, the citywide plan is a unique setting where residents and different interest groups alike exercise power to influence what the city will look like in the future. In the modern era, Daniel Burnham's 1909 *Plan of Chicago* is often cited as a seminal example of a citywide plan (Burnham, 2009). It established a vision and guidelines for the future growth and development of the US city of Chicago – including infrastructure, green space, civic and cultural institutions, transportation, and more – while also embedding the process of larger-scale planning into the DNA of modern cities for the next century and beyond. Much of this aspirational vision from over 100 years ago can be observed in the city's built environment today. A citywide plan is important not only for setting a vision for the future development of a city, but it also serves as a foundation for the many legal mechanisms that dictate urban development, such as building and zoning codes and many other built environment guidelines.

Much has changed since the 1909 *Plan of Chicago*. Urban planning has evolved to include many different types of plans and settings. Urban landscapes across the globe have developed in ways that continue to improve well-being and population health, but they have done so unevenly. Nowhere is this more apparent than in Chicago, which is one of the most racially and economically segregated cities in the US. As with most metropolitan areas across the world, much of this inequality can be traced back to yesterday's planning and policy decisions. The power to participate in planning decisions has historically been concentrated among elite and wealthy interests, resulting in many of today's most pressing urban challenges and inequities: segregation, environmental injustice, displacement, and a lack of transportation and affordable housing, to name just a few. Urban planning, and citywide plans more specifically, have the potential to reshape the built environment in ways that address these historical inequities, but they are highly contested settings that feature struggles for power and influence. This chapter examines power and empowerment within urban planning settings, with a particular focus on attempts to establish participatory planning processes. First, it reviews the history and evolution of participation in planning efforts in cities across the globe. It then considers how power and empowerment manifest within these settings, with examples drawn from the recently adopted *We Will Chicago* citywide plan (https://wewillchicago.com). Finally, it concludes with reflections on how urban planning settings can more effectively reduce power imbalances within cities rather than amplify them.

A Brief History of Planning and Participation

Public participation has long been a component of urban planning theory and practice, and most planning endeavors aspire to engage the public, at least to some degree, in strategies and decisions. Arnstein's (1969) ladder of citizen participation outlined a spectrum of participation in planning that is still frequently used today. The typology ranges from nonparticipation, or empty rituals of participation (where officials, at worst, engage participants in a manipulative manner), to token forms of participation (e.g., consultation with citizens whose input does not actually influence outcomes), all the way up to full resident power and control over policy and development decisions. Full resident power and control remain elusive aspirations in most planning processes given the complexities and power structures within and across communities and the broader citizenry. Nonetheless, resident control remains an important aspiration for many communities, especially given a long history in which residents – particularly low-income residents of color – have not had a seat at the table where planning and policy decisions are made.

Early city planning efforts in the modern era were less exercises in democratic expression and participation than they were top-down visions from architects, engineers, and city boosters. Barcelona's 1859 plan is often cited as the first modern city plan. It helped integrate the medieval city with its modern expansion through a vast street grid system and uniform building heights (Urbano, 2016). Although the plan was envisioned as a response to the growing social problems resulting from urbanization, its vision and policy mechanisms were entirely expert-driven.

Similarly, the 1909 *Plan of Chicago*, despite often being lauded as an inspiring vision that helped shape the future of Chicago, was largely driven by elite interests who stood to benefit from the plan's strategies and central goal of making the city more economically competitive. It was a top-down approach that sought to establish order and social control at a time when cities were experiencing rapid growth in immigrant populations, laborers were organizing for more power, and unfettered development created squalid conditions right alongside the rapidly growing centers of capital and commerce (Smith, 2006). Although the plan did envision a city where all residents had access to open spaces, it ignored the many challenges experienced by residents, such as overcrowded housing, poverty, and the growing inequalities apparent in everyday life (McCabe, 2016). Decades later, renowned US urban theorist Jane Jacobs would criticize the plan for the degree to which it ignored the human scale and the vibrancy experienced every day by people in neighborhoods (Jacobs, 1961). Nevertheless, it helped establish the importance of the larger-scale citywide plan, as much of Chicago's subsequent development can be traced back to the plan's vision.

Over time, planning evolved to encompass much more than citywide frameworks and visions to include more specific regulations about land use. Many of the most consequential decisions related to development concern land-use planning. These decisions and plans can be comprehensive in scale or concerned with individual parcels of land. The rules and regulations that dictate what type of land use is allowed have outsized influence on how the built environment develops over time. They are ultimately responsible for "districts" with a predominant use (e.g., manufacturing) and the character of a neighborhood (e.g., single-family homes with yards). Land-use regulations – which include tools such as zoning that dictate what density, structures, and features are allowable – are also the mechanisms through which many of the racial disparities in the built environment were historically codified, with little or no possibility for participation and community voice. For example, Chicago's first comprehensive zoning ordinance, passed in 1923, has been shown to be responsible for the sorting of non-White residents into industrial areas of the city – early development patterns that shaped land value and wealth accumulation potentials over time and led to disparate generational health outcomes (Shertzer et al., 2018).

Challenges to top-down planning for communities eventually emerged – notably, in the US, in response to inequitable urban renewal projects that disproportionately impacted low-income communities of color. US civil rights movements ushered in an era of new demands for community participation and control of planning and development decisions. Federal urban policy in the middle of the twentieth century ultimately served to abandon Black neighborhoods, first through redlining – the refusal of banks to lend to Black homeowners – and then through urban renewal projects that decimated Black urban neighborhoods and left inner US cities in decline (Metzger, 2010). Federal subsidies, investments, and planning efforts focused on the newly sprawling suburbs, subsidizing the flight of White families away from urban neighborhoods. Civil rights organizing efforts developed in response to these inequitable investment and development practices. At the same time, in Latin America, people's and Indigenous movements increasingly rejected top-down planning policies that were often characterized by nonexistent or token forms of community participation, instead seeking self-management of development but also more political power (Guaraldo Choguill, 1996).

Community participation and empowerment became increasingly embedded in the language of urban planning during this time, as the field began to embrace ideas of equity, advocacy, and pluralism (Davidoff, 1965). Planning efforts with an advocacy orientation were often built around the idea that the role of the planner in civil society was to help build capacity and empower communities by incorporating more collaborative processes. Empowerment was seen as both a precursor to successful planning and an outcome of a successful planning process (Bailey, 2010; Sager, 2022). Although there are examples of advocacy planning achieving some positive outcomes for poor and marginalized communities and using planning methods that creatively engage participants (e.g., design workshops), such approaches do not typically build sustainable power and influence (Forester & Krumholz, 2003; Sager, 2022). Nonetheless, equity and advocacy planning marked an important turn toward institutionalizing the focus on equitable outcomes for poor and marginalized communities.

Meanwhile, outside of the US, other important trends related to participation in planning and development decisions were also occurring. Porto Alegre, Brazil, became the first city to implement participatory budgeting in 1989, where residents participated in democratic exercises to determine how the city would allocate its resources (Marquetti et al., 2012). Participatory budgeting has since spread to cities all over the world, with Latin America accounting for the largest share (see Chapter 8). Although largely heralded as a successful innovation in city governance, successfully engaging the poorest and most marginalized populations, and shifting power away from traditionally dominant groups are challenges that nonetheless remain for participatory budgeting and planning efforts (Kuruppu et al., 2016).

If it is true that the historical arc of urban planning has continued to bend toward aspirations of deeper participation and collaboration, it is also true that participation has not historically resulted in many changes to power structures in cities or equitable outcomes for low-income communities of color. Planning efforts often fail to acknowledge the long history of well-intentioned engagement and numerous plans that have resulted in little progress on deep-seated inequities in the built environment (Mitlin, 2021). Not only do most participatory planning processes not acknowledge this history, but they also often simply reproduce power differentials. Participation in local government and planning policies in the US skews toward older, Whiter, male, homeowner populations, who are more likely to oppose policies such as new affordable housing construction that could benefit lower-income residents of color (Levine Einstein et al., 2018). In setting after setting where participatory planning takes place, this trend holds true. Whiter, more socioeconomically advantaged residents use participatory planning processes to wield influence in ways that preserve the status quo, whether it be zoning exclusively for single-family homes in neighborhoods with pricey real estate or opposition to any other type of land use that is deemed undesirable.

Negative Consequences of Planning Decisions

For all the common good that city planning efforts have aspired to do, they have, in the past, also helped create many of the social and racial inequities that are a common feature of modern cities. Racial segregation in the US has long been a function of land- use regulations made in the service of protecting the property values of White homeowners (Massey & Rugh, 2017; Trounstine, 2018). Early zoning laws in US cities were used as methods for segregating families of color into slums, excluding them from wealthier suburbs, and ultimately transferring wealth from Black urban neighborhoods to White suburbs (Rothstein, 2014). During the period of urban renewal in the middle of the twentieth century, there were few (in some places no) opportunities for Black residents to participate in planning processes that might result in neighborhood improvements. Instead, top-down decisions were made by policymakers and planners about neighborhood demolitions to make way for new highways. In city after city, highways were disproportionately built through Black neighborhoods, leaving many families displaced and otherwise cut off from downtown business centers (Mallach, 2018). Zoning then became a tool to locate undesirable land uses in poor neighborhoods of color. In many cities across the US, manufacturing and polluting industries were permitted disproportionately near Black neighborhoods, resulting in myriad health disparities (Brulle & Pellow, 2006; Maantay, 2002).

Segregation, baked into the urban landscape from years of planning and policy decisions, has itself, over time, become a predictor of continued divestment, leaving many neighborhoods stuck in cycles of decline. City governments have shown little appetite for addressing this historical problem. In fact, there is evidence that they are less inclined to do so and actually spend less on public goods that could improve the lives of low-income residents of color in segregated places where minority populations have made gains in representation on city councils (Trounstine, 2016). Although these historical inequities are a well-known feature of the built environment and planning history, planning practices and settings have largely failed to provide pathways to meaningfully correct past injustices. Indeed, many planning processes continue to reproduce longstanding inequities. For example, many of the same communities of color that were the sites of slum clearance during the period of urban renewal and decades of long-standing disinvestment are now the sites of new zoning changes and developments that threaten to displace long-term residents who have remained (Papazekos, 2022). Without planning policies that break the cycles of disinvestment caused by segregation and the outsized influence of advantaged homeowning populations, equity in planning will remain elusive.

Current Planning Settings and Structures

Planning settings in cities are so numerous, diverse, and opaque that one of the first challenges residents must navigate is figuring out how and where to participate. Little uniformity exits, and each setting features a constellation of organizations and stakeholders who exert power and influence. One common feature is that most settings are hyperlocal in nature, are facilitated by formal government, and are often spaces where conflict is prevalent. Even larger-scale plans, such as citywide or comprehensive plans, when they happen, invite participation through neighborhood-level settings. It is very common for cities to create and regularly update comprehensive plans aimed at influencing land use, zoning, and transportation at a citywide scale. But there are many other local planning settings for community participation and input on built environment decisions. For example, new developments that require a change in zoning – necessary when a property owner wants to build a structure with a different type of density or use than is currently allowed by the zoning code – often require notification to nearby residents and, potentially, provide a forum for residents to express their support or opposition. Such forums, however, are inconsistent across and within cities. Similarly, major transportation projects often include public input sessions to consult with residents who will be impacted by planned changes. Decision-making authority in such settings typically rests somewhere within local or regional government – a planning department, planning commission, city council member, or transportation authority, for example. Community residents exert power and influence as stakeholder participants or through formal and informal organizations. Although this type of setting may feature tokenistic forms of participation, it is often where the power of socioeconomically advantaged residents is exercised. So-called NIMBY ("not in my backyard") interests are consistently effective at exercising sufficient opposition to block certain projects from happening in their neighborhood by generating organized pressure on local officials (Payton Scally & Tighe, 2015).

Neighborhood plans provide another setting in which residents participate and exercise power over built environment decisions. Neighborhood plans may or may not be a part of a larger citywide-scale plan, and they can be facilitated by government and nonprofit and private organizations alike. These local "neighborhood," "community," or "area" planning settings are highly variable in terms of structure, participation, and influence. Local plans led by a nonprofit community organization may engage residents with the goal of more influence and control but lack the institutional power and influence for recommendations to be formally implemented (Chaskin, 2005). Some cities have successfully incorporated local neighborhood planning into larger-scale plans. For instance, Sirianni (2007) documented how Seattle's comprehensive planning effort in the 1990s effectively built relationships and neighborhood planning infrastructure that resulted in the adoption of thirty-seven new neighborhood plans, with some measure of successful implementation. Participatory budgeting processes, noted earlier, are yet another setting where residents have the opportunity to influence the allocation of resources for built environment improvements, which may or may not be associated with other local plans (Lehtonen, 2022).

Equity-Focused Trends in Planning and Participation

As cities across the world continue to produce and update both local and comprehensive plans, several important broad trends have emerged with the potential to correct past planning injustices. One is the emergence of health impact assessments (HIAs). Generally, HIAs are processes used to examine the likely effects of policies, programs, or projects on the health of a population (Collins & Koplan, 2009). Increased recognition of how the built environment affects health and health disparities has led to increased use of HIA in urban planning decision-making (Moore et al., 2018). Closely related to HIAs, there has been a proliferation of equity goals, policies, and metrics in urban plans (Pineo et al., 2018). Whereas plans in the past have published goals for growth or sustainability (e.g., producing new housing units or increasing transportation access), more planning efforts are now incorporating HIAs, health indicators, and equity goals. These typically focus on matching strategies and policies with goals to reduce racial health disparities and close equity gaps in areas such as housing, transportation, and other measures of economic and health well-being (Heller et al., 2014; Ross et al., 2012).

Regarding community participation, many cities strive to improve their community engagement and outreach practices. Although this is a common trend, very few cities have worked to standardize engagement practices across all departments and settings, although many have recognized the importance of equitable engagement across all neighborhoods (Sirianni, 2007). Truly inclusive and standardized community engagement requires significant resource allocation and commitment to iterative processes of community input. Additional community engagement trends in US planning include ensuring opportunities for resident voices that have historically been marginalized, creating governance structures that allow residents to define their roles in the process, and providing accessible and consistent engagement processes. Other features include proactive outreach to community organizations regarding any proposed land-use changes, as well as participatory budgeting to determine neighborhood-level investments (Metropolitan Planning Council, 2020).

Power and Empowerment in Participatory Urban Planning

Community influence over development decisions may be an aspirational goal of participatory urban planning, but such efforts are often set up in ways that simply reproduce existing inequitable power structures within communities. Plans do not always influence the totality of laws, policies, and practices that shape the development of the built environment. They also rarely acknowledge power structures, let alone seek to transform them. What is more, there are many policy mechanisms, government entities, and processes adjacent to planning that are ultimately responsible for development changes, all with unique pathways of power and influence. For example, even though a government planning department may establish principles related to the development of new affordable housing, zoning and land-use decisions made by a separate set of actors can ultimately dictate where such development does and does not take place (often granting exceptions to specific developers or landowners). All of this adds up to a complex relationship between citizen participation, empowerment, and power in planning settings. For participatory planning to succeed in shifting power and influence toward residents, and particularly toward marginalized and disadvantaged communities, an important starting point is an understanding and acknowledgment of how power has historically operated in planning settings and processes.

Christens (2019) presents a conceptual model for studying how empowerment processes can lead to more collective social power for marginalized groups, which can create systems and policy changes that ultimately improve population health and well-being. Urban planning efforts represent a unique category of setting to examine how these pathways to social power and equitable outcomes can play out. Critical to the understanding of this model in a planning context is both the theoretical pathways as well as the myriad ways that power is enacted in an oppositional manner to preserve the status quo at each step of the way. This begins with opportunity structures that allow more equitable and democratic participation of traditionally marginalized groups, to the building of relationships and social power, all the way through the crafting of rules and policies that govern development. Along this continuum, various actors and systems wield power in ways that can serve to minimize the potential influence of marginalized groups.

The term "empowerment" in urban planning settings is frequently centered on the ability of citizens to participate in built or natural environment planning and the extent of decision-making authority these opportunities provide (UN-Habitat, 2018). The International Association of Public Participation (IAP2) adapted Arnstein's (1969) original participation model into a condensed five-level framework (inform, consult, involve, collaborate, empower) to rate public participation in urban planning efforts (IAP2, 2018). The fifth level of participation, "empower," involves placing final decision-making fully into the hands of the community or participants – for example, through ballots or delegated decision authority. One systematic international literature review of public participation in urban planning efforts found that participation did not rise to the level of the "empowerment" by this definition in any of the more than 100 planning case studies reviewed (Foroughi et al., 2023). The most frequent level of participation was level 3, "involve." These processes typically employ methods like workshops, collecting preference input through polling, and working directly with stakeholders to understand concerns but not necessarily allowing participants to build sustainable relationships with each other that result in increased social power (Garcia et al., 2017).

The literature on participation in urban planning is rich with discussions of participation methods, including novel uses of technology, but comparatively light on analysis of whether processes are empowering, and even lighter on tying such efforts to building durable resident power and influence. Scholars have also acknowledged that efforts to involve citizens in planning often fall well short of their intended goals in terms of both resident engagement and influence (Bailey et al., 2011). Traditionally marginalized groups often do not perceive there to be sufficient opportunities for participation in planning processes and feel that outcomes do not center their interests (Silverman et al., 2019). Studies often focus on how to improve the processes and experiences of participation, such as improving outreach and communication methods, accessibility, and the use of visual and analytical tools (Munster et al., 2017). Some go a step further and consider how citizen participation improves the civic knowledge and skills of participants, which are ultimately building blocks of a healthy deliberative democracy (Michels & De Graaf, 2010). Others have identified the many barriers to equitable participation that exist for citizens, including the stage at which participation is solicited, the types of participation sought, the commitment and availability of local authorities, and the convenience of participation structures (MacLaran et al., 2018). Such features of planning processes are ultimately critical precursors to more equitable participation. For instance, when stakeholders are engaged late in a process, after much of the planning framework and goals have already been established, there may be little room for meaningful power and influence.

Gaps clearly exist in both theory and practice related to power-building in planning settings. One of the reasons for this is an inherent tension and contradiction in processes that are typically designed, developed, and facilitated by government institutions rather than grassroots organizations or organized citizens. That is, participation structures are almost always formal rather than spontaneous or organized (Romariz Peixoto et al., 2022). Citywide-scale plans add another level of complexity in that they are often focused on high-level systems and principles and have long time frames between the forming of the plan and when development actually occurs. If participation opportunities are structured only to solicit input into the formation of the plan, without continuous involvement and follow-up evaluation and accountability, any social power and influence that could be built among participants is not likely to be sustainable.

Participation in planning efforts, like any social change setting involving policymakers, carries with it a paradox for participants, who have to choose between cooperation and opposition. Successfully collaborating with planning professionals, policymakers, local organizations, and other citizens is critical for establishing the relationships necessary to build power and effect change. However, pushing to dismantle any inequitable status quo that benefits powerful interests will necessarily involve conflict when those interests inevitably push back (Speer, 2008). Building social power involves competency in navigating how to successfully collaborate at times and organize in opposition at others (Christens & Inzeo, 2015). In some planning settings, the opportunities to participate can be prescriptive and limited (e.g., a finite number of meetings with residents to gather input on proposed design concepts). If urban planning efforts are to create pathways for power-building, opportunity structures for deeper participation are necessary across the life of an effort and in terms of structures, processes, and outcomes.

Transforming planning and policy systems to be more responsive to the needs of marginalized communities and populations is a critical step on the pathway to greater health and well-being. The evidence is clear on how the built environment and corresponding policies influence population health: Zoning and land-use policies in urban areas have historically led to negative economic and health outcomes for low-income communities of color (Rothstein, 2014; Walz & Fron, 2018). Bachrach and Baratz's (1970) conceptualization of the two faces of community power and Lukes' (2005) three-dimensional model of power are particularly useful in describing how power is wielded in ways to prevent systems from being more responsive to low-income communities of color. The most recognizable or first "face" of community power is the broader and observable ecosystem of institutions and actors who have influence in urban policies. Elite business groups, homeowners, and government officials, as well as coalitions of such actors, have historically had outsized power to influence policies that shape the built environment (Gilens & Page, 2014; Trounstine, 2018). This dimension of power is where the most visible conflicts take place – for example, homeowner groups who show up to a public forum and loudly voice their concern about affordable housing negatively impacting their neighborhood in an attempt to block a new development. Such a scenario is common in participatory planning efforts.

The second, less visible face of power, however, is perhaps even more important in preserving the status quo. Here lies a web of rules and processes that can effectively limit input, debate, and development possibilities. For example, zoning and land-use laws dictate what can be built on a parcel of land, who approves any changes to those regulations, and who has input into any changes. The public face of governmental authority may be the specific actor who has the power to approve or deny a proposed development, but planning rules and policies – special planning districts and tax-increment finance districts, to name a few, all with different public input processes that are prescriptive – limit the potential scope of public input and power. Finally, Lukes' (2005) notion of a third dimension (or "face") of power concerning pervasive narratives and myths is also critical to understanding how the status quo of power is maintained in planning settings. This third dimension can reliably be observed across US cities with new proposed affordable housing developments. Myths about public safety, traffic, and parking are often centered in the public discourse despite a lack of evidence or evidence to the contrary, and government bodies often reject new developments on the basis of such negative and fear-based narratives (National Fair Housing Alliance, 2019; Trounstine, 2018). Further, efforts to enact any progressive urban development policies are likely to be confronted with similar narratives and myths (i.e., it is common for investors and developers to threaten to refuse to make new investments if new affordable housing requirements are proposed by a city government).

No single participatory planning effort can change the totality of policies, structures, and processes that limit the power of marginalized communities to build power and influence over built environment decisions. However, a citywide planning process can help lay a foundation for more opportunity structures for residents and communities that have historically borne the brunt of racist and inequitable planning decisions and policies. It can broaden the scope of the types of principles and outcomes a plan seeks to change, broaden the continued opportunities for community input into development decisions, and identify the rules and processes that need to be changed to be more responsive and restorative to communities historically harmed by planning policies. The next section provides a case example of a recently completed citywide plan in Chicago, including the mechanisms of participation, the dynamics of power and influence within the planning process, and its potential blueprint to change planning and development policies in the future to center equitable outcomes for marginalized communities.

Case Example: *We Will Chicago* Citywide Plan

Background and Historical Reckoning

At a citywide scale, comprehensive plans represent one of the most common planning practices in US cities and ultimately influence land-use regulations across entire cities. Most cities produce and update such plans at least every decade. Chicago is an outlier in the sense that its most recent comprehensive plan was completed more than half a century ago (in 1966) and was never actually adopted formally by the city. It was a top-down vision aimed at guiding new development that was hoped to result from a large flow of federal investments in cities at the time. Although it may have served as an internal framework to guide some city decisions, its influence on the development of the city was marginal. Federal funds to cities dried up shortly thereafter, and the city's planning efforts were largely regulatory ever since. There have been many plans produced since then, but no citywide-scale plans, and none at such a large scale that sought deep resident input (Bailly & Harris, 2020).

In 2020, the City of Chicago began to develop a framework for a new citywide plan. In preparation for the effort, they, alongside the Metropolitan Planning Council (MPC), a nonprofit planning organization, established a participatory process for deciding how to shape the planning framework – that is, *preplanning*, or how to invite participation, and the methods for how participation would shape the final plan. The MPC and the City's Department of Planning and Development convened workshops featuring staff from different US peer cities to help Chicago stakeholders – planning officials and community, civic, and private-sector stakeholders – learn about the challenges and successes faced in creating citywide plans elsewhere. Among the topics discussed was how each planning process engaged residents and built trust, evaluated the equity impacts of plans and policies, and collaborated across agencies. Findings and recommendations from this pre-planning phase were summarized by the MPC in a public report, and these key themes were used to guide the development of how Chicago's citywide planning process would be structured (Metropolitan Planning Council, 2020). Three of the themes most central to the focus of the citywide plan were Historical Reckoning and Trust Building, Systematic Evaluation of Equity Impacts, and Accessible and Meaningful Community Engagement. These were core to how the City of Chicago would approach the work of creating the citywide plan in collaboration with stakeholders.

The City of Chicago then worked with a consultant team to invite broad swaths of community-based organizations, interest groups, and residents to take part in virtual discussions around a range of different topics. These online conversations helped inform participants about citywide planning processes and provided a platform for input into the topics on which the City of Chicago should structure its citywide plan. Participants ultimately provided recommendations through interviews, structured conversations, and surveys for what the city should focus on. Many of the interactions took place online, as the COVID-19 pandemic had ushered in a new era of remote work and events. More than 600 Chicago residents weighed in on what they thought the plan should accomplish, and these conversations ultimately formed the basis of the key "pillar areas" of the plan. During preplanning, the consultant team also reviewed more than 300 past plans authored by the city and other institutions to better understand the topic areas these plans focused on to provide some continuity. The vast majority of these plans were released in the past twenty years and ranged from neighborhood or area, to specific issues (e.g., transportation, housing), to regional in scale. The plans were authored by more than thirty different agencies or entities. Of these plans, none had proposed major goals that were specific to equity, resiliency, or acknowledged past injustices related to planning and policy.

Moving out of the preplanning phase into active planning, the City of Chicago convened seven distinct research teams by topic, or "pillar area," with the purpose of collaborating to help shape the objectives and recommendations of the plan and identify past harms and inequitable outcomes that resulted from government planning and policy decisions. They also convened an overall Advisory Committee that helped provide greater structure and accountability to the planning process by serving as a sounding board and reviewing the work of the research teams. These research teams consisted of 115 volunteer resident participants, 25 community-based organizations, and approximately 100 city staff, all with specific interests or expertise. Volunteer participants were selected via an open application process, with selection criteria focused on ensuring broad and diverse representation across the city's communities and interest groups. The final plan includes objectives and goals that were developed in collaboration with the research teams as well as a detailed historical overview, or *reckoning*, of all the past planning inequities, which echoed one of the five themes of the preplanning process. Equity, as one of the guiding principles of the overall planning process, was also firmly centered in all the plan's recommendations so that the goals and objectives were targeted to address and reverse some of these past harms. The acknowledged historical harms included land stolen from Indigenous people, historical treatment of Native Americans, urban renewal, destruction of public housing, redlining, housing covenants and contract buying, school closures in neighborhoods of color, over-policing in neighborhoods of color, industrial pollution, downtown development at the expense of neighborhoods, and race-related data exclusion.

Participation, Equity, and Power in the *We Will Chicago* Citywide Plan

Along with the volunteer research teams who helped guide research into each of the plan's "pillar areas," seventy-two local in-person and virtual events were convened by volunteer organizers and Chicago artists, attracting more than 5,000 participants who weighed in with specific policy recommendations (see Figure 9.1). Critically, partnering with stakeholders and organizations at events across different communities resulted in greater participation by communities of color, who had traditionally been underrepresented. Once the plan's potential goals, objectives, and policy recommendations were drafted, they were presented to the public to review and comment on electronically over the course of 2022. Overall, more than 10,000 comments were received, with a reported 90 percent of respondents expressing support for the planning framework, which was officially adopted by the Chicago Planning Commission in early 2023.

There are several participation features in the *We Will Chicago* plan that were unique among planning settings. The first was that a significant amount of collaborative work took place to establish the opportunity structures for

Figure 9.1 *Participatory planning workshop in Chicago.*
Photo credit: *Matt Altstiel, Metropolitan Planning Council.*

participation in the actual planning process. The opportunity to learn from peer cities and the ability of a broad range of stakeholders (community-based organizations, philanthropy, etc.) to provide input into how the City of Chicago should ultimately structure all aspects of its planning process were unique features of the *We Will Chicago* plan. This preplanning phase of collaboration allowed more forums for stakeholders to voice concerns and convey desires about aspects of the planning process. The need for a "historical reckoning" with past planning and policy decisions was a theme that emerged during this phase and was determined to be of critical importance to stakeholders. It was not enough to just publish a new plan with lofty goals. Stakeholders wanted an acknowledgment of inequitable past planning and policy decisions to inform future priorities and commitments and an opportunity to frame the discussion of such past inequities. The work of the different volunteer research teams in identifying past planning injustices was compiled and included as its own section in the final plan.

Additionally, the City of Chicago included outside reviewers as part of its process to ensure that its compilation of historic planning inequities matched the perspectives of the communities harmed. As part of its efforts, the MPC convened a Historical Acknowledgment Working Group to provide feedback on its inclusion in the citywide plan. This group reviewed an initial draft copy of the Historical Reckoning section and provided recommendations on the representation of events and information that should be included but was missing. As a result, the City of Chicago made changes to the plan to better reflect community concerns, including adding in a section that more extensively documented the harms to Native American populations, which was originally absent.

A second important feature was that participating stakeholders worked to identify methods and processes for addressing the historical planning harms and for ensuring that new goals and policies had equitable impacts. An example of how this ultimately manifested in the final plan is in the proposed use of health and racial equity impact assessments to ensure that future policy decisions are likely to facilitate positive health benefits and, in general, to positively impact communities of color that were the victims of past built environment injustices (Gurin-Sands, 2022). The City of Chicago had already been one of the first US cities to utilize a racial equity impact assessment to analyze and determine its policy goals (Chicago Department of Housing, 2021), and the recently published citywide plan calls for further institutionalizing the practice, along with publishing data and metrics to determine progress on racial equity across multiple dimensions.

A final unique feature of the plan is that the City of Chicago, late in the process, added an eighth "pillar" for civic and community engagement to prioritize it just as much as any other area of focus (other pillar areas included housing, economic development, and transportation, which are more typical of a citywide plan). This was largely the result of participants and stakeholders repeatedly requesting a deeper focus on engagement and the City responding to this feedback. Further, this also largely resulted from the City's efforts to engage more stakeholders in the planning process in the first place. Community partners received stipends to participate on research teams as well as host their own events so that more residents could ultimately provide input into the plan. The MPC also helped the City create a meeting toolkit, translated into multiple languages, so that anyone could host a community planning session on their own with input that would influence the plan's goals and objectives. In the end, broader participation early on led to the deeper prioritization of civic and community engagement in the final published plan, with the Advisory Committee helping to define its recommendations.

The final plan outlines a number of goals, objectives, and policy ideas in this area. Highlights included creating stronger long-term partnerships with organizations and coalitions to continue to build more participation opportunities, standardizing engagement across City departments, providing more equitable virtual and in-person access to all City business, and establishing standards and structures for community-driven decision-making, among many others. The policy recommendations for civic and community engagement, if fully implemented, have the potential to transform how plans and policies are developed in the City of Chicago in the future. The commitment to regularly publish data and metrics that track progress on racial equity in the city – including participation and engagement – could also help stakeholders organize around a shared understanding of goals and challenges.

In terms of social power, the *We Will Chicago* planning process engaged residents, organizations, and stakeholders who are not the elite economic interests that have traditionally wielded the most influence over the development of cities. This is reflected in the plan's guiding principle of equity, its focus on a historical reckoning with past racial inequities, and its identification of approaches to address them. In this sense, the plan broadened the frame from what had typically been considered in urban planning processes. The process included new opportunity structures for historically marginalized stakeholders to participate and shape the final goals, objectives, and policy recommendations, including stipends to community organizations for their participation. The final plan also has the potential to shift narratives about the purpose of urban planning and how success should be measured. Rather than reinforcing elite narratives about development, the plan advances the notion that the mechanisms of urban planning should, at least in part, identify and address previously inequitable policies and establish methods and goals to ensure equitable impacts of policies in the future. Applying Lukes' (2005) three-dimensional power framework, the planning process involved shifts in the second and third "faces" of power, which can often be determinative of dynamics in the first dimension.

In applying the IAP2 "ladder of participation" to *We Will Chicago*, it is clear that in many respects the process went beyond merely "involving" residents, which is the most common type of participation in such endeavors (IAP2, 2018). What remains to be seen is whether Chicago's comprehensive plan will have any enduring influence over the myriad mechanisms that comprise the second "face" of power. Citywide plans are aspirational frameworks that seek to guide the future development of cities. However, there nonetheless remain many rules, policies, and practices that are ultimately responsible for both large and small changes to the built environment. Although citywide plans can help create new opportunity structures for participation and social power, they do not, alone, ensure sustainable shifts in influence, power, and built environment policy. Reforms to the many adjacent urban planning policies and practices – the second face of power – are needed for any deep-seated equitable changes to take place, and such changes are likely to take place over a much longer time horizon.

Discussion and Conclusions

Urban areas across the globe share many features. One of the most common such features is that planning and development decisions have historically favored wealthy and powerful interests, resulting in stark inequalities in the built environment and negative impacts and disparate outcomes for low-income, marginalized communities. City planning efforts by themselves may not challenge the broader political economy and capitalist forces that drive urban inequality, but they do influence some of the mechanisms that shape and maintain it. More opportunity structures for civic and community engagement in establishing citywide goals is, at the very least, a first step in transforming some of these mechanisms. Many practitioners in the field of urban planning have aspired to provide opportunity structures for residents to build social power and exert greater control over built environment policies that affect their lives, yet most planning efforts fail to live up to promises of empowerment and local control. The case example of Chicago's *We Will* citywide plan illustrates that progress in shifting power and influence away from the status quo in urban planning settings is complex and will likely happen slowly, over increments. A citywide plan can provide an important ideological blueprint, but it is only a starting point – a roadmap to identify the myriad processes and policies that need to be changed if planning settings are to facilitate equitable outcomes. Implementing the goals and objectives of a plan in an equitable manner requires continued opportunity structures for deeper civic and community participation.

Social movements have often been wary of city government. Decisions, both local and citywide, provide an impetus for reactive organizing. Participation in a comprehensive or citywide plan places residents and organizations in a difficult position of navigating the tension of cooperation versus confrontation. On the one hand, collaborating with public officials provides opportunities for building relationships and influence with city government. On the other hand, participation may not always be a route to building more collective, oppositional community power. However, the risks of the latter are lower in a citywide planning process, as the final product is an aspirational framework rather than a final policy implementation. It can be argued that the relationships built across stakeholders and public officials could ultimately be useful in future organizing efforts. If future policies do not reflect the vision of the plan, for example, relationships and power built throughout the planning process could prove instrumental in organizing to hold government officials accountable.

One area where participatory citywide planning can have an impact is shaping the third dimension of power, or the long-held myths and narratives that effectively limit what changes can be made in planning settings. Chicago's *We Will* plan made strides in acknowledging the historically unjust and racist outcomes that came from the planning efforts of decades past. This seemingly small victory is important to ensuring that the goals and outcomes of a plan are not limited from the beginning. In many planning efforts, the second face of power operates in ways that limit goals and leave status quo processes in place, which narrows the scope of outcomes that can be considered by participating in planning. Acknowledging the unjust outcomes of previous planning processes opens the door for centering equitable outcomes in the future. Chicago's *We Will* plan does just this, setting the stage for transforming opportunity structures for residents at many different levels. It is, however, just a first step. Building sustainable social power will necessarily involve continuous changes to adjacent planning processes such as zoning and participation structures at neighborhood-levels, with outcomes always explicitly centering equity.

Finally, it is clear that more research is needed to understand the relationship between planning processes, social power, the ways that they affect decision-making about the built environment, and the ways that this ultimately affects community well-being. In particular, basic evaluation processes need to be built into planning efforts to understand not only participant-level outcomes but also the degree to which residents are effectively building relationships with planners and other decision-makers as well as with each other and with grassroots organizations. Methods such as social network analysis could be helpful in mapping power and relationships to help hold decision-makers accountable to more equitable planning goals. Without clear mechanisms for evaluating plans against the lofty goals of repairing the harm of past plans, there is always a risk of continuing to reinforce the status quo.

References

Arnstein, S. A. (1969). A ladder of citizen participation. *Journal of the American Institute of Planners, 35*(4), 216–224.

Bachrach, P., & Baratz, M. S. (1970). *Power and poverty: Theory and practice*. Oxford University Press.

Bailey, K., Blandford, B., & Ripy, J. (2011). Planning, technology, and legitimacy: Structured public involvement in integrated transportation and land-use planning in the United States. *Environment and Planning B: Urban Analytics and City Science, 38*(3), 447–467.

Bailey, N. (2010). Understanding community empowerment in urban regeneration and planning in England: Putting policy and practice in context. *Planning Practice and Research, 25*(3), 317–332.

Bailly, J., & Harris, C. (2020, October 19). *Looking back to move forward: Chicago's planning landscape defined*. Metropolitan Planning Council. www.metroplanning.org/news/9947/Looking-back-to-move-forward-Chicagos-planning-landscape-defined

Brulle, R. J., & Pellow, D. N. (2006). Environmental justice: Human health and environmental inequalities. *Annual Review of Public Health, 27*, 103–124.

Burnham, D. (2009). *Plan of Chicago* (centennial ed.). Great Books Foundation.

Chaskin, R. J. (2005). Democracy and bureaucracy in a community planning process. *Journal of Planning Education and Research, 24*(4), 408–419.

Chicago Department of Housing. (2021). *Racial equity impact assessment: Qualified action plan*. City of Chicago. www.chicago.gov/content/dam/city/depts/doh/qap/qap_2021/draft_reia_qap.pdf

Christens, B. D. (2019). *Community power and empowerment*. Oxford University Press.

Christens, B. D., & Inzeo, P. T. (2015). Widening the view: Situating collective impact among frameworks for community-led change. *Community Development, 46*(4), 420–435.

Collins, J., & Koplan, J. P. (2009). Health impact assessment. *JAMA: The Journal of the American Medical Association, 302*(3), 315–317.

Davidoff, P. (1965). Advocacy and pluralism in planning. *Journal of the American Institute of Planners, 31*(4), 331–338.

Forester, J., & Krumholz, N. (2003). *Making equity planning work: Leadership in the public sector*. Temple University Press.

Foroughi, M., de Andrade, B., Pereira Rodgers, A., & Wang, T. (2023). Public participation and consensus-building in urban planning from the lens of heritage planning: A systematic literature review. *Cities, 135*, 104235.

Garcia, X., Benages-Albert, M., Pavon, D., Ribas, A, Garcia-Aymerich, J., & Vall-Casas, P. (2017). Public participation GIS for assessing landscape values and improvement preferences in urban stream corridors. *Applied Geography, 87*, 184–196.

Gilens, M., & Page, B. (2014). Testing theories of American politics: Elites, interest groups, and average citizens. *Perspectives on Politics, 12*(3), 564–581.

Guaraldo Choguill, M. B. (1996). A ladder of community participation for underdeveloped countries. *Habitat International, 20*(3), 431–444.

Gurin-Sands, C. (2022, March 21). *We Will Chicago: Translating policies into actions through HREIA*. Metropolitan Planning Council. www.metroplanning.org/news/10326/We-Will-Chicago-translating-policies-into-actions-through-HREIA

Heller, J., Givens, M., Yuen, T., Gould, S., Jandu, M., Bourcier, E., & Choi, T. (2014). Advancing efforts to achieve health equity: Equity metrics for health impact assessment practice. *International Journal of Environmental Research and Public Health, 11*(11), 11054–11064.

IAP2. (2018). *IAP2 spectrum of public participation*. International Association of Public Participation. http://cdn.ymaws.com/www.iap2.org/resource/resmgr/pillars/Spectrum_8.5x11_Print.pdf

Jacobs, J. (1961). *The death and life of great American cities*. Random House.

Kuruppu, C., Adhikari, P., Gunarathna, V., Ambalangodage, D., Perera, P., & Karunarathna, C. (2016). Participatory budgeting in a Sri Lankan urban council: A practice of power and domination. *Critical Perspectives on Accounting, 41*, 1–17.

Lehtonen, P. (2022). Policy on the move: The enabling settings of participation in participatory budgeting. *Policy Studies, 43*(5), 1036–1054.

Levine Einstein, K., Palmer, M., & Glick, D. M. (2018). Who participates in local government? Evidence from meeting minutes. *Perspectives on Politics, 17*(1), 28–46.

Lukes, S. (2005). *Power: A radical view* (2nd ed.). Palgrave Macmillan.

Maantay, J. (2002). Zoning law, health, and environmental justice: What's the connection? *Journal of Law, Medicine, and Ethics, 30*(4), 572–593.

MacLaran, A., Clayton, V., & Brudell, P. (2018). *Empowering communities in disadvantaged urban areas: Towards greater community participation in Irish urban planning? Final report*. Palala Press.

Mallach, A. (2018). *The divided city: Poverty and prosperity in urban America*. Island Press.

Marquetti, A., Schonerwald da Silva, C. E., & Campbell, A. (2012). Participatory economic democracy in action: Participatory budgeting in Porto Alegre, 1989–2004, *Review of Radical Political Economics, 44*(1), 62–81.

Massey, D. S., & Rugh, J. (2017). The intersections of race and class: Zoning, affordable housing, and segregation in U.S. metropolitan areas. In G. D. Squires (Ed.), *The fight for fair housing* (2nd ed.) (pp. 245–265). Routledge.

McCabe, M. P. (2016). Building the planning consensus: The plan of Chicago, civic boosterism, and urban reform in Chicago, 1893 to 1915. *The American Journal of Economics and Sociology, 75*(1), 116–148.

Metropolitan Planning Council. (2020). *We Will Chicago: Co-creating an inclusive process.* Metropolitan Planning Council. www.metroplanning.org/uploads/cms/documents/peerworkshops_wewillchicago_appendix_new.pdf

Metzger, J. (2010). Planned abandonment: The neighborhood life-cycle theory and national urban policy. *Housing Policy Debate, 11*(1), 7–40.

Michels, A., & De Graaf, L. (2010). Examining citizen participation: Local participatory policy making and democracy. *Local Government Studies, 36*(4), 477–491.

Mitlin, D. (2021). Editorial: Citizen participation in planning: From the neighbourhood to the city. *Environment & Urbanization, 33*(2), 295–309.

Moore, T. H. M., Kesten, J. M., López-López, J. A., Ijaz, S., McAleenan, A., Richards, A., Gray, S., Savović, J., & Audrey, S. (2018). The effects of changes to the built environment on the mental health and well-being of adults: Systematic review. *Health and Place, 53*(June), 237–257.

Munster, S., Georgi, C., Heijne, K., Klamert, K., Rainer Noennig, J., Pump, M., Stelzle, B., & van der Meer, H. (2017). How to involve inhabitants in urban design planning by using digital tools? An overview on a state of the art, key challenges and promising approaches. *Procedia Computer Science, 112*, 2391–2405.

National Fair Housing Alliance. (2019). *Defending against unprecedented attacks on fair housing: 2019 fair housing trends report.* National Fair Housing Alliance. https://nationalfairhousing.org/wp-content/uploads/2019/10/2019-Trends-Report.pdf

Papazekos, T. (2022). Power play goal: Analyzing zoning law and reparations as remedies to historic displacement in Pittsburgh's Hill District. *Georgetown Journal on Poverty Law and Policy, 29*(3), 407–430.

Payton Scally, C., & Tighe, J. R. (2015). Democracy in action?: NIMBY as impediment to equitable affordable housing siting. *Housing Studies, 30*(5), 749–769.

Pineo, H., Glonti, K., Rutter, H., Zimmermann, N., Wilkinson, P., & Davies, M. (2018). Urban health indicator tools of the physical environment: A systematic review. *Journal of Urban Health, 95*(5), 613–646.

Romariz Peixoto, L., Rectem, L., & Pouleur, J. A. (2022). Citizen participation in architecture and urban planning confronted with Arnstein's ladder: Four experiments into popular neighbourhoods of Hainaut demonstrate another hierarchy. *Architecture, 2*(1), 114–134.

Ross, C. L., Leone de Nie, K., Dannenberg, A. L., Beck, L. F., Marcus, M. J., & Barringer, J. (2012). Health impact assessment of the Atlanta Beltline. *American Journal of Preventive Medicine, 42*(3), 203–213.

Rothstein, R. (2014). *The color of law: A forgotten history of how our government segregated America.* Norton.

Sager, T. (2022). Advocacy planning: Were expectations fulfilled? *Planning Perspectives, 37*(6), 1205–1230.

Shertzer, A., Twinam, T., & Walsh, R. P. (2018). Zoning and the economic geography of cities. *Journal of Urban Economics, 105,* 20–39.

Silverman, R. M., Louis Taylor, Jr., H., Yin, L., & Miller, C. (2019). Are we still going through the empty ritual of participation? Inner-city residents' and other grassroots stakeholders' perceptions of public input and neighborhood revitalization. *Critical Sociology, 46*(3), 1–16.

Sirianni, C. (2007). Neighborhood planning as collaborative democratic design: The case of Seattle. *Journal of the American Planning Association, 73*(4), 373–387.

Smith, C. (2006). *The plan of Chicago: Daniel Burnham and the remaking of the American city.* University of Chicago Press.

Speer, P. W. (2008). Social power and forms of change: Implications for psychopolitical validity. *Journal of Community Psychology, 36*(2), 199–213.

Trounstine, J. (2016). Segregation and inequality in public goods. *American Journal of Political Science, 60*(3), 709–725.

Trounstine, J. (2018). *Segregation by design: Local politics and inequality in American cities.* Cambridge University Press.

UN-Habitat. (2018). *SDG indicator 11.3.2 training module: Civic participation in urban planning and management.* United Nations Human Settlement Programme (UN-Habitat). https://unhabitat.org/sites/default/files/2021/08/indicator_11.3.2_training_module_civic_participation.pdf

Urbano, J. (2016). The Cerdà plan for the expansion of Barcelona: A model for modern city planning, *Focus: The Journal of Planning Practice and Education, 12*(1), 13.

Walz, K., & Fron, P. (2018). The color of power: How local control over the siting of affordable housing shapes America. *DePaul Journal for Social Justice, 12*(1), 3.

10 Youth Policy Advocacy in Municipal Governance

Astraea Augsberger and Mary Elizabeth Collins

Introduction

Youth participation in community life is important for youth, the community, and the broader society. There are many different ways for youth to participate. In this chapter we focus on the specific model of youth participation in policy advocacy through the mechanism of municipal youth councils. Youth councils are generally connected to ongoing governmental institutions. This characteristic distinguishes them from other ways by which youth provide input to community decision-making.

Although there is great variation among youth councils (Martin et al., 2007), Taft and Gordon (2013, p. 4) identify the following commonalities: Youth councils connect young people to policymakers, participating youth are considered experts on youth issues, councils work on issues of policy related to youth (but not typically other policy areas), they are formalized and usually part of the government structure, they are authorized by statute or executive order, they have adult staff to support the work, and they meet on a regular basis. Although we will use the term "youth council," which we find to be the most common name, these entities might be known by names such as "youth commission," "youth advisory board," "youth task force," or something similar (Collins et al., 2016). We provide primary attention to youth councils attached to municipal governments but will also comment on their utility in other settings and for specialized populations.

All societies have some structures and norms for how youth are integrated into community life and how they can appropriately participate. Zeldin et al. (2007) provide some context for the discussion of young peoples' role in governance in the US. Young people have had a diminished role in society as a result of industrialization, and the consequences include an increased emphasis on formal schooling and a decreased emphasis on youth employment. This has led to young people and adults operating in separate domains for large parts of their time. As a result, "society loses the contribution that all youth could make to the well-being of communities, and many adolescents lose adult guidance and the opportunities for personal development that emanate from taking on valued community roles and responsibilities" (Zeldin et al., 2007, p. 78).

There are many ways in which the voices of young people can be included in governance. Our focus on municipal youth councils does not negate the importance of other venues for youth civic engagement. Taft and Gordon (2013), in their comparison of the youth council model to youth activism, have articulated some of the criticisms of a youth council model: mainly that youth councils are not designed to promote empowerment but rather "produce and reproduce a particular political order and particular types of citizens" (p. 88). The authors report that (1) while youth are given voice on youth councils, they are limited in terms of their overall impact on community and social problems, (2) youth councils are "elite" spaces that are not representative of all youth and, in particular, youth who are disadvantaged by political institutions, and (3) youth are limited in terms of power-sharing with adults and having agency in decision-making.

Despite these criticisms, research has identified some important benefits to the youth council model. Specifically, young people are brought into munici-pal buildings, given opportunities to learn how policymaking works, asked to consult on or contribute to policy decision-making, and gain access to poten-tial career paths and mentors (Collins et al., 2016). This type of engagement can influence a young person's understanding of government and potentially increase their motivation for future political engagement, including careers in government service (Augsberger et al., 2017b; Cohen & Chaffee, 2013). In reflecting on the benefits and criticisms of the youth council model, it is critical that efforts to engage youth in community governance recognize these tensions and take steps to address them (e.g., in terms of training adults, their power structure, and their decision-making opportunities), as will be discussed later in the chapter.

Although much research on youth involvement in community governance has focused on the impacts on youth in terms of their own development (e.g., Finlay, 2010), the argument for robust youth engagement is the potential for its organized youth impact to benefit the wider population of youth, such as in local planning decisions (e.g., Mansfield et al., 2021) and in building a healthy and inclusive democracy (Nairn et al., 2006). For example, youth councils can represent the voices of the wider youth community to key governmental and community decision-makers. This can result in, for example, improvements in youth recreational spaces, increased job opportunities for youth, and youth-centered communications about local events (Collins et al., 2016).

Very limited research has been conducted to determine the effect of youth engagement in policy advocacy on the community and/or larger society. For the most part, scholars have demonstrated the limitations of these efforts, suggesting that there has been little impact on policy outcomes (e.g., Adu-Gyamfi, 2013). We will return to this important point in a discussion of further research later in this chapter. Here we note a few potential explanations for such limited impact. In a multiple-case study (Feringa & Tonkens, 2017) conducted in the Netherlands that was specifically focused on various participation styles in local youth councils, the researchers found that youth participation was predominantly "internally focused" rather than focused on deliberation about civic issues or issues affecting other young people. The researchers concluded that the councils "do not at present meet the purposes of international policy" (p. 55): that is, increasing young people's participation in democracy by representing the needs of young people more broadly. As another example, Nir and Perry-Hazan (2016) studied eight Israeli youth councils and found that the council activities were largely confined to the specific municipal department responsible for youth and mostly comprised the organization of parties, performances, and trips for youth. Contacts with other municipal staff outside of the specific youth department were determined to be sporadic and concerned with the leisure activities that the youth councils organized. The authors characterized this as "framed participation," which confined the power of youth councils only to a delimited area of decision-making (Nir & Perry-Hazan, 2016).

It is evident and notable that youth councils are rarely developed at the initiative of youth themselves. In our earlier work studying twenty-four youth councils in the Boston Metropolitan Area, we found that none were formed by young people. Rather, adults typically raised concerns about a youth-focused issue in the community (e.g., substance use, suicide, community violence) and formed youth councils to help address these issues (Collins et al., 2016). This is consistent with other research on youth councils (Matthews & Limb, 1998) noting that youth engagement is directly related to the interest of adults.

Organizational Structure

Collins et al. (2016) studied twenty-four municipal youth councils in the Boston area. The purpose of the youth councils was generally similar across the twenty-four sites: to give a voice to youth in the community so that youth issues can be identified and addressed. But attributes such as size, membership, selection processes, and activities were variable. Variation in the structure, scope, functioning, and activities of youth councils is supported by additional research (Matthews & Limb, 1998; Richards-Schuster & Checkoway, 2009). In part, this great variation is related to the localized nature of youth councils in the US. They rely on the local context in regard to structure, recruitment methods, access to decision-makers, and many other factors. Thus, the extent to which young people have authentic political agency and decision-making power also relies on the specifics of a locality.

Many city youth councils are operated by the municipal government in similar ways to other councils, typically with an adult municipal worker who serves as liaison to the youth council (Collins et al., 2016). In some cases, municipal governments contract with a local community-based agency that has youth expertise to organize and staff the youth council with some mechanism of liaison with the city. Another model might utilize a school-based student council to be tapped to serve in an advisory capacity for the city government. Richards-Schuster and Checkoway (2009) specifically examined organizational structures by providing examples from three Michigan cities. They found that one council had agency advocates that were not formalized as part of the government structure, another had strong mayoral support and a formal charter, and a third was affiliated with a community foundation. In sum, there is no standard youth council model. The structure, function, and activities vary depending on the context, membership, and community needs.

Youth councils also vary in terms of how well their members represent the broader community. Processes of selecting youth council members require significant attention if members are meant to represent the youth of the community. Augsberger et al. (2018) raised cautions about the potential for youth councils to reinforce social inequalities. In their case study of one city's youth council, they found that although there were efforts to achieve proportional representation in terms of race, gender, and neighborhood, the youth council members were all in high school, and many of them were in high-achieving exam schools (Augsberger et al., 2018). Overall, a major criticism of youth councils is that they tend to select academically oriented, often White youth and those already engaged in multiple organized activities. This potentially further marginalizes the voices of disengaged youth and youth of color (Freeman et al., 2003; Matthews, 2001; Nairn et al., 2006; Wyness, 2009).

Prevalence and Trends

To our knowledge, the Manhasset Youth Council (Jostyn, 1945) represents the first written account of a youth council in the US, dating back to 1943. The council was a part of the municipal Recreation Committee and developed as a space for youth to engage in positive leisure activities to prevent them from engaging in delinquent behaviors. No data source exists to identify the number of existing youth councils and determine whether that number is growing or declining. We do know that their existence is not always stable and is often dependent on the commitment of adults in municipal government who value the engagement of youth through this mechanism (Collins et al., 2016).

The National League of Cities compiled a report in 2007 that documented 120 youth councils (including city and state levels) in nineteen states (Martin et al., 2007). They defined youth councils as "formal bodies made up of youth (typically ages 16–18) who advise high-level decision makers and elected officials" (p. 8). Additionally, they identified youth engagement in youth councils as important to identifying youth-relevant issues and determining effective solutions to these issues.

The majority of research on youth councils has involved qualitative case studies of one or a few youth councils. It is therefore challenging to draw firm conclusions from the knowledge base. Cushing and van Vliet (2017) conducted the only study of which we are aware that assessed the state of youth councils across the US. This study collected data from 139 cities using an online survey. Most of the youth councils surveyed (57 percent) had been formed since 2000. Common reasons for forming included to solicit youth input on community issues (62 percent), to provide skills-building and leadership opportunities for youth (41 percent), and to address specific youth-related problems (17 percent). The study also found that the youth councils with longer histories were more likely to indicate that the reason for forming the council was to address youth problems (Cushing & van Vliet, 2017). More recently formed youth councils tended to be informed by the positive youth development and civic engagement literatures and focused on youth assets (e.g., skills-building, leadership development, critical consciousness) rather than deficits.

Although youth councils vary in scale and structure, some research has sought to develop insights into the characteristics that make them effective at engaging young people in local civic and political issues. For instance, Martin et al. (2007) provide several descriptive examples of a range of youth councils at city and state levels, concluding that there is not a "right" way to promote youth participation in local government. They do note that young people who are actively engaged in social change efforts have three core strengths: capacity (knowledge, leadership, and action skills), motivation (understanding and awareness of issues and root causes, systems, strategies for change, commitment, and a sense of responsibility), and opportunity (chances to act on passions, use skills, and generate change through relevant sustained action; p. 11). Youth councils provide opportunities and can facilitate both capacity and motivation.

Youth councils may be more visible in other countries in comparison to the US (e.g., Feldmann-Wojtachnia et al., 2010; Matthews, 2001). This is likely due to the United Nations Convention on the Rights of the Child (UNCRC), which requires attention to be given to the voice and perspectives of young people. This has led many countries to develop formal councils as a means to implement this requirement. The US is not a signatory to the UNCRC and so has not made the same concerted effort to formally engage young people. Several scholars of youth councils outside the US explicitly link the UNCRC to the formation and operation of youth councils even while noting the barriers that still exist (e.g., Nir & Perry-Hazan, 2016).

It is not known how many youth councils are in existence around the globe. Although the references are now somewhat dated, Sant and Davies (2018) summarized the following: At least thirty countries have some sort of national, regional, or local council (Wall, 2011), 1,600 children's city councils were reported in France (Casas et al., 2008), and about 700 councils were found in other individual European countries (e.g., Portugal, Belgium, Italy, Germany, Poland; Hart, 2013). Given the linkage of youth councils with democracy, they are likely to be more prominent in countries with democratic traditions.

Zeldin et al. (2007) argued that "[t]he notion that youth should, or even can, be engaged in community governance is not embedded within the United States culture or policy" (p. 85). We agree with this statement but also suggest that municipal settings may have the best potential for youth engagement in governance. Our anecdotal experience, supported by the practice literature (e.g., National League of Cities, 2020), suggests that many US municipalities have some form of youth council or are interested in developing a youth council. As we noted earlier, interest in developing a youth council rarely comes from youth themselves (Matthews, 2001). Rather, adults may perceive a need to develop a youth council for a variety of reasons (e.g., a rise in youth mental health issues in the community). Furthermore, adults vary in the extent to which they perceive young people as policy actors and have skills to engage with youth on these types of issues. Some adults value this work deeply and can be strong advocates in city government to be more inclusive of youth. Additionally, as principles of positive youth development have taken hold in many governmental systems, funding agencies may now require some mechanism of youth voice. This would be a strong incentive for municipalities to form these councils and provide needed infrastructure to support them.

Another trend is the spreading of the youth council model beyond municipal government to a variety of specialized arenas, such as child welfare (Forenza & Happonen, 2016; Havlicek et al., 2016), health care (Haddad et al., 2020; Moreno et al., 2021), and police services (Komel, 2018). These specialized arenas may have specific benefits in allowing for more focused youth activities (and potentially more direct impact) as well as allowing young people to work on issues of greatest interest to them. As an example, Augsberger et al. (2020) examined youth participation in policy advocacy in the context of the New England Youth Coalition, a group of current and former foster care youth from across New England who advise the commissioners and directors of those states. Youth members of the Coalition identified policy issues specific to youth in foster care (e.g., sibling rights, permanency, and normalcy), gathered information from diverse youth in their respective states, and developed policy and practice solutions that were subsequently adapted by several states. Augsberger et al. (2020) documented key aspects of youth engagement in this context, including direct contact with high-level decision-makers (commissioners and directors), positive relationships with peers who have similar lived experience, support from adult facilitators and allies, focus on meaningful policy projects, and the collective power of working with multiple states to influence policy outcomes.

Exemplar: Boston Mayor's Youth Council

The Boston Mayor's Youth Council was founded in 1994 by Mayor Menino's administration as an advisory board to the Mayor. According to the Council's website (City of Boston, n.d.), it was the first Mayor's youth council in the US and "has spurred cities across the nation, and even internationally to examine how they include youth in local government." The goal of the council is to "connect, engage and empower Boston's diverse youth through government and civic participation."

Membership on the Council is intended to be representative of all neighborhoods in Boston. In 2022, there were three neighborhood working groups that represented youth from nineteen areas of the city (City of Boston, n.d.). There is an application process that uses US Census data to ensure proportional representation of high school-aged youth from all Boston neighborhoods. Council members are selected by youth members and adult allies, confirmed by the Mayor, and are responsible for representing their peers within the Mayor's office, with city officials, and with other community leaders.

The Council initially consisted of thirty-six youth in their junior and senior years of high school. In 2014, there was a redesign of the Council. The redesign began with brainstorming exercises with youth council members focused on the qualities of the council, youth members, adult staff, and the Mayor. The identified goals were more robust engagement of youth and an increase in membership. Three objectives were identified: (1) strengthen communication with neighborhoods (e.g., build community partnerships, conduct regular check-ins with community partners, increase the number of slots (n = 86) to be proportionate with number of youths in neighborhoods), (2) cultivate youth leaders (e.g., drop age requirement to sophomores so they have the opportunity to be on the council longer), and (3) refocus the agenda to develop subcommittees formatted around the city cabinet.

Today, the Council conducts various activities to engage youth in policy advocacy. The Council meets monthly as a larger group and has various subcommittees organized around the Mayor's cabinet that engage in diverse activities. The subcommittees include Art and Culture, Education, Civic Engagement, Climate Action, Public Health, Public Peace, Workforce and Economic Development, and Youth Lead the Change. Each subcommittee has defined goals and establishes projects associated with those goals.

Regarding policy advocacy, youth council members decide which issues to prioritize and work toward positive solutions. One example was the creation of a "one ID" for youth, a photo ID that can be used on the public transportation system, as student ID, for school lunch, and in Boston public libraries. Another example is the Participatory Budgeting Project. Since 2013, the Mayor's Youth Council has engaged in *Youth Lead the Change: Participatory Budgeting Boston*, the first youth-led participatory budgeting

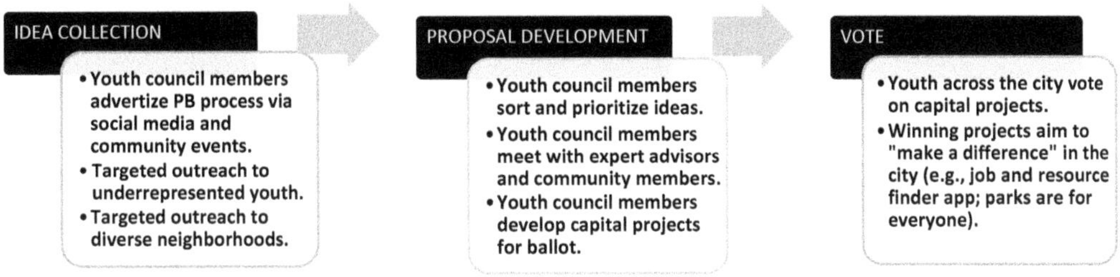

IDEA COLLECTION	PROPOSAL DEVELOPMENT	VOTE
• Youth council members advertize PB process via social media and community events. • Targeted outreach to underrepresented youth. • Targeted outreach to diverse neighborhoods.	• Youth council members sort and prioritize ideas. • Youth council members meet with expert advisors and community members. • Youth council members develop capital projects for ballot.	• Youth across the city vote on capital projects. • Winning projects aim to "make a difference" in the city (e.g., job and resource finder app; parks are for everyone).

Figure 10.1 *Boston's participatory budgeting (PB) process.*

(PB) process in the US. Participatory budgeting is a process that allows citizens to determine how to allocate money from a governmental budget (see Chapter 8). Since the 2013–2014 fiscal year, the Mayor of Boston has set aside $1 million of the capital budget for youth aged twelve to twenty-five to brainstorm/collect issues and priorities, develop capital projects, and vote on the proposals. As a function of their role on the Mayor's Youth Council, youth council members – with the support of adult allies – oversee the PB process.

Figure 10.1 is a visual representation of the three stages of Boston's PB process: idea collection, proposal development and voting, and the role of youth engagement at each stage.

During 2015–2016, we conducted a year-long evaluation of Boston's PB process that included interviews with adult stakeholders, focus groups with youth, observations of youth council meetings, and a review of documents (Augsberger et al., 2017b). We identified key themes related to youth engagement in policy advocacy. The first theme was the *role of adult facilitators* in training, preparing, and supporting youth in the PB process. The adult facilitator in this case was a full-time City Hall staff member assigned to oversee the youth council. He had prior civic engagement experience, including serving as a member of the Boston Mayor's Youth Council. He organized and attended each youth council meeting, providing training and guidance throughout the PB process. In interviews with youth council members, they noted their reliance on the adult facilitator in training and supporting them during each phase of the PB process. Another important theme was the *direct communication* with individuals in leadership positions, including the Mayor and City Hall staff, throughout the PB process. The youth experienced this interaction with key leaders to be both instructional (e.g., in determining which capital projects were feasible and understanding city government processes) and legitimized their role as advisors to the Mayor. Another key theme was the importance of *capturing diverse youth voices*, and in particular the perspectives of youth who have been marginalized from governmental decision-making. Youth council members engaged in multiple forms of community outreach to court involved, homeless or housing insecure, undocumented, and LGBTQ+ youth. This included youth council members going into the community to describe and promote the PB process, holding community listening sessions to gather youth perspectives, conducting outreach via social media, and reaching out to their social networks. A final theme was the importance of *providing input* into how city government spends its public budget. Youth viewed the allocation of $1 million from the capital budget as evidence that they had influence in determining priorities for the city.

In addition to the themes listed above, stakeholder interviews identified the importance of *social networking opportunities*. Through participation in the council, the youth were able to meet peers, adult allies, and political leaders across the city and build their networks. Youth developed an understanding of how local government works and were given exclusive access to information regarding employment opportunities to enhance their resumes and engage in career development opportunities. At times this resulted in employment in governmental-related positions. Examples of Mayor's Youth Council alumni include the Co-Executive Director at the Participatory Budgeting Project (www.participatorybudgeting.org) and the founder of Pipeline to Power and 2021 Obama Scholar (www.obama.org/scholars).

Youth who participated in the PB process also had the opportunity to develop skills including teamwork, public speaking, communications, decision-making, and time management (Augsberger et al., 2017c). While our research has identified individual and community benefits of youth participation in policy advocacy, there remained questions about the degree to which youth engagement has influenced policy decision-making and/or outcomes. As part of the PB process, the youth collected data on youth policy priorities, but many perceived a lack of influence on policy outcomes (Augsberger et al., 2017c).

In sum, the Boston Mayor's Youth Council provides a case exemplar of policy advocacy in the context of a youth council model. The strength of the council included the opportunities to develop skills and knowledge regarding the governmental processes, to network with youth and adults in key leadership positions, and to engage in a project that can positively impact the community. The challenges included member representation (whether youth council members represented all voices), ongoing communication with the Mayor and other City Hall staff, and the limitation of capital projects in influencing policy.

Power and Empowerment Processes in Youth Policy Advocacy

The mission, goals, and activities of youth councils center around engaging youth voice in policy and program decision-making. While there are criticisms of youth engagement on youth councils (Taft & Gordon, 2013), there is also research documenting their impact on various components of psychological and community empowerment (Richards-Schuster &

Checkoway, 2009). As we noted earlier, primary criticisms of youth councils focus on their potential role in inculcating youth into the norms of democratic societies that perpetuate existing formalized structures, including power relations and the status quo. In this way, youth's participation preserves the existing political order (Andersson, 2017; Matthews, 2001; Sant & Davies, 2018). In other words, youth civic engagement at the governmental level is framed by what is and is not allowed, as defined by the institution (Nir & Perry-Hazan, 2016). Nonetheless, Sant and Davies (2018) also noted, however, that youth's participation can be understood as being empowering, "offering possibilities to challenge, if necessary, the political order" (p. 373).

We begin this section with a review of the literature on psychological empowerment, then we review the literature on community empowerment, including specific elements of youth councils that can facilitate community power.

Psychological Empowerment Processes

Richards-Schuster et al. (2018) note, "at its core, youth empowerment concentrates on the processes of young people reducing powerlessness by gaining power, over their own lives, within the agencies and institutions that serve them, in their communities, or in the broader society" (p. 3). Research on youth participation in policy advocacy has largely focused on the individual benefits to youth (Checkoway, 2011). These benefits include the development of skills such as decision-making, problem-solving, and conflict resolution (Akiva et al., 2014). Participation can lead to feelings of enhanced self-esteem and self-efficacy (Blanchet-Cohen et al., 2014; Matthews, 2001; Zeldin et al., 2007). Participation may also increase youth's critical consciousness and understanding of local government (Checkoway et al., 2005; Forenza, 2017; Matthews, 2001) or interest and motivation to participate in community service, political action, or other forms of public engagement (Cohen & Chaffee, 2013; Harada, 2021; Matthews, 2001).

Research shows that youth councils can provide an opportunity to develop positive relationships with peers, adult allies, and political leaders. These relationships can assist youth in building social networks and social capital (Augsberger et al., 2018). They may also lead to exclusive access to information or employment opportunities that may not have otherwise been available (Augsberger et al., 2018). For specialized populations, such as systems-involved youth, these relationships may facilitate youth's understanding that they are not alone in dealing with bureaucratic systems, and that they can collectively advocate for improved policies and programs (Augsberger et al., 2019b; Collins et al., 2022).

Our case exemplar of Boston's PB process demonstrates multiple aspects of psychological empowerment (Augsberger et al., 2019a). *Intrapersonal empowerment* involves the relationship youth hold to the environment and their perceived ability to make change in the environment. Youth reported feeling in control of the process, stating that they developed confidence in their ability to communicate with key stakeholders, prioritize their ideas, and design capital projects. Key aspects that contributed to intrapersonal empowerment included the support and guidance the youth received from peers and adult allies, as well as the training they received regarding PB. *Interactional empowerment* includes youth's understanding of community issues and priorities in their environment, the resources available to them, and how to utilize the resources to implement change. Youth noted the role of adult allies in assisting them in developing the skills (e.g., leadership, decision-making, problem-solving) and knowledge needed to carry out the PB process. They also stated the importance of meeting directly with adults who held the power to make decisions for the city (e.g., Mayor, City Hall staff) as a critical component of understanding how city government works and developing feasible projects that could be implemented. *Behavioral empowerment* includes engaging in activities that can lead to community change. Youth noted the importance of the Mayor allocating $1 million of the capital budget to carry out the PB process as a factor in moving forward positive community change. Youth felt agency in terms of identifying and targeting specific issues when developing the capital projects. They also felt that the projects could "make a difference" in their community.

Community Power

In comparison to other groups, young people are rarely a top priority of policymakers because they usually cannot vote and they lack the financial resources to contribute to campaigns. Classic scholarship by Schneider and Ingram (1993) identified characteristics of different target populations that were associated with their treatment in policy processes; children were classified as "dependent," requiring the beneficial actions of others (Schneider & Ingram, 1993). Collins and Mead (2021) expanded this work with a specific focus on various populations of children and youth. Notably, they identified that children and youth can be contenders for power when they are supported by adults (e.g., parents) and organized to express their voice in policy processes focused on securing resources or policy changes that benefit them (Collins & Mead, 2021). This often occurs at the local level because in the US children and youth lack a coordinated national constituency on many policy matters (Youniss & Levine, 2009).

We have noted that the US differs from other nations because it has not ratified the UNCRC. Thus, the policy infrastructure for youth councils is more visible and widespread in other countries, particularly those in Europe, Canada, and Australia. One report, produced by Finnish and German scholars, states that the national reporting obligations required by the UNCRC have "triggered a worldwide best practice movement in child and youth participation" (Feldmann-Wojtachnia et al., 2010, p. 15). The report further states that it is "hard to overestimate" the role of the UNCRC in strengthening youth rights to participation. In the US, there is some excellent work on youth engagement, and many cities have developed strong infrastructure to support youth councils, but without the guidance of the UNCRC these efforts tend to be very specific to individual localities.

Scholarship on youth participation in decision-making has identified several models articulating various levels of youth engagement that range from the symbolic tokenism of engaging youth in adult-led initiatives to a robust engagement of youth in leadership and decision-making roles (Hart, 1992; Shier, 2001; Wong et al., 2010). For example, Augsberger et al.'s (2018) typology was specifically focused on municipal youth councils, offering a continuum from adult-centric to youth-centric practice. Though often not stated explicitly, the inherent assumption of such typologies is that more robust youth-led initiatives, with the support of adult allies, would be more capable of exerting community power.

Earlier, we noted that the extant research has not identified a strong effect of youth councils on policy changes, although there are anecdotal reports of policy impacts from the case studies of these councils (Checkoway et al., 2005; Collins et al., 2016; Richards-Schuster & Checkoway, 2009). These case-specific impacts are important and speak to the need to identify key salient issues within the locality on which youth can achieve policy victories. This can be an important role for adult allies or the adult liaison to the youth council. Without muting youth voice or disempowering youth engagement, committed adult allies can partner with youth to help hone youth ideas to make them more feasible and likely to result in success. The core caution is to avoid adultism (Hart, 2013). Rather, just like any other form of citizen engagement in policymaking, young citizens new to the process of governance can learn as well as advocate. This includes educating youth regarding the reality that most policymaking is incremental.

In our study of twenty-four youth councils (Collins et al., 2016), we identified seven common activities of such councils: education and prevention activities, youth summits, recreational activities, community service, community assessments, counseling, and policy-specific actions. Our focus here is on the policy-specific actions. Thirteen youth councils engaged in activities that involved the young people engaging in policy change efforts. A few of these examples include: working to raise community awareness of the importance of transportation for youth by working with the local transit authority to create a "youth route" that linked some of the critical places that youth wanted to go; working to pass tobacco regulations by making presentations to the Board of Health and the City Council; and creating a "one ID" for youth (a photo ID that can be used as a student ID and for school lunch service, on public transportation, and in public libraries). In addition to these "policy-specific" activities, some of the other activities had policy components. For example, education and prevention activities aimed to educate youth, parents, teachers, or other community audiences on important youth concerns (substance use, mental health, violence prevention). Also, the community assessment activities generally were aimed at collecting data in the community (e.g., on the range of services available to youth) that might then be used in an advocacy capacity (e.g., to seek more support).

We have described the PB process in Boston earlier (Augsberger et al., 2019a). The City of Boston website identifies selected projects including expanded Wi-Fi in youth settings, more shared bike programs, making parks more accessible, a job resource app, a space for the performing and visual arts, installing fans in schools that lack air-conditioning, more trash and recycling bins, and investing in local urban farms. Generally, the central themes of these projects include establishing/upgrading city spaces, technology enhancements, and beautification efforts.

Cushing and van Vliet's (2017) study of 139 youth councils in the US reports the frequencies of youth council activities from a list of nineteen such activities. Most frequently mentioned was participating in community service and/or outreach projects (84 percent). Other common responsibilities include organizing events (79 percent), providing feedback and advice on community initiatives (78 percent), and seeking informal feedback from other young people to advocate on their behalf (76 percent). Most relevant to our focus on policy activities, the authors state: "Noticeably absent are significant responsibilities in helping shape local government decisions" (p. 8).

One key element of engaging in government decisions is that issues must be relevant to the youth population and optimally are driven by youth interests (rather than adult interests). Additionally, it is important that the policy focus be of manageable scope by a youth-led group within a specific period of time. Many young people who participate in a youth council might do so only for one term (typically a year) because they have other important life tasks in which they are engaged. While multiyear projects are possible, there is a very real risk of loss of momentum as membership of the group changes. Furthermore, like any other policy interest group, small victories in the policy process can be instrumental for both individuals' and group members' continued engagement in policy work. By contrast, policy defeats can discourage people from further engaging in the process. In summary, specific policy issues relevant to youth interests with short time horizons are important to the success of municipal youth councils. Successes can demonstrate the relevance of the youth council model, further building its capacity and reputation in the community as an important component of policy development.

Youth councils can engage in more complex policy activities of longer duration and more ambitious scope. To do so effectively, however, mechanisms should be built into the structure and process. These might include, for example, multiyear terms of youth councilors, project teams composed of senior and newer councilors, staff continuity over multiple years, and documentation of steps and milestones achieved that are parts of longer-term policy goals. Under these conditions, youth participants can continue to view their participation in a positive light and as contributing to a long-term goal, even when the goal is not achieved during their term of service.

In addition to the importance of selecting youth-identified specific policy issues rather than adults deciding on the area of focus – which has been a documented tension in prior research (see Augsberger et al., 2018) – we have also described several core elements of youth councils (diverse representation, youth–adult partnerships, etc.) that can build community power. These key attributes are discussed further in the next section.

Features That Facilitate Community Power

In our own research, we have identified key features of youth councils that can function as facilitators and/or barriers to community power: youth voice, youth–adult partnerships, engaged leadership, meaningful activities, and community impact (Figure 10.2). In addition, it is critical to strive for diverse representation, including intentionally recruiting youth who represent the demographics of the community. In this section, we elaborate on these features of youth councils that can build youth/community power.

The National League of Cities (2020) offers a general framework for authentically engaging youth in civic life. They propose four interrelated elements of active youth civic engagement: setting, structure, strategy, and support. Building the *setting* includes creating a warm and welcoming environment where youth are viewed as assets (rather than problems) and are provided with opportunities for meaningful engagement in policy, planning, and decision-making. This includes political leaders believing that youth are competent constituents who are capable of promoting policies and programs that can enhance the city. It also includes establishing *infrastructure* that

Figure 10.2 *Key themes of youth councils.*

promotes meaningful *youth voice* and participation, including examining the opportunities for engagement and ensuring that they are youth-friendly and not driven exclusively by adult priorities. The *strategy* includes providing diverse activities that youth find meaningful and can result in positive community impact. Finally, youth need to be *supported* by adult allies both inside and outside local government.

These features are similar to those emerging from research on youth empowerment. For example, Richards-Schuster et al. (2018, p. 8) describe core practices of youth empowerment based on a review of the youth political empowerment literature that are consistent with the report from the National League of Cities (2020). The first core practice is the *setting* – "creating a welcoming space that promotes meaningful and authentic youth engagement" (Richards-Schuster et al., 2018, p. 9) – which includes examining the environment to ensure it is youth-friendly, culturally and ethnically responsive, and offers a physical space for youth to convene and converse. The second core practice is *adult allies* who support youth in political engagement and share power in policy processes. The third core practice is *critical reflection and analysis*, which includes opportunities for youth to reflect on multilevel factors that influence their situations and develop a critical consciousness (e.g., understanding of systems of inequality). The fourth core practice, tied to critical reflection, is that youth are provided with *opportunities for action*, including capacity-building activities and activities that can address systems of inequality and promote positive community change. The practices described here are consistent with the literature reviewed throughout this chapter related to features of youth councils that can lead to community power.

Youth–Adult Partnerships

Research supports the importance of youth–adult partnerships: youth partnering with adults who share power and support them at each stage of decision-making (Blanchett-Cohen et al., 2014; Zeldin et al., 2007). However, there remain questions regarding adults' ability to view youth as assets (rather than problems) and share power with them in the civic realm (Bessell, 2009). Zeldin et al. (2013) define youth–adult partnerships as "the practice of multiple youth and multiple adults deliberating and acting together, in a collective fashion, over a sustained period of time, through shared work, intended to promote social justice, strengthen an organization and/or affirmatively address a community issue" (p. 388).

The youth engagement research often identifies power imbalances when engaging youth in policy advocacy in the context of youth councils. As reported by Adu-Gyamfi (2013), youth participation alone does not automatically lead to empowerment, especially when youth do not influence decision-making and/or outcomes. Adult allies are critical in providing information, support, and guidance (Checkoway, 2011; Ramey et al., 2017). Many councils dedicate at least one adult to facilitating youth council activities (Collins et al., 2016). Ideally, these adults should be trained in principles of positive youth development, civic engagement, and social justice (Collins et al., 2018) and understand their role in creating a supportive social context where youth are provided with the opportunity to develop knowledge and skills with the training and support of adults (Augsberger et al., 2020). Checkoway (2011) further notes the important role of youth leaders (e.g., individuals who take on leadership roles in the council) who can mentor and support youth and provide a bridge between youth and adults. In addition, youth noted the importance of *engaged leadership*, including ongoing communication with the Mayor and/or other municipal staff.

Our own research (Augsberger et al., 2018) identified key areas to consider when thinking about power-sharing in the context of youth councils, including the ratio of youth to adults (e.g., we favor majority youth supported by adult allies), opportunities for youth to share leadership and decision-making with adults (e.g., planning a community event, selecting agenda items), youth's ability to identify and decide upon the priorities and issues of the council, and instituting democratic processes (e.g., voting) that ensure all voices are heard.

Diverse Representation

The research on youth councils shows that youth who participate are often White youth who are academically oriented and well connected to various institutions and organizations (Augsberger et al., 2018; Freeman et al., 2003; Matthews, 2001; Nairn et al., 2006; Wyness, 2009). Godfrey and Cherng (2016) suggest that historically marginalized youth may possess greater societal awareness, and thus these youth have a great deal to offer their communities and society. There is a need to intentionally recruit youth with multiple identities, including youth of color, immigrant youth, low-income youth, youth with disabilities, and youth who identify as LGBTQ+ (Augsberger et al., 2018). As much as possible, youth who become members of youth councils should represent the demographics of the community (Matthews, 2001). Outreach efforts to specific groups may be needed to support the goals of enhancing diversity. Systems-involved youth are those young people with strong connections to services systems – for example, youth with lived experience of foster care, juvenile justice, or housing instability and homelessness (Collins et al., 2022). As previously noted, youth council models have been identified specifically for engaging systems-involved youth in policy advocacy (e.g., Augsberger et al., 2020; Forenza & Happonen, 2016; Havlicek et al., 2016), but it is also important that they be included in opportunities for serving on municipal youth councils, where they can engage with a wider community of young people.

Meaningful Activities (and Impact)

A core feature that can contribute to the building of community power is ensuring that there is a range of activities for engaging with local government and that the activities are meaningful to youth (Collins et al., 2016; Richards-Schuster & Checkoway, 2009). Meaningful activities might be those characterized as stemming from youth interests, focused on the community (particularly for youth populations), and having potential impact.

Our case exemplar highlighted PB, which meets these criteria of being "meaningful" to youth members. Generation of ideas for the budget came directly from youth, had wide community reach, and offered the potential for sustained impact. Other potentially meaningful activities that were discerned from the literature include presentations to city council members about youth-focused issues such as transportation needs, community events, or trainings related to health issues and antiviolence measures and data-gathering activities with youth to inform community decision-making (Collins et al., 2016; Richards-Schuster & Checkoway, 2009).

Youth councils often engage in other activities that may be more recreational, focused on development of youth skills, or aimed at providing peer support (Collins et al., 2016). While these are important activities for youth councils to engage in and may build a sense of community among the participants, their linkage to community power may be more indirect.

Research shows that youth who engage in policy advocacy want to "make a difference" in their community. As noted by Zaff et al. (2010), active and engaged citizenship includes the component of working together "for the greater good." There are several case examples reviewed throughout this chapter that demonstrate opportunities to promote community change (e.g., Richards Schuster & Checkoway, 2009). However there remains a critical need for additional information on the degree to which youth engagement in policy advocacy results in community impact.

Application and Future Research

Application

The knowledge base regarding municipal youth councils offers several implications for practitioners, leaders, policymakers, funders, and other stakeholders engaged in this work or contemplating entering this field of practice. First, we recognize youth to be the primary constituency who might benefit from existing knowledge about municipal youth councils. Ironically, it is likely that youth are not aware of these opportunities (either the possibility of forming a youth council or the ability to join a youth council) unless they are informed about the opportunities by an adult. We noted that we have no information about youth councils that were initiated by youth; instead, they are typically developed by adults in the community who see a need for a youth council. To support youth-led efforts, mechanisms of communicating directly with youth, not through adult intermediaries, might be particularly fruitful. This may be especially necessary in the US because it is not a signatory to the UNCRC and lacks the youth-focused infrastructure that is available in some other countries.

Second, certainly adults working in youth-oriented positions in municipal government or in the community represent an important constituency for information about youth councils. As noted earlier, adults often serve as gatekeepers of youth councils. For these groups, practical information about how to form and support youth councils is usually the primary interest. Resources such as those from the National League of Cities (2020) provide the kind of practical guidance that would be helpful. We emphasize three core components:

(1) *Youth development principles:* Youth development is a strengths-based empowerment perspective that views youth as assets and aims to support youth in achieving optimal development. The youth development perspective supports youth in developing relationships with peers, adults, and their community. Youth development principles provide a core overarching approach to empowering youth.

(2) *Youth–adult partnerships:* In order to achieve effective youth–adult partnerships that do not tokenize youth, it is important for adults working with youth to recognize youth as experts on youth issues and priorities and to collaborate with them in all phases of the work. These relationships center power-sharing in decision-making processes. As previously noted, ideally there should be at least one adult facilitator assigned to the youth council. This individual should have expertise in civic engagement and be trained in practices of positive youth development, youth empowerment, and social justice.

(3) *Policy engagement:* Because the model of municipal youth councils situates youth within government, it would be worthwhile if young people received robust training on the real-world practice of policy engagement. Enhanced efforts in this direction might demonstrate more lasting system-level effects of municipal youth councils than are typically seen. Practice principles would include ongoing access to decision-makers, paired or group mentoring by government officials, and project-based work focused on a youth-driven issue. The PB process in Boston is a good exemplar of this, but these principles could also exist in other kinds of initiatives.

Third, policymakers are not often the specific audience for research on municipal youth councils, yet the availability of good information might be particularly helpful to them. There is some evidence that mayors of American cities do value youth as a constituency; a nationally representative survey of mayors identified youth as a constituency that local government needs to do more to help (Einstein et al., 2017). Yet youth (and children) rarely receive significant attention because they are disadvantaged in political processes due to their age (being ineligible to vote or run for office) and their lack of financial resources (Collins & Mead, 2021). Nonetheless, policymakers might be inclined to value youth councils when they serve a critical purpose in representing youth of the community and as partners in addressing complex youth-oriented problems.

Fourth, funders need up-to-date information on best practices of youth councils to inform funding decisions. In particular, funders should be encouraged to fund those youth councils that demonstrate adherence to the principles we have outlined. Foundations and other funders of research also must contribute to sponsoring research and evaluations that can further develop the evidence base regarding effective youth councils.

Future Research

Unfortunately, there has been limited progress in developing, funding, and executing a robust research agenda to understand municipal youth councils (and other youth councils) and their community and policy impacts. The research literature is dominated by cross-sectional descriptive case studies. These have been helpful as guides to practice, but additional research is needed to develop this as a mature research field. We offer some suggestions to this end in this section.

First, research should study whether and to what extent youth councils have impact on community power and policy decisions. We have repeatedly identified that there is a dearth of information on how youth councils have impact in these areas. There is some modest information about how youths themselves are impacted (e.g., skills-building, civic efficacy, critical consciousness). But key questions to be answered include: Are youth councils effective in bringing a pro-youth perspective to the community? Do the projects in which youth engage have positive impacts on the community? Is youth policy advocacy achieving key policy effects that improve the lives of young people? To answer these questions, more rigorous research methods are needed than are typically used in the case study documentation of youth councils.

Second, research should engage multiple sites and study them simultaneously. This can offer opportunities for comparative analysis to address key questions. Cross-site analysis would be able to demonstrate how various structures (size, activities, schedule) may be related to outcomes. It would provide the ability to examine the role of context in impacting youth council operations and outcomes. Contextual variables that could be examined in cross-site analyses include the size of the municipality, the form of government, the level of integration of the youth council in government operations, and youth-focused community challenges.

Third, longitudinal designs would be useful in understanding youth councils. Questions about the origins (how they start), representation (diverse participation), ongoing operations (needed structural elements), development over time (e.g., growth, mission change), and impact on outcomes might be addressed through longitudinal designs. Augsberger et al. (2017a) described youth council origins, identified that some ended, and suggested that many may become more youth-driven over time. But more research is needed to examine these processes. Ideally, this research would employ participatory methods, engaging youth and communities in the development of research questions, methods, data collection and analysis, and dissemination.

Conclusion

These are exciting times in the US and across the globe, as we are witnessing multiple efforts by young people to have their voices heard on topics such as climate change, racial justice, and inequality of opportunities. Along with other scholars focused on youth empowerment, we value the importance of youth perspectives and believe that young people can provide leadership toward a more just society. Youth councils provide one potential mechanism to this end. This chapter has aimed to summarize key aspects of the extant knowledge base and also to call for significantly more research on this topic.

References

Adu-Gyamfi, J. (2013). Can children and young people be empowered in participatory initiatives? Perspectives from young people's participation in policy formulation and implementation in Ghana. *Children and Youth Services Review*, *35*(10), 1766–1772.

Akiva, T., Cortina, K. S., & Smith, C. (2014). Involving youth in program decision-making: How common and what might it do for youth? *Journal of Youth and Adolescence*, *43*(11), 1844–1860.

Andersson, E. (2017). Young people's political participation: A public pedagogy challenge at the municipal level. *Young*, *26*(2), 179–195.

Augsberger, A., Collins, M. E., & Gecker, W. A. (2017a). Engaging youth in municipal government: Moving towards a youth centric practice. *Journal of Community Practice*, *26*(1), 41–62.

Augsberger, A., Collins, M. E., Gecker, W., & Dougher, M. (2018). Youth civic engagement: Do youth councils reduce or reinforce social inequality? *Journal of Adolescent Research*, *33*(2), 187–208.

Augsberger, A., Collins, M. E., Gecker, W. A., Lusk, K., & Dougher, M. (2017b, January 25). *Youth lead the change: Participatory budgeting Boston 2016*. Boston University, Initiative on Cities. https://open.bu.edu/handle/2144/20263

Augsberger, A., Collins, M. E., Gecker, W., Lusk, K., & Zhao, Q. J. (2017c). "She treated us like we bring valid ideas to the table": Youth experiences of a youth-led participatory budgeting process. *Children and Youth Services Review, 76*(C), 243–249.

Augsberger, A., Gecker, W., & Collins, M. E. (2019a). "We make a direct impact on people's lives": Youth empowerment in the context of a youth-led participatory budgeting project. *Journal of Community Psychology, 47*(3), 462–476.

Augsberger, A., Springwater, J. S., Hilliard-Koshinsky, G., Barber, K., & Sprague-Martinez, L. (2019b). Youth engagement in policy-advocacy: Examination of a multi-state former and current foster care youth coalition. *Children and Youth Services Review, 107*, 104491.

Augsberger, A., Toraif, N., Springwater, J., Hilliard-Koshinsky, G., & Sprague Martinez, L. (2020). Strategies for engaging current and former foster care youth in policy advocacy: Lessons from the New England Youth Coalition. *Child Welfare, 97*(6), 251–270.

Bessell, S. (2009). Children's participation in decision-making in the Philippines: Understanding the attitudes of policy-makers and service providers. *Childhood, 16*(3), 299–316.

Blanchet-Cohen, N., Manolson, S., & Shaw, K. (2014). Youth-led decision making in community development grants. *Youth & Society, 46*(6), 819–834.

Casas, F., González, M., Montserrat, C., Navarro, D., Malo, S., Figuer, C., & Bertran, I. (2008). *Informe sobre experiencias de participación social efectiva de niños, niñas y adolescentes [Childhood and young people's effective social participation report]*. Observatorio de la infancia.

Checkoway, B. (2011). What is youth participation? *Children and Youth Services Review, 33*(2), 340–345.

Checkoway, B., Allison, T., & Montoya, C. (2005). Youth participation in public policy at the municipal level. *Children and Youth Services Review, 27*(10), 1149–1162.

City of Boston. (n.d.). *Mayor's Youth Council*. City of Boston. www.boston.gov/departments/youth-engagement-and-employment/mayors-youth-council

Cohen, A. K., & Chaffee, B. W. (2013). The relationship between adolescents' civic knowledge, civic attitude, and civic behavior and their self-reported future likelihood of voting. *Education, Citizenship and Social Justice, 8*(1), 43–57.

Collins, M. E., & Mead, M. (2021). Social constructions of children and youth: Beyond dependents and deviants. *Journal of Social Policy, 50*(3), 493–510.

Collins, M. E., Augsberger, A., & Gecker, W. A. (2016). Youth councils in municipal government: Examination of activities, impact and barriers. *Children and Youth Services Review, 65*, 140–147.

Collins, M. E., Augsberger, A., & Gecker, W. A. (2018). Identifying policy and practice components of youth councils: Contributions of theory. *Child and Adolescent Social Work Journal, 35*, 599–610.

Collins, M. E., Augsberger, A., & Kerzner-Sirois, L. (2022). Examining civic engagement opportunities for system-involved youth: A comparative analysis. *Journal of Youth Studies, 25*(4), 416–432.

Cushing, D. F., & van Vliet, W. (2017). Children's right to the city: The emergence of youth councils in the United States. *Children's Geographies, 15*(3), 319–333.

Einstein, K. L., Glick, D., & LeBlanc, C. (2017, January 10). *2016 Menino Survey of Mayors*. Boston University, Initiative on Cities. http://hdl.handle.net/2144/19829

Feldmann-Wojtachnia, E., Gretschel, A., Helmisaari, V., Kiilakoski, T., Matthies, A., Meinhold-Henschel, S., Roth, R., & Tasanko, P. (2010). *Youth participation in Finland and in Germany – Status analysis and data based recommendations*. The Finnish Youth Research Network and Forschungsgruppe Jugend & Europa am CAP, Ludwig Maximilians Universität.

Feringa, D., & Tonkens, E. (2017). How the participation style in local youth councils contributes to the civic engagement of young people. *Journal of Social Intervention: Theory and Practice, 26*(2), 43–59.

Finlay, S. (2010). Carving out meaningful spaces for youth participation and engagement in decision-making. *Youth Studies Australia, 29*(4), 53–59.

Forenza, B. (2017). Awareness, analysis, engagement: Critical consciousness through foster care youth advisory board participation. *Child Adolescent Social Work Journal, 35*(2), 119–126.

Forenza, B., & Happonen, R. (2016). A critical analysis of foster youth advisory boards in the United States. *Child & Youth Care Forum, 45*(1), 107–121.

Freeman, C., Nairn, K., & Sligo, J. (2003). "Professionalising" participation: From rhetoric to practice. *Children's Geographies, 1*(1), 53–70.

Godfrey, E. B., & Cherng, H.-Y. S. (2016). The kids are all right? Income inequality and civic engagement among our nation's youth. *Journal of Youth and Adolescence, 45*, 2218–2232.

Haddad, K., Lindquist-Grantz, R., Vilvens, H., Boards, A., Jacquez, F., & Vaughn, L. (2020). Empowering youth to build BRIDGES: Youth leadership in suicide prevention. *Collaborations, 3*(1), 10.

Harada, A. (2021). How to involve a diverse group of young people in local government decision making: A case study of Danish youth councils. *Compare: A Journal of Comparative and International Education, 53*, 820–836.

Hart, R. A. (1992). *Children's participation: From tokenism to citizenship* (Innocenti Essay No. 4). International Child Development Centre. www.unicef-irc.org/publications/100-childrens-participation-from-tokenism-to-citizenship.html

Hart, R. A. (2013). *Children's participation: The theory and practice of involving young citizens in community development and environmental care*. Routledge.

Havlicek, J., & Samuels, G. M. (2018). The Illinois state foster youth advisory board as a counter-space for well-being through identity work: Perspectives of current and former members. *Social Services Review, 92*(2), 241–289.

Havlicek, J., Lin, C.-H., & Villalpando, F. (2016). Web survey of foster youth advisory boards in the United States. *Children and Youth Services Review, 60*, 109–118.

Jostyn, J. (1945). The Manhasset Youth Council. *The Journal of Educational Sociology, 18*(3), 417–425.

Komel, R. (2018). *"Never about them without them": The Ottawa Police Service's youth advisory committee as an opportunity for youth civic engagement* [Doctoral dissertation]. Université d'Ottawa/University of Ottawa.

Mansfield, R. G., Batagol, B., & Raven, R. (2021). "Critical agents of change?": Opportunities and limits to children's participation in urban planning. *Journal of Planning Literature, 36*(2), 170–186.

Martin, S., Pittman, K., Ferber, T., & McMahon, A. (2007). *Building effective youth councils: A practical guide to engaging youth in policy making*. The Forum for Youth Investment.

Matthews, H. (2001). Citizenship, youth councils and young people's participation. *Journal of Youth Studies, 4*(3), 299–318.

Matthews, H., & Limb, M. (1998). The right to say: The development of youth councils/forums within the UK. *Area, 30*(1), 66–78.

Moreno, M. A., Jolliff, A., & Kerr, B. (2021). Youth advisory boards: Perspectives and processes. *Journal of Adolescent Health, 69*(2), 192–194.

Nairn, K., Sligo, J., & Freeman, C. (2006). Polarizing participation in local government: Which young people are included and excluded? *Children, Youth, and Environments, 16*(2), 248–273.

National League of Cities. (2020). *Authentic youth engagement: A guide for municipal leaders*. National League of Cities. www.youthlead.org/resources/authentic-youth-civic-engagement-guide-municipal-leaders

Nir, T., & Perry-Hazan, L. (2016). The framed right to participate in municipal youth councils and its educational impact. *Children and Youth Services Review, 69*, 174–183.

Ramey, H. L., Lawford, H. L., & Vachon, W. (2017). Youth–adult partnerships in work with youth: An overview. *Journal of Youth Development, 12*(4), 38–60.

Richards-Schuster, K., & Checkoway, B. (2009). Youth participation in public policy at the local level: New lessons from Michigan municipalities: Youth participation in public policy at the local level. *National Civic Review, 98*(4), 26–30.

Richards-Schuster, K., Pritzker, S., & Rodriguez-Newhall, A. (2018, May 24). *Youth empowerment*. Encyclopedia of Social Work. https://doi.org/10.1093/acrefore/9780199975839.013.1077

Sant, E., & Davies, I. (2018). Promoting participation at a time of social and political turmoil: What is the impact of children's and young people's city councils? *Cambridge Journal of Education, 48*(3), 371–387.

Schneider, A., & Ingram, H. (1993). Social construction of target populations: Implications for politics and policy. *American Political Science Review, 87* (2), 334–347.

Shier, H. (2001). Pathways to participation: Openings, opportunities and obligations. *Children & Society, 15*(2), 107–117.

Taft, J. K., & Gordon, H. R. (2013). Youth activists, youth councils, and constrained democracy. *Education, Citizenship and Social Justice, 8*(1), 87–100.

Wall, J. (2011). Can democracy represent children? Toward a politics of difference. *Childhood, 19*, 86–100.

Wong, N. T., Zimmerman, M. A., & Parker, E. A. (2010). A typology of youth participation and empowerment for child and adolescent health promotion. *American Journal of Community Psychology, 46*(1–2), 100–114.

Wyness, M. (2009). Children representing children: Participation and the problem of diversity in UK youth councils. *Childhood, 16*(4), 535–552.

Youniss, J., & Levine, P. (2009). *Engaging young people in civic life*. Vanderbilt University Press.

Zaff, J., Boyd, M., Li, Y., Lerner, J. V., & Lerner, R. M. (2010). Active and engaged citizenship: Multi-group and longitudinal factoral analysis of an integrated construct of civic engagement. *Journal of Youth and Adolescence, 39*, 736–750.

Zeldin, S., Camino, L., & Calvert, M. (2007). Toward an understanding of youth in community governance: Policy priorities and research directions. *Analise Psicologica, 1*(XXV), 77–95.

Zeldin, S., Christens, B. D., & Powers, J. L. (2013). The psychology and practice of youth–adult partnership: Bridging generations for youth development and community change. *American Journal of Community Psychology, 51*(3–4), 385–397.

PART III

Civil Society and Coalitions

11 Community Leadership Development

Wilson Majee, Sarah Hultine Massengale,
Claire Rippel, and Johanna Reed Adams

Introduction

Over the last few decades, significant resources have been channeled toward improving human well-being throughout the world, and many professions have witnessed huge returns on this investment. The medical profession has made significant progress in combating disease (Gawande, 2010) that has enhanced the scientific breakthroughs in COVID-19 vaccine development (Forman et al., 2021). In the realms of communication technology, significant strides such as the development and use of the Internet, Zoom, Twitter, and Facebook have also been noted. In overcoming global poverty, the world has also made huge advances, reducing the percentage of those surviving on $1.90 a day or less from 36 percent in 1990 to 9.2 percent in 2017 (World Vision, 2021). Despite these gains, success in reducing economic, social, and health disparities has not been remarkable overall. Poor health outcomes, shrinking economic opportunities, and inequitable access to resources are made worse by increasingly disengaged citizens, contentious public discourse, and racial inequality (Kent & Ricketts, 2020; National Academies of Sciences, Engineering, and Medicine, 2020). COVID-19 is also contributing additional adverse impacts on individuals and communities. Globally, the World Bank estimates the number of people living in extreme poverty to be 659 million as of March 2023 (Baah et al., 2023).

These complex issues cannot be solved solely by individual leaders at the top but will require the leadership of diverse community members working collectively to make progress on these issues (Heifetz et al., 2009; Ospina & Foldy, 2016). Community leadership development (CLD) remains a key area requiring investment to build community capacity to address community issues in a sustainable manner. We must acknowledge people as the fundamental assets in a community and engage them in community activities that affect their health and socioeconomic well-being (Blanchard, 2012).

Community Leadership Development

Community leadership development programs are community-based programs that generally focus on community-identified priorities and are commonly organized, sponsored, and delivered through diverse local entities such as chambers of commerce, university extension services, community action agencies, faith-based organizations, and other not-for-profit organizations (Pigg et al., 2015). These initiatives are different from management-style leadership training programs. Community leadership development programs are often focused on local residents and work to build group processes that are inclusive and collaborative to enhance local capacities, individually and collectively, to accomplish community change (Apaliyah et al., 2017; Komives & Wagner, 2016; Pigg et al., 2015). Overall, such programs are aimed at creating and sustaining local leadership to encourage and maintain sustainable community development.

Cooperative extension, community organizations, corporations, local government entities, and foundations are, independently or collaboratively, devoting tremendous resources to help improve the vitality and wealth of individuals and communities through the development of local leadership capacities (Goodman et al., 2018; Majee et al., 2012, 2014, 2017). Many of these programs, in the US and abroad, use an asset-based approach to CLD that highlights how engaged residents can affect change using resources already existing in their communities, especially people, relationships, and networks (Kirk & Shutte, 2004; Krietzman & McKnight, 1993; Nel, 2018; Sandfort & Bloomberg, 2012). A study of asset-based versus needs-based leadership programs in South Africa (Nel, 2018) noted that while both training styles created community changes and engagement, the asset-based programs had more grassroots, team-based leadership among community residents that engaged and created empowering environments for community members to participate in affecting change.

In the past few decades, there has been an expansive movement in CLD focused on target populations, including professionals from community organizations or businesses, ordinary community members, youth, and low-income community members. Project planning and networking are two common areas of CLD programs that provide critical skills and learning for participants but can be leveraged in different ways depending on the program audience.

On one hand, many community-based organizations focus on the grassroots community level and are intentional about involving local residents, particularly low-income residents and youth, in leadership development programs. Community leadership development programs targeting low-income community residents tend to acknowledge the disenfranchisement of low-income community members and encourage them to gain the leadership skills needed to fully participate in shaping their communities. These programs tend to focus on motivating participants to self-learn, share their experiences, and identify and nurture their passion. Thus, the curriculum covers general topics that often resonate with individuals in underserved communities. Examples include sessions on planning for one's passion, understanding diversity, embracing diversity, and organizing and running a meeting. Participants are given the opportunity to engage in activities and assignments that complement curriculum topics and focus on applying new skills to design and implement individual or group community projects. The goals of these CLD programs focus on developing participants' self-awareness and interpersonal skills while increasing their capacity to participate in their communities' decision-making processes (Reed Adams et al., 2005). The first exemplar described in this chapter, Neighborhood Leadership Academy (NLA), will highlight a grassroots-level leadership program.

On the other hand, there is the movement in CLD targeting business or organizational professionals within a community, which stems from employers who are increasingly acknowledging the connection between organizational success and sustainability and community outreach and engagement (Mattioli, 2009). There is interest among organizations to invest in leadership development that strengthens employees' organizational and community understanding (Alexander et al., 2001; Theleman, 2011). Industry leaders are realizing that addressing community-based health and well-being concerns requires more resources than a single organization, such as a community hospital or community bank, can provide. With this realization, community stakeholders may need to collaborate in addressing mutually identified concerns to successfully engage community members' demands that professionals look strategically beyond the organization and view the wider community as their consumer (Rubino et al., 2018). When multiple entities collaborate to address a community issue, "leader skills that facilitate effective team operation and function are required" (Alexander et al., 2001). Participants in business-focused community leadership programs are usually existing or emerging professionals in the community, such as business managers, educators, faith-based organization leaders, and local government officials (Brungardt & Seibel, 1995; Langone & Richard Rohs, 1995; Wituk et al., 2005). Although curricula vary by program and location, emphasis is generally placed on understanding community history, local economy, and networking opportunities (Maltsberger & Majee, 2012). Community leadership development programs for the broader community also help participants to understand the different sectors in their community, such as health, education, agriculture, and other industries. Such a community- and sector-focused approach enriches participants' community knowledge, which, in turn, motivates people to accept community leadership roles. While not necessarily limited to business professionals, often the timing of such programs assumes commitment from an employer to participate during regular work hours. The Experience in Community Enterprise and Leadership (EXCEL) program, described later in this chapter as the second exemplar, highlights how this form of CLD program can be created at the community level.

Community leadership development programs, whether for professionals or any community members, have been found to offer many benefits: increased confidence and leadership skills (Walker & Gray, 2009), development of collective efficacy (Kirk & Shutte, 2004; Ohmer, 2016), increased citizen involvement and volunteer activity (Aref & Ma'rof, 2008), sense of ownership and responsibility (Foster-Fishman et al., 2007), and better familial relations (Majee et al., 2018). Collective efficacy happens when community members trust one another and are more willing to work toward a common agenda in addressing community concerns (Sampson et al., 2009). However, CLD programs have been criticized for operating independently of each other. While there is value in training professionals and citizens in leadership skills, much lies in promoting inclusive and collaborative projects among graduates from these independent programs at the community/local level (Majee et al., 2017; Pigg et al., 2015).

Evolution of Leadership Development

Trends in leadership theory have paralleled the complexity of past and emergent community challenges and suggest the need for collective effort in addressing community issues. Broadly, leadership theories have shifted from a leader-centric paradigm to collective perspectives of leadership (Ospina & Foldy, 2016). Leader-centric theories posit that traits such as intelligence, self-confidence, and integrity and particular skills (e.g., conceptual skills) and behaviors (e.g., task or relationship behaviors) are key characteristics of leaders (Nelson & Squires, 2017; Northouse, 2021). Rost (1993) critiqued leader-centric perspectives of leadership as having leaders with "certain preferred traits [who] influence followers to do what the leader(s) wish(es) in order to achieve group/organizational goals" (Rost, 1993, p. 97), arguing that a new kind of leadership is needed for today's society. He advanced the notion of leadership as "an influence relationship among leaders and their collaborators who intend real changes that reflect their mutual purposes" (p. 99). Today, leadership has evolved to where many scholars now view it as a property of the collective, not the individual (Cullen-Lester & Yammarino, 2016; Ospina & Foldy, 2016). Although this paradigm shift is still evolving, CLD as a form of adaptive leadership has potential for activating community members for community change.

As leadership educators in higher education and cooperative extension who work collaboratively with students and community members, our aim in discussing CLD is to (1) highlight the barriers and facilitators to effective CLD, (2) demonstrate the potential efficacy of CLD programs to activate community members to work together toward a shared vision, and (3) document the importance of interorganizational collaboration. We do this using two in-depth cooperative extension programs in Missouri, specifically examining their sponsorship, content, structure, and impact. Through examination of these exemplars, the chapter offers a vision for how to reimagine community leadership programs so that they are more responsive to the complexity of current and emergent community challenges. An argument is made that cooperative extension, because of its strong ties to local communities and networks nationwide and links to university researchers, is well placed to support CLD that promotes community-identified strategies to address a wide range of local issues among diverse stakeholders.

Cooperative Extension and Community Leadership Development

In the US, land grant universities were created by Congress in 1862 through legislation in which the federal government gave land to states in exchange for creating institutions of higher learning. Additional land grants were created in 1890 (historically Black colleges and universities) and 1994 (tribal institutions). Cooperative extension programs were formalized in 1914 to extend university knowledge to all residents of the state, not just students, and historically focused on agriculture and home economics programs (University of Missouri Extension, 2021). Today, the federal government partners with one hundred and thirteen 1860, 1890, and 1994 land grant universities (National Institute of Food and Agriculture, 2021) to provide extension services to US residents. Cooperative extension programs have also expanded beyond agriculture to include educational programs and outreach for youth and families, businesses, and communities. Cooperative extension programs work in partnership with federal, state, county, and local government agencies, organizations, and residents to identify community needs and match them to the research and resources of the university to address pressing community issues. While these operate differently between states, one common characteristic of extension services is a presence on the ground in communities, which builds networks between local residents and extension specialists. For instance, University of Missouri Extension (MU Extension) has a county presence in all 114 counties of the state of Missouri. Additionally, at the local level in Missouri, extension programs are advised by local extension councils. Extension councils are established by state statute and are composed of locally elected and appointed members who have authority to fund and operate the local county extension office. They allow for direct connection and input from local community members into the administration and programmatic activities of university extension, in partnership with their local extension specialist in their county office.

Community leadership development programs have been a core component within cooperative extension for a significant portion of extension's history. A study by the National Extension Task Force (1977) analyzed community leadership programs throughout US state extension services and studied the workforce and value of investment in providing leadership training and resources. It also focused on core objectives for CLD programs, including encouraging local initiative, self-determination and local citizen participation in community development (National Extension Task Force, 1977). The study recommended that community leadership be continued as a core component of cooperative extension community resource development programs and that investments in staff and time for those programs be increased. While resources have not increased proportionally with the need for CLD, having even dwindled in some areas, there is still a continued focus on leadership development programs in some form in many state cooperative extension programs. In Missouri, the MU Extension Community Development Program, in partnership with University of Missouri–St. Louis (UMSL), provides community and economic development educational resources that build the civic capacity of Missouri communities to create thriving places (University of Missouri–St. Louis, 2023). A significant focus of programming includes leadership development, provided through a variety of educational formats and resources designed to target specific audiences and address identified leadership needs. Two of MU Extension's leadership programs will be highlighted. Key outcomes measured for these programs regardless of format or audience include the number of new leaders trained and new leadership roles undertaken as a result of participating in an MU Extension community development leadership program.

Exemplar: Neighborhood Leadership Academy

Since 2002, MU Extension has partnered with UMSL to facilitate NLA – a program that uses project-based curricula to train community members invested in creating positive change in their neighborhoods.

Structure and Content

Neighborhood Leadership Academy is a ten-week, thirty-hour course in which participants receive in-depth training following a set of community-building principles that emphasize community-driven processes. The program uses Gallup's Clifton Strengths assessment to instill a strengths-focused approach to leadership on a personal level and provides an asset-based community development (McKnight & Kretzmann, 1993) framework for working with one's community. After facilitators lay the foundations of thinking about both self and community from a place of strength, the curriculum walks participants through the steps of developing a community improvement project. Program curricula include topics such as visioning, goal setting, stakeholder analysis, action planning, running successful meetings, consensus-building, inclusive community engagement, and evaluation. During the final session of the program, participants present their project to the class and

Figure 11.1 *A cohort of participants in the University of Missouri Extension and University of Missouri–St. Louis Neighborhood Leadership Academy.*

submit a written overview of the project. Facilitators provide comments and feedback after the program.

Every participant that attends eight out of the ten sessions receives a Chancellor's Certificate from UMSL (see Figure 11.1). The university's intent is for this credentialing to add value and significance to the program for participants, particularly those without college degrees. To date, the program has graduated nearly 600 neighborhood and organization leaders. For the first eighteen years of its existence, NLA focused on the St. Louis region, although in 2020 the program expanded across the state of Missouri. Graduates include neighborhood association members, community leaders, resident volunteers, community-based organization staff, business owners, local government staff, and municipal elected officials. Cohorts typically number twenty to twenty-five individuals. While recruiting is extremely time-consuming, MU Extension adds the benefit of faculty with strong ties to the local community and deep relationships with stakeholders. These long-term community relationships, coupled with the academic credibility of extension professionals serving local communities, result in well-respected research-based programs such as NLA that are empowering environments in which community members can address local issues. According to 2020 NLA graduate Tysha, "I had confidence joining NLA because of MU Extension's reputation. I knew if it was some-thing they were involved in, it would be a quality opportunity for me."

Participant diversity varies with each cohort. Cohorts have ranged between 50 percent and 90 percent representation of people of color. The majority of participants every year are women. Participants often cite the diversity of backgrounds and experiences as the most important component of the program. One participant summed up the value of diversity in this way: "Everybody came from different places and had different goals, but in general [because of NLA], you could kind of see that you weren't alone, you know, that other people were in the same boat, trying to improve their areas or their communities. And I think that was encouraging, too, because you didn't feel like you were the only one trying to fight for something" (Dorner et al., 2009). This sense of "togetherness" is critical for the sustainability of community projects. It is commonly said: If you want to go fast, go alone, but if you want to go far, go together.

Neighborhood Leadership Academy is a fee-based program, with tuition ranging from $390 to $425. Some discounts are offered for early registration. Program administrators have engaged in discussion over the years about whether tuition excludes potential participants, but they work to build in inclusivity by offering partial and full scholarships through an application process and encouraging individual participant sponsorships by partnering with neighborhood associations, churches, community development corporations, and businesses. Sponsorships give these community partners the opportunity to invest in community leadership alongside the university system. Program leaders believe that fee-based models help to sustain these programs, which has contributed to NLA's longevity.

Impacts

Neighborhood Leadership Academy has established itself as a valuable community asset in St. Louis and more recently throughout the state of Missouri. A longitudinal evaluation from 2010 demonstrated that many NLA graduates take on leadership roles in their communities and take actions that positively impact their neighborhoods (Dorner et al., 2009). The evaluation assessed impact using three primary questions: Were program graduates taking up leadership roles? Were they implementing their projects? And were the projects having impact in their communities? Results showed that program graduates engage in diverse activities following completion of training (e.g., forming neighborhood associations to encourage more community involvement; establishment of community gardens; planning and obtaining funding for neighborhood parks; and forming a school-based youth coding program).

Data were collected from the first eight cohorts of the program (n = 133) using interviews and focus group discussions. The study noted that the majority of NLA alumni respondents developed some plans (90 percent), with 53 percent planning to create a community project, 30 percent to lead a community organization in a specific task, and 8 percent to lead a community organization at the end of the program. About 70 percent of these projects or plans were implemented in St. Louis.

Most respondents (76 percent) reported that they had increased their involvement as a leader in community volunteer or service work. Following participation in NLA, 68 percent reported that they had started new community or leadership roles. These new roles included: founder, leader, or key member of a neighborhood association/block or garden (11); coordinator or member of a nonprofit or community association (6); board chair/member of a nonprofit organization (4); leader or pastor at a church (3); leader of a coalition of agencies or company (3); volunteer or community spokesperson (2); and public leader (mayor) or public service worker (2).

The evaluation highlighted NLA's value in that it instills important leadership skills that improve how NLA alumni are implementing community improvement projects and that, overall, these projects are positively impacting their communities. Neighborhood Leadership Academy graduates go on to start and execute additional projects and assume new leadership roles.

In 2018, the University of Missouri Public Policy and Research Center conducted a follow-up study, but the response rate was low (n = 16) and therefore the results are not included here. However, impactful community leaders continue to share their stories of success from the NLA experience. For example, Gretchen (NLA 2017) started her NLA project called the Neighbor Helping Neighbor Community Coalition, which serves to connect social services to residents in crisis in Bridgeton, a municipality in St. Louis County. As she became more involved and understood the strengths and challenges in her community, she was elected to the Bridgeton City Council. Erica (NLA 2018) came to NLA seeking technical assistance and networking opportunities to benefit her newly formed nonprofit organization A Red Circle, focused on community betterment and racial equity in north St. Louis County. Through NLA she developed and launched a monthly Healthy Community Market with fresh produce, fitness activities, and nutrition resources. She developed connections in NLA with other like-minded food justice advocates with whom she partnered to launch a two-day Good Food Summit in summer 2021.

As community development continues to grow as a field and in the face of diverse community challenges (e.g., poverty, shrinking economic opportunities, growing population of disconnected youth, and health), residents are demonstrating a commitment to taking leadership roles to address these challenges locally in a way that collaboratively improves their neighborhoods and places from the ground up.

Recommendations: Pivoting and Growing

While the longitudinal evaluations demonstrated positive outcomes from NLA, the team realized the continued need to respond to the complexity of current and emergent community challenges. Several key insights were gleaned from the 2010 study. First, program administrators should provide additional instruction on fundraising and grant writing or connections to financial resources for community benefit. Fewer than 50 percent of participants surveyed felt successful in developing funds or resources. Second, participants surveyed described needing more information and practice with engaging others, connecting with others across diverse interests, and using social media. Considering this, facilitators developed an advanced neighborhood leadership program to both adequately cover the fundraisingand community connectivity concerns while also acknowledging the need for a program focused on communities in St. Louis facing the most severe challenges.

Pivot #1: Adding an Advanced Program

In 2018, MU Extension and UMSL partnered with the St. Louis Economic Development Partnership to launch an advanced follow-up leadership program called Neighborhood Leadership Fellows (NLF). This nine-month, 100-hour curriculum targets a yearly cohort of twenty-five residents from the St. Louis Promise Zone, an area designated by the federal government as needing additional investment given disadvantages including high rates of poverty (30 percent), low average life expectancy rates (64.6 years), and high property vacancy (22.5 percent; St. Louis Economic Development Partnership, 2021). In contrast to NLA, NLF provides a $2,000 stipend (funded by a local foundation) to every participant upon completion to enable community members from all socioeconomic backgrounds to participate and to acknowledge their investment of time in community-building and leadership programs.

In NLF, Fellows learn the advocacy skills and strategies needed to gain access to civic leadership tables and halls of power. This program is focused on power and how residents who are often excluded from halls of power can play a major role in leading the conversations about systemic change in their neighborhoods and municipalities. Given that the Promise Zone comprises 88 percent African American residents (and the NLF alumni closely mirror this figure at 92 percent), the curriculum addresses the structural racism built into the culture and environment of the region and how to dismantle the entrenched institutional policies that disproportionally affect people of color. Each Fellow creates a ten-year Individualized Personal Leadership Plan. They also work in groups to develop a policy-focused project aimed at addressing more equitable regional policies for neighborhoods and preventing violence in the community. At the end of the program, project groups can submit a request for up to $2,500 to continue their project after the program. This element of the program is in direct response to the feedback from the NLA 2010 evaluation identifying the challenge of raising funds. Qualitative feedback collected from participants in 2020 acknowledged the benefits of this additional community leadership opportunity:

> Prior to NLF, all I knew was I wanted to help the community. After NLF, I am able to define what community I am referencing and specific disparities I want to work towards addressing. Before NLF, all I knew was I wanted to make a difference but didn't know how. During NLF, I was appointed to a St. Louis County Board where I was able to network with additional change agents in St. Louis and now, I have an opportunity to work towards closing the digital divide in St. Louis after graduation. I would have never considered applying for a board if it wasn't for NLF. I would recommend this program to anyone who is serious about improving their community.   (NLF 2020 graduate)

One of the greatest challenges in this advanced program came through the shift from individual projects to group projects. Working together on pressing equity policy issues facing their communities generated a great deal of friction between Fellows, despite facilitators employing team-building strategies and conflict-resolution workshops. Facilitators witnessed continued communication breakdowns outside the confines of the leadership program when passionate individual grassroots leaders experienced very public conflict with neighbors that ultimately impeded collective action against those in power with opposing agendas. Over the past three years the facilitators added in sessions on reframing, active listening, and understanding different conflict styles using the Thomas–Kilmann instrument. This is a chronic challenge that sustained coaching and relationship-building may address but that has no clear resolution.

Pivot #2: Moving Online and Statewide

In 2020, the NLA faced a quandary of how to move forward during the global COVID-19 pandemic. With the understanding that leadership was more important than ever in times of crisis, NLA decided to continue virtually. While this posed significant challenges with regard to modifying the existing curriculum to an online format, an unintended benefit of COVID-19 to the virtual program has been growth in class participation due to the fact that participants do not have to drive to the program site but rather tune in from their homes or workplaces. Transitioning to online also met a preexisting need from among MU Extension community development faculty to offer the program in other communities outside of St. Louis. For the first eighteen years of its existence, the program had only been offered in St. Louis. Given this interest, NLA expanded to a statewide footprint and simultaneously migrated the ten three-hour sessions to an online Zoom format. The NLA facilitators accomplished this expansion by assembling a team of twelve MU Extension faculty with deep community ties embedded in cities, counties, and small towns across Missouri. Faculty recruited interested emerging leaders in their respective areas and then supported their local participants through the virtual course with technical assistance and individualized project feedback. The statewide team of MU Extension faculty collaborated on curriculum updates to ensure that the materials and guest speakers reflected the diversity of the state.

The 2020 cohort had fifty-eight participants from St. Louis and a wide variety of smaller rural communities from around the state. The participants were divided into four cohorts based on region to contextualize/localize the training and provide the opportunity for them to meet other people for networking opportunities. Reflecting on their experiences, some NLA online graduates stated:

> I'm so happy I was able to be a part of the state-wide virtual NLA class. It has made a lasting impression on me; how I look at my community, cultivate relationships, and understand what I'm good at and can bring to the table so I can be of better use to my community.

In the fall of 2020, extension received a $475,000 grant from Missouri Foundation for Health to continue the NLA statewide expansion and the NLF program, as well as a youth component. The 2021 NLA program grew to eighty-five participants, demonstrating evidence of increasing interest in this kind of program from both participant and sponsor perspectives, and evaluations show increases in learning and skill-building comparable to those from in-person courses based on pre–post tests.

Exemplar: Experience in Community Enterprise and Leadership Program

The EXCEL approach to CLD was first implemented in 1982–1983 in Randolph County, Missouri, a rural county in central Missouri with a population of 24,878 people in 2019. Today, the county has a median household income of $47,740 and a poverty rate of 16.4 percent (DataUSA, 2021). The program was developed in response to residents noting that leadership roles in the community were often held by the same people. The process, designed to be a flexible, adaptable model that can be adjusted to fit local needs and circumstances, was developed with community member input and MU Extension community development specialists. EXCEL, which today stands for Experience in Community Enterprise and Leadership, was originally an acronym for Experiment in Community Enterprise and Leadership. The approach developed as an experiment to determine whether a particular form of education for citizenship, offered to a significant number of community members, could increase the effectiveness of local civic systems and the vitality of rural communities. Each of the early approaches was an experiment because it was based on a new and innovative model of leadership education –

locally based, inclusive, future-oriented, and participatory – and because each was uniquely designed to specifically meet the challenges and circumstances of the sponsoring community. The program's goal was to "create a critical mass" of community leaders. Specifically, the EXCEL program's purpose is to increase the capacity of individuals and organizations to address community problems effectively by mobilizing people and social networks in the community toward common goals.

Structure and Content

The EXCEL program is not a prepackaged program but is instead a process for community leadership. The primary elements of the model focused on adult participation and adult learning strategies, concentrated and extensive learning opportunities, community as the vehicle for learning, producing leaders for community development, inviting all emerging leaders to participate, and a need for curriculum decisions to be made by a local planning committee.

What distinguishes EXCEL from other approaches to leadership development is its high degree of flexibility, local control, inclusiveness, and focus on the future of community governance. A local planning committee of existing county leaders and numerous University of Missouri faculty members as well as personnel from state and local government agencies assisted in the implementation.

This approach was intended to ensure local relevancy and community support/buy-in and to provide incentives for participation as community members would feel empowered to collectively address common concerns (Pigg, 2001). Key components of EXCEL programs include: a Kickoff Event and Graduation, Introduction to Community, County History, Getting to Know One Another, Team-Building Retreat, Vision and Action Planning, and Topical Sessions, such as education, natural resources, local government session and study tours, state government session and study tours, health services and study tours of local health-care facilities, community economic development and business and industry tours, social services, community study tours, and closure/evaluation sessions.

The EXCEL program helps participants increase personal growth and self-efficacy, community commitment, shared future and purpose, community knowledge, and civic engagement. Program participants are drawn from all sectors of a community if they are interested in developing strategies to help the community, improving their ability to work with groups, discovering what influences community politics, recognizing the impact of cultural and socio-economic values on the community, developing and implementing action plans, and participating in community decision-making processes. Each participant is both a teacher and student; EXCEL is an active experience in which participants are responsible for both their own learning and sharing their knowledge with others.

As in any true partnership, the cost is shared. Local funding is necessary to cover expenses such as travel, supplies, and general program administration. Total costs vary depending on the program that is developed. Potential participants are asked to submit a concise application and pay a portion of the total cost in the form of a fee, which usually covers about a third of the program's cost. This gives them a stake in the program and helps ensure their commitment to participate. An attendance policy is put in place to encourage their regular participation. The rest of the operational costs are usually covered by local firms, organizations, and government groups. Formation of a local steering committee is a critical factor in developing and implementing a successful EXCEL program. The steering committee is the heart, soul, and manager of the program. A local facilitator from MU Extension typically provides ongoing support and assistance during the process in collaboration with a chamber of commerce, a community betterment organization, and/or other interested parties.

Impacts

The EXCEL program expanded after receiving interest from community members and extension faculty members, and subsequently the program was replicated in thirty-eight of Missouri's 114 counties and, in some instances, repeated annually with different participants (University of Missouri Extension, 2000). Since 1984, more than 7,500 citizens from a third of Missouri's counties and communities have participated in community leadership programs using the EXCEL approach. In his 2001 program evaluation, Pigg summarized that CLD education should address the central driving force in community development: leaders who can address community problems effectively by mobilizing the human and social capital in the community to common purposes (Pigg, 2001). Most change in the community, good or bad, is attributed to the quality of community leadership. Rarely does research analysis identify factors that explain more than a small portion of the change that occurs in a community directly; the balance of the explanatory effect is often attributed to "leadership quality." "Leadership quality" is an elusive term that is hard to measure reliably, with observers differing as to what constitutes quality and leadership. Pigg's (2001) evaluation acknowledged these difficulties and, in its design, made choices that emphasize the variability that is likely to exist in the way people understand what leadership is and what leaders contribute to the community.

The evaluation reported that the EXCEL program had produced substantial and significant outcomes that transcend the individuals that participate and reflect changes in and impacts on the community where the participants live (Pigg, 2001). Benefits to individual participants include increased confidence and self-efficacy to participate in public affairs, public dialogue, and civic action, a better understanding of city and county functions and their local economy, and an ability to communicate with one another in a more inclusive manner (Apaliyah et al., 2017). Communities investing in an EXCEL program see new, younger, and more diverse people running for public office, more Missourians involved in community activities and organizations, improved community appearance, better-functioning boards and commissions, and community groups developing effective partnerships and coalitions (Apaliyah et al., 2017; Pigg et al., 2015).

Effective citizen leaders translate the knowledge they have gained and commitment they feel into hands-on action and participate in meeting the challenges facing their communities. They can convert words and ideas into action. They use insights and skills learned in programs like EXCEL to engage in building community networks, making well-informed community decisions, and finding real solutions to real problems (Pigg, 2001).

A graduate of Leadership Phelps County (LPC) commented:

> I have greatly benefited from my experience with Leadership Phelps County. During my class year, I had the opportunity to learn more about my community, the services provided, and what I could do to be of better service to the region. This leadership class also connected me with individuals that I possibly wouldn't have known if it were not for the LPC opportunity.   (Marketing interview, 2020)

Recommendations from EXCEL

Community leadership development programs have a concrete, positive effect on the community that sponsors them. Community leadership development participants take on and complete a variety of projects and activities that they feel will benefit their community. They employ a variety of community resources to achieve their goals. These activities appear to be self-organizing, in that individual who feel empowered as a result of their CLD experience are brought together through interactions that focus on a shared purpose or objective without any apparent intervention, encouragement, or approval by formal authorities in the local community. These civically activated residents may take on problems that range from conserving natural resources and green spaces for environmental reasons or for leisure activities, to raising money to support health objectives in creating spaces in which the arts can flourish, to organizing community events that may attract tourists and supplement the local economy, and more (Pigg et al., 2015).

In over twenty-five years of EXCEL programs in the state of Missouri, some best practices have emerged. The most successful and long-standing programs have created a strong local leadership committee that makes the decisions about content, and often these programs develop into their own 501 (c)(3) (i.e. nonprofit) organizations to fully run and fund the program from the community level. While MU Extension still serves as a partner (as ad hoc members of the board or content teachers), the community organizations build on local partnerships, often with chambers of commerce, to plan and implement the annual program.

Often graduates of the program are invited to serve on the planning committee or to help facilitate or speak to the next class of leaders. Alumni of programs also are encouraged to help recruit future participants, speak on behalf of the program to businesses and elected leaders, and provide mentoring relationships to new participants. These efforts build and strengthen a culture of leadership and value, contributing to the growth of future leaders.

The focus on a specific community or county for this program provides in-depth learning and networking that builds social capital and appreciation for other assets in the community. While communities need relationships and networks that extend beyond the community boundaries, often a significant first step for new leaders is to strengthen their knowledge and networks locally to better represent their local community when working beyond its borders.

Discussion

Our exemplars show that community residents can benefit from training and experiences that strengthen their personal leadership abilities and create skills and relationships to address community issues collectively. Community members can realize collective impact when they become engaged in discussing and mitigating community issues that are important to them and build relationships with others who have common concerns. They become energized and enabled to be a part of building a better community. The collaborative framework enshrined in CLD programs provides a mindset, a set of principles, and problem-solving and decision-making processes that enable community members to work together in ways that build the community's capacity and resilience.

The EXCEL model and its primary substantive focus on networking and building a bench of new leaders compares directly to many other cooperative extension-sponsored leadership development education programs offered across the US. Given demographic trends of baby boomers and youth leaving rural communities, many communities can ill afford to ignore the transitional problem faced when a generation of leaders retire from public life and new leaders are expected to replace them (Moore, 1988). Without conscious effort to prepare and "legitimate" such a cadre of new leaders, communities can drift and decline in ways that may be preventable. Further, the notion of "critical mass" recognizes that it takes a lot of people working together collaboratively to make community development work well. Other states have similar programs; many of those establish more specific learning goals for participants such as "learning how to conduct effective meetings" or "learning how to establish a vision for the community" (Littrell & Littrell, 2000).

In a six-state study of community leadership programs completed in 2015 that included Missouri's EXCEL program, Pigg et al. (2015) found that "leadership in the community is individual and collective behavior that is intended to keep the community viable" (p. 31). The study found that CLD programs not only created or increased leadership capacity but also prepared individuals to behave as effective community leaders. According to the 2015 study, people who participated in CLD programs displayed significantly greater scores compared to the "four-treatment" communities, for a total of twenty-four sites, in the six leadership outcome indices used in the study (personal growth and efficacy, community knowledge, community commitment, shared future and purpose, social cohesion, and civic engagement). The researchers concluded that personal leadership development of community residents to engage civically – supported by networks of bridging social capital (social cohesion) – is what provides the connecting link between individual attributes and the immediate effects of CLD programs on individuals and the more distal effects on communities (Pigg et al., 2015). These outcomes highlight why MU Extension invests significantly in CLD to create the conditions for strong personal leadership development, deep social networks, and civic engagement. The exemplars show different ways of achieving those goals.

The two exemplars provided, and CLD programs in general, have processes in place that are based on a set of principles that include inclusivity, mutual respect, open communication, transparent processes, understanding of others' interests, identification of shared interests, and consensus-building. For community members from different stakeholder organizations to work together, they must first come together, speak openly, and listen to one another. Community leadership programs provide this opportunity. Open conversations help in exploring options and creating solutions to community issues. The exemplars demonstrate that collaborative efforts have many important steps, and the CLD literature suggests that four are critical: leadership, stakeholders, processes for problem-solving, and common goals and action (Robinson Jr & Green, 2011). Community leadership development programs aim to educate participants on these steps.

- *Leadership:* Successful community initiatives require leaders who have the courage to take on difficult issues and model the use of shared power and mutual respect for all perspectives. It is important that leaders can encourage and facilitate broad participation and unite people around a common issue. Throughout the leadership training, these traits are learned and nurtured by people as they work together. Training in facilitating difficult conversations, goal setting, and other skills that participants practice can strengthen their confidence in leading through shared power and respect.
- *Stakeholders:* Equitable communities ensure that every resident has the opportunity and voice to contribute to decision-making in their community. Stakeholders include individuals and organizations with the formal power to

make or block a decision or the informal power to influence the decisions of those who will be affected by the decision and those with relevant information or expertise (Straus, 2002). Many community leadership programs invite key stakeholders to be part of the program either as instructors, funders, or participants. The two exemplars effectively leverage relationships between MU Extension specialists and local community members, partnerships with program alumni, local elected leaders, foundations, and agencies to recruit participants, serve as program advisors and speakers, and advocate for program enhancements based on community needs.

- *Processes of problem-solving:* In most leadership development programs, participants are educated on the importance of identifying how the group will address issues and make decisions and how it will involve people in these processes. In practice, community initiatives always find themselves at this decision-making crossroads. Goal setting, project development, and resources to support project implementation can have a positive impact on the community needs identified by program participants.

- *Common goals and action:* When addressing community issues, people need to feel that their time has been well spent and see the potential for change to occur. Community leadership development programs train participants to identify common goals and celebrate milestone accomplishments to keep collaborative efforts moving forward. Community leadership development programs can provide opportunities for participants to learn from each other, discuss and collaborate on shared goals, and recognize accomplishments during the program and through ongoing communication with alumni after graduation.

Thus, CLD is intentional about creating the conditions for self-empowerment that then contribute to collaborative efforts in a community. The processes of self- empowerment that happens within the exemplars – and CLD programs more broadly – contribute to the development of the individual's control over their life, increase their sense of responsibility for their broader community, and support community-led efforts to address complex social issues.

Around the world, people are participating in CLD programs to be empowered to tackle a variety of community issues, including energy projects, HIV/AIDS issues, education, and access to food concerns, among other issues. For example, around HIV/AIDS, evidence suggests that disempowerment is a root source of vulnerability to HIV (e.g., Blankenship et al., 2008), making the empowerment of marginalized groups critical (Cornish et al., 2012). Empowerment, in this context, is understood not only in the narrow sense of people gaining greater control over their health-related behaviors but also in a broad sense of gaining greater control in their everyday lives (Dworkin & Ehrhardt, 2007). In the example of NLA, leaders not only gain tools and strategies but psychological empowerment to succeed in community development. As a result of their involvement in such programs, many people mention changes in themselves, such as "confidence" or "hope." This is especially true for those residents who live in communities that have experienced a great deal of disinvestment and trauma. They are used to seeing the deficits in their communities, and as Nel (2018) pointed out, using an asset-based approach can enhance community engagement and project impact. Looking instead for assets, both in individual participants and community activities like asset mapping, alters the way individuals approach community-building and how they see themselves as agents of change in the process. The other contributor to psychological empowerment is simply being in a room with other community advocates and change-makers. Often people feel lonely and isolated doing this work – that they are the only ones who care about their neighborhood. Knowing that others are also invested in improving their community and having potential collaborators or sources for support in the process give people a psychological boost.

Community leadership development can improve self-efficacy and provides participants with skills to create community change from the project idea stage through planning to implementation – important skills for any community effort to succeed and be sustainable. However, to build community capacity, the issues that community leaders elect to address should more closely align with collective paradigms rather than leader-centric paradigms. Thus, it is critical that community leadership programs do not perpetuate the leader-centric paradigm of leadership through programs that are meant to only network those with existing privilege. This argument is what Majee et al. (2017) write on when they proposed their "WE-Lead" community leadership model that anchors coalitions as representing relational leadership. The model views coalitions as responding to problems through a social ecological lens by assessing community issues from multiple perspectives and through enacting and putting in place multilayered strategies. The key is that these coalitions should not operate in isolation of each other but, rather, must be coordinated to focus on the grander whole of building vibrant communities. Thus, coalitions formed under the proposed approach will provide a mechanism capable of connecting the interactions occurring in different parts of the community into a collective whole. It is generally understood that the strongest communities do not have a single strong leader but rather a *network of leaders* who come from, are part of, and affirm the community. WE-Lead realizes that no single issue exists in a vacuum and acknowledges that issues are contextual, varying from one community to another and even among subgroups in one community. Kirk and Shutte (2004) proposed similar recommendations from their work in South Africa for relationship leadership based on processes and roles instead of individual leaders. The exemplars in this chapter focus on local context by allowing for community input into program design and implementation and arranging for local or regional cohorts to support networking for addressing broader community challenges. It is, therefore, critical that coalition activities mutually reinforce one another and that open communication is maintained and upheld. We need CLD opportunities where diverse stakeholders can come together around common issues alongside leadership educators to enhance the practice of collective leadership in order to address complex social issues.

While this is an ideal status to attain, facilitating impactful CLD programs is easier said than done – it can be messy. First, selecting program participants can further fragment the community if the process is not transparent and inclusive. On the other hand, welcoming everyone to the program can also derail efforts as community members fail to bond and work together during the program. Second, facilitation of leadership development requires awareness of the community's cultural norms and values and other socioeconomic factors affecting the livelihoods of potential program participants. Facilitators can influence the effectiveness of a program. In community-based programs such as leadership development, how the facilitator makes participants feel can be more impactful than what they say and do. Thus, in cases where training programs are designed and delivered by people outside of the target community, facilitators must make the effort to integrate with that community's culture. This practice can facilitate a collaborative environment between program participants and facilitators, which in turn fosters trust that can be leveraged to motivate participants to engage in the training and in community practice with open minds. Finally, funding project ideas developed during training can be a challenge that potentially alienates community members if those whose ideas were not funded harbor feelings of resentment. Enhancing leadership programs with skills and knowledge of other ways to access resources and funding for projects can help to reduce this challenge.

Conclusion

As evidenced in this chapter, leadership development has a long history as an approach to addressing community issues, especially as a program of US university extension services. As communities evolve, so must the approaches to developing strong community leaders who can support the process of community change. Effective CLD programs must continually adapt and refresh their methods of teaching and learning to respond to changing community needs and evaluations of effectiveness of the program. This chapter highlights two models of community leadership programs developed by MU Extension in partnership with other agencies and local communities that prioritize the empowerment of residents within their communities, focus on processes and content that allow for adaptations to local contexts and needs, and emphasize collective, collaborative leadership to address social issues. The two programs highlighted demonstrate the value and impact of CLD programs that leverage and connect partners (such as the relationship between the MU Extension specialists and local communities), focus on individual and community assets, and respond to ongoing feedback from participants. These types of CLD programs can effectively support communities to collectively respond to complex social challenges and improve outcomes for all members of their communities.

While a lot of work has been done around CLD, there are still grey areas that future research should address. No studies have examined how demographic characteristics of participants such as age, gender, race/ethnicity, geographic location, and socioeconomic status may explain the type and extent of benefits participants may derive from such programs. In their study, Majee et al. (2018) acknowledged that women tend to participant more in CLD than men. However, this research falls short of articulating how men and women benefit from participating in a leadership development program. The role of facilitators during CLD is a key component of the training. There is a need for future research to examine the association between facilitator skills and program outcomes: Do programs facilitated by multiple people produce better outcomes? How does a facilitator's gender influence program outcomes? Do program participants prefer certain facilitators based on gender, education, race/ethnicity, socioeconomic status, length of stay, and position in the community? Additionally, in a post-COVID-19 world, new research and ongoing evaluation of programs to document impacts on new community issues and challenges will be critical to continue to produce strong, vibrant community leaders who are able to respond and adapt to a changing global context.

References

Alexander, J. A., Comfort, M. E., Weiner, B. J., & Bogue, R. (2001). Leadership in collaborative community health partnerships. *Nonprofit Management and Leadership*, *12*(2), 159–175.

Apaliyah, G. T., Martin, K. E., Gasteyer, S. P., Keating, K., & Pigg, K. (2017). Community leadership development education: promoting civic engagement through human and social capital. In N. Walzer & S. Cordes (Eds.), *Innovative community change practices* (pp. 40–57). Routledge.

Aref, F., & Ma'rof, R. (2008). Barriers to community leadership in tourism development in Shiraz, Iran. *European Journal of Social Sciences*, *7*(2), 172–178.

Baah, S. K. T., Aguilar, R. A. C., Diaz-Bonilla, C., Fujs, T., Lanker, C., Nguyen, M. C., & Viveros, M. (2023). *March 2023 global poverty update from the World Bank: the challenge of estimating poverty in the pandemic*. World Bank Blogs. https://blogs.worldbank.org/opendata/march-2023-global-poverty-update-world-bank-challenge-estimating-poverty-pandemic

Blanchard, A. (2012). People transforming communities. For good. In *Investing in What Works for America's Communities* (pp. 140–149). Federal Reserve Bank of San Francisco.

Blankenship, K. M., West, B. S., Kershaw, T. S., & Biradavolu, M. R. (2008). Power, community mobilization, and condom use practices among female sex workers in Andhra Pradesh, India. *AIDS*, *22*, S109–S116.

Brungardt, C. L., & Seibel, N. (1995). *Assessing the effectiveness of community leadership programs*. Kansas Leadership Forum.

Cornish, F., Campbell, C., Shukla, A., & Banerji, R. (2012). From brothel to boardroom: Prospects for community leadership of HIV interventions in the context of global funding practices. *Health & Place*, *18*(3), 468–474.

Cullen-Lester, K. L., & Yammarino, F. J. (2016). Collective and network approaches to leadership: Special issue introduction. *The Leadership Quarterly*, *27*(2), 173–180.

DataUSA. (2021). *Randolph County, MO*. DataUSA. https://datausa.io/profile/geo/randolph-county-mo

Dorner, L., Layton, A., & Hager, E. (2009). An evaluation of the neighborhood leadership academy: From individual to community effects. *Journal of Community Psychology*, *37*(8), 975–986.

Dworkin, S. L., & Ehrhardt, A. A. (2007). Going beyond "ABC" to include "GEM": Critical reflections on progress in the HIV/AIDS epidemic. *American Journal of Public Health*, *97*(1), 13–18.

Forman, R., Shah, S., Jeurissen, P., Jit, M., & Mossialos, E. (2021). COVID-19 vaccine challenges: What have we learned so far and what remains to be done? *Health Policy*, *125*(5), 553–567.

Foster-Fishman, P. G., Cantillon, D., Pierce, S. J., & Van Egeren, L. A. (2007). Building an active citizenry: The role of neighborhood problems, readiness, and capacity for change. *American Journal of Community Psychology*, *39*(1–2), 91–106.

Gawande, A. (2010). *Complications: A surgeon's notes on an imperfect science*. Profile Books.

Goodman, L., Majee, W., & Reed Adams, J. (2018). Building community leaders in underserved communities: An exploration of the role of seed-funding for community projects by program graduates. *Journal of Community Practice*, *26*(3), 358–376.

Heifetz, R. A., Heifetz, R., Grashow, A., & Linsky, M. (2009). *The practice of adaptive leadership: Tools and tactics for changing your organization and the world*. Harvard Business Press.

Kent, A. H., & Ricketts, L. R. (2020, December 2). *Has wealth inequality in America changed over time? Here are key statistics*. Federal Reserve Bank of St. Louis. www.stlouisfed.org/open-vault/2020/december/has-wealth-inequality-changed-over-time-key-statistics

Kirk, P., & Shutte, A. M. (2004). Community leadership development. *Community Development Journal*, *39*(3), 234–251.

Komives, S. R., & Wagner, W. (2016). *Leadership for a better world: Understanding the social change model of leadership development*. John Wiley & Sons.

Krietzman, J., & McKnight, J. (1993). *Building communities from the inside out: A path towards finding and mobilizing a community's assets*. Center for the Urban Affairs & Policy Research.

Langone, C. A., & Richard Rohs, F. (1995). Community leadership development: Process and practice. *Community Development*, *26*(2), 252–267.

Littrell, D., & Littrell, D. (2000). *EXCEL, an approach to community leadership handbook*. University of Missouri Extension.

Majee, W., Goodman, L., Reed Adams, J., & Keller, K. (2017). The WE-Lead model for bridging the low-income community leadership skills–practice gap. *Journal of Community Practice*, *25*(1), 126–137.

Majee, W., Long, S., & Smith, D. (2012). Engaging the underserved in community leadership development: Step up to leadership graduates in northwest Missouri tell their stories. *Community Development*, *43*(1), 80–94.

Majee, W., Maltsberger, B. A., Johnson, L. K., & Adams, J. R. (2014). Collaboration: Finding the place for cooperative extension in the intersection of community development and health promotion. *Community Development*, *45*(1), 90–102.

Majee, W., Thullen, M. J., & Goodman, L. (2018). Community leadership development: Perspectives of graduates of a low-income leadership development program on family relations. *Journal of Community Practice*, *26*(2), 143–161.

Maltsberger, B., & Majee, W. (2012). Building regional networking capacity through leadership development: The case of leadership northwest Missouri. *Journal of Extension*, *50*(4), 1–11.

Mattioli, D. (2009). Despite cutbacks, firms invest in developing leaders. *The Wall Street Journal*, *9*, B4.

McKnight, J., & Kretzmann, J. (1993). *Building communities from the inside out. A path toward finding and mobilizing a community's assets.* ACTA Publications.

Moore, C. M. (1988). *A colorful quilt: The community leadership story.* National Associations of Community Leadership Organizations.

National Academies of Sciences, Engineering, and Medicine. (2020). *Social isolation and loneliness in older adults: Opportunities for the health care system.* National Academies Press.

National Institute of Food and Agriculture. (2021). *National Institute of Food and Agriculture FACTSHEET.* National Institute of Food and Agriculture. https://nifa.usda.gov/sites/default/files/resource/NIFA-Fact-Sheet-2019.pdf

National Extension Task Force. (1977). *An evaluation of community organization and leadership development in cooperative extension's community development program: A National Task Force report.* Cooperative Extension Service, Mississippi State University.

Nel, H. (2018). Community leadership: A comparison between asset-based community-led development (ABCD) and the traditional needs-based approach. *Development Southern Africa*, *35*(6), 839–851.

Nelson, T., & Squires, V. (2017). Addressing complex challenges through adaptive leadership: A promising approach to collaborative problem solving. *Journal of Leadership Education*, *16*(4), 111–123.

Northouse, P. G. (2021). *Leadership: Theory and practice.* Sage.

Ohmer, M. L. (2016). Strategies for preventing youth violence: Facilitating collective efficacy among youth and adults. *Journal of the Society for Social Work and Research*, *7*(4), 681–705.

Ospina, S. M., & Foldy, E. G. (2016). Collective dimensions of leadership. In A. Farazmand (Ed.), *Global encyclopedia of public administration, public policy, and governance* (pp. 1–6). Springer.

Pigg, K. (2001). *EXCEL: Experience in Community Enterprise and Leadership.* University of Missouri Extension.

Pigg, K., Gasteyer, S., Martin, K., Apaliyah, G., & Keating, K. (2015). *Community effects of leadership development education: Citizen empowerment for civic engagement*. West Virginia University Press.

Reed Adams, J., Donahue, G., & Duncan, M. (2005). *A facilitator's guide to Step Up to Leadership*. University of Missouri Extension.

Robinson Jr, J. W., & Green, G. P. (2011). *Introduction to community development: Theory, practice, and service-learning*. Sage.

Rost, J. C. (1993). Leadership development in the new millennium. *Journal of Leadership Studies*, *1*(1), 91–110.

Rubino, L. G., Esparza, S. J., & Chassiakos, Y. (2018). *New leadership for today's health care professionals*. Jones & Bartlett Learning.

Sampson, R., Raudenbush, S. W., & Earls, F. (2009). Neighborhoods and violent crime: A multilevel study of collective efficacy. In H. P. Hynes & R. Lopes (Eds.), *Urban health: Readings in the social, built, and physical environments of US cities* (pp. 79–97). Jones & Bartlett Learning.

Sandfort, J. R., & Bloomberg, L. (2012). InCommons: supporting community-based leadership. *Community Development*, *43*(1), 12–30.

St. Louis Economic Development Partnership. (2021, February). *St. Louis Promise Zone Progress Report*. St. Louis Economic Development Partnership. https://stlpartnership.com/wp-content/uploads/2021/03/2021-annual-reportv8.pdf

Straus, D. (2002). *How to make collaboration work: Powerful ways to build consensus, solve problems, and make decisions*. Berrett-Koehler Publishers.

Theleman, B. (2011). *Closing the gaps in leadership development*. UNC Kenan-Flagler Business School. www.kenan-flagler.unc.edu/executive-development/custom-programs/~/media/D38ECCA30B1341A18E65F85D150E1104.ashx

University of Missouri Extension. (2021). *History of extension*. University of Missouri Extension. https://extension.missouri.edu/about-us/history-of-extension

University of Missouri–St. Louis. (2023). *Economic and community development*. University of Missouri–St. Louis Office of Research and Economic and Community Development. www.umsl.edu/recd/economic-and-community-development/building-civic-capacity-for-thriving-communities/index.html

Walker, J., & Gray, B. (2009). Community voices: A leadership program making a difference in rural underserved counties in North Carolina. *Journal of Extension*, *47*(6), 1–11.

Wituk, S., Ealey, S., Clark, M. J., Heiny, P., & Meissen, G. (2005). Community development through community leadership programs: Insights from a state-wide community leadership initiative. *Community Development*, *36*(2), 89–101.

World Bank. (2021, October 7). *COVID-19 to add as many as 150 million extreme poor by 2021*. World Bank. www.worldbank.org/en/news/press-release/2020/10/07/covid-19-to-add-as-many-as-150-million-extreme-poor-by-2021

World Vision. (2021). *Global poverty: Facts, FAQs, and how to help*. World Vision. www.worldvision.org/sponsorship-news-stories/global-poverty-facts

12 Community Coalitions and Empowerment

Michelle C. Kegler and Lauren M. Bigger

Introduction

Community coalitions are a form of strategic association character-ized by constituencies and organizations from a range of sectors within a community agreeing to work together toward a common goal (Feighery & Rogers, 1990). Coalitions are action-oriented and provide a mechanism for diverse sectors to collaboratively address a community problem by assessing and analyzing the issue, identifying and implementing relevant and culturally appropriate intervention strategies, and creating community change that could not have been achieved by a single group or agency alone (Butterfoss & Kegler, 2009). Community coalitions differ from short-term advocacy coalitions that come together for a narrowly defined purpose in that they tend to be more formal and longer-lasting, typically for several years and often much longer.

Community coalitions are based in geographic areas with a shared identity, such as small towns, counties, cities, and multicounty regions. Ideally, members reflect the diversity within a community and include both grassroots residents and representatives from a range of organizations that serve the community. In effective coalitions, members are actively engaged in decision-making, problem-solving, and the implementation of collaboratively developed action plans. Additionally, they pool and expand available resources, adapt intervention approaches to local contexts, and create collaborative synergy that leads to better solutions (Butterfoss & Kegler, 2009).

Coalitions, also commonly called community partnerships, are now a mainstay of community-based public health. Thousands of coalitions have formed over the past four decades across the US to address a broad range of public health and social issues (Chin & Abesamis-Mendoza, 2012; Choy et al., 2016; Hussaini et al., 2018; Kegler et al., 2020; Lee et al., 2012; Sirdenis et al., 2019; Toumbourou et al., 2019; van den Berg et al., 2019). Coalitions of health agencies, schools, faith-based organizations, recreation centers, food justice advocates, and neighborhood groups have come together to increase access to healthy foods and environments that support active living. Tobacco control advocates, public health agencies, and local residents have formed coalitions to pursue smoke-free ordinances and tax increases on tobacco products. Civic and faith-based groups have formed coalitions to expand affordable housing. Social service providers, veterans' groups, the military, and families are working together through coalitions to prevent suicide. Youth-focused coalitions have formed to address concerns around tobacco use, adolescent health, substance use, and sexual equity. Multisectoral coalitions have formed to increase childhood immunization and COVID-19 vaccination. And the list goes on.

The growth of coalitions occurred alongside the progression and evolution of community-wide health promotion over the past few decades. In the US, several large-scale community demonstration projects were launched in the 1980s to combat cardiovascular disease. Funded by the National Institutes of Health, these projects were viewed as state-of-the-art community-based public health, and they employed community advisory boards to plan and implement a range of prevention strategies, including some innovative approaches focused on environmental change (Mittelmark, 1999). At about the same time, the Centers for Disease Control and Prevention (CDC) was funding state and local health departments to engage in the Planned Approach to Community Health, which involved the formation of community coalitions and a formal assessment, planning, and implementation process. In the 1990s, major federally funded tobacco and antidrug initiatives mandated community coalitions (Butterfoss & Kegler, 2009; Manley et al., 1997). Since then, CDC and the Substance Abuse and Mental Health Services Administration continued to require community coalitions in many of their large-scale community health promotion initiatives (Bunnell et al., 2012; Flewelling & Hanley, 2016; Giles, 2010; Soler et al., 2016; Tucker et al., 2006; Yarnoff et al., 2019), as have several large foundations (Brennan et al., 2012; Brownson et al., 2015; Cheadle et al., 2018).

Outside of the US, the World Health Organization initiated the Healthy Cities movement, also in the 1980s. The model operationalized a broad view of health and emphasized the critical role city governments play in "establishing the conditions for health" (Ashton et al., 1986; World Health Organization, 2019). The movement evolved to include a broader range of geographic boundaries and government entities as it spread globally to thousands of communities. These initiatives are characterized by a set of principles that continue to emphasize a broad view of health, a shared vision, improving equity and quality of life, diverse resident participation and widespread community ownership, a focus on systems change, development of local assets and resources, and ongoing evaluation (Norris & Pittman, 2000; World Health Organization, 2019). Community participation, empowerment, and capacity-building have been emphasized throughout, along with multisectoral partnerships and a health-in-all-policies perspective (Dooris & Heritage, 2013). Additional international examples include the adaptation of a coalition-based approach to address adolescent health problems in Australia (Toumbourou et al., 2019), coalitions to address homelessness in Canada (Fleury et al.,

2014), and smoke-free air coalitions in Armenia and Georgia (Berg et al., 2019; Kegler et al., 2023a).

Part of the reason why coalitions have gained such deep traction as a community change mechanism is that they provide a structure through which communities can organize to change policies, systems, and environments. Coalition-based approaches align well with the social-ecological model that acknowledges the complexity of major public health and social problems and that levers of change exist at multiple levels, from individual to policy (McLeroy et al., 1988; Solar & Irwin, 2010). Community coalitions can engage multiple sectors within a community to implement an interrelated and synergistic set of interventions, including those aimed at policies and environments, to improve prioritized outcomes. Additional benefits include increased coordination, decreased duplication of effort, and increased community ownership and likelihood of sustained community changes. The application of pooled skills and expertise toward collective efforts aligns well with community empowerment.

Exemplar: California Healthy Cities and Communities

Because coalitions usually form to address a public health or social problem, they are rarely evaluated systematically for the purpose of documenting whether and how empowerment occurs. A few initiatives, such as California Healthy Cities and Communities (CHCC), have been evaluated to assess processes and outcomes at individual, civic participation, organizational, interorganizational, and community levels (Kegler et al., 2000). Given the strong correspondence between these levels and empowerment, we describe this initiative as an excellent example of how coalitions can lead to empowerment processes and outcomes.

The purpose of the CHCC was to enhance the capacity of recognized and Indigenous leaders in communities with underserved or vulnerable populations to understand and address environmental and structural determinants of community well-being. Twenty communities participated, ranging from rural regions within counties to urban neighborhoods. The first year of each three-year local effort was devoted to developing a governance structure for the coalition, engaging a broad cross-section of the community to produce a shared vision, conducting a community assessment, identifying a priority community improvement focus, and developing an action plan. The second and third years were spent implementing and evaluating the action plan. The initiative was supported by technical assistance on governance, coalition-building, systems reform, sustainability, and evaluation, as well as conferences and workshops for skill-building, and membership in a statewide network for sharing best practices.

The evaluation was mixed methods and employed a coalition member survey, focus groups, key informant interviews, and program records as the major data sources. The results reported here pull heavily from the Initiative's Final Report (Kegler et al., 2003).

Resident Engagement in the Planning Phase

The early steps in the planning process were to develop a community vision and conduct a community assessment. Large participatory workshops were a common approach to visioning. Grassroots residents, often the priority for empowerment-focused efforts, were involved as coalition members, although not without some challenges, and through surveys, community forums, focus groups, and community dialogues. In some of the communities, a concerted effort was made to ensure that prioritized residents were able to provide input in the process despite challenges (e.g., people with no phones, immigrants with limited English skills). Additionally, in some of the communities, residents and youth were trained to collect assessment data by going door to door for community surveys or through photovoice projects.

Through this process, coalitions selected priority focus areas. A number of the priority areas aligned well with community empowerment. Civic capacity-building activities involved a range of strategies to strengthen the ability of community residents to meet their needs in a fair and equitable way, with an emphasis on leadership development and community cohesion. Neighborhood improvement included strategies to improve municipal infrastructure, neighborhood appearance, and public safety. Economic development also focused on physical infrastructure, along with affordable housing, technology, and economic opportunities. Volunteerism involved ways of leveraging contributions from individuals, organizations, and institutions toward community well-being, and intergroup relations attempted to improve communication, relationships, and opportunities for culturally diverse groups within communities.

Facilitators and Barriers to Resident Engagement

The coalition member survey asked members whether coalition leadership made an effort to involve people who were broadly representative of the community, and the majority of coalition members strongly agreed. A smaller proportion were very satisfied with how well the coalition represented the diversity of the community. The survey also documented that the coalition membership was similar to that of many coalitions across the US, with the majority of adult coalition members being aged forty-five to sixty-four, with a college or graduate degree, White, and women.

While a significant number of barriers inhibited the ability of the coalitions to deeply engage grassroots residents, many of these were overcome. Barriers included competing demands related to family, work, and day-to-day survival, limited time to participate in community efforts, language barriers, difficulty

with transportation to meetings and events due to age or distance, profession-
ally dominated meetings (often with bureaucratic jargon), and challenges in
finding meeting times that worked well for both agency professionals and
residents. Additional barriers included cultural differences or conflicts in the
community, an emphasis on process over action in coalition meetings, and a
culture of independence, with the latter being especially prominent in
rural areas.

These barriers were overcome, at least partially, by creating a welcoming
environment and supporting grassroots residents with transportation, day-
care, translation, meeting reminders, and meeting times that were convenient.
Well-connected coordinators and coalition members with preexisting relationships with diverse groups within a community were additional facilitators, as
was partnering with organizations who were already trusted by disenfranchised segments of the community. Commitment to an inclusive community-
driven process and structuring meetings to allow for everyone to be heard were
also key to facilitating grassroots engagement, in addition to taking the time to
get to know people in the community. Distributing funds to local groups to
address their own needs was another useful strategy in supporting grassroots
resident involvement. Notably, grassroots resident involvement increased in
the implementation years that were more action-focused.

Empowerment-Related Outcomes at the Individual Level

The coalition member survey assessed *skills that were strengthened or gained*
by coalition members. Of the planning and action skills assessed, about a third
of respondents reported a great deal of improvement for assessing needs and
assets and for developing and/or advocating for policy change. Of the group
process and community-building skills assessed, about a third reported a great
deal of improvement in understanding different perspectives, defining health
broadly, using an empowering style, facilitating groups, and communicating
effectively in groups.

New civic leadership opportunities were also examined as part of the evaluation. Leadership opportunities provide mechanisms through which current
and potential leaders can contribute their talents and build and strengthen new
skills through exposure to new ideas, perspectives, and experiences. Over 1,100
new civic leadership roles were created over the course of the initiative. These
included formal leadership positions within the coalitions and their subcommittees, such as chairs or officers, with a much higher proportion related to
implementation of the action plan and/or spin-off community health improvement efforts. Many of these were youth leadership- and service-oriented, with
others involving the coordination and provision of services for children,
youth, and families.

The evaluation also sought to identify examples of individuals who
developed skills, confidence, or connections through participation in a

coalition and affiliated activities that they were able to apply in civic engagement opportunities outside of the initiative. These examples included helping to establish a volunteer fire department, joining the Parent–Teacher Association, volunteering to be a block captain for an early childhood development project, and writing grant proposals.

Empowerment-Related Outcomes at the Organizational Level

Organizations such as schools, faith-based organizations, and city governments serve as the dominant vehicle through which people engage within their communities. Across the twenty coalitions, over 200 organization-based *programs and services were newly created or expanded*. Examples include block clubs and civic education programs, time exchange/barter programs, community gardens, code enforcement, graffiti and neighborhood cleanup, small business plans and website development classes, fine and performing arts programs, new facilities such as teen centers and skateboard parks, new funding for public recreation, and diversity training.

Organizational policy and practice change was defined as administrative actions with the potential to improve community health, with both public institutions and private organizational changes considered. Although not an explicit goal in most initiatives, organizations changed how they "do business." Some of the practice changes stemmed from a broadened definition of health. Changes in this domain involved the adoption of new strategies aimed at social determinants of health, shifting away from health care and traditional health education. Another type of change increased community input in decision-making, including new structures for input and increased diversity or action, as well as mechanisms for new populations to provide input (e.g., youth, Latinos, representation from remote parts of counties). Thirdly, government and private entities expanded and institutionalized new forms of interorganizational collaboration.

The coalitions also *leveraged considerable funds*, bringing substantial resources into the participating communities. Collectively, the twenty coalitions were able to leverage $21 million from twelve different sources, ranging from federal, state, county, and city governments to state tobacco tax funds, private-sector donations, and fund-raising.

Collaboration between Organizations

Organizational representatives were asked whether they *increased interorganizational relationships* through their involvement in the coalition. The vast majority reported increased sharing of information with partners and increased cosponsoring of events, coordination of services, and collaborative initiatives. An example was a new partnership between a teen center and a sheriff's office for court-mandated community service placement and supervision.

Community-Level Outcomes

More than thirty *policy changes* were documented, with most of them directly and significantly influenced by the coalition. The others were a result of the coalition playing a supportive role in a larger advocacy effort. Policies covered restructuring of government, new public financing, integration of coalition goals into public plans, retention of services scheduled for elimination, and changes in land-use/zoning policies.

Community leaders and coordinators were asked to reflect on whether community problem-solving norms and values had changed as a result of the initiative. The majority described a shift with respect to *valuing diversity more than before*. The most compelling examples of changed norms were increased breadth and depth of people involved in community problem-solving and examples of powerful constituencies within communities displaying more openness to new ideas and people.

Physical changes in the community involved the construction, expansion, and renovation of facilities (e.g., expansion of community center space, construction of skate parks and bike trails). Additionally, improvements in public utilities and public safety were attributed to the coalitions, such as repairs to streets, the installation of new street lighting and traffic control features, and repairs to water mains. Changes were also made related to neighborhood and community beautification (e.g., trash removal, murals, and mosaics) and environmental improvements (e.g., stream restoration).

Current Initiative Assessing Similar Outcomes

The evaluation framework for CHCC, with its emphasis on empowerment and capacity-related outcomes, informed the evaluation questions for the *Two Georgias Initiative* (2017–2022), which focused on health equity in rural Georgia. Evaluation methods are similar, with the addition of a community change-tracking tool to document policy, systems, and environmental (PSE) changes and serial cross-sectional population-based surveys. Many of the evaluation questions and associated indicators provide insights into empowerment processes and outcomes, such as: the proportion of leadership positions filled by residents and/or members of the prioritized populations; opportunities provided to give diverse demographics, grassroots residents, and nontraditional sectors a voice in planning, priority-setting, implementation, and evaluation; personal and/or interorganizational networks expanded and/or linked; and evidence of community power redistributed toward equity (Kegler et al., 2023b).

Research on Coalitions as a Mechanism for Power-Building and Empowerment

Coalitions are typically created when a nonprofit organization or local government agency responds to an opportunity, such as a funding announcement, that requires a coalition (Butterfoss & Kegler, 2009). Threats (e.g., a pandemic or natural disaster) or a mandate can also catalyze coalition formation. The convening organization often initiates a coalition by engaging formal and informal community leaders, agency professionals, and sometimes grassroots residents for an initial meeting to assess interest in forming a coalition. Coalitions typically start with a core group that then actively recruits to expand the coalition membership to reflect the diversity of the community in terms of demographic composition and to ensure representation from relevant community sectors (e.g., faith, health, recreation, housing, education, business). Many of the coalitions created across the US are in response to federal, state, or foundation funding initiatives. They may or may not evaluate their work beyond providing progress reports to their funding agencies and/or outcomes specific to the prioritized public health or social problem they were funded to address. As such, they are deeply grounded in practice, with the vast majority not evaluated for power-building or empowerment processes and outcomes.

Additionally, scholars writing about coalitions represent a range of disciplines, including community psychology, public health, nursing, and sociology, among others. While this variety provides broad perspectives and can promote interdisciplinary collaboration, it also results in inconsistency in the approaches to studying and assessing the work of coalitions. This makes it challenging to achieve consensus on the predominant theories and constructs used to understand the factors influencing coalition effectiveness and appropriate indicators of coalition success (Zakocs & Edwards, 2006). Despite this, discussion of empowerment in the literature on coalitions is slowly becoming more common, driven in part by increased attention to social determinants of health and structural racism as drivers of persistent inequities (Domlyn & Coleman, 2019; Plough, 2018; Wolff, 2016; Wolff et al., 2017). Commentaries on a popularized approach to coalition-building (i.e., Collective Impact) and racial injustice in police violence and COVID-19 have deepened discussions about resident participation and power-sharing with those most affected by the prioritized community problem (Christens et al., 2019; Kegler et al., 2019; Wolff, 2016; Wolff et al., 2017). Recent summaries of Community Coalition Action Theory, a comprehensive theory on coalition formation and the process through which coalitions create change, include increased attention to resident engagement in coalitions, meaningful roles for residents to enable leadership development, and an ongoing focus on building community capacity and changing policies, systems, and environments (Butterfoss et al., 2022).

The concept of empowerment is no different. For example, similar concepts are described in the coalition literature but often under the rubric of "community capacity" in public health spheres. Community capacity is defined as "the characteristics of communities that affect their ability to identify, mobilize, and address social and public health problems" (Goodman et al., 1998,

p. 259). Conceptualizations of community capacity identify a number of dimensions that influence capacity, with commonalities across models including skills, resources, participation, and leadership (Norton et al., 2002; Wendel et al., 2009) Community empowerment, while occasionally used interchangeably with community capacity, typically has a more explicit focus on the process through which communities gain control and self-agency (Christens, 2019; Israel et al., 1994).

While mentioned fairly often, empirical research on community coalitions does not measure capacity or empowerment frequently, comprehensively, or consistently. When capacity and/or empowerment are mentioned explicitly, it is typically in the introduction or discussion section of a paper to provide context rather than being discussed in depth in terms of methodological approaches or employed as a measured construct under study. It is more common that coalition literature will acknowledge that the distribution of power (among other factors) plays a critical role in creating health inequities in the first place, prompting the need for health-focused coalition work (Brady et al., 2018). In some cases, a coalition's success is described as dependent upon the ability to build partnerships that are strength-based, responsive, and facilitate empowerment (Truiett-Theodorson et al., 2015). In the global health literature on partnerships, the imbalance of power is also discussed between visiting (e.g., outsiders) and local stakeholders (Yiu et al., 2018).

Coalition Research Explicitly Using Empowerment as a Theoretical Lens

Empowering processes and outcomes are often conceptualized at the individual, organizational, and community levels, and discussion of empowerment and related concepts in the coalition literature spans these multiple levels of analysis.

Research on Psychological Empowerment through Coalitions

In general, empowerment at the individual level or psychological empowerment refers to gaining a sense of control and actively participating in community efforts (Israel et al., 1994). The public health literature touches on this concept through discussion of the acquisition of skills essential for community problem-solving (e.g., root cause and power mapping, fundraising, and policy advocacy), as well as member influence in coalition decision-making and playing an active role in the coalition more broadly. Psychological empowerment is reflected through competence (e.g., applying skills), self-efficacy, and a sense of control (Peterson & Reid, 2003; Zimmerman et al., 1992). A qualitative study of coalition members documented that participation in the coalition was a way for community members to gain power and use their own voices to meet their community's needs (Lardier et al., 2021).

Empowerment is also discussed as an individual outcome resulting from specific coalition-based initiatives, such as activating "the power of parent advocacy" to address childhood obesity (Hussaini et al., 2018) or increasing access to the housing market, which was described as "a landmark of freedom of choice and empowerment for the homeless population living with mental health disorders" (Fleury et al., 2014, p. 45). In these cases, empowerment was not measured as an outcome per se but was noted as a result of the coalitions' work. Viewing empowerment as an outcome for program participants can be consistent with empowerment theory, but it can also contradict it in situations where one group "empowers" another with no attention given to power redistribution (Christens, 2019).

Research on Organizational-Level Empowerment through Coalitions

At the organizational level, empowerment in the coalition context can be understood as building power within individual member organizations. It can operate through organizations developing their abilities to cultivate policy influence, sharing coalition leadership responsibilities, competing successfully for resources, networking more effectively, and/or exerting influence in coalition- or community-level decision-making (Israel et al., 1994). Similarly to the individual level, organizational empowerment can take place both among coalition member organizations and among those influenced by coalition efforts. In some examples, coalitions have worked to cultivate power through information and education to program providers in their community, essentially equipping them with the knowledge and resources to be more effective. The LiveWell Greenville Initiative, for example, sought to "inform, educate, and empower" afterschool program providers who they partnered with to address childhood obesity (Kemper et al., 2018).

While coalitions can be empowering for participating organizations, there may also be some downsides to coalition participation that may affect community power distribution. Depending on the formality of a coalition, there may be a loss of autonomy and control for an organization if it joins forces with other organizations that have very different cultures and/or embrace dissimilar approaches, such as consensus versus conflict. Additionally, by taking staff time for meetings and coalition activities, coalitions can divert energy and resources from an organization's own priorities (Butterfoss & Kegler, 2009). In some cases, a coalition may take positions that do not align well or are contrary to a member organization's own agenda or policies. For activist-oriented organizations, the consensus-making process may be viewed as too slow and cumbersome, and the coalition may not take as strong a position on certain issues due to compromises made to maintain harmony within the coalition or broader community power structure.

Research on Coalition-Level and/or Interorganizational Empowerment

Although interorganizational networks are conceptualized as an outcome in the empowerment literature, empowering processes and outcomes can apply to the coalition as an entity (Israel et al., 1994). Coalitions can gain standing and influence in the community through their work, or in some cases partnerships between researchers and coalitions provide opportunities for coalition empowerment. In a study that employed an empowerment framework, university evaluators facilitated the empowerment of the coalition itself (framed as increasing organizational capacity). The university evaluators approached the evaluation process from a strengths-based lens, believing that community coalitions could be equipped to engage in rigorous research and evaluation methods. They equipped the community coalitions with scaffolded support so that, through the process, they would gain the skills to evaluate their community-based work, thereby increasing the coalition's capacity (Schweinhart & Raffle, 2021).

Research on Community-Level Empowerment

While empowerment and the development of community power are rarely measured in coalition work, empowerment and community power undergird the concept of coalition formation and the outcomes many coalitions seek to accomplish, which are often policy-based, systems-based, environmental, and structural in nature. Realmuto et al. (2021) considered the empowerment of local community leaders to be a structural outcome consistent with a systemic, community-building approach to change. Lead Local, a collaborative research project bringing together well-respected local power-building leaders in the fields of community organizing, advocacy, and research, defines community power as "[t]he ability of communities most impacted by structural inequity to develop, sustain and grow an organized base of people who act together through democratic structures to set agendas, shift public discourse, influence who makes decisions, and cultivate ongoing relationships of mutual accountability with decision makers that change systems and advance health equity" (Speer et al., 2020, p. 4). In the context of health-focused coalitions, building community power is a process that can be studied and also an outcome to be measured and reported. Conceptualizations of community empowerment list access to resources, open governing structures, and tolerance for diversity as processes and organizational coalitions, pluralistic leadership, and participatory skills among residents as outcomes (Israel et al., 1994). Building and sustaining community power requires long-standing coalitions that leverage their networks and assets beyond a single issue and ideally result in long-standing alliances in the community (Farhang & Gaydos, 2021). Coalitions have the potential to facilitate all of these conceptualizations of community empowerment, along with concrete changes in policies, environments, and systems.

Mechanisms through Which Coalitions Build Community Capacity and Community Empowerment

Engaging Residents in Community Coalitions

As conceptualized by Goodman et al. (1998), community capacity is greater when there is a strong participant base among residents who are involved in defining and resolving needs. Norton et al. (2002) describe community capacity as requiring "participatory mechanisms" that allow for constituencies within communities to have a seat at the table and provide input into community and governmental decision-making. Greater capacity is achieved when all segments of a community are engaged or have mechanisms for engagement and when a range of opportunities exist to create linkages and build trust across groups within a community. Mediating structures such as community coalitions can provide a vehicle for participation opportunities and the building of such trust across diverse factions of a community. This takes intentional and concerted efforts to actively engage the community beyond service providers and the removal of participation barriers for those who have been historically disenfranchised.

Community coalitions, in theory, strive to include community residents as coalition members in addition to professionals from a broad range of community sectors. Success in balancing resident voice with that of organizational representatives varies across coalitions and has been a challenge for some. The theory underlying coalitions is rooted in the notion that coalitions are able to achieve more than an individual or single organization can accomplish on its own through the creation of synergy (Butterfoss & Kegler, 2009; Lasker et al., 2001). The mechanism for improved approaches and outcomes is the pooling of diverse and complementary knowledge and resources. Diverse perspectives and the mobilization of a broad array of community assets and resources are thought to produce a deeper and more contextualized understanding of community problems and allow for concurrent action on several determinants of a problem. Involving grassroots residents in this process is viewed as essential as they have deep knowledge of the problems that coalitions are trying to address as well as a much more nuanced and personal understanding of the community context in which solutions are implemented. Numerous studies have documented that coalition members tend to be agency professionals who serve the communities that coalitions are focused on, although sometime these professionals also live in the community. Engaging grassroots residents in addition to professionals is an ongoing challenge for many coalitions (Christens et al., 2019; Grêaux et al., 2021; Kegler et al., 2019).

By providing a collaborative environment to facilitate equitable engagement between residents, community leaders, and organizations, coalitions align with both individual and organizational levels of empowerment (McMillan et al., 1995). Residents can participate in coalition work in a variety of ways, ranging from completing surveys that are used to inform the work to actively choosing and implementing change strategies (Kegler et al., 2009). Especially promising are approaches in which the coalition purposefully centers resident engagement in their work. The Go! Austin/Vamos! Austin (GAVA) coalition initiative focused on low-income communities experiencing disparities in access to healthy food and physical activity. Through resident-led teams, the coalition activated residents by providing a structure for them to address barriers in their community. They found that this resident-led approach built community capacity and self-governance (van den Berg et al., 2019). Similarly, Reid et al. (2019) found that tools from the Robert Wood Johnson Foundation-funded Spreading Community Accelerators through Learning and Evaluation (SCALE) initiative, which facilitated collaborative coalition processes, allowed for shared aim-setting and decision-making with residents that fostered relationship-building within and across coalitions. Additionally, SCALE was intentionally designed to build leadership capability, and it required that those with lived experience (i.e., persons directly impacted by inequities), called "community champions," be members of the core coalition team. While successful in doing so, numerous challenges to resident engagement arose, such as limited time for coalition meetings and struggles with issues of day-to-day living (e.g., health problems, unstable housing) that made participation difficult.

Engaging and Nurturing Community Leadership

Community coalitions offer opportunities to engage formal and informal community leaders to work together in new ways to solve community problems. Within the original conceptualization of community capacity, leadership was described in terms of who was involved in leadership roles (i.e., inclusion of formal and informal leaders), how they provided leadership (e.g., encouraged diverse community representation, implemented procedures for ensuring participation for all), and leadership traits (e.g., receptive to prudent innovation and risk-taking, responsive and accessible style, focused on both task and process details). Cultivating new leaders and an ability to transition from old to new were also mentioned as leadership characteristics associated with community capacity (Goodman et al., 1998; Norton et al., 2002). Norton et al. (2002) discuss identifying leadership through positional and reputational positions, with the former referring to the talents of those in management or formal office-holders and the latter to more informal but well-known and respected individuals within specific community constituencies.

Coalitions, when intentionally structured to do so, can strengthen the natural abilities of community residents to take on leadership roles and gain experiences essential for growth (Kegler et al., 2008). In a qualitative study of participation in an active living coalition, Barnes et al. (2015) identified different levels of participation, from silent participation to connector, visionary resource sharer, worker bee, and helper. Structuring opportunities for various types of participants to move to the next level of leadership requires concerted effort. As described in the CHCC case study earlier, Kegler et al. (2008) documented a range of leadership development opportunities, with many of these roles related to specific program activities in which volunteers were given a position of responsibility (e.g., coordinating a play group or organizing a neighborhood beautification project). Leveraging coalitions to replenish the pool of new leaders, particularly from groups that have traditionally been excluded from community power structures, has potential to further strengthen community capacity (Kegler et al., 2008). Specifically, coalition leaders can actively work toward increased community capacity by structuring coalition processes for meaningful participation and the emergence of new leaders, especially among those with "lived experience," and to nurture connections to informal and formal leaders from sectors and groups often excluded from community power structures. In some literature this is referred to as "catalytic leadership," where informational and instrumental support is provided to those involved in the work, whether as individuals, organizations, or institutions. This type of multidimensional leadership facilitates cross-sector collaboration and is particularly vital for large-scale change efforts that result in the enactment and sustainability of PSE changes (Tsuchiya et al., 2018).

Strengthening Knowledge and Skills for Community Change

Community health improvement requires strategic action and community mobilization, both of which depend on a set of skills that includes community assessment, strategic planning, resource mobilization, group facilitation, conflict management, power mapping, policy advocacy, and evaluation, among others. The collaborative nature of the coalition setting places unique demands on participants either to already have this wide range of specialized skills or to acquire them during the coalition's initiatives. Therefore, the coalition's capacity is greatly influenced by both the existing skills/knowledge that leaders, organizations, and residents bring to the table and the members' willingness to acquire new skills to meet the demands of the work ahead. This can lead to a power imbalance within the membership. Some coalitions have taken special efforts to include skills development in their work to increase equitable involvement from their membership. Coalitions develop community capacity and can equalize power dynamics within their initiatives by leveraging resources to provide training to their membership. Recognizing the critical role that skills play in a coalition's success, many rely on technical assistance to further develop the knowledge and skills of their local community (Foster-Fishman et al., 2001).

Community assessment is an essential skill to a community coalition, and it is frequently mentioned in the recent literature as either a skill that was relied upon for the essential early work leading up to the prioritization of initiatives or a skill that was rapidly acquired (Hussaini et al., 2018; Lee et al., 2012; Mendel et al., 2021; Ochtera et al., 2018; Toumbourou et al., 2019). In the SCALE initiative, community coalitions focused on improving health, well-being, and equity in their communities; power mapping and root cause analysis took a central role in the coalitions' work. Racism and structural inequities were centered as root causes of poor health, and coalition members were taught how to use tools such as implicit bias tests and how to facilitate challenging conversations on racism in their coalitions and communities (Reid et al., 2019). Others have recognized the need for more specialized knowledge at certain time points in their projects and focused skill development in areas such as community engagement (Mendel et al., 2021), community survey analysis and evaluation methods (Lee et al., 2012; Schweinhart & Raffle, 2021), and policy advocacy and media relations (Chin & Abesamis-Mendoza, 2012; Hare et al., 2000; Ochtera et al., 2018).

Many coalitions that involve youth place a special emphasis on developing knowledge and skills in an effort to equalize power dynamics between age demographics in the coalition. The Michigan Forward in Enhancing Research and Community Equity (MFierce) coalition was formed as an intergenerational, collaborative, multisector partnership of public health practitioners and researchers, community-based organizations, health departments, and gay, bisexual, and transgender youth (GBTY). Their work targeted improving sexual health equity for GBTY. Over the course of their initiative, the coalition held trainings on topics including advocacy, leadership, presentations, sexual health, and digital media for members of their Youth Advocacy Board. The coalition also sought to develop the knowledge and skills of external partners, thereby increasing the community's overall capacity (Sirdenis et al., 2019).

Expanding and Linking Personal and Interorganizational Networks

Coalitions, by their very nature, expand and strengthen networks for both individual coalition members and organizations represented in the coalition. Goodman et al. (1998) characterize networks that foster community capacity as having frequent, supportive, and reciprocal linkages across the network, overlap with or linkages to other networks, and an openness and ability to form new associations such as expanding the network and/or linking to other networks. Capacity may be greatest when networks have high levels of trust within as well as ties to other networks for resource mobilization and information flow. Granovetter (1973) argued that weak or bridging ties are essential for the latter. Using social capital as a theoretical lens, capacity will be higher when coalitions can build and strengthen both bonding and bridging social capital, the latter referring to linkages across networks (Kreuter & Lezin, 2002; Putnam, 2000). While strengthened and expanded network ties occur naturally through community coalitions, coalitions can also be structured to purposely strengthen relationships among coalition members. Chin and Abesamis-Mendoza (2012) describe a day-long retreat early in a coalition's formation with the explicit purpose of team-building and developing a shared vision.

Numerous studies have examined the network characteristics of coalitions (Ken-Opurum et al., 2019; Mendel et al., 2021; Yiu et al., 2018). Some of these have examined network characteristics and how these evolve over time within coalitions. Others have employed network analysis methodologies to study the patterns of relationship development and expansion due to coalition work. For example, Yiu et al. (2018) identified the role of "key players" among the coalition membership, which they termed "boundary spanners," who informally facilitated communication and programmatic alignment with community needs and priorities. Ken-Opurum et al. (2019) conducted network analyses that suggested that a coalition's structure, including opportunities for power-sharing among coalition members, likely influences coalition effectiveness. Finally, Bess (2015) studied how interorganizational relationships changed over time in a large system of youth-serving organizations in which a subset participated in a community coalition.

Leveraging Resources for Community Change

Collaborative processes catalyzed by coalitions can foster relationships, both internal and external, which provide pathways to resources essential to achieving coalition goals (Foster-Fishman et al., 2001; Lin, 1999). While emphasis is often placed on the resources and assets internal to the community and/or coalition membership such as space for events, access to policymakers, or deep understanding of the community context, access to external resources may be of equal importance to a coalition accomplishing their goals (e.g., technical assistance, external funding) (McKnight & Kretzmann, 1993). Technical assistance resources in particular may be especially important for coalition effectiveness. In one example, a community team was connected to appropriate education and prevention resources at a university through state-level extension prevention coordinators, who provided a wide variety of technical assistance to the community coalition (Chilenski et al., 2016). The transfer of expertise is key; access should be fluid and not promote dependency (Norton et al., 2002). If the coalition remains dependent on external resources, then that may be counterproductive, as it promotes reliance rather than empowerment and self-agency.

Research on Coalitions as Mechanisms for Community Change

Community change is frequently sought as the outcome for coalitions, whether this comes in the form of robust sustainable programs or broader changes in policy, systems, and environments. Community coalitions usually seek to facilitate larger-scale change in a community beyond the implementation of a single program. They often seek to adapt evidence-based programs for their local context and/or foster changes in policy, systems, and environments that serve as drivers or determinants of their prioritized concern. A large number of studies have documented a wide range of PSE change resulting from community coalition efforts, including tobacco control policies, access to healthy foods, community–clinical linkages, government-issued IDs, renovated parks and new walking trails, safe routes to schools, and many, many more (Bunnell et al., 2012; Evenson et al., 2012; Hahn et al., 2015; LeBrón et al., 2019; Roussos & Fawcett, 2000; Soler et al., 2016). A recent review of methods to evaluate coalition outcomes documented that new programs as well as changes to policy, systems, and environments were very common coalition outcomes, along with changes in some aspect of community capacity such as increased linkages across organizations (Kegler et al., 2020). Study designs tended to be descriptive and to focus on one coalition. Attribution to the coalitions was based on clear connections to coalition goals and advocacy efforts and, in some cases, an effort to document the role of the coalition in creating the change (i.e., networking/creating linkages, staffing or leading the effort, or providing financial support; Cheadle et al., 2010). More rigorous studies used quasi-experimental designs or cluster-randomized trials with behavioral or health outcomes being reported in addition to changes in policies, systems, environments, and programs.

There are myriad ways to approach community-identified priorities through coalition efforts to create community change. Many coalitions are able to build and marshal power within their communities to achieve PSE changes. Following an assessment of community strengths, communities typically utilize the assets and levers available to them in their local community context to work toward their aims. Intervention tools and models (e.g., best practices) can serve as a strong facilitator in the pursuit of PSE change by providing a framework to keep all the pieces moving toward a common goal. Other tools and strategies around advocacy, including public and political will-building and technical skills such as power mapping and evaluation methods, also support successful sought-after community change. Increasingly, community coalitions recognize that facilitating residents in a way that elevates community voices to engage with and within existing community power structures is a critical element of PSE change that addresses health equity.

Application and Future Research

Coalitions can strengthen psychological empowerment by providing a mechanism through which residents can participate in community life, apply and gain new skills, grow through successive leadership roles with increased responsibilities over time, and play a role in creating community change. The extent to which these empowerment outcomes are realized, and for whom, depends on who initiates the coalition, who is invited to join the coalition, how the coalition is structured to accommodate diverse voices and life experiences, removal of barriers to participation for those who cannot participate as part of their work responsibilities, and the intentional creation of opportunities for skill development and leadership opportunities. Coalitions have been criticized by some for their tendency to be dominated by agency professionals that may have a stake, consciously or unconsciously, in maintaining the status quo and seeking incremental and nonthreatening community change (Wolff, 2016; Wolff et al., 2017). With a strengthened emphasis on health equity and structural racism as pervasive and powerful social determinants of health (Ford & Airhihenbuwa, 2010), future coalition research should examine whether and how coalitions are able to address more deeply rooted causes of inequity. This necessitates the psychological, organizational, and community empowerment of those most affected by unfair practices and policies as opposed to professionals affiliated with organizations and participating in a professional capacity. This chapter documented some of the challenges to resident participation in coalitions, as well as some of the opportunities. Future research should evaluate different models for integrating grassroots community residents – particularly those with lived experience – more fully into coalition processes. Better understanding of the community change process is also needed through clear articulation of how empowerment and/or capacity-building, including redistribution of power, theoretically lead to change, as is empirical support for various pathways across a range of public health and social challenges and community contexts.

References

Ashton, J., Grey, P., & Barnard, K. (1986). Healthy cities – WHO's new public health initiative. *Health Promotion International*, *1*(3), 319–324.

Barnes, P. A., Schaefer, S., Middlestadt, S., & Knoblock, H. (2015). Who's who in the crew? Exploring participant involvement in the Active Living Coalition. *Evaluation and Program Planning*, *50*, 88–95.

Berg, C. J., Dekanosidze, A., Torosyan, A., Grigoryan, L., Sargsyan, Z., Hayrumyan, V., Topuridze, M., Sturua, L., Harutyunyan, A., Kvachantiradze, L., Maglakelidze, N., Gamkrelidze, A., Abovyan, R., Bazarchyan, A., & Kegler M. C. (2019). Examining smoke-free coalitions in Armenia and Georgia: Baseline community capacity. *Health Education Research*, *34*(5), 495–504.

Bess, K. D. (2015). Reframing coalitions as systems interventions: A network study exploring the contribution of a youth violence prevention coalition to broader system capacity. *American Journal of Community Psychology*, *55*(3), 381–395.

Brady, S. S., Parker, C. J., Jeffries, E. F., Simpson, T., Brooke-Weiss, B. L., & Haggerty, K. P. (2018). Implementing the Communities That Care Prevention System: Challenges, solutions, and opportunities in an urban setting. *American Journal of Preventive Medicine, 55*(5 Suppl. 1), S70–S81.

Brennan, L. K., Brownson, R. C., & Hovmand, P. (2012). Evaluation of Active Living by Design: Implementation patterns across communities. *American Journal of Preventive Medicine, 43*(5 Suppl. 4), S351–S366.

Brownson, R. C., Kemner, A. L., & Brennan, L. K. (2015). Applying a mixed-methods evaluation to Healthy Kids, Healthy Communities. *Journal of Public Health Management and Practice, 21*(Suppl. 3), S16–S26.

Bunnell, R., O'Neil, D., Soler, R., Payne, R., Giles, W. H., Collins, J., & Bauer, U. (2012). Fifty communities putting prevention to work: Accelerating chronic disease prevention through policy, systems and environmental change. *Journal of Community Health, 37*(5), 1081–1090.

Butterfoss, F. D., & Kegler, M. C. (2009). Community Coalition Action Theory. In: R. DiClemente, R. Crosby, & M. Kegler (Eds). *Emerging theories in health promotion practice and research* (2nd ed., pp. 237–276). Jossey-Bass.

Butterfoss, F. D., & Kegler, M. C. (2022). Community Coalition Action Theory: Designing and evaluating community collaboratives. In M. Minkler & P. Wakimoto (Eds.), *Community organizing and community building for health and social equity* (4th ed., pp. 307–324). Rutgers University Press.

Cheadle, A., Atiedu, A., Rauzon, S., Schwartz, P. M., Keene, L., Davoudi, M., Spring R, Molina M., Lee L., Boyle K., Williamson, D., Steimberg, C., Tinajero, R., Ravel, J., Nudelman, J., Azuma, A., Kuo, E., & Solomon L. (2018). A community-level initiative to prevent obesity: Results From Kaiser Permanente's Healthy Eating Active Living Zones Initiative in California. *American Journal of Preventive Medicine, 54*(5 Suppl. 2), S150–S159.

Cheadle, A., Egger, R., LoGerfo, J. P., Schwartz, S., & Harris, J. R. (2010). Promoting sustainable community change in support of older adult physical activity: Evaluation findings from the Southeast Seattle Senior Physical Activity Network (SESPAN). *Journal of Urban Health, 87*(1), 67–75.

Chilenski, S. M., Perkins, D. F., Olson, J., Hoffman, L., Feinberg, M. E., Greenberg, M., Welsh, J., Crowley, D., & Spoth, R. (2016). The power of a collaborative relationship between technical assistance providers and community prevention teams: A correlational and longitudinal study. *Evaluation and Program Planning, 54*, 19–29.

Chin, J. J., & Abesamis-Mendoza, N. (2012). Project CHARGE: Building an urban health policy advocacy community. *Progress in Community Health Partnerships, 6*(1), 17–23.

Choy, L. B., Maddock, J. E., Brody, B., Richards, K. L., & Braun, K. L. (2016). Examining the role of a community coalition in facilitating policy and environmental changes to promote physical activity: The case of Get Fit Kaua'i. *Translational Behavioral Medicine, 6*(4), 638–647.

Christens, B. D. (2019). *Community power and empowerment.* Oxford University Press.

Christens, B. D., Butterfoss, F. D., Minkler, M., Wolff, T., Francisco, V. T., & Kegler, M. C. (2019). Learning from coalitions' efforts to promote equity and justice. *Health Education & Behavior, 46*(1 Suppl.), 110S–114S.

Domlyn, A. M., & Coleman, S. (2019). Prioritizing equity: Exploring conditions impacting community coalition efforts. *Health Equity*, *3*(1), 417–422.

Dooris, M., & Heritage, Z. (2013). Healthy Cities: Facilitating the active participation and empowerment of local people. *Journal of Urban Health*, *90*(Suppl. 1), 74–91.

Evenson, K. R., Sallis, J. F., Handy, S. L., Bell, R., & Brennan, L. K. (2012). Evaluation of physical projects and policies from the Active Living by Design partnerships. *American Journal of Preventive Medicine*, *43*(5 Suppl. 4), S309–S319.

Feighery, E., & Rogers, T. (1990). *Building and maintaining effective coalitions. How-to guides on community health promotion*. Health Promotion Resource Center, Stanford Center for Research and Disease Prevention.

Farhang, L., & Gaydos, M. (2021). Shifting and sharing power: Public health's charge in building community power. *NACCHO Exchange*, *20*(1), 15–19.

Fleury, M. J., Grenier, G., Vallée, C., Hurtubise, R., & Lévesque, P. A. (2014). The role of advocacy coalitions in a project implementation process: The example of the planning phase of the At Home/Chez Soi project dealing with homelessness in Montreal. *Evaluation and Program Planning*, *45*, 42–49.

Flewelling, R. L., & Hanley, S. M. (2016). Assessing community coalition capacity and its association with underage drinking prevention effectiveness in the context of the SPF SIG. *Prevention Science*, *17*(7), 830–840.

Ford, C. L., & Airhihenbuwa, C. O. (2010). Critical race theory, race equity, and public health: Toward antiracism praxis. *American Journal of Public Health*, *100*(S1), S30–S35.

Foster-Fishman, P. G., Berkowitz, S. L., Lounsbury, D. W., Jacobson, S., & Allen, N. A. (2001). Building collaborative capacity in community coalitions: A review and integrative framework. *American Journal of Community Psychology*, *29* (2), 241–261.

Giles, W. H. (2010). The US perspective: lessons learned from the Racial and Ethnic Approaches to Community Health (REACH) program. *Journal of the Royal Society of Medicine*, *103*(7), 273–276.

Goodman, R. M., Speers, M. A., McLeroy, K., Fawcett, S., Kegler, M., Parker, E., Smith, S., Sterling, T., & Wallerstein, N. (1998). Identifying and defining the dimensions of community capacity to provide a basis for measurement. *Health Education & Behavior*, *25*(3), 258–278.

Granovetter, M. S. (1973). The strength of weak ties. *American Journal of Sociology*, *78*(6), 1360–1380.

Grêaux, K., de Vries, N., Bessems, K., Harting, J., & van Assema, P. (2021). Does partnership diversity in intersectoral policymaking matter for health promoting intervention packages' composition? A multiple-case study in the Netherlands. *Health Promotion International*, *36*(3), 616–629.

Hahn, E. J., Rayens, M. K., Adkins, S., Begley, K., & York, N. (2015). A controlled community-based trial to promote smoke-free policy in rural communities. *Journal of Rural Health*, *31*(1), 76–88.

Hare, M. L., Orians, C. E., Kennedy, M. G., Goodman, K. J., Wijesinha, S., & Seals, B. F. (2000). Lessons learned from the PMI case study: The community perspective. *Social Marketing Quarterly*, *6*(1), 54–65.

Hussaini, A., Pulido, C. L., Basu, S., & Ranjit, N. (2018). Designing place-based interventions for sustainability and replicability: The case of GO! Austin/VAMOS! Austin. *Frontiers in Public Health*, *6*, 88.

Israel, B. A., Checkoway, B., Schulz, A., & Zimmerman, M. (1994). Health education and community empowerment: Conceptualizing and measuring perceptions of individual, organizational, and community control. *Health Education Quarterly*, *21*(2), 149–170.

Kegler, M. C., Dekanosidze, A., Torosyan, A., Grigoryan, L., Rana, S., Hayrumyan, V., Sargsyan, Z., & Berg, C. J. (2023a). Community coalitions for smoke-free environments in Armenia and Georgia: A mixed methods analysis of coalition formation, implementation and perceived effectiveness. *PLoS ONE*, *18*(8), e0289149.

Kegler, M. C., Halpin, S., & Butterfoss, F. D. (2020). Evaluation methods commonly used to assess effectiveness of community coalitions in public health: Results from a scoping review. *New Directions for Evaluation*, *2020*(165), 139–157.

Kegler, M. C., Hermstad, A., Haardörfer, R., Arriola, K. J., Gauthreaux, N., Tucker, S., & Nelson, G. (2023b). Evaluation design for The Two Georgias initiative: Assessing progress toward health equity in the rural South. *Health Education & Behavior*, *50*(2), 268–280.

Kegler, M. C., Norton, B. L., & Aronson, R. (2003). *Evaluation of the five year expansion program of California Healthy Cities and Communities (1998–2003)* [Unpublished document]. Rollins School of Public Health, Emory University.

Kegler, M. C., Norton, B. L., & Aronson, R. E. (2008). Strengthening community leadership: Evaluation findings from the California Healthy Cities and Communities program. *Health Promotion Practice*, *9*(2), 170–179.

Kegler, M. C., Painter, J. E., Twiss, J. M., Aronson, R., & Norton, B. L. (2009). Evaluation findings on community participation in the California Healthy Cities and Communities program. *Health Promotion International*, *24*(4), 300–310.

Kegler, M. C., Twiss, J. M., & Look, V. (2000). Assessing community change at multiple levels: The genesis of an evaluation framework for the California Healthy Cities Project. *Health Education & Behavior*, *27*(6), 760–779.

Kegler, M. C., Wolff, T., Christens, B. D., Butterfoss, F. D., Francisco, V. T., & Orleans, T. (2019). Strengthening our collaborative approaches for advancing equity and justice. *Health Education & Behavior*, *46*(1 Suppl.), 5S–8S.

Kemper, K. A., Pate, S. P., Powers, A. R., & Fair, M. (2018). Promoting healthy environments in afterschool settings: The LiveWell Greenville Afterschool Initiative. *Preventing Chronic Disease*, *15*, E144.

Ken-Opurum, J., Lynch, K., Vandergraff, D., Miller, D. K., & Savaiano, D. A. (2019). A mixed-methods evaluation using effectiveness perception surveys, social network analysis, and county-level health statistics: A pilot study of eight rural Indiana community health coalitions. *Evaluation and Program Planning*, *77*, 101709.

Kreuter, M. W., & Lezin, N. (2002). Social capital theory: Implications for community-based health promotion. In R. DiClemente, R. Crosby, & M.

Kegler (Eds.), *Emerging theories in health promotion practice and research* (1st ed., pp. 228–254) Jossey-Bass.

Lardier, D. T., Jr., Merrill, E. A., & Cantu, I. N. (2021). Psychological sense of community and motivation toward collective social change among community coalition members of color in the southwestern United States. *Journal of Community Psychology*, *49*(2), 547–563.

Lasker, R. D., Weiss, E. S., & Miller, R. (2001). Partnership synergy: A practical framework for studying and strengthening the collaborative advantage. *Milbank Quarterly*, *79*(2), 179–205, iii–iv.

LeBrón, A. M. W., Cowan, K., Lopez, W. D., Novak, N. L., Ibarra-Frayre, M., & Delva, J. (2019). The Washtenaw ID Project: A government-issued ID coalition working toward social, economic, and racial justice and health equity. *Health Education & Behavior*, *46*(1 Suppl.), 53s–61s.

Lee, J. P., Lipperman-Kreda, S., Saephan, S., & Kirkpatrick, S. (2012). Youth-led tobacco prevention: Lessons learned for engaging Southeast Asian American youth. *Progress in Community Health Partnerships*, *6*(2), 187–194.

Lin, N. (1999). Building a network theory of social capital. *Connections*, *22*(1), 28–51.

Manley, M., Lynn, W., Payne Epps, R., Grande, D., Glynn, T., & Shopland, D. (1997). The American Stop Smoking Intervention Study for cancer prevention: An overview. *Tobacco Control*, *6* (Suppl. 2), S5–S11.

McKnight, J., & Kretzmann, J. (1993). *Building communities from the inside out. A path toward finding and mobilizing a community's assets.* ACTA Publications.

McLeroy, K. R., Bibeau, D., Steckler, A., & Glanz, K. (1988). An ecological perspective on health promotion programs. *Health Education Quarterly*, *15*(4), 351–377.

McMillan, B., Florin, P., Stevenson, J., Kerman, B., & Mitchell, R. E. (1995). Empowerment praxis in community coalitions. *American Journal of Community Psychology*, *23*(5), 699–727.

Mendel, P., O'Hora, J., Zhang, L., Stockdale, S., Dixon, E. L., Gilmore, J., Jones, F., Jones, A., Williams, P., Sharif, M., Masongsong, Z., Kadkhoda, F., Pulido, E., Chung, B., & Wells, K. B. (2021). Engaging community networks to improve depression services: A cluster-randomized trial of a community engagement and planning intervention. *Community Mental Health Journal*, *57*(3), 457–469.

Mittelmark, M. B. (1999). Social ties and health promotion: Suggestions for population-based research. *Health Education Research*, *14*(4), 447–451.

Norris, T., & Pittman, M. (2000). The healthy communities movement and the coalition for healthier cities and communities. *Public Health Reports*, *115*(2-3), 118–124.

Norton, B. L., McLeroy, K. R., Burdine, J. N., Felix, M. R., & Dorsey, A. M. (2002). Community capacity. In R. DiClemente, R. Crosby, & M. Kegler (Eds.), *Emerging theories in health promotion practice and research* (1st ed., pp. 194–227). Jossey-Bass.

Ochtera, R. D., Siemer, C. J., & Levine, L. T. (2018). Supporting community-based healthy eating and active living efforts in sustaining beyond the funding cycle. *American Journal of Preventive Medicine*, *54*(5 Suppl. 2), S133–S138.

Peterson, N. A., & Reid, R. J. (2003). Paths to psychological empowerment in an urban community: Sense of community and citizen participation in substance abuse prevention activities. *Journal of Community Psychology, 31*(1), 25–38.

Plough, A. L. (2018). *Advancing health and well-being: Using evidence and collaboration to achieve health equity*. Oxford University Press.

Putnam, R. D. (2000). *Bowling alone: America's declining social capital*. Simon & Schuster.

Realmuto, L., Weiss, L., Masseo, P., Madondo, K., Kumar, R., Beane, S., & Pagán, J. A. (2021). "Hey, we can do this together": Findings from an evaluation of a multi-sectoral community coalition. *Journal of Urban Health, 98*(5), 687–694.

Reid, A., Abraczinskas, M., Scott, V., Stanzler, M., Parry, G., Scaccia, J., Wandersman, A., & Ramaswamy, R. (2019). Using collaborative coalition processes to advance community health, well-being, and equity: A multiple-case study analysis from a National Community Transformation Initiative. *Health Education & Behavior, 46*(1 Suppl.), 100s–109s.

Roussos, S. T., & Fawcett, S. B. (2000). A review of collaborative partnerships as a strategy for improving community health. *Annual Review of Public Health, 21*, 369–402.

Schweinhart, A., & Raffle, H. (2021). Productive struggle: How community coalitions developed capacity to conduct qualitative research through CBPR. *Health Promotion Practice, 22*(6), 735–740.

Sirdenis, T. K., Harper, G. W., Carrillo, M. D., Jadwin-Cakmak, L., Loveluck, J., Pingel, E., Benton, A., Peterson, A., Pollard, R, & Bauermeister, J. A. (2019). Toward sexual health equity for gay, bisexual, and transgender youth: An intergenerational, collaborative, multisector partnerships approach to structural change. *Health Education & Behavior, 46*(1 Suppl.), 88s–99s.

Solar, O., & Irwin, A. (2010). *A conceptual framework for action on the social determinants of health. Social determinants of health discussion. Paper 2 (policy and practice)*. World Health Organization.

Soler, R., Orenstein, D., Honeycutt, A., Bradley, C., Trogdon, J., Kent, C. K., Wile, K., Haddix, A., O'Neil, D., & Bunnell, R. (2016). Community-based interventions to decrease obesity and tobacco exposure and reduce health care costs: Outcome estimates from communities putting prevention to work for 2010–2020. *Preventing Chronic Disease, 13*, E47.

Speer, P. W., Gupta, J., Haapanen, K., Balmer, B., Wiley, K., & Bachelder, A. (2020). *Developing community power for health equity: A landscape analysis of current research and theory*. Vanderbilt University.

Toumbourou, J. W., Rowland, B., Williams, J., Smith, R., & Patton, G. C. (2019). Community intervention to prevent adolescent health behavior problems: Evaluation of communities that care in Australia. *Health Psychology, 38*(6), 536–544.

Truiett-Theodorson, R., Tuck, S., Bowie, J. V., Summers, A. C., & Kelber-Kaye, J. (2015). Building effective partnerships to improve birth outcomes by reducing obesity: The B'more Fit for healthy babies coalition of Baltimore. *Evaluation and Program Planning, 51*, 53–58.

Tsuchiya, K., Howard Caldwell, C., Freudenberg, N., Silver, M., Wedepohl, S., & Lachance, L. (2018). Catalytic leadership in food & fitness community partnerships. *Health Promotion Practice, 19*(1 Suppl.), 45S–54S.

Tucker, P., Liao, Y., Giles, W. H., & Liburd, L. (2006). The REACH 2010 logic model: An illustration of expected performance. *Preventing Chronic Disease, 3*(1), A21.

van den Berg, A., Nielsen, A., Akhavan, N., Pulido, C. L., Basu, S., Hussaini, A., Jovanovic, C., Janda K., Denis, L., & Ranjit N. (2019). Design and evaluation of a coalition-led obesity initiative to promote healthy eating and physical activity in low-income, ethnically diverse communities: The Go! Austin/Vamos! Austin initiative. *Archives of Public Health, 77*, 25.

Wendel, M. L., Burdine, J. N., McLeroy, K. R., Alaniz, A., Norton, B., & Felix, M. R. (2009). Community capacity: Theory and application. In R. DiClemente, R. Crosby, & M. Kegler (Eds.), *Emerging theories in health promotion practice and research* (2nd ed., pp. 277–302). Jossey-Bass.

Wolff, T. (2016). Ten places where collective impact gets it wrong. *Global Journal of Community Psychology Practice, 7*(1), 1–13.

Wolff, T., Minkler, M., Wolfe, S. M., Berkowitz, B., Bowen, L., Butterfoss, F. D., Christens, B. D., Francisco, V. T., Himmelman, A. T., & Lee, K. (2017). Collaborating for equity and justice: Moving beyond collective impact. *Nonprofit Quarterly, 9*, 42–53.

World Health Organization. (2019). *Implementation framework for phase VII (2019–2024) of the WHO European Healthy Cities Network: Goals, requirements and strategic approaches.* World Health Organization.

Yarnoff, B., Bradley, C., Honeycutt, A. A., Soler, R. E., & Orenstein, D. (2019). Estimating the relative impact of clinical and preventive community-based interventions: An example based on the Community Transformation Grant Program. *Preventing Chronic Disease, 16*, E87.

Yiu, K., Dimaras, H., Valdman, O., Franklin, B., Prochaska, J., & Loh, L. (2018). Characterizing a community health partnership in Dominican Republic: Network mapping and analysis of stakeholder perceptions. *Canadian Medical Education Journal, 9*(2), e60–e71.

Zakocs, R. C., & Edwards, E. M. (2006). What explains community coalition effectiveness? A review of the literature. *American Journal of Preventive Medicine, 30*(4), 351–361.

Zimmerman, M. A., Israel, B. A., Schulz, A., & Checkoway, B. (1992). Further explorations in empowerment theory: An empirical analysis of psychological empowerment. *American Journal of Community Psychology, 20*(6), 707–727.

13 Youth-Infused Community Coalitions

Jessica J. Collura, Holly Raffle, Meagan R. Joseph, and Mollie F. Stevens

Many of the issues communities face – such as climate change, substance use disorder, or homelessness – are wicked problems (Rittel & Webber, 1973) that require complex, comprehensive responses. No single entity can effectively address these problems alone; the participation and engagement of a diverse group of citizens are essential to develop a solution set to address such issues (Rittel & Webber, 1973). Community coalitions are mechanisms for addressing complex issues at the local level. Coalitions involve representatives from diverse organizations and constituencies (e.g., social service agencies, businesses, faith organizations, parents) who collaborate around a shared interest and work together to achieve a common goal (Butterfoss & Kegler, 2002; Feighery & Rogers, 1990). Community coalitions bring people and the organizations they represent together to have a larger impact on identified local issues. Wolff (2001) identified several criteria for groups to be considered community coalitions, including: focusing primarily on local issues rather than national issues; being composed of community members; helping to resolve local problems through collaboration; having representatives from multiple sectors; and being citizen-influenced, though not necessarily citizen-driven.

The work of community coalitions typically focuses on three primary tasks: negotiated coordination, knowledge coordination, and action coordination (Lawlor et al., 2021). Negotiated coordination involves establishing governance structures, such as identifying roles and responsibilities and creating bylaws, to facilitate consensus-building processes and the sharing of resources. To coordinate knowledge, coalitions often establish data collection processes and administer surveys to monitor the behaviors, beliefs, and attitudes of local community members (Shapiro et al., 2013). Coalitions may utilize these collected data to identify community issues and determine contributors to local issues. This information often drives the development of logic models and strategic plans that guide the selection of actions taken in their community. Once a logic model and strategic plan have been created, coalitions implement actions in their local community ranging from providing services as a group to mobilizing communities to create policy change.

Community coalitions can focus on a wide variety of local issues, from homelessness to violence prevention. Youth-infused community coalitions, which are community coalitions that engage young people, tend to focus on public health issues (particularly issues pertaining to youth behavioral or mental health) or community youth development (e.g., Camino & Zeldin, 2002; Campbell & Erbstein, 2011), although there are some documented examples of youth-infused coalitions that focus on the foster care system (e.g., Augsberger et al., 2019; Forenza, 2016) or juvenile justice (Ford et al., 2013). Although all community issues inherently affect young people, the trend is to engage young people in coalitions primarily when the issue that the group seeks to address explicitly or directly impacts youth. The young people recruited to serve on community coalitions tend to be high-achieving students or young people who are recognized as leaders within their school environment. Depending on the purpose of the coalition, adult participants range from professionals representing a variety of sectors (e.g., business, law enforcement, religious agencies) or those representing primarily youth-serving professionals (e.g., schools, community-based youth programs). While there is a lot of rhetorical support for youth engagement in community coalitions, examples remain relatively limited, particularly of effective youth-infused community coalitions (Campbell & Erbstein, 2011; Price, 2020) or those in international contexts. Entities that fund coalition work have noticed the gap in youth representation in community coalitions and have attempted to course correct through funding requirements, training, or technical assistance. Campbell and Erbstein (2011) found that nascent coalitions that engaged young people from their inception were more effective at engaging youth but struggled to establish a broader working coalition or infrastructure to achieve short-term goals. Paradoxically, these researchers found that established coalitions were better able to achieve short-term goals but struggled to effectively integrate youth.

Community coalitions, including youth-infused community coalitions, have expanded over the past forty years in the US (Butterfoss & Kegler, 2002; Butterfoss et al., 1993; Wolff, 2001). There are several reasons for this rapid growth. A devolution of federal programs to state and local entities, combined with cuts in government funding for human services and needs, is one contributing factor (Christens & Inzeo, 2015; Wolff, 2001). With less funding, government agencies began to invite nonprofits to compete for short-term funding, reducing government costs and long-term obligations to provide services (Christens & Inzeo, 2015). Coalitions, however, have been successful at creating measurable change to improve the health outcomes and overall quality of life in communities, which has also fueled their expansion (Janosky et al., 2013). Community coalitions are particularly effective at addressing issues at the policy, systems, and environmental level as opposed to the individual level (Bermea et al., 2019; Janosky et al., 2013). Their ability to identify and implement community-level interventions to promote health and well-being at the population level contributes to their growth and expansion. Coalitions have also risen in popularity because they are mechanisms for increasing civic engagement and involvement in civil society (Mayan et al., 2013; Wolff, 2001). The Canadian government, for example, funds multicultural coalitions designed to increase ethnic minorities' participation in civic society (Mayan et al., 2013).

Given the breadth of issues that coalitions address and the variety of reasons for which they may form, it is difficult to identify how many exist in the US and globally. In addition, there is little literature on youth-infused community coalitions in contexts outside of the US and Canada. Community coalitions exist primarily in democratic countries, and research suggests that contextual factors in various countries, even democratic ones, may affect their functioning. For example, in a comparative study of substance use prevention coalitions in the US and Mexico, researchers found that Mexican coalitions operated in a substantially more challenging environment than US coalitions (Brown et al., 2016). Specifically, the researchers found that Mexican coalition members perceived significantly more community problems than those in the US and also perceived a lower sense of community, along with a belief that the general population did not value prevention efforts. Contextual factors, therefore, influence not only the development but also the functioning of coalitions.

Substance Abuse Prevention Coalitions

One of the first national initiatives that relied on community coalitions was through the Office of Substance Abuse Prevention's Community Partnership Program (Wolff, 2001). In the field of substance use prevention, federal funding for the Drug-Free Communities (DFC) Support Program, administered by the White House Office of National Drug Control Policy (ONDCP) and managed through a partnership between the ONDCP and the Centers for Disease Control and Prevention, has helped support the development and expansion of community coalitions to prevent youth substance use (Centers for Disease Control and Prevention, 2021). Drug-Free Communities funding began in 1997 through the Drug-Free Communities Act with the goal of establishing locally driven community-based coalitions that provide informed and culturally appropriate prevention intervention strategies in their communities (Center for Substance Abuse Prevention, 2009; Centers for Disease Control and Prevention, 2021; Price, 2020). In federal fiscal year 2021, more than 700 DFC coalitions were awarded DFC grants, and the Centers for Disease Control and Prevention (2021) estimate that, since 2005, about half (51 percent) of the population in the US has lived in a community with a DFC coalition. Through this initiative, community members with diverse perspectives use local data to identify risk and protective factors and implement prevention strategies to reduce youth substance use (Perkins et al., 2011). The primary work of substance use prevention coalitions (i.e., negotiated coordination, knowledge coordination, and action coordination) is the same as coalition work in other areas of focus.

In addition to the Centers for Disease Control and Prevention, ONDCP engages other partners to help implement the DFC Support Program. One partner, the Community Anti-Drug Coalitions of America (CADCA), provides training and technical assistance to build and strengthen local coalitions. In addition to the support and training it provides in the US, CADCA also has an international program that has helped establish 305 coalitions in twenty-eight countries globally (CADCA, 2022). CADCA emphasizes that if the entire community is to benefit from prevention efforts, then the coalitions need to be reflective of the whole community. They recommend twelve key sectors (e.g., media, school, religious, law enforcement) be represented in all community coalitions. Two demographic groups are identified as "sectors" by CADCA: parents and young people. Because young people are identified as a demographic group that should participate in substance use prevention coalitions, there are some examples of youth-infused community coalitions in the field of substance use prevention. However, as Price (2020) notes, "many coalitions, not just those that receive DFC funding, neglect to engage the very youth they intend to reach" (p. 177). In short, although there are examples of youth-infused community coalitions, the practice of engaging young people in community coalitions is still not widespread.

Youth-Infused Community Coalitions in Ohio

In our work in Ohio providing training and technical assistance to community coalitions composed of youth and adults, we have found two theoretical frameworks to be particularly useful: the Community Coalition Action Theory (CCAT; Butterfoss & Kegler, 2002) and the Youth Empowerment Conceptual Framework (YECF; Holden et al., 2004b). The CCAT is a theoretical framework for understanding coalitions and coalition-building. It can be used as both an evaluation tool and as a resource to educate coalitions on core processes and structures, including the roles of staff, shared and formalized decision-making processes, and member engagement. Akin to the CCAT, the YECF (Holden et al., 2004b) conceptualizes the core structures and processes needed for youth-led coalitions to impact change in their communities; it also can be used as both an evaluative framework and a resource for educating facilitators of youth-led coalitions. The CCAT proposes that broad-based, diverse community participation strengthens a coalition's capacity to identify and address complex issues. One core proposition of the CCAT is that, during the formation state of a community coalition, the lead agency typically recruits a core group of people, but over time effective coalitions result when the core group expands to include participants that represent diverse interest groups and organizations (Butterfoss & Kegler, 2002). However, we have often found that young people are not a constituency that is engaged in community coalition work when agencies work solely from the CCAT framework. The YECF, therefore, is a useful complementary tool for community coalitions that are specifically interested in also engaging young people in their work. Taken together, these two frameworks support lead agencies in successfully facilitating youth-infused community coalitions. The exemplar discussed in the next section highlights one lead agency that has successfully utilized these two frameworks to establish a countywide youth-infused community coalition that seeks to promote the health and well-being of local residents.

Exemplar: River Hills Prevention Connection Coalition

The River Hills Prevention Connection (RHPC) coalition, located in Appalachia, serves the southernmost area of Ohio bordering Kentucky and West Virginia. Consistent with the literature on coalitions (e.g., Wolff, 2001), RHPC serves as a hub for local efforts that seek to promote the health and well-being of community members; the broad mission of the coalition is to encourage residents to build a healthier, more connected community. RHPC defines its community as those residents living in Lawrence County, which has a population of approximately 58,000. The community has seen economic downturn and loss of work due to closing of local industries, which is leading to a growing divide between the "haves" and "have-nots," a disappearing middle class, and a recent increase in overdose deaths and suicide. Given this context, one of the coalition's primary goals is to reduce substance misuse and increase mental health promotion.

IMPACT Prevention, a community-based nonprofit located in a low-income housing complex, serves as the backbone organization (Kania & Kramer, 2011) for the coalition; it provides paid staff and manages all grants that fund the coalition. Several funding sources support the work of RHPC, including the Substance Abuse and Mental Health Services Administration's (SAMHSA) Strategic Prevention Framework – Partnerships for Success (SPF-PFS) grant. In 2015, the agency received funding from a statewide nonprofit to engage in training and technical assistance to ground their youth-led initiative in the YECF (Collura et al., 2019; Holden et al., 2004b). Then, in federal fiscal year 2021, with funding from another statewide nonprofit, leaders from IMPACT Prevention engaged in a training and technical assistance process to ground their coalition in the CCAT.

RHPC has members from each of the twelve CADCA sectors, and their membership is reflective of county demographics, including age, education, and recovery status. Members are expected to attend 70 percent of the coalition meetings, which are held monthly, to be considered active. Rather than simply having young people as the population their work seeks to affect, IMPACT Prevention has a long history of involving young people directly in their community work. Today, young people engage in their coalition in a variety of manners: Youth-led prevention groups lead their own activities that are connected to RHPC's work, youth serve on advisory boards to provide feedback on RHPC's proposed activities, and young people serve directly alongside adults in the coalition.

Youth-led prevention groups were initially established in Lawrence County in the early 1990s, but the work evolved over time. Early youth-led prevention groups were primarily school-based and focused on implementing programs as opposed to creating policy or systems change. Over the years, the groups transformed by broadening both the issues they addressed (e.g., bullying, conflict resolution, self-image, tobacco and alcohol use) and the strategies they used (e.g., began using more policy and systems change strategies).

In 2015, IMPACT Prevention began structuring and facilitating a county-wide youth-led initiative as a "youth-led coalition." The nonprofit had already established youth-led prevention groups in most school districts throughout Lawrence County, as well as groups in a few of the neighboring county's school districts. Young people from the school-based youth-led prevention groups were recruited to serve on a countywide youth-led coalition; this structure ensured representation from school districts across the county and allowed for a coordinated effort to evolve in the region. The countywide youth-led coalition was structured as a community-based process (Hogan et al., 2003) in which young people came together to determine an issue of focus, identify the root causes of those issues, and then select and implement evidence-based strategies to address those root causes. All youth who wished to become a positive influence in their schools and communities were welcomed and encouraged to join. Program staff intentionally sought to recruit a mixture of students from a variety of backgrounds and experiences.

The countywide youth-led coalition became responsible for reviewing county-level data to determine issues affecting local youth. Once the county-wide group identifies an issue of focus, school-based groups then review their local school data to identify the root causes of the issue and select and implement strategies to address the issue in their school. Most recently, the countywide group identified mental health, specifically depression and anxiety, as their issue of focus. This approach galvanizes the local efforts and ensures a broader impact in the county.

Simultaneously, IMPACT Prevention became responsible for coordinating RHPC. Grounded in a belief that young people have a right to be heard on the matters impacting their lives, the staff at IMPACT Prevention saw an opportunity to involve young people in the broader coalition work occurring in the county. Initially, the young people serving on the countywide youth coalition were consulted as an advisory board for RHPC. As the coalition was making decisions about the prevention activities to initiate in the community, IMPACT Prevention staff would present these ideas to the countywide youth-led coalition for feedback.

Figure 13.1 *Youth and adult subcommittee members review data from the Ohio Healthy Youth Environments Survey.*

As the work of the coalition expanded, it began to operate under a subcommittee structure, with subcommittees meeting more frequently to make decisions and complete work in between whole group coalition meetings. In this process, a subcommittee for youth was established as part of the structure of the larger coalition. Young people involved in the countywide youth-led coalition were invited to participate directly on this subcommittee as their time and interest allowed. Over time, youth involvement also expanded to the other subcommittees and to direct representation during RHPC coalition meetings. Young people now participate in partnership with adults on all six subcommittees and during general coalition meetings (see Figure 13.1). As members of the coalition, young people also engage in all professional development opportunities, including attending national conferences on substance abuse prevention. This structure allows for the broad-based participation of young people throughout the county and allows youth to represent themselves as the priority population, ensuring that they are involved in policies and services that impact them in the county.

Program staff emphasize that young people feel confident in participating in RHPC subcommittee meetings and general coalition meetings because they have an initial foundation from their school-based youth-led prevention program and the countywide youth coalition. Through their participation in these opportunities, young people develop the knowledge, skills, and attitudes needed to participate directly in RHPC. The youth that engage with RHPC are selected through a competitive application process, but all young people in the county have an opportunity to develop the skills needed to participate by engaging in their school-based youth-led prevention program. Prior to their first meeting with adult coalition members, program staff also meet with the youth to prepare them for the meeting structure and answer any questions they may have.

Equally important, program staff spend time preparing adult coalition members for partnering with young people and have established certain customs to help welcome youth members. At each coalition meeting when new members are present – regardless of age – the meeting begins with introductions to give new members context and help them feel welcomed. At every subcommittee meeting, icebreakers are utilized to familiarize members with each other and help the youth–adult relationships solidify.

Through the established structure and processes, IMPACT Prevention has created multiple avenues for young people to participate in their community and ensure youth representation. Program staff note that the initial youth involvement has led to greater involvement from other youth and community members over time.

Youth participants also note the power and importance of their participation in the coalition. Coalition leaders ask young people to reflect on their experience serving on the coalition at the end of their term. Feedback is collected both in writing and verbally. The following quote from one youth participant was selected by program staff as representative of the feedback they receive regarding the impact of serving in the coalition:

> I believe that being part of a coalition has allowed me to develop a greater understanding of the value of working together to achieve a common goal. I began attending the River Hills Coalition meetings as a youth representative. Although I was first intimidated by the professionalism and discipline-based terminology that seemed to be common knowledge, I was honored to be given the opportunity to represent the youth's perspective of what positive change looks like in the context of the community. The more I was able to interact with people who are passionate about positively impacting the community, the more connected I felt to the community and the more I was motivated to actively seek positive change.

Program staff also report that, as a result of participation in the coalition, young people's capacity to engage in other community efforts is enhanced. Many of the young people who were involved in these initiatives continue to work in the community as elected officials, teachers, officers of mental health agencies, faith-based leaders, and police officers. Currently, a former youth coalition member is engaging in RHPC as a paid staff member, and other past participants now serve as board members for IMPACT Prevention.

Community Power

Effective community coalitions can provide a vehicle for community empowerment (Wolff, 2001). A core concept in empowerment theory is that psychological empowerment and community empowerment are inextricably linked (Christens, 2019; Zimmerman, 2000). Individuals become empowered by participating in empowering settings and vice versa. While the components of psychological empowerment have become more clearly defined and measured over time, the conceptualization of community empowerment has received less attention (Christens, 2019). Christens (2019), drawing on the work of Lukes (1974), recently posited a framework for community power and empowerment that includes three primary components: situational, institutional, and systemic. In this section, we review the literature on youth involvement in community coalitions as it relates to these components of community empowerment.

Situational

The situational dimension of community power directs attention to who wins and who loses in public debates over policies and resources (Christens, 2019). A key indicator of this dimension is broad-based participation, as participation is both a precursor to and expression of community empowerment and collective action. IMPACT Prevention's approach to engaging young people in change efforts at multiple levels throughout the county therefore demonstrates one aspect of the situational dimension of power. Given the structure that IMPACT Prevention has established, youth throughout the county have opportunities to engage in change-making processes in their local schools, at the county level, and in partnerships with adults in RHPC. This type of approach builds power from the base up and gives young people opportunities for participation in many different settings, broadening their impact and reach in the county.

In the public health and substance abuse prevention literature, Mothers Against Drunk Driving (MADD) provides a rich case study for community power and youth participation (Fell & Voas, 2006; Weed, 1987). In the early 1990s, as MADD sought to expand its agenda to focus on underage drinking, it recognized the need to have youth members partner with local adults – including law enforcement and school leaders – to implement environmental prevention strategies to strengthen the enforcement of underage drinking laws and policies (Fell & Voas, 2006; Pentz, 2003). More than forty teams of youth and adults have been created in communities across the country. Although MADD has also become a national organization, these local teams function as youth-infused community coalitions and specifically address the issue of underage drinking in their local communities. As Fell and Voas (2006) note, young people are particularly effective in drawing attention to the issue of underage drinking in their local communities and recruiting other youth to engage in this work. More contemporary qualitative studies also find that when youth participate in community coalitions, they can mobilize networks of other young people to support the change effort (Campbell & Erbstein, 2011).

Collective efficacy – the belief that by working together groups can create change – is also a feature of the situational dimension of community power (Holden et al., 2004b; Zimmerman, 2000). This is often demonstrated by having distributed power and leadership in a group setting, though Christens (2019) is careful to note that this may look different when operating in nondemocratic contexts. Distributed power is both a goal and a challenge for many community coalitions, as engaged partners may rely heavily on the backbone organization to complete activities and work instead of sharing the workload across partners. In the context of youth-infused community coalitions, this tension is often felt in the distribution of power and responsibility between youth and adults. As Camino (2005) noted, adults working alongside youth frequently opt to "get out of the way" and fail to provide the support needed for young people to successfully engage in change efforts.

Institutional

Agenda-setting that lifts up or prevents community issues from being discussed in public debates is the focus of the institutional dimension of power (Christens, 2019). Features of this dimension include mobilization networks and the ability of these networks to assess and understand community problems. Having youth participate in agenda-setting when they are the intended beneficiaries of the coalition's efforts may improve the relevance and acceptability of the proposed solutions (Powers & Tiffany, 2006; Prilleltensky, 2010). A youth-infused community coalition focused on changing the food system in their local community of Holyoke, Massachusetts, provides an example of the institutional dimension of power (Sands et al., 2016). The coalition sought to improve access to healthy, affordable, locally grown food in the school and community. After installing a salad bar in the school setting, youth and adult coalition members kept track of salad bar participation and conducted a photovoice project to document local food sources and how they were used and consumed in the school setting (Sands et al., 2016). Their ability to document and assess the successes and challenges of having fresh, local vegetables available in the school setting allowed them to advocate for more options by presenting their findings to the school board. These efforts helped to provide a deeper understanding of the local food system and highlighted access to healthy foods as an issue worthy of attention.

As community coalitions and youth-infused community coalitions focused on substance use prevention began to shift to a comprehensive approach to prevention based upon guidance from the 1993 federal Alcohol and Drug Abuse and Mental Health Service Block Grant (45 CFR § 96.125), mass media campaigns became a useful and effective tool to meet the Block Grant's charge for population-level change (Jernigan & Wright, 1996). Although media campaigns are not likely to change behavior alone, they are a valuable strategy in substance use prevention through media advocacy

(Hogan et al., 2003). Wallack (1994) defines media advocacy as a "hybrid tool combining advocacy approaches with the strategic and innovative use of media to better pressure decision makers to support changes for healthy public policies" (p. 421). In their systematic review of the effectiveness of mass media campaigns for reducing alcohol-impaired driving, Elder et al. (2004) noted that mass media campaigns likely have indirect effects on population health due to the agenda-setting role that they play by influencing the public's perception of public health issues. This agenda-setting, in turn, garners support for community coalitions to take additional actions (such as policy and enforcement changes) or build community readiness (Oetting et al., 2014) to address public health issues.

Systemic

The systemic dimension of community power is the most foundational and the most difficult to document empirically; it refers to the ways that power shapes the public's beliefs, desires, and perceptions of an issue (Christens, 2019). For example, when MADD began, the dominant belief was that only heavily intoxicated drivers were a risk for public safety. As MADD began to expand its policy agenda to include lowering the legal blood alcohol limit for driving in the 1990s, it was met with resistance from the hospitality and alcohol industries, who feared that the lowered limit would affect social drinking and thus their revenues (Fell & Voas, 2006). Resistance from the hospitality and alcohol industries slowed the policy agenda of MADD, as these industries leveraged their power to shape the public's perceptions of the meaning of drunk driving and propelled a narrative that MADD advocates were "prohibitionists."

Contemporary coalitions, including youth-infused community coalitions, focused on substance use prevention often utilize environmental strategies to create change. Examples of environmental strategies in the context of substance use prevention include price interventions (e.g., excise taxes), minimum-purchase-age interventions (e.g., using decoy or sting operations to determine whether sellers are in compliance with purchase-age laws), deterrence interventions (e.g., alcohol-impaired driving laws), interventions addressing the location and density of retail outlets (i.e., through zoning or licensing limitations), restrictions on use (e.g., smoke-free workplace policies), server-and-seller-oriented interventions (e.g., server and seller training to check identification of patrons prior to tobacco and/or alcohol purchases), and counter-advertising (e.g., warning labels on alcohol and cigarettes; Brounstein et al., 1998). Planning and implementing environmental strategies such as these require public support to be successful because they are often related to changes in systems via policies and perceptions. When influencing systems, public support is essential in all stages of the policymaking cycle, as detailed by Lasswell (1956; e.g., intelligence, recommendation, prescription, invocation, application, appraisal, and termination). For example, a smoke-free workplace law or policy can be rendered ineffective if there is no enforcement of it. As such, community coalitions are often purposeful and intentional in how they frame issues to garner the support necessary to successfully implement environmental strategies aimed at creating systems changes (Hogan et al., 2003).

At times, action is needed to change dominant beliefs and perceptions. In the case of Holyoke, Massachusetts, members of the youth-infused community coalition solicited funding from the W.K. Kellogg Foundation to launch a prototype salad bar in the high school. The coalition was aware of the existing food narrative perpetuated by school food services – and more generally in US culture – that children and youth, particularly from low-income backgrounds, do not like to eat fresh fruit and vegetables and prefer processed foods (Sands et al., 2016). This dominant perception limited the school's efforts to provide healthy foods to students. The coalition sought the funding for the salad bar and then documented its use to change the narrative and demonstrate that children and youth will eat healthy food when it is offered consistently.

Psychological Empowerment

Participation in community coalitions that seek to address local community issues is theorized to facilitate psychological empowerment for young people (Holden et al., 2004b; Zeldin et al., 2013). The YECF (Holden et al., 2004b), for example, posits that young people become empowered by participating in organized, collective action with others. In the context of youth-infused community coalitions, young people engage in partnership with adults as they work together to address a community issue. Youth–adult partnerships, characterized by a mutuality and respect among youth and adults, with an emphasis on shared learning and leading (Camino, 2005), are similarly theorized to contribute to psychological empowerment (Zeldin et al., 2013). In this section, we review the extant studies that demonstrate psychological empowerment as an outcome associated with youth participation in community coalitions and partnerships with adults.

Emotional

Most of the research on psychological empowerment has focused on the emotional component (Christens, 2012; Peterson et al., 2011). In their evaluation of young people's participation in youth-led tobacco control efforts in Canada, Holden et al. (2004a) found that taking a leadership role, engaging in group discussions, and trying to recruit others to attend the group were all positively associated with perceived sociopolitical control, an indicator of the emotional component of psychological empowerment. A qualitative study of coalitions that engaged youth and adults in planning and implementing community change strategies found that youth participants developed public-speaking skills and learned how to organize and lead meetings (Campbell & Erbstein, 2011).

Youth-infused community coalitions engage young people in partnership with adults. Youth–adult partnerships may be a setting-level driver of psychological empowerment in the coalition setting. Research has found a relationship between youth–adult partnerships and psychological empowerment in other settings. For example, quantitative studies with international samples in the context of afterschool programs have found an association between engaging in youth–adult partnerships and perceived sociopolitical control. A study of Malaysian youth found that partnerships with adults, in the form of supportive adult relationships and youth voice in decision-making, were significant predictors of young people's perceived sociopolitical control (Krauss et al., 2013). Similarly, a cross-national study of Malaysian, Portuguese, and American youth who engaged in partnership with adults found that partnerships were a strong predictor of empowerment, specifically the emotional component of psychological empowerment (Zeldin et al., 2017).

Cognitive

The cognitive component of psychological empowerment – the critical awareness and knowledge needed to change systems (Zimmerman, 2000) – is also theorized to develop through participation in youth-infused community coalitions. Evaluators of a youth-led tobacco control effort found that taking on leadership roles was positively associated with knowledge of resources, an indicator of the cognitive component of psychological empowerment (Holden et al., 2004a). More contemporary qualitative studies have found that participation in community coalitions facilitates cognitive empowerment by fostering participants' understanding of power and systems. For example, in one study of a coalition that involved youth who had aged out of the foster care system, Forenza (2016) found that young people learned how to identify those in power within the local systems. This is illustrated by the following comment from a youth participant: "I've learned the chain of command at [the Department of Children and Families] – who to talk to and who to go over" (Forenza, 2016, p. 282). Another in-depth case study of a multistate coalition composed of youth and adults impacted by the foster care system found that, by meeting with other young people, participants began to realize the issues and barriers that they experienced were not unique to them but rather represented systemic barriers (Augsberger et al., 2019). The researchers reported that the young people became less likely to focus on individual problems and more focused on identifying systemic issues and understanding the broader systems that were affecting lives. Interestingly, research (e.g., Christens et al., 2011) suggests that it is possible to understand how to pursue community change without actually feeling capable of making change. In other words, it is possible for young people to demonstrate components of cognitive empowerment without demonstrating components of emotional empowerment (Christens et al., 2013).

Behavioral

The actions taken to impact or exert influence on the social and political environ-ment are the focus of the behavioral component of psychological empowerment (Zimmerman, 2000). In the research base, this component is most often referred to as community participation. Studies with adult populations consistently find that individuals who have a higher degree of sociopolitical control participate in more community activities and are more likely be critically aware of how to exert power to create change (Speer, 2000; Speer et al., 2001). More recently, Christens and Lin (2014) found that community participation increased leadership drive and furthered involvement in community programs. The notion of coalition participation furthering involvement in other community work is evident in the young person's quote provided in the exemplar earlier.

For young people, community participation may encompass a variety of activities, ranging from volunteering with organizations or speaking at a school board meeting, to buy-cotting and protesting. Indeed, participation in a community coalition is itself an example of the behavioral component of empowerment (Forenza, 2016) and has been theorized as a pathway to the development of sociopolitical skills in youth (Camino & Zeldin, 2002). In their seminal evaluation of youth-led tobacco control efforts, Holden et al. (2004a) found that taking a leadership role, engaging in group discussions, taking responsibility for getting things done, and making an effort to recruit others to attend the group were all positively associated with advocacy, an indicator of the behavioral component of psychological empowerment.

In Ohio, youth coalitions and youth-infused community coalitions such as RHPC engage in data-driven planning processes to select and implement evidence-based prevention strategies in their communities (Collura et al., 2019). The actions young people take in their community by participating in a coalition therefore may involve advocating to reduce youth access to regu-lated substances (i.e., alcohol, tobacco, and, in some states, marijuana) and drugs with the potential for misuse (e.g., over-the-counter and prescription drugs) through supporting the creation of enforcement of laws and policy or seeking to change community norms through the development of social marketing or social norms campaigns (Haines et al., 2005).

Relational

The relational component of psychological empowerment focuses on young people's collaborative competence and ability to facilitate others' empowerment (Christens, 2012, 2019). Studies suggest that participating in community coalitions does foster relational empowerment. In a qualitative study of a substance use prevention coalition, researchers found that adult coalition members' desire to connect with and influence young people was a motivation for their continued engagement on the coalition (Bermea et al., 2019). The ability to involve young people in the community and in preventing substance misuse fostered the continued participation of adult members. Similarly, a qualitative study of a youth-infused community coalition focused on HIV prevention in youth populations found that young people's participation in the coalition made the adult members perceive the coalition as worthwhile (Reed et al., 2012). Adults who engage in partnership with young people report feelings of generativity and increased confidence in their ability and desire to work with youth (Zeldin, 2004).

Youth who engaged in partnership with adults in a multistate coalition pertaining to foster care described the collaborative process of working with others, sharing information, and developing joint presentations for state leaders as an empowering process (Augsberger et al., 2019). In this case study, the coalition established a "buddy system" that allowed more experienced youth participants an opportunity to mentor newer participants. This helped create a welcoming environment while also supporting the youth's ability to facilitate others' empowerment. Relatedly, in their study of young people involved in high school gay–straight alliances (GSAs), youth spoke to the importance of relational processes as part of empowerment (Russell et al., 2009). Youth acknowledged that group membership was associated with feelings of confidence and solidarity, expressed a commitment to passing on the GSA legacy and a desire to facilitate others' empowerment in the organization. For youth-infused community coalitions, this suggests the importance of creating a culture and processes committed to fostering relationships and supporting others' growth. The relational aspects of engaging in the community may be particularly relevant for adolescents (Chiman & Linney, 1998).

Setting Features

Youth-infused community coalitions offer participants unique opportunities for community involvement and collective action. Three setting features – member representation, decision-making processes, and opportunity role structure – are critical to facilitating community power and psychological empowerment in these settings. Core to the functioning of a community coalition is the participation of individuals who represent various organization and stakeholder perspectives within the community. *Diverse membership* allows coalitions to develop and increase public support for issues or actions more broadly within the community and enhances a coalition's effectiveness (Butterfoss et al., 1993; Zakocs & Edwards, 2006). Coalitions that collaborate across race and class generate the possibility for broad systems change (Sands et al., 2016). Ensuring diverse representation and having structures in place to welcome and onboard new members are crucial for both the immediate and long-term effectiveness of coalitions. For example, in their study of community-based prevention coalitions, Perkins et al. (2011) found new member integration to be strongly related to the coalition's sustainability. Given that opportunities for participation and civic engagement are not evenly distributed by race, social class, ability, or age (Flanagan & Levine, 2010), careful consideration must be given to ensuring that the individuals selected to participate in the coalition are reflective of the local community. The presence of young people in a community coalition helps to diversify membership in terms of age. However, in youth-infused community coalitions, selection of youth participants frequently relies on identifying exemplary student leaders in schools or districts. Coalition members must be cognizant of the characteristics of the young people they are recruiting and how representative the young people are of the local youth population. Like other community coalitions, youth-infused community coalitions tend to function more as planning and coordinating entities than as grassroots mobilizers (Miller et al., 2012). Youth-infused coalitions that mobilize broad-based grassroots participation tend to have structures similar to RHPC, in which youth representatives are connected to other local groups that can be mobilized for action.

When young people are involved in a coalition, intergenerational relationships need to be established and nurtured as part of the coalition's processes. In RHPC, coalition leaders ensure young people and adults have time for relationship-building during subcommittee meetings. This forms the foundation for them to be able to engage in meaningful community change efforts together. Equally important are the structures that guide *decision-making processes*. Core to youth–adult partnerships and intergenerational relationships in community change efforts is the opportunity for authentic voice in decision-making processes (Camino, 2005; Zeldin et al., 2013). Empowering settings engage members in deliberations (Hess, 2009; Hess & McAvoy, 2015) and seek to reach consensus through knowledge-sharing and discussion. Coalitions engage in a multitude of decisions – such as which issue to focus on, why the issue is occurring in their community, and what strategies to implement – before they take collective action. As opposed to simply presenting options and moving to a vote, empowering settings foster rich discussions and deliberations in which members exchange information and opinions to reach a decision. Adults and youth demonstrate respect and a mutuality in teaching and learning from each other during these discussions and deliberations (Zeldin et al., 2013). Notably, past research has found that coalitions led by service delivery organizations sometimes struggle to engage youth as cocreators since this approach counters their traditional orientation of engaging with youth as service recipients (Campbell & Erbstein, 2011). On the other hand, adult allies or lead organizations grounded in community organizing were more willing to embrace youth voice but struggled with finding developmentally appropriate ways of engaging youth.

Finally, both the YECF and CCAT models indicate the importance of *opportunity role structure* (Butterfoss & Kegler, 2002; Holden et al., 2004b; Maton, 2008). Empowering settings offer members opportunities to take on new roles and responsibilities as their skills and interest increase. IMPACT Prevention and RHPC established an expansive, multilevel structure that allows for broad-based participation among county youth. All youth interested in making a change in their community are able to participate through the school-based groups, and as their interest and skills develop over time they are able to engage in the countywide youth coalition or directly in RHPC. This structure allows for a broad youth engagement movement in the county while providing unique opportunities for young people to grow and expand their contributions based on their interest and availability.

Application

Youth-infused community coalitions are powerful contexts that promote psychological empowerment and positive youth development while also effectively creating population-level changes in local communities. Young people who serve on community coalitions engage in empowering settings that fuel their own positive development. Simultaneously, the actions that the coalition takes lead to changes in local communities that help create more positive and nurturing environments for the broader population of youth and adults. Given these benefits, youth-infused community coalitions are worthy of time and investment.

Effectively engaging young people in community coalitions and change efforts requires skilled facilitators capable of creating a culture of shared learning, decision-making, and action. As other scholars have noted (e.g., Campbell & Erbstein, 2011; Christens & Zeldin, 2016; Perkins et al., 2011), these skills are in short supply. To expand and support effective youth-infused community coalitions, we recommend that funders and policymakers invest in training and technical assistance designed to support coalition leaders in simultaneously engaging young people in a developmentally appropriate manner while taking collective action. Training and technical assistance should offer practitioners safe spaces to learn from each other and bolster the foundational knowledge and skills – including knowledge of community organizing, change management, and youth development – needed to create a culture that supports intergenerational relationships based on mutual respect. Funders should also be mindful that requiring the inclusion of young people in community coalitions does not ensure that young people are participating in an equitable manner. In many ways, the system is not currently built to support the engagement of youth, and therefore time and resources must be dedicated to intentionally educating and supporting coalition leaders, with an understanding that successful inclusion may take time and could temporarily delay the actions of the coalition. Investing in strong membership and an inclusive environment ultimately contributes to coalition effectiveness (Butterfoss et al., 1993; Zakocs & Edwards, 2006) but does take time.

Regardless of their access to technical assistance, coalition leaders should be aware that there are tools and resources available to support their work. Both the YECF (Holden et al., 2004b) and CCAT (Butterfoss & Kegler, 2002) provide theoretical foundations for youth-infused community coalitions. When used together as intentional planning and reflection tools, practitioners can identify and focus on the core elements needed to effectively implement youth-infused community coalitions.

Coalition leaders should think strategically about how to build broad-based youth engagement in their coalition over time. In the example of Lawrence County and RHPC, the lead agency had a strong history of facilitating school-based youth-led prevention programs. Eventually, a countywide youth coalition was developed with representatives from each of the school-based groups. This countywide youth coalition remains responsible for coordinating the work of youth-led programs across the county and, through the review of local data, identifying issues for all school-based programs to focus on. Today, selected youth-led coalition members serve directly in RHPC to ensure that the coalition is infused with youth voice and perspectives. This multifaceted approach has resulted in broad-based youth participation and voice, built over time. As illustrated in this example, the involvement started with small, local school groups and expanded over time. Young people sometimes need their own space to work collaboratively with other youth on community change efforts before they feel comfortable engaging with adults. Creating initial spaces for young people to lead and work collaboratively may be a critical starting point.

Future Research

Much of the research on youth-infused community coalitions – and youth community engagement more broadly – does not precisely identify and distinguish the settings in which young people are participating. This is a challenge for the current literature base, as different models of community engagement (e.g., youth organizing, youth governance, youth participatory action research) may lead to differential outcomes for youth and communities. When reviewing the literature on youth engagement in community change efforts, much of the contemporary research focuses on youth organizing; however, as Conner notes in Chapter 1, by 2013, 77 percent of youth organizing initiatives were reporting involvement in networks or coalitions. Broad-based movements often encompass a variety of organizations and community groups in their change efforts, and different models may be utilized or embraced at various points during their efforts. This further challenges the ability of researchers to precisely define the type of setting or context young people are engaged in and to decipher how their participation impacts their own development and the community's development. As others have noted (e.g., Christens & Lin, 2014), most studies on psychological empowerment do not make distinctions among the ways in which people engaged in the organization or community setting. At the very least, scholars should be mindful of the variety of change efforts young people may engage in and seek to precisely define organizational and coalition settings and their attributes when conducting research on psychological empowerment.

Recent studies have validated measures of cognitive empowerment among young people (Speer et al., 2019), but a validated measure for the relational component of empowerment for youth is still needed. A measure of relational empowerment has recently been validated in adult populations (Peterson et al., 2021), but further testing is needed with a youth sample. Relatedly, most studies on youth-infused community coalitions focus on the individual outcomes – specifically developmental outcomes for youth – associated with participation. More research is needed at the community level, along with research on the outcomes for adults who engage with youth as partners in this setting. Finally, although there are examples of community coalitions working to address health disparities in international contexts, examples of *youth-infused* community coalitions in international environments are still limited. This is therefore an area where applied research could make important contributions.

References

Augsberger, A., Springwater, J. S., Hilliard-Koshinsky, G., Barber, K., & Martinez, L. S. (2019). Youth participation in policy advocacy: Examination of a multistate former and current foster care youth coalition. *Children and Youth Services Review, 107,* 104491.

Bermea, A. M., Lardier, D. T., Forenza, B., Garcia-Reid, P., & Reid, R. J. (2019). Communitarianism and youth empowerment: Motivation for participation in a community-based substance abuse prevention coalition. *Journal of Community Psychology, 47*(1), 49–62.

Brounstein, P., Zweig, J., & Gardner, S. (1998). *Science-based practices in substance abuse prevention: A guide.* Center for Substance Abuse Prevention, Division of Knowledge Development and Evaluation.

Brown, L. D., Chilenski, S. M., Ramos, R., Gallegos, N., & Feinberg, M. E. (2016). Community prevention coalition context and capacity assessment: Comparing the United States and Mexico. *Health Education & Behavior, 43*(2), 145–155.

Butterfoss, F. D., & Kegler, M. C. (2002). Toward a comprehensive understanding of community coalitions: Moving from practice to theory. In R. J. DiClemente,

R. A. Crosby, & M. C. Kegler (Eds.), *Emerging theories in health promotion practice and research: Strategies for improving public health* (pp. 157–193). Jossey-Bass.

Butterfoss, F. D., Goodman, R. M., & Wandersman, A. (1993). Community coalitions for prevention and health promotion. *Health Education Research, 8*(3), 315–330.

CADCA. (2022, August). *International programs: Where we work*. CADCA. www.cadca.org/international/home

Camino, L. (2005). Pitfalls and promising practices of youth–adult partnerships: An evaluator's reflections. *Journal of Community Psychology, 33*(1), 75–85.

Camino, L., & Zeldin, S. (2002). From periphery to center: Pathways for youth civic engagement in the day-to-day life of communities. *Applied Developmental Science, 6*(4), 213–220.

Campbell, D., & Erbstein, N. (2011). Engaging youth in community change: Three key implementation principles. *Community Development, 43*(1), 63–79.

Center for Substance Abuse Prevention. (2009). *Identifying and selecting evidence-based interventions revised guidance document for the Strategic Prevention Framework State Incentive Grant Program* (HHS Publication No. SMA09-4205). Center for Substance Abuse Prevention, Substance Abuse and Mental Health Services Administration.

Centers for Disease Control and Prevention. (2021, January 22). *Drug-Free Communities Support Program*. Centers for Disease Control and Prevention. www.cdc.gov/drugoverdose/drug-free-communities/about.html

Chinman, M. J., & Linney, J. A. (1998). Toward a model of adolescent empowerment: Theoretical and empirical evidence. *Journal of Primary Prevention, 18*, 393–413.

Christens, B. D. (2012). Toward relational empowerment. *American Journal of Community Psychology, 50*(1–2), 114–128.

Christens, B. D. (2019). *Community power and empowerment*. Oxford University Press.

Christens, B. D., & Inzeo, P. T. (2015). Widening the view: Situating collective impact among frameworks for community-led change. *Community Development, 46*(4), 420–435.

Christens, B. D., & Lin, C. S. (2014). Influences of community and organizational participation, social support and sense of community on psychological empowerment: Income as moderator. *Family & Consumer Sciences Research Journal, 42*(3), 211–223.

Christens, B. D., & Zeldin, S. (2016). Community engagement. In R. J. R. Levesque (Ed.), *Encyclopedia of adolescence* (2nd ed., pp. 483–487). Springer International.

Christens, B. D., Collura, J. J., & Tahir, F. (2013). Critical hopefulness: A person-centered analysis of the intersection of cognitive and emotional empowerment. *American Journal of Community Psychology, 52*(1–2), 170–184.

Christens, B. D., Speer, P. W., & Peterson, N. A. (2011). Social class as a moderator of the relationship between (dis)empowering processes and psychological empowerment. *Journal of Community Psychology, 39*(2), 170–182.

Collura, J., Raffle, H., Collins, A., & Kennedy, H. (2019). Creating spaces for young people to collaborate to create community change: Ohio's youth-led initiative. *Health Education and Behavior, 46*(1 Suppl.), 44S–52S.

Elder, R. W., Shults, R. A., Sleet, D. A., Nichols, J. L., Thompson, R. S, & Rajab, W. (2004). Effectiveness of mass media campaigns for reducing drinking and driving and alcohol-involved crashes: A systematic review. *American Journal of Preventive Medicine, 27*(1), 57–65.

Feighery, E., & Rogers, T. (1990). *Building and maintaining effective coalitions.* Health Promotion Resource Center, Stanford Center for Research in Disease Prevention.

Fell, J. C., & Voas, R. B. (2006). Mothers Against Drunk Driving (MADD): The first 25 years. *Traffic Injury Prevention, 7*(3), 195–212.

Flanagan, C., & Levine, P. (2010). Civic engagement and the transition to adulthood. *Future of Children, 20*(1), 159–179.

Ford, R., Hershberger, S., Glenn, J., Morris, S., Saez, V., Togba, F., Watson, J., & Williams, R. (2013). Building a youth-led movement to keep young people out of the adult criminal justice system. *Children & Youth Services Review, 35I*(8), 1268–1275.

Forenza, B. (2016). Psychological empowerment and pursuit of social change. *Journal of Public Child Welfare, 10*(3), 274–290.

Haines, M. P., Perkins, H. W., Rice, R. M., & Barker, G. (2005). *A guide to marketing social norms for health promotion in schools and communities.* National Social Norms Resource Center.

Hess, D. E. (2009). *Controversy in the classroom: The democratic power of discussion.* Routledge.

Hess, D. E., & McAvoy, P. (2015). *The political classroom: Evidence and ethics in democratic education.* Routledge.

Hogan, J. M., Gabrielsen, K. R., Luna, N., & Grothaus, D. (2003). *Substance abuse prevention: The intersection of science and practice.* Pearson Education.

Holden, D. J., Crankshaw, E., Nimsch, C., Hinnant, L. W., & Hund, L. (2004a). Quantifying the impact of participation in local tobacco control groups on the psychological empowerment of involved youth. *Health Education & Behavior, 31*(5), 615–628.

Holden, D. J., Messeri, P., Evans, W. D., Crankshaw, E., & Ben-Davies, M. (2004b). Conceptualizing youth empowerment within tobacco control. *Health Education & Behavior, 31*(5), 548–563.

Janosky, E., Armoutliev, E. M., Benipal, A., Kingsbury, D., Teller, J. L., Snyder, K. L., & Riley, P. (2013). Coalitions for impacting the health of a community: The Summit County, Ohio experience. *Population Health Management, 16* (4), 246–254.

Jernigan, D. H., & Wright, P. A. (1996). Media advocacy: Lessons learned from community experiences. *Journal of Public Health Policy, 17*(3), 306–330.

Kania, J., & Kramer, M. (2011). Collective impact. *Stanford Social Innovation Review, 9*(1), 36–41.

Krauss, S. E., Collura, J., Zeldin, S., Ortega, A., Abdullah, H., & Sulaiman, A. H. (2013). Youth–adult partnership: Exploring contributions to empowerment, agency and community connections in Malaysian youth programs. *Journal of Youth and Adolescence, 43*(9), 1550–1562.

Lasswell, H. D. (1956). *The decision process: Seven categories of functional analysis.* Bureau of Governmental Research.

Lawlor, J. A., Metta, K. R., & Neal, Z. P. (2021). What is a coalition? A systematic review of coalitions in community psychology. *Journal of Community and Applied Social Psychology*, *32*(3), 3–18.

Lukes, S. (1974). *Power: A radical view*. Humanities Press.

Maton, K. I. (2008). Empowering community settings: Agents of individual development, community betterment, and positive social change. *American Journal of Community Psychology*, *41*(1–2), 4–21.

Mayan, M., Turner, A. T., Ortiz, L., & Moffatt, J. (2013). Building a multicultural coalition: Promoting participation in civic society among ethnic minority communities. *Canadian Ethnic Studies*, *45*(1–2), 157–178.

Miller, R. L., Reed, S. J., Francisco, V. T., Ellen, J. M., & The ATN 079 Protocol Team for the Adolescent Medicine Trials Network for HIV/AIDS Interventions. (2012). Conflict transformation, stigma, and HIV-preventive structural change. *American Journal of Community Psychology*, *49*(3–4), 378–392.

Oetting, E. R., Plested, B. A., Edwards, R. W., Thurman, P. J., Kelly, K. J., Beauvais, F., & Stanley, L. R. (2014). *Community readiness for community change: Tri-Ethnic Center for Community Readiness handbook* (2nd ed.). Colorado State University.

Pentz, M. A. (2003). Evidence-based prevention: Characteristics, impact, and future direction. *Journal of Psychoactive Drugs*, *35*(Suppl. 1), 143–152.

Perkins, D. F., Feinberg, M. E., Greenberg, M. T., Johnson, L. E., Chilenski, S. M., Mincemoyer, C. C., & Spoth, R. L. (2011). Team factors that predict to sustainability indicators for community-based prevention teams. *Evaluation and Program Planning*, *34*(3), 283–291.

Peterson, N. A., Lardier, D. T., Powell, K. G., Mankopf, E., Rashid, M., Morton, C. M., & Borys, S. (2021). Psychometric properties of a recovery empowerment scale: Testing emotional, cognitive, behavioral, and relational domains. *Journal of Community Psychology*, *49*(7), 2874–2891.

Peterson, N. A., Peterson, C. H., Agre, L., Christens, B. D., & Morton, C. M. (2011). Measuring youth empowerment: Validation of a sociopolitical control scale for youth in an urban community context. *Journal of Community Psychology*, *39*(5), 592–605.

Powers, J. L., & Tiffany, J. S. (2006). Engaging youth in participatory research and evaluation. *Journal of Public Health Management and Practice*, *12*, 79–87.

Price, A. W. (2020). Lessons learned working with drug-free community coalitions and collaboratives. *New Directions for Evaluation*, *165*, 171–180.

Prilleltensky, I. (2010). Child wellness and social inclusion: Values for action. *American Journal of Community Psychology*, *46*, 238–249.

Reed, S. J., Miller, R. L., & The Adolescent Medicine Trials Network for HIV/AIDS Interventions. (2014). The benefits of youth engagement in HIV-preventive structural change interventions. *Youth & Society*, *46*(4), 529–547.

Rittel, H. W., & Webber, M. (1973). Dilemmas in a general theory of planning. *Policy Sciences*, *4*(2), 155–169.

Russell, S. T., Muraco, A., Subramaniam, A., & Laub, C. (2009). Youth empowerment and high school gay–straight alliances. *Journal of Youth and Adolescence*, *38*(7), 891–903.

Sands, C., Stewart, C., Bankert, S., Hillman, A., & Fries, L. (2016). Building an airplane while flying it: One community's experience with community food transformation. *Journal of Agriculture, Food Systems and Community Development, 7*(1), 89–111.

Shapiro, V. B., Oesterle, S., Abbott, R. D., Arthur, M. W., & Hawkins, J. D. (2013). Measuring dimensions of coalition functioning for effective and participatory community practice. *Social Work Research, 37*(4), 349–359.

Speer, P. W. (2000). Intrapersonal and interactional empowerment: Implications for theory. *Journal of Community Psychology, 28*(1), 51–61.

Speer, P. W., Jackson, C. B., & Peterson, N. A. (2001). The relationship between social cohesion and empowerment: Support and new implications for theory. *Health Education & Behavior, 28*(6), 716–732.

Speer, P. W., Peterson, N. A., Christens, B. D., & Reid, R. J. (2019). Youth cognitive empowerment: Development and evaluation of an instrument. *American Journal of Community Psychology, 64*(3–4), 528–540.

Wallack, L. (1994). Media advocacy: A strategy for empowering people and communities. *Journal of Public Health Policy, 15*(4), 420–436.

Weed, F. J. (1987). Grass-roots activism and the drunk driving Issue: Survey of MADD chapters. *Law & Policy, 9*(3), 259–278.

Wolff, T. (2001). Community coalition building – Contemporary research and practice: Introduction. *American Journal of Community Psychology, 29*(2), 165–172.

Zakocs, R., & Edwards, E. (2006). What explains community coalition effectiveness? A review of the literature. *American Journal of Preventive Medicine, 30*(4), 351–361.

Zeldin, S. (2004). Youth as agents of adult and community development: Mapping the process and outcomes of youth engaged in organizational governance. *Applied Developmental Science, 8*(2), 75–90.

Zeldin, S., Christens, B., & Powers, J. (2013). The psychology and practice of youth–adult partnership: Bridging generations for youth development and community change. *American Journal of Community Psychology, 51*(3–4), 385–397.

Zeldin, S., Gauley, J., Krauss, S. E., Kornbluh, M., & Collura, J. (2017). Youth–adult partnership and youth civic development: Cross-national analyses for scholars and field professionals. *Youth & Society, 49*(7), 851–878.

Zimmerman, M. A. (2000). Empowerment theory: Psychological, organizational, and community levels of analysis. In J. Rappaport & E. Seidman (Eds.), *Handbook of community psychology* (pp. 43–63). Kluwer Academic Publishers.

14 Neighborhood Associations and Community Change

Kayla M. Anderson and Brian D. Christens

Introduction

Throughout history populations have organized into clusters as a way to survive and feel connected within larger, often hostile geographies (Talen, 2018; Wargent & Talen, 2021). When these clusters promote intensive social interaction and/or serve as administrative units they are typically classified as neighborhoods (Smith, 2010). Neighborhoods, as a form of spatial and social organization, have played integral roles throughout urban history. For example, archaeologists have described the presence and critical function of neighborhoods in ancient civilizations in Mesopotamia (cities of Ur and Nippur), Mesoamerica (Mayan and Aztec), and Europe (Greek and Roman; Smith, 2010; Talen, 2018). The spatial division of cities into neighborhoods has also been traced to preindustrial cities such as Marseille (France) during the fourteenth century, Addis Ababa (Ethiopia) during the late nineteenth century, Ilesha (Nigeria) during the late nineteenth and early twentieth centuries, and Bhaktapur (Nepal) during the twentieth century (Smith, 2010).[1] Within all of these cities, neighborhoods were fundamental to the social and political organization of urban residents.

A modern understanding of neighborhoods developed during the eighteenth and nineteenth centuries alongside industrialization and urbanization. During this time, increases in industry and densely built housing drew populations across Europe (starting in the UK), the US, and Japan into cities. With the sudden influx of migrants, people often clustered together based on similar cultural backgrounds and values as a way to provide support and mutual aid (Talen, 2018). However, these homophilic clusters also established spatial divisions and exclusion based on differences (i.e., religion, ethnic background, and/or class).

During the nineteenth century in England and the US, the expansion of the streetcar challenged the neighborhood as a social and spatial unit. As streetcars proliferated, cities became spaces designed for roads, on which people moved through urban space, often making it harder to define specific urban neighborhoods. Additionally, with the rise of affordable mass transit, middle- and upper-class residents increasingly left the city for the suburbs, where their

---

1 For a detailed account of ancient neighborhoods, see Talen (2018).

understanding of a neighborhood shifted from that of support and mutual aid to status and aesthetics (Talen, 2018). Many of those who remained in urban neighborhoods found their neighborhood spaces drastically disrupted due to increased development (e.g., of transportation infrastructure and industry).

It was around this same time that early modern neighborhood organization movements – such as the settlement house movement – formed to address pressing social issues as a result of the increased industrialization and rapid population influx in urban areas (Chaskin, 1997; Lohmann, 2002). The settlement house movement originated in England in 1885 with the founding of Toynbee Hall in East London (Reinders, 1982), then quickly expanded to other nations around the world (Köngeter, 2021). The goals of settlement houses, though different depending on context, were to provide direct services to meet immediate needs, increase the sense of community within neighborhoods, and build collective action to address social issues (Koerin, 2003).

The important role of neighborhood organizations, like settlement houses, was identified early on by scholars and practitioners alike. In 1918, US-based social worker and management theorist Mary Parker Follet asserted that neighborhood organizations were fundamental for democratic governance (Mathews, 2021). Follet wrote:

> First, every neighborhood must be organized; the neighborhood groups must then be integrated, through larger intermediary groups, into a true state. Neither our cities nor our states can ever be properly administered until representatives from neighborhood groups meet to discuss and thereby to correlate the needs of all parts of the city, of all parts of the state. (Follet, 1918, as cited in Mathews, 2021, p. 821)

Despite Follet's assertion and concerted efforts by neighborhood groups around the world, Follet's vision for the role of neighborhood organizations in local governance would not become widespread until decades later.[2]

The Rise of Neighborhood Associations

Neighborhood associations can be defined as geographically bound, grassroots organizations that rely on volunteer membership and direct participation to identify and address issues within their neighborhood (Mesch & Schwirian, 1996; Moore & McGregor, 2021; Pekkanen & Tsujinaka, 2008). Often these groups serve as intermediaries between residents and local decision-makers, such as government officials and developers (Chaskin & Greenberg, 2015; Pekkanen, 2003).

Beginning in the immediate post-World War II period, neighborhood associations became more prevalent in cities across much of the US, western

---

2 Apart from in some locations such as Japan, where incredible growth took place in the presence and prevalence of neighborhood associations starting in the 1920s (Pekkanen, 2003).

Europe, Asia, and Latin America (Avritzer, 2009a; Lama-Rewal, 2007; Lohmann, 2002; Ruef & Kwon, 2016). In the US, Europe, and Turkey, many neighborhood associations developed as a response to urban renewal (1950s to early 1970s in the US and western Europe and 2000s in Turkey), serving as mechanisms that residents could use to protect their economic and social interests against encroaching development, as well as to maintain and improve quality of life in their neighborhoods (Ay, 2019; Foell & Foster, 2022; Moore & McGregor, 2021; Scheller & Yerena, 2017). In Turkey and some South Asian and South American countries, neighborhood associations formed after the adoption of decentralized governance policies that prompted increased citizen participation in governance (Ay, 2019; Kohl & Farthing, 2008; Lama-Rewal & Zérah, 2011). In Brazil, the prominence of neighborhood associations rose in the 1970s, and sharply so in the 1980s, alongside the liberalization of the former authoritarian regime and as a reaction against authoritarianism broadly (Avritzer, 2009b). In the US, Mesch and Schwirian (1996) identified four primary reasons for the development of neighborhood associations: gentrification, urban redevelopment, community engagement initiated by local government, and crime. They argue that these four contextual factors prompted the organization and mobilization of residents into formally organized groups to protect neighborhoods' identities and advocate on behalf of their neighborhoods' economic, social, and political interests.

Characteristics and Roles of Neighborhood Associations

One basic defining feature of neighborhood associations around the world is that they are geographically bound to particular neighborhoods (Florin & Wandersman, 1990; Mesch & Schwirian, 1996), distinguishing them from other issue-oriented grassroots organizations. Defining their organizations' purview and membership geographically allows neighborhood associations to focus on hyperlocal issues that affect particular social and environmental segments of a larger urban area (Lama-Rewal, 2007; Moore & McGregor, 2021). These issues include but are not limited to concerns around safety, improvements to facilities (parks, sidewalks, shopping centers) or services (garbage collection, health care), neighborhood appeal (cleanliness, housing conditions, visual appeal), and development (Logan & Rabrenovic, 1990; Zérah, 2007).

Homeowner associations (HOAs) can play some similar roles to neighborhood associations, but they also have important differences. Like neighborhood associations, HOAs are also geographically bound and focus on local issues. However, HOAs are usually developed as restrictive covenants linked to the deeds of properties with some level of collective investment (e.g., condominiums; Ruef & Kwon, 2016), whereas neighborhood associations typically derive from more inclusive, locally initiated grassroots efforts (Chaskin, 1997; Florin & Wandersman, 1990; Pratt, 1971). As their name indicates, HOAs are unlikely to represent renters, and they are typically smaller in scale than neighborhood associations.

In addition to focusing on local issues, neighborhood organizations can play critical roles in brokering relationships between neighborhood residents and local government entities (Chaskin & Greenberg, 2015). In some instances, this entails a neighborhood association advocating on behalf of residents or establishing relationships with policymakers that allow residents to have increased access to decision-making spaces (Koschmann & Laster, 2011; Logan & Rabrenovic, 1990). In other cases, local governments play a central role in the development of neighborhood associations, assisting in the formation of these groups across cities (Moore & McGregor, 2021). However, regardless of the level of support that neighborhood associations receive from local government agencies, studies have found that participation in these organizations tends to increase local residents' ability to influence policy and play an engaged role in the governance of their communities (King, 2004).

Organizational Structures

Neighborhood associations tend to have loose organizational structures with little or no hierarchy; however, they can vary in complexity depending on the larger contexts in which they are embedded (Oropesa, 1995). As previously noted, membership is typically voluntary (Scheller & Yerena, 2017) and limited to those residing and, at times, working in the geographical confines of the neighborhood (Pekkanen & Tsujinaka, 2008). Additionally, neighborhood organizations rarely have paid leadership positions and rely heavily on volunteer labor (Oropesa, 1995). The reliance on volunteer labor can be an obstacle for many associations, as they are often competing for members' time and resources and therefore are only as productive as members are committed (Koschmann & Laster, 2011). Associations can overcome this challenge by having strong leadership that is committed to the goals of the group and is willing to put in the work needed to organize people and resources to effectively mobilize (Rich, 1980). Certain organizational structures may provide better contexts for the emergence of strong leadership. For example, Austin (1991) argues that neighborhood organizations with complex leadership structures, such as multiple differentiated leadership roles, may be better situated to address the ever-changing availability of resources (i.e., people and money) within neighborhoods. However, excessive complexity of organizational structures can also make associations rigid and less capable of quickly adapting to contextual changes and responding to pressing issues.

Trends in Participation

It is difficult, if not impossible, to determine the number of active neighborhood associations throughout the world (Lama-Rewal, 2007). In some cities, such as Portland, Oregon (De Morris & Leistner, 2009), Seattle, Washington (Sirianni, 2007) and Birmingham, Alabama (Portney & Berry, 1997), in the US, Calgary, Alberta, and Vancouver, British Columbia (Moore & McGregor, 2021), in Canada, Delhi and Mumbai in India, and in cities across Japan (Pekkanen, 2003), neighborhood associations are supported by local governments, often making it possible to determine the number of active associations. In Japan, where neighborhood associations play important roles in civil society, it has been estimated that there are nearly 300,000 active neighborhood associations across the county (Pekkanen & Tsujinaka, 2008). In many other cities around the world, however, less formal networks of neighborhood associations exist, making it difficult to gauge their prevalence.

The same can be said about participation within individual neighborhood associations. Due to the voluntary and loosely structured nature of these organizations, it is hard to capture membership sizes and participation rates. Studies conducted on neighborhood association membership in the US in the late 1980s and 1990s by Oropesa (1989, 1995) found that neighborhood associations typically had around thirty-four active members with about 6 percent of all adults within the neighborhood boundaries identifying as members of the association. Additionally, among those who identified as members, only 26 percent were actively participating. More recently, Ruef and Kwon (2016) found that about a quarter of respondents in a US national sample identified as being a member of a neighborhood association. This is much lower than in Japan, where it is anticipated that nearly all individuals or households are members of a neighborhood association (Pekkanen, 2003). Across all contexts, however, membership does not equate to participation.

The likelihood that an individual or household is a member of a neighborhood association is related to a range of factors, such as home ownership (Ruef & Kwon, 2016), neighborhood tenure (Wandersman et al., 1987; Zérah, 2007), marital status, age, retirement status, and having children (Oropesa, 1992; Wandersman et al., 1987), occupying the middle class (Lama-Rewal, 2007; Oropesa, 1992; Zérah, 2007), and feeling positively about the neighborhood (Carr et al., 1976). As a result, neighborhood association membership is typically not representative of neighborhood sociodemographics and interests. Zérah's (2007) work on the role of middle-class neighborhood associations or Advanced Locality Management (ALM) units in politics in Mumbai, India, found that ALM units were primarily composed of new middle-class professionals, or "traditional English educated elite" (p. 63), who had access to political actors and were able to clearly articulate their views. Furthermore, in their study on the representativeness of neighborhood associations in two Canadian cities, Moore and McGregor (2021) found that neighborhood associations were typically composed of members who were older, Whiter, and more educated than the general neighborhood population. As a result, neighborhood organizations with limited representativeness may only be advocating on behalf of a particular subset of residents while ignoring the concerns of other segments of the neighborhood (Lama-Rewal, 2007). This issue of breadth of representation is a crucial determinant of how associations relate to local power structures that shape and affect conditions within the neighborhood.

Case Example: Minneapolis Neighborhood Revitalization Program

The Minneapolis Neighborhood Revitalization Program (NRP; launched in 1990) is a notable long-standing attempt to bolster the role of neighborhood associations in municipal governance. In the 1970s and 1980s, Minneapolis had a rapidly decreasing population (e.g., more than 14 percent decline in population during the 1980s) due in large part to White suburban flight and associated disinvestment in urban neighborhoods.[3] Prior efforts at urban revitalization had been focused primarily on downtown development to the detriment of neighborhoods. In the late 1980s, a new group of neighborhood-oriented Minneapolis leaders devised a plan to allocate $400 million to neighborhood revitalization. The initial funding was drawn from a tax increment financing district in downtown Minneapolis.

The program required each neighborhood association to engage in deliberative processes to determine their own priorities for revitalization in collaboration with local government agencies. The initial plan designated eighty-one distinct neighborhoods. Some neighborhoods, however, chose not to cooperate, resulting in sixty-seven participating neighborhood associations in the city (many of the neighborhoods represented by these associations are pictured in Figure 14.1). Each neighborhood association is required to be formally incorporated as a nonprofit organization that interfaces with the NRP office and other local governmental entities (e.g., city and county governments, local public schools, the parks/recreation board) and bears primary responsibility for convening neighbors, determining priorities, planning projects, allocating funding, and implementing/executing plans. Although the participating neighborhood associations have a high degree of autonomy in how they accomplish these tasks, their processes and plans are reviewed and approved by the NRP office, which also provides technical assistance (e.g., around how to broaden and diversify resident participation or how to seek additional funds). During the program's first decade, neighborhood plans and expenditures focused on (in descending order by amount of expenditures) housing, economic development, parks and recreation, human services, community-building/arts

---

3 Minneapolis' 2020 municipal population stands at 429,954 residents, an increase from 368,383 residents in 1990 (Minneapolis anchors the larger metropolitan area often referred to as the Twin Cities, with a 2020 population of nearly 3.7 million residents, up from about 2.6 million residents in 1990; US Census Bureau, 2020).

Figure 14.1 *Minneapolis neighborhood markers.*
Source: *Image created by MinnesotanUser, licensed under CC BY-SA 4.0.*

and culture, crime and security, schools and libraries, transportation, and environmental projects (Martin & Pentel, 2002).

The NRP has received scholarly attention not only from the disciplines typically interested in neighborhood associations (i.e., urban planning, urban affairs, and community development; e.g., Fainstein et al., 1995; Goetz & Sidney, 1994), but also from political scientists and sociologists as a case study of *empowered participatory governance* and as a model for *democracy from below* (Fagotto & Fung, 2006; Wright & Rogers, 2011). It is credited with stabilizing and reviving many of the neighborhood associations in the city and with the creation of some associations in neighborhoods where none had existed previously. In addition to the physical revitalization of neighborhoods (housing, transportation infrastructure, parks, etc.), the NRP has engaged a greater proportion of Minneapolis residents in local decision-making, leading to gains in their knowledge, skills, and collective capacity. Some believe that this has altered the city's power structure, since elected officials and city agency staff have come to expect that residents will be more informed, engaged, and capable of holding them accountable to the priorities that their neighborhoods have determined.

Many of the complexities and difficulties of neighborhood association functioning described elsewhere in this chapter, however, are evident in these studies of the NRP. Some of these challenges may have been exacerbated by the amplification of the role that neighborhood associations play in municipal governance through the NRP. For instance, Fagotto and Fung (2006) list a set of critiques and caveats that were described by local actors in Minneapolis:

(1) That the NRP – by dispersing decision-making processes to the neighborhood level – can lead to parochial decision-making without the benefits of aggregate or centralized planning.
(2) That low levels of participation in many neighborhood associations mean that they overrepresent some interests (e.g., homeowners and/or businesses) over others (e.g., renters or residents with lower incomes).
(3) Some perceived that neighborhood associations had been given too much authority and therefore had unrealistic expectations of what they could accomplish.
(4) Some perceived that local politicians now found it difficult to get "credit" for making projects happen due to the increased involvement of residents.
(5) That funding had been reduced over time, and that some projects, particularly in wealthy neighborhoods, had been perceived as wasteful.
(6) That there was a lack of parallel transformation in many local government agencies, which at least in some cases had little or no obligation or accountability to adapt their practices to the expanded role of the neighborhood associations.

Among these critiques, the concerns over low levels of participation and over/underrepresentation of different groups of residents have received the most scrutiny. Early in the project's history, fewer than 2 percent of Minneapolis residents attended neighborhood association meetings on average (Fainstein et al., 1995). Thanks in part to greater emphasis and technical assistance focused on resident engagement by the NRP office, however, participation expanded over time (Fagotto & Fung, 2006). Of greater concern than the overall levels of participation, though, has been the tendency for meetings and association leadership roles to be dominated by homeowners to the exclusion of renters (who are disproportionately non-White and have lower average incomes than homeowners).

This overrepresentation of homeowners is due in part to their greater availability of time to engage in (often time-intensive) voluntary roles within the neighborhood associations. Other social and structural dynamics, however, play roles too. For instance, neighborhood associations are required to report on their financial activities in detail to the NRP office, creating a particular need for association members with financial expertise. "Neighborhood meetings all too often are dominated by those who have a mastery of organizational finances, regardless of their vision (or lack thereof) for the neighborhood. In board meetings, for example, those who have financial expertise dominate the conversation while those with little or no knowledge of the process are ignored" (Filner, 2006, p. 72).

Homeowners may also be incentivized to participate in funding allocation because they are more likely to financially benefit by the process of making neighborhood improvements. Some homeowners, moreover, feel entitled to a greater say in the neighborhood than renters thanks to their greater "investment" in it. In describing this class-biased ideology of homeownership, Goetz and Sidney (1994) provide this quote from a homeowner active in a Minneapolis neighborhood association: "Renters in the inner-city generally regard their living as a temporary situation ... it is that attitude that, 'this is only temporary, I'm going to leave.' That means you don't get a person who's committed to doing something to improve the quality of life in that neighborhood" (p. 325).

In some cases, the overrepresentation of homeowners has resulted in neighborhood associations that were unsupportive of plans that would increase residential density or subsidized rental housing in the neighborhood. In some Minneapolis neighborhood associations with more active renters, differences in the preferences of homeowners and renters resulted in conflicts, in some cases even leading to power struggles that restructured or replaced the neighborhood associations themselves. For example, in the Whittier neighborhood – a racially/ethnically diverse neighborhood two miles south of downtown Minneapolis – a long-standing neighborhood association endured intense conflicts early in the NRP's implementation as groups of homeowners and landlords sought to capture board seats so that they could exercise greater control and tilt the plan away from subsidized housing and social services and toward increasing homeownership (Goetz & Sidney, 1994).

When neighborhood associations submit their reports and plans, they are required to describe their outreach and engagement efforts, but these vary considerably, based in part on how the associations have chosen to structure themselves. For instance, some use NRP resources to pay for staff who focus specifically on neighbor engagement. Others choose not to allocate resources to staff time in order to save resources for allocation to other priorities. There is therefore wide variation in the extent to which the neighborhood associations are inclusive of the diversity in race/ethnicity, class/income, and opinion that their neighborhoods contain in terms of who participates and who holds influence. Nevertheless, despite the inconsistencies in inclusiveness and the disproportionate levels of homeowner involvement in some neighborhood associations, the allocation of NRP funding has not tended to disproportionately benefit homeowners (Fagotto & Fung, 2006). This is at least in part due to the progressive allocation of funds across neighborhood associations – with more disadvantaged neighborhoods receiving more funding per resident than more advantaged neighborhoods.

The NRP in Minneapolis has been influential, with some other cities (e.g., Milwaukee, Wisconsin) designing similar initiatives (Ghose, 2005). Most evaluators, scholars, and observers of the Minneapolis NRP, however, have not come away with exclusively or overwhelmingly positive or negative depictions of the project. Instead, they have wrestled with its complexities and trade-offs. For instance, Elwood (2002) examined the NRP as an instance of neoliberalization of city government – pushing what had been city agencies' responsibilities onto numerous neighborhood-level nonprofit organizations that are beholden to the city for their funding and therefore disincentivized to challenge government-defined priorities. Although Elwood identified plenty of such features of neoliberal governance at the program level, she also observed that the neighborhood associations frequently devised and pursued alternative goals and strategies and sometimes exerted pressure for city and state policy changes. Likewise, although the NRP can be credited with building organizational infrastructure for engaging a greater number of people in local decision-making by pushing political debates to the most local level, it has also contributed to fragmentation and neighborhood-based parochialism that have been barriers to consensus on larger-scale projects such as mass transit (Steel et al., 2014).

Power and Empowerment Processes in Neighborhood Associations

Community Power

Neighborhood associations seek to play active roles in local decision-making processes and often must contend with other powerful actors and institutions.

Their ability to build and exercise power depends on their ability to organize and mobilize residents. Variance in associations' capacities to build power depends both on features of the associations themselves and on contextual factors in their cities and metropolitan areas. Scholars have developed frameworks for community power to guide inquiry into collective actions to address power imbalances and community issues. Drawing on Lukes (1974) and Alford and Friedland (1985), Christens (2019) describes three dimensions of community power: situational, institutional, and systemic. Situational power – the most easily observed dimension – refers to public contestations and their outcomes. Institutional power is the ability to control the public agenda by determining what is and what is not brought to public debate/contestation. And systemic power – the least easily observed dimension – is the ability to shape public perception and ideology. All three dimensions of power are interrelated, but examining them in parallel can yield valuable insights into power dynamics (e.g., Gaventa, 1980). How do neighborhood associations tend to operate in each of these three dimensions of power?

Situational

Situational power refers to associations' ability to win public contestations. Much of the literature on this topic ties the success of neighborhood associations to broad participation and their ability to leverage resources (Koschmann & Laster, 2011; Mesch & Schwirian, 1996). Some research has investigated why people become involved and stay involved in neighborhood associations. Neighbors' initial involvement has been attributed to personal interactions and invitations from current members, suggesting that neighborhoods with stronger social ties will have greater levels of involvement (Hays, 2007). In a study conducted on six neighborhoods in the Netherlands, for instance, Lelieveldt (2004) found that "social capital is an important stimulant of neighborhood-oriented forms of participation that include the prevention and tackling of problems by citizens themselves" (p. 547). Others have found that a sense of duty or a desire to be neighborly leads to participation (Hays, 2007). Initial participation is important for building an active neighborhood association that is capable of exercising community power. However, if neighborhood associations aim to prompt longer-term changes, participation must remain high over a sustained period of time (Koschmann & Laster, 2011). In a study on the perceived effectiveness of neighborhood and community organizations in Seattle, Washington, Coats (2019) found that neighborhood associations that were able to develop greater levels of trust and collective efficacy among residents were seen as more effective.

The relationships between neighborhood association participation and local community power structures are complex. In a study on the effectiveness of neighborhood associations in Columbus, Ohio, Mesch and Schwirian (1996) found that increases in neighborhood association participation led to greater awareness of local problems and the ability to effectively organize, thus leading to a greater ability to influence local politics and address social problems. They also found that neighborhood associations located in wealthier neighborhoods were perceived to be more effective than those located in neighborhoods with fewer resources. They interpreted this as a reflection of the fact that city governments favored wealthier neighborhoods (Mesch & Schwirian, 1996). Other factors linked to the perceived effectiveness of neighborhood associations included effective communication strategies (i.e., widely circulated newsletters) and links to other neighborhood-based organizations like businesses and churches, which provided associations with additional resources (i.e., money, people, and material goods) and increased organizations' perceived legitimacy within the community.

Neighborhood associations vary in the extent to which they participate in coalitions, alliances, and other interorganizational networks. The study of Columbus, Ohio, neighborhood associations by Mesch and Schwirian (1996) did not find connections or alliances with other neighborhood associations to be associated with greater perceived association effectiveness, leading to the conclusion that associations that are not a part of a larger system of organizations are no less effective than those that are. Anderson et al. (2018) however, assert that neighborhood association alliances may help increase individual groups' political and social capital, thus potentially expanding the influence of these associations (Lama-Rewal, 2007). King (2004) likewise suggests that participation in neighborhood association coalitions could increase the influence and power of individual neighborhood associations. Zérah (2007) came to similar conclusions in work on neighborhood associations in Mumbai, finding that associations were part of a larger "civic network" that allowed them to have greater access to and prominence in decision-making spaces (p. 63). It is possible that there are some circumstances in which associations may benefit from operating independently and others in which their goals may be better accomplished by working in coalition with other organizations.

In addition to developing relationships with other local nonprofit organizations and neighborhood associations, relationships with local government entities can play an important role in neighborhood associations' ability to accomplish their goals (Lama-Rewal, 2007; Zérah, 2007). Like proponents of the Minneapolis NRP, King (2004) argues that formal partnerships between neighborhood associations and local government can "systematize and institutionalize citizen input" (p. 394) and increase resources received from local government agencies. Likewise, Chaskin and Greenberg (2015) claim that neighborhood associations may be more effective if they have close ties to elected officials. In their study on the allies and opponents of neighborhood associations in the Capital District of New York State, Logan and Rabrenovic (1990) found that neighborhood associations saw local government just as much as an ally as an opponent. The authors state that when addressing issues around quality of life, services, and facilities, neighborhood associations were more likely to work alongside local government; however, when addressing issues concerning development and land use, neighborhood associations were more likely to be at odds with local officials. However, like Mesch and Schwirian (1996), Logan and Rabrenovic (1990) warn that local government entities may be more inclined toward working alongside upper- and middle-class neighborhoods than with lower- and working-class ones, thus limiting the direct influence some associations may have when seeking a collaborative relationship with local governments. Indeed, studies have found that associations in neighborhoods with fewer resources are more likely to engage in direct action and use conflict to bring about change (e.g., Dierwechter & Coffey, 2010).

Institutional

Institutional power is exercised by neighborhood associations when they shape public agendas, elevating issues and concerns of neighborhood residents to public debate in the city. Neighborhood associations are often well positioned to do this because of the intermediary roles they can play between residents and local government entities (Chaskin & Greenberg, 2015). However, the nature of these relationships can influence how associations aim to shape public agendas and their success in doing so. In cases when neighborhood associations are closely tied to government entities, they may be less likely to push agendas that contradict the goals of public officials for fear of jeopardizing the relationships and benefits that accompany them. In these instances neighborhood associations are more likely to uphold the status quo than challenge it. In other cases in which neighborhood associations are more independently constituted, they may conversely be limited in their ability to gain access to spaces where they can shape the public agenda. As a result, many observers suggest that neighborhood associations need to walk a fine line between courting and challenging local government and elected officials in order to take full advantage of their unique position within local governance structures. For example, in their study on relationships between neighborhood associations and local governance, Chaskin and Greenberg (2015) explain that neighborhood associations operate "betwixt and between the state and civil society, in which they have a foot in and a foot out of government, sometimes effectively wielding direct influence on public decision-making and resource allocation and representing the interests of the neighborhood" (p. 257). Balancing their involvement with city government with their independence and grassroots leadership development can thus be crucial to associations' ability to exercise power.

In addition to navigating the priorities of the local government, neighborhood associations must negotiate the sometimes conflicting agendas of their own members. Since neighborhoods are diverse geographic entities, the values, views, motiviations, and priorities of residents also vary, at least on some issues. As a result, neighborhood associations themselves often contain diverging and sometimes conflicting agendas. In a study on the communicative tensions in neighborhood associations in a midsize city in the southwestern US, Koschmann and Laster (2011) found that, due to the complexity and diversity of neighborhood association participants, there were often conflicts in how members framed social issues and consequently varying beliefs on how these issues should be addressed. These researchers concluded that although too much conflict could derail the work of associations and limit their effectiveness, some conflict within associations was often beneficial, leading to more creative solutions.

When it comes to neighborhood associations setting and promoting public agendas, there is also the concern that they may not adequately represent the diversity of the neighborhood and thus not accurately depict the goals of the neighborhood's residents. As previously mentioned, neighborhood association participants tend to be wealthier on average and have more formal education than the general neighborhood population. As a result, neighborhood issues that associations find to be most pressing may not actually be what other residents would identify as top priorities. Of course, some associations do a better job of representing the agendas of their neighborhoods than others. In a study on issue representation in neighborhood associations in Indianapolis, Indiana, Swindell (2000) found that neighborhood associations that represent neighborhoods with larger and more stable populations are able to better represent the concerns of their residents. However, Swindell explains that this could be a result of strong social cohesion among long-term residents in more stable neighborhoods and that neighborhoods representing larger areas may be representing suburban neighborhoods, which tend to have more homogeneous populations and potentially fewer issues to address than urban neighborhoods.

Systemic

Neighborhood associations can be influential in shaping public perceptions and narratives about urban spaces, infrastructure, policies (e.g., zoning), and institutional practices (e.g., police, schools). Their influence on narratives can sometimes alter power relations in the systemic dimension. For instance, associations can shape public perceptions of the desirability of various potential urban futures and shift public narratives regarding who and what different spaces should be for. Neighborhood associations often operate at the interface between private property rights and the public's ability to regulate and restrict what can be done with privately owned land and buildings. The struggles that neighborhood associations undertake and/or mediate therefore influence the broader public's understanding of residents' rights and potential claims regarding how different spaces in cities and regions should be shaped and used.

Some neighborhood groups operate as sites of contestation and resistance to manifestations of inequality. They can amplify the perspectives and claims of poorer, less powerful, and/or marginalized groups. By demanding and broker-ing redistributive policies (e.g., community benefits agreements), for instance, they can shape public perceptions of fairness and what wealthy landowners and developers owe to their neighborhoods and cities (or, often, the cities where they are investing in real estate development). However, even in cases in which they are acting as vehicles for resistance and contestation by poorer residents, associations can adopt arguments that fit neatly within a neoliberal framework and may thereby reinforce elements of this dominant ideology that serve to perpetuate inequality. For example, in a study of two Istanbul neighborhoods' (Başıbüyük and Sulukule) resistance to state-led urban renewal projects and associated threats of displacement, Karaman (2014) noted associations' vacillation between uncompromising opposition and nego-tiating with the state on its terms, implicitly accepting the rationale and inevitability of the urban renewal projects.

In wealthy neighborhoods, on the other hand, some associations take actions that more directly exacerbate urban inequality. Many, for instance, have fought to prevent increases in residential density, the construction of affordable housing, and the provision of social services in or adjacent to their neighborhoods (Scally & Tighe, 2015). These efforts often reinforce narratives that are implicitly racist and/or classist (Nguyen et al., 2013; Tighe, 2012). Neighborhood associations can thus operate across a broad ideological spec-trum, ranging from vigilant maintenance of existing sociospatial inequities to assiduous challenges to imbalances in local power relations. Even neighbor-hood associations representing the interests of wealthier neighborhoods, how-ever, sometimes provide highly visible enactments of collective claims to control over what can be done with private property. In this sense, paradoxic-ally, they may also complicate and counteract purely libertarian notions of the rights of private property owners.

Finally, in cities across many postcolonial contexts, poorer neighborhoods have often taken shape through self-organization processes that have recently been described as *popular urbanization* (Streule et al., 2020) but have more often been described as urban informal settlements. These labels (and others such as "slum" and "blight") can become important dimensions to power struggles involving neighborhoods. In Egypt, for example, the current regime has announced a policy of eliminating informal urban areas, which it represents as threats to the nation. Sharp (2022) traces the political processes through which this label of "informality" has been produced and applied to specific places – often places where residents have taken part in protests against the regime. The definitions of informality and the places to which it is applied are therefore central to the current power struggles between neighborhoods and political and military actors. When neighbor-hood associations engage in efforts to resist, complicate, and supplant nar-ratives and terms such as these, they are exercising power in the systemic dimension.

Psychological Empowerment

Engaging in collective action and exercising community power also involve psychological empowerment among participants in neighborhood associations (Zimmerman & Rappaport, 1988). Drawing from Rappaport (1987), Christens (2019) describes psychological empowerment as "the psychological aspects of processes through which people, organizations, and communities are developing critical awareness of their environments, building social networks and social movements, and gaining greater control over their lives" (p. 63). The process of psychological empowerment can be understood as a set of interrelated affective, behavioral, cognitive, and relational processes. Next, we will examine how each of these components of psychological empowerment can occur within neighborhood associations.

Affective and Behavioral

The affective component of psychological empowerment refers to the feelings and belief that one is capable, through collective action, of influencing decision-making processes and working with others to effect social and political change. The behavioral component refers to the associated actions of participation and engagement. Participation and perceived sociopolitical control are closely related, and both are crucial elements of neighborhood associations' capacity (Chong et al., 2013; Foster-Fishman et al., 2007, 2013).

Some research has found that perceptions of sociopolitical control and self-efficacy/community efficacy can lead people to participate in neighborhood organizations (Checkoway & Zimmerman, 1993). When studying the impacts of a community-building initiative in Battle Creek, Michigan, for instance, Foster-Fishman and colleagues found that increases in collective efficacy led to greater participation in neighborhood and community efforts (Foster-Fishman et al., 2013) and was predictive of citizen participation (Foster-Fishman et al., 2007). The authors explain that participation in neighborhood activities led to a greater sense of control and helped individuals to develop skills, build knowledge, and strengthen connections to their community. Likewise, Chong et al.'s (2013) work in the Klang Valley of Malaysia reports that increases in sociopolitical control led to greater participation in community activities.

Reciprocally, others have found that increased participation in neighborhood organizations can lead to a greater sense of sociopolitical control and self-efficacy (Zimmerman & Rappaport, 1988). In research on neighborhood associations in Pittsburgh, Pennsylvania, for instance, Ohmer found that increased participation in decision-making processes and everyday activities led to a greater sense of sociopolitical control (Ohmer, 2007) and self-efficacy (Ohmer, 2008). Likewise, in a study in Tel Aviv, Israel, Itzhaky and York (2000) found that participation – specifically participation in decision-making processes – was associated with the development of sociopolitical control.

Participation in neighborhood associations can take many different forms, and engagement in types of processes (and/or playing different roles in those processes) likely contributes differentially to psychological empowerment. For instance, Checkoway and Zimmerman (1993), in their study of neighborhood organizations in Detroit, Michigan, found that neighborhood associations frequently engaged in some activities (education on neighborhood issues, planning a neighborhood program, contacting public officials about needs, organizing groups for social action, and developing coalitions with other groups) while engaging less frequently in other activities (advocating with business or government entities, testifying at a public hearing, developing social service organizations, encouraging voter turnout, and mobilizing for a protest demonstration). They explored which of these activities were most often used by groups reporting higher-quality participation versus groups reporting lower-quality participation. Associations reporting higher-quality participation were more likely to be engaged in both external (i.e., testifying at hearings) and internal (i.e., developing service organizations) activities, whereas groups reporting lower-quality participation were more likely to engage mainly in internal activities. A mix of internally and externally focused activities may provide participants with space to grow their leadership capabilities and confidence that can then be utilized in outward-facing activities (Foster-Fishman et al., 2009).

Relational

The relational component of psychological empowerment refers to collaborative competencies that enable people to come together and effectively work toward achieving common goals. Stronger relationships with neighbors can help facilitate neighborhood collective efficacy and have been found to be associated with greater levels of sociopolitical control (Chavis & Wandersman, 1990; Ohmer, 2007). Additionally, neighborhood relationships can contribute to increased participation in neighborhood associations and activities, as these relationships serve as informal mechanisms for communicating about events and providing information about outside resources (Chavis & Wandersman, 1990).

Although little research has directly examined relational empowerment processes in neighborhood associations, many have explored the role that the psychological sense of community has played in facilitating engagement between neighborhood associations and residents (Perkins & Long, 2002; Perkins et al., 1990). Chavis and Wandersman (1990), for example, studied the sense of community among neighborhood association participants in Nashville, Tennessee, finding that a stronger sense of community can increase participation in neighborhood associations, encourage neighboring relationships, and increase one's sociopolitical control. They explain that "in the neighborhood environment a sense of community can be both a cause and effect of local action" (Chavis & Wandersman, 1990, p. 73). Similarly, Foster-Fishman and colleagues (2007, 2009, 2013) studied the role of a sense of community in facilitating participation and developing empowerment among residents in neighborhoods in Battle Creek, Michigan, finding that a sense of community increased the involvement of residents and that residents were more likely to engage in community efforts when there was a stronger sense of belonging and interdependence with their neighbors. They explain that residents who felt more connected to their community were more likely to believe change was possible (affective) and to engage in neighborhood associations (behavioral). They conclude that "interventions aimed at building strong connections between neighbors may be more important for fostering norms for activism" (Foster-Fishman et al., 2009, p. 566) than, for instance, those focused on developing collective efficacy.

Cognitive

The cognitive component of psychological empowerment involves a critical understanding of social problems and the role of power in change processes. Cognitive aspects have been less studied in neighborhood associations than other aspects of psychological empowerment processes. Some studies, however, showcase some of the possibilities for participants in neighborhood associations to learn about the complexities of the structures that affect their lives and to gain understanding of how power can be used to both defend and challenge the status quo.

Within the limited literature related to the cognitive component of psychological empowerment, much of it concerns the development of social norms that promote citizen engagement and the understanding that change requires collective (rather than individual) actions. Chong et al. (2013) suggests that neighborhood organizations can serve as a source of education and socialization; they can cultivate norms that prompt individuals to engage in civic life. Foster-Fishman et al. (2013) argue that the development of neighborhood norms for activism can lead to increased participation by previously uninvolved residents as it sets an expectation for collective engagement.

Neighborhood associations that engage in community organizing and participatory decision-making in advocacy efforts are often especially capable of fostering this kind of learning. Neighbors who participate in these activities learn about policies and other decision-making processes that affect neighborhood quality of life (e.g., transportation, housing, education, policing, parks, and other infrastructure). Disagreements within the neighborhood can promote learning (Koschmann & Laster, 2011), as can power struggles with other organizations and actors in city politics (Fagotto & Fung, 2006). Some associations partner with universities to study these issues and advance shared goals around, for example, sustainability (Hidayat & Stoecker, 2021). Associations can also join with other institutions in their cities to take part in larger citywide organizing initiatives (e.g., Warren, 2013) and can function as anchor institutions for smaller-scale organizing and participatory action research efforts (Tang Yan et al., 2019).

Features That Facilitate Empowerment Processes

Taking a broad view of research on neighborhood associations, some key features are apparent that affect their capacity to facilitate empowerment processes. High-quality, broad participation as well internal and external relationship-building are key programmatic features that can lead to the development of psychological empowerment and community power among neighborhood associations and their members. Additionally, the research on neighborhood associations consistently reports that strong leadership and clear organizational structures are important for facilitating these processes.

High-Quality, Broad Participation

High participation levels in neighborhood associations are crucial for establishing the broad-scale support needed to exercise situational power through collective actions (Koschmann & Laster, 2011; Wandersman & Florin, 2000). Ohmer (2007) asserts that neighborhood associations can encourage diverse and committed participation by engaging residents in "small-scale projects" that achieve "small successes" (p. 118). These small wins can unite residents and facilitate the development of self- and collective efficacy, helping neighborhood groups to feel equipped to address more challenging problems in the future. By tackling smaller-scale projects, neighborhood associations can increase their perceived legitimacy by proving their effectiveness. Consequently, a neighborhood association's perceived effectiveness has been shown to increase meaningful participation, contribute to increased knowledge and skills, and develop a stronger sense of collective efficacy and sense of community (Ohmer, 2008). As discussed earlier, however, associations are often not representative of their neighborhoods (with homeowners, for example, being overrepresented among active members when compared to renters). Associations that are composed disproportionately of more advantaged neighbors may be more likely to exacerbate power imbalances rather than work to counter them (by, for instance, opposing the construction of subsidized/affordable housing within the neighborhood).

Strong Internal and External Relationships

Much depends on the strength of relationships within neighborhoods and organizations. Relationships within neighborhoods play a fundamental role in the recruitment of members to neighborhood associations (Hays, 2007).

Likewise, a strong sense of community within neighborhoods and neighborhood associations has been found to increase meaningful participation in the neighborhood associations and aid in the development of sociopolitical control and self-efficacy (Chavis & Wandersman, 1990; Foster-Fishman et al., 2009). A strong sense of community within neighborhood associations and the neighborhoods in which they reside has been linked to increases in neighborly relationships and the sharing of information about neighborhood activities (Chavis & Wandersman, 1990). It can also lead to a stronger sense of belonging and interdependence among residents, which in turn can develop a shared understanding about neighborhood concerns (Foster-Fishman et al., 2013). It is through these relationships that participants may develop a more critical understanding of the social problems their neighborhoods face and the role collective action can play in addressing them, thus facilitating cognitive aspects of psychological empowerment.

Relationships outside the neighborhood may be equally important. Research has shown that balanced relationships with external actors such as government entities and policymakers are critical for the success of neighborhood associations and can allow participants to engage in activities that promote psychological empowerment (Logan & Rabrenovic, 1990). Forming relationships with policymakers and local government actors can help increase the legitimacy of neighborhood associations within the public arena as well as increase their level of access to decision-making spaces (King, 2004). By having access to these spaces, neighborhood groups may have more opportunity to influence and shape the public agenda, thus exercising institutional power (Chaskin & Greenberg, 2015). In turn, the development of relationships with government entities may serve as an empowering process for neighborhood association participants; by engaging with policymakers in decision-making spaces participants may experience an increased perception of sociopolitical control, self-efficacy, and collective efficacy. However, as described earlier in this chapter, neighborhood associations must be cautious when engaging with local officials, understanding that access to direct influence may at the same time limit their flexibility and ability to engage in contentions challenges to elite interests.

Clear and Robust Organizational Structures

Neighborhood associations with clear organizational structures and concrete opportunities for involvement have been found to have greater organizational capacity and the ability to maximize the benefits of participation for members (Ohmer, 2008; Wandersman & Florin, 2000). Organizational climate (including diverse opportunities for involvement), organizational order and efficiency, and diversity in roles have all been linked to increased success in influencing policy (McMillan et al., 1995) and greater political efficacy (Dougherty, 1988). Researchers have also found that these same organizational features – sometimes collectively referred to as "opportunity role structure" – can increase participant satisfaction and enjoyment (Florin & Wandersman, 1990; Giamartino & Wandersman, 1983), thus prolonging engagement with associations.

Neighborhoods are often conglomerates of a wide range of individuals and families who may possess unique skills and experience and have varying amounts of time to commit to neighborhood-based activities, providing neighborhood associations with a diverse pool of potential participants to draw from. Recognizing and leveraging the various assets that residents can contribute to the association can further develop the capacity of the organization and lead to wider neighborhood change (Chaskin et al., 2001). To do this, neighborhood associations must provide diverse and concrete opportunities for meaningful participation (Florin et al., 1992, as cited in Wandersman & Florin, 2000). These opportunities can take the form of outward-facing neighborhood activities such as leading educational seminars on community problems or speaking at city council meetings, or they can involve inward-facing activities such as trainings on community organizing or leadership development (Ohmer, 2008). Research has shown that participation in these various types of activities can lead to increased sociopolitical control, self-efficacy, and collective efficacy and to the development of a stronger sense of community among neighborhood residents.

Strategies for Leadership Development

Because neighborhood associations are typically volunteer-run, effective voluntary leadership is important for the success of the association (Chaskin, 2001; Ohmer, 2008). Rich (1980) asserts that having strong leadership enables neighborhood organizations to mobilize resources and engage in collective action. Ohmer (2008) echoes Rich's claim, stating that building leadership among residents is needed for neighborhood associations to make tangible neighborhood improvements. However, despite general recognition of the need for strong leadership within neighborhood associations, there is little research that indicates the best ways to engage in these processes. Ohmer (2007, 2008) asserts that increased participation in the daily activities and decision-making processes of neighborhood associations can help facilitate leadership competency, which in turn increases self-efficacy and sociopolitical control. Foster-Fishman et al. (2009) suggest that neighborhood organizations need to provide structured opportunities for individuals to develop leadership skills and that, through engaging in these activities, participants will develop self-efficacy and be more likely to take on leadership roles.

Application

There are numerous factors that neighborhood associations must consider to play an effective role in promoting neighborhood quality of life and representation of neighborhood interests in local decision-making processes. First, neighborhood associations need to include a diverse array of residents who represent different backgrounds and experiences within the neighborhood. Research has found that neighborhood association membership in the US and Canada tends to be Whiter, older, and wealthier than the general population of the neighborhood (Moore & McGregor, 2021). Associations also tend to be composed primarily of homeowners, with very little participation from renters. However, if neighborhood associations are to build strong organizations that accurately represent the values and needs of their neighborhoods, they must find ways to expand their reach to all residents. To do this, many neighborhood associations may need to rethink strategies for recruitment and involvement and develop opportunities for involvement that accommodate the schedules of those who do not work a nine-to-five job.

Second, to develop and wield community power, neighborhood associations should consider building and taking part in coalitions with other neighborhood associations. Anderson et al. (2018) and Zérah (2007) have found that the development of neighborhood coalitions can serve as a tool for increasing social and political capital as well as community power. Additionally, by navigating these complex relationships, participants can develop collaborative competencies that equip them to work more effectively with others to achieve collective goals. At the same time neighborhood associations should seek to build relationships with government entities and elected officials; however, they must do so with caution to avoid being coopted by more powerful actors (Chaskin & Greenberg, 2015). Developing balanced relationships with people in positions of power can help neighborhood associations access institutional and situational power as well as provide avenues for participants to develop psychological empowerment. However, neighborhood associations must be aware that by focusing attention on developing external relationships with either other neighborhood associations or government entities they may be taking time and attention away from local neighborhood activities (King, 2004).

Third, as neighborhood associations seek to develop community power, the focus of neighborhood association actions should vary between internal and external activities (Checkoway & Zimmerman, 1993). Neighborhood associations that focus exclusively on inward-facing activities such as neighborhood watches or block parties silo themselves from engaging in the larger political landscape, preventing them from developing and wielding the community power needed to address larger systemic social issues. However, when neighborhood associations focus too much attention on addressing larger social issues like advocating for citywide policy change they can lose focus on neighborhood-specific issues like development and land use and can fail to provide vital leadership development and community-building activities that can help increase participation and long-term commitment (Foster-Fishman et al., 2009). As a result, neighborhood associations need to be intentional about deeply engaging residents in neighborhood-specific activities while also seeking to influence the larger political arena.

Finally, in addition to balancing these internal and external actions, it is also crucial for neighborhood associations to provide spaces for participants to reflect on their involvement in these activities. By incorporating a model of praxis, or a continuous cycle of action and reflection (Kieffer, 1984), neighborhood associations can help participants translate their actions into a more critical understanding of systems and environments, further developing systemic power and enhancing the cognitive component of psychological empowerment.

Future Research

As studies described throughout this chapter have shown, the breadth and quality of participation drastically impact the effectiveness of neighborhood associations in exercising community power. As a result, research on participation trends as well as forms of participation is foundational for understanding the potential of neighborhood associations. The landscape and residential makeup of urban spaces are perpetually being altered (e.g., through gentrification, rising housing costs, and consequent displacement within many urban neighborhoods). This likely means that participation patterns within many neighborhood associations are also changing. Additionally, widespread use of neighborhood-focused social media platforms (e.g., neighborhood Facebook groups or Nextdoor) have potentially changed what participation can and does look like. To build better understanding of the roles neighborhood associations play in exercising community power and engaging in local democratic processes, research designed to yield insights into broad participation patterns and changes in the nature of participation in these groups is needed.

Our synthesis of the research on power and empowerment processes in neighborhood associations identified some substantial gaps. For instance, few have examined the ways in which neighborhood associations exercise power in the systemic dimension. This gap in the literature prevents the development of a deeper understanding of how neighborhood associations critically examine social problems and shape public perceptions and ideology. These aspects of empowerment processes are fundamental for identifying root causes of social problems and imagining alternative realities that can fuel collective action. By understanding how neighborhood associations develop and deploy systemic power, a richer understanding of the roles neighborhood associations play in democratic processes can be developed.

Similarly, there is scant extant research exploring how neighborhood associations facilitate civic learning and critical reflection (cognitive aspects of psychological empowerment processes). This could be a result of limited capacity within neighborhood associations for providing spaces for reflection that allow for more complex understandings of social issues to develop. Alternatively, it could also reflect a gap within the neighborhood association research literature. Regardless, considering how pervasive neighborhood associations are within urban areas around the world, it is important to understand when and how involvement in neighborhood associations leads to deeper understanding of social problems and social change strategies.

References

Alford, R., & Friedland, R. (1985). *The powers of theory: Capitalism, the state, and democracy*. Cambridge University Press.

Anderson, G., Blair, R., & Shirk, J. (2018). Neighborhood associations and community development: Differences in needs and strategies. *Community Development, 49*(5), 504–521.

Austin, D. M. (1991). Community context and complexity of organizational structure in neighborhood associations. *Administration & Society, 22*(4), 516–531.

Avritzer, L. (2009a). Participatory publics in Brazil and Mexico: The compatibility of public deliberation and complex administration. In L. Avritzer (Ed.), *Democracy and the public space in Latin America* (pp. 135–164). Princeton University Press.

Avritzer, L. (2009b). The transformation of the Latin American pubic space. In L. Avritzer (Ed.), *Democracy and the public space in Latin America* (pp. 77–102). Princeton University Press.

Ay, D. (2019). Diverging community responses to state-led urban renewal in the context of recentralization of planning authority: An analysis of three urban renewal projects in Turkey. *Habitat International, 91*, 102028.

Carr, T. H., Dixon, M. C., & Ogles, R. M. (1976). Perceptions of community life which distinguish between participants and nonparticipants in neighborhood self-help organization. *American Journal of Community Psychology, 4*(4), 357–366.

Chaskin, R. J. (1997). Perspectives on neighborhood and community: A review of the literature. *Social Service Review, 71*(4), 521–547.

Chaskin, R. J. (2001). Building community capacity: A definitional framework and case studies from a comprehensive community initiative. *Urban Affairs Review, 36*(3), 291–323.

Chaskin, R. J., & Greenberg, D. M. (2015). Between public and private action: Neighborhood organizations and local governance. *Nonprofit and Voluntary Sector Quarterly, 44*(2), 248–267.

Chavis, D. M., & Wandersman, A. (1990). Sense of community in the urban environment: A catalyst for participation and community development. *American Journal of Community Psychology, 18*(1), 55–81.

Checkoway, B., & Zimmerman, M. A. (1993). Correlates of participation in neighborhood organizations. *Administration in Social Work, 16*(3–4), 45–64.

Chong, S. T., Ten, W. K., Er, A. C., & Koh, D. (2013). Neighbourhood participation as a proxy to civic engagement. *Pertanika Journal of Social Science and Humanities, 21*, 143–154.

Christens, B. D. (2019). *Community power and empowerment*. Oxford University Press.

City of Minneapolis. (n.d.). *Neighborhood Revitalization Program*. City of Minneapolis. www2.minneapolismn.gov/government/departments/ncr/neighborhood-programs/neighborhood-revitalization-program/

Coats, J. (2019). Assessing perceptions of effectiveness for a third sector: A study of organized neighborhood associations and community clubs and the people they serve. *International Social Science Review, 95*(2), 1–22.

De Morris, A. A., & Leistner, P. (2009). From neighborhood association system to participatory democracy: Broadening and deepening public involvement in Portland, Oregon. *National Civic Review, 98*(2), 47–55.

Dierwechter, Y., & Coffey, B. (2010). Assessing the effects of neighborhood councils on urban policy and development: The example of Tacoma, Washington. *The Social Science Journal, 47*(3), 471–491.

Dougherty, D. (1988). *Participation in community organizations: Effects on political efficacy, personal efficacy, and self-esteem* [Doctoral dissertation]. Boston University.

Elwood, S. (2002). Neighborhood revitalization through "collaboration": Assessing the implications of neoliberal urban policy at the grassroots. *GeoJournal, 58* (2/3), 121–130.

Fagotto, E., & Fung, A. (2006). Empowered participation in urban governance: The Minneapolis Neighborhood Revitalization Program. *International Journal of Urban and Regional Research, 30*(3), 638–655.

Fainstein, S., Hirst, C., & Tennebaum, J. (1995). *An evaluation of the Minneapolis Neighborhood Revitalization Program*. Center for Urban Policy Research Policy Report No. 12. Rutgers, The State University of New Jersey.

Filner, M. F. (2006). The limits of participatory empowerment: Assessing the Minneapolis Neighborhood Revitalization Program. *State and Local Government Review, 38*(2), 67–77.

Florin, P., & Wandersman, A. (1990). An introduction to citizen participation, voluntary organizations, and community development: Insights for empowerment through research. *American Journal of Community Psychology, 18*(1), 41–54.

Foell, A., & Foster, K. A. (2022). "We roll our sleeves up and get to work!": Portraits of collective action and neighborhood change in Atlanta's West End. *Urban Affairs Review, 58*(6), 1652–1688.

Foster-Fishman, P. G., Cantillon, D., Pierce, S. J., & Van Egeren, L. A. (2007). Building an active citizenry: The role of neighborhood problems, readiness, and capacity for change. *American Journal of Community Psychology, 39*(1–2), 91–106.

Foster-Fishman, P. G., Collins, C., & Pierce, S. J. (2013). An investigation of the dynamic processes promoting citizen participation. *American Journal of Community Psychology, 51*(3–4), 492–509.

Foster-Fishman, P. G., Pierce, S. J., & Van Egeren, L. A. (2009). Who participates and why: Building a process model of citizen participation. *Health Education & Behavior, 36*(3), 550–569.

Gaventa, J. (1980). *Power and powerlessness: Quiescence and rebellion in an Appalachian Valley*. University of Illinois Press.

Ghose, R. (2005). The complexities of citizen participation through collaborative governance. *Space and Polity, 9*(1), 61–75.

Giamartino, G. A., & Wandersman, A. (1983). Organizational climate correlates of viable urban block organizations. *American Journal of Community Psychology, 11*(5), 529–541.

Goetz, E. G., & Sidney, M. (1994). Revenge of the property owners: Community development and the politics of property. *Journal of Urban Affairs, 16*(4), 319–334.

Hays, R. A. (2007). Community activists' perceptions of citizenship roles in an urban community: A case study of attitudes that affect community engagement. *Journal of Urban Affairs, 29*(4), 401–424.

Hidayat, D., & Stoecker, R. (2021). Collective knowledge mobilization through a community–university partnership. *Journal of Higher Education Outreach and Engagement, 25*(2), 95–110.

Itzhaky, H., & York, A. S. (2000). Sociopolitical control and empowerment: An extended replication. *Journal of Community Psychology, 28*(4), 407–415.

Karaman, O. (2014). Resisting urban renewal in Istanbul. *Urban Geography, 35*(2), 290–310.

Kieffer, C. H. (1984). Citizen empowerment: A developmental perspective. In J. Rappaport & R. Hess (Eds.), *Studies in empowerment: Steps toward understanding and action* (pp. 9–36). Haworth Press.

King, K. N. (2004). Neighborhood associations and urban decision making in Albuquerque. *Nonprofit Management and Leadership, 14*(4), 391–409.

Koerin, B. (2003). The settlement house tradition: Current trends and future concerns. *Journal of Sociology and Social Welfare, 30*(2), 53–68.

Kohl, B., & Farthing, L. (2008). New spaces, new contests: Appropriating decentralization for political change in Bolivia. In V. A. Beard, F. Miraftab, & C. Silver (Eds.), *Planning and decentralization: Contested spaces for public action in the Global South* (pp. 69–85). Routledge.

Köngeter, S. (2021). A brief transnational history of the settlement house movement. In J. Gal, S. Köngeter, & S. Vicary (Eds.), *The settlement house movement revisited: A transnational history* (pp. 15–33). Bristol University Press, Policy Press.

Koschmann, M., & Laster, N. M. (2011). Communicative tensions of community organizing: The case of a local neighborhood association. *Western Journal of Communication, 75*(1), 28–51.

Lama-Rewal, S. T. (2007). Neighbourhood associations and local democracy: Delhi municipal elections 2007. *Economic and Political Weekly, 42*(47), 51–60.

Lama-Rewal, S. T., & Zérah, M.-H. (2011). Introduction. Urban democracy: A South Asian perspective. *South Asia Multidisciplinary Academic Journal, 5*, 5.

Lelieveldt, H. (2004). Helping citizens help themselves: Neighborhood improvement programs and the impact of social networks, trust, and norms on neighborhood-oriented forms of participation. *Urban Affairs Review, 39*(5), 531–551.

Logan, J. R., & Rabrenovic, G. (1990). Neighborhood associations: Their issues, their allies, and their opponents. *Urban Affairs Quarterly, 26*(1), 68–94.

Lohmann, R. A. (2002). *Neighborhood associations: The foundation of community development.* West Virginia University Faculty & Staff Scholarship. https://researchrepository.wvu.edu/faculty_publications/2579/

Lukes, S. (1974). *Power: A radical view* (2nd ed.). Macmillan.

Martin, J. A., & Pentel, P. R. (2002). What the neighbors want: The Neighborhood Revitalization Program's first decade. *Journal of the American Planning Association, 68*(4), 435–449.

Mathews, M. A. (2021). Understanding the roles and contributions of neighborhood organizations in civic governance. *VOLUNTAS: International Journal of Voluntary and Nonprofit Organizations, 32*(4), 821–829.

McMillan, B., Florin, P., Stevenson, J., Rerman, B., & Mitchell, R. E. (1995). Empowerment praxis in community coalitions. *American Journal of Community Psychology, 23*, 699–727.

Mesch, G. S., & Schwirian, K. P. (1996). The effectiveness of neighborhood collective action. *Social Problems, 43*(4), 467–483.

Moore, A. A., & McGregor, R. M. (2021). The representativeness of neighbourhood associations in Toronto and Vancouver. *Urban Studies, 58*(13), 2782–2797.

Nguyen, M., Basolo, V., & Tiwari, A. (2013). Opposition to affordable housing in the USA: Debate framing and the responses of local actors. *Housing, Theory & Society, 30*(2), 107–130.

Ohmer, M. L. (2007). Citizen participation in neighborhood organizations and its relationship to volunteers' self- and collective efficacy and sense of community. *Social Work Research, 31*(2), 109–120.

Ohmer, M. L. (2008). The relationship between citizen participation and organizational processes and outcomes and the benefits of citizen participation in neighborhood organizations. *Journal of Social Service Research, 34*(4), 41–60.

Oropesa, R. S. (1989). The social and political foundations of effective neighborhood improvement associations. *Social Science Quarterly, 70*(3), 723–743.

Oropesa, R. S. (1992). Social structure, social solidarity and involvement in neighborhood improvement associations. *Sociological Inquiry, 62*(1), 107–118.

Oropesa, S. R. (1995). The ironies of human resource mobilization by neighborhood associations. *Nonprofit and Voluntary Sector Quarterly, 24*(3), 235–252.

Pekkanen, R. (2003). Molding Japanese civil society: State-structured incentives and the patterning of civil society. In F. J. Schwartz & S. J. Pharr (Eds.), *The state of civil society in Japan* (1st ed., pp. 116–134). Cambridge University Press.

Pekkanen, R., & Tsujinaka, Y. (2008). Neighbourhood associations and the demographic challenge. In F. Coulmas, H. Conrad, A. Schad-Seifert, & G. Vogt (Eds.), *The demographic challenge: A handbook about Japan* (pp. 707–720). Brill.

Perkins, D. D., & Long, D. A. (2002). Neighborhood sense of community and social capital. In A. T. Fisher, C. C. Sonn, & B. J. Bishop (Eds.), *Psychological sense of community* (pp. 291–318). Springer.

Perkins, D. D., Florin, P., Rich, R. C., Wandersman, A., & Chavis, D. M. (1990). Participation and the social and physical environment of residential blocks: Crime and community context. *American Journal of Community Psychology, 18*(1), 83–115.

Portney, K. E., & Berry, J. M. (1997). Mobilizing minority communities: Social capital and participation in urban neighborhoods. *American Behavioral Scientist, 40* (5), 632–644.

Pratt, R. B. (1971). Parties, neighborhood associations, and the politicization of the urban poor in Latin America: An exploratory analysis. *Midwest Journal of Political Science, 15*(3), 495–524.

Rappaport, J. (1987). Terms of empowerment/exemplars of prevention: Toward a theory for community psychology. *American Journal of Community Psychology, 15*(2), 121–148.

Reinders, R. C. (1982). Toynbee Hall and the American settlement movement. *Social Service Review, 56*(1), 39–54.

Rich, R. C. (1980). A political-economy approach to the study of neighborhood organizations. *American Journal of Political Science, 24*(4), 559.

Ruef, M., & Kwon, S.-W. (2016). Neighborhood associations and social capital. *Social Forces, 95*(1), 159–190.

Scally, C. P., & Tighe, J. R. (2015). Democracy in action?: NIMBY as impediment to equitable affordable housing siting. *Housing Studies, 30*(5), 749–769.

Scheller, D. S., & Yerena, A. (2017). Neighborhood concerns and mobilization patterns of homeowners and neighborhood associations. *Journal of Public Management & Social Policy, 24*(2), 82–99.

Sharp, D. (2022). Haphazard urbanisation: Urban informality, politics and power in Egypt. *Urban Studies, 59*(4), 734–749.

Sirianni, C. (2007). Neighborhood planning as collaborative democratic design: The case of Seattle. *Journal of the American Planning Association, 73*(4), 373–387.

Smith, M. E. (2010). The archaeological study of neighborhoods and districts in ancient cities. *Journal of Anthropological Archaeology, 29*(2), 137–154.

Steel, R., Shelton, E., & Warren, C. (2014, June). *Community engagement in transit-related planning in the Twin Cities: Final report on strategies, impact, and potential sustainability*. Wilder Research. www.wilder.org/sites/default/files/imports/CET_2014_Report_6-14.pdf

Streule, M., Karaman, O., Sawyer, L., & Schmid, C. (2020). Popular urbanization: Conceptualizing urbanization processes beyond informality. *International Journal of Urban and Regional Research, 44*(4), 652–672.

Swindell, D. (2000). Issue representation in neighborhood organizations: Questing for democracy at the grassroots. *Journal of Urban Affairs, 22*(2), 123–137.

Talen, E. (2018). *Neighborhood*. Oxford University Press.

Tang Yan, C., Moore de Peralta, A., Bowers, E., & Sprague Martinez, L. (2019). Realmente tenemos la capacidad: Engaging youth to explore health in the Dominican Republic through photovoice. *Journal of Community Engagement and Scholarship, 12*(1), 54–67.

Tighe, J. R. (2012). How race and class stereotyping shapes attitudes toward affordable housing. *Housing Studies, 27*(7), 962–983.

US Census Bureau. (2020). *QuickFacts: Minneapolis city, Minnesota*. US Census Bureau. www.census.gov/quickfacts/minneapoliscityminnesota

Wandersman, A., & Florin, P. (2000). Citizen participation and community organizations. In J. Rappaport & E. Seidman (Eds.), *Handbook of community psychology* (pp. 247–272). Kluwer Academic/Plenum.

Wandersman, A., Florin, P., Friedmann, R., & Meier, R. (1987). Who participates, who does not, and why? An analysis of voluntary neighborhood organizations in the United States and Israel. *Sociological Forum*, *2*(3), 534–555.

Wargent, M., & Talen, E. (2021). Rethinking neighbourhoods. *Town Planning Review*, *92*(1), 89–95.

Warren, M. R. (2013). Public schools as centers for building social capital in urban communities: A case study of the Logan Square Neighborhood Association in Chicago. In R. M. Silverman & K. L. Patterson (Eds.) *Schools and urban revitalization: Rethinking institutions and community development* (pp. 167–184). Taylor & Francis.

Wright, E. O., & Rogers, J. (2011). *American society: How it really works*. W. W. Norton & Company.

Zérah, M.-H. (2007). Middle class neighbourhood associations as political players in Mumbai. *Economic and Political Weekly*, *42*(47), 61–68.

Zimmerman, M. A., & Rappaport, J. (1988). Citizen participation, perceived control, and psychological empowerment. *American Journal of Community Psychology*, *16*(5), 725–750.

15 State-Led Community (Dis)empowerment in China

Ming Hu, Xiaoyun Wang, and Yulong Lian

Introduction

The neighborhood is considered to be at the base of the highly centralized administrative system in China. Consequently, it has been given great attention by the authoritarian state that pursues state legitimacy through strong control over society and seeks to maintain its power over neighborhoods where the reach of the formal government system ceases. On the other hand, the state has to allow room for neighborhoods and residents to manage their internal affairs and to win their support for the state's rule by backing neighborhood development (Heberer, 2009; Midgley et al., 1986). After all, putting neighborhoods under absolute state control proved to be disastrous politically, economically, and morally, as seen in China's totalitarian era between the 1950s and 1970s. But the control and support strategy of managing neighborhood affairs often raises a contradiction in public policies: Does it empower or disempower the neighborhoods? Or is this necessarily an either-or question? This chapter aims to answer these questions by reviewing the extant literature on state-led neighborhood development in contemporary China.

This chapter unveils the nature of state-led community development and examines its performance from a community empowerment perspective. It also presents an example of how community empowerment may be pursued in an authoritarian state context like China.

The Neighborhood and Its Management in China's Political System

In brief, the Chinese Communist Party (hereafter "the Party") founded the People's Republic of China by winning the 1940s civil war and has since served as the only ruling party. The Party's committees are established in each of the five levels of the formal government system: national, provincial (and direct-administered municipalities), municipality, county (or district in a municipality), and township (or subdistrict). At each level, the Party committee acts as the principal decision-maker in public policies and oversees government departments. In this sense, government departments can be seen approximately as the Party's executive/government wing (Zheng, 1997). The Party itself is also highly centralized, following the Leninist party principle: "[L]ower-level Party organizations defer to higher-level Party organizations, and all organizations and members of the Party defer to the National Congress and the Central Committee of the Party" (The Chinese Communist Party's 19th Congress, 2017, para. 71). The neighborhood level under the downtown government had no government agency but had the Party's grassroots organizations. Usually, a township consists of fifteen or so neighborhoods (*shequ* or *xingzhengcun*), each of which comprises around 800 households (about 2,000 residents). There were nearly 628,000 neighborhoods across the country in 2017.[1]

During the Mao era (1949–1978), the state controlled nearly every aspect of neighborhood life: economy, political participation, culture, and even social life. When the "Reform and Open-Up" grand policy began in 1978, the state retracted power from neighborhoods. Neighborhood leaders faced significant growth in resident needs but had limited resources to meet these needs, which led to shortages of public services and social disorder in neighborhoods across the country. The state also felt the weakening of its ruling power at the grassroots. In response, between the 1990s and 2000s, the state greatly enhanced neighborhood investments to improve social security, public health, public safety, and culture and education while supporting the development of a variety of neighborhood-based organizations, including both state-affiliated organizations and relatively independent nonprofit organizations (Xia, 2019). In the early 2010s, the state launched the "Neighborhood Governance" (*shequ zhili*) campaign nationwide to further enhance public administration, social services, and public safety in all urban and rural neighborhoods. The campaign has since been a prominent part of the social and political policy landscape in contemporary China. This chapter will review the campaign from a community empowerment perspective.

The Goal, Structure, and Characteristics of State-Led Neighborhood Governance

The mid-term goal of the Neighborhood Governance campaign was described in the 2017 Opinions on Enhancing and Refining Urban and Rural Neighborhoods' Governance made by The CCP Central Committee and the State Council (2017):

> [The goal is], by the year of 2020, to preliminarily form a rural and urban neighborhood governance system in which the Party's grassroots

---

1 Please refer to the portal of the National Bureau of Statistics (www.stats.gov.cn/tjsj/).

organization leads, the grassroots-level government administers, and multiple parties participate to govern. Consequently, the institutions and policies become more sophisticated, the neighborhoods' governance capacity will be greatly enhanced, and public services, public management, and public safety get well guaranteed.

According to the 2017 Opinions, the campaign had at least five main fields of work: (1) improving the physical environment and developing sophisticated infrastructure in urban and rural neighborhoods; (2) improving public services provision and reducing the urban–rural gap in the scope and standards of neighborhood services; (3) improving cultural and social mores that include the promotion of socialist core values and role models, volunteering, and the preservation and exhibition of cultural relics; (4) encouraging residents' neighborhood participation and cultivating residents' deliberative capacity in managing neighborhood affairs; and (5) resolving social conflicts such as improving psychological support for disadvantaged individuals, improving the institutions that assist residents' expression of interests and conflict resolution, and reinforcing the measures and workforces of neighborhood policing. Apparently, such neighborhood governance covered more than governance issues: It involved almost every basic aspect of neighborhood development.

An improved neighborhood governance system should contain four major actors (The CCP Central Committee and the State Council, 2017). First, the Party's organizations at the grassroots level served as the core of leadership. The 2017 Opinions stated, "[We] should reinforce and improve the township- and neighborhood-level Party organizations' leadership on various neighborhood organizations and fields of work, and ensure the effective implementation of the Party's guidelines and policies in all urban and rural neighborhoods" (para. 9). Second, the township government took responsibility for administration, including enhancing public policies, providing financial and material support, undertaking capacity-building for urban and rural neighborhood governance, and better instructing and regulating residents' self-governing organizations. Third, the Residents' Committee served as a special task force. As the only so-called residents' self-governing organization that was legitimized by law, the Residents' Committee supposedly was established through resident election, enabling the Residents' Committee to self-govern neighborhood affairs on behalf of all residents of the neighborhood. The Residents' Committee responsibilities included four categories: government-instructed services such as conflict resolution, public safety, public health, and family planning; economic work such as managing neighborhood-owned assets and the physical environment; neighborhood welfare services for disadvantaged residents; and other work to improve *jingshen wenming* (spiritual civilization) in terms of cultural, educational, moral, and rule-of-law development (The People's Congress, 2018a, 2018b). Finally, the social (nongovernmental) organizations assisted in neighborhood governance.

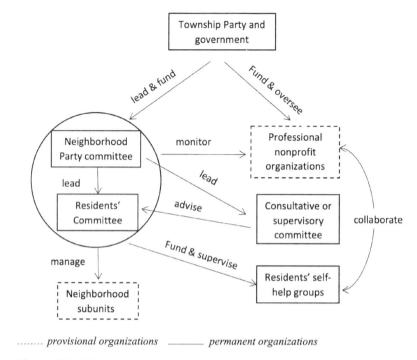

.... *provisional organizations* ———— *permanent organizations*

Figure 15.1 *The typical structure of neighborhood governance in China.*

They included professional nonprofit organizations, residents' self-help groups, cooperatives, and sometimes neighborhood-based small enterprises. The state especially encouraged social organizations to assist in conflict resolution, eldercare, poverty alleviation, disaster prevention and mitigation, recreation, education and training, and technological development.

The typical relations between the main actors in neighborhood governance are shown in Figure 15.1. First of all, the township Party committee directly led the neighborhood Party committee according to the Party's centralized structure. In addition, the township Party committee often oversaw the nonprofit organizations working in the neighborhood through the Party cells that were established in the nonprofit organizations. According to the Opinions on Reinforcing Party Building in Social Organizations (The CCP Central Committee, 2015), each social organization should establish a Party branch or cell under the leadership of the Party committee at the township level or higher. At the neighborhood level, the Party committee led the Residents' Committee's work. In fact, the leaders of both organizations often overlapped, and they put together what were often called *liangwei* ("the two committees"). In addition, many neighborhoods founded a supervisory or consultative committee that was intended to consult with or oversee the Residents' Committee's work, but still under the neighborhood Party committee's leadership. Some large neighborhoods were further divided into several subunits (*wangge*), each of which consisted of around 300 households living close by. The *liangwei* supervised the subunits' management, which was also funded by the township government. Some professional nonprofit organizations could also enter the neighborhood to assist in neighborhood development by working closely with the *liangwei*, residents' self-help groups, and families, but their work was often monitored by the neighborhood leadership.

Nearly all of the neighborhoods across the country have been engaged in the Neighborhood Governance policy campaign, which has been made a top priority in the Party and state's ruling agenda. But their specific structures and contents varied a lot according to the neighborhood's geographic traits, residents' livelihoods, local economic growth, and local politics.

Generally, the campaign had the following characteristics. The first was the predominant leadership of the Party. Following the political principle "the Party leads everything" that had been founded in the 1960s and recovered by the new administration in 2017 (Xi, 2017, para. 46), the Party has greatly reinforced its power in the neighborhoods. Each kind of organization was required to establish a Party cell and follow the Party's policies so that the Party's organizational structure could cover every corner of the society. In addition, the neighborhood Party committee was institutionally supported to co-opt the Residents' Committee, though the latter supposedly was elected by neighborhood residents. In addition, the Party committee was assigned to "unanimously lead various organizations and fields of work" in the neighborhood (The CCP Central Committee and the State Council, 2021, para. 5).

Second, the campaign strengthened the executive power of the township and neighborhood leadership. Township governments had served as deputies of the county or district government. The 2021 Opinions stated that "[the state] authorizes township [and subdistrict] governments the power of integrated management, planning and coordination, and emergency management" (para. 8), which was reserved by higher governments. Consequently, the number of township government employees and their budgets have been greatly increased over recent decades (Chen, 2009). The township governments in turn enhanced political and financial support for their neighborhood-level deputies – the neighborhood *liangwei*. Some neighborhoods established subunits (*wangge*) to assist in managing their numerous government-assigned responsibilities. To staff the neighborhood work, more *liangwei* members who had received merely limited allowances from the government became full-time government employees (Wu, 2019). Occasionally they were promoted to become civil servants.

Third, the deliberative participation of residents played a supplementary role in the campaign. Some forms of supervisory or consultative committees composed of both cadres and ordinary residents had been widely established to participate in making major decisions on neighborhood affairs. Sometimes residents' self-help groups, neighborhood-based firms, and others were also engaged. But the actual influence of such deliberation varied across neighborhoods.

Fourth, nonprofit organizations participated in neighborhood development. The central government has, since 2013, promoted government procurement from service-oriented nonprofit organizations, particularly social work organizations, and encouraged them to work in neighborhoods to enhance social welfare provision and engage residents in neighborhood governance. Volunteer organizations, self-help groups, and other voluntary organizations were also welcomed, provided that they would work under the *liangwei* leadership.

Fifth, the administration was project-based. Except in some basic fields of work such as office expenses and social security, the townships and higher levels of government allocated neighborhood grants in the form of projects that usually would last one to three years, have clear objectives, and be evaluated and paid according to performance. Some projects were noncompetitive and others competitive so that neighborhood cadres had to work hard to apply for the projects and finish them satisfactorily to win adequate resources for their neighborhoods.

Finally, Internet-based management tools were intensively used. Numerous photographic, audio, and video recorders were installed to collect and communicate resident and neighborhood information, which nevertheless was weakly regulated by the state. Numerous apps, websites, digital communication platforms, and social media instruments have been widely used to realize "intelligent, accurate, professional governance" under the banner of "the Internet-empowered neighborhood" (The CCP Central Committee and the State Council, 2019, para. 16).

Since its launch in the early 2010s, the Neighborhood Governance campaign has ever been stoked by the central Party and state (Wang, 2018; Wu, 2019). The 2021 Opinions even claimed that "enhancing the governance of townships [and subdistricts] and urban and rural neighborhoods is the fundamental project for realizing the modernization of the national governance system and governing capacity" (The CCP Central Committee and the State Council, 2021, para. 1). Consequently, nearly all neighborhoods claimed to undertake neighborhood governance, and countless "innovative models" have been spawned and promoted across the country in the past decade (e.g., Song, 2017). The Sichuan Provincial Government (2021) even developed a special five-year plan on neighborhood governance.

Despite the predominantly state-led nature of neighborhood governance, a handful of rights-based nonprofit organizations did seek to pursue resident-led neighborhood governance, taking a bottom-up empowerment approach including participatory development and governance. They tried to find some gray zone to work independently or steer clear of state-led neighborhood governance to genuinely empower residents and their voluntary organizations. But most such initiatives experienced constraints and opposition from local governments and their neighborhood deputies, ending in the withdrawal of these organizations from the neighborhood or adapting their initiatives to focus on social welfare issues through cooperation with the neighborhood leadership. Some examples included Hu and Zhu (2021), Song (2017), Wang and Meng (2015), Xu and Huang (2020), and Zhang (2017).

An Example of Neighborhood Governance

The Zung Neighborhood (Figure 15.2) is located in suburban Yangzhou, a large city in east China. Its gated territory of 0.8 square kilometers accommodates more than 4,100 households (about 12,000 residents). Most residents had been peasants but were resettled here by the municipal government about fifteen years ago. After losing their land due to the displacement, many residents worked in nearby factories, public services, and shops or started small businesses. About a third of the neighborhood population consists of elders. The income per capita was RMB 20,000 (approximately USD 3,077), about 60 percent of the mean in Yangzhou. However, no households lived below the poverty line thanks to the local state's antipoverty policies of recent years.

The Zung Neighborhood shows how a typical neighborhood community is governed and administered in China. The neighborhood *liangwei* had eleven

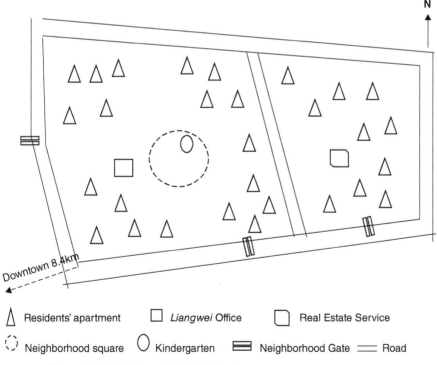

Figure 15.2 *The Zung Neighborhood.*

members, including seven Party committee members and eight Residents' Committee members (four belonged to both committees). The Party secretary also served as chair of the Residents' Committee. The Zung Neighborhood was divided into five subunits (*wangge*), each of which was managed by a special cadre who reported to the *liangwei*. Given the heavy workload in the neighborhood, the township government recruited four cadres to base in Zung Neighborhood to assist the *liangwei* in managing neighborhood affairs. Taken together, fourteen people, including the *liangwei* members and the special neighborhood cadres (one also joined the *liangwei*), worked full time in the neighborhood and were paid by the township Party and government. The neighborhood leadership also asked the households living in the same building to elect a building head to work with neighborhood cadres on their behalf, but the building head job was voluntary.

With respect to neighborhood budgeting, Zung Neighborhood had three major sources of revenue, all from local government. First, the government gave a regular grant of RMB 320,000 to pay for the overheads of the neighborhood leadership. Second, the government allocated some special grants for neighborhood development. Such grants were arranged by the government and could last no more than five years. For example, the Party made a Party-building grant of RMB 200,000 to Zung Neighborhood and required them to spend it on strengthening Party organizations and improving residents' well-being. Third, the government also made available some competitive grants for which they invited the neighborhoods to apply. An example was the *hongse chuangtou* ("Red Venture Fund") that the district government set up in 2020 in an attempt to enhance the well-being of elders, children, and the disabled through Party-building activities.[2] The proposals from three neighborhoods, including Zung Neighborhood, were finally selected to share the grant of RMB 90,000. Finally, sometimes the government would establish rewards for those neighborhoods achieving excellent performance.

The neighborhood leadership had two basic categories of work. The first category was the tasks assigned by the townships and higher government, which included two subcategories: regular neighborhood services and mobilizational projects. Regular neighborhood services involved neighborly conflict resolution, public safety, public health, welfare services, and others. Mobilizational projects were temporary but intensive. Some examples included Party-building activities, population censuses, *chuangjian wenming chengshi* ("building a civilized city," a comprehensive assessment of a city's economic development, government, mores, and environment by the national government), and COVID-19 prevention and control activities (see Figure 15.3), the latter of which being top priorities recently.

---

2 The "Red Venture Fund" is so named to indicate its relation to the Party because the Party's flag is red. The same goes for "Red Real Estate Management" mentioned later.

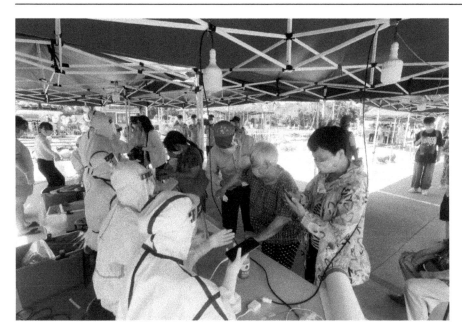

Figure 15.3 *Health workers assisted by neighborhood cadres testing residents for COVID-19.*

The second category involved self-determined projects in regard to neighborhood governance. In the past three years, the Zung Neighborhood leadership focused on three projects. The first was to upgrade a small and old neighborhood center. With a special grant from the government, a new center was built to accommodate neighborhood meetings, on-site service provision, and cultural and educational activities and to host a government-funded nonprofit incubator that aimed to foster neighborhood-based nonprofit organizations. The second project involved garbage classification, including constructing special facilities and providing incentives for residents to classify their garbage. The third project was *hongse wuye* ("Red Real Estate Management"), in which the neighborhood Party committee founded a special Party cell consisting of Party members from the *liangwei*, the real estate firm, and the homeowner association to play a coordinator role in real estate management.

The neighborhood *liangwei* made major decisions on neighborhood affairs with the authorization of the township and higher government. It also set up a supervisory committee to oversee neighborhood governance, but the committee existed merely on paper. Sometimes the *liangwei* convened a temporary consultative session and invited residents to discuss neighborhood affairs and communicate their opinions. However, most residents had no interest in attending these sessions: They believed that what the *liangwei* could address was trivial and of little value, and they attended these sessions only when they were focused on their private interests. Consequently, the attendees were

Figure 15.4 *Neighborhood cadres attending a training course on nonprofit management at the Zung Neighborhood Center.*

mainly resident volunteers and building heads in addition to neighborhood cadres. Zung Neighborhood had thirty to forty active volunteers who were warm-hearted senior residents. They assisted neighborhood cadres in managing garbage classification, neighborhood patrols, neighborly conflict resolution, and other issues. They were also invited to attend a variety of neighborhood events to highlight resident participation.

Zung Neighborhood had two categories of nonprofit organization. Five nonprofit organizations – a neighborhood college, a youth service center, a disability service center, a drawing and painting institute, and a volunteer association – were registered with the district government. They sometimes received special grants that were provided by the local government to encourage government–nonprofit partnerships in neighborhood governance (see Figure 15.4). However, due to the shortage of organizational capacity, the grants were managed primarily by neighborhood cadres who also sat on the boards of directors of the organizations. In addition, Zung Neighborhood had seven unregistered nonprofit organizations that were supervised by the *liangwei*. However, these existed merely on paper: They could not receive government grants and organized hardly any activities. In fairness, the establishment of the two categories of neighborhood-based organization was done to meet a local government policy that each neighborhood should have five registered nonprofit organizations and ten *liangwei*-supervised nonprofit organizations. However, in recent years, the district government introduced an independent nonprofit organization to manage a nonprofit incubator that was located in Zung Neighborhood and was intended to foster grassroots nonprofit organizations across the district. The nonprofit incubator has now started activity and hopefully can foster in the years to come a few nonprofit organizations that are relatively independent of the neighborhood leadership and capable of assisting in neighborhood governance and services.

Literature Review of Community Empowerment in the State-Led Neighborhood Governance Campaign

The state claimed that the purpose of the Neighborhood Governance campaign was "building the urban and rural neighborhoods as the happy homes that are harmonious and orderly, green and civilized, innovative and inclusive, commonly built and owned" (The CCP Central Committee and the State Council, 2017, para. 2). But to what extent has the campaign really contributed to neighborhood development? In what follows, we review the extant literature on the campaign from a community empowerment perspective.

Community Empowerment/Disempowerment

The campaign has increased neighborhoods' control over their internal affairs in the following ways. First, neighborhoods have gained more resources to improve their physical environment and social services provision. For example, national spending on social services was RMB 481 billion in 2020, an increase of 30 percent compared to 2012 (Ministry of Civil Affairs, 2020). There were 511,000 or so neighborhood centers across the country that provided neighborhood-based social services, a 2.5-fold increase over the number in 2012. All urban neighborhoods and 65.7 percent of rural neighborhoods established a neighborhood center. Moreover, there were more than 669,000 certificated social workers in China in 2020, most of whom worked in neighborhoods. Some special grants were also founded by townships and higher government to fund neighborhood organizations in addressing neighborhood-specific concerns such as the physical environment, eldercare services, cultural development, and neighborhood inclusion (Chen, 2015; Li, 2020; Xue & Sun, 2017).

Second, deliberative neighborhood governance has been widely promoted and extended by the local state, which enhanced residents' engagement in neighborhood affairs. For example, some neighborhoods established a consultative committee that met seasonally to discuss and make decisions on major neighborhood projects (Ren et al., 2018). Other neighborhoods set up temporary committees composed of *liangwei* members, representatives of homeowner associations and neighborhood-based firms, and active residents to address their common concerns (Zhang, 2020). Some neighborhoods invited local elites to form a supervisory board to consult on neighborhood affairs (Ren et al., 2018).

Third, the partnership with nonprofit organizations facilitated the growth of residents' self-help groups, volunteering, and decision-making on neighborhood affairs and thus improved their collective efficacy (Song, 2019; Xu, 2018). For example, a nonprofit organization promoted Robert's Rules of Order for modern meetings in neighborhoods to improve democratic neighborhood governance (Zhang, 2017). Residents learned the skills of deliberation and decision-making, built neighborhood-based groups to start and manage small projects to solve neighborhood problems, and improved neighborhood services. In another case, a nonprofit organization organized many neighborly recreation activities such as flea markets, sports contests, and festivals, which greatly mobilized resident volunteers and enhanced residents' engagement with their neighbors (Ji, 2017). Occasionally, resident-driven initiatives leveraged neighborhood resources and stimulated institutional change at the neighborhood level for better governance (Wu et al., 2019).

Despite these factors that may contribute to community empowerment, some other factors have been rather detrimental to neighborhoods' control of internal affairs.

First, the local Party and state have reinforced their control over neighborhood affairs through the Neighborhood Governance campaign. By strengthening and extending the Party's organizational structure in the neighborhood and practicing the Party's centralization principle, the state has unprecedentedly strengthened its grasp on neighborhoods by placing all kinds of organizations under its direct control. So, when the higher-level Party organizations made neighborhood policies, all of the lower-level Party organizations had to follow, which left very limited room for neighborhoods' self-governance (Xu & Chen, 2017). In addition, by funding the neighborhood *liangwei* and subunits, the government actually converted neighborhood self-governing bodies into their neighborhood deputies, which fostered the bureaucratization of neighborhood governance (Wu, 2019). Government grants for neighborhood governance had similar effects when they were competitive, contract-based, standardized, and monitored by the township and higher government (Huang, 2015). In addition, the widespread use of Internet instruments greatly facilitated the local state to directly intervene in neighborhood affairs and monitor organizations and residents (Huang & Ji, 2016).

Second, resident participation has been marginalized in reality. Despite the variety of deliberative institutions in the neighborhood, the Party committee played a predominant role in decision-making (Ren et al., 2018; Wu, 2019). Residents' participation was primarily restricted to the small projects focused on the neighborhood services of gardening, eldercare, and neighborhood patrols, but their voice was often ignored or absent when making major decisions involving politics or economic development (Wu, 2019; Xu, 2018). In some cases, residents' participation served merely to ceremonially approve the neighborhood *liangwei*'s decisions and meet government requirements on resident participation. The majority of participants in neighborhood events were retirees, students on leave, and receivers of the minimum income guarantee because they had time, needed financial support from the *liangwei*, or genuinely wanted to contribute to neighborhood interests and realize their self-worth (Song, 2019). But most residents seldom participated. The feeling of powerlessness and low participation thus remained great challenges to neighborhood governance across the country (Wu, 2019; Zhou, 2016).

Third, nonprofit and voluntary organizations were absorbed into the state-led neighborhood governance system. By encouraging and funding service-based nonprofits but restricting rights-based nonprofits, the state has managed to incorporate most nonprofit organizations into its centralized social control regime. Especially as the previous "preserving social stability" strategy has shifted toward a new "preserving national safety" strategy in recent years, voluntary organizations and residents' collective actions struggled to cope with the greater supervision and constraints. Most voluntary and nonprofit organizations had to avoid rights issues and empowerment approaches and instead focus on social welfare delivery, being funded and monitored by the township and neighborhood leadership (Wu, 2019; Xu, 2018; Xu & Huang, 2020).

Many scholars have used a model of community power with three dimensions: situational, institutional, and systemic (e.g., Christens, 2019; Gaventa, 1980). The situational dimension of power involves who wins and who loses in public contests over issues. The institutional dimension of power determines which issues are brought to the table in public debate and which are not. And the systemic dimension of power concerns how ideology and public opinion are shaped. Following this model, it may reasonably be argued that in the Neighborhood Governance campaign residents' situational power might have been increased in some cases. They gained more resources for social services provision, have been better informed of public policies and government procedures, and had Internet-based instruments to help voice their opinions that were more easily heard by decision-makers within and beyond the neighborhood.

But their institutional power generally declined. Residents seemingly gained access to deliberative governance (at least in nonpolitical, noncritical fields), had more rights granted through legislation and public policies, and developed their capacity in volunteer and self-help groups. However, they were often marginalized in neighborhood governance when the Party reinforced its political and organizational control over neighborhood-based organizations, and the government extended its bureaucratic system to neighborhood affairs by incorporating neighborhood cadres into the government staff and funding neighborhood development projects. Some studies simply claimed resident participation to be false (e.g., Zhang, 2016; Zhou, 2016).

More importantly, the state strongly exerted and reinforced its systemic power over neighborhood organizations and residents. Neighborhood governance has been seen as the foundation of so-called national governance (i.e., the state's governance over the country), such that it must serve to consolidate state power at the grassroots. As the Ministry of Civil Affairs (2009) clearly stated, "the center for reinforcing social management is the neighborhood, the basis for improving people's livelihood is the neighborhood, and the foundation of preserving social stability is the neighborhood" (para. 2). Neighborhood governance has therefore been transformed into another government level that was incorporated into the centralized government system to complete state control over society. Residents' participation, following this political philosophy, was designed to produce people's consent to and even voluntary support for the exclusive and permanent rule of the authoritarian state rather than to enhance neighborhood autonomy (Wu, 2019; Zhou, 2016). In the face of a mighty, centralized, and ever-present state, the participation that disallowed competitive interests and contentions within the neighborhood reinforced state power through residents' collective submission and active engagement. As a result, the state has seemed like the only solution to neighborhood problems.

Psychological Empowerment/Disempowerment

While most previous studies focused on the structure and management of the Neighborhood Governance campaign, only a few studies investigated resident participation and psychological empowerment. The campaign might enhance psychological empowerment in the following respects.

First, some residents experienced satisfaction due to higher incomes and better neighborhood services. For example, the disposable income per capita in China in 2020 was RMB 32,189, a 1.6-fold increase compared to 2010 (The State Council News Office, 2021). Nearly all citizens, including those living in the most impoverished regions, became exempt from absolute poverty in 2020. Some 80 percent of adults had access to old-age benefits, and 96.8 percent of Chinese citizens had some form of medical care insurance. Nearly all townships and neighborhoods across the country had access to concrete pavements and roads. Neighborhood services involving electricity, drinking water, housing, health care, preschool and primary education, eldercare, and others were also greatly enhanced over the past decade. The improved quality of life generally enhanced people's feeling of happiness and confidence in the prospects for their future life (Zhang, 2018).

Second, some residents experienced a greater sense of self-worth and efficacy through their neighborhood participation. By joining volunteer groups and attending neighborhood events that the local state greatly promoted and sponsored during the campaign, residents built more connections within and outside the neighborhood. Retirees, especially those with social service expertise, overcame social exclusion and realized their self-worth by volunteering to serve their neighbors (Wu et al., 2019; Yang, 2007). In particular, the connections with the Party's grassroots organizations helped some individuals to gain political capital and improve their self-efficacy (e.g., Tang & Hu, 2016). Some enhanced their identification with the neighborhood and the Party and state by assisting the neighborhood leadership with public affairs, especially when their efforts were acknowledged by state agencies and other residents. The enhancement of political efficacy was salient, especially among the Party members who were retired or disadvantaged in terms of social status: The Party's reinforced leadership in the neighborhood gave them the psychological and organizational support to strengthen their political identity.

Third, residents have improved their awareness of rights and gained more capacity to voice their opinions on public policies and administration. Despite their lack of public and political interests in general, neighborhood residents in China have developed a strong sense of individual freedom and private rights over the past decades (e.g., Heberer, 2009; Wang & Meng, 2015), which was partly corroborated during the Neighborhood Governance campaign. They often skirted or broke through the state's constraints and took collective action to defend their interests, as can be seen in the homeowner rights movement (Xiao, 2011). In addition, when neighborhood governance became more transparent due to the development of deliberative institutions, the top-down requirements for transparency, and the improved access to government information, residents had more capacity to voice their views on neighborhood affairs.

However, psychological disempowerment also occurred during the campaign. First, when a handful of residents actively took part in neighborhood governance, most residents kept their distance from it or participated only when required to by the neighborhood leadership. Only a small proportion of residents regarded the Residents' Committee as an autonomous organization representing neighborhood interests (Heberer, 2009; Yang, 2007). Turnout rates in the neighborhood elections remained relatively low, such that the *liangwei* sometimes had to offer small gifts to encourage residents' attendance. Some Party members perfunctorily attended neighborhood events when they were mobilized by Party organizations, but their ceremonial participation disappeared immediately in the absence of top-down mobilization (Liu, 2020).

Second, some residents became dependent on the neighborhood and government leadership. They felt powerless, growing used to the state's rigorous control over neighborhood affairs and the marginalization of resident participation. Some tended to appeal to top-down state intervention rather than organizing residents' collective action, or they turned to neighborhood cadres and government officials to seek personal support (Chen, 2018). Such behavior in turn reinforced state power but resident disempowerment in the neighborhood (Wu, 2020).

Application

These dynamics around neighborhood-based governance in China have implications for public policymakers, neighborhood leaders, and researchers.

The first implication involves the nature of the Neighborhood Governance campaign, which has long been controversial in the researcher community.

Taking a state–society relation perspective, the extant literature develops three threads of theory regarding the nature of the campaign (Chen, 2015). The first thread argues for state-led neighborhood governance on the grounds that the state should reinforce its ruling power at the grassroots to solve the social conflicts that have accumulated during China's economic reform over recent decades and would otherwise pose a great challenge to state legitimacy. In addition, the strong state tradition was carried over from the communist era, meaning that the state was used to state control over society, not to mention that the weak civil society could not practice self-governance in the neighborhood. The second thread argues for authentic neighborhood self-governance for the reasons of democratization and government performance. Practicing self-governance is necessary to nurture people's public participation and foster civil society to organize and represent the differentiated interests that formed during China's economic reform. Neighborhood self-governance can also reduce the state's expenses in terms of public administration. The third thread of the literature suggests some mixture of the first two approaches from a practical and balanced perspective.

It is noted that the authoritarian state took the first approach in reality, despite its political rhetoric about neighborhood self-governance in numerous policy documents. Some researchers argue that the state has not abandoned the goal of neighborhood self-governance but defined it from a rather restrictive and instrumental perspective: Self-governance meant that neighborhood leaders and residents self-managed – under the leadership of the local state – the neighborhood affairs that are assigned by the state (Bray, 2006; Heberer, 2009). In this sense, self-governance was a secondary and supplementary component in the state-led neighborhood governance structure, serving to strengthen of national governance at the neighborhood level (Wu, 2019; Zhou, 2016). In addition, there has been a lack of institutional bases and practical spaces for neighborhood self-governance in the authoritarian state apparatus (Zhou, 2017). Wu (2019) even argues that the neighborhood has become a "poli-community" in which the state has attempted to integrate its three primary functions – political leadership, social service delivery, and social control – to reinforce state power at the grassroots level. Given the all-encompassing state control of the neighborhood and the voluntary sector as demonstrated in this chapter, some researchers warn of the return to totalitarianism in China (Kang, 2018; Wu, 2019).

The second implication concerns the great challenges of the Neighborhood Governance campaign. One great challenge was simply financial unsustainability (Wu, 2019). The campaign has led to the rapid expansion of government budgeting. Some townships recruited temporary government employees at twice the number of full-time government employees to assist in dealing with public administration (Zhou & Zhao, 2010). At the neighborhood level, the average number of government-paid employees has increased from three to ten or so over the past decade, as seen in the case of Zung Neighborhood, not to mention the rapidly growing expenses regarding physical environment improvement and social services provision. Such huge expenses have become increasingly unsustainable during China's economic recession in recent years.

The second challenge derives from the ever-growing managerial complexity and the risks of bureaucratic failure. In using *liangwei* and other organizations as extensions of the state in the neighborhood, the local state demanded that they also share government responsibilities regarding neighborhood affairs. Hu and Cao (2018) found that the neighborhood *liangwei* managed more than 130 projects, only ten of which pertained to neighborhood self-governance, and the *liangwei* staff spent more than 80 percent of their time on the projects assigned by the township Party committee and government. The heavy workload of the township and neighborhood leadership has become so salient that the central state even named the year of 2019 "the year for alleviating the grassroots level's burden" (The CCP Central Committee, 2019, para. 1) and promulgated several policies to hopefully reduce their workload. In addition, the overextended administrative structure at the township and neighborhood levels produced complex management procedures and mechanisms and a bulky grassroots bureaucracy, which in turn greatly reduced government efficiency and performance (Xu & Chen, 2017; Zhou, 2016). Some studies (e.g., Liu, 2020) even found significant burnout in the Party-building field, which was seen as the powerhouse of the campaign: The highly demanding requirements on Party-building from the higher-level Party organizations have led to much political rhetoric and ceremonial participation in lower-level Party organizations and by ordinary Party members. Practically, the over-extension of the state system to the neighborhoods may in some ways finally damage rather than improve the state's ruling capacity.

The third implication involves resident participation. The state-led neighborhood governance reduced the agency of residents and neighborhood-based organizations and led to widespread political alienation and faked participation. Despite the increasing government procurement from nonprofit organizations and the state's welcoming of volunteer service, these are incorporated into the state-controlled system to strengthen social control. The growing constraints on voluntary actions and organizations have resulted in the actual disempowerment of neighborhoods during the campaign that claimed to foster a community in which "everyone has responsibilities, everyone fulfills responsibilities, and everyone owns and benefits" (The CCP Central Committee and the State Council, 2021). It is time to rethink the role and functioning of community empowerment in the interest of sustainable neighborhood development.

Future Research

We suggest three productive avenues for future research on community empowerment in the state-led Neighborhood Governance campaign.

First, the field will benefit from the measurement of community empowerment and disempowerment during the campaign. Though several previous studies investigated community empowerment, most relied on theoretical analysis to identify the nature and direction of neighborhood participation. The absence of reliable measurements of neighborhood community empowerment hinders future explorations of the campaign. Efforts at measuring community empowerment have proved to be diverse, controversial, and challenging (Laverack & Pratley, 2018; Taylor, 2003) because empowerment involves both value and practice and both process and consequence. But the effort will still be worthwhile and necessary when monitoring the performance of neighborhood participation. A possible solution might be to develop neighborhood empowerment indicators that are comparable to the general indicators and methods used in the developing world (e.g., Laverack & Pratley, 2018) but are adaptable to the neighborhood context in China, where the neighborhood has long been incorporated into the state apparatus. Another solution might be to develop the indicators from community empowerment practices at the neighborhood level through the collaborative work of stakeholders, including residents, practitioners, researchers, and local policymakers (Christens, 2019).

Second, the field will benefit from additional scholarly exploration of community disempowerment mechanisms during the campaign. While rich strands in the literature scrutinize community empowerment processes, little research examines in detail how community disempowerment occurs in the neighborhood context. This progressive approach of community research obscures the changing horizon of neighborhood practice, especially in authoritarian states where state power and local elites manipulate neighborhood residents and voluntary organizations to serve their purposes. Sometimes such disempowerment occurs under the cloak of capacity-building, social services provision, public safety, or neighborly solidarity. In the case of the Neighborhood Governance campaign in China, future research could aim to answer the following questions: How does the exclusive leadership of the Party that seeks to aggregate and represent the common interests of all parties dampen people's genuine interest in politics and public affairs? How does the over-extension of the bureaucratic system of the government undermine the development of public and voluntary participation in the neighborhood? And how does the incorporation of nonprofit and voluntary organizations weaken state power in the long run by smothering social autonomy, destroying cultural diversity, and weakening social innovations? The role of technology is also noteworthy: How are Internet-based instruments used by the political elite to disempower neighborhoods and residents? Future investigations of these community disempowerment issues could help practitioners better understand their challenges and find counteractive methods.

Third, regardless of the seemingly insurmountable challenges, whether genuine community empowerment can emerge from the Neighborhood Governance campaign still deserves further inquiry. For example, the financial unsustainability of the policy campaign may force the local state to retract from the neighborhood or at least loosen its direct control, which might create spaces for voluntary organizations to advance community empowerment. In some other cases, voluntary organizations ceremonially conformed to the requirements of the local state but kept their organizational autonomy, or even proactively developed connections and partnerships with the Party organizations to manipulate political support in the pursuit of their mission (Shen & Yu, 2016). Scrutinizing nonprofit organizations' empowerment practices during the campaign could help us to identify the factors in and chances for counteracting or even transforming state-led disempowerment, especially as the public policy environment changes quickly in the years to come.

References

Bray, D. (2006). Building "community": New strategies of governance in urban China. *Economy & Society, 35*, 530–549.

Chen, W. (2015). *Fuquan shequ: jumin zizhi de yizhong kexingxing lujing* [Empowering community: A route to residents' self-governance]. *Shehui kexuejia, 6*, 8–14.

Chen, W. (2018). *Shequ xingdongzhe luoji: pojie shequ zhili nanti* [The logic of neighborhood actors and the solution of predicament in neighborhood governance]. *Zhengzhixue yanjiu, 1*, 103–106.

Chen, X. (2009). *Cong jiejuzhi dao shequzhi: chengshi jiceng zhili moshi de zhuanbian* [From "*jiejuzhi*" to "*shequzhi*": A pattern shift of urban grassroots governance]. *Huadong jingji luntan, 23*, 92–98.

Christens, B. D. (2019). *Community power and empowerment*. Oxford University Press.

Gaventa, J. (1980). *Power and powerlessness: Quiescence and rebellion in an Appalachian Valley*. University of Illinois Press.

Heberer, T. (2009). Evolvement of citizenship in urban China or authoritarian communitarianism? Neighborhood development, community participation, and autonomy. *Journal of Contemporary China, 18*(61), 491–515.

Hu, M., & Zhu, J. (2021). Fostering civil society through community empowerment: An extended case of the Sichuan Earthquake in China. *Administration & Society, 53*(1), 13–35.

Hu, X., & Cao, H. (2018). *Shequ zhili tixi he zhili nengli xiandaihua de sikao* [Thoughts on the modernization of neighborhood governance structure and capacity]. *Jingji wenti, 1*, 8–14.

Huang, X. (2015). *Dangdai zhongguo shehui zuzhi de zhidu huanjing yu fazhan* [The institutional environment and the development of social organizations in contemporary China]. *Zhongguo shehui kexue, 9*, 146–164.

Huang, X., & Ji, X. (2016). *Jishu zhili de juxian ji qi chaoyue* [The upper limit of technological governance and its transformation]. *Shehui kexue, 11*, 72–79.

Ji, Y. (2017). *Cong shuangxiang qianru dao shuangxiang fuquan: yi N shi shequ shehui zuzhi weili* [From bidirectional embeddedness to bidirectional empowerment: A case study of social organizations in City N]. *Zhejiang xuekan, 1*, 49–56.

Kang, X. (2018). Moving toward neo-totalitarianism: A political-sociological analysis of the evolution of administrative absorption of society in China. *Nonprofit Policy Forum, 9*(1), 20170026.

Laverack, G., & Pratley, P. (2018). *What quantitative and qualitative methods have been developed to measure community empowerment at a national level?* World Health Organization. https://apps.who.int/iris/handle/10665/326225

Li, X. (2020). *Shuanggui dongyuan: xiangmuzhi shequ zizhi de shijian luoji ji qi yingxiang* [Double-tracked mobilization: The practical logic and impact of the project-based neighborhood self-governance]. *Tianjin xinzheng xueyuan xuebao, 22*, 60–69.

Liu, X. (2020). *Dangzhi shehui: quyuhua dangjian guocheng zhong de neijuanhua qingxiang yanjiu* [Party-governed society: A study of the involution of Party building]. *Shehui kexue, 6*, 46–57.

Midgley, J., Hall, A., Hardiman, M., & Narine, D. (1986). *Community participation, social development and the state*. Methuen.

Ministry of Civil Affairs. (2009, November). *Guanyu jinyibu tuijin hexie shequ jianshe gongzuo de yijian* [Opinions on further improving the building of harmonious neighborhoods]. Ministry of Civil Affairs. www.gov.cn/gzdt/2009-11/26/content_1473425.htm

Ministry of Civil Affairs. (2020). *2020 nian minzheng shiye fazhan tongji gongbao* [Statistics of civil affairs development in 2020]. Ministry of Civil Affairs. http://images3.mca.gov.cn/www2017/file/202109/1631265147970.pdf

Ren, K., Hu, P., & Nie, W. (2018). *Shequ xieshang minzhu de jiben moshi ji qi zhili chengxiao* [The basic patterns of neighborhood-based deliberative democracy and their performance]. *Nanjing zhengzhi xueyuan xuebao, 34*, 72–77.

Shen, Y., & Yu, Z. (2016). *Shehui zuzhi dangjian dongli jizhi wenti: zhidu qihe yu ziyuan tuozhan* [The issue on the promoting mechanism of social organizations' Party building: Institutional coincidence and resource development]. *Beijing xingzheng xueyuan xuebao, 6*, 13–21.

Song, D. (2017). *Zhuanxing zhongguo de shequ zhili: guojia zhili de jishi* [Neighborhood governance as the cornerstone of national governance in a transitional China]. *Fudan xuebao, 3*, 172–179.

Song, X. (2019). *Shehui zuzhi canyu chengshi shequ zhili de zhidu huanjing yu xingdong celue* [The institutional environment and strategy of social organizations in urban neighborhood governance]. *Jiangsu shehui kexue, 2*, 155–164.

Tang, Y., & Hu, B. (2016). *Shequ zhili zhong de gongzhong canyu: guojia rentong yu shequ rentong de shuangchong qudong* [Public participation in neighborhood governance: The double drives of national identity and neighborhood identity]. *Yunnan shifan daxue xuebao, 48*, 63–69.

Taylor, M. (2003). *Public policy in the community*. Palgrave.

The CCP Central Committee. (2015). *Guanyu jiaqiang shehui zuzhi dangde jianshe gongzuo de yijian* [Opinions on strengthening Party building in social organizations]. The CCP Central Committee. www.gov.cn/xinwen/2015-09/28/content_2939936.htm

The CCP Central Committee. (2019). *Guanyu jiejue xingshi zhuyi tuchu wenti wei jiceng jianfu d tongzhi* [Notice on solving formalistic problems and reducing the grassroots level's workload]. The CCP Central Committee. www.gov.cn/zhengce/2019-03/11/content_5372964.htm

The CCP Central Committee and the State Council. (2017). *Guanyu jiaqiang he wanshan chengxiang shequ zhili de yijian* [Opinions on enhancing and refining urban and rural neighborhoods' governance]. The CCP Central Committee and the State Council. www.gov.cn/zhengce/2017-06/12/content_5201910 .htm

The CCP Central Committee and the State Council. (2019). *Guanyu jiaqiang he gaijin chengxiang zhili de zhidao yijian* [Guiding opinions on strengthening and enhancing urban and rural governance]. The CCP Central Committee and the State Council. www.gov.cn/zhengce/2019-06/23/content_5402625.htm

The CCP Central Committee and the State Council. (2021). *Guanyu jiaqiang jiceng zhili tixi he zhili nengli xiandaihua jianshe de yijian* [Opinions on strengthening the building of a modernized grassroots governance system and governing capacity]. The CCP Central Committee and the State Council. www.gov.cn/ zhengce/2021-07/11/content_5624201.htm

The Chinese Communist Party's 19th Congress. (2017). *Zhongguo gongchandang zhangcheng* [Constitution of the Chinese Communist Party]. The Chinese Communist Party's 19th Congress. www.qstheory.cn/dukan/qs/2017-11/01/ c_1121886219.htm

The People's Congress. (2018a). *Chengshi jumin weiyuanhui zuzhi fa* [Organizational law of the residents' committee in urban neighborhood]. The People's Congress. www.mca.gov.cn/article/gk/fg/jczqhsqjs/201911/20191100021349.shtml

The People's Congress. (2018b). *Cunmin weiyuanhui zuzhi fa* [Organizational law of the villagers' committee]. The People's Congress. www.mca.gov.cn/article/gk/fg/ jczqhsqjs/201911/20191100021350.shtml

The Sichuan Provincial Government. (2021). *Sichuansheng shisiwu chengxiang shequ fazhan zhili guihua* [The 14th five-year plan on rural and urban neighborhood development and governance in Sichuan]. The Sichuan Provincial Government. www.sc.gov.cn/10462/c108551/2022/1/19/609181bfec29470096 841f8ba796a2cf.shtml

The State Council News Office. (2021). *Zhongguo de quanmian xiaokang* [Building an all-encompassing *xiaokang* society in China]. The State Council News Office. www.gov.cn/zhengce/2021-09/28/content_5639778.htm

Wang, H., & Meng, Q. (2015). *Shehui zuzhi canyu chengzhongcun shequ zhili de guocheng yu jizhi yanjiu* [The process and mechanisms for social organizations' participation in neighborhood governance in urban villages]. *Chengshi fazhan yanjiu, 22,* 114–119.

Wang, K. (2018). *Zhongguo chengshi shequ zhili chuangxin de tezheng dongyin ji qushi* [The characteristics, contributing factors, and trends in the innovative governance of urban neighborhoods in China]. *Chengshi wenti, 284,* 67–76.

Wu, X. (2019). *Zhiquan tonghe fuwu xiachen yu xuanzexing canyu: gaige kaifang sishinian chengshi shequ zhili de fuhe jiegou* [Integration of governance power, gravity down of services and selective participation: The form of "policommunity complexity" of urban community governance in China]. *Zhongguo xingzheng guanli, 409,* 54–61.

Wu, Y. (2020). *Shehui ruhe bei shengchan: chengshi jiceng shequ de zhili shijian* [How is society reproduced? A review of urban neighborhood governance]. *Huanan shifan daxue xuebao, 5,* 70–82.

Wu, Y., Chen, A., & Ni, R. (2019). *Zhuanye zhengzhi yu dangjian shehui gongzuo de zengneng moshi* [Professionalism, politics, and empowerment in Party-building social work]. *Shehui gongzuo, 5*, 76–87.

Xi, J. (2017). *Zai zhongguo gongchandang di shijiuci quanguo daibiao dahui shang de jianghua* [Presidential speech on the CCP's 19th National Congress]. CNR. http://news.cnr.cn/native/gd/20171027/t20171027_524003098.shtml

Xia, J. (2019). *Cong shequ fuwu dao shequ jianshe zaidao shequ zhili: woguo shequ fazhan de sange jieduan* [From Neighborhood service to neighborhood building to neighborhood governance: The three stages of neighborhood development in China]. *Gansu shehui kexue, 6*, 24–32.

Xiao, L. (2011). *Shequ yanjiu yu shequ yanjiu: jinnianlai woguo chengshi shequ yanjiu pingshu* [Community-based research and research of community: A literature review of urban neighborhoods in China]. *Shehuixue yanjiu, 4*, 185–208.

Xu, B., & Chen, W. (2017). *Jumin zizhi neijuanhua de genyuan* [Root causes of the involution of neighborhood self-governance]. *Chengshi wenti, 6*, 83–89.

Xu, X. (2018). *Shehui zuzhi qianru shequ zhili de xieshang liandong jizhi yanjiu* [A study on the cooperative and deliberative mechanisms of social organizations in neighborhood governance]. *Gonggong guanli xuebao, 15*, 96–107.

Xu, X., & Huang, J. (2020). *Cong zhengshe guanxi dao dangshe guanxi: shehui gongzuo jieru shequ zhili de qingjing bianqian yu lilun zhuanxiang* [From the government–nonprofit relationship to the Party–nonprofit organization relationship: The change to the context and theory of the application of social work in neighborhood governance]. *Shehui kexue, 3*, 68–85.

Xue, Z., & Sun, R. (2017). *Fenceng xiangmuzhi: shanghaishi tuijin zhengfu goumai gonggong fuwu de jingyan yu qishi* [Layered project-based management: Experience and lessons of promoting government procurement of public services in Shanghai]. *Shanghai xingzheng xueyuan xuebao, 18*, 50–58.

Yang, M. (2007). *Zuowei guojia zhili danwei de shequ* [Community as state governance unit]. *Shehuixue yanjiu, 4*, 137–164.

Zhang, C. (2018). *Zhongguo jumin shehui zhili manyidu jiqi wenti yanjiu* [Chinese citizens' satisfaction on social governance and the problems]. *Huadong shifan daxue xuebao, 6*, 144–152.

Zhang, D. (2020). *Dangling qunyi: xieshang xitong zhong shequ zhili de yinlingshi xieshang* [Mass deliberation under the Party's leadership: Exploring deliberation in neighborhood governance]. *Zhongzhou xuekan, 10*, 75–82.

Zhang, J. (2016). *Cong xingzheng fuquan dao falv fuquan: canyushi zhili chuangxin jiqi tiaoshi* [From administrative empowerment to legal empowerment: The innovation of local participatory governance and its adjustment]. *Sichuan daxue xuebao, 6*, 20–29.

Zhang, N. (2017). *Zhengfu shequ feizhengfu zuzhi hezuo de chengshi shequ canyushi zhili jizhi yanjiu* [Participatory governance in urban neighborhood: Building collaboration between the government, neighborhood, and nonprofit organizations]. *Zhongguo renmin daxue xuebao, 6*, 89–97.

Zheng, S. (1997). *Party vs. state in post-1949 China: The institutional dilemma.* Cambridge University Press.

Zhou, M., & Zhao, Z. (2010). *Jiceng zhengfu renyuan bianzhi yinxing pengzhang wenti yanjiu* [A study of hidden inflation of government staff at the grassroots]. *Zhongguo xingzheng guanli, 12,* 65–68.

Zhou, Q. (2016). *Lun zhongguo shequ zhili: cong weiquanshi zhili dao canyushi zhili* [Neighborhood governance in China: From authoritarian governance to participatory governance]. *Xuexi yu tansuo, 6,* 38–48.

Zhou, Q. (2017). *Lun jiceng shehui zizhi* [On society's self-governance at the grassroots]. *Huazhong shifan daxue xuebao, 56,* 1–11.

PART IV

Enterprise

16 A New Generation of Worker Cooperatives

Joan S. M. Meyers, Sanjay Pinto, Laura Hanson Schlachter, and Olga Prushinskaya

Introduction

Worker cooperatives are businesses collectively owned and democratically operated by their employees, functioning to address some of the basic problems of paid labor under capitalism, including: capital's extraction of the value produced through labor; the alienation arising from having one's labor directed by others; inequities based on race/ethnicity, gender, sexuality, national origin, dis/ability; and long-term damage to the natural environment for the sake of short-term economic gain. Worker cooperatives sit at the nexus of two organizational worlds. On the one hand, they are generally for-profit enterprises designed to generate value within capitalist markets. On the other, they challenge the extractive logic of capitalism by distributing ownership and control over the enterprise to their members. Like other businesses, worker cooperatives produce goods or services for financial benefit. However, the benefits derived from producing these goods or services are shared equitably among worker-owners rather than being transferred to external owners of capital. At their best, worker cooperatives allow individuals and communities to build wealth, stabilize social connections, and make informed decisions about economic activity while enriching the field of spaces in which democracy can be practiced.

Democratic worker ownership is relatively uncommon in a vastly capitalist world, and worker cooperatives are a smaller feature of the economic landscape in the US today than in many other parts of the world (Esim & Katajamaki, 2017). Yet worker cooperatives have a history dating back to the seventeenth century in the US (Knapp, 1968), and they were an important part of the US labor movement in the nineteenth century (Leikin, 2004). US worker cooperatives have often been founded in reaction to the inequities and instabilities of capitalist market development: for example, as a response to ongoing economic marginalization of African Americans during the century after the Civil War (Gordon Nembhard, 2014; White, 2018) and in different generational cohorts responding to periods of economic crisis including the Long Depression in the late 1800s, the 1930s Great Depression, financial and economic restructuring of the 1970s, and the Great Recession of the 2010s (Dickstein, 1991).

As a means of empowerment, worker cooperatives have historically offered not just material but also conceptual support for newly emerging social collectivities of waged workers (Gourevitch, 2013), Black Americans seeking greater autonomy within a structurally racist labor market (Du Bois, 1907), the involuntarily unemployed (Kerr & Taylor, 1935), feminists (Iannello, 1992), countercultural youth (Jackall & Crain, 1984), and many who straddle these and other categories simultaneously. Yet their record in addressing different forms of social inequality and marginalization has been uneven. For example, nineteenth-century labor republican cooperatives often excluded people of color and women (Gerteis, 2002; Marti, 1984). Self-help cooperatives of the Depression era relied on neighborhood labor pools and then-dominant family logics of a masculine provider and a feminine homemaker that reinforced white supremacy and patriarchy at least as much as they advanced ethnoracial and gender inclusion (Mitchell, 1973; Rose, 1990). And the countercultural collectives of the 1970s and 1980s replaced bureaucratic rules with friendship ties and unspoken assumptions that subtly yet unassailably reproduced White, middle-class norms and patterns of control (Davis, 2017; Mansbridge, 1980).

In this chapter, we start by describing the current landscape of worker cooperatives in the US. We then look at two contemporary worker cooperatives in New York City, identifying key differences in organizational structure and worker experience despite similar organizational goals and worker demographics: Golden Steps, a small and direct-democratic home care cooperative in the private-pay sector; and Cooperative Home Care Associates, a unionized agency in the public-pay sector that is the largest worker cooperative in the US, coupling representative democracy with a more conventional managerial structure. We then explore what these cooperatives tell us about empowerment of individuals and communities. Finally, we identify some lessons for both researchers and practitioners in terms of: how economic democracy can work within a capitalist economic and social order; what worker cooperatives can reveal about workplace diversity, equity, and inclusion; and what potential worker cooperatives hold for a more broadly imagined workers' movement.

Worker Cooperatives Today

Worker cooperatives hire waged and/or salaried employees like other firms but act as a form of collective self-employment. Most worker cooperatives follow the International Cooperative Alliance (2017) principle of voluntary and open membership in the ownership and democratic organizational control of their enterprise. Ownership is achieved through the purchase of *equity* in the cooperative, often in the form of a single member share, which can range in cost from the equivalent of an hour's to several months' earnings. Through this investment, workers share in the financial reward and risk of

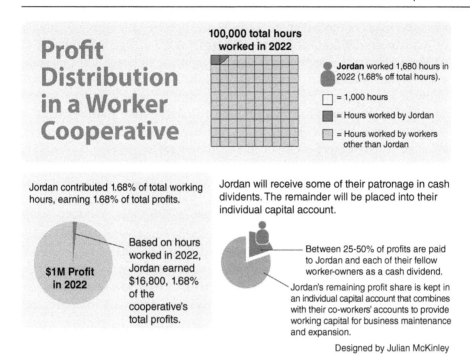

Figure 16.1 *Profit distribution in a worker cooperative.*

their cooperative. In this regard, worker cooperatives are similar to employee stock ownership plans (ESOPs), the most common form of worker ownership in the US, which benefit a firm's workers regardless of rank or title. But there are fundamental differences: ESOPs usually hold a minority share of companies traded on markets among nonemployee shareholders, generally allocate shares unequally (usually based on pay), and do not link ownership to wide-ranging governance rights.

Worker cooperative members derive economic benefits both in the form of wages or salaries based on their labor and profits from their role as owners. Wages or salaries may be equally apportioned or based on a mix of weekly hours, duties, and expertise. However, annual member profit-sharing, or *patronage*, tends to derive entirely from the proportion of hours each worker contributes to the collective whole (see Figure 16.1). Worker cooperatives typically bank a significant portion of collective profits in workers' individual *capital accounts*, using a portion of these funds as working capital for maintenance, improvements, or expansion and distributing the rest (typically between 20 and 50 percent of annual profits) as annual cash dividends.

Democratic control is typically distributed on a one-person, one-vote basis. Many worker cooperatives have fewer than ten members, and, in these organizations, democratic power is often exercised directly through flat management, where all major (and sometimes minor) decisions are made together either through a consensus or majoritarian process. Some cooperatives, including many of those that are larger in size, operate by more representative or parliamentarian forms of democratic governance, delegating authority to an elected board of directors or member committee. In larger firms, management of the enterprise is frequently separated from governance, but with ultimate authority still residing with the general membership: The general membership elects and can recall the board of directors, and the board of directors exerts ultimate hiring and firing power over upper management. Whether through more direct or representative routes, worker cooperatives transfer economic and political rights from capital to labor (Safri, 2020), challenging the typical worker/owner distinction (Ellerman, 1988). But there may be trade-offs between scale and depth. The 2021 national Cooperative Governance Research Initiative survey from the University of Wisconsin–Madison Center for Cooperatives found fairly equal numbers of worker cooperatives practicing direct versus representative democracy. Direct-democratic cooperatives were somewhat smaller in terms of total worker-owners, and somewhat more likely to report that internal discussions allow for healthy dissent and for workers to cultivate interpersonal dynamics that support effective decision-making.

Worker cooperatives are formed when workers pool resources to create a new collectively owned enterprise as a *start-up*, or buy out and reorganize an existing one as a *conversion*. Often these processes occur with the support of one of the many local, regional, or national cooperative development organizations located around the country, which provide various forms of technical assistance on incorporation, mobilizing capital and developing a business plan, and establishing organizational structures and bylaws. In the US, the legal-institutional framework for cooperative ownership is not currently standardized nationally. Depending on local laws and the needs of workers, worker cooperatives may be limited liability corporations, nonprofits, simple corporations, or cooperatives (Safri, 2020). While some worker cooperatives are co-owned by consumers or state entities, such multistakeholder enterprises are rare in the US (Martins Rodrigues & Schneider, 2021).

There are concentrations of worker cooperatives in South America (particularly Argentina and Venezuela), the South Asian subcontinent (particularly Bangladesh and India), Europe (particularly Italy and Spain), and, to a lesser extent, the US in North America (Eum, 2017). Although worker cooperatives are distributed across the US, the 2021 Economic Census of Worker Cooperatives and Democratic Workplaces indicates particularly high numbers in three geographic regions and four sectors: The San Francisco Bay Area, New York City, and Puerto Rico have the largest geographic clusters of worker cooperatives; and food and beverage, technology, consulting, and cleaning services have the highest industry concentrations (Democracy at Work Institute & US Federation of Worker Cooperatives, 2022). A total of 612 worker cooperatives and democratic workplaces were identified in the 2021 Economic Census, although the actual number of worker cooperatives in the US may be closer to 1,000. Worker cooperatives surveyed in the 2021 Economic Census employed an estimated 5,996 workers and produced over $283 million in revenue in the 2020 fiscal year. While these figures account for a small proportion of the estimated 32.5 million small businesses employing close to half of all US workers (Office of Advocacy, 2021), the total number of worker cooperatives has grown by 30 percent since the last census conducted in 2019 and by 100 percent since the first worker cooperative census effort in 2013 (Palmer, 2014). The 2021 Economic Census also indicates that most contemporary worker cooperatives are fairly new (started or converted less than five years earlier) and fairly small (median workforce of six, with gross annual earnings of $300,000).

In contrast to the historical underrepresentation of people of color in worker cooperatives in the US and the underrepresentation of White women prior to the countercultural cooperative wave of the 1970s, workers from these groups are somewhat overrepresented in US worker cooperatives today. Fifty-two percent identify as women compared to 47 percent in the US workforce as a whole, 25 percent as Hispanic or Latino/a/x compared to 18 percent of the US workforce, and 13 percent as Black or African American compared to 12 percent of the US workforce (Democracy at Work Institute & US Federation of Worker Cooperatives, 2022; US Bureau of Labor Statistics, 2022). This can be explained in part by the growth of worker cooperatives in areas of the labor market where, due to patterns of gender, racial, and ethnic segmentation, large numbers of women and people of color – particularly Latinas – are employed (Reibstein & Schlachter, 2022). There is also some evidence that contemporary worker cooperative members are more likely to come from working-class backgrounds (Meyers, 2022).

It remains unclear how the COVID-19 pandemic will affect worker cooperatives and their members over the long term. However, early research focusing on the first year of the pandemic indicates that cooperatives facing similar stresses as other small businesses were nonetheless more likely to prioritize worker safety and well-being, give and receive support from other local cooperatives and the community, and use non-layoff strategies to retain staff (Prushinskaya et al., 2021). The findings on retention accord with a robust body of historical evidence on the behavior of worker-owned enterprises during economic downturns (Burdín, 2014).

Examples from Home Care

Due to longer lifespans, the aging of the baby boomer generation, and the growing desire of many seniors to "age in place," demand for home care services – health assistance provided to seniors and persons with disabilities within their homes – has increased rapidly, with employment more than doubling in the past ten years and having the highest occupational growth projections in the US (PHI, 2020). Yet workers in this sector – disproportionately women of color, often from immigrant backgrounds – confront meager earnings, exclusion from basic labor and employment rights, and a lack of visibility connected to the long-standing racialized and gendered devaluation of care work (Berry & Schneider, 2011; Covington-Ward, 2021). In turn, these conditions contribute to high turnover and hamper the ability of workers to organize collectively, despite growing gaps between client demand and home care worker availability.

In this context, formation of worker cooperatives provides a vehicle for solidarity, mutualism, and empowerment. Throughout the post-2008 period of cooperative expansion, health care has continued to comprise 7 percent of US worker cooperatives (Palmer, 2014; Schlachter & Prushinskaya, 2021), and a recent report identified fourteen active home care worker cooperatives employing 2,640 workers in the US in 2020 (ICA Group, 2021), or roughly 0.1 percent of the home care workforce (PHI, 2020). This report found that these cooperatives had higher wages and job tenure than the industry average and lower rates of worker turnover, and they were mainly servicing public-pay clients (although private-pay markets were growing). In what follows, we focus on two home care worker cooperatives in the New York City area: Golden Steps, a small private-pay cooperative; and Cooperative Home Care Associates, by far the largest US worker cooperative, which primarily serves public-pay clients. Both cooperatives also embody the increased representation of women of color in the US worker cooperatives movement during recent years. These examples allow us to consider the potential of worker cooperatives for advancing voice and empowerment while addressing long-standing ethnoracial and gender inequities in the economy.

Golden Steps: Dignity and Protection for Immigrant Workers

Founded in 2012, Golden Steps is a Brooklyn-based worker cooperative of immigrant women of color, all of whom have roots in Central and South America and the Caribbean. Providing services to those who do not qualify for Medicare or need more than what Medicare will pay for, Golden Steps operates in a part of the market where home care workers are hired directly by private-pay clients and their families. Workers in this arena continue to labor under exclusions dating back to the 1930s, when Southern Democrats intent on maintaining the subjection of Black workers blocked the coverage of domestic workers in landmark New Deal labor and employment protections (Berry & Bell, 2018; Valocchi, 1994). In this context, forming worker cooperatives has proved to be one of the few available vehicles for organizing collectively and building a shared support structure.

Golden Steps, legally structured as a marketing referral cooperative, launched with the support of the Cooperative Development Program of the Center for Family Life, a social service organization that has helped develop twenty-one worker cooperatives since 2006 (Bransburg, 2011). Formed as part of the wave of worker cooperatives developed in the wake of the Great Recession, with particular clustering in New York City and other metro regions (Hudson, 2021), several members were already working in home care when they formed Golden Steps, while others joined the cooperative after being displaced by the closure of a local factory. By 2020, Golden Steps had fourteen members who provided home care services across the five boroughs of New York City. Although the COVID-19 pandemic made it difficult to maintain a private-pay clientele and the cooperative dropped to six members, in early 2022 Golden Steps started actively recruiting new members again.

Golden Steps members pay a monthly cooperative membership fee of $100 for access to ongoing training and back-office administrative services, keeping the rest of the hourly wages they earn from clients. Golden Steps uses direct democratic governance and management in its bimonthly general membership meetings and task-specific committees that allow – and require – all members to have a say in day-to-day and long-term operations. This democratic organization is a selling point for many clients. Of course, home care clients also act as employers in some sense, and Golden Steps' democratic structure cannot fully compensate for power imbalances underpinning these worker–client relationships. However, Golden Steps provides training in communication with clients and their families and a community in which members can share insights on building strong client relationships and establishing fair workplace conditions.

In addition to training and education on workers' rights and being a member of a cooperative enterprise, Golden Steps provides new members with much of the training that home health aides working in the publicly funded system receive. Through Golden Steps, members are certified in key skill areas (e.g., adult CPR and first aid, nutrition and food preparation, and preventing falls) that home care providers in the independent, private market must typically seek out and pay for on their own. Further, mirroring its commitment to internal equity and inclusion, the cooperative has also taken steps to better serve a diverse client base, including the specific needs of LGBTQ+ seniors. According to one Golden Steps member, this broad training and the ability to tailor services help attract clients, including many who qualify for publicly funded support but nevertheless pay out of pocket to engage Golden Steps.

Cooperative Home Care Associates: Scale and Unionization

Typically referred to by its acronym CHCA, Cooperative Home Care Associates was founded in 1985 with the goal of providing stable and dignified livelihoods for women in the home care field and offering a "high road" model for the industry. Home care services supported by Medicaid, Medicare, and other publicly funded programs – the terrain in which CHCA operates – are more highly regulated than those in the private-pay market and thus ensure a higher hourly base pay. However, workers in this arena also confront a variety of challenges. For example, policymakers have set reimbursement rates at low levels based in part on the assumption that women of color can provide these services cheaply, which holds down rates of pay. Indeed, it has been estimated that more than half of all public-pay home care workers must rely on social welfare programs themselves (PHI, 2020).

CHCA was founded by twelve worker-owners with support from an antipoverty nonprofit, the Community Service Society of New York City, as a worker cooperative to increase workers' organizational commitment, lower its operating costs, and improve its members' economic standing. CHCA has sought to reduce the scheduling volatility endemic in the industry and thus provide its more than 2,000 current workers with steadier paychecks (Berry & Schneider, 2011), leading to lower turnover rates than the industry norm. It offers profit-sharing to the half of its workforce who have elected to become members through the purchase of a $100 equity share, often paid off over extended payroll deductions (Pinto, 2021).

CHCA's approach from the outset has been to combine scale with representative democratic governance, and it has found new ways to advance worker voice and empowerment. In many ways, it is structured like a typical home care agency, with a hierarchical managerial structure and centralized administrative unit that today directs the work of some 2,000 care workers. However, unlike a traditional agency, management is accountable to a board of directors on which workers have a majority of seats (Pinto, 2023). CHCA also spends around 80 percent of its revenue on wages and benefits for frontline workers, and 45 percent of current administrative staff are former home care workers – figures that CHCA managers believe are higher than those of their competitors. Worker interests are also centered through its collective bargaining agreement with the health-care union 1199SEIU, which signed its first contract with CHCA in 2003.

Unionization gave cooperative members access to 1199SEIU's substantial fringe benefits and enabled CHCA to align itself with another important actor in the struggle to improve conditions for frontline health-care workers. While there were some initial challenges in reconciling the advocacy role of a union with the cooperative enterprise structure, the partnership has gelled and deepened over time. A labor management committee with representation from management, the union, and the general workforce now serves as a venue for problem-solving and conflict resolution. Unionization has solidified what Mandiberg and Kim (2021) describe as a "mutualist logic" of solidarity and decentralized support for workers. Recently, CHCA and 1199SEIU worked together in a "Fair Pay for Home Care" campaign in New York State, with the active involvement of several CHCA/1199SEIU members. Although the campaign did not achieve all of its demands, it won a $3 per hour pay increase for home care workers across the state.

Over time, CHCA has inspired other cooperative efforts in the long-term care arena. With PHI, the think tank it spawned in 1991, CHCA supported the development of a similar home care worker cooperative in Philadelphia and recently advised on the creation of a new "Trust for Workers" to jointly employ home care workers across Washington State. An exploratory committee within 1199SEIU is looking to extend the CHCA model to nursing homes. Amid the economic restructuring that is undercutting the position of the union in the long-term care arena, the committee sees worker cooperatives as part of a strategy to deepen worker voice and solidify the position of the union over the long run (Pinto, 2021).

Different Structures, Different Benefits

Situated in the same sector within the same city, Golden Steps and CHCA have fought to create financial stability and improved work life in an industry characterized by near-poverty wages and everyday indignities. Both have benefited from private and/or state funding for initial capitalization and the technical assistance of cooperative developers, and both were founded to empower low-income women of color through organizational forms that amplify their voice and leadership. Indeed, similar to recent trends in union growth (Milkman, 2006), historically marginalized and excluded workers may drive the growth of worker cooperatives in the US (Berry & Bell, 2018).

The two cooperatives have nonetheless followed distinct paths. Operating in the part of the market where individuals and households engage and pay for services directly, Golden Steps is more representative of the broader landscape of worker cooperatives in the US: relatively small, fairly new, and governed by the kind of direct democracy that provides a degree of collective voice rarely found in low-wage work in the informal sector. Its members appreciatively describe the sense of community and support developed in this small and personalistic kind of organization, and of learning not only caregiving skills but also leadership and business management. Yet sudden shifts in the physical and economic environment pose a real danger to the survival of smaller firms, as Golden Steps' significant staffing reductions during the pandemic show.

CHCA's management and governance, in contrast, are more similar to conventional managerial firms, reducing its members' workplace control but making it more legible to and congruent with the insurance companies that dominate the market in which it operates. CHCA's size also makes it an outlier among worker cooperatives, with its membership accounting for nearly one third of the total US worker cooperative workforce. Its scale makes it better able to absorb challenging market conditions by distributing lower revenues or lower demand across a much wider population than smaller cooperatives and to help shape debates about the future of the home care industry beyond the confines of the worker cooperative community. However, working in such a large organization may also generate the interpersonal estrangement typical of large firms. Further, as worker cooperative scholarship has observed with historical regularity (Kasmir, 1996; Kerr, 1939; Webb & Webb, 1897), the bureaucratization that seems to be required of large organizations can be at odds with the democratic character of cooperatives, allowing the inequalities of the capitalist labor market to be reproduced in terms of how pay, power, and autonomy are distributed.

Worker Cooperatives as Individual and Community Empowerment Strategies

Far from being merely a "boutique" approach to workplace and community problems – small, nonreplicable, and primarily serving elites – worker cooperatives like Golden Steps and CHCA demonstrate that worker cooperatives are flexible in form, provide reproducible egalitarian workplace models, and offer an important tool for marginalized communities. Worker cooperatives can advance community empowerment by providing direct benefits to individual community members, by transforming the ways in which critical goods and services are delivered within local communities, and by embodying alternatives to exploitation and powerlessness.

Empowerment of Individuals: Time and Money

As we see at Golden Steps and CHCA, worker-owners are invested with democratic workplace control (albeit to varying degrees) over how they set pay rates, interact with clients, schedule their shifts, solicit new business, increase their skills and capacities, and protect their safety. Many worker cooperatives give workers a fair degree of control over their scheduling, which both stabilizes weekly or biweekly earnings (Berry & Bell, 2018) and allows worker-owners precious time for family responsibilities, creative activities, or pure leisure (Meyers, 2022). In the broader universe of worker cooperatives, worker-owners exercise direct and/or representative democratic control over organizational processes such as production, distribution, sourcing, investment, and personnel policies – a form of empowerment often referenced by worker-owners as a key source of personal pride and feelings of efficacy (Berry, 2013). Compared to other enterprises, worker cooperatives are less likely to have the production process dictated by managers and more likely to elicit participative management in day-to-day work routines (Hoffmann, 2012). While the degree to which managers determine outcomes varies between a direct-democratic organization like Golden Steps and a representative-democratic one like CHCA, the one-person, one-vote democratic authority of the worker cooperative inverts the power hierarchy of investor-owned firms and makes it more likely that even managerial decisions are based in a logic of prioritizing the needs of workers.

In addition, collective ownership of their enterprises entitles worker-owners like those at Golden Steps and CHCA to receive the value of their labor via wages and profit-sharing. Worker-owners are also more likely to receive medical and retirement benefits than similar workers in noncooperative firms, as well as training in income-boosting skills (Berry & Bell, 2018). They are also less likely to be laid off. Having no outside investors or corporate boards demanding short-term profit distributions over long-term reinvestment, worker cooperatives are more likely to choose work-hour reductions over layoffs, reduced profit-sharing over closure, and – with the notable exception of the Mondragón Corporation[1] – local employment over offshore relocation (Craig & Pencavel, 1992). That both Golden Steps and CHCA survived the COVID-19 pandemic – when each care worker visit to a client's home was fraught with mutual concern about infection – suggests that this cooperative logic is well-suited to preserving both jobs and services in times of crisis (Prushinskaya et al., 2021).

Community Empowerment: Anchoring a Solidarity Economy

Yet individual empowerment is not the only – or perhaps even best – unit of analysis by which to assess empowerment; at the organizational level, worker cooperatives improve residential and occupational communities, industrial sectors, and the organization of work more generally. When worker cooperatives like Golden Steps and CHCA anchor jobs in specific places, they also anchor a community's wealth (Gordon Nembhard, 2014). When individual workers have more time for family, creative, and leisure pursuits, the community as a whole benefits from the love, art, and joy that are added to it (Jackall & Crain, 1984). When parents and grandparents are alive, healthy, and able to retire from paid labor, their unpaid caring weaves a net that can catch those knocked down by capitalism (Wilson, 1996). Worker cooperatives have also innovated and tested versions of distributed and participative workplace management that later showed up in mainstream workplaces as "high-performance work systems" (Appelbaum et al., 2000) or "holacracy" (Kumar & Mukherjee, 2018), developing now-common forms of workplace voice, self-efficacy, and dignity with noncooperative workers. The 1970s worker cooperative focus on "right livelihood," or activity that does not harm others (Schumacher, 1973), paved the way for the "benefit corporation," a legal entity that is required to

---

[1] The Mondragón Corporation of originally Basque cooperatives has pursued the incorporation of industries beyond its region since the 1960s, beyond its country since the 1990s, and beyond its continent since the 2000s, all in aid of increased competitiveness in a rapidly globalizing world and its mission of spreading worker ownership (Flecha & Ngai, 2014). However, to avoid dilution of its highly local cooperative culture, not all new international subsidiary workers have the same workplace rights as the core Basque cooperative members, which has raised concerns about the disconnect between the discourse and practice of workplace democracy (Bretos & Errasti, 2018). This example has had a chilling effect on cooperatives in other parts of the world considering international expansion.

consider the effects of their actions beyond corporate shareholders – which has in turn become an attractive designation for certain worker cooperatives (Berry & Bell, 2018).

At present, worker cooperatives have been engaging unions and social movements in what can be considered a broader "solidarity economy" – sometimes also called "social and solidarity economies" (Laville, 2015) or "community economies" (Gibson-Graham et al., 2017) – that conceptualizes an organization of economic activity rooted in anticapitalist logics, mutual support between oppressed groups, and environmental sustainability. CHCA was only one of several worker cooperatives that have unionized or been formed through union partnerships (Ji, 2016; Schlachter, 2017). The density of worker cooperatives in local solidarity economies may create better community resiliency (Schneiberg, 2021) and support activism (Roth, 2016), provide fresh food access in Black and Brown low-income urban and rural areas (Figueroa & Alkon, 2017; White, 2018) and more generally reduce institutional racism (Bell et al., 2018), and increase sustainable energy practices (Alperovitz et al., 2010) and reduce environmental harms (Wright, 2010).

Spillover or Selection? The Question of Political Engagement

For decades, scholars have looked to worker cooperatives as "schools of democracy" with the potential to generate attitudes and skills that support political engagement beyond the workplace (Pateman, 1970). Some empirical studies of the broader democracy-building effects of worker cooperatives have found support for this "civic spillover" hypothesis (Greenberg, 1986), and others have found that worker control in noncooperative firms also supports civic engagement outside the workplace (Budd et al., 2018). Yet, overall, this body of research is inconclusive: The majority of studies report mixed results (Greenberg 2008) or attribute a relationship between engagement on and off the clock to self-selection rather than spillover. For instance, Schlachter and Már (2022) find that activism is often a pathway to worker ownership, motivating individuals to opt into or create workplaces that allow them to pursue civic goals "on the clock."

However, even if worker cooperatives do not broadly transform their membership into more active participants in their communities, the cooperative itself provides examples and actions that can transform its economic and political environs. The examples of Golden Steps and CHCA show that workers form cooperatives for their economic and social empowerment, but these cooperatives also reveal dramatic shifts in how work and workers are conceptualized. As noted earlier, the larger labor movement as well as the worker cooperative movement historically battled over who was and was not included in the categories of workers and work: whether explicitly by race, gender, and nationality or implicitly in terms of whether work was traditionally waged (like increasingly masculinized and White-dominated factory labor) or unwaged (like both consistently feminized care work and the share-cropping agricultural labor that segregation forced the majority of Black adults to take up). Contemporary worker cooperatives are not merely less White and less dominated by men than the workforce as a whole but more explicitly expand the range of what legitimately counts as workers' interests to include environmental sustainability, scheduling autonomy to balance family responsibility, and practices to create gender and ethnoracial justice. That is, contemporary worker cooperatives such as Golden Steps and CHCA aim for empowerment – albeit differently – across individuals and communities.

Application and Future Research

There are, of course, limitations to what worker cooperatives offer: There is no single solution to the nexus of capitalism, managerialism, racism, sexism, and anti-immigrant state and community actions. As relatively uncommon enterprises that are rarely on business school syllabi (Parker, 2018), new worker cooperatives struggle to find funding and may be doomed by starting out undercapitalized (Hoover, 2018). Democratic workplace governance and/or management require skills most people never learn in schools or civic organizations (Mansbridge, 1980), and shifting the logic of profit as the singular goal of an economic enterprise requires significant discursive work (Gibson-Graham et al., 2017). The deep penetration of assumptions about gender, ethnicity and race, and class into the division of labor and the very essence of what it means to be a worker can easily become reproduced within cooperatives (Meyers & Vallas, 2016), and the state's construction of citizenship as central to employment may put cooperative workers at odds with each other (Alvarez, 2017).

Yet worker cooperatives have an important role in discussions of economic empowerment and community economic development. They have persistently been at the center of debates regarding the benefits of democratic engagement and workplace egalitarianism. And, while largely absent from labor movement conversations since the turn of the twentieth century, they have lately been returning to that fold (Ji, 2016).

Capitalism and Democratic Egalitarian Enterprises

Despite noted economic advantages to both workers and firms when democratic control is linked to worker ownership (Dube & Freeman, 2010) and when both are linked to social justice (Burdín, 2014), such combinations also produce tensions between a business ethos of efficient management for profit and a social ethos of self-rule and egalitarian distributions of wealth. For over 100 years, even supportive observers have noted how difficult it can be for worker cooperatives to preserve workplace democracy and egalitarianism and resist self-exploitation within a society and market predicated on inequality (Webb & Webb, 1920; Luxemburg, 2006). Indeed, the success of worker cooperatives seems to require confronting tough questions: Does compensating workers for the true value of their labor leave an enterprise undercapitalized and vulnerable to shifts in the market? Does the slower decision-making process of direct-democratic firms undermine their ability to compete with nondemocratic and hierarchical ones? The success of worker cooperatives depends in part on addressing such questions.

Along with the more than 100 US worker cooperatives in operation for more than twenty years (Palmer, 2020), Golden Steps and CHCA offer a resounding "no" to both questions. For these two cooperatives, part of the reason may be that the care work market has always been characterized by a tension between, on the one hand, the routinization and impersonal standardization of care that results from a cost-cutting model (Boris & Klein, 2012) and, on the other, a desire by clients and workers to cultivate authentically caring relations (Stacey, 2011). Some cooperatives in the publicly funded system such as CHCA have married the streamlining of bureaucracy to the connection of participatory workplace control in a nonhierarchical but formalized "participatory bureaucracy" (Meyers, 2022), while others such as Golden Steps, operating in the private-pay system, have countered the isolation of this context through smaller-scale collectivism. Rather than trying and failing to approximate non-worker-controlled firms, worker cooperatives have developed new forms of economic democracy that provide material, social, and development support for their members. For those seeking to understand worker participation – scholars as well as workforce developers and employer consultants – this underscores the necessity of including worker cooperatives in all considerations of the topic. Although worker cooperatives are a small fraction of workplaces and employ an even smaller fraction of workers, they offer "real utopian" (Wright, 2010) visions of how economic activity could be practically coordinated for the broader empowerment of workers and the communities in which they are embedded. In the US, worker cooperatives are critical models for how labor can be coordinated, worker skills and capacities can be developed, and social connections that are too often stripped away in typical jobs, particularly low-wage employment, can be restored.

Both Golden Steps and CHCA were founded with the help of nonprofit workforce development agencies, lending empirical support to claims that worker cooperative development is a viable solution to employment issues among the urban poor (Berry & Bell, 2018) and suggesting that the mobilization of philanthropic investment could expand the footprint of cooperatives in the future (Pinto et al., 2021). Organizations that help to incubate worker cooperatives might do well, of course, to absorb the histories of damages wrought by professional do-gooders and proceed with caution (Funicello, 1993). However, the success and social impact of worker cooperatives such as Golden Steps and CHCA suggest the benefits of municipal, state, and federal policies that could encourage workers to form their own cooperatives: not only legal structures to streamline incorporation across those different levels of tax codes, but also tax credits and rebates for cooperative start-ups and succession, loan policies written with cooperative ownership in mind, preferential status for those whose goods and services are purchased through government-supported programs, and municipal investment in cooperative "ecosystems" of mutually supportive private and public institutions such as the Cleveland Model (Alperovitz et al., 2010) or the Los Angeles Union Cooperative Initiative.

Modeling Workplace Approaches to Diversity, Equity, and Inclusion

Research shows that contemporary worker cooperatives have also taken decades of critique regarding workplace gender, ethnicity/race, class, and sexuality inequality to heart (e.g., Bell et al., 2018). The Diversity, Equity, & Inclusion Trends in the Cooperative Community study (Schlachter, 2021) found that worker cooperatives are more likely than other types of cooperatives to systematically track data about members' demographic characteristics, evaluate their organizational culture of inclusion, and adopt statements in support of diversity, equity, and inclusion. They are also more likely to change organizational practices to recruit from excluded and marginalized groups, offer the kinds of paid leave that can compensate for gendered inequalities of caretaking responsibilities, and provide material support or partnership with local community social justice campaigns and organizations. Exemplified by Golden Steps and CHCA, contemporary worker cooperatives have preserved their high rates of labor force participation by women, are (as noted earlier) more ethnoracially diverse than either previous cooperative generations or the US labor force, and are also more likely to include people from working-class backgrounds than worker cooperatives of the past fifty years.

Both Golden Steps and CHCA are largely composed of immigrant women of color, part of a larger wave of women and BIPOC-led organizations that have contributed to the diversity of the contemporary US worker cooperative movement. Many individual worker cooperatives are also diverse along ethnoracial and other lines and have made explicit commitments to equity and inclusion, providing a refutation of earlier claims that worker cooperative success requires demographic homogeneity (e.g., Pencavel, 2001). A growing number of practitioners and policymakers are recognizing that worker cooperatives can be vehicles for greater diversity, equity, and inclusion – of race and ethnicity, yes, but also of class, gender, sexuality, citizenship status, and dis/ability – and can also promote more egalitarian conditions within capitalism.

At the same time, given the historical inequalities of US worker cooperatives described earlier in this chapter, researchers must attend to the degree to which inclusion and equity follow demographic diversity. Yes, this post-2008 "solidarity" generation of worker cooperatives is far more rooted in working-class occupations and in Black and Brown communities than the counter-cultural collectivist generation of the 1970s and 1980s. And, yes, this generation is far more integrated by race/ethnicity and gender than either the enduring African American tradition or the White- and male-dominated self-help generation of the 1930s or the labor republican generation of the 1870s–1890s. But it is still too early to tell whether more inclusion and less segregation will reduce or reproduce the workplace inequalities of earnings, autonomy, and/or power that attach to strong divisions of labor and the gendered and ethnoracialized valuation of "skill" (Tomaskovic-Devey & Avent-Holt, 2019). Future scholarship can explore how and under what conditions worker cooperatives are capable of disrupting the central role workplaces play in maintaining and exacerbating the unequal and unjust social order in which we live.

Unions and Worker Cooperatives Return to the Roots

One place where the current generation of worker cooperatives may address these complex and intersectional inequalities is with the labor movement. CHCA's unionization is not unique: Contemporary worker cooperatives are also more likely to be connected to organized labor than any generation of worker cooperatives since they emerged as a force within the late nineteenth-century era of labor republicanism. Recently, cooperatives and unions have been reaching across the historic divides of both Samuel Gompers' trade-specific and wage-oriented unionism (Polletta, 2002) and the postwar business–labor accord (Lichtenstein, 2012) to explore the common ground of workers' rights and workplace voice (Pinto, 2021). From the 2009 collaboration agreement of the United Steelworkers with the Mondragón Corporation (Witherell, 2013), to the New Era Windows and Doors cooperative collectively bargained by United Electrical, Radio, and Machine Workers of America in Chicago (Mulder, 2015), to the multiunion food and sustainable energy cooperatives of Co-op Cincy (Schlacter, 2017), to Maine's Lobster 207 producer cooperative supported by the International Association of Machinists (Arvins et al., 2018), to half a dozen taxi and ride-hailing cooperatives supported by national and local unions (Borowiak & Ji, 2019), unions and cooperators are collaborating toward shared goals of empowering workers and preserving good jobs within local communities.

There are other areas of new growth in union cooperatives, some of which incorporate the lessons of scale learned from CHCA. These include: AlliedUp, a health-care staffing worker cooperative developed with support from the Service Employees International Union (SEIU) United Healthcare Worker West; Community Safety Specialists, a community safety cooperative in Minneapolis developed with support from SEIU Local 26 as an alternative to traditional policing; and a newly forming immigrant construction worker cooperative in Central Falls, Rhode Island, developed through a partnership between the Fuerza Laboral, a local worker center, and District Council 11 of the International Union of Painters and Allied Trades. These new models seek to combine the benefits of scale and standardization with deep democracy at the local level.

Such a folding of worker cooperatives back into the labor movement has the potential to cement their status as a form of resistance to modes of capitalist development that have increased social inequalities and eroded the foundations of local communities. As the established labor movement seeks new ways to retain its foothold while expanding worker voice, the scaled-up union model provided by CHCA may offer a reconception of the labor movement as existing beyond the borders of unions. For cooperative developers, union partnerships can provide political might as well as access to health-care benefits, but perhaps more importantly they preserve the "worker" orientation of the worker-owner model. Solidarity is built through a movement that encompasses multiple kinds of people, organizations, and strategies for a more just world.

As these new models of worker cooperative/union partnership emerge and evolve, it will be important for labor scholarship to watch whether and how they blend logics of direct and representative democracy while negotiating the rigors of contemporary capitalist markets. Scale has become an increasingly central concern among cooperative developers (Spicer & Kay, 2022) – although not without some contestation (Alperovitz, 2011) – and challenges have been mounted to the claim that the bureaucratic apparatus required to manage large organizations inherently undermines democracy and egalitarian distributions of power and wealth (Malleson, 2014; Meyers, 2022). While tethering wealth to the communities that generate it is valuable in itself, the protection and promotion of grassroots democratic action has the additional benefit of normalizing community control of the institutions that shape people's lives, including the institution of work.

Worker cooperatives are economic entities that offer vast potential for social transformations: how resources are allocated, how recognition is granted, and what labor means and does in a given society. While worker ownership does not guarantee greater and more egalitarian empowerment, it provides opportunities not available elsewhere. Historically and in the present moment, worker cooperatives widen the repertoire of workplace and community empowerment.

References

Alperovitz, G. (2011). The new-economy movement. *The Nation 292*(24), 20–24.
Alperovitz, G., Howard, T., & Williamson, T. (2010). The Cleveland model. *The Nation*, *290*(8), 21–24.

Alvarez, A. (2017). Lawyers, organizers, and workers: Collaboration and conflict in worker cooperative development. *Georgetown Journal on Poverty Law & Policy*, *24*(3), 353–380.

Appelbaum, E., Bailey, T., Berg, P., & Kalleberg, A. L. (2000). *Manufacturing advantage: Why high-performance work systems pay off*. Cornell University Press.

Arvins, J., Larcom, M., & Weissbourd, J. (2018). *New forms of worker voice in the 21st century*. Harvard Kennedy School of Government and MIT Sloan School of Management Working Paper. https://mitsloan.mit.edu/shared/ods/documents? DocumentID=4475

Bell, M. P., Leopold, J., Berry, D., & Hall, A. V. (2018). Diversity, discrimination, and persistent inequality: Hope for the future through the solidarity economy movement. *Journal of Social Issues*, *74*(2), 224–243.

Berry, D. (2013). Effects of cooperative membership and participation in decision making on job satisfaction of home health aides. In D. Kruse (Ed.), *Sharing ownership, profits, and decision-making in the 21st century* (pp. 3–25), Emerald Group.

Berry, D., & Bell, M. P. (2018). Worker cooperatives: Alternative governance for caring and precarious work. *Equality, Diversity and Inclusion: An International Journal*, *37*(4), 376–391.

Berry, D. P., & Schneider, S. (2011). Improving the quality of home health aide jobs: A collaboration between organized labor and a worker cooperative. In E. J. Carberry (Ed.), *Employee ownership and shared capitalism: New directions in research* (pp. 59–89). Labor and Employment Relations Association.

Boris, E., & Klein, J. (2012). *Caring for America: Home health workers in the shadow of the welfare state*. Oxford University Press.

Borowiak, C., & Ji, M. (2019). Taxi co-ops versus Uber: Struggles for workplace democracy in the sharing economy. *Journal of Labor and Society*, *21*(1), 1–21.

Bransburg, V. (2011, April 19). *The Center for Family Life: Tackling poverty and social isolation in Brooklyn with worker cooperatives*. Grassroots Economic Organizing (GEO) Newsletter. https://geo.coop/articles/center-family-life-tackling-poverty-and-social-isolation-brooklyn-worker-cooperatives

Bretos, I., & Errasti, A. (2018). The challenges of managing across borders in worker cooperatives: Insights from the Mondragon Cooperative Group. *Journal of Co-operative Organization and Management*, *6*(1), 34–42.

Budd, J., Lamare, R., & Timming, A. (2018). Learning about democracy at work: Cross-sectional evidence on individual employee voice influencing political participation in civil society. *ILR Review*, *71*(4), 956–985.

Burdín, G. (2014). Are worker-managed firms more likely to fail than conventional enterprises? Evidence from Uruguay. *ILR Review*, *67*(1), 202–238.

Covington-Ward, Y. (2021). Bodily burdens: Physical abuse, workplace injury, and understanding intersectionality through the experiences of African immigrant direct care health workers. *Transforming Anthropology*, *29*(2), 115–126.

Craig, B., & Pencavel, J. (1992). The behavior of worker cooperatives: The plywood companies of the Pacific Northwest. *The American Economic Review*, *82*(5), 1083–1105.

Davis, J. C. (2017). *From head shops to whole foods: The rise and fall of activist entrepreneurs*. Columbia University Press.

Democracy at Work Institute, & US Federation of Worker Cooperatives. (2022). *2021 State of the sector: Worker cooperatives in the U.S.* Democracy at Work Institute. https://institute.coop/resources/2021-worker-cooperative-state-sector-report

Dickstein, C. (1991). The promise and problem of worker cooperatives. *Journal of Planning Literature, 6*(1), 16–33.

Du Bois, W. E. B. (1907). *Economic co-operation among Negro Americans.* Atlanta University Press.

Dube, A., & Freeman, R. B. (2010). Complementarity of shared compensation and decision-making systems: Evidence from the American labor market. In D. L. Kruse, R. B. Freeman, & J. R. Blasi (Eds.), *Shared capitalism at work: Employee ownership, profit and gain sharing, and broad-based stock options* (pp. 167–199). University of Chicago Press.

Ellerman, D. P. (1988). The legitimate opposition at work: The union's role in large democratic firms. *Economic and Industrial Democracy, 9*(4), 437–453.

Esim, S., & Katajamaki, W. (2017). Rediscovering worker cooperatives in a changing world. *IUSLabor, 3*, 1–8.

Eum, H. (2017, January 26). *Cooperatives and employment: Second global report 2017.* CICOPA. www.cicopa.coop/publications/second-global-report-on-cooperatives-and-employment/

Figueroa, M., & Alkon, A. H. (2017). Cooperative social practices, self-determination, and the struggle for food justice in Oakland and Chicago. In A. H. Alkon & J. Guthman (Eds.), *The new food activism* (1st ed., pp. 206–231). University of California Press.

Flecha, R., & Ngai, P. (2014). The challenge for Mondragon: Searching for the cooperative values in times of internationalization. *Organization, 21*(5), 666–682.

Funicello, T. (1993). *Tyranny of kindness: Dismantling the welfare system to end poverty in America.* Atlantic Monthly Press.

Gerteis, J. (2002). The possession of civic virtue: Movement narratives of race and class in the Knights of Labor. *American Journal of Sociology, 108*(3), 580–615.

Gibson-Graham, J., Cameron, J., Dombroski, K., Healy, S., & Miller, E. (2017). *Cultivating community economies: Tools for building a liveable world.* The Next System Project. https://thenextsystem.org/cultivating-community-economies

Gordon Nembhard, J. (2014). *Collective courage: A history of African American cooperative economic thought and practice.* Pennsylvania State University Press.

Gourevitch, A. (2013). Labor republicanism and the transformation of work. *Political Theory, 41*(4), 591–617.

Greenberg, E. S. (1986). *Workplace democracy: The political effects of participation.* Cornell University Press.

Greenberg, E. S. (2008). Spillovers from cooperative and democratic workplaces: Have the benefits been oversold? In B. Sullivan, M. Snyder, & J. Sullivan (Eds.), *Cooperation: The political psychology of effective human interaction* (pp. 219–239). Wiley-Blackwell.

Hoffmann, E. A. (2012). *Co-operative workplace dispute resolution: Organizational structure, ownership, and ideology.* Gower.

Hoover, M. (2018). Converting employees to owners: Deeper investment for deeper impact. In C. E. V. Horn (Ed.), *Investing in work* (pp. 115–128). W.E. Upjohn Institute for Employment Research.

Hudson, L. (2021). New York City: Struggles over the narrative of the solidarity economy. *Geoforum, 127*, 326–334.

Iannello, K. P. (1992). *Decisions without hierarchy: Feminist interventions in organization theory and practice*. Routledge.

ICA Group. (2021). 2020 homecare cooperative benchmarking report: By the numbers: Successes and continuing challenges. ICA Group. https://icagroup .org/wp-content/uploads/2021/09/5465_HC_2020-BenchmarkingReport_9.20 .21.pdf

International Cooperative Alliance. (2017, January 3). *Guidance notes to the co-operative principles*. International Cooperative Alliance. www.ica.coop/en/ media/library/research-and-reviews/guidance-notes-cooperative-principles

Jackall, R., & Crain, J. (1984). The shape of the small worker cooperative movement. In R. Jackall (Ed.), *Worker cooperatives in America* (pp. 88–104). University of California Press.

Ji, M. (2016). Revolution or reform? Union–worker cooperative relations in the United States and Korea. *Labor Studies Journal, 41*(4), 355–376.

Kasmir, S. (1996). *The myth of Mondragón: Cooperatives, politics, and working-class life in a Basque town*. State University of New York Press.

Kerr, C. (1939). *Productive enterprises of the unemployed: 1931–1938*. University of California.

Kerr, C., & Taylor, P. S. (1935). *The self-help cooperatives in California*. Regents of the University of California.

Knapp, J. G. (1968). *The rise of American cooperative enterprise: 1620–1920*. Interstate Printers and Publishers.

Kumar, V. S., & Mukherjee, S. (2018). Holacracy – The future of organizing? The case of Zappos. *Human Resource Management International Digest, 26*(7), 12–15.

Laville, J.-L. (2015). Social and solidarity economy in historical perspective. In P. Utting (Ed.), *Social and solidarity economy: Beyond the fringe* (pp. 41–56). Zed Books.

Leikin, S. B. (2004). *The practical utopians: American workers and the cooperative movement in the Gilded Age*. Wayne State University Press.

Lichtenstein, N. (2012). *State of the Union: A century of American labor*. Princeton University Press.

Luxemburg, R. (2006). *Reform or revolution and other writings*. Dover Publications, Inc.

Malleson, T. (2014). *After Occupy: Economic democracy for the 21st century*. Oxford University Press.

Mandiberg, J. M., & Kim, S. M. (2021). A matrix form of multi-organizational hybridity in a cooperative–union venture. In K. K. Chen & V. T. Chen (Eds.), *Organizational imaginaries: Tempering capitalism and tending to communities through cooperatives and collectivist democracy* (Research in the Sociology of Organizations, Vol. 72, pp. 141–162). Emerald Publishing Ltd.

Mansbridge, J. J. (1980). *Beyond adversary democracy*. Basic Books, Inc.

Marti, D. B. (1984). Sisters of the Grange: Rural feminism in the late nineteenth century. *Agricultural History*, *58*(3), 247–261.

Martins Rodrigues, J., & Schneider, N. (2021). Scaling co-operatives through a multi-stakeholder network: A case study in the Colorado solar energy industry. *Journal of Entrepreneurial and Organizational Diversity*, *10*(2), 29–53.

Meyers, J. S. M. (2022). *Working democracies: Managing inequality in worker cooperatives*. ILR Press, an imprint of Cornell University Press.

Meyers, J. S. M., & Vallas, S. P. (2016). Diversity regimes in worker cooperatives: Workplace inequality under conditions of worker control. *The Sociological Quarterly*, *57*(1), 98–128.

Milkman, R. (2006). *LA story: Immigrant workers and the future of the US labor movement*. Russell Sage Foundation.

Mitchell, H. L. (1973). The founding and early history of the Southern Tenant Farmers Union. *The Arkansas Historical Quarterly*, *32*(4), 342–369.

Mulder, C. P. (2015). *Transcending capitalism through cooperative practices*. Palgrave Macmillan.

Office of Advocacy. (2021). *2021 Small business profile*. US Small Business Administration.

Palmer, T. C. (2014). *Democratic workplace ownership after the Great Recession: An economic overview of U.S. worker cooperatives in 2013*. Democracy at Work Institute.

Palmer, T. C. (2020). *2019 Worker cooperative state of the sector report*. Democracy at Work Institute. https://institute.coop/resources/2019-worker-cooperative-state-sector-report

Parker, M. (2018). *Shut down the business school: What's wrong with management education*. Pluto Press.

Pateman, C. (1970). *Participation and democratic theory*. Cambridge University Press.

Pencavel, J. (2001). *Worker participation: Lessons from the worker co-ops of the Pacific Northwest*. Russell Sage Foundation.

PHI. (2020, September 8). *Direct care workers in the United States: Key facts*. PHI. www.phinational.org/resource/direct-care-workers-in-the-united-states-key-facts/

Pinto, S. (2021). Economic democracy, embodied: A union co-op strategy for the long-term care sector. In K. K. Chen & V. T. Chen (Eds.), *Organizational imaginaries: Tempering capitalism and tending to communities through cooperatives and collectivist democracy* (Research in the Sociology of Organizations, Vol. 72, pp. 163–184). Emerald Publishing Ltd.

Pinto, S. (2023). Cooperative home care associates. In A. Scharf (Ed.), *Just health: Case studies of worker cooperatives in health and care sectors* (pp. 40–47). Institute for the Study of Employee Ownership and Profit Sharing, Rutgers School of Management and Labor Relations.

Pinto, S., Kerr, C., & Criscietello, R. (2021, December). *Shifting power, meeting the moment: Worker ownership as a strategic tool for the labor movement*. Rutgers School of Management and Labor Relations. https://cleo.rutgers.edu/articles/shifting-power-meeting-the-moment-worker-ownership-as-a-strategy-tool-for-the-labor-movement

Polletta, F. (2002). *Freedom is an endless meeting: Democracy in American social movements*. University of Chicago Press.

Prushinskaya, O., Pockrandt, J., McKinley, J., & Hoover, M. (2021). When workers matter most: A study of worker cooperatives and the prioritization of workers through COVID-19. *Journal of Participation and Employee Ownership, 4*(2), 106–115.

Reibstein, S., & Schlachter, L. H. (2022). *Gender- and race-based inequalities in democratic worker-owned firms: Evidence from the first national survey of the sector*. Rutgers School of Management and Labor Relations. https://cleo.rutgers.edu/articles/gender-and-race-based-inequalities-in-democratic-worker-owned-firms-evidence-from-the-first-national-survey-of-the-sector/

Rose, N. E. (1990). Discrimination against women in New Deal work programs. *Affilia, 5*(2), 25–45.

Roth, S. (2016). Professionalisation and precariousness: Perspectives on the sustainability of activism in everyday life. *Interface: A Journal for and about Social Movements, 8*(2), 29–58.

Safri, M. (2020). Worker cooperatives. In J. K. Gibson-Graham & K. Dombroski (Eds.), *Handbook of diverse economies* (pp. 40–47). Edward Elgar Publishing.

Schlachter, L. H. (2017). Stronger together? The USW–Mondragon union co-op model. *Labor Studies Journal, 42*(2), 124–147.

Schlachter, L. H. (2021). *Diversity, equity, and inclusion trends in the cooperative community*. National Cooperative Business Association CLUSA International. https://ncbaclusa.coop/diversity-equity-inclusion-trends-in-the-cooperative-community/

Schlachter, L. H., & Már, K. (2022). *Spillover or enrichment? Workplace and civic participation in democratic firms*. SocArXiv. https://osf.io/preprints/socarxiv/684tf/

Schlachter, L. H., & Prushinskaya, O. (2021). *How economic democracy impacts workers, firms, and communities: The census of individual workers in worker cooperatives*. Democracy at Work Institute. https://institute.coop/resources/how-economic-democracy-impacts-workers-firms-and-communities

Schneiberg, M. (2021). Organizational infrastructures for economic resilience: Alternatives to shareholder value-oriented corporations and unemployment trajectories in the US during the Great Recession. In K. K. Chen & V. T. Chen (Eds.), *Organizational imaginaries: Tempering capitalism and tending to communities through cooperatives and collectivist democracy* (Research in the Sociology of Organizations, Vol. 72, pp. 187–228). Emerald Publishing Ltd.

Schumacher, E. F. (1973). *Small is beautiful: Economics as if people mattered*. Harper & Row.

Spicer, J., & Kay, T. (2022). Another organization is possible: New directions in research on alternative enterprise. *Sociology Compass, 16*(3), e12963.

Stacey, C. L. (2011). *The caring self: The work experiences of home care aides*. ILR Press, an imprint of Cornell University Press.

Tomaskovic-Devey, D., & Avent-Holt, D. (2019). *Relational inequalities: An organizational approach*. Oxford University Press.

US Bureau of Labor Statistics. (2022). *Household data averages: Employed persons by detailed occupation, sex, race, and Hispanic or Latino ethnicity*. US Bureau of Labor Statistics. www.bls.gov/cps/cpsaat11.htm

Valocchi, S. (1994). The racial basis of capitalism and the state, and the impact of the New Deal on African Americans. *Social Problems, 41*(3), 347–362.

Webb, S., & Webb, B. P. (1897). *Industrial democracy*. Longmans, Green and Co.

Webb, S., & Webb, B. P. (1920). *A constitution of the socialist commonwealth of Great Britain*. Longmans, Green and Co.

White, M. M. (2018). *Freedom farmers: Agricultural resistance and the Black freedom movement*. University of North Carolina Press.

Wilson, W. J. (1996). *When work disappears: The world of the new urban poor*. Alfred A. Knopf.

Witherell, R. (2013). An emerging solidarity: Worker cooperatives, unions, and the new union cooperative model in the United States. *International Journal of Labour Research, 5*(2), 251–268.

Wright, E. O. (2010). *Envisioning real utopias*. Verso.

17 Employment Social Enterprises

Kymberly L. Byrd and Rasheda L. Weaver

Introduction

Social enterprises can be broadly defined as mission-driven organizations that utilize market-based strategies to achieve a social aim (Martin & Osberg, 2007). The organizations have both a social and economic bottom line, which involve creating social value (e.g., reducing unemployment) and generating revenue to fund the social enterprise's programs and services (Austin et al., 2006; Fruchterman, 2011; Weaver, 2016). Social enterprises can operate as not-for-profit organizations or for-profit businesses (Martin & Osberg, 2007). Those that combine not-for-profit and for-profit models are often labeled "hybrid organizations" (Battilana et al., 2012; Murray, 2012; Weaver, 2016).

This chapter focuses on a particular type of social enterprise called employment social enterprises (ESEs), which provide employment opportunities to individuals experiencing marginalization and exclusion in the labor market (Mandiberg, 2016). It is not known exactly what proportion of social enterprises are ESEs, but Weaver's 2019 study of 115 US social enterprises found that 30 percent were focused on providing employment opportunites to marginalized populations. Employment social enterprises across the US employ chronically unemployed and underemployed individuals, including formerly incarcerated individuals, immigrants, opportunity youth, individuals experiencing mental health issues, individuals in recovery, and individuals with disabilities (Hazenberg et al., 2012; Spear & Bidet, 2005; Vilà et al., 2007; Warner & Mandiberg, 2006). Many ESEs also provide wraparound services to their employees, which are individualized services "wrapped" around an individual to address their needs in a comprehensive manner (Lysaght et al., 2018; Stambaugh et al., 2007). In the social enterprise literature, these organizations are also referred to as work integration social enterprises (WISEs) (Cooney 2013, 2015), social firms (Lysaght et al., 2018), affirmative businesses (Warner & Mandiberg, 2006), and social purpose businesses (Cooney, 2011b). Nomenclature differs across different countries. Outside of the US, many of these terms are used interchangeably. In the US, the label of "employment social enterprise" helps to describe the function and aim of these organizations.

Sheltered workshops – the earliest form of ESEs – first emerged in the US in the late nineteenth century. They operated on the assumption that individuals with intellectual and physical disabilities needed separate, sheltered alternatives to the labor market (Cooney, 2016). These models relied on private charity instead of public subsidies and were "shaped by normative beliefs about the inherent value of work, concerns about idleness, and beliefs about the lower productivity levels of intellectually and physically disadvantaged populations" (Cooney, 2016, p. 441). The sheltered workshop model has since evolved amid concerns about discrimination and efforts focused on community integration (Cooney, 2016; Mandiberg, 1999; Mandiberg & Warner, 2012).

A newer model of ESEs gained traction in the 1980s and expanded in the succeeding decades during the neoliberal restructuring of the welfare state. This restructuring resulted in the erosion of income supports for individuals receiving welfare (Brenner & Theodore, 2002; Cooney, 2016; Garrow & Hasenfeld, 2014). This policy shift is encapsulated by the 1996 Personal Responsibility and Work Opportunity Reconciliation Act (PRWORA), which replaced Aid to Families with Dependent Children (AFDC) with Temporary Aid for Needy Families (TANF). Under PRWORA, cash entitlement programs were transformed and replaced with a welfare-to-work program that had lifetime limits for aid (Cooney, 2016; Danziger & Lehman, 1996; Riccio & Orenstein, 1996).

The ESEs that emerged during this era were often not-for-profit retailers, restaurants, and custodial or landscaping businesses focused concurrently on revenue generation and workforce development (Cooney, 2011a, 2016). They often targeted chronically unemployed and underemployed populations, such as individuals in recovery, formerly incarcerated individuals, and opportunity youth. These organizations were deemed innovators for merging commercial activity with social service delivery and heralded for offering employment opportunities during a time when welfare policies began to require employment (Cooney, 2016; Shore, 2003).

Data on the number and types of social enterprises within and across countries are scarce. A study by Spear and Bidet (2005) identified more than 14,000 WISEs across twelve European countries. In 2017, approximately 70 percent of Hong Kong's 600 social enterprises could be categorized as WISEs (Leung et al., 2019). While data are not available on the exact number of ESEs in the US, examining the Roberts Enterprise Development Fund's (REDF) work provides a glimpse into the impacts of these organizations. The REDF is a venture philanthropy organization that has invested in 219 ESEs in thirty states since 1997. These ESEs have employed over 73,000 people, who have earned over $68 million in collective wages. On average, these employees earn 123 percent of the minimum wage in their first job after working in the ESE. These organizations return $2.23 to society for every dollar invested in the ESE (REDF, 2021b). The REDF calculates this impact using social return on investment (SROI), which "identifies the various cost savings, reductions in spending, and related benefits" generated by ESEs and monetizes these cost savings and related benefits (Emerson et al., 2000, p. 139). As these data from the REDF suggest, ESEs can help to combat unemployment and under-employment by supporting the personal and professional development of individuals marginalized in and excluded from the labor market.

Exemplars

In an effort to illustrate the design and potential impacts of ESEs, we now describe two exemplary ESEs. These organizations are exemplars given their scope and scale. While there are many ESEs with similar aims offering similar services, few rival the scope and scale of these organizations. Specifically, the scope of UTEC's service delivery and the scale of the Center for Employment Opportunities' (CEO) operations demonstrate the potential of ESEs to combat unemployment and underemployment.

UTEC

Founded in 1999 in Lowell, Massachusetts, UTEC's "mission and promise is to ignite and nurture the ambition of our most disconnected young people to trade violence and poverty for social and economic success" (UTEC, 2021a). The United Teen Equality Center[1] was founded in response to youth organizing efforts to establish a teen center that could combat gang violence in Lowell. UTEC has evolved over the past twenty years and now provides streetworker outreach, transitional coaching, workforce development, educational programming, social justice and civic engagement opportunities and cultural enrichment programming, and it also runs an early childhood education center. UTEC's three social enterprises include a mattress recycling factory, food services, and a woodworking shop. The organization targets "impact" young adults, which they define as individuals aged seventeen to twenty-five with proven risk factors such as criminal records, gang involvement, and no high school credentials (UTEC, 2021d). UTEC has been nationally recognized for its efforts to serve justice-involved young adults.

UTEC recognizes that young adults encounter many barriers that can impede their success, such as poverty, limited employment opportunities, and low-quality education. UTEC's three target communities – Lowell, Lawrence, and Haverhill – have high poverty rates and low educational attainment levels. Of the 168 young adults that UTEC served in fiscal year 2020, 89 percent had a criminal record, 75 percent were gang involved, 70 percent did not have high school credentials, and 36 percent were parenting or expecting children. In fiscal year 2020, 97 percent of UTEC participants had no new convictions or technical violations of probation or parole,

---

[1] The organization now uses the name UTEC instead of United Teen Equality Center.

88 percent had no new arrests, and 76 percent attempted a High School Equivalency Test (HiSET) (UTEC, 2021e).

One of UTEC's strategies to promote social and economic success for young adults is providing employment in a social enterprise. Of the 168 young adults served in fiscal year 2020, 79 percent were employed in a social enterprise. In its mattress recycling factory, UTEC reuses and recycles mattress and box spring components. The UTEC employees hand-cut the mattresses and recycle the steel, foam, wood, and cotton. The mattress recycling factory is the first paid work experience for the impact young adults, who later transition to the food services or woodworking social enterprises. In the food services social enterprise, employees learn transferable culinary and hospitality skills. They have the option to work in retail food service at Café UTEC, work for UTEC's catering business, or work in UTEC's Community Kitchen supporting their food manufacturing operations. In the woodworking shop, employees develop basic design and construction skills to create cutting boards, salad tongs, merchandising displays, and other items (UTEC, 2021c). UTEC's 2020 impact report describes the social enterprises' triple bottom line as: (1) facilitating positive youth development, along with paid work experience; (2) generating earned revenue to support the mission of the organization; and (3) supporting the community's economic development (UTEC, 2021e).

The Center for Employment Opportunities

The CEO is the largest employer of formerly incarcerated individuals in the US. It currently operates in eleven states and thirty cities and serves more than 8,000 participants annually. A majority of CEO participants are on probation or parole. Over half (56 percent) have no prior work experience. A majority (87 percent) of the participants are male, 81 percent are people of color, and 51 percent are between the ages of eighteen and thirty. The CEO aims to reduce recidivism and increase employment through job-readiness training, transitional employment, job coaching and placement, and retention services (Center for Employment Opportunities, 2021a). The scale of the CEO's operations and their sustained success are unique in the field.

The job-readiness training consists of a weeklong course that prepares individuals to enter or reenter the workforce. After completing the training, participants begin paid transitional work. Participants work four days a week with their transitional work crews while receiving on-the-job coaching from their site supervisor. The transitional work consists of outdoor services (e.g., groundskeeping, snow removal, and construction), indoor services (e.g., janitorial work, renovation, and weatherization) and event set-up and clean-up. Participants are paid at the end of each shift. They spend approximately two to four months on the transitional work crew before securing employment in the mainstream labor market. While working on the transitional work crew, participants receive comprehensive vocational services to prepare them for the labor market. Participants are assigned a job coach who assists them with resume-building, mock interviews, and the job search process. Job coaches also refer participants to social service providers as needed. Once participants feel prepared to enter the labor market, CEO staff refer participants to employers for interviews based on employer needs and participant skills. Once participants secure employment, they begin receiving personalized job retention services from the CEO. These services include workplace counseling, crisis management, and career planning. These services are designed to support participants experiencing long-term success in the labor force (Center for Employment Opportunities, 2021a).

The CEO describes itself as a "reliable, comprehensive staffing solution" for organizations in need of an on-demand workforce (Center for Employment Opportunities, 2021a). It pays and manages the transitional work crews and is responsible for insurance, payroll, and benefits, which saves the employer time and money. Many see the CEO as an exemplar because of this innovative staffing model. Compared to an ESE that operates a restaurant, designs products, or runs a similar brick-and-mortar business, the CEO can provide transitional employment to a much larger number of individuals. Furthermore, their outdoor services, indoor services, and event set-up and clean-up allow transitional employees to gain diverse skills. This staffing model is more scalable and sustainable than that of a brick-and-mortar ESE, which is evidenced by the fact that the CEO launched in New York City and expanded to twenty-five more cities in fewer than twenty-five years.

The CEO is also an exemplar because of its commitment to evidence-based practices. Few ESEs conduct rigorous evaluations of their programs and services, making it difficult to assess their effectiveness in achieving their desired outcomes. The CEO is an exception and is a data-informed organization that frequently releases reports detailing the findings of their external evaluations. In 2012, MDRC published the findings of "More than a Job," a three-year evaluation of the CEO (Redcross et al., 2012). The study used random assignment to determine whether the CEO's job-readiness training, transitional employment, job coaching and placement, and retention services were more effective than job search assistance. In the first year of the evaluation, the program group had higher employment rates, but these effects faded over time. This increase was a result of their employment with the transitional work crew, meaning that these effects faded when individuals left these positions. Over the three-year follow-up period, however, individuals in the program group were significantly less likely to have been convicted of a crime and/or be incarcerated.

In 2010, the New York State Division of Criminal Justice Services (DCJS) launched an evaluation of reentry providers. Evaluators used a quasi-experimental design to match individuals participating in a CEO transitional work crew with a similar quasi-control group matched on forty-five variables, such as demographics, socioeconomic status, and criminal background.

At twelve months postenrollment, individuals in the treatment group were 52 percent more likely to be employed than their counterparts in the comparison group. At thirty-six months postenrollment, individuals in the treatment group were 48 percent more likely to be employed and 19 percent less likely to be rearrested or reconvicted for a felony than their counterparts in the comparison group (Center for Employment Opportunities, 2019). The CEO's sustained success in serving the formerly incarcerated demonstrates the potential of ESEs to promote both social and economic opportunity.

Community Power

UTEC and the CEO are two of many ESEs aiming to build community power. The employment opportunities that ESEs provide boost economic resources among individuals, families, and communities. This economic development can help support the flourishing of communities that are often plagued by underinvestment. Employment social enterprises also recognize that structural and systemic changes must occur for these communities to thrive. In fact, many ESEs also engage in various advocacy and organizing efforts to facilitate this transformation. For example, UTEC's youth organizing efforts include social justice workshops, candidate forums, and youth-led policy campaigns. Their policy platform includes youth violence prevention funding, young adult justice reform, ending multigenerational poverty, and improving social enterprise workforce development (UTEC, 2021b). Likewise, the CEO has a dedicated policy team engaged in local, state, and national policymaking. The organization engages with policymakers to advocate for the removal of punitive barriers to employment for formerly incarcerated individuals. Their policy efforts focus on eliminating legal and regulatory barriers to employment and increasing the number of employment opportunities for individuals with a criminal conviction (Center for Employment Opportunities, 2021b). The CEO's systems change efforts also involve the criminal justice system. The organization engages with policymakers to advocate for increased public investment in evidence-based reentry employment programs, and they partner with state and national organizations to advance systems change in the criminal justice system. The CEO believes that investing resources back into the communities most impacted by incarceration can begin to undo the harms of mass incarceration (Center for Employment Opportunities, 2021b).

The REDF (the venture philanthropy organization mentioned previously that supports more than 200 ESEs) also engages local, state, and federal policymakers to advance economic opportunity. They have played key roles in legislative and budgetary successes, including the development of workforce development programs for limited English-proficient individuals, the removal of barriers to occupational licensing for individuals with criminal convictions, the extension of the Ban the Box law to private employers (prohibiting employers from including a question about criminal history on applications), and an expansion of the California earned income tax credit (REDF, 2021a).

Though organizations like UTEC, the CEO, and the REDF are engaged in advocacy and organizing, not all social enterprises are engaged in similar ways, and this sector therefore has untapped potential to build community power. A study examining the characteristics of 115 social enterprises illuminates this potential (Weaver, 2020). The study surveyed individuals in executive leadership positions in social enterprises throughout the US. When asked to indicate which strategies they engage in to advance social change, 55 percent indicated capacity-building, which aims to equip individuals, organizations, or communities with the tools, skills, and knowledge to help themselves. A quarter (23 percent) indicated advancing a social movement, which consists of group actions aiming to advance social change. About a tenth (13 percent) indicated resource provision, which refers to the provision of resources or services that can help individuals, organizations, or communities meet their needs. Only 9 percent indicated systemic change, which involves collaborating with governing institutions to transform the systems that govern society.

Social enterprises may utilize one or more social change strategies within one organization, but many focus on only one strategy. For instance, a social enterprise focused on systemic change may also develop a capacity-building strategy that involves organizing community members to address a need in the community. Social enterprises may also start with one social change strategy (e.g., capacity-building) and develop others over time (e.g., launch a social movement focused on capacity-building; Weaver, 2020).

While Weaver's 2020 study explores how social enterprises are engaging in social change efforts, ESEs have been critiqued for embodying neoliberal logics (Cooney, 2016; Garrow & Hasenfeld, 2014). The argument posits that ESEs legitimize the marketization of the welfare state and the commodification of the poor through the merging of commercial activity and social service delivery (Cooney, 2016). This hybridization reinforces the belief that the welfare state fosters dependency and detachment from the labor market. Because of this dependency and detachment, public assistance must be contingent on participation in the labor market (Garrow & Hasenfeld, 2014). Employment social enterprises rely on commercial revenue to further their social mission, which reduces their dependence on government funding and exposes them to market forces. Garrow and Hasenfeld (2014) assert that this approach upholds the neoliberal belief that privatization and marketization of the social safety net will reduce costs and increase efficiency in the production and distribution of social services (Garrow & Hasenfeld, 2014; Somers, 2008).

Critics posit that ESEs shift the problem of unemployment from the state to the individual. These organizations "embrace the ideology that poverty and detachment from the labor market are caused by individual deficiencies and moral failings, that labor market participation is a desired end, and that any work is better than no work" (Garrow & Hasenfeld, 2014, p. 1481). This ideology screens out discourse examining structural and systemic issues such as income inequality, workplace discrimination, and exploitative working conditions. Instead, the discourse shifts to identifying individuals who are detached from the labor market because of personal circumstances, moral deficiencies, or poor work ethic and how to modify this behavior with sanctions or incentives (Garrow & Hasenfeld, 2014).

While it is imperative for ESEs to contend with these tensions, further examination of UTEC (described earlier) helps to counter these critiques. In fiscal year 2019, government grants and contracts contributed to 45 percent of UTEC's revenue stream, individuals contributed 29 percent, corporate and private foundations contributed 10 percent, social enterprise revenue contributed 10 percent, and the remaining 6 percent came from interest and other sources (UTEC, 2021e). UTEC is in fact merging commercial activity and social service delivery, but commercial activity comprises very little of its revenue stream. Instead of an embrace of privatization and marketization, this hybrid approach could be described as an attempt to diversify UTEC's revenue stream. Both scholars and practitioners argue that nonprofit organizations that cultivate revenue from disparate sources are less vulnerable than those that generate revenue from a single type of source (Hung & Hager, 2019). Revenue diversification provides more flexibility for nonprofit organizations and can protect against financial uncertainty (Carroll & Stater, 2009). For example, a decrease in government contracts could be offset by an increase in revenue from Café UTEC. While UTEC's financial profile may not be representative of all ESEs, this information adds important nuance to the critiques described earlier. Employment social enterprises are using innovative approaches to improve social and economic opportunity while navigating tensions between social service provision and enterprise.

Psychological Empowerment Processes

In addition to their roles in promoting community development, ESEs seek to improve the lives of the people who are participating as employees. Although evidence is limited, some existing studies provide insights into their effectiveness in this regard. Studies conducted in Australia, Scotland, Hong Kong, and several other countries have examined the relationship between ESEs and well-being and demonstrated promising findings (Elmes, 2019; Ho & Chan, 2010; Macaulay et al., 2018). For instance, in a longitudinal study of an Australian ESE, participants reported improved health, increased social support, and increased sense of purpose, confidence, and community (Elmes, 2019).

In the US, most such research has focused on economic opportunity among individuals participating in ESEs. In 2015, Mathematica Policy Research

Table 17.1 *Employment outcomes.*

Employed at least one month	93%
Employed at least three months	84%
Employed at least six months	67%
Employed at least nine months	51%
Employed at least twelve months	35%

published findings from a study of 436 individuals across seven different ESEs (Rotz et al., 2015). Researchers conducted a baseline survey when the individual was hired by the ESE and a follow-up survey twelve months after their hire date. Prior to their employment at the ESE, 25 percent of respondents had never been employed, 37 percent had not been employed in the previous year, and 84 percent were not currently employed (Maxwell et al., 2013). Table 17.1 highlights their employment outcomes twelve months from the start of their ESE employment.

Less than a quarter (23 percent) of respondents were employed at the ESE at the time of follow-up, which means that the majority of respondents who reported being employed found opportunities in the mainstream labor market. Since research suggests that six months of employment improves wages, long-term job retention, and labor force attachment for individuals with barriers to employment (Sattar, 2010), this distribution suggests that two-thirds of respondents experienced these gains after leaving the ESE. The findings from this study also suggest that individuals experienced increased stability following their ESE employment. One year from the start of their ESE employment, their total monthly income increased by 91 percent. The percentage of respondents renting or owning a home or apartment increased from 49 to 81 percent and the percentage who reported stable housing increased from 15 to 53 percent, increases that were statistically significant. These findings on employment outcomes demonstrate the role of ESEs in establishing financial stability, which may relate to psychological empowerment in other domains (Johnson, 2021).

Although most research on ESEs has focused on economic opportunity, some research has explored the impact of ESEs on youth development. The Social Enterprise Intervention (SEI) model, developed collaboratively by social work professor Kristin M. Ferguson and a community-based, homeless youth agency, targets young people experiencing homelessness and consists of vocational and business training, small business development, supportive mentorship, and clinical services that utilize a harm reduction approach to improve mental health, prosocial behaviors, social support, and service utilization among this population (Ferguson, 2012; Tyler & Johnson, 2006). The model was first implemented at a homeless youth drop-in center in Los Angeles (Ferguson, 2007). Individuals participating in SEI meet weekly with a clinical social worker to identify, evaluate, and treat their areas of need (Cook, 2006; Ferguson, 2012). The intensity and focus of the clinical services are tailored according to the severity of the individual's conditions. Individuals participating in SEI experienced increases in mental health status, social support, and service utilization and decreases in high-risk sexual behaviors and substance use (Ferguson, 2012). The SEI model demonstrates the potential of ESEs to promote psychological empowerment.

Although ESEs differ in the populations that they serve and the types of enterprise that they operate, research suggests that many are functioning as settings that promote not just employability but human development more broadly. For instance, in a qualitative study of a technology-focused social enterprise targeting high school and college-age youth, outcomes included improved academic performance, self-confidence, leadership capacity, work habits and communication skills and healthier peer and familial relationships (O'Donnell et al., 2012). Taken together, these findings from various ESEs suggest that they provide a context not only for improved economic opportunities but also for the development of skills, knowledge, and connections. Since ESEs tend to serve marginalized populations, they can therefore play a valuable role in building individual and community capacity.

Setting Features

To understand the mechanisms through which ESEs are building capacity, we scanned the literature for articles on WISEs, social firms, affirmative businesses, and social purpose businesses to assess existing research on ESEs. In doing so, we aimed to identify ESE models that emerging evidence suggests practitioners may consider applying. After reviewing the literature on this topic, two models that emerged were *open hiring* and *targeted hiring* (see Table 17.2). Weaver's Social Enterprise Directory was used to identify and highlight examples of social enterprises throughout the US that employ this strategy. Weaver's Social Enterprise Directory is a national, public directory that provides information on more than 1,200 social enterprises in the US (Mbacke et al., 2020; Weaver, 2021; Weaver et al., 2021).

As shown in Table 17.2, different organizations employ different ESE strategies. While the research does not outline the rationale behind these strategies, many entrepreneurs are inspired to launch social enterprises because of their lived experiences (Bornstein & Davis, 2010). The mission of many social enterprises is driven by needs in the local community (Eversole et al., 2014), which means community context can also dictate which model the organization employs. The following subsections outline each strategy in detail.

Open Hiring

With open hiring, anyone that seeks employment is offered a job. New York-based Greyston Bakery utilizes open hiring. This hiring process requires no

Table 17.2 *Employment social enterprise models.*

	Strategy	Target population	Social enterprise examples
Open hiring	Hires anyone willing to work without any questions asked about their experience or background	The general public, but they focus on individuals facing difficulties securing employment	Greyston Bakery (New York, NY) Hot Chicken Takeover (Columbus, OH) Ovenly (New York, NY) CK Cafe (Camden, NJ) Venice on Vine (Cincinnati, OH) Drive Change Foods (Brooklyn, NY)
Targeted hiring	Hires from particular groups, usually in order to address issues impacting these individuals (e.g., youth, formerly incarcerated individuals)	Specific populations (e.g., women, people living with disabilities)	Women's Bean Project (Denver, CO) South Camden Farms (Camden, NJ) Peace Coffee (Minneapolis, MN) Perky Planet Coffee and Social Revolution (Burlington, VT)

interviews, resumes, background checks, or applications. With open hiring, anyone willing to work is hired – no questions asked. Open hiring helps to reduce recruitment and retention costs. According to a 2016 report from the Society for Human Resource Management, organizations in the US spend an average of $4,129 per hire (Society for Human Resource Management, 2016). With open hiring, Greyston Bakery can shift human resources to focus on training, benefits, and employee support. The turnover rate at Greyston Bakery is 12 percent, compared to a turnover rate of 30–70 percent for similar industries. In 2018, Greyston Bakery launched the Center for Open Hiring, a learning space that evaluates, improves, and defines open hiring best practices (Greyston Bakery, 2021). Organizations that engage in open hiring are discussed less frequently in the social enterprise literature, but assessing their impact can help us to determine whether the model is worth replicating.

Targeted Hiring

A number of organizations target individuals from specific populations in an effort to address the issues impacting them. Since social enterprises often have a local orientation (Eversole et al., 2014), the organization may focus on an issue that is prominent in its community and that affects particular groups of individuals. Many of these organizations provide wraparound services to address needs that extend beyond the workplace. The Colorado-based Women's Bean Project offers financial education, digital literacy courses, high school equivalency courses, mental health services, and other supports. South Camden Farms in Camden, New Jersey, provides employment opportunities to youth in a city with rampant unemployment. The youth grow habanero peppers, make hot sauce from the peppers, and sell the hot sauce throughout the state (Cope, 2018). Though South Camden Farms provides employment opportunities, it is important to note that the parent company of South Camden Farms – the Center for Environmental Transformation – does not identify as an ESE. It is not uncommon for ESEs to be housed in organizations where job training is one of many organizational strategies to promote social change. Thus, it is helpful to examine these hiring practices both inside and outside organizations that identify as ESEs.

Organizations that engage in this work or support ESEs (e.g., funders, technical assistance providers) should assess the impacts of these two models on the individuals they employ and the communities they serve. Since ESEs are a popular social enterprise model, conducting research on the short- and long-term impacts of ESEs could help to assess each model's efficacy. In general, enthusiasm for ESEs among government agencies, nonprofit social service providers, and philanthropists has outpaced the evidence on which models are likely to have the greatest impacts.

Future Research and Application

Research on ESEs has thus far primarily examined the influence of ESEs in combating unemployment and underemployment. Drawing on our review of current research, we suggest the following topics for future research.

Influence of Mission on Organizational Impact

Future research should explore the influence of an organization's overarching mission on the impacts of ESEs. For example, impacts may differ in an organization where open hiring or targeted hiring is central to the mission compared to an organization where these hiring practices are one of many strategies utilized to promote social change. While these two models appear to each be promising strategies for reducing chronic unemployment and underemployment, it is important to explore the operational boundaries of such models. Research should examine the organizational and contextual factors contributing to the success of these hiring practices and their potential impacts on organizational sustainability. These questions are important for assessing the replicability of these approaches.

Community-Wide Benefit Assessments

Some research has demonstrated that social enterprises can have positive impacts on the communities where they are located (Eversole et al., 2014), although more research is needed to examine the potential benefits of ESEs on local communities and to compare the effects of different ESE models. The capability approach – a multidimensional framework for assessing human development – is one framework for examining the impacts of these organizations (Kato et al., 2018; Sen, 1992). Weaver (2018) has used this approach to outline thirteen different dimensions of social value, some of which include employment, education, and mental health. Using the capability approach for these assessments can provide more specific insights into how ESEs affect individuals and communities and can create greater consistency across the research literature on ESEs.

Influence of Organizational Structure

Given the many options for incorporating ESEs under different legal entities (e.g., benefit corporations, nonprofit organizations), future research should explore the role of legal structure in creating and sustaining ESEs. While many ESEs are incorporated as nonprofit organizations, some research suggests that for-profit businesses may be more suitable for this model (Cooney, 2011b; Teasdale, 2010). More research is needed to assess the role of legal structures in the effectiveness of ESEs, in addition to other contextual factors (e.g., mix of services/supports offered alongside employment, combining services with advocacy/organizing).

Application

Employment social enterprises have the potential to impact individuals, families, and communities by promoting the personal and professional well-being of individuals marginalized in and excluded from the labor market. Practitioners can help these individuals flourish by attending to their holistic needs. As these organizations provide employment opportunities, participants also must address housing, health care, education, and other needs. Funders can provide the resources to help these organizations expand in scope (e.g., UTEC) and in scale (e.g., CEO). With more financial support, ESEs can better meet their social and economic missions. Funding can also be allocated to assess the social and economic impacts of these organizations, helping to grow the evidence base, which currently has significant gaps. UTEC, the CEO, and the REDF have demonstrated the importance of advocacy and organizing in these organizations. These efforts can go beyond individual-level intervention to help drive lasting structural and systemic change and build a world in which all can thrive.

References

Austin, J., Stevenson, H., & Wei-Skillern, J. (2006). Social and commercial entrepreneurship: Same, different, or both? *Entrepreneurship Theory and Practice, 30* (1), 1–22.

Battilana, J., Lee, M., Walker, J., & Dorsey, C. (2012). In search of the hybrid ideal. *Stanford Social Innovation Review, 10*(3), 51–55.

Bornstein, D., & Davis, S. (2010). *Social entrepreneurship: What everyone needs to know*. Oxford University Press.

Brenner, N., & Theodore, N. (2002). Cities and the geographies of "actually existing neoliberalism." *Antipode, 34*(3), 349–379.

Carroll, D. A., & Stater, K. J. (2009). Revenue diversification in nonprofit organizations: Does it lead to financial stability? *Journal of Public Administration Research and Theory, 19*(4), 947–966.

Center for Employment Opportunities. (2019, February). *Improving long-term employment outcomes: Promising findings from New York state*. Center for Employment Opportunities. https://ceoworks.org/assets/images/CEO-Improving-Long-Term-Employment_042319_print.pdf

Center for Employment Opportunities. (2021a). *Our approach*. Center for Employment Opportunities. https://ceoworks.org/

Center for Employment Opportunities. (2021b). *Policy & advocacy*. Center for Employment Opportunities. https://ceoworks.org/policy-advocacy

Cook, J. A. (2006). Employment barriers for persons with psychiatric disabilities: Update of a report for the President's Commission. *Psychiatric Services, 57* (10), 1391–1405.

Cooney, K. (2011a). The business of job creation: An examination of the social enterprise approach to workforce development. *Journal of Poverty, 15*(1), 88–107.

Cooney, K. (2011b). An exploratory study of social purpose business models in the United States. *Nonprofit and Voluntary Sector Quarterly, 40*(1), 185–196.

Cooney, K. (2013). Examining the labor market presence of US WISEs. *Social Enterprise Journal, 9*(2), 147–163.

Cooney, K. (2015). *Social enterprise in the United States: WISEs and other worker-focused models*. ICSEM Working Papers, No. 09. The International Comparative Social Enterprise Models (ICSEM) Project.

Cooney, K. (2016). Work integration social enterprises in the United States: Operating at the nexus of public policy, markets, and community. *Nonprofit Policy Forum, 7*(4), 435–460.

Cope, S. (2018, October 5). *In Camden, a hot sauce is helping young urban entrepreneurs fight poverty*. Cornell Small Farms Program. https://smallfarms.cornell.edu/2018/10/in-camden-a-hot-sauce-is-helping-young-urban-entrepreneurs-fight-poverty/

Danziger, S., & Lehman, J. (1996). How will welfare recipients fare in the labor market? *Challenge, 39*(1), 30–35.

Elmes, A. I. (2019). Health impacts of a WISE: A longitudinal study. *Social Enterprise Journal, 15*(4), 457–474.

Emerson, J., Wachowicz, J., & Chun, S. (2000). *Social return on investment: Exploring aspects of value creation in the nonprofit sector*. Roberts Enterprise

Development Fund. https://redf.org/wp-content/uploads/REDF-Box-Set-Vol .-2-SROI-Paper-2000.pdf

Eversole, R., Barraket, J., & Luke, B. (2014). Social enterprises in rural community development. *Community Development Journal*, *49*(2), 245–261.

Ferguson, K. M. (2007). Implementing a social enterprise intervention with homeless, street-living youths in Los Angeles. *Social Work*, *52*(2), 103–112.

Ferguson, K. M. (2012). Merging the fields of mental health and social enterprise: Lessons from abroad and cumulative findings from research with homeless youths. *Community Mental Health Journal*, *48*(4), 490–502.

Fruchterman, J. (2011). For love or lucre. *Stanford Social Innovation Review*, *9*(2), 42–47.

Garrow, E. E., & Hasenfeld, Y. (2014). Social enterprises as an embodiment of a neoliberal welfare logic. *American Behavioral Scientist*, *58*(11), 1475–1493.

Greyston Bakery. (2021). *Inclusive hiring services*. Greystone Bakery. www.greyston .org/employers/

Hazenberg, R., Seddon, F., & Denny, S. (2012). Investigating the outcome performance of a WISE delivering employability programmes to the unemployed. *Journal of Leadership, Accountability and Ethics*, *9*(6), 40–50.

Ho, A. P., & Chan, K. (2010). The social impact of work-integration social enterprise in Hong Kong. *International Social Work*, *53*(1), 33–45.

Hung, C., & Hager, M. A. (2019). The impact of revenue diversification on nonprofit financial health: A meta-analysis. *Nonprofit and Voluntary Sector Quarterly*, *48*(1), 5–27.

Johnson, L. (2021). Increasing financial empowerment among survivors of intimate partner violence: A growth curve analysis. *American Journal of Community Psychology*, *68*(1–2), 29–46.

Kato, S., Ashley, S. R., & Weaver, R. L. (2018). Insights for measuring social value: Classification of measures related to the capabilities approach. *VOLUNTAS: International Journal of Voluntary and Nonprofit Organizations*, *29*(3), 558–573.

Leung, Z. C. S., Ho, A. P. Y., Tjia, L. Y. N., Tam, R. K. Y., Chan, K. T., & Lai, M. K. W. (2019). Social impacts of work integration social enterprise in Hong Kong – Workfare and beyond. *Journal of Social Entrepreneurship*, *10*(2), 159–176.

Lysaght, R., Roy, M. J., Rendall, J. S., Krupa, T., Ball, L., & Davis, J. (2018). Unpacking the foundational dimensions of work integration social enterprise: The development of an assessment tool. *Social Enterprise Journal*, *14*(1), 60–70.

Macaulay, B., Mazzei, M., Roy, M. J., Teasdale, S., & Donaldson, C. (2018). Differentiating the effect of social enterprise activities on health. *Social Science & Medicine*, *200*, 211–217.

Mandiberg, J. M. (1999). The sword of reform has two sharp edges: Normalcy, normalization, and the destruction of the social group. *New Directions for Mental Health Services*, *1999*(83), 31–44.

Mandiberg, J. M. (2016). Social enterprise in mental health: An overview. *Journal of Policy Practice*, *15*(1–2), 5–24.

Mandiberg, J. M., & Warner, R. (2012). The value of mutual support through client community in the design of psychiatric treatment and rehabilitation programs. In A. Azzopardi & S. Grech (Eds.), *Inclusive communities* (pp. 149–165). Sense Publishers.

Martin, R., & Osberg, S. (2007). Social entrepreneurship: The case for definition. *Stanford Social Innovation Review, 5*(2), 29–39.

Maxwell, N., Rotz, D., Dunn, A., Rosenberg, L., & Berman, J. (2013). *The structure and operations of social enterprises in REDF's social innovation fund portfolio: Interim report.* Mathematica Policy Research.

Mbacke, M., Gallagher, K., & Weaver, R. L. (2020). Reflections on applied social enterprise education: Using Weaver's Social Enterprise Directory to teach social entrepreneurship. *The International Undergraduate Journal For Service-Learning, Leadership, and Social Change, 10*(1), 1–9.

Murray, J. H. (2012). Choose your own master: Social enterprise, certifications, and benefit corporation statutes. *American University Business Law Review, 2*(1), 1–20.

O'Donnell, J., Tan, P. P., & Kirkner, S. L. (2012). Youth perceptions of a technology-focused social enterprise. *Child and Adolescent Social Work Journal, 29*(5), 427–446.

Redcross, C., Millenky, M., Rudd, T., & Levshin, V. (2012, January). *More than a job: Final results from the evaluation of the Center for Employment Opportunities (CEO) Transitional Jobs Program.* United States Department of Health and Human Services. www.acf.hhs.gov/sites/default/files/documents/opre/more_than_job.pdf

REDF. (2021a). *Creating opportunity at a systems level.* Roberts Enterprise Development Fund. https://redf.org/what-we-do/policy/

REDF. (2021b). *The impact.* Roberts Enterprise Development Fund. https://redf.org/the-impact/

Riccio, J. A., & Orenstein, A. (1996). Understanding best practices for operating welfare-to-work programs. *Evaluation Review, 20*(1), 3–28.

Rotz, D., Maxwell, N., & Dunn, A. (2015). *Economic self-sufficiency and life stability one year after starting a social enterprise job.* Mathematica Policy Research.

Sattar, S. (2010). *Evidence scan of work experience programs.* Mathematica Policy Research.

Sen, A. (1992). *Inequality reexamined.* Clarendon Press.

Shore, B. (2003). *Powering social change: Lessons on community wealth generation for nonprofit sustainability.* Community Wealth Ventures.

Society for Human Resource Management. (2016, August 3). *Average cost-per-hire for companies is $4,129, SHRM survey finds.* Society for Human Resource Management. www.shrm.org/about-shrm/press-room/press-releases/pages/human-capital-benchmarking-report.aspx

Somers, M. R. (2008). *Genealogies of citizenship: Markets, statelessness, and the right to have rights.* Cambridge University Press.

Spear, R., & Bidet, E. (2005). Social enterprise for work integration in 12 European countries: A descriptive analysis. *Annals of Public and Cooperative Economics, 76*(2), 195–231.

Stambaugh, L., Mustillo, S. A., Burns, B. J., Stephens, R. L., Baxter, B., Edwards, D., & Dekraai, M. (2007). Outcomes from wraparound and multisystemic therapy in a Center for Mental Health Services system-of-care demonstration site. *Journal of Emotional and Behavioral Disorders, 15*(3), 143–155.

Teasdale, S. (2010). Explaining the multifaceted nature of social enterprise: Impression management as (social) entrepreneurial behaviour. *Voluntary Sector Review*, *1*(3), 271–292.

Tyler, K. A., & Johnson, K. A. (2006). Pathways in and out of substance use among homeless-emerging adults. *Journal of Adolescent Research*, *21*(2), 133–157.

UTEC. (2021a). *Mission and values*. UTEC. https://utecinc.org/who-we-are/mission/

UTEC. (2021b). *Organizing and policymaking*. UTEC. https://utecinc.org/what-we-do/organizing-policy/

UTEC. (2021c). *Our social enterprises*. UTEC. https://utecinc.org/what-we-do/social-enterprises/

UTEC. (2021d). *Our young adults*. UTEC. https://utecinc.org/what-we-do/impact-young-adults/

UTEC. (2021e). *Outcomes & impact*. UTEC. https://utecinc.org/our-impact/impact/

Vilà, M., Pallisera, M., & Fullana, J. (2007). Work integration of people with disabilities in the regular labour market: What can we do to improve these processes? *Journal of Intellectual & Developmental Disability*, *32*(1), 10–18.

Warner, R., & Mandiberg, J. (2006). An update on affirmative businesses or social firms for people with mental illness. *Psychiatric Services*, *57*(10), 1488–1492.

Weaver, R. L. (2016). Social enterprise self-employment programs: A two-dimensional human capital investment strategy. *Social Enterprise Journal*, *12*(1), 4–20.

Weaver, R. L. (2018). Re-conceptualizing social value: Applying the capability approach in social enterprise research. *Journal of Social Entrepreneurship*, *9*(2), 79–93.

Weaver, R. L. (2019). Social enterprise and the capability approach: Exploring how social enterprises are humanizing business. *Journal of Nonprofit & Public Sector Marketing*, *32*(5), 427–452.

Weaver, R. L. (2021). The utilization, benefits, and challenges of online social enterprises directories. *Social Innovations Journal*, *5*, 1–18.

Weaver, R. L., Mbacke, M., & Gallagher, K. (2021). Weavers Social Enterprise Directory: A tool for teaching social enterprise and entrepreneurship. In C. Matthews & E. Liguori (Eds.), *Annals of entrepreneurship education and pedagogy – 2021* (pp. 408–414). Edward Elgar Publishing.

PART V

Participatory and Community Arts

18 Participatory Arts for Vulnerable Populations

Emily A. Hennessy, Anise Gold-Watts, Agata Z. Pietrzak, Sam Lapoint, and Ana Bess Moyer Bell

Introduction

Empowerment is the mechanism by which people, groups, and communities can gain control over their actions and the situations that influence them (Rappaport, 1984). It is an iterative process (Cattaneo & Chapman, 2010) that can positively nurture youth development and provide young people with skills to engage as genuine participants in the larger society (Camino, 2000; Chinman & Linney, 1998; Christens & Peterson, 2012; Wallerstein, 2006). Programs that seek to cultivate empowerment among young people should create a space for youth to build self-efficacy, gain knowledge about their world, learn skills, engage in meaningful activities, and learn how to be agents of change (Chinman & Linney, 1998; Deutsch & Jones, 2008). From a developmental perspective, adults' roles in organizations can be pivotal in this process (Chinman & Linney, 1998; Gambone et al., 2006; Gil & Rhodes, 2006; Lind, 2007; Zeldin et al., 2013); yet, adults often view youth as passive recipients of knowledge, include youth in name but not in action (tokenism), or exclude youth from decision-making processes altogether (Nygreen et al., 2006; Zeldin et al., 2005). Thus, careful attention to these issues, and to balancing adult and youth roles, is necessary in these spaces.

There are a variety of specific program modalities that may involve youth empowerment as a process or outcome (e.g., youth organizing; see Chapter 1), and there are many youth programs or activities that could also encourage youth empowerment processes. One such opportunity is the use of art – specifically, participatory arts. Participatory arts are gaining recognition worldwide for the management and promotion of health and well-being (Corbin et al., 2021), and they can include a variety of modalities, such as community/cultural festivals, fairs, and events, literature, online, digital, and electronic arts, performing arts, and visual arts, design, and craft (Davies et al., 2012; O'Donnell et al., 2022). Participatory art can be transformative in its ability to expose current systems of oppression while also providing a conceptual avenue for imagining and planning for a different system (Hardt & Negri, 2009; Raynor, 2019; Urke et al., 2021). In the enaction of participatory arts, the lines between the art space "as a designated liminal space and everyday life can become blurred; moving the performance ... beyond the confines of the stage" (Hatala & Bird-Naytowhow, 2020, p. 259). In addition, art may offer a useful medium through which one can reflect on and discuss sensitive topics that may otherwise be viewed as taboo. The arts can provide a space for advocacy and amplify silenced voices, thereby leveraging power (Corbin et al., 2021; Sloman, 2012). Indeed, Bell and Desai (2011) argue that arts should be considered a critical form of social justice practice. Thus, participatory arts may be both an approach to and a process for building empowerment and community power.

This chapter will describe how participatory arts may create a unique opportunity for youth empowerment and will discuss ways by which participatory arts have the potential to address barriers to empowerment. Our objectives for this chapter are as follows: (1) Provide an overview of the empowerment process and challenges to it, specifically for youth with marginalized identities; (2) use a case example of a community-based program known as 2nd Act, which focuses on drama therapy and theatrical performances, to demonstrate how this type of participatory arts programming can be especially valuable for youth with additional vulnerabilities such as addiction and mental health recovery; and (3) review and discuss how the literature on participatory arts using drama and theater demonstrates the capability for these methods to enable broader community-level engagement and empowerment.

Process and Challenges of Youth Empowerment within Community-Based Programs

Power differentials can often exist in programs that address youth but still grant adults some form of power, whether that is in the form of types of knowledge, access to resources, or by the nature of their program role (Nygreen et al., 2006). This authority over youth participants will impact youth actions, even in settings where empowerment is a desired process or goal (Laverack, 2005). Youth empowerment in a program led by an adult can be particularly challenging because of social and cultural power dynamics, which influence the relationship between youth and adults. This dynamic can be especially prevalent in the Global South or contexts in which generational hierarchies are traditionally and culturally preserved. Thus, youth in a program led by an adult could follow the adults' directions for many reasons, including out of fear of punishment or rejection, even if they feel different action should be taken or do not fully comprehend what they are being asked to do. Youth will also often view the adult leaders as experts and simply absorb what adults tell them instead of engaging in critical thinking. In settings seeking empowerment as a process and/or outcome, adult staff and leaders must maintain self-awareness of their power to be able to perceive, understand, and contemplate how and when to use or diffuse the power they hold (Bess, 1988; Deutsch & Jones, 2008; Scheve et al., 2008).

These challenges to youth empowerment may be even more striking when working with vulnerable or marginalized populations, such as those struggling with mental health or substance use issues, those with uncertain citizenship or refugee status, and those perceived as minority populations in relation to the predominant group demographic or in relation to the demographic of the group leaders (e.g., minority status by gender, sexual orientation, race, ethnicity, ability, or other characteristics). Youth in recovery from mental health and substance use issues may be especially vulnerable in program settings as they often have had adverse childhood experiences or trauma, issues that they may still be in the process of healing from (Nash et al., 2019; Tanner-Smith et al., 2018). While adolescents are influenced by several physical and psychosocial developmental transitions that change aspects of their emotional regulation and cognitive processing (Leffert et al., 1998), early adverse experiences in particular may contribute to delayed or underdeveloped emotional regulation and cognitive development skills. Related deficits in stress management, problem-solving, and conflict resolution skills are all factors that could get in the way of an empowering process (Clark et al., 2008; Shono et al., 2018; Squeglia et al., 2014; Wilson et al., 2015; Witt, 2010). In addition, youth in recovery from mental health and substance use issues may feel shame or have directly experienced stigma as a result of their struggles (Brousseau et al., 2020; Earnshaw et al., 2018; Schoenberger et al., 2022). Whether actual or perceived, this stigma may render youth even less likely to express their individuality or voice their feelings or opinions, opting instead to engage in ways that allow them to blend in with the group.

Participatory Arts: Unique Empowerment Opportunity

Empowerment models that utilize a fluid approach (i.e., an approach in which practitioners make frequent adjustments based on the context) seem necessary for adults to engage with youth as colearners in a project (Bruun Jensen & Simovska, 2005; Camino, 2000; Cattaneo & Chapman, 2010; Chinman & Linney, 1998; Jennings et al., 2006; Wong et al., 2010). As suggested in the Introduction, participatory arts may offer several unique empowerment opportunities to utilize such a fluid approach. Participatory arts and arts-based methods represent an emerging field among the published literature, demonstrating growth in the evidence base over the last few decades. This literature indicates that participatory arts-based approaches are applied globally among different age groups in a variety of settings using different types of methods, such as performing arts, visual arts, and creative writing (Bell & Desai, 2011; Toma et al., 2014).

Although participatory arts can take a wide variety of forms, in our example we focus specifically on drama therapy[1] and its use of community-based theater

---

[1] Different cultures appear to use the term "drama therapy" or similar terms in slightly different ways, including "community drama" (Kewley & Van Hout, 2022) or "therapeutic theater" (Sajnani et al., 2019). This chapter will not go into the nuances of all the ways that "drama

performances. We have chosen to focus on these art forms because they offer unique avenues "for reflection and subversion – using the body (with and without words) in and through the strange theatre-making process" (Raynor, 2019, p. 703).

Drama Therapy

The theory that underpins the majority of drama therapy in practice is role theory: It assumes that "life is dramatic … a central feature of existence is dramatic action" (Landy, 2008, p. 102). Dramatic action leads to a particular role, which leads to dramatic action, back to a particular role, and so on. Thus, individuals are a taxonomy, a combination of roles that they consciously and unconsciously put on and take off throughout daily life, and roles that are conceptualized in "discrete patterns of behavior that suggest a particular way of thinking, feeling or acting" (Landy, 2009, p. 67). In this way, each role serves a function and contains unique characteristics, and in totality creates the whole person. Within the taxonomy exist roles that can aid individuals in overcoming obstacles or can hold them back from their most resilient and dynamic selves. Drama therapy recognizes that each person has a unique taxonomy or collection of roles or personas they access frequently, and it works with individuals to explore these roles.

Effective drama therapy involves several process phases: identify, explore, present, and evaluate (Baim, 2017; Kewley & Van Hout, 2022). The *identify* phase involves the practitioners or facilitators laying the foundation for the later creative work: forming groups and building initial trust, identifying an individual's goals and needs, creating boundaries, and developing an action plan. Next, the *explore* phase involves participants in a variety of creative activities and exercises, sharing stories, creating scenes and characters, practicing theater skills, and eventually having rehearsals (i.e., using the participants' experiences to drive the exploration, which can lead to the generation of the content for a performance). The *present* phase then involves presenting the created works to the target audience. Depending on the readiness of the participants, this could mean simply presenting to the internal group (e.g., likely early in the drama therapy process) or to those larger groups that might have been identified during the identify phase (e.g., likely later in the drama therapy process and after full development and rehearsal of the piece). Finally, the *evaluate* phase is where the group has an opportunity to debrief, reflect, decide on the next steps, and, in some settings, measure the effects of their work. These phases are exemplified in the following core activity components undertaken during the drama therapy experience: play, dramatic projection, embodiment, personification and impersonation, interactive audience and witnessing, life–drama connection, therapeutic performance, drama-therapeutic empathy, distancing, and transformation (Jones, 2007).

---

therapy" versus other iterations of the term are used; instead, we will use the term as our example, 2nd Act, intended it.

For those working with marginalized populations, the Drama Spiral is one tool to use for decision-making by practitioners and facilitators when planning meeting sessions. This tool can allow them to tailor the activities and methods to participants' specific experiences and situations (Baim, 2017). The Drama Spiral has six rings, each of which suggest closer (or farther) situations from the participant's lived experience (Figure 18.1). In using this tool, practitioners and facilitators must constantly be critically reflexive and adaptive; they must consider to what degree group work should be personalized, what degree of distance regulation might be needed, and the level of sensitivity needed in developing characters or scenarios. For example, the outermost ring is the most removed from the participant's lived experiences and involves games and creative activities. As the rings in the Drama Spiral move toward the middle, the activities will become closer to their experiences (e.g., moving from fictionalized personal stories to stories of unresolved difficulties).

Community-Based Theater

Community-based theater is a type of grassroots theater that takes a critical stance on social issues. Unlike other forms of theater, which often imitate professional settings, produce well-known plays, and focus on the entertainment value of the production, community-based theater participants seek to create original theater with the aims of raising awareness, promoting discourse, and advocating for new ways of knowing and being in the community (Faigin & Stein, 2010; Sloman, 2012). Indeed, as Raynor (2019) argues, the theatrical performance process provides multiple opportunities for those marginalized "to become visible, present, excessive, in performance, but also processes through which we can attune to, explore and perhaps even intervene in, the conditions of marginality" (p. 703). Furthermore, as suggested by Sloan (2021), participatory theater may be a way of building an alliance by joining in a "common understanding of the precariousness of life" (p. 19).

Faigin and Stein (2010) delineate seven core elements inherent to community-based theater that likely contribute to positive change: (1) processes of group cohesion and affiliation, (2) common goals, (3) common experiences, (4) setting characteristics of openness and inclusion, (5) opportunities for community connections and integration, (6) flexibility, and (7) ownership. As will be discussed in the context of our case example, community-based theater is a part of the drama therapy experience for its youth participants.

Overview of Our Example, 2nd Act

2nd Act is a new organization resulting from a merger of two separate nonprofit organizations: Creating Outreach About Addiction Support Together (COAAST) and Improbable Players. Founded in 1984 by Lynn

The Drama Spiral

Clark Baim 2015

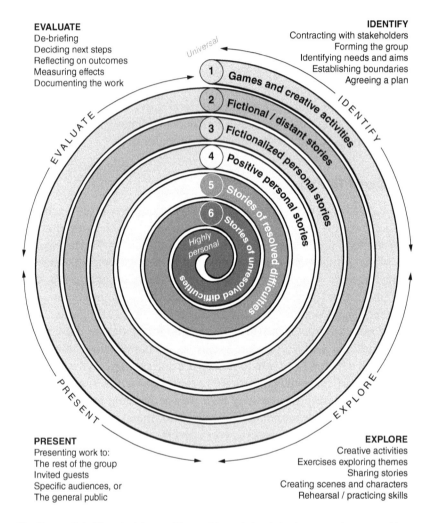

EVALUATE
De-briefing
Deciding next steps
Reflecting on outcomes
Measuring effects
Documenting the work

IDENTIFY
Contracting with stakeholders
Forming the group
Identifying needs and aims
Establishing boundaries
Agreeing a plan

Universal

EVALUATE
IDENTIFY

1 Games and creative activities
2 Fictional / distant stories
3 Fictionalized personal stories
4 Positive personal stories
5 Stories of resolved difficulties
6 Stories of unresolved difficulties

Highly personal

PRESENT
EXPLORE

PRESENT
Presenting work to:
The rest of the group
Invited guests
Specific audiences, or
The general public

EXPLORE
Creative activities
Exercises exploring themes
Sharing stories
Creating scenes and characters
Rehearsal / practicing skills

The Drama Spiral is a decision-making tool intended to help theatre and arts practitioners to work safely and ethically along the continuum from the fictional to the highly personal. In the outer rings, participants are involved in creative activities and work at the metaphorical and fictional level. As one 'spirals in' towards the centre, the rings represent stories that are increasingly personal and sensitive for the participants. Each ring of the Spiral includes four important processes: *Identify, Explore, Present and Evaluate.*

Figure 18.1 *The Drama Spiral.*
Source: *Reprinted from Baim (2017).*

HIGH

↑ FICTIONAL DISTANCE ↓

1

Games and creative activities

- Group-building; warm-ups; theatre games; communication and performance skills.
- Creative activities including dance, music, song, art, writing, rhythmic movement and percussion, social and communal customs and pastimes where everyone participates.

2

Fictional / distant stories

- Enacting stories and plays that are already written. Can include myths, fables, fairy tales and other well-known stories. Can also include watching a play / interacting with characters.
- Ensemble-created plays or improvised dramas that are wholly fictional or based on historical / news events.

3

Fictionalized personal stories

- Ensemble-created drama with fictionalized scenes and characters; can include stories and themes that have arisen from more personal work.
- Metaphor is frequently used to create distance from personal stories and to contain powerful themes.

4

Positive personal stories

- Participants enact directly personal stories focusing on neutral, positive, safe or non-troubling topics.
- Participants may also enact situations they desire or may face in the future, i.e. 'rehearsals for life.'

5

Stories of resolved difficulties

- Participants enact directly personal stories about troubling issues that are resolved – for example, stories of healing, growth, or triumph over adversity. The rehearsal process itself may be a part of the healing and growth.
- Important processes include informed consent, group support, sharing experiences, validation and witnessing.

6

Stories of unresolved difficulties

- Participants enact directly personal, unresolved stories for the purpose of therapy or growth. Important processes include informed consent, confidentiality, witnessing, group sharing and follow-up support.
- The focus on unresolved personal stories can make participants highly vulnerable and requires experienced facilitators and the guidance or supervision of a qualified therapist with relevant training, e.g. psychodrama, drama therapy.

LOW

Figure 18.1 (*cont.*)

Bratley (MEd, Tufts University), an arts educator in long-term recovery, Improbable Players tells true stories about addiction recovery, strength, and hope (Snyder-Young et al., 2022). COAAST was founded in 2006 by drama therapist Ana Bess Moyer Bell (MA, New York University), who also created and produced ethnodramas[2] about the impacts of opioid use disorder and the opioid epidemic. 2nd Act's mission is to change the way people and communities respond to the impacts of substance use through theater and drama therapy. Throughout their theatrical performances, drama therapy, and theater-based educational interventions, 2nd Act programs are performed and facilitated by actors, teaching artists, and drama therapists, all of whom are recovering from addiction or share close personal experiences of addiction. Since its initiation, 2nd Act has performed for over 1 million people, sustaining a record of excellence in presenting performances and drama workshops in schools, rehabilitation centers, and community organizations in the New England region of the US, and more recently in New York City and Cleveland through satellite programs.

Although the target populations for the drama therapy and educational interventions of 2nd Act are often reflective of the critical preadolescent, adolescent, and young adult years, the performances and educational workshops are designed to be inclusive of the adult audiences that play a role in the neighborhood or community settings in which youth live, attend school, and play. These theatrical performances seek to help young people and adults recognize how addiction affects people's lives, families, and communities. Furthermore, the theater-based workshops engage participants in topics that intersect with recovery in a creative way, providing participants and audiences with the language and resources that can unite students, teachers, staff, and other partners working to build a collective community response to addiction and resilience for the recovery process.

Both organizations that preceded 2nd Act began with ethnodramas from Ms. Bratley's and Ms. Moyer Bell's lived experience of addiction. The two cornerstone scripts, *I'll Never Do That* and *Four Legs to Stand On*, tell stories about how one character's struggle with addiction impacts their family and point to the importance of community-involved recovery. The performances run for about thirty-five to fifty minutes and are followed by a period for discussion between the audience and performers. The discussion includes time for actors to briefly share their own personal experience with addiction, and the audience can ask questions regarding their experience and the stories that were performed (Snyder-Young et al., 2022). The performances coupled with the discussions serve to destigmatize the topic and help audience members identify when they need to ask for help for themselves or a loved one and who/how to ask for support.

---

[2] Ethnodrama: dramatic playscript for a live, public theatrical performance that has been generated from ethnographic research data (Given, 2008).

Creative Container: Drama Therapy as a Tool to Cultivate Creativity, Connections, and Positive Learning

The main goal of the drama therapy program is to create a positive learning environment in which participants feel both seen and validated in shared experiences. 2nd Act refers to this positive environment as the *Creative Container* (Sajnani et al., 2019). This is a space where 2nd Act works with participants to build self-awareness, self-management, relationship skills, social awareness, and responsible decision-making. It is also a space where participants can explore and examine sensitive themes related to their experience of addiction recovery.

The Creative Container is facilitated by a structured approach to the drama therapy group, which includes a check-in ritual, warm-up activity, embodiment curriculum, a period of processing, and a closing ritual (Figure 18.2); this general structure is followed for each of the sessions. These elements of the drama therapy are viewed as key to working with vulnerable youth in their recovery process and addressing potential areas of risk for returning to substance use. The initial activities (check-in and warm-up) set the foundation and tone for the day and create a safe space for the active work of the group: creative embodiment and processing. The *embodiment* seeks to engage participants in the expressive arts medium to unearth unconscious feelings through metaphor and storytelling. The *processing*, which follows the embodiment, is essential to the 2nd Act group experience as it helps participants make a conscious connection between their artistic expression and their cognitive understanding of that expression. Finally, the *closing ritual* allows participants to exit the Creative Container with a sense of supportive closure.

The drama therapy group is meant to occur regularly (typically twice per week) for approximately thirty weeks. This period of time is needed to build relationships, establish rapport, and deepen connections among participants. The program is facilitated by an adult teacher artist and an adult drama therapist.

Empowerment and Community Power in the Participatory Arts

There is a range of global research that demonstrates how participatory arts can be used for psychological empowerment and to build community power; it may support self-reflection, increase self-esteem, cognitive function, and problem-solving skills, and help individuals process emotional experiences. In addition, these efforts can enable broader advocacy and, in theatrical performances, prompt the audience to focus on an issue in a different way and to create new alliances with the performers (Faigin & Stein, 2010; Roy et al., 2021; Sloan, 2021). Figure 18.3 is a visualization of how participatory arts programs could work toward individual empowerment and community power using the 2nd Act experience as the example.

CREATIVE CONTAINER

Figure 18.2 *The Creative Container.*

Check-in
- Participants share their name, how they are feeling, and answer a question of the day. This ritual is designed to connect each participant with themselves and with the wider group.

Warm-up
- This activity will orient the participants to the theme of the group through developmentally appropriate theater games to connect group members.

Creative Embodiment
- This will vary but can include storytelling by participants, improvisation, and other theatrical activities.

Processing
- The facilitators help the participants make connections between the embodiment (scene work, character creation, storytelling) and their story.

Closing
- A chance for participants to reflect on all they have experienced in the group and to select one thing to take with them into their day.

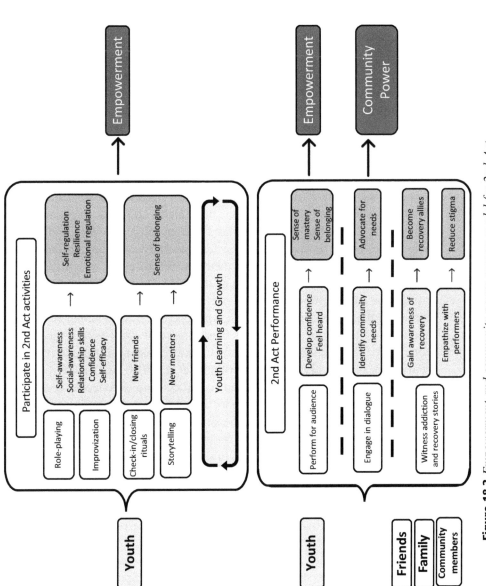

Figure 18.3 *Empowerment and community power process model for 2nd Act.*

Psychological Empowerment

Psychological empowerment covers several salient domains of adolescent development and life experience: affective/emotional, behavioral, cognitive, and relational (Christens, 2019). Several systematic reviews of research among youth and adults suggest that involvement in performing arts can affect these various domains in several ways. First, these reviews suggest that participatory arts can improve mental health and specific targeted behavioral outcomes through meaning-making, redefining identity, personal growth, increasing self-concept (internal outcomes), and the creation of spaces for connectedness, thereby increasing social skills and team-building (interpersonal outcomes; Daykin et al., 2008; O'Donnell et al., 2020).

There is a strong theoretical rationale with varying levels of research support for the use of participatory arts to enable empowerment among youth and to address specific barriers among youth recovering from addiction. In the drama therapy exercises used by 2nd Act, the use of games, role-play, impersonation, and storytelling altogether provided an opportunity to learn how to identify an emotion, use that emotion without experiencing negative consequences, and develop a new perspective on that emotion (Larson & Brown, 2007). Indeed, coping with emotions is a necessary skill for youth recovering from addiction, especially considering that negative emotional states can trigger a return to substance use (Nash et al., 2019). Research also suggests that participatory arts can help individuals process emotions from highly traumatic experiences. For example, in Puerto Rico, one group used theater, music, drawing, and dance to help gender-based violence service providers and advocates process the primary and vicarious trauma resulting from their experience dealing with the aftermath of Hurricane Maria (Ramírez-Ayala et al., 2021). During this initiative, participants were guided through ways of processing trauma at multiple levels. This facilitated the processing of their own experiences of trauma and increased their ability to return to or to continue their important work within the broader community. As youth in recovery often report a history of trauma (Hennessy et al., 2021; Nash et al., 2019; Tanner-Smith et al., 2018), using participatory art to help them process feelings related to difficult life experiences is especially relevant. Participatory art can support their recovery and facilitate empowerment by allowing youth to take ownership of their healing process.

The use of theater games as a warm-up activity can also give participants a break from the more serious aspects of their day-to-day lives and simply enjoy the experience of fun with others (Andvig & Hummelvoll, 2016; Mohler, 2012). Research on a UK theater group working with adults in recovery also suggests that theater games represent a fun and nonthreatening approach to strengthening cognitive function, as they encourage participants to rely on their memory, abstract reasoning, or skills of organization (Kewley, 2019; Kewley & Van Hout, 2022), aspects that have also been linked to the emotional and cognitive components of psychological empowerment.

Returning to the concept of the Creative Container space that is utilized in the 2nd Act project (Sajnani et al., 2019), this space can facilitate the emergence of unconscious thoughts and feelings, offering further opportunities for critical reflection and intervention. This opportunity to voice one's experience can result in increased emotional empowerment as one feels heard as well as increased cognitive empowerment in the process of learning how to voice this experience most effectively, ultimately resulting in a sense of responsibility and ownership for themselves and the narrative they present (Larson & Brown, 2007). For example, interviews of "at-risk" Norwegian youth (i.e., not in school or employed) who participated in a yearlong theater project suggested that they not only experienced a change in their self-image during this time but also developed increased self-confidence, feelings of responsibility, and coping skills and felt more connection to others and to society (Andvig & Hummelvoll, 2016).

The opportunity to create a new character and envisage a new type of self in a situation or a new reaction to a situation can also be healing and empowering. For example, the Circle of Voices theater program in Saskatoon, Saskatchewan, Canada, used a strength-based approach that focused on supporting Indigenous youth in learning how to enact, protest, and play with a range of social identities that could challenge their racially and culturally stereotyped identities. Youth who participated in the program described enjoying being able to try out these different identities, including being able to be "weird" and change their own ways of moving in the world through these theatrical activities (Hatala & Bird-Naytowhow, 2020). It was this aspect of theater that Hatala and Bird-Naytowhow (2020) suggested could lead to empowerment: "Rather, these experiences helped young people feel more in control of how they can perform, project themselves, or engage with their social worlds, constructing their stories and lives in more desirable, wellness-promoting ways" (p. 256). Indeed, having control of one's narrative in one's community, such as when one is performing onstage, has been shown to lead to feelings of empowerment (Christens & Peterson, 2012).

The use of film rather than a live theatrical performance has also been shown to promote psychological empowerment among marginalized youth. For example, US-based participatory research involving transgender and gender-nonconforming youth of color culminated in the making of a film in which youth shared their unique stories (Marx & Regan, 2021). This initiative invited participants to address misconceptions about their own communities, and, through collaboratively directing the production of this film, they envisioned themselves as agents of change. In Canada and England, participatory film allowed youth to reproduce experiences of homelessness and closely examine interrelated themes, such as mental health and substance use (Roy et al., 2021). By assuming leadership roles within both projects, which involved aspects of participatory arts beyond performance, youth could engage in decision-making, problem-solving, team-building, and self-reflection. While the example of film diverges from conventional, theater-based drama therapy, it allows for a collaborative space that provides opportunities to "promote positive change among youth, increase interpersonal connections and provide greater self-awareness and social awareness" (Burch et al., 2019, p. 117).

The group that is engaged together in the Creative Container is also key to the process and outcomes. While the games employed may help to establish a new kind of community with peers based on the common experience of having fun (Andvig & Hummelvoll, 2016; Mohler, 2012), other theatrical activities can cause youth to feel vulnerable. Yet, with the right leadership in place and in a critically reflective, safe space the bonds developed can be stronger than in a program in which there is less vulnerability (Larson & Brown, 2007; Mohler, 2012). Zeldin et al. (2013) posit that in these collective spaces, as youth exercise their agency with each other they will develop psychological empowerment and "mastery, skill development, confidence, identity exploration, initiative, and emotional well-being" (p. 390). In addition, experience from a theater program in US high schools suggests that youth who participate learn how to better recognize the emotions of others, understand their emotional responses to situations, and differentiate these responses from personality traits (Larson & Brown, 2007).

Thus, even from this brief review of the literature, evidence from a variety of contexts suggests that participatory arts can provide many opportunities to gain psychological empowerment among youth across all of its domains: affective/emotional, behavioral, cognitive, and relational (Christens, 2019). In addition, some of these opportunities can work in tandem to contribute to different domains of psychological empowerment simultaneously. As youth gain affective/emotional skills and empowerment, they may improve their interpersonal skills, leading to a greater sense of belonging and improvements in the relational domain of psychological empowerment.

Community Power

Youth in recovery – and other marginalized youth – may often be viewed within the dominant stereotypical lens that serves to dehumanize them (Kelly, 2004); in other words, that they are "derelict and criminogenic to charitable cases without agency of their own" (Roy et al., 2021, p. 960). In their day-to-day experiences, they may be asked to conform to and present as an identity that does not represent their true self but rather results from the dominant lens that oppresses and marginalizes them (Hatala & Bird-Naytowhow, 2020). Through theatrical experience, participants have the opportunity to change their collective self-image and become active members of the larger society by making art to influence their surroundings (Andvig & Hummelvoll, 2016); that is, they can be "the influencer" rather than "one under the influence" (Reynolds, 2017, p. 75). Importantly, these public performances turn the narrative of addiction and recovery on its head: Rather than being anonymous in one's substance use, performing one's recovery subverts the larger narrative (Reynolds, 2017).

Audience members who experience and witness art as a collective may gain a deeper shared understanding of addiction as well as of the problems that the community faces around addiction and potential opportunities for addressing these issues from a community or structural perspective (Andvig & Hummelvoll, 2016; Urke et al., 2021). As a result, audience members may take on a sense of responsibility or ownership for addressing the issue in collaboration with the actors (Sloman, 2012). For example, in Timor-Leste, a displaced persons camp for two different ethnic groups in Bibi Bulak was experiencing local gang attacks (Sloman, 2012). The camp staff implemented theatrical performances and workshops as a way to encourage people to develop and implement their own ways to create a peaceful environment; as a result of these activities, camp leaders were able to begin a dialogue with the warring parties. Eventually there was a peaceful resolution, and structures were put into place to manage further conflicts. Another study that examined participatory theater as a mechanism to change stigmatizing attitudes toward LGBTQ+ people in Swaziland and Lesotho found that the audience reported a deeper understanding of the pain that resulted from the stigmatizing attitudes and that community members identified the need to create change in their own communities (Logie et al., 2019). The findings suggest, in support of Raynor's argument, that the act of viewing and engaging in these performances as willing audience members can make the experience "visceral" for those who have not experienced the situations presented (Raynor, 2019, p. 694). This experience can then increase feelings of connection with those previously othered and increase feelings of empathy for them (Corbin et al., 2021; Madsen et al., 2021), potentially leading to a reduction in stigma (Gaiha et al., 2021). Activist and writer Qwo-Li Driskill, who is Cherokee and two-spirit, proposed that the act of participating in theater can be a "suture" to heal the wounds left by historical trauma among Indigenous peoples (2008, cited in Hatala & Bird-Naytowhow, 2020). These performances can also be healing for audience members who may themselves have experienced addiction and stigma from addiction; in these cases, sharing with a performer that their show was helpful can reinvent the performer's identity as one of a helper and so work to combat the actor's stigmatized identity (Snyder-Young et al., 2022).

Participatory arts can develop community power in part by strengthening the bonds between participants and the predominant social environment. For instance, Madsen et al. (2021) describe a theatrical production in Australia on the topic of domestic violence that utilized a script written from excerpts of interviews with victims of domestic violence. The audience not only developed empathy for the victims who endured this stigmatized violence but also reflected on their own relationships with more nuanced comprehension. Similarly, Raynor (2019) discusses a fiction production in the UK that portrayed experiences of women living in poverty and attending a family support service. In each case, the discussion between the audience and participants that followed the show fostered deeper connection between the two groups. Focusing on another marginalized group, Deleo et al. (2021) describe the experience of a self-managed social movement to promote mental health and reduce stigma around mental illness through the use of dance (Biodanza) and art therapy in the Psychosocial Hospital of Managua, Nicaragua. The program has provided improved behavioral and psychological outcomes for people who utilized the hospital, while the local youths who got involved in the program developed a more empathetic and sophisticated understanding of mental illness, which they brought with them out into the community at large.

This advocacy can lead to change beyond a single audience or community. In recent years, documentary films have been used to challenge views regarding individuals in recovery, such as *Anonymous People* (Williams, 2013) and *Generation Found* (Williams & Reilly, 2016). These films have been used at the state and national level for advocacy and activism to shape the larger conversation about addiction recovery and to prompt a focus on funding for recovery services. For example, at the national level, the films were used to mobilize people to advocate for the passage of the Comprehensive Addiction and Recovery Act, the first major federal legislation on addiction in forty years that authorized over $181 million a year in new funding for prevention and treatment infrastructure and programming (Whitehouse, 2016). There is also evidence that these films challenged local community leaders to see the problem of substance use and addiction and invest in more treatment and recovery services that their constituents could access (Juvenile Justice Information Exchange, 2014).

In sum, there is evidence to suggest that the act of performance can lead to a variety of positive interpersonal outcomes, which, if harnessed, can ultimately translate into advocacy and activism efforts, leading to change beyond the performance space and larger than the single community. Modalities such as film may have greater potential than theatrical stage performances as they can be more widely shared; yet, after the COVID-19 pandemic and related in-person restrictions we may have gained new opportunities for greater advocacy with online modalities of sharing content from performances.

Features of Participatory Arts That Can Foster Power and Empowerment

These examples show that several features must be in place for empowerment and power to be fostered. Sloman (2012) argues that the most important ingredient is having an extensive amount of time. This is necessary for the foundational work of developing strong relationships and understanding the community's experience and needs: Thus, the focus of such projects should be more on the process and less on the product.

For developing youth empowerment, the programs must attend to the youths' developmental situations and meet those needs. The programs must also reflect the specific additional needs of a young person struggling with addiction and recovery and have trained and experienced staff. The Drama Spiral, or other similar tools, may be useful for the practitioner in gauging the readiness and skills of the youth. In terms of building community power, the theatrical performances must be engaging so that they grab audience members' attention. They must also be delicately provocative, challenging boundaries without repelling audiences. Achieving these goals is quite a feat for a theatrical performance to achieve as, unlike film, the performance narrative cannot be "fixed" mid-show. Fortunately, engaging in multiple rehearsals and having a dry run (or two) of the performance with external viewers in advance could mitigate this issue.

Application and Future Directions

Despite the potential of participatory arts, there still remain challenges; just engaging youth in a participatory arts project without consistent reflection and action regarding these challenges could actually lead to disempowerment (Roy et al., 2021). Indeed, with theater performances, as Raynor (2019) argues, "simply gathering, assembling, and staging stories may reproduce institutional colonisations of voice and re-assert norms and conventions" (p. 695). Thus, careful attention must be paid to these issues throughout the planning and implementation phases by practitioners and facilitators. For theatrical performances to be transformative, audience members must also be open to reflective listening as opposed to token listening (Roy et al., 2021). Although some of their openness may be shaped by the advertising, setting, and space created, much of that is beyond the reach of the performers. Importantly, empowerment does not happen inside of a vacuum but is influenced by the larger context. That is, although a program can facilitate processes of empowerment, it is still important to be considerate of the overwhelming and oftentimes influential systems of oppression external to the immediate context that continuously disempower youth, especially those in marginalized and/or vulnerable populations. Indeed, Sloman (2012) reviews several case examples in Ghana, Kenya, Tanzania, and Uganda in which groups used the label of "participatory theater" for their performances but, given the preset agendas of the government and/or nongovernmental organization supporting the group, these activities were anything but participatory: Audiences were not challenged to make changes and grew bored with the rote, didactic performances, and participants became discouraged by the process.

As with any work involving vulnerable or at-risk populations, the practitioners and facilitators involved must have a deep understanding of the particular challenges and potentially triggering dynamics or situations faced by their population. They must also have systematic plans in place for addressing these issues as they arise and the ability to empathize and build trust with their participants (Andvig & Hummelvoll, 2016; Kewley & Van Hout, 2022; Mohler, 2012). To avoid creating further silencing, they may also need to conduct outreach and planning to ensure that they do not "exclude those who do not feel the desire, the right, or the capacity to speak or perform with others" (Raynor, 2019, p. 694).

Finally, there is a need for more rigorous research in this area. Although drama therapy has been suggested to be effective for a variety of populations, there is a vast amount of variability in the type and quality of studies assessing it (Feniger-Schaal & Orkibi, 2020), making it difficult to come to firm conclusions on its exact mechanisms that could lead to empowerment and community power.

Conclusion

In sum, the participatory arts hold wide promise for building empowerment and power for youth. Participatory arts can be a useful tool for enhancing psychological empowerment and community power through empowerment processes that support self-reflection, agency, cognitive function, problem-solving skills, and processing emotional experiences in different contextual settings globally. More rigorous research should seek to develop methodologies specifically for the unique environment of theater and other participatory arts. Although this chapter emphasizes the specific use of drama therapy and theatrical performances for youth with mental health and substance use disorders, there is a wide variety of work to suggest that participatory arts can be relevant in many contexts and for various population groups (Urke et al., 2021).

References

Andvig, E., & Hummelvoll, J. K. (2016). "I dare": Experiences of young adults at risk participating in a one-year inclusive-theatre project in Norway. *Nordic Journal of Social Research, 7*, 46–65.

Baim, C. (2017). The Drama Spiral: A decision-making model for safe, ethical, and flexible practice when incorporating personal stories in applied theatre and performance. In A. O'Grady (Ed.), *Risk, participation, and performance practice: Critical vulnerabilities in a precarious world* (pp. 79–109). Palgrave Macmillan.

Bell, L. A., & Desai, D. (2011). Imagining otherwise: Connecting the arts and social justice to envision and act for change: Special issue introduction. *Equity & Excellence in Education, 44*(3), 287–295.

Bess, M. (1988). *Power, moral values and the intellectual: An interview with Michel Foucault.* History of the Present. https://monoskop.org/images/e/e2/Foucault_Michel_1988_Power_Moral_Values_and_the_Intellectual.pdf

Brousseau, N. M., Earnshaw, V. A., Menino, D., Bogart, L. M., Carrano, J., Kelly, J. F., & Levy, S. (2020). Self-perceptions and benefit finding among adolescents with substance use disorders and their caregivers: A qualitative analysis guided by Social Identity Theory of Cessation Maintenance. *Journal of Drug Issues*, *50*(4), 410–423.

Bruun Jensen, B., & Simovska, V. (2005). Involving students in learning and health promotion processes – Clarifying why? What? And how? *Promotion & Education*, *12*(3–4), 150–156.

Burch, D., Summer, D., Ward, E., Watt, C., & Feldman, D. (2019). Qualitative data from a mixed methods study of resilience in ENACT's therapeutic theatre process Show UP! *Drama Therapy Review*, *5*(1), 117–138.

Camino, L. A. (2000). Youth–adult partnerships: Entering new territory in community work and research. *Applied Developmental Science*, *4*(Suppl. 1), 11–20.

Cattaneo, L. B., & Chapman, A. R. (2010). The process of empowerment: A model for use in research and practice. *American Psychologist*, *65*(7), 646–659.

Chinman, M. J., & Linney, J. A. (1998). Toward a model of adolescent empowerment: Theoretical and empirical evidence. *Journal of Primary Prevention*, *18*(4), 393–413.

Christens, B. D. (2019). *Community power and empowerment*. Oxford University Press.

Christens, B. D., & Peterson, N. A. (2012). The role of empowerment in youth development: A study of sociopolitical control as mediator of ecological systems' influence on developmental outcomes. *Journal of Youth and Adolescence*, *41*(5), 623–635.

Clark, D. B., Thatcher, D. L., & Tapert, S. F. (2008). Alcohol, psychological dysregulation, and adolescent brain development. *Alcoholism: Clinical and Experimental Research*, *32*(3), 375–385.

Corbin, J. H., Sanmartino, M., Urke, H. B., & Hennessy, E. A. (2021). Arts, health promotion, and social justice: Synergy in motion. In J. H. Corbin, M. Sanmartino, E. A. Hennessy, & H. B. Urke (Eds.), *Arts and health promotion: Tools and bridges for practice, research, and social transformation* (pp. 345–356). Springer International Publishing.

Davies, C. R., Rosenberg, M., Knuiman, M., Ferguson, R., Pikora, T., & Slatter, N. (2012). Defining arts engagement for population-based health research: Art forms, activities and level of engagement. *Arts & Health*, *4*(3), 203–216.

Daykin, N., Orme, J., Evans, D., Salmon, D., McEachran, M., & Brain, S. (2008). The impact of participation in performing arts on adolescent health and behaviour: A systematic review of the literature. *Journal of Health Psychology*, *13*(2), 251–264.

Deleo, A., Romero, R., & Zelaya, E. A. (2021). Movimiento Ventana: An alternative proposal to mental health in Nicaragua. In J. H. Corbin, M. Sanmartino, E. A. Hennessy, & H. B. Urke (Eds.), *Arts and health promotion: Tools and bridges for practice, research, and social transformation* (pp. 295–311). Springer International Publishing.

Deutsch, N. L., & Jones, J. N. (2008). "Show me an ounce of respect": Respect and authority in adult–youth relationships in after-school programs. *Journal of Adolescent Research*, *23*(6), 667–688.

Earnshaw, V. A., Bogart, L. M., Menino, D. D., Kelly, J. F., Chaudoir, S. R., Reed, N. M., & Levy, S. (2018). Disclosure, stigma, and social support among young people receiving treatment for substance use disorders and their care-givers: A qualitative analysis. *International Journal of Mental Health and Addiction, 17*(6), 1535–1549.

Faigin, D. A., & Stein, C. H. (2010). The power of theater to promote individual recovery and social change. *Psychiatric Services, 61*(3), 306–308.

Feniger-Schaal, R., & Orkibi, H. (2020). Integrative systematic review of drama therapy intervention research. *Psychology of Aesthetics, Creativity, and the Arts, 14*(1), 68–80.

Gaiha, S. M., Salisbury, T. T., Usmani, S., Koschorke, M., Raman, U., & Petticrew, M. (2021). Effectiveness of arts interventions to reduce mental-health-related stigma among youth: A systematic review and meta-analysis. *BMC Psychiatry, 21*(1), 364.

Gambone, M. A., Yu, H. C., Lewis-Charp, H., Sipe, C. L., & Lacoe, J. (2006). Youth organizing, identity-support, and youth development agencies as avenues for involvement. *Journal of Community Practice, 14*(1–2), 235–253.

Gil, C. E., & Rhodes, J. E. (Eds.). (2006). *Mobilizing adults for positive youth develop-ment* (Vol. 4). Springer US.

Given, L. (Ed.). (2008). Ethnodrama. In *The SAGE encyclopedia of qualitative research methods* (pp. 283–285). SAGE Publications, Inc.

Hardt, M., & Negri, A. (2009). Of love possessed. *Artforum International, 48*(2), 180–264.

Hatala, A. R., & Bird-Naytowhow, K. (2020). Performing *pimâtisiwin*: The expression of Indigenous wellness identities through community-based theater. *Medical Anthropology Quarterly, 34*(2), 243–267.

Hennessy, E. A., Tanner-Smith, E., Nichols, L. M., Brown, T. B., & Mcculloch, B. J. (2021). A multi-site study of emerging adults in collegiate recovery programs at public institutions. *Social Science & Medicine, 278*, 113955–113955.

Jennings, L. B., Parra-Medina, D. M., Hilfinger-Messias, D. K., & McLoughlin, K. (2006). Toward a critical social theory of youth empowerment. *Journal of Community Practice, 14*(1–2), 31–55.

Jones, P. (Ed.). (2007). *Drama as therapy volume 1: Theory, practice and research* (2nd ed.). Routledge.

Juvenile Justice Information Exchange. (2014, February 24). *The great hidden secret: How "The Anonymous People" is changing recovery culture*. Juvenile Justice Information Exchange. https://jjie.org/2014/02/24/the-great-hidden-secret-how-the-anonymous-people-is-changing-recovery-culture/

Kelly, J. F. (2004). Toward an addictionary: A proposal for more precise terminology. *Alcoholism Treatment Quarterly, 22*(2), 79–87.

Kewley, S. (2019). Changing identities through Staging Recovery: The role of commu-nity theatre in the process of recovery. *The Arts in Psychotherapy, 63*, 84–93.

Kewley, S., & Van Hout, M. C. (2022). "I'd Probably Be Dead Now": Evaluating the impact of theatre practitioners working on a recovery-based community drama project. *International Journal of Mental Health and Addiction, 20*, 1212–1230.

Landy, R. J. (2008). *The couch and the stage: Integrating words and action in psycho-therapy*. Jason Aronson.

Landy, R. J. (2009). Role theory and the role method of drama therapy. *Current Approaches in Drama Therapy, 2*, 65–88.

Larson, R. W., & Brown, J. R. (2007). Emotional development in adolescence: What can be learned from a high school theater program? *Child Development*, *78*(4), 1083–1099.

Laverack, G. (2005). *Public health: Power, empowerment and professional practice.* Palgrave Macmillan.

Leffert, N., Benson, P. L., Scales, P. C., Sharma, A. R., Drake, D. R., & Blyth, D. A. (1998). Developmental assets: Measurement and prediction of risk behaviors among adolescents. *Applied Developmental Science*, *2*(4), 209–230.

Lind, C. (2007). The power of adolescent voices: Co-researchers in mental health promotion. *Educational Action Research*, *15*(3), 371–383.

Logie, C. H., Dias, L. V., Jenkinson, J., Newman, P. A., MacKenzie, R. K., Mothopeng, T., Madau, V., Ranotsi, A., Nhlengethwa, W., & Baral, S. D. (2019). Exploring the potential of participatory theatre to reduce stigma and promote health equity for lesbian, gay, bisexual, and transgender (LGBT) people in Swaziland and Lesotho. *Health Education & Behavior*, *46*(1), 146–156.

Madsen, W., Redman-MacLaren, M., Saunders, V., O'Mullan, C., & Judd, J. (2021). Reframing health promotion research and practice in Australia and the Pacific: The value of arts-based practices. In J. H. Corbin, M. Sanmartino, E. A. Hennessy, & H. B. Urke (Eds.), *Arts and health promotion: Tools and bridges for practice, research, and social transformation* (pp. 179–196). Springer International Publishing.

Marx, R. A., & Regan, P. V. (2021). Lights, camera, (youth participatory) action! Lessons from filming a documentary with trans and gender non-conforming youth in the USA. In J. H. Corbin, M. Sanmartino, E. A. Hennessy, & H. B. Urke (Eds.), *Arts and health promotion: Tools and bridges for practice, research, and social transformation* (pp. 123–140). Springer International Publishing.

Mohler, C. E. (2012). How to turn "a bunch of gang-bangin' criminals into big kids having fun": Empowering incarcerated and at-risk youth through ensemble theatre. *Theatre Topics*, *22*(1), 89–102.

Nash, A. J., Hennessy, E. A., & Collier, C. (2019). Exploring recovery capital among adolescents in an alternative peer group. *Drug and Alcohol Dependence*, *199*(1), 136–143.

Nygreen, K., Ah Kwon, S., & Sanchez, P. (2006). Urban youth building community: Social change and participatory research in schools, homes, and community-based organizations. *Journal of Community Practice*, *14*(1–2), 107–123.

O'Donnell, J. M., Jelinek, G. A., Gray, K. M., De Livera, A., Brown, C. R., Neate, S. L., O'Kearney, E. L., Taylor, K. L., Bevens, W., & Weiland, T. J. (2020). Therapeutic utilization of meditation resources by people with multiple sclerosis: Insights from an online patient discussion forum. *Informatics for Health & Social Care*, *45*(4), 374–384.

O'Donnell, S., Lohan, M., Oliffe, J. L., Grant, D., & Galway, K. (2022). The acceptability, effectiveness and gender responsiveness of participatory arts interventions in promoting mental health and Wellbeing: A systematic review. *Arts & Health*, *14*(2), 186–203.

Ramírez-Ayala, H., Silva-Martínez, E., & Vázquez-Pagán, J. M. (2021). CuidarNos: Art and social work to address trauma among gender-based violence advocates after Hurricane María in Puerto Rico. In J. H. Corbin, M. Sanmartino, E. A. Hennessy, & H. B. Urke (Eds.), *Arts and health promotion: Tools and bridges for practice, research, and social transformation* (pp. 85–102). Springer International Publishing.

Rappaport, J. (1984). Studies in empowerment. *Prevention in Human Services, 3*(2–3), 1–7.

Raynor, R. (2019). Speaking, feeling, mattering: Theatre as method and model for practice-based, collaborative, research. *Progress in Human Geography, 43*(4), 691–710.

Reynolds, J. (2017). Outside Edge's theatre for recovery: Reshaping influence and the addict identity. *Performance Research, 22*(6), 73–82.

Roy, A., Kennelly, J., Rowley, H., & Larkins, C. (2021). A critical discussion of the use of film in participatory research projects with homeless young people: An analysis based on case examples from England and Canada. *Qualitative Research, 21*(6), 957–974.

Sajnani, N., Mayor, C., Burch, D., Feldman, D., Davis, C., Kelly, J., Landis, H., & McAdam, L. (2019). Collaborative discourse analysis on the use of drama therapy to treat trauma in schools. *Drama Therapy Review, 5*(1), 27–47.

Scheve, J. A., Perkins, D. F., & Mincemoyer, C. (2008). Collaborative teams for youth engagement. *Journal of Community Practice, 14*, 219–234.

Schoenberger, S. F., Park, T. W., dellaBitta, V., Hadland, S. E., & Bagley, S. M. (2022). "My life isn't defined by substance use": Recovery perspectives among young adults with substance use disorder. *Journal of General Internal Medicine, 37*(4), 816–822.

Shono, Y., Edwards, M. C., Ames, S. L., & Stacy, A. W. (2018). Trajectories of cannabis-related associative memory among vulnerable adolescents: Psychometric and longitudinal evaluations. *Developmental Psychology, 54*(6), 1148–1158.

Sloan, C. (2021). The "pop-up" recovery arts café: Growing resilience through the staging of recovery community. *Research in Drama Education: The Journal of Applied Theatre and Performance, 26*(1), 9–23.

Sloman, A. (2012). Using participatory theatre in international community development. *Community Development Journal, 47*(1), 42–57.

Snyder-Young, D., Houston, A., Bell, A. B. M., Short, A., & Lincoln, A. (2022). Recovery capital and collaborative theatre making: How actors in recovery from substance addiction value their participation in addiction prevention plays. *Research in Drama Education: The Journal of Applied Theatre and Performance, 27*, 121–136.

Squeglia, L. M., Rinker, D. A., Bartsch, H., Castro, N., Chung, Y., Dale, A. M., Jernigan, T. L., & Tapert, S. F. (2014). Brain volume reductions in adolescent heavy drinkers. *Developmental Cognitive Neuroscience, 9*, 117–125.

Tanner-Smith, E. E., Finch, A. J., Hennessy, E. A., & Moberg, D. P. (2018). Who attends recovery high schools after substance use treatment? A descriptive analysis of school aged youth. *Journal of Substance Abuse Treatment, 89*, 20–27.

Toma, M., Morris, J., Kelly, C., & Jindal-Snape, D. (2014). *The impact of art attendance and participation on health and wellbeing: Systematic literature review* (work package 1). Glasgow Centre for Population Health.

Urke, H. B., Hennessy, E. A., Sanmartino, M., & Corbin, J. H. (2021). Exploring the potential for the arts to promote health and social justice. J. H. Corbin, M. Sanmartino, E. A. Hennessy, & H. B. Urke (Eds.), *Arts and health promotion: Tools and bridges for practice, research, and social transformation* (pp. 3–15). Springer International Publishing.

Wallerstein, N. (2006, February). *What is the evidence on effectiveness of empowerment to improve health?* [Health Evidence Network]. WHO Regional Office for Europe. www.dors.it/alleg/0000/Doc_empowerment_OMS2006.pdf

Whitehouse, S. (2016, July 22). *Text – S.524 – 114th Congress (2015–2016): Comprehensive Addiction and Recovery Act of 2016* (2015/2016) [Legislation]. US Congress. www.congress.gov/bill/114th-congress/senate-bill/524/text

Williams, G. (2013). *Anonymous people* [Documentary]. Gathr Films.

Williams, G., & Reilly, J. (2016). *Generation found* [Documentary]. Gathr Films.

Wilson, S., Malone, S. M., Thomas, K. M., & Iacono, W. G. (2015). Adolescent drinking and brain morphometry: A co-twin control analysis. *Developmental Cognitive Neuroscience, 16*, 130–138.

Witt, E. D. (2010). Research on alcohol and adolescent brain development: Opportunities and future directions. *Alcohol, 44*(1), 119–124.

Wong, N. T., Zimmerman, M. A., & Parker, E. A. (2010). A typology of youth participation and empowerment for child and adolescent health promotion. *American Journal of Community Psychology, 46*(1–2), 100–114.

Zeldin, S., Christens, B. D., & Powers, J. L. (2013). The psychology and practice of youth–adult partnership: Bridging generations for youth development and community change. *American Journal of Community Psychology, 51*, 385–397.

Zeldin, S., Larson, R., Camino, L., & O'Connor, C. (2005). Intergenerational relationships and partnerships in community programs: Purpose, practice, and directions for research. *Journal of Community Psychology, 33*(1), 1–10.

19 Community Arts, Decoloniality, and Epistemic Justice

Christopher C. Sonn, Rama P. Agung-Igusti, Roshani J. Jayawardana, Amy F. Quayle, and Samuel P. Keast

Introduction

Using arts for social change is not a new phenomenon. In different countries using arts for social change has its origins in liberation struggles and developed alongside other movements such as the civil rights movement in the US and Indigenous land and feminist movements that were advocating against colonialism, patriarchy, and White supremacy (Kasat, 2020). At Victoria University, our research group, which is part of the Community, Identity and Displacement Research Network, has been collaborating with community arts practitioners (creatives) and agencies that use community arts practice as a method for individual, community, and social change (Agung-Igusti & Sonn, 2020). Through these collaborations, we have developed long-term relationships built on our intersecting social locations, lived experiences, and shared commitments to social justice for marginalized groups suffering the brunt of intersecting structures of oppression. From these settings we have sought to research *alongside* and *with* and shape praxis that is attuned to circuits of power expressed through various dichotomies such as researcher/researched and hegemonic institutional and disciplinary knowledges and practices, and move toward mutual forms of accompaniment and solidarity. In this chapter, we draw on examples from community arts projects to illustrate practices that support community power through epistemic justice. This form of power centers agency for people who are excluded or marginalized and brings people together in settings to deconstruct and create new narratives that counter radicalization as well as affirm personal, cultural, and community identities.

Community Arts and Social Change

In various disciplines, there is a growing trend advocating for community arts as modes of cultural production to create settings, organize and build community, and support narrative change (Madyaningrum & Sonn, 2011; Watkins & Shulman, 2008). Community arts practice is a collaborative process between artists and/or art workers and community members where diverse modalities of arts are used as a platform for communities to express, contest, and elevate identity, concerns, and aspirations. The practice is context-bound, critical, and generative, and it "inevitably responds to the current social conditions; the work is grounded in social critique and imagination" (Goldbard, 2006, p. 22). Thomas and Rappaport (1996) argued that community arts could be an important site to promote the goals of empowerment. They noted that "[e]ngagement in local arts projects is a way for communities that are typically excluded from control over the means to uncover, interpret and create their own identity to obtain access to a powerful resource" (Thomas & Rappaport, 1996, p. 317). For Thomas and Rappaport (1996), community arts practices are linked to cultural rights, including the right to tell existing stories about self and community and to create new ones. Telling stories through arts practice, they argue,

> [is] about reclaiming a history and filling in a past that helps to make a whole person. Restorations of community histories are important for forming and informing the human subject and developing community solidarity. Not only exercises in nostalgia or feeling good.   (p. 330)

Importantly, it is also a means through which typically marginalized communities can contest dominant cultural narratives (Rappaport, 2000) and engage in counter-storytelling.

Feminist scholars (e.g., Anzaldua & Keating, 2015; Collins, 2000; hooks, 1990) and critical race scholars (e.g., Ladson-Billings, 2003; Solórzano & Yosso, 2002) have shown how arts and cultural practice can facilitate engagement or participation but can also involve counter-storytelling. Arts and cultural practice are ways of knowing and doing that are vital to resistance and survival; they can be sites for understanding experiences of oppression and igniting emancipatory actions. By providing opportunities for narrative and voice, arts and cultural practice can create empowering settings to help "build new forms of relationships across diverse populations and social positions to conceptualise and create better settings and worlds" (Stewart, 2011, p. 203). Lykes (2002) noted that arts practice involves the creation of "spaces and times for being, doing and thinking in ways that promote social change that improve the material, spiritual, and psychological lives of those marginalised from power and resources" (p. 387). In this way, community art can be understood as a political project aimed at cultural transformation, because culture is a site of power that is "situated and always-contested" and "possesses material and symbolic consequences that are pertinent to psycho-social-historical projects of emancipation" (Malherbe, 2020, p. 204). Culture is therefore understood as a site for (re)producing coloniality or, alternatively, creating possibilities for decoloniality, reflected in the renewed ways in which people understand the matrix of power and how this influences their understanding of self, other, and the social world.

Decoloniality and Epistemic Justice

The colonial matrix of power (Quijano, 2000), which constructs some people as above the line of the human and others as less deserving and below the line of the human (Fanon, 1967), persists in the present. The coloniality of power, consisting of various intersecting systems of oppression, including colonialism, patriarchy, sexism, and racism,

> is maintained alive in books, in the criteria for academic performance, in cultural patterns, in common sense, in the self-image of peoples, in aspirations of self, and so many other aspects of our modern experience. In a way, as modern subjects we breathe coloniality all the time and every day. (Maldonado-Torres, 2007, p. 243)

Scholars and activists alike have drawn attention to various ways in which assumptions informing research and practice (re)produce epistemic violence (Teo, 2005). These assumptions, with their roots in colonialism and discourses of modernity, include a focus on universalizing and normalizing individualism, the separation of the human and nonhuman world, and mind–body dualism. These assumptions find expression in modes of inquiry that favor a mechanistic worldview and methodologies that center objectivity, expert voice, and reductionism, which have been the dominant approaches informing research (Adams et al., 2015; Mignolo & Walsh, 2018; Sloan, 2018).

Decolonial approaches call for epistemic parity and inclusion and bring to attention how epistemic violence is enacted through hegemonic assumptions about ways of being and knowledge practices that produce erasure, absences, and silences in knowledge archives (Smith, 2012; Teo, 2005). Various authors have conceptualized epistemic justice and injustice (e.g., Dotson, 2012; Fricker, 2006). Pohlhaus (2017, p. 44) proposed that epistemic injustices can be conceptualized in three differing but interconnected ways: Firstly, they serve to "wrong particular knowers as knowers," which can include suppression of testimony or by "making it difficult for particular knowers to know what it is in their interest to know." Secondly, the injustices cause "epistemic dysfunction" by impeding or distorting inquiry. Thirdly, the previous harms are accomplished through the use of "epistemic practices and institutions in ways that systematically ignore, distort, and/or discredit particular intellectual traditions." These forms of epistemic injustice involve not only individuals as knowers but also how they can be embedded within institutions, organizations, and a range of epistemic activities such as knowing, creating, and imagining. This also means that mitigating such injustices is not achieved merely by affording or increasing participation in epistemic communities. For where there are disempowering structures and systematic breakdowns in trust, epistemic injustice prevails. Importantly, conceptualizing epistemic injustice in this way is not to reify or intellectualize these issues but rather to understand how structures, places, and practices disempower, devalue, and harm people and communities, as proposed by Shotwell

(2017): "The collective epistemic resources on which we depend to make sense of and engage the world may be both impoverished and harmed by systemic oppression" (p. 193).

An important area of work then is creating settings (Sarason, 1972) to respond to what Fricker (2006) described as hermeneutical injustice, "the injustice of having some significant area of one's social experience obscured from collective understanding owing to a structural identity prejudice in the collective hermeneutical resource" (p. 100), and what others have referred to as "epistemologies of ignorance" (Mills, 1997; Sullivan & Tuana, 2007) or simply dominant cultural narratives in the context of asymmetrical power relations (Rappaport, 2000). These settings enable communities to come together to tell their own stories and center their voices, perspectives, knowledge, and ways of being in the world. These can also be settings for healing from the pain that comes from the experiences of oppression and epistemic injustice and spaces to engage in resistance through speaking back to and critiquing the deficiencies of social knowledge (see also Case & Hunter, 2012). In creating settings through community arts, marginalized communities can retrieve through remembering and create archives of stories and counter-stories that have the potential to contest dominant hermeneutical resources and surface the plurality of narratives reflective of diverse communities' histories, cultures, and experiences. This means recognizing that "marginalized groups can be silenced relative to dominant discourses without being prevented from understanding or expressing their own social experiences" (Mason, 2011, p. 294; see also Dotson, 2012). This process is focused on healing from below, but it also problematizes the "epistemically and ethically blameworthy ignorance perpetrated by members of dominant groups" (Mason, 2011, p. 294; Sullivan & Tuana, 2007).

Practices to Foster Epistemic Justice

Given the continuity of coloniality in the present and the structural, discursive, symbolic, and cultural means through which power is produced and maintained, arts and cultural practice can be understood as sites to make visible the dynamics of oppression and as means to create intentional settings from which to foster personal, relational, and community power toward resistance and liberation (Agung-Igusti & Sonn, 2020; Haapanen & Christens, 2021; Quayle & Sonn, 2019). There is a long history of often-overlooked critical scholarship that informs current efforts to reimagine the world and to promote just, humanizing, and inclusive applied social psychologies (Fine, 2021; Hodgetts & O'Doherty, 2019). In this writing, several practices aimed at challenging absences and the coloniality of Eurocentric knowledge and ways of being are put forward to achieve epistemic justice, such as relational knowledge practices, retrieving and expanding knowledge archives, and counter-storytelling.

Relational Knowledge Practices

A decolonial frame for creating settings centers on relationality and reciprocity and pays attention to how privilege and power are expressed in these settings and to how these can be transformed and used to promote community empowerment. Relational practices involve accompaniment and the creation of settings that are participatory, transformative, situated, and culturally safe and affirming (Fine, 2018; Montero, 2009). They entail coming together in contact zones of contestation with different tasks for people who are differently positioned within the context of power relations (Huygens, 2011). As noted by Fernández et al. (2019), decoloniality requires "that meaningful relationships and coalitions of co-intentional solidarity be formed and sustained" (para. 10). Importantly, this is recognized as ongoing and dynamic work, never final or taken for granted but reflective of the contingent nature of maintaining and being in "good relations" (Moreton-Robinson, 2020). Critical reflexivity is thus at the core of participatory and accompanying praxis – that is, efforts to engage ethically with and alongside differently positioned communities in the pursuit of liberation from oppressive social relations that shape lived experiences, subjectivities, and relationships in everyday contexts (Fernández et al., 2021).

Archival Retrieval

The retrieval and expansion of archives entail the elevation and embrace of ways of knowing, being, and doing that have been othered or silenced but that have served communities by providing sources of meaning, cultural values and continuity, and a sense of community. This process entails the recovery of historical memory and deepening awareness of sources of oppression and future horizons. Malherbe (2020) referred to this process as cultural re-membering, which "seeks to enable communities to return back to themselves by remaining attentive to the psycho-material constitution of historical narrative" (p. 11). The recovery of historical memory provides the basis for cultural reparation, restoration, and healing (Martín-Baró, 1994). There are numerous examples of archival retrieval and expansion, such as the Apartheid Archive Project in South Africa that brought everyday people's experiences of apartheid into the public sphere (Stevens et al., 2013). The Aboriginal History Archive in Australia is another example of Aboriginal people telling their own history, correcting the partial and biased history informing the present (Aboriginal History Archive, 2021).

Storytelling and Counter-Storytelling

Biographical and storytelling approaches center the lived experiences of those who are marginalized by intersecting systems of oppression (Ladson-Billings,

2003; Montero, 2009). Dutta et al. (2022) argued that counter-storytelling is a vehicle for epistemic justice. Counter-storytelling through community arts "involves an interruption of dominant narratives, and awakening to silences, an articulation of the modes of forgetfulness that prevent dialogue" (Watkins & Shulman, 2008, p. 233). Community arts can be an important site for the recovery of historical and cultural memories and the production of counter-memories that challenge and resist both "passive and active" forms of forgetting (Watkins & Shulman, 2008). Community arts practices generate opportunities for the conscientization, problematization, and deideologization of oppressive social realities and the generation of intercultural and intergenerational empathy through dialogue (Freire, 1972; Martín-Baró, 1994; Montero, 2009). In our work, we have documented how coming together in settings to engage in dialogue that is mediated by arts-based processes and practices can contribute to experiences and capacities such as connectedness, a sense of hope, and critical literacies about the social and structural roots of sources of oppression. The immediate personal and interpersonal transformations lay the foundations for broader activism that is evident in the publicly exhibiting arts products such as performances, images, and sound portraits. These exhibitions insert voices from the margins as counternarratives into the public sphere (Agung-Igusti & Sonn, 2020; Segalo, 2016), thereby opening possibilities for broader engagement and awareness-raising. Next we draw on two recent projects to illustrate the ways in which community arts praxis contributes to epistemic justice and the enactment of community power.

Examples of Community Arts, Decoloniality, and Epistemic Justice

Next In Colour and Brimbank LIVE are community-engaged projects that emerge from and are in collaboration with social actors in different settings. We draw from these current projects to illustrate the various interconnected aspects of liberation-oriented social and cultural practices. These practices include community-engaged and participatory methods, archival retrieval, and the production of counter-stories and narratives. The combination of these practices produces personal, relational, and community power among differently positioned social actors and opens up possibilities to work in solidarity through liberation-oriented community arts practice against epistemic injustice.

Next In Colour: "We're Creating a Space Where... you can Deconstruct Stuff for Yourself"

Next In Colour is an initiative developed by a collective of creatives from the African diaspora in Melbourne, Australia. The members of the collective draw on various creative modalities in their work such as film, photography, poetry, dance, and design, and they have variously engaged in a range of community arts and development projects largely centered on the lands of the Woi Wurrung and Boon Wurrung people of the Kulin Nation in the western suburbs of Melbourne. The initiative was conceived as a response to the forms of racialized structural exclusion experienced by the collective members and their communities within the creative industries but also felt across their lives more broadly. Individually and across other projects, the collective had been engaging in transformative community and cultural work that mobilized arts and creative practices in powerful ways, but it faced barriers either through the lack of resources or the need to work within the context of human services organizations that constrained their ability to self-determine. Through the Next In Colour initiative, they were able to apply for public funding, enabling them to attain important resources and work *with* a supporting organization rather than *within* an organization. The funding would enable the creation of various platforms to develop networks of support across communities of the African diaspora in Melbourne and of important vocational pathways within the creative industries. Further, the initiative sought to facilitate critical conversations and dialogues within and across their communities encompassing identity, belonging, and community, as well as building solidarities with other racialized communities. Importantly for the collective, these platforms and spaces would "[reflect] the communities we come from, and we are able to call our own, as well as ensuring that we continue to create a map for the next generations to come" (Colour Between the Lines, n.d.a). It was central for Next In Colour that, alongside leveraging and developing material resources and opportunities, important forms of meaning-making, recognition, and epistemic justice would occur.

For Next In Colour, self-determination was central to their aspirations: to self-determine in their ways of organizing, to self-determine over the activities they engaged in, the settings they created, and the work they produced, and to self-determine over their stories and ways of being represented. Self-determination is the counter to the material and symbolic forms of marginalization experienced by communities of the African diaspora in Australia, whom often are positioned as beneficiaries, whose subjectivities are constrained in limiting ways (Kwansah-Aidoo & Mapedzahama, 2018; Majavu, 2018; Udah, 2018), and whose stories and histories are silenced and erased (Pybus, 2006). Thus, the collective would infuse the settings they created and their practices and structures of organizing and coming together with ways of being, doing, and knowing that sought to realize these desires for self-determination. However, the path to self-determination is not easy. Despite having access to material resources through the grant and a clear vision of the spaces they would create and practices they would foster, many of the structural conditions they sought to challenge shaped the necessary relationships that the collective had with various organizational power-holders. This

Figure 19.1 *Space secured by Next In Colour.*

created barriers to self-determination for Next In Colour that would need to be navigated. Alternative settings such as Next In Colour are always situated within a network of contexts and relationships that can be impacted on but also may limit the utilization of power.

However, finding a physical space to house the initiative, to hold workshops and exhibitions, for the collective to work from, and to be an accessible community resource was an important step toward resisting external pulls of power that sought to create relationships of dependence. The collective was able to secure a space (Figure 19.1) that had previously been a community arts studio and was located in the heart of the inner western suburbs, which have important histories and ties to many African diaspora communities. As one of the collective members shared:

> Creating a space or allowing a space to be created collectively by community is so important because it's not only operated and run by a collective of people that understand the language of being marginalized and the importance of having a space to just be, it's like we're creating a sense of home. We're creating a space where you can be vulnerable and where you can deconstruct stuff for yourself.

This yearning for a sense of home evokes the idea of a "home-place" (hooks, 1990), a place of respite and healing for the collective and their communities from the experiences of oppression and marginalization that structured their lives. This space would also be an important *counterspace* (Case & Hunter, 2012) that created opportunities for meaning-making and resistance, deconstructing and reconstructing their worlds and identities. Through self-determination the limits placed on subjectivity and collective identity-making are troubled, as myriad possibilities emerge to renarrate selves and lives.

However, for the transformative and restorative potentialities of such a space to be realized, it must emerge from a shared set of values and orientations that are fundamentally relational. This relationality is what creates a space that is culturally safe, where one can be vulnerable or feel empowered to (re)imagine one's world. Within the Next In Colour initiative an ethic of relatedness was manifest in reciprocity and interconnectedness, and the respect and responsibility they held for their communities and one another. The collective and the initiative were not apart from but instead constituted by their communities. Driving intentions for the initiative were to create a structure that served as a hub to connect creatives and communities of the African diaspora, organize resources and create opportunities, and respond to community needs. For one person involved in a creative project through Next In Colour, this interconnectedness is how Next In Colour embodies a "true" definition of community arts:

> [Community arts is] where people who are in relation with each other, who try to support each other, who are connected to each other and share, not only certain elements of our identities and our experiences, but we share place, we share resources ... we're just in genuine community relationship with each other and we are arts workers. And those things combine, and [Next In Colour] is the culmination of those things. And that's what defines it, as community arts ...

They also noted that this community-making and being in relation with one another both preceded and would exist long after Next In Colour. It is not this setting that engenders such an orientation but rather a communal orientation from which the setting can spring. This ethic of relationality would also need to be the foundation of the research relationship from which to shape our own relational knowledge practices and engage in forms of accompaniment. This meant engaging critical reflexivity as researchers to think through how our research practices impacted on the efforts of the collective to self-determine. It meant finding opportunities for reciprocity, whether through coauthoring or contributing in meaningful ways to the activities of the initiative. It meant finding ways to ensure that co-constructed knowledges were created and shared democratically and not disenfranchised from the contexts and settings through which they were generated.

Through a commitment to relationality, Next In Colour itself then becomes a sustaining and generative space. Collective members spoke about the opportunities that were not available to them across their lives as young people of African heritage in Australia, whether these were spaces to come together and be, resources to bring projects to life, or seeing their stories represented. Beyond addressing these conditions, Next In Colour is also fundamentally oriented toward envisioning a different future, one in which the next generations of young people of African heritage may be free from traversing the same experiences and can grow and build on the foundations laid in the present – a "road map" for the future.

In building these foundations, to imagine different futures and possibilities entails an engagement with the past and a remembering and accounting for the absences found in dominant narratives. The creative and intellectual work produced by Next In Colour also constitutes an important archive, connecting the past, present, and future. In the following quote, a collective member, Ruth, speaks to the importance of cultural and historical remembering and preservation:

> I think a lot of it is just … the experience of like, you know, me as a South Sudanese person. Not a lot of my history is really archived, because of war, because of displacement, because of colonialism, there's not much of … information that I know about, you know, about my people. So I think that importance of archiving something, is to, you know what I mean, is to look back in fifty years, and be like this is what the narrative is, and also for like the future generations to compare the realities and the themes that we're experiencing and exploring …

The imperative to archive meets an "ethical obligation to witness, record, reclaim and acknowledge the historical experiences of others, so as to ensure that present and future generations are able to come to terms with this history, integrate it, learn from it" (Stevens et al., 2013, pp. 36–37). Curating a record serves as testimony, as representation, and as a powerful tool for transformation. Understanding the past becomes an important tool for naming the world and understanding the sources of oppression and exclusion faced by marginalized communities.

Remembering also plays an important healing and restorative function. The following is a quote from Ez Eldin, a collective member, director, and photographer, who was interviewed on the radio show Diaspora Blues (www.3cr.org.au/diasporablues) about his photography being exhibited as part of the Next In Colour initiative:

> I went back to South Sudan in Africa … for the first time and then when I went there first of all I had a culture shock, I'd never been there since I was a little kid and … I was intrigued seeing so many Black people in one place, you know what I mean, and everybody is walking around with their heads up, everybody was wearing colorful clothes, music, cars all over the place. So for me it was unreal, so after one week I was like, "I'm just gonna start taking photographs" … [I]t was healing for me, also it will be a way for me to connect with the young people who are living in Australia who have never been to Southern [sic] Sudan before who lost their cultural identity, who lost their sense of belonging, but through those photographs they get to see themselves and hopefully they will connect.   (Chuol & Ayan, 2021)

Disconnection from historical and cultural memory has profound effects, especially when harmful dominant narratives constrain subject formation (Fanon, 1967). In the previous excerpt, photography was described as an important healing practice for Ez Eldin to reengage with ancestral place and to provide a vision of a world where he did not exist as a racialized other. But it also was an important medium to convey this same sense of belonging and identity to young South Sudanese people in Australia. His photography (e.g., Figure 19.2) was not only a story of connection to ancestral place but also of migration and diaspora – connecting past and present.

Figure 19.2 *Photograph by Ez Eldin Deng.*

The archival material documented and created through the Next In Colour initiative surfaces important counter-stories that work to center lived experience and interrupt dominant narratives. These counter-stories are important cultural resources from which new and complex subjectivities can emerge. The insertion of these counter-stories into the epistemic economies of our social worlds provides important meanings for how others come to "know" people of African heritage in Australia and how they come to know themselves (Agung-Igusti & Sonn, 2020). To tell and to listen to stories are fundamentally healing processes and acts of psychic self-preservation, precipitating the development of collective consciousness as the threads of individual stories are woven into a shared understanding that provides a framework for understanding the systemic antecedents of racialized oppression and structural exclusion (Delgado, 1989; Martín-Baró, 1994). Importantly, coming to these stories through relational acts and community-making is essential, as these practices foreground trust, respect, and the politics of representation needed to hold and share others' stories ethically. Du Ve (2020) examined the narratives within *The Colouring Book*, a digital zine produced through Next In Colour that "[deconstructs] bla(c)k[1] and brown existence" (Colour Between the Lines, n.d. b) through imagery, poetry, and prose. Across these different forms were *narratives of self-determination*, in which dreaming is a space where new meanings of Blackness, family, and gender could be imagined and through which self-determination over stories decentered the dominant White and colonial narratives of indigeneity and the African diaspora in Australia. The zine also contained *narratives of ancestors*, through which connection to cultural and ancestral memories was maintained. Lastly, *narratives of self-love*

---

[1] The term "blak," originally used by Aboriginal artist Destiny Deacon in 1994, has come to be used to differentiate between the racialized experiences of Aboriginal and non-Aboriginal communities of color (Latimore, 2021).

unsettled the Eurocentric and colonial strictures on beauty and the body. Across the work that Next In Colour both creates and supports are also broader narratives that speak to the *complexity of Black identities and experiences*, countering the singular stories told of the African diaspora as criminal or refugee and the flattening of experience into a homogeneous conception of "Blackness" or "Africanness" (Kwansah-Aidoo & Mapedzahama, 2018; Majavu, 2018). Other narratives serve as *celebrations of Black excellence*, recognizing and valuing the knowledges, products, practices, and achievements that have emerged from the African diaspora and Black culture. The following is an excerpt from a spoken-word piece by Geskeva Komba showcased through Next In Colour. The excerpt shows some of the powerful counter-stories that constitute these different narratives.

Geskeva

Meaning: Removing the suffrage of being alone

I am because you are
A reality that is stronger than any dream we could ever have
Because you are an affinity so strong it's in the world so deep
Because you are one of the foundations for the vision of us standing together for radical change

You are because I am
Able to find peace amongst others who have the same vision
Because I am the reflection you had dreamed of for you had faith
Because I am the child of a nation of beasts that aren't weak
Because I am the future you saw grow with hope for a better tomorrow
Because I am continuing that long walk to freedom side by side with kin
Because I am part of a generation who will always speak
Because I am one of the single bursts of liberation that you saw when you were alone
Because I am empowered by your grace and the courage of our people
Because I am one of thousands of beacons that'll bring all that havoc that you could not reap
I am because you are and you are because I am

> Source: *Spoken-word excerpt from "Name the Word" by Geskeva Komba, full recording available at www.nextincolour.com/events/virtual-spotlight-2.*

The piece evokes ancestral and cultural memory, speaking back to family and community and a sense of lineage. It evokes a strength, grace, and courage that is carried on across time. It evokes an interconnectedness and communality in which radical change and collective action are grounded. The line "the child of a nation of beasts" is reminiscent of the words of Fela Kuti (1989) and connects into a rich history of African art and resistance. Embodied here is self-determination, history, excellence, self-love, and complex personhood within a piece that is deeply personal and reflective of an individual story yet offers a mirror for others to see their own stories in.

These stories, across their varied platforms and mediums, also radiate beyond the communities of the African diaspora as public pedagogy and sites of intercultural contact. Other projects we have documented, created by members of the creative collective responsible for Next In Colour, have shown the ways differently positioned audiences engage with such stories in acts of witnessing. Creative mediums can create an aesthetic distance, a traversal between fiction and reality, which enables conditions for both resonance and critical reflection – and the surfacing of opportunities for solidarity (Agung-Igusti & Sonn, 2020). The insertion of counter-stories into public discursive space can work to unsettle the comfort that dominant groups find in stock stories (Bell, 2010). Such unsettling challenges the complacency and willful ignorance of dominant groups that perpetuate and are perpetuated by deficient collective hermeneutical resources and "ethically bad affective investments in negatively stereotyping another group" (Dotson, 2012, p. 27). The broadening of repertoires of representation from which to construct our understandings of the world creates new possibilities for thought and action for differently positioned groups. For some, this becomes the basis of solidarity and recognition; for others, such interventions into the public sphere are less welcome. However, the presences of these counter-stories and narratives grounded in lived experience serve to highlight the incongruences and absences that have been intimately felt by communities of the African diaspora in Australia – and they become much harder to deny when preserved in archival work.

Brimbank LIVE: "It Gave Me the Opportunity to Talk About Things I Wanted to Talk About … Things Important to Me"

Brimbank LIVE is a youth-led digital radio station produced and presented by young people in the western suburbs of Melbourne, Australia. The project was created in the context of disempowerment experienced by youth in the local government area of Brimbank, which stemmed from forms of marginalization and discrimination. Brimbank is characterized by a high number of migrants and refugees who have reported lower levels on indicators of health, wealth, education, and employment opportunities (Brimbank Youth Strategy, 2019; Brotherhood of St Laurence, 2019; Paulsen, 2018). Young people within Brimbank, particularly those from migrant and refugee backgrounds, are often raced, racialized, and negatively stereotyped based on their youth and area of residence within local and institutional spaces (Brimbank Youth Strategy, 2019; Koob & Pearson, 2020). The Brimbank LIVE space was created by a group of young people from ancestral and ethnic backgrounds of South Sudan, Ethiopia, The Democratic Republic of the Congo, Samoa, Macedonia, Greece, and Croatia as an intentional site to make dynamics of oppression visible. The young people worked in solidarity to carve their own digital community radio setting and curate their own radio shows to unpack their lived experiences creatively, dialogically, and publicly. This example case illustrates how the community radio setting and output produced cultural strength and power for young people to collaboratively contest and speak back to dominant framings and author their own self-determined narratives.

Curating the Youth-Led and Digital Setting of Brimbank LIVE

In light of COVID-19 restrictions and given the closure of physical and community spaces, young people of Brimbank pitched a digital setting as an alternative space to connect, build their skills, and platform their experiences through conversational dialogue and music. According to the Community Broadcasting Association of Australia (2015), community radio provides a diverse space that platforms services and perspectives relevant to local and community-specific audiences, which are often overlooked by commercial or mass-media broadcasters. Community radio also challenges traditional ideas of delivering and consuming content as it grants community members – particularly those on the margins – social capital and resources to become media creators, contributors, and broadcasters, and it gives listeners entry points to understand and engage with their lives (Community Broadcasting Association of Australia, 2015; Sarmah & Lama, 2017). Arguably, through community radio, opportunities are created for sharing stories that are largely absent from dominant community and cultural narratives.

During the process of building Brimbank LIVE, the young team was supported by youth workers and community team leaders affiliated with a council-run community center, Brimbank Neighbourhood House, and a radio producer from a local broadcasting network, LIVE FM. One of the authors (Roshani J. Jayawardana), a young person who was born and raised in the Brimbank area, adopted ethnographic methods and also worked alongside the young team as a participant. These variously privileged and positioned individuals utilized their access to resources to make tools and opportunities available to the young people to curate their radio shows. Youth were provided radio training, studio time, and radio equipment such as devices, headsets, and microphones. The youth workers, community leaders, radio producer, and researcher also advocated and mentored youth when guidance was requested and helped promote the space publicly. Using these resources and tools, the young team collectively made decisions about the content of their radio shows and the conversations, guests, and music they would have on air. The engagement of community members through Brimbank LIVE challenged traditional spaces of knowledge production, as adult allies relinquished control and made way for youth while providing resources to enable them to become active agents in driving and leading their own space.

On his radio show, Charlie spoke of how resources and mentorship from the youth workers, community leaders, radio producer, and researcher in the process of building the radio space were enriching, encouraging, and reciprocal:

> They [the adult allies] spend so much money and effort in putting everything together. Like they bought a Mac computer for 3,200 [Australian] dollars even though we just needed a little laptop, they bought speakers that we're using, the mics that we're using, the mixer. Everything, and they're even paying for a producer . . . . Not many programs or people who run them would be like "here have a 3,200-dollar computer" . . . . They sat us down and told us what needed to be done [to create radio] and what they were going to do for us in exchange . . . . This space has changed our lives . . . and it's given me a chance to pursue what I want to do.

Hosting space, sharing expertise, and providing tools and access to youth are how adult allies can use their capital to enable and make way for those at the margins (Cammarota & Fine, 2008; Fox & Fine, 2015). They also demonstrate trust and belief in young people's ideas and voice, which are pivotal given the general mistrust and invalidation of youth experience within public spaces. Community members working collaboratively to support youth in the process of making their space sparked meaningful encounters and relationships and exemplified a contact zone (Pratt, 1991). Through the building of solidarity and working toward the same cause, adult allies supported the empowerment processes reflected in youth agency to imagine and control their visions and to make their stories known in their own curated spaces (Rappaport, 2000).

Young People as Authors and Broadcasters

Individuals reveal and make sense of themselves in the stories they tell, and there is power in stories when they are told by those who live them (Lieblich et al., 1998). Young people creating their own radio content through Brimbank LIVE showed how youth can lead knowledge production and become authors of their own stories, thereby positioning young people as knowers. Young people used their radio space to voice their stories of constraining categorizations and the discrimination that it harbors to create new narratives about their lives. Lee conveyed how the youth-led space of Brimbank LIVE permitted the process of young people telling their stories from their perspectives:

> There's so many circumstances where dominant media can be doing better, and so I feel like circumstances like this . . . with the radio. . . [and] little forms of media are kinda good because it gets more people's opinions out . . . . Being part of this program . . . I've been able to . . . have a proper voice, and I really appreciate the opportunity to have a voice.

Through this opportunity to have a "proper voice," radio broadcasting also disseminated and amplified youth's stories into the public sphere for consumption, reaching approximately 10,000 podcast and live listeners. This signals how the platform of community radio positioned youth as epistemic agents, as narratives were heard through the voice of the storyteller, and how the digital element of broadcasting gave these stories their "wings" (Copeland & De Moor, 2018). Additionally, as radio shows were archived in a public and online space, youth's stories could be accessed and engaged with even after broadcasting ceased. This demonstrates not only how youth lead knowledge production and author their own stories through community radio but also how community radio is a vessel for stories to be dispersed to the community and preserved through digital archives.

Speaking Back to Dominant Stories to Re-Exist and Narrate Complex Subjectivities

Youth used their radio platform as an alternative setting to talk about their histories and lived experiences and to speak back to dominant narratives that often misrepresented youth as delinquent, inadequate, or incompetent (Fu et al., 2021; Tiller et al., 2020). Young people conveyed that speaking within the radio space allowed them to showcase their knowledge and capabilities. This is conveyed by Grace as she spoke of how young people in her community are positioned:

> I feel in general being a young person ... [y]ou just feel like you don't have a say in some things because they [the world] sees you as this young person who doesn't have experience or much knowledge ...

In light of silencing those who live and know their own truths, young people used their radio shows to speak about how dominant stories often paint them through the fixed lens of their categorizations, such as their race or ethnicity, and often diminish other aspects of their lives or contributions. This is relayed by Ali, who spoke of how her Blackness is homogenized, the perceptions attached to it are negatively framed, and the positive contributions made by her community are often excluded from dominant media constructions:

> Being South Sudanese ... we're vilified in the media, we're vilified by politicians, we're a scapegoat for violence and all things that have to do with Black people. A couple of weeks ago they [the media] said that South Sudanese people had a[n illegal] house party, but it was actually a group of West Africans. So, they [the dominant media] don't care, Black is Black, and Black could be anything to them. ... It's a double-edged sword being a young South Sudanese person .... The media only portrays the bad things .... But I see them [the South Sudanese community] doing a lot of great things.

Young people also recalled the ways in which aspects of their social and political identities mark them as "deficient" or how their past experiences blacklist them. For example, Charlie recalled his encounters with the police and described how his ethnic background and experience of being in the justice system are often used to diminish his progression toward rehabilitating and flourishing:

> I get pulled up just because I'm who I am, cos of what I did in the past and most people don't even care about what I'm doing now, they just see my record and think "you're still that person" …. I'm not even the worst one, but when you come from a background with all that shit, and you still get pulled up because of your past …. It's hard to make a change when they won't let you.

This commentary shows how young people understand and critically analyze through naming the systems and limiting discourses attached to their intersections of age, race, ethnicity, and past experiences. Mignolo and Walsh (2018) convey that naming dominant narratives illustrates resistance to them, and they discuss how the process of this resistance is intricately linked to re-existing and rebuilding new stories.

In dissecting dominant narratives and their impacts, young people reclaimed and retold complex stories about themselves, which they broadcasted as new narratives. The radio space enabled them to platform their perspectives into the public sphere and engage in dialogue about what is important to them and their lives. This showed not only that the radio content reached the community but also that the process of doing radio allowed the young people to be enriched individually. For example, Ali said:

> This [radio space] gave me the opportunity to talk about things I wanted to talk about, and things important to me … the radio show, it amplified my voice and it was something that I originally wanted to have in my community, which was really nice.

They also used the radio space to trouble dominant narratives, actively challenging perceptions of young people from the west of Melbourne. For Grace, involvement in the radio space gave her the opportunity to show that she is more than the homogenizing stereotypes imposed on her through dominant cultural narratives:

> I want to show people [through radio] that even when you're young you're capable of many, many things, and I feel like I'll be a great example myself because knowing what type of person I am – shy, really scared to like step out and like do these things [radio] – I'm really trying to push myself and show people that if I can step out and like do these things … then you can as well …

She also spoke of the personal power and confidence she gained through the process, which she hopes will be recognized by community and global listeners consuming her radio content.

As young people wanted to use the space to openly speak and defy what is expected of them, they mobilized this public resistance by engaging in dialogue about their aspirations and specific goals. Alluding to socioeconomic struggles, racial profiling, and exclusion from traditional and institutional spaces, Edward spoke on air about his aspirations of pursuing music and how being able to platform his music through his radio show built a new trajectory for him:

> At school not many people understood me and the way I was coming across. I was struggling at school, trying to learn, struggling with money. It was rough growing up the way I did, but I got through it . . .. And music helped . . . [music] has been part of my life since birth . . .. Having music is not a hobby . . .. Through this program – talking about my music on radio, writing songs – it's like a job for me, and this program has given me a chance to pursue what I want to do.

As young people created new narratives about their lives through sharing their complex subjectivities and aspirations through radio, they also articulated that there was value in the process of storytelling. Matt explained how storytelling was important in conveying his story on radio and shaping his future goals:

> I'm trying hopefully to make a cricket career and I'm working towards it, I made the Victorian team, so hopefully that happens. But if it doesn't [I'd] probably be a journalist to really share stories about people and try to use my voice to influence society. That's my ultimate goal to be able to write things and put it out there and for people to read and hear, and they can be influenced by that . . .. Like what we're doing with radio . . .. That's my ultimate goal . . . to share people's stories and to influence.

Brimbank LIVE illustrates the processes and outcomes of young people from various ethnic and racial backgrounds coming together with the support of adult allies to gain resources for and control over curating an intentional, inclusive space of resistance and mobilization and to create counter-stories and new narratives about their lives creatively and dialogically. Through the participatory processes of community radio, the young people spoke their stories of struggle, identity, and aspiration into existence. In so doing, they built solidarity and acquired community power. Brimbank LIVE shows how community spaces and radio-making as a political activity can enable young people to exercise their cultural rights and articulate their knowledge and social experiences. This process was deemed empowering and produced empowered outcomes reflected in youth's complex subjectivities and critical consciousness.

Summary and Implications

Epistemic justice is central to the goals of emancipatory praxis, which centers the lived experiences of those at the margins whose knowledge and cultural practices have been devalued and distorted, such as knowledge and cultural practices that are central to healing, dignity, and belonging (Reyes Cruz & Sonn, 2015). In this chapter we drew on theoretical and conceptual resources from decolonial writing to suggest that community arts practice can contribute to liberation-oriented projects for communities that are racialized, othered, excluded, or marginalized. The concepts coloniality of power, knowledge, and being bring into focus how colonial practices have diminished knowledge and cultures of colonized/racialized groups and how these effects continue in the present. We outlined three epistemic practices – archival retrieval, relational knowledge practices, and counter-storytelling – that can contribute to epistemic justice. Through the examples of Next In Colour and Brimbank LIVE we sought to present efforts to enact these epistemic practices with and alongside communities, highlighting the dominant cultural narratives young people contested as well as the counter-stories young people wanted to tell about their lives. Engaging with culture as a process means contesting and resignifying meanings. These processes are expressions of agency and resistance and have material and symbolic effects for people and others in their lifeworld.

Next In Colour and Brimbank LIVE illustrate these practices, and both attest to the importance of creating empowering settings that create opportunities for narrative and voice (Stewart, 2011). Community arts represent a vehicle for meaning-making and imagination, for recovery of historical memory, and for creating new narratives. As noted by Anzaldua and Keating (2015), "Imagination opens the road to both personal and societal change – transformation of self, of consciousness, community, culture, society. Without imagination transformation is not possible" (p. 44). Through participatory processes, cultural practice can be empowering, as people develop skills, problematize dominant narratives, build relationships and networks, and create new narratives about themselves. Community arts outputs elevated into the public sphere through radio, exhibitions, or performances can assert the marginalized group's status as knowers, as counter-storytelling lays the ground for an aesthetic of resistance (Teo, 2015) to harmful and oppressive dominant group narratives.

There is great responsibility held by those who are sustained by the hegemonic systems and institutions of knowledge production to seek our own forms of unsettling and find opportunities to both dream and act together. The task of being in good relations in various settings, roles, and change-oriented activities requires critical reflexivity and deliberate and deep rethinking as well as equitable access to material and symbolic resources to engage in decolonial and antiracist work. Anzaldua and Keating (2015) put it this way: "To be in conocimiento with another person or group is to share knowledge, pool resources, meet each other, compare liberation struggles and social movement histories, share how we confront institutional power, and process and heal wounds" (p. 91). Problematization and the embrace of complexity and plurality in research and practice are necessary to challenge ignorance and oppressive practices in everyday contexts.

References

Aboriginal History Archive. (2021, August 10). *Aboriginal History Archive*. Victoria University. www.vu.edu.au/about-vu/university-profile/moondani-balluk-indi

genous-academic-unit/aboriginal-research-researchers/aboriginal-history-arch
ive-aha

Adams, G., Dobles, I., Gómez, L. H., Kurtiş, T., & Molina, L. E. (2015). Decolonizing
psychological science: Introduction to the special thematic section. *Journal of
Social and Political Psychology*, *3*(1), 213–238.

Agung-Igusti, R. P., & Sonn, C. C. (2020). African-diaspora in Australia narrating
stories of belonging through community theatre: Enacting decolonial aesthetics toward epistemic justice. In J. A. Inzunza, B. O. Espinoza, Ma. V. M.
Álvarez, P. G. Corbalán, & F. J. Birth (Eds.), *Diálogos contemporáneos en
psicología comunitaria: escenarios, problemas y aprendizajes* (pp. 44–70).
University of Chile.

Anzaldúa, G., & Keating, A. (2015). *Light in the dark: Luz en lo oscuro: Rewriting
identity, spirituality, reality*. Duke University Press.

Bell, L. A. (2010). *Storytelling for social justice: Connecting narrative and arts in
antiracist teaching*. Taylor & Francis.

Brimbank Youth Strategy. (2019). *Brimbank Youth Strategy 2020–2024*. Brimbank
City Council. www.brimbank.vic.gov.au/plans-policies-and-strategies/strat
egies/brimbank-youth-strategy-2020-24

Brotherhood of St Laurence. (2019). *Smashing the avocado debate: Australia's youth
unemployment hotspots*. Brotherhood of St Laurence. www.bsl.org.au/
research/publications/smashing-the-avocado-debate/

Cammarota, J., & Fine, M. (Eds.). (2008). *Revolutionizing education: Youth participatory action research in motion*. Routledge.

Case, A. D., & Hunter, C. D. (2012). Counterspaces: A unit of analysis for understanding the role of settings in marginalised individual's adaptive responses to
oppression. *American Journal of Community Psychology*, *50*, 257–270.

Chuol, B., & Ayan, S. (2021, June 21). *Ez Eldin Deng* [radio broadcast]. 3CR. www.3cr
.org.au/diasporablues/episode-202106211430/ez-eldin-deng

Collins, P. H. (2000). Gender, black feminism, and black political economy. *The
Annals of the American Academy of Political and Social Science*, *568*(1),
41–53.

Colour Between the Lines. (n.d.a). *About*. Next In Colour. www.nextincolour.com/
about

Colour Between the Lines. (n.d.b). *About the zine*. Next In Colour. www.nextincolour
.com/about-the-zine

Community Broadcasting Association of Australia. (2015). *About community broadcasting*. Community Broadcasting Association of Australia. www.cbaa.org
.au/about/about-community-broadcasting

Copeland, S., & De Moor, A. (2018). Community digital storytelling for collective
intelligence: Towards a storytelling cycle of trust. *AI & Society*, *33*(1),
101–111.

Delgado, R. (1989). Storytelling for oppositionists and others: A plea for narrative.
Michigan Law Review, *87*(8), 2411–2441.

Dotson, K. (2012). A cautionary tale: On limiting epistemic oppression. *Frontiers:
A Journal of Women Studies*, *33*(1), 24047.

Du Ve, E. (2020). *Curating counter narratives: A case study of The Colouring Book zine
project* [Unpublished honors thesis]. Victoria University.

Dutta, U., Azad, A. K., & Hussain, S. M. (2022). Counterstorytelling as epistemic justice: Decolonial community-based praxis from the Global South. *American Journal of Community Psychology, 69*(1–2), 59–70.

Fanon, F. (1967). *Black skin, White masks*. Grove Press.

Fernández, J. S., Sonn, C. C., & Carolissen, R. (2019). Mapping in and for decolonial transnational community psychologies. *The Community Psychologist, 524*(4), 4–7.

Fernández, J. S., Sonn, C. C., Carolissen, R., & Stevens, G. (2021). Roots and routes toward decoloniality within and outside psychology praxis. *Review of General Psychology, 25*(4), 498–511.

Fine, M. F. (2018). *Just research in contentious times: Widening the methodological imagination*. Teachers College Press.

Fine, M. F. (2021). Decolonizing critical knowledges borne in the borderlands: From "morbid symptoms" to critical solidarities. In G. Stevens & C. C. Sonn (Eds.), *Decoloniality and epistemic justice in contemporary global community psychology* (pp. 59–78). Springer.

Fox, M., & Fine, M. (2015). Leadership in solidarity: Notions of leadership through critical participatory action research with young people and adults. *New Directions for Student Leadership, 148*(1), 45–58.

Freire, P. (1972). *Pedagogy of the oppressed*. Penguin Books.

Fricker, M. (2006). Powerlessness and social interpretation. *Episteme: A Journal of Social Epistemology, 3*(1–2), 96–108.

Fu, J., Wyn, J., & Churchill, B. (2021, June). *Young Australians' confidence in political institutions and their civic engagement*. University of Melbourne. https://education .unimelb.edu.au/__data/assets/pdf_file/0007/3820660/Youth-confidence-and-c3ivi cs-Eric-report.pdf

Goldbard, A. (2006). *New creative community: The arts of cultural development*. New Village Press.

Haapanen, K. A., & Christens, B. D. (2021). Community-engaged research approaches: Multiple pathways to health equity. *American Journal of Community Psychology, 67*(3–4), 331–337.

Hodgetts, D., & O'Doherty, K. C. (2019). Introduction: Applied social psychology – An evolving tradition. In K. C. O'Doherty & D. Hodgetts (Eds.), *The SAGE handbook of applied social psychology* (pp. xxv–xxxviii). SAGE Publications.

hooks, b. (1990). *Yearning: Race, gender, and cultural politics*. South End Press.

Huygens, I. (2011). Developing a decolonisation practice for settler colonisers: A case study from Aotearoa New Zealand. *Settler Colonial Studies, 1*(2), 53–81.

Kasat, P. A. (2020). *Singing the women back up: Art for social change and the empowerment of women* [Unpublished doctoral thesis]. Curtin University.

Koob, S. F., & Pearson, E. (2020, June 18). *BDK, 97, Brotherhood: Police aware of "ongoing gang issue" in western suburbs*. The Age. www.theage.com.au/ national/victoria/bdk-97-brotherhood-police-aware-of-ongoing-gang-issue-in-western-suburbs-20200618-p553v6.html

Kuti, F. A. (1989). *Beasts of No Nation* [recorded by F. A. Kuti & Egypt 80]. *On Beasts of No Nation* [Digital recording]. Shanachie Records.

Kwansah-Aidoo, K., & Mapedzahama, V. (2018). "There is really discrimination everywhere": Experiences and consequences of everyday racism among the new Black African diaspora in Australia. *Australasian Review of African Studies*, *39*(1), 81–109.

Ladson-Billings, G. (2003). It's your world, i'm just trying to explain it: Understanding our epistemological and methodological challenges. *Qualitative Inquiry*, *9*(1), 5–12.

Latimore, J. (2021, August 30). *Blak, Black, Blackfulla: Language is important, but it can be tricky*. The Sydney Morning Herald. www.smh.com.au/national/blak-black-blackfulla-language-is-important-but-it-can-be-tricky-20210826-p58lzg.html

Lieblich, A., Tuval-Mashiach, R., & Zilber, T. (1998). *Narrative research: Reading, analysis, and interpretation*. SAGE Publications.

Lykes, M. (2002). Possible contributions of a psychology of liberation: Whither health and human rights? In D. F. Marks (Ed.), *The health psychology reader* (pp. 352–372). SAGE Publications.

Madyaningrum, M. E., & Sonn, C. (2011). Exploring the meaning of participation in a community art project: A case study on the seeming project. *Journal of Community & Applied Social Psychology*, *21*(4), 358–370.

Majavu, M. (2018). The Whiteness regimes of multiculturalism: The African male experience in Australia. *Journal of Asian and African Studies*, *53*(2), 187–200.

Maldonado-Torres, N. (2007). On the coloniality of being: Contributions to the development of a concept. *Cultural Studies*, *21*(2–3), 240–270.

Malherbe, N. (2020). Articulating liberation psychologies of culture. *Journal of Theoretical and Philosophical Psychology*, *40*(4), 203–218.

Martín-Baró, I. (1994). *Writings for a liberation psychology*. Harvard University Press.

Mason, R. (2011). Two kinds of unknowing. *Hypatia*, *26*(2), 294–307.

Mignolo, W., & Walsh, C. E. (2018). *On decoloniality: Concepts, analytics, praxis*. Duke University Press.

Mills, C. W. (1997). *The racial contract*. Cornell University Press.

Montero, (2009). Methods for liberation: Liberation psychology beyond Latin America. In M. Montero & C. C. Sonn (Eds.), *Psychology of liberation: Theory and applications* (pp. 73–92). Springer.

Moreton-Robinson, A. (2020, September 2). *Broadly speaking: Aileen Moreton-Robinson: 20th anniversary of talkin' up to the White woman*. Wheeler Centre. www.wheelercentre.com/events/aileen-moreton-robinson-20th-anniversary-of-talkin-up-to-the-white-woman

Paulsen, I. K. (2018). Relationships, relationality and schooling: Opportunities and challenges for Pacific Islander learners in Melbourne's western suburbs. *International Education Journal: Comparative Perspectives*, *17*(3), 39–54.

Pohlhaus, G. (2017). Varieties of epistemic injustice. In I. Kidd, J. Medina, & G. Pohlhaus (Eds.), *The Routledge handbook of epistemic injustice* (pp. 39–58). Routledge.

Pratt, M. L. (1991). Arts of the contact zone. *Profession*, *1991*, 33–40.

Pybus, C. J. (2006). *Black founders: The unknown story of Australia's first Black settlers*. UNSW Press.

Quayle, A. F., & Sonn, C. C. (2019). Amplifying the voices of Indigenous elders through community arts and narrative inquiry: Stories of oppression, psychosocial suffering, and survival. *American Journal of Community Psychology, 64*(1–2), 46–58.

Quijano, A. (2000). Coloniality of power and Eurocentrism in Latin America. *International Sociology, 15*(2), 215–232.

Rappaport, J. (2000). Community narratives: Tales of terror and joy. *American Journal of Community Psychology, 28*(1), 1–24.

Reyes Cruz, M., & Sonn, C. C. (2015). (De)colonizing culture in community psychology: Reflections from critical social science. In: R. Goodman & P. Gorski (Eds.), *Decolonizing "multicultural" counseling through social justice.* Springer.

Sarason, S. B. (1972). *The creation of settings and the future societies.* Brookline Books.

Sarmah, B., & Lama, S. (2017, December 16–17). *Radio as an educational tool in developing countries: Its evolution and current usages* [Conference presentation]. International Conference on Developmental Interventions and Open Learning for Empowering and Transforming Society. Krishna Kanta Handiqui State Open University, Assam, India.

Segalo, P. (2016). Using cotton, needles and threads to break the women's silence: Embroideries as a decolonising framework. *International Journal of Inclusive Education, 20*(3), 246–260.

Shotwell, A. (2017). Forms of knowing and epistemic resources. In I. J. Kidd, J. Medina, & G. Pohlhaus (Eds.), *The Routledge handbook of epistemic injustice* (1st ed., pp. 179–197). Routledge.

Sloan, T. (2018, July). *On waking up to coloniality: An invitation.* Parkmore Institute. www.parkmoreinstitute.org/on-waking-up-to-coloniality-an-invitation/

Smith, L. T. (2012). *Decolonizing methodologies: Research and Indigenous peoples* (2nd ed.). Zed Books.

Solórzano, D. G., & Yosso, T. J. (2002). Critical race methodology: Counter-storytelling as an analytical framework for education research. *Qualitative Inquiry, 8*(1), 23–44.

Stevens, G. E., Duncan, N. E., & Hook, D. E. (2013). *Race, memory and the apartheid archive: Towards a transformative psychosocial praxis.* Palgrave Macmillan.

Stewart, E. (2011). On voice: Difference, power, change. In M. S. Aber, K. I. Maton, & E. Seidman (Eds.), *Empowering settings and voices for social change* (pp. 193–206). Oxford University Press.

Sullivan, S., & Tuana, N. (Eds.). (2007). *Race and epistemologies of ignorance.* Suny Press.

Teo, T. (2005). *The critique of psychology: From Kant to postcolonial theory.* Springer.

Teo, T. (2015). Essay on an aesthetics of resistance. In J. Cresswell, A. Haye, A. Larrain, M. Morgan, & G. Sullivan (Eds.), *Dialogue and debate in the making of theoretical psychology* (pp. 303–310). Captus.

Thomas, R. E., & Rappaport, J. (1996). Art as community narrative: A resource for social change. In M. B. Lykes, R. Liem, A. Banuazizi, & M. Morris (Eds.), *Unmasking social inequalities: Victims, voice and resistance* (pp. 317–336). Temple University Press.

Tiller, E., Fildes, J., Hall, S., Hicking, V., Greenland, N., Liyanarachchi, D., & Di Nicola, K. (2020). *Youth survey report 2020*. Mission Australia. www .missionaustralia.com.au/what-we-do/research-impact-policy-advocacy/ youth-survey

Udah, H. (2018). "Not by default accepted": The African experience of othering and being othered in Australia. *Journal of Asian and African Studies, 53*(3), 384–400.

Watkins, M., & Shulman, H. (2008). *Toward psychologies of liberation*. Palgrave Macmillan.

PART VI

Education and Engaged Research

20 Action Civics

Kathryn Y. Morgan and Parissa Jahromi Ballard

Introduction

The goal of civic education is to support youth's knowledge, beliefs, commitments, and actions as participants in society (Crittenden & Levine, 2018). Through civic curricula, schools prepare young people for relating to one another, their communities, institutions, and the nation state in constructive ways (Dewey, 1923; Rebell, 2018). However, school reform, standardization, and disinvestment in civic education have disrupted youth's civic development (Levine & Kawashima-Ginsberg, 2017). As schools face competing pressures in allocating time and resources, students lose opportunities to engage in civic life. The civic opportunities that remain are unequally distributed across schools and neighborhoods (Levinson, 2012).

For the past twenty years educators have looked to action-oriented curricula to address the disparity in civic opportunity that their students face (Gingold, 2013). Evidence that youth in the US were experiencing political polarization and civic disengagement at unprecedented rates illuminated the need for school-based interventions to support students' authentic civic development (Levinson, 2012; Youniss, 2011). This sparked the creation of a new form of civic curriculum that drew on strengths-based approaches, positive youth development, and Deweyan experiential education (CIRCLE, 2013). This novel approach to civic education became known as *action civics*, a broad term that describes learning opportunities that go beyond traditional civics education by viewing youth as assets in their community and engaging youth in addressing local issues (CIRCLE, 2013). To build this emerging field, a community of educators and researchers convened in 2010 to create the National Action Civics Collaborative (NACC), a network of curriculum providers, educators, and practitioners committed to supporting experiential civic education for all youth (NACC, n.d.). Action civics proliferated in 2012 when then-US Secretary of Education Arne Duncan described it as "the new generation of civic education" (Duncan, 2012; Gingold, 2013). The field has since expanded to include over thirty NACC member organizations who lead the charge in expanding action civics across the United States through curriculum development and legislative advocacy (NACC, n.d.). Action civics has continued to gain prevalence as an immersive alternative to traditional civic education, which has been critiqued for failing to address the shortcomings of the US political system and the structural forces that shape students' experiences in US civic life (Abramowitz et al., 2018). Although action civics is US-centric, it has developed alongside similar participatory approaches to engaging youth in social change efforts that have gained international traction over the past twenty years (Ballard et al., 2019b). As global youth populations surge, more organizations view youth participation as "critical to global stability, economic growth, and development" and are supporting youth engagement in local decision-making accordingly (USAID, n.d., para. 4).

Action civics is a promising instructional model rooted in experiential learning that offers an asset-based approach to civic education (Warren, 2019). Through action civics, youth "engag[e] in a cycle of research, action, and reflection about problems they care about personally while learning about deeper principles of effective civic, and especially political, action" (Levinson, 2012, p. 224). In this chapter, we define action civics and outline inherent challenges; describe action civics intermediary organizations and discuss two examples; place action civics within a community power framework; discuss how action civics may promote psychological empowerment; explore specific setting features that make action civics programs ripe settings for empowerment; and describe implications for practice and future directions for research about action civics as settings for empowerment.

Action civics curricula follow a multistep framework that emphasizes youth voice, youth expertise, collective action, and reflection (CIRCLE, 2013). Action civics' emphasis on the *collective* distinguishes it from traditional civic education, which has primarily sought to develop *personally responsible* civic agents who obey laws, pay taxes, and act morally (Westheimer & Kahne, 2004). Action civics instead seeks to foster *participatory* and *justice-oriented* civic agents (Westheimer & Kahne, 2004). In action civics, students practice participatory civic agency by selecting a local issue and addressing it through active community engagement. Students practice justice-oriented civic agency by critically analyzing their selected issue's root cause to consider it structurally. This root cause analysis is a defining feature of the action civics model. Although action civics is a justice-oriented model, action civics programs do not necessarily prepare justice-oriented civic agents or result in more just realities. However, action civics calls for a level of criticality and attention to systems change that goes beyond participatory civic agency. Through interrogating systemic injustice, students can move closer to disrupting unjust patterns in their communities

Disparity in the amount and quality of opportunities for civic engagement creates a *civic opportunity gap* that disproportionately impacts historically marginalized youth, who are significantly less likely to be offered high-quality civic education in school (Levinson, 2010; Shapiro & Brown, 2018). Across the lifespan, students who experience a civic opportunity gap engage in voting, volunteering, advocacy, and activism far less frequently than their peers who receive high-quality civic education in school (Gaby, 2017; Youniss, 2011). The impact of policies such as standardization and high-stakes testing may contribute to this gap. Furthermore, many youth live in *civic deserts* or communities without civic engagement opportunities that cater to youth, such as out-of-school youth programming, arts and culture organizations, and religious spaces (Atwell et al., 2017). Exclusion from forms of civic life and civic engagement in multiple settings contributes to a *civic empowerment gap* (Levinson, 2010). Given the links between earlier civic engagement on later developmental outcomes such as well-being and socioeconomic status (e.g., Ballard et al., 2019a), inadequate early civic instruction and lack of local, meaningful opportunities for civic engagement may contribute to disparities over the long term. Empowering community settings like action civics have the potential to reach far beyond the classroom and offer entry points into civic life (Ballard et al., 2016). Such civic opportunities can profoundly shape sociopolitical environments, with implications not only for youth empowerment but also for creating a thriving society (Flanagan & Christens, 2011).

Challenges in Action Civics

Action civics curricula face a range of barriers to implementation that limit the field's efficacy as an empowering community setting. Many challenges to action civics implementation are rooted in the same inequitable policies and practices that action civics aims to address. First, action civics is a complex approach that requires flexibility, which is often at odds with the realities of accountability and standardization within the US public school system (Morgan et al., 2022). In some instances, action civics is limited to enrichment and elective courses, meaning only academically advanced students are offered the curriculum while their peers participate in courses aimed at improving standardized test scores. Constraints on time and pressure to align instruction to testable material may result in students' final projects being cut short, reducing or eliminating the action portion of the curriculum. Priorities are ever-evolving in the US education policy landscape, and schools have many competing requirements that can require teachers to abandon the curriculum in order to fulfill a new mandate from their principal or district. Learning about root causes of inequitable social conditions without opportunities to address these conditions may ultimately result in students' disempowerment as students reflect on injustice without scaffolded opportunities to act (Christens et al., 2013; Watts & Hipolito-Delgado, 2015). When projects are cut short, students' opportunities for action are stifled.

Additionally, the types of systemic change that action civics promotes rarely fit neatly within the confines of the academic calendar, which may lead to students in school-based action civics programs struggling to situate themselves as viable actors in addressing social issues (Morgan et al., 2022). This creates an important tension, as many action-oriented projects fail to bring about concrete changes or to generate lasting campaigns for change, particularly when they are not coupled with out-of-school opportunities to build on the momentum generated in schools. However, without in-school curricula, the pool of youth who have access to action civics would be inequitably limited to those who are already active in extracurricular organizations aimed at fostering social change. For these reasons, school-based action civics programming may be a conduit for long-term systems change efforts happening outside of schools.

Action civics may appear to be an uncontroversial approach to closing the civic opportunity gap, as promoting active citizenship has considerable bipartisan support (Rebell, 2018). However, action civics has recently faced critiques for being too politically progressive, despite many action civics intermediary organizations espousing nonpartisanship. As action civics gained traction as a viable response to addressing gaps in civic education, conservative groups criticized the field and deemed action civics as radical and politically divisive (Kurtz, 2021). Such critique may create barriers to implementation in the US's increasingly polarized climate if school administrators believe families might not support action civics for political reasons.

Challenges also arise when adult action civics facilitators are unprepared to engage students in addressing systemic injustice. Action civics engages students in exploring deep-rooted community issues requiring complex solutions. Teachers may feel unprepared to facilitate an open classroom climate in which youth can discuss complex topics relevant to their communities (Godfrey & Grayman, 2014; Hess, 2009). Teachers may also feel unprepared to share power with youth through experiential project-based civic education (Abramowitz et al., 2018). As action civics seeks to bring youth voice into otherwise-adult spaces, both groups may struggle to navigate shared decision-making and the promotion of youth–adult partnerships. Despite a renewed focus on the part of some action civics intermediaries to enhance their adult training processes to aid youth in taking on new responsibilities within the civic sphere, action civics has implications for creating social change only to the extent that adults with power respect and value youth's funds of knowledge and their local expertise.

Action Civics Intermediary Organizations

Action civics is often facilitated through partnerships between schools and action civics intermediary organizations. Although some educators and youth-serving professionals independently enact action civics in their classrooms and community programs, intermediary organizations enhance practitioners' capacity to support high-quality civic education through providing a

Figure 20.1 *An action civics class mapping assets, opportunities, and challenges in their neighborhood.*

standards-aligned curriculum, teacher training and coaching, volunteer training and coordination, and curricular extension opportunities. Intermediary organizations support youth by brokering youth–adult partnerships that can advance student-led policy and advocacy solutions and by mobilizing their networks to build public will and garner public support for student projects. Partnerships between schools and intermediary organizations are particularly beneficial for schools in civic deserts. Such partnerships position schools as civic hubs where youth have the resources needed to enact social change. For these reasons, intermediary networks make up the bulk of NACC organizations and play a crucial role in the growth of the field through providing direct curricular support to teachers and advocating for the expansion of action civics education to legislators and school administrators (NACC, n.d.).

Two examples of action civics intermediary organizations with vast differences in size and scope are *Generation Citizen*, a nationwide organization and leader in action civics, and *Design Your Neighborhood*, a small organization fusing action civics and urban design in Nashville, Tennessee (see Figure 20.1). Generation Citizen and Design Your Neighborhood are not representative of all action civics intermediary organizations, but they offer a unique case study due to key differences between the two approaches (e.g., program scale, project issue selection) while sharing a theory of change that unites the field. We briefly describe each organization before highlighting the organizational aspects that provide empowering settings for youth.

Generation Citizen

Generation Citizen (GC) is a nonprofit and nonpartisan organization that administers a semester-long civics curriculum designed for middle and high school students. Launched in 2009, GC is a founder of the action civics field. Generation Citizen has operated in over ten states and has engaged over 90,000 students in action civics projects (Generation Citizen, 2020b). Through their expansive scope, GC aims to close the civic engagement gap in under-resourced school districts. To that end, GC prioritizes working with students in historically marginalized communities who are likely to be excluded from the political process (Generation Citizen, 2020b).

The GC curriculum includes fourteen lessons implemented in social studies or elective classes. During GC's in-class program, students think broadly about issues impacting their community, choose one local issue to focus on, evaluate the root cause(s) of the problem they have identified, develop a focused and strategic plan to address the issue, take action by implementing a campaign to address the issue, and reflect on their process (Generation Citizen, n.d.b).

The original GC model relied on partnerships between classroom teachers and Democracy Coaches cofacilitating the curriculum. Democracy Coaches were typically college student volunteers who received training in the GC model from GC staff. Generation Citizen has recently adjusted its model and launched an exclusively teacher-led curriculum. The teacher-led model allows GC to expand support, training, and leadership development to teachers to support them in fostering a democratic school environment that continues beyond the project (Generation Citizen, 2020b).

Each GC classroom follows a common framework known as the Advocacy Hourglass. This theory of change helps students promote systemic change through "political engagement, which we define as interaction with power" (Generation Citizen, n.d.c, p. 2). Students are trained to deliberate and build consensus as they work together to choose a single issue to address as a collective. Some classes focus on in-school issues (e.g., school lunch programs, dress codes), while others address community issues (e.g., access to part-time employment, community violence; Ballard et al., 2016; Pope et al., 2011). The selected issue's scope impacts students' Action Plans, including appropriate intervention targets (e.g., institutions, community groups, policymakers) and tactics for achieving their desired social change. For example, one GC class engaged in a campaign addressing on-campus vaping. Students analyzed advertising strategies that tobacco companies use to encourage young people to vape, contacted legislators with their findings, and presented their research to a state representative (Generation Citizen, 2019). Their representative then integrated students' testimony into a bill to limit vaping product sales in youth-accessible stores.

Generation Citizen culminates with a Civics Day during which representatives from GC classrooms in each city present their plans to other GC students, community members, public officials, GC staff, political stakeholders, and community members. These stakeholders share feedback and insights with students and serve as volunteer judges to recognize outstanding projects, teachers, and students. Generation Citizen awards prizes for top presentations, and students get to see what their peers at other schools have done. Ultimately, Civics Day encourages students to continue working toward social change after their time in the program ends (Generation Citizen, n.d.a).

Generation Citizen also provides program alumni with opportunities to join student leadership committees within the organization. These groups advocate for funding and legislation to bolster civic education across the country. Generation Citizen is also creating compensated fellowships for alumni in political, advocacy, and governmental offices to encourage them to remain involved in policy and advocacy after completing the curriculum.

Design Your Neighborhood

Design Your Neighborhood (DYN) is a place-based action civics curriculum that engages students in addressing disparities in the built environment. Design Your Neighborhood is situated within the Civic Design Center, a participatory community development nonprofit organization in Nashville, Tennessee. The Civic Design Center has a long history of grassroots urbanist action, combining principles of community development and grassroots organizing to address equity issues in the urban environment. In 2017, DYN set out to produce a middle school curriculum in partnership with the Metro Nashville Public School District. The curriculum is modeled after two books on Nashville's urban environment published by the Civic Design Center (Gaston & Kreyling, 2015; Kreyling, 2005). These books propose changes in Nashville's urban policies, systems, and environments that are key to reducing structural inequality in the city.

To build the curriculum, DYN assembled a team of high-impact teachers who had a history of engaging their students in social justice-oriented experiential learning. These teachers cowrote action civics curricula with community development and urban planning professionals from the Civic Design Center. Together, they crafted five three-week standards-aligned units for English, social studies, math, science, and visual arts classes. The units function independently within each content area but are combined to offer an interdisciplinary exploration of locally specific urban design issues that have exacerbated inequality in Nashville.

Teachers sign up with their grade-level teaching teams to implement DYN's curriculum in their classrooms. Before implementation, teachers are trained in the basics of equitable urban design and prepared to help their students address a community issue through action civics. A daylong teacher training session introduces teachers to the curriculum and provides a crash course in Nashville's history of neighborhood displacement, White flight, blockbusting, systemic disinvestment in public transit, highway construction, pollution within historically Black neighborhoods, and school bussing policies (Erickson, 2016).

The DYN curriculum first offers students a brief urban design education that presents essential factors for a healthy built environment (e.g., affordable housing, active transit, parks and open spaces, food resources). The curriculum then provides a shared language to describe systemic issues (e.g., displacement, gentrification, redlining) rooted in histories of oppression. Students then learn policy tactics and community responses (e.g., place-keeping, community land trusts, tenant protections) that could increase equity in Nashville's built environment. The rest of the curriculum uses the action civics theory of change to engage youth in collaborative local decision-making processes that address the structural barriers entrenched in Nashville's built environment. Students work to address disparities in the city's urban design policies and systems in each core subject. For instance, students in English classes might create a podcast to introduce their issue to other youth by interviewing neighbors, reaching out to government officials, or spotlighting community organizations, while art classes focus on community development and place-keeping processes, like creating a mural or building a small free library. Students are supported by local volunteers from relevant fields, including architects, urban planners, community organizers, engineers, government officials, and artists.

At the end of each school year, DYN hosts a Youth Design Exhibition to showcase students' action civics projects. Students invite community stakeholders (e.g., business leaders, school and government officials, community organizers, design professionals) to attend. At the Exhibition, students set up stations to share their projects with attendees, lead panel discussions to address topics relevant to the curriculum, and brainstorm ways to build on their action civics experiences.

Design Your Neighborhood has established partnerships with eighteen of thirty-three middle schools in Metro Nashville Public Schools, reaching over 7,000 students. Design Your Neighborhood aims to eventually partner with all thirty-three schools to allow every young person in Nashville to learn how an equitable built environment supports a thriving city. Additionally, DYN engages "graduates" of the curriculum in ongoing action civics projects through the Nashville Youth Design Team. The Team uses community development, youth organizing, participatory mapping, and action research to understand and address factors in the built and natural environment that contribute to youth well-being (Morgan et al., 2022).

Community Power

Generation Citizen and Design Your Neighborhood are unique school-based programs that are meant to empower youth. However, these programs are contextually bound and therefore influenced by societal, institutional, organizational, and interpersonal factors that can constrain community power (Nasir & Kirshner, 2003; Rubin & Jones, 2007). *Community power* is a multidimensional construct that accounts for how individuals work to address issues in their community through collective action. Community

Table 20.1 *Features of the action civics model that support multidimensional youth community power.*

Dimensions of community power	Features of the action civics model
Situational	Scaffolds youth-led collective action
	Alters structural and social conditions in communities and organizations
	Supports youth–adult partnerships and coalition-building
Institutional	Facilitates youth agenda-setting power
	Prioritizes youth voice in organizational decision-making
	Reduces gatekeeping, adultism, and tokenization of youth
Systemic	Cultivates youth's critical consciousness through root cause analysis and reflection on action
	Shifts dominant narratives that maintain traditional civics education to include more experiential and liberatory possibilities

power is contested, negotiated, and enacted in action civics settings. Next, we review the situational, institutional, and systemic dimensions of community power and propose how features of the action civics model might support them (see Table 20.1; Christens, 2019; Lukes, 2005).

Situational Power

Situational power is exercised in the public realm through debates or conflicts over community issues (Christens, 2019). Action civics projects have the potential to alter communities' structural and social conditions (Ballard & Syme, 2016). The most tangible, visible outcomes produced as youth enact community power through action civics are in the situational domain (Christens, 2019). Youth enact situational power through collective action, challenging the status quo, addressing equity issues within the institutions that serve them, and fighting for new public policy that supports their thriving.

Situational power-building often occurs through cross-sector youth–adult partnerships. Through action civics, youth identify and broker partnerships with neighborhood coalitions, government offices, and organizing groups to advocate for, fund, and carry out equity-oriented community projects. For example, when a DYN cohort took on the issue of activating an underutilized park in their neighborhood, they collaborated with a local neighborhood association to host a community design charette. They worked with a team of architects and landscape engineers to generate a community-informed masterplan of the park and then partnered with the Metro Nashville Parks Department to fund and carry out the plan. Similarly, one GC class addressed police violence through a series of community meetings with stakeholders from the local police department and district attorney's office (Generation Citizen, 2020a). From these meetings, students deepened their understanding of the criminal justice system. They narrowed their project's focus to a policy and advocacy campaign. They successfully advocated reallocating funds to community policing, updating community outreach practices, and improving relationships between residents and police officers.

These examples illuminate the ways that action civics programs allow youth to practice building situational power. However, the goal of action civics is not necessarily for students to change public policy or disrupt oppressive institutions in one semester but rather to support youth in building on their experiences in the future through lifelong civic engagement (Pope et al., 2011; Warren, 2019). Through exercising situational power in action civics classrooms, youth develop the collective efficacy and leadership skills needed to remain involved in systems change efforts across their lifespans (Christens, 2019).

Institutional Power

Institutional power is exercised through allowing, disallowing, prioritizing, and selecting issues that are open for public debate. Institutional power in local decision-making is often purposefully hidden from public view. When organizations reproduce the status quo by setting the agenda, tempering public participation, and acting as gatekeepers, they exercise institutional power to prevent transformative change (Bachrach & Baratz, 1962; Christens, 2019). Action civics programs exist within communities and institutions such as schools, community centers, and other youth-serving organizations with well-established hierarchies and norms that dictate who has the right to participate and how (Kohfeldt et al., 2011). These settings may have histories of precluding youth participation, tokenizing youth, or excluding them from decision-making about issues that impact them (Akiva & Petrokubi, 2016; Hart, 1992).

Action civics can support settings in which youth exercise institutional power. For example, through action civics, youth leverage agenda-setting power as they select issues to address. Youth are experts over their own lives. When youth expertise is recognized, it disrupts adultism and creates opportunities for more expansive participation in civic life (Kohfeldt et al., 2011). Action civics supports youth decision-making, agency, and power in the organizations they are part of. The value action civics places on youth expertise and local knowledge can disrupt adultist tendencies that engage youth in tokenistic roles or co-opt youth's voices to support an adult agenda. Instead, through action civics, participation is youth-led, youth are integral to the direction of the work, and decision-making is shared with adults (Hart, 1992). For example, Mikva Challenge employs more than 110 youth across five youth-led councils. Each council addresses ongoing local issues (e.g., health, school climate, juvenile justice) that coincide with committees within Chicago's city government. Youth councils work directly with local city officials to make policy recommendations, resulting in nineteen shifts in state and local policies that support and expand action civics in 2020 (Mikva Challenge, 2020). Similarly, in Philadelphia, high school students in Presenting Our Perspectives on Philly Youth News (POPPYN) are "working to alter the landscape of local media by highlighting the missing perspectives, contributions and concerns of young people" (University Community Collaborative n.d.b, para. 2). Youth partner with journalists to product short films and television segments in which they explore issues of importance to youth in their city, bringing this crucial perspective to a broader audience.

Sharing power in this way is a core tenet of action civics. This is a radical shift in normative structures in most schools, where teachers, administrators, and policymakers determine the scope and sequence of a class period with little input from students. By giving youth agenda-setting power as they prioritize and select the local issue that their class will address collectively, youth expand the scope of what can be addressed in schools to include issues that were previously not up for debate (Christens, 2019).

Systemic Power

Systemic power is enacted through disrupting dominant narratives – the pervasive and widely accepted cultural stories that reify the social status quo. Dominant narratives often justify existing distributions of resources and opportunities that benefit dominant groups. These limiting, harmful narratives sustain normative distributions of power. The creation of more just, liberatory narratives requires unlearning, introspection, and interrogation of inequitable distributions of power (Christens, 2019).

Dominant narratives in education settings reinforce socially reproductive forms of civic education and minimize the role of young people in civic life. For example, civic education has historically involved promoting the knowledge and skills that youth need to pledge their allegiance and demonstrate loyalty to the nation state through engaging in political processes, adhering to law and order, and trusting that civic institutions are fair and just (Gutmann, 1995). These narratives normalize adults as civic *actors* and youth as civic *learners*. This negates youth's position as "already civic beings with identities and experiences that inform their ideas about what problems matter and how they can be solved" (Swalwell & Payne, 2019, p. 127). These dominant narratives justify youth's exclusion from decision-making, agency, and power in addressing issues that impact their lives.

Action civics can disrupt dominant narratives about civic education at two levels. The act of engaging in root cause analysis can illuminate narratives that justify the unequal distribution of resources and opportunities. For example, students participating the in the iEngage Summer Action Civics Institute examine diverse perspectives on their issues of choice, which range from youth homelessness to pollution, to identify root causes and propose potential solutions (Blevins et al., 2021; iEngage, n.d.). The Street Law action civics curriculum similarly leads students through the process of analyzing root causes of injustice in the US legal system so that youth can advocate for their rights and work toward creating a more just and fair society (Street Law, n.d.). Through action civics, youth learn about the interlocking systems of oppression that result in social inequities, and many action civics projects seek to address such inequities. This gives students space to interrogate the dominant narratives they were socialized into and increases their critical consciousness.

Although many educators and administrators are unsatisfied with traditional civic education, they are entrenched within a system that constrains social change. When educators and administrators adopt action civics in their schools, it may serve to normalize more expansive, liberatory forms of civic education and disrupt the status quo. For example, schools that engage students in the Earth Force action civics curriculum reject normative forms of environmental education that focus on personal behavior change and instead engage students in contributing to systemic solutions for community sustainability through action-oriented and project-based learning (Earth Force, n.d.). When educators and administrators interrogate the influence of dominant narratives on their civics instruction and choose to engage their students in action civics, they exercise systemic power.

Psychological Empowerment

Psychological empowerment is an ecological and contextually oriented construct that youth develop as they work together to build power within community settings (Cattaneo et al., 2014; Christens, 2013; Zimmerman, 2000). Through psychological empowerment, youth experience positive developmental processes that allow them to exert control over their own lives, have a voice in community decisions, and critically evaluate their sociopolitical environments (Ballard & Ozer, 2016). Here, we consider research that aligns action civics with several components of psychological empowerment. We also discuss the promise of action civics as an empowering process and address tensions that arise as youth develop psychological empowerment.

The action civics field has produced a small but growing body of research addressing the impacts of program participation on psychological empowerment among youth. Overall, quantitative evaluations of action civics interventions reveal modest gains in constructs related to psychological empowerment. Qualitative evaluations have provided students with opportunities to share their experiences of engaging with action civics curricula and their perceptions of how action civics projects impact communities (Ballard et al., 2016; Cohen et al., 2018; Hart & Wandeler, 2018; Lecompte et al., 2020; Pope et al., 2011).

Community participation – which is a behavioral component of psychological empowerment – has been considered in several action civics studies. The accumulation of civic experiences through prolonged community participation is fundamental to psychological empowerment (Itzhaky & York, 2000). Community participation is a precursor to gains in other components of psychological empowerment, such that youth gain psychological empowerment through experiences in empowering community settings. For example, studies of GC frequently inventory or describe youth community participation (Ballard et al., 2016, 2019b), and studies of the iEngage summer civics camp have demonstrated gains in youth's perceived readiness for community participation (Blevins et al., 2021), but research has not yet studied long-term changes in the behavioral component by measuring community participation years after experiences in action civics programs.

Some research has assessed the emotional component of psychological empowerment among participants in action civics. This component is typically operationalized as the feeling that one's active participation and involvement can influence civic decision-making. Studies of GC have shown that engaging in action civics is associated with gains in civic self-efficacy (Ballard et al., 2016). Longitudinal studies of iEngage have also demonstrated that gains in civic competence – a construct related to the emotional component of empowerment – are most pronounced after students' first exposure to action civics but continue to increase as students engage in additional action civics projects (LeCompte et al., 2020).

The relational component of psychological empowerment addresses the way relationships facilitate the development and exercise of power at multiple levels (Christens, 2011). Action civics has been found to support listening, empathy, trust, and deliberation, particularly between groups of students with differing views, attitudes, and experiences who were engaging in Project Soapbox, an action civics program in which students engage in public speaking to address issues that impact their communities (Andolina & Conklin, 2020; Mikva Challenge, n.d.a). This may be conceptually related to relational empowerment, particularly the *bridging social divisions* element, which "refers to the set of competencies necessary for building trust and reciprocity across lines of differences" (Christens, 2019, p. 71).

Finally, the cognitive component of psychological empowerment involves developing a critical awareness of community power. This includes understanding how systemic and institutional forces shape society and how social change occurs (Christens, 2019). Research on the cognitive component is emergent and particularly limited in studies of youth (Speer et al., 2019). Studies of critical consciousness development in DYN found that school-based action civics supports critical reflection and critical motivation but has limited efficacy in facilitating critical action (Morgan & Christens, 2023), and a study of GC suggests five key ways that the curriculum aligns with critical consciousness development, such as emphasizing action and incorporating critical reflection (Ballard & Cohen, 2023). This suggests that action civics may be particularly well-suited to fostering the psychological components of critical consciousness and supporting the development of cognitive empowerment, given the conceptual overlap between these two constructs (Christens et al., 2016).

While the literature suggests that participating in action civics may help to cultivate psychological empowerment, disempowerment can still occur. Given that action civics projects occur in an education system with a legacy of perpetuating inequity (Noguera, 2017), youth might be hesitant to attempt systems change from within the system. Additionally, psychological empowerment requires critical analysis of social injustice, and while some youth might find power in consciousness-raising, it may also illuminate painful and difficult realities. This may be particularly salient among students from marginalized communities (Ballard & Ozer, 2016; Rubin & Jones, 2007; Watts & Flanagan, 2007). However, *critical hopefulness* may also position youth as particularly capable of working within this paradox, affecting social change within broken systems (Christens et al., 2018).

Setting Features

Youth experience different levels of empowerment in different settings (Zimmerman & Zahniser, 1991). Empowering community settings offer youth opportunities for active participation and collective power-building (Christens, 2013; Maton, 2008; Zimmerman, 2000). Here, we apply Maton's (2008) framework of organizational characteristics in empowering community settings to discuss features of action civics programs that facilitate community power and empowerment. We illustrate each feature: (1) a common belief system, (2) core activities, (3) the relational environment, (4) opportunity role structure, (5) leadership, and (6) setting maintenance and change, with an example from GC or DYN.

First, a *common belief system* in empowering community settings allows for a shared vision and theory of change that is collective, strengths-based, and mission-aligned. The common belief system in action civics centers youth collectively exercising transformative power to address a locally relevant issue in ways that simultaneously shape their developmental pathways (Ballard & Ozer, 2016; Speer, 2008). Generation Citizen's Advocacy Hourglass is a well-known example of action civics' commitment to a shared theory of change. First, it gives youth a common lens for problem-solving. The framework asks that students "approach the challenge politically – instead of thinking about solving hunger by serving at soup kitchens, think about it by broaching structural issues that enable hunger, such as lack of funding for adequate school breakfast programs" (Generation Citizen, n.d.c). Additionally, reviews indicate that many action civics intermediary organizations have adopted a theory of change similar to the Advocacy Hourglass adjusted for their curriculum's timeline and scope, (Fitzgerald, 2020; Gingold, 2013), unifying the field's commitment to transformative change through collective action. This is true for organizations like the Youth Engage Summer Civics Institute, which draws on the action civics Advocacy Hourglass model to direct campers through the process of identifying the root cause of a community issue, considering ways to address the issue, and proposing sustainable solutions to community organizers and activists in order to address the issue collaboratively (Magill et al., 2020).

These common beliefs are reinforced through a set of *core activities* associated with empowering community settings, including active learning, opportunities for reflection, innovative activities, and quality instruction. As a form of experiential, problem-based learning, action civics is particularly attuned to these features. For example, GC frequently updates its curriculum to include timely, relevant social issues for youth to examine collectively. A recently added lesson guided students through synthesizing historical and contemporary examples of voter suppression and brainstorming ways to advocate for greater access to voting for all. Students then explored current barriers to voting and learned from local experts about how they can participate in advocacy to overcome voter suppression. iCivics, a national provider of digital action civics curricula, also offers unique core activities aligned with the action civics model. Their curriculum is a series of online games in which students simulate civic participation, creating opportunities to practice meaningful civic participation "in a range of key civic roles: the President, a judge, a news editor, a community organizer, an informed voter, etc." (iCivics, 2021, p. 12). Action civics courses typically culminate with an opportunity for students to share what they have learned with an audience, as demonstrated by GC's Civics Day and DYN's Youth Design Exhibition, which helps students translate their ideas into action (see Figure 20.2).

The *relational environment* in empowering community settings attends to the quality and nature of relationships fostered within the setting and the extent to which students feel they belong both within and beyond the setting. Psychological empowerment and civic development are relational processes (Christens, 2019; Youniss, 2011), and school climate plays a significant role in contributing to the relational environment in action civics classrooms. Design Your Neighborhood's place-based curriculum is particularly interested in fostering a sense of community to support empowerment. For example, In March 2020, Nashville was hit by a tornado that devastated many of DYN's students' neighborhoods and schools. Weeks later, the COVID-19 pandemic shuttered schools across the city indefinitely. Design Your Neighborhood immediately began restructuring the curriculum for a virtual

Figure 20.2 *An action civics student discusses their project with community stakeholders.*

learning environment, altering the focus to allow youth to consider how these new realities impacted their communities and giving students space to build and maintain community while physically distanced. Some action civics organizations have demonstrated that curricular participation supports positive teacher–student and peer-to-peer relationships. For example, 95 percent of Mikva Challenge students report that they are more likely to actively listen to peers, even when they have differing viewpoints, and 95 percent of teachers report that they are more likely to have positive relationships with their students after completing the curriculum (Mikva Challenge, 2020).

An *opportunity role structure* in empowering community settings allows youth to "take on new roles and responsibilities as their skills and interest increase" (Maton, 2008, p. 12). In action civics, youth select roles that are developmentally appropriate and share power across roles (Ozer et al., 2010; Watts & Flanagan, 2007). Role choice helps youth build new skills (e.g., research, collaboration) and draw on personal strengths (e.g., public speaking, research). For example, graduates of DYN are invited to remain involved in the Nashville Youth Design Team as they progress through high school. Over time, team members can choose to take on larger, more demanding roles with increased autonomy and leadership opportunities. When team members graduate high school, they have had opportunities to develop skills in action research, youth organizing, and community development, carrying out projects of profound local importance from beginning to end. Similarly, when participants in University Community Collaborative action civics programs graduate high school, they are invited to join the Leader Corps, where they facilitate youth programs for the Collaborative and engage in professional development to support them in "working in the nonprofit and public sectors … pursuing policy-oriented graduate and law school programs … and helping to inspire a new generation of social justice leaders" (University Community Collaborative, n.d.a, para. 2).

Leadership in empowering community settings is "shared and delegated, rather than resting solely with one person, and open to expansion as new leaders emerge" (Maton, 2008, p. 13). Generation Citizen's decentralized leadership structure, including a Teacher Leadership Board, a Student Leadership Board, and a Local Leadership Board, reflects this approach. Each group brings a crucial perspective, with teachers advising on curriculum development, students sharing their experiences in the program, and local leaders supporting networking, fundraising, and public relations. Some action civics organizations, like Youth on Board, ground their understanding of leadership in antiadultist terms, functioning as a "youth-led, adult supported program where young people have the space and tools to recognize and utilize the power they hold to dismantle political and economic structures that reinforce inequity" (Youth on Board, n.d., para. 2).

Finally, *setting maintenance and change* refer to an organization's ability to adapt, form external partnerships, and gain legitimacy. In action civics, external linkages to community stakeholders who serve as classroom volunteers and consult on student projects are highly generative and provide resources to fund, market, or otherwise support student projects. These help youth gain political access, center issues relevant to youth, and support youth legitimacy to outside groups who might not yet recognize youth as change agents (Camino & Zeldin, 2002). For example, DYN is situated within the Civic Design Center, a local participatory community development nonprofit with a long history of grassroots urbanist action. The Civic Design Center legitimates DYN to city stakeholders and brokers partnerships with influential leaders working to address local issues. An association with the Civic Design Center credentials youth in DYN, which often helps city leaders reorient their professional identities to make room for youth's knowledge and local expertise. At the height of the COVID-19 pandemic and the movement for racial justice, Mikva Challenge supported youth in creating local response teams and then convened these groups through a National Youth Response Movement that "crafted policy recommendations for building more just, equitable and student focused schools" that youth then presented to Members of Congress (Mikva Challenge, 2020, p. 6).

Implications for Practice

To improve the field, stakeholders and practitioners should consider investing in action civics education and extending positive youth development opportunities.

Now is the time for a grassroots movement for equitable, antiracist, strengths-based, action-oriented civic education led by young people. At the cusp of the 2020 presidential election, a regressive political undercurrent introduced patriotic education as a replacement for civic education rooted in American exceptionalism. While this effort was ultimately nullified, patriotic education threatened to upend any progress that had been made to promote experiential civic education. Action civics intermediary organizations can take a multiscalar approach to ensure that action civics is prioritized in future civic education legislation and funding. For example, GC is carrying out a five-year federal policy campaign to ensure that action civics is properly resourced through "funding for teacher professional development, student led projects, evaluation and accountability, and state and district-level support" (Generation Citizen, 2020b, p. 21), while iCivics is lobbying for federal action civics funding to double by 2026 (iCivics, 2021). Smaller intermediary organizations like DYN and the University Community Collaborative can also advocate for state policy that promotes and prioritizes experiential and action-oriented civic education. Action civics alumni are positioned to lead these policy and advocacy campaigns using the skills they learned through participating in these curricula.

Additionally, action civics creates structures in which grassroots and community engagement can exist both in and beyond classrooms simultaneously. Social change does not follow the academic calendar, but traditional education structures limit the depth and duration of school-based action civics. To address this, educators and intermediary organizations can act as bridges to other opportunities for youth civic engagement and development (Morgan et al., 2022). This includes connecting alumni to local positive youth development programs through which they can build upon their classroom projects and hone their skills, as Mikva Challenge has demonstrated through their Youth-Led Advocacy programming, including their neighborhood leadership initiative that centers issues of youth violence, their student voice committees that foster youth–adult partnerships, and their citywide youth councils that bring youth voices to local public policy decision-making (Mikva Challenge, n.d.b). Many positive youth development processes align with the action civics model, allowing alumni to easily integrate into less bounded forms of youth-oriented civic participation. For example, action civics and youth organizing share a commitment to interrogating and deconstructing power to destabilize systems of oppression that are at work in society (Westheimer & Kahne, 2004). In both youth organizing and action civics, youth identify pressing issues in their communities, research the root causes and impacts of these issues, and employ policy and advocacy strategies to address these issues and their root causes (Christens & Kirshner, 2011). Youth participatory action research follows a similar model of enacting change, with a particular emphasis on knowledge production (Kornbluh et al., 2015). Action civics alumni might find that participating in these related positive youth development settings helps them further develop skills in local civic engagement and build community with other youth who are committed to civic participation (Ballard et al., 2019b).

Future Research

Future research in the action civics field should attend to civic development over time, expand youth outcomes of interest, employ cross-group comparisons, collect data from teachers, and assess multilevel change.

Action civics intermediary organizations are not yet systematically tracking long-term impacts among participants. This limits the field's ability to understand how action civics participation impacts youth's civic outcomes across their lifespan. Studies of sustained psychological empowerment over time are needed (Andolina & Conklin, 2018), as are studies of action civics' community impacts over time. Additionally, programs like GC and DYN are transitioning to models with sustained alumni engagement. Longitudinal research following these youth from the classroom to the community could identify civic growth trajectories and support program improvement.

Action civics programs employ many of the same measures to assess student civic outcomes (Gingold, 2013). Few studies address outcomes beyond civic knowledge, skills, and dispositions. What exists points to positive associations between civic development and other positive youth development outcomes, including self-reported physical health (Ballard et al., 2019a). More research should consider including measures beyond those historically used in traditional civics evaluative assessments to reflect the expansive learning and youth development that happens in action-oriented civics programming. Potential constructs of interest include psychological empowerment, critical consciousness, sociopolitical control, place attachment, school importance, and youth–adult partnership quality. Additionally, these studies should account for variance in effects across groups to address the ways that action civics education may differentially impact youth based on age, gender, race/ethnicity, and socioeconomic status.

Additionally, most action civics programs employ the same theory of change – the Advocacy Hourglass – to drive student projects. However, most of the existing empirical evidence about the effectiveness of action civics evaluates programs independently from one another. Cross-group comparisons (especially comparisons that include a control group) of youth involved in different action civics programs might reveal significant programmatic differences (e.g., program duration, facilitation structure, topic refinement, program setting) that impact youth outcomes.

Variations in action civics project approaches have been found to be associated with variance in civic outcomes (Ballard et al., 2016), but little evidence documents variation in curriculum implementation style among teachers. Additionally, as action civics intermediary organizations like GC and DYN

invest in teachers as the most important adult partners in school-based programming, the field needs to explore the impacts of action civics programs on
teachers' practices, pedagogies, levels of empowerment, and civic dispositions.

Finally, Kirshner and Ginwright (2012) called for research on youth organizing to conceptualize and evaluate change at three levels: individual, community, and society. We believe that research on action civics would benefit from
such an approach, as it would illuminate setting features that are particularly
suited to promoting youth empowerment and civic identity development.
By assessing settings-level features associated with empowerment, we can push
the field past a focus on individual positive youth development toward creating the conditions for collective action and social change (Rappaport, 1987).

References

Abramowitz, M. J., Blinken, A., & Kuzmich, H. (2018). *The Democracy Project final
report*. Freedom House. www.democracyprojectreport.org/sites/default/files/
2018-06/FINAL_POLL_REPORT_Democracy_Project_2018_v5.pdf

Akiva, T., & Petrokubi, B. (2016). Growing with youth: A lifewide and lifelong
perspective on youth–adult partnership in youth programs. *Children and
Youth Services Review, 14*, 248–258.

Andolina, M. W., & Conklin, H. G. (2018). Speaking with confidence and listening
with empathy: The impact of Project Soapbox on high school students.
Theory & Research in Social Education, 46(3), 374–409.

Andolina, M. W., & Conklin, H. G. (2020). Fostering democratic and social-emotional
learning in action civics programming: Factors that shape students' learning from
Project Soapbox. *American Educational Research Journal, 57*(3), 1203–1240.

Atwell, M. N., Bridgeland, J., & Levine, P. (2017, October 19–20). *Civic deserts:
America's civic health challenge* [Conference presentation]. 2017 National
Conference on Citizenship, Jonathan M. Tisch College of Civic Life, Tufts
University, Medford, MA, USA.

Bachrach, P., & Baratz, M. S. (1962). Two faces of power. *The American Political
Science Review, 56*(4), 947–952.

Ballard, P. J., & Cohen, A. K. (2023). Critical consciousness development in the
context of a widespread school-based civics intervention. In E. B. Godfrey
& L. J. Rapa (Eds.), *Developing critical consciousness in youth: Contexts and
settings* (pp. 41–59). Cambridge University Press.

Ballard, P. J., & Ozer, E. J. (2016). Implications of youth activism for health and well-
being. In J. Conner & S. M. Rosen (Eds.), *Contemporary youth activism:
Advancing social justice in the United States* (pp. 223–244). Praeger.

Ballard, P. J., & Syme, S. (2016). Engaging youth in communities: A framework for
promoting adolescent and community health. *Journal of Epidemiology and
Community Health, 70*(2), 202–206.

Ballard, P. J., Cohen, A. K., & Duarte, C. (2019a). Can a school-based civic empowerment intervention support adolescent health? *Preventive Medicine Reports,
16*, 100968.

Ballard, P. J., Cohen, A. K., & Littenberg-Tobias, J. (2016). Action civics for promoting civic development: Main effects of program participation and differences by project characteristics. *American Journal of Community Psychology, 58*(3–4), 377–390.

Ballard, P. J., Suleiman, A. B., Hoyt, L. T., Cohen, A. K., Ayenekulu, M., & Ebuy, G. (2019b). Participatory approaches to youth civic development in multicultural societies. In P. F. Titzman & P. Jugert (Eds.), *Youth in superdiverse societies: Growing up with globalization, diversity, and acculturation* (pp. 251–267). Routledge.

Blevins, B., LeCompte, K. N., Riggers-Piehl, T., Scholten, N., & Magill, K. R. (2021). The impact of an action civics program on the community & political engagement of youth. *The Social Studies, 112*, 146–160.

Camino, L., & Zeldin, S. (2002). From periphery to center: Pathways for youth civic engagement in the day-to-day life of communities. *Applied Developmental Science, 6*(4), 213–220.

Cattaneo, L., Calton, J., & Brodsky, A. (2014). Status quo versus status quake: Putting the power back in empowerment. *Journal of Community Psychology, 42*(4), 433–446.

Christens, B. D. (2011). Toward relational empowerment. *American Journal of Community Psychology, 50*, 114–128.

Christens, B. D. (2013). In search of powerful empowerment. *Health Education Research, 28*(3), 371–374.

Christens, B. D. (2019). *Community power and empowerment.* Oxford University Press.

Christens, B. D., & Kirshner, B. (2011). Taking stock of youth organizing: An interdisciplinary perspective. *New Directions for Child and Adolescent Development, 134*, 27–41.

Christens, B. D., Byrd, K., Peterson, N., & Lardier Jr., D. (2018). Critical hopefulness among urban high school students. *Journal of Youth and Adolescence, 47*(8), 1649–1662.

Christens, B. D., Collura, J. J., & Tahir, F. (2013). Critical hopefulness: A person-centered analysis of the intersection of cognitive and emotional empowerment. *American Journal of Community Psychology, 52*(1–2), 170–184.

Christens, B. D., Winn, L. T., & Duke, A. M. (2016). Empowerment and critical consciousness: A conceptual cross-fertilization. *Adolescent Research Review, 1*(1), 15–27.

CIRCLE. (2013, June). *Civic learning through action: The case of Generation Citizen.* Tufts University. https://circle.tufts.edu/sites/default/files/2019-12/civic_learning_action_generation_citizen_2013.pdf

Cohen, A. K., Littenberg-Tobias, J., Ridley-Kerr, A., Pope, A., Stolte, L. C., & Wong, K. K. (2018). Action civics education and civic outcomes for urban youth: An evaluation of the impact of Generation Citizen. *Citizenship Teaching & Learning, 13*(3), 351–368.

Crittenden, J., & Levine, P. (2018, August 31). Civic education. In E. Zalta (Ed.), *The Stanford Encyclopedia of Philosophy.* https://plato.stanford.edu/archives/fall2018/entries/civic-education/

Dewey, J. (1923). *The school and society and the child and the curriculum.* University of Chicago Press.

Duncan, A. (2012, January 10). *Secretary Arne Duncan's remarks at "For Democracy's Future" forum at the White House* [Speech]. www.ed.gov/news/speeches/secretary-arne-duncans-remarks-democracys-future

Earth Force. (n.d.). *Our Model*. Earth Force. https://earthforce.org/caps/

Erickson, A. T. (2016). *Making the unequal metropolis: School desegregation and its limits*. University of Chicago Press.

Fitzgerald, J. (2020). Civic thinking and public policy analysis: A comparative approach to political decision-making. *Journal of International Social Studies, 10*(2), 12–36.

Flanagan, C., & Christens, B. (2011). Youth civic development: Historical context and emerging issues. *New Directions for Child and Adolescent Development, 2011*(134), 1–9.

Gaby, S. (2017). The civic engagement gap: Youth participation and inequality from 1976 to 2009. *Youth & Society, 49*(7), 923–946.

Gaston, G., & Kreyling, K. (2015). *Shaping the healthy community: The Nashville plan*. Vanderbilt University Press.

Generation Citizen. (2019). *2019 Annual report*. Generation Citizen. https://generationcitizen.org/wp-content/uploads/2019/12/GC-Report-2019-FINAL-WEB.pdf

Generation Citizen. (2020a). *2020 Annual report*. Generation Citizen. https://generationcitizen.org/wpcontent/uploads/2020/12/GC_2020_Annulal_Report_FINAL_300dpi.pdf

Generation Citizen. (2020b). *Generation Citizen strategic plan*. Generation Citizen.

Generation Citizen. (n.d.a). *Civics Day*. Generation Citizen. https://generationcitizen.org/our-approach/civics-day/

Generation Citizen. (n.d.b). *Framework for action*. Generation Citizen. https://generationcitizen.org/our-approach/framework-for-action/

Generation Citizen. (n.d.c). *Our curriculum*. Generation Citizen. https://generationcitizen.org/our-programs/our-curriculum/

Gingold, J. (2013, August). *Building an evidence-based practice of action civics: The current state of assessments and recommendations for the future (CIRCLE Working Paper No. 78)*. CIRCLE. https://circle.tufts.edu/sites/default/files/2019-12/WP78_BuildingCaseActionCivics_2013.pdf

Godfrey, E., & Grayman, J. (2014). Teaching citizens: The role of open classroom climate in fostering critical consciousness among youth. *Journal of Youth and Adolescence, 43*(11), 1801–1817.

Gutmann, A. (1995). Civic education and social diversity. *Ethics, 105*(3), 557–579.

Hart, R. A. (1992). Children's participation: From tokenism to citizenship. *UNICEF Essays, 92*(6), 1–12.

Hart, S., & Wandeler, C. (2018). The impact of action civics service-learning on eighth-grade students' civic outcomes. *International Journal of Research on Service-Learning and Community Engagement, 6*(1), 1–17.

Hess, D. E. (2009). *Controversy in the classroom: The democratic power of discussion*. Routledge.

iCivics (2021). *iCivics FY21–25 strategic plan*. iCivics. https://issuu.com/icivics0/docs/final_long_form_strategic_plan

iEngage. (n.d.). *Student projects*. iEngage Summer Civics Institute. https://blogs.baylor
.edu/iengage/2019-student-projects/

Itzhaky, H., & York, A. (2000). Sociopolitical control and empowerment: An extended
replication. *Journal of Community Psychology, 28*(4), 407–415.

Kirshner, B., & Ginwright, S. (2012). Youth organizing as a developmental context for
African American and Latino adolescents. *Child Development Perspectives, 6*
(3), 288–294.

Kohfeldt, D., Chhun, L., Grace, S., & Langhout, R. D. (2011). Youth empowerment
in context: Exploring tensions in school-based yPAR. *American Journal of
Community Psychology, 47*(1–2), 28–45.

Kornbluh, M., Ozer, E. J., Allen, C. D., & Kirshner, B. (2015). Youth participatory
action research as an approach to sociopolitical development and the new
academic standards: Considerations for educators. *The Urban Review, 47*(5),
868–892.

Kreyling, K. (Ed.). (2005). *The plan of Nashville: Avenues to a great city*. Vanderbilt
University Press.

Kurtz, S. (2021, January 26). *"Action civics" replaces citizenship with partisanship*. The
American Mind: A Publication of the Claremont Institute. https://
americanmind.org/memo/action-civics-replaces-citizenship-with-
partisanship/

LeCompte, K., Blevins, B., & Riggers-Piehl, T. (2020). Developing civic competence
through action civics: A longitudinal look at the data. *The Journal of Social
Studies Research, 44*(1), 127–137.

Levine, P., & Kawashima-Ginsberg, K. (2017). *The republic is (still) at risk – And
civics is part of the solution*. Tufts University. www.civxnow.org/sites/default/
files/resources/SummitWhitePaper.pdf

Levinson, M. (2010). *The civic empowerment gap: Defining the problem and locating
solutions*. John Wiley and Sons.

Levinson, M. (2012). *No citizen left behind*. Harvard University Press.

Lukes, S. (2005). *Power: A radical view* (2nd ed.). Palgrave Macmillan.

Magill, K. R., Davis Smith, V., Blevins, B., & LeCompte, K. N. (2020). Beyond the
invisible barriers of the classroom: iEngage and civic praxis. *Democracy and
Education, 28*(1), 1–11.

Maton, K. I. (2008). Empowering community settings: Agents of individual development, community betterment, and positive social change. *American Journal
of Community Psychology, 41*, 4–21.

Mikva Challenge. (2020). *2020 Annual report*. Mikva Challenge. https://
mikvachallenge.org/wp-content/uploads/2021/02/2020-Annual-Report.pdf

Mikva Challenge. (n.d.a). *Project Soapbox*. Mikva Challenge. https://mikvachallenge
.org/our-work/programs/project-soapbox/

Mikva Challenge. (n.d.b). *Youth Led Advocacy*. Mikva Challenge. https://mikvachallenge
.org/our-work/programs/youth-led-advocacy/

Morgan, K. Y., & Christens, B. D. (2023). Critical consciousness development in
place-based action civics. In E. B. Godfrey & L. J. Rapa (Eds.), *Developing
critical consciousness in youth: Contexts and settings* (pp. 60–82). Cambridge
University Press.

Morgan, K. Y., Christens, B. D., & Gibson, M. (2022). Design Your Neighborhood: The evolution of a city-wide urban design learning initiative in Nashville, Tennessee. In R. Stoecker & A. Falcón (Eds.), *Handbook on participatory action research and community development* (pp. 282–301). Edward Elgar Publishing.

NACC. (n.d.). *History.* National Action Civics Collaborative. https://actioncivicscollaborative.org/about-us/history/

Nasir, N. I., & Kirshner, B. (2003). The cultural construction of moral and civic identities. *Applied Developmental Science, 7*(3), 138-147.

Noguera, P. A. (2017). Introduction to "Racial inequality and education: Patterns and prospects for the future." *The Educational Forum, 81*(2), 129–135.

Ozer, E. J., Ritterman, M. L., & Wanis, M. G. (2010). Participatory action research (PAR) in middle school: Opportunities, constraints, and key processes. *American Journal of Community Psychology, 46*(1), 152–166.

Pope, A., Stolte, L., & Cohen, A. (2011). Closing the civic engagement gap: The potential of action civics. *Social Education, 75*(5), 265–268.

Rappaport, J. (1987). Terms of empowerment/exemplars of prevention: Toward a theory for community psychology. *American Journal of Community Psychology, 15*(2), 121–148.

Rebell, M. A. (2018). *Flunking democracy: Schools, courts, and civic participation.* University of Chicago Press.

Rubin, B., & Jones. C. (2007). "There's still not justice": Youth civic identity development amid distinct school and community contexts. *Teachers College Record, 109*(2), 449–481.

Shapiro, S., & Brown, C. (2018, February 21). *The state of civics education.* Center for American Progress. https://files.eric.ed.gov/fulltext/ED586237.pdf

Speer, P. (2008). Social power and forms of change: Implications for psychopolitical validity. *Journal of Community Psychology, 36*(2), 199–213.

Speer, P., Peterson, N., Christens, B., & Reid, R. (2019). Youth cognitive empowerment: Development and evaluation of an instrument. *American Journal of Community Psychology, 64*(3-4), 528–540.

Street Law. (n.d.). *About us.* Street Law. www.streetlaw.org/who-we-are/offices

Swalwell, K., & Payne, K. A. (2019). Critical civic education for young children. *Multicultural Perspectives, 21*(2), 127–132.

University Community Collaborative. (n.d.a). *Leaders Corps.* University Community Collaborative. www.uccollab.org/leaders-corps

University Community Collaborative. (n.d.b). *POPPYN.* University Community Collaborative. www.uccollab.org/copy-of-programs

USAID. (n.d.) *Youth impact.* USAID. www.usaid.gov/youthimpact

Warren, S. (2019). *Generation Citizen: The power of youth in our politics.* Counterpoint Press.

Watts, R. J., & Flanagan, C. (2007). Pushing the envelope on youth civic engagement: A developmental and liberation psychology perspective. *Journal of Community Psychology, 35*(6), 779–792.

Watts, R. J., & Hipolito-Delgado, C. P. (2015). Thinking ourselves to liberation?: Advancing sociopolitical action in critical consciousness. *The Urban Review, 47*(5), 847–867.

Westheimer, J., & Kahne, J. (2004). What kind of citizen? The politics of educating for democracy. *American Educational Research Journal, 41*(2), 237–269.

Youniss, J. (2011). Civic education: What schools can do to encourage civic identity and action. *Applied Developmental Science, 15*(2), 98–103.

Youth on Board. (n.d.). *Our vision.* Youth on Board. www.youthonboard.org/our-vision

Zimmerman, M. A. (2000). Empowerment theory: Psychological, organizational, and community levels of analysis. In J. Rappaport & E. Seidman (Eds.), *Handbook of community psychology* (pp. 43–63). Kluwer Academic Publishers.

Zimmerman, M. A., & Zahniser, J. (1991). Refinements of sphere-specific measures of perceived control: Development of a sociopolitical control scale. *Journal of Community Psychology, 19*(2), 189–204.

21 Gender–Sexuality Alliances

V. Paul Poteat, Robert A. Marx, Michael D. O'Brien, and Megan K. Yang

Introduction

Over the past two decades, there have been tempered improvements in the school-based experiences of LGBTQ+ youth. On the one hand, trends suggest that overall rates of victimization on account of sexual orientation and gender identity or expression have decreased (Goodenow et al., 2016). On the other hand, schools are a setting wherein many LGBTQ+ youth continue to experience discrimination and witness it with ubiquity (Kosciw et al., 2020). Disparities in victimization between LGBTQ+ youth and their heterosexual cisgender peers persist, as do disparities in corresponding health concerns (Russell & Fish, 2019). If left unaddressed, schools will continue to be a source of stress and adversity for LGBTQ+ youth.

Nevertheless, LGBTQ+ youth can thrive when schools are supportive and affirming in their policies, practices, and pedagogy. Encouraging advances have been made in schools to protect and affirm LGBTQ+ students. Schools have adopted enumerated antibullying or antidiscrimination policies that afford explicit protections to LGBTQ+ students (Kull et al., 2016; Seelman & Walker, 2018). A number of schools use inclusive curricula representative of LGBTQ+ people and topics (Snapp et al., 2015). There are also growing numbers of LGBTQ+-affirming school clubs for students, often referred to as gender–sexuality alliances (GSAs), to which we turn our attention.

Gender–sexuality alliances have strong potential to harness youth's community power and facilitate empowerment processes among LGBTQ+ youth and their allies. As we go on to detail, GSAs are key spaces in schools for youth to access LGBTQ+-affirming support and resources, as well as providing opportunities to counteract discrimination through advocacy (Griffin et al., 2004). In some schools, they may represent the only explicitly affirming space for LGBTQ+ people. In some communities, they may be one of few accessible LGBTQ+-oriented spaces for youth.

In this chapter, we provide a brief historical overview of GSAs; describe how they tend to be structured and function; present examples of GSA efforts to amplify social power among youth to engender change; elaborate on youth empowerment within the context of GSAs; highlight group characteristics that may foster community power in GSAs; and discuss implications for GSAs and future research.

The Historical and Contemporary Context of GSAs

Historical Underpinnings of GSAs

The origins of GSAs in the US can be traced back to relatively independent and localized efforts among schoolteachers and counselors in the mid-1980s to early 1990s to provide a supportive space to LGBTQ+ students in a largely hostile and stigmatizing school setting. Project-10 is one of the earliest examples, formed in a Los Angeles high school by several students and their science teacher and counselor, Virginia Uribe (Uribe & Harbeck, 1992). Similar groups later came to be formed, largely organically. The first of these groups to be called a "GSA" (an acronym originally for "gay–straight alliance") was one formed at a school in Concord, Massachusetts, by Kevin Jennings, then an educator at the school (Wong, 2019). The primary focus of these groups tended to be to provide social and emotional support to members who experienced discrimination, as well as a place for conversation and learning about current social issues faced by LGBTQ+ communities (Lee, 2002; Uribe & Harbeck, 1992). In this way, GSAs were founded on the premise of supporting the empowerment of a community that was historically marginalized in schools.

From the start, these groups faced backlash and hostility from school administrators and conservative religious groups that sought to prohibit their formation or to restrict students' abilities to participate in them (Mayo, 2008; Miceli, 2005). Legal cases have offered mixed support for students' rights to form GSAs, and even now GSAs face barriers in their efforts (Graybill et al., 2015; Mayo, 2008; Miceli, 2005).

Contemporary GSAs

Despite these challenges, there has been a major expansion in the number of schools in the US with GSAs and comparable clubs for LGBTQ+ students and their allies. At present, these clubs are in about 38 percent of US secondary schools and in 54 percent of schools in large urban districts (Centers for Disease Control and Prevention, 2019). Their presence does vary across specific states, however, from 14 percent of secondary schools in Mississippi to 72 percent in Rhode Island. Whereas historically most GSAs were formed in high schools, increasingly they are being formed in middle schools and elementary schools. A 2015 report indicated that 5.3 percent of elementary schools had a GSA or comparable club (Centers for Disease Control and Prevention, 2015). In some areas, the growth in the number of GSAs has come with the coordinated support of nongovernmental organizations (e.g., the GSA Network) or from state education departments and local school districts themselves (e.g., the Massachusetts GSA Leadership Council, supported in part by the Massachusetts Department of Elementary and Secondary Education).

Gender–sexuality alliances and comparable LGBTQ+ youth-centered clubs and groups also have been established outside the US. For instance, IGLYO (International LGBTQI Youth & Student Organisation) is an expansive European-based organization for LGBTQ+ youth and students offering opportunities similar to GSAs (though not necessarily in schools) for LGBTQ+ youth and allies across multiple countries (Vella et al., 2009). More broadly, there have been efforts to address the school-based experiences of LGBTQ+ youth globally, some of which have included efforts to support LGBTQ+ youth empowerment within groups similar to GSAs (Kosciw & Pizmony-Levy, 2013). Still, to our knowledge, GSAs and comparable school-based groups remain less expansive or visible within other countries relative to the US and at times may first form in postsecondary education settings. The preponderance of GSA research – and research on such comparable groups – has been conducted among youth in North American schools and principally among those within the US. Consequently, much of this chapter draws on LGBTQ+ youth and ally experiences within either the US or North American context more broadly.

Although GSAs are not standardized programs, contemporary GSAs tend to share similar aspirations and show some similarities in how they are structured and function. Gender–sexuality alliances have several primary aims, which include providing settings for youth to socialize and build community with one another, seek and provide social-emotional support, access LGBTQ+-affirming resources or to learn about LGBTQ+ topics, and engage in collective action against discrimination and to promote justice for LGBTQ+ people (Griffin et al., 2004). In this respect, GSAs have both inward-facing goals (e.g., support and community-building among members) and outward-facing goals (e.g., advocacy to promote justice in their schools).

As reflected in their name, GSAs constitute a space for LGBTQ+ youth as well as their heterosexual and cisgender allies to work collectively to address issues around sexual orientation and gender diversity. Many members identify with a range of sexual orientation and gender-diverse identities other than heterosexual or cisgender (Lapointe, 2017). Yet, representation can vary across GSAs, with some including predominantly LGBTQ+ members and others predominantly cisgender heterosexual members. Likewise, the racial and ethnic diversity of GSAs can vary, sometimes reflective of the racial or ethnic composition of the larger school (Poteat et al., 2015).

Gender–sexuality alliances tend to meet from twenty minutes up to one hour each week, either after school, during lunch, or during an elective period. Meeting times and their frequency can depend on factors such as school and student resources (e.g., availability of after-school bussing, students' employment, or other school commitments), advisor availability, or other logistical constraints.

Many GSAs are youth-led and adult-supported by one or more advisors (Poteat et al., 2015; Russell et al., 2009). Youth members in some GSAs hold formal leadership positions (e.g., as president or secretary), while members of other GSAs share informal leadership roles and responsibilities over the school year. Adult advisors are often teachers, counselors, or nurses at the school.

Early GSA Research

Adding to the initial descriptive work on GSAs and youth's experiences in them, early research focused on comparing the well-being of youth in schools based on GSA presence. Cross-sectional comparisons of youth in schools with or without GSAs generally found that youth in schools with GSAs reported greater perceived safety and well-being than youth in schools without GSAs (Davis et al., 2014; Marx & Kettrey, 2016; Walls et al., 2010). These findings underscore the importance of GSA access and suggest that their presence could contribute to broader efforts to improve school climate, safety, and inclusion for LGBTQ+ students.

Some studies have made similar comparisons based on GSA membership. Their findings have been mixed in identifying differences between youth who have ever versus never been members of their school's GSA. One possibility for these less consistent differences is that the benefits of certain GSA efforts (e.g., their advocacy) could extend beyond the immediate GSA membership to benefit the larger school population. Another possibility, and one we revisit in later sections, is that comparing members to nonmembers masks variability among GSA members in their reasons for joining, their level of involvement, and the range of their experiences in the GSA.

The progressive expansion of GSAs in schools across the US and more recently in other countries as well, combined with the growth in GSA research, has underscored the need to consider GSAs and their members more carefully and contextually. Doing so could capture greater nuance in their members' experiences. Historically, GSA research has treated GSAs as monolithic (e.g., comparing schools based on GSA presence) and their members as homogeneous (e.g., comparing members to nonmembers). Scholars examining youth's involvement in other extracurricular groups have noted that such binary comparisons offer limited information and that research should move to consider variability among members along different dimensions of their involvement in these groups (Bohnert et al., 2010; Busseri & Rose-Krasnor, 2009). There has been recent movement to identify variability between GSAs in how they are structured and function, variability in GSA members' experiences, and how GSAs support youth's resilience and thriving. In doing so, research also has begun to give attention to how GSAs may be more inclusive and responsive to members with different constellations of privilege and marginalization, to address the range of needs and interests of members, and to capitalize on the strengths that they bring.

Community Power in GSAs

Gender–sexuality alliances provide a space for members to organize and advocate for change in their schools and communities (Fetner et al., 2012; Griffin et al., 2004; Miceli, 2005). In fact, when asked what they most want from their GSAs, a number of students indicate that they desire advocacy opportunities (Calzo et al., 2020). Advocacy in GSAs can take many forms with varying goals. Examples of GSA advocacy include addressing individual instances of discrimination, raising awareness of and providing information on LGBTQ+ identities and heterosexism or cissexism in schools, petitioning for changes to discriminatory school policies, or planning and attending political events (Griffin et al., 2004; Mayberry et al., 2013; Mayo, 2015).

These broad-ranging efforts are fairly consistent in their outward focus and push for more equitable treatment of LGBTQ+ youth and communities (Griffin et al., 2004). In this respect, advocacy is one way in which GSAs come to build and harness their collective power to shape their schools and communities and to promote equity and justice for LGBTQ+ people. In this section, we discuss some of these efforts, grouped according to their targets for change: (1) promoting individual attitude and behavior change; (2) seeking equity for LGBTQ+ students in school and district policies; and (3) building coalitions to address broader and intersectional issues around equity and social justice.

Actions for Individual Attitude and Behavior Change

Many GSA advocacy efforts aim to promote attitude and behavior change among students and adults at school. For instance, GSAs create awareness and education campaigns within their schools to share information about LGBTQ+ identities and examples of heterosexism and cissexism and how they affect LGBTQ+ students (Calzo et al., 2020; Fetner et al., 2012; Griffin et al., 2004; Hamby, 2007). These campaigns can include public outreach in school spaces such as in the use of bulletin boards, the lunchroom, and daily announcements for sharing information; hosting annual events (e.g., Day of Silence, Transgender Awareness and Remembrance Day); and providing panels or workshops for school personnel (Hamby, 2007; Mayberry et al., 2013; Mayo, 2015). Gender–sexuality alliance members may also serve as consultants, offering insights to adults on their experiences as LGBTQ+ members of the school community (Hamby, 2007).

These initiatives generally operate on an expectation that promoting greater awareness and knowledge about LGBTQ+ identities and experiences will lead other students and adults at school to express more LGBTQ+-affirming attitudes and behaviors. Furthermore, there is an expectation that more affirming attitudes and behaviors among students and adults will foster more welcoming and inclusive school norms and climates. At times, GSA research has alluded to this possible process to explain why students in schools with GSAs tend to perceive safer environments and greater support and report less victimization than students in schools without GSAs (Baams & Russell, 2021; Day et al., 2020; Marx & Kettrey, 2016). This process is one compelling approach that GSAs might use in their efforts to promote safer and more welcoming climates in their schools.

Actions Around School and District Policies

Many GSAs also use their collective power to challenge school and district policies and practices that discriminate against LGBTQ+ students (Macgillivray, 2005; Stonefish & Lafreniere, 2015). Such policy interventions are of broad importance to LGBTQ+ youth. Some discriminatory policies target GSAs directly. For example, GSAs in Mexico City, Ontario, and in parts of the US have resisted policies aimed at preventing their formation (Kosciw et al., 2020; Lapointe, 2018; Macgillivray, 2005). Other policies affect LGBTQ+ students in schools more broadly. As examples, GSAs have petitioned against policies preventing the discussion of LGBTQ+ identities in schools (Mayberry et al., 2013) or have advocated for enumerated anti-discrimination policies (Griffin et al., 2004).

These GSA initiatives aim to challenge heterosexist and cissexist power structures in schools by leveraging the collective efforts of GSA members (Mayberry et al., 2013; Poteat et al., 2020b). For example, members may advocate to update school dress codes prohibiting students from freely expressing their gender or may lead initiatives to allow students to change their names on school documents. Gender–sexuality alliances may also work to change rules that limit who they can bring as a date to a dance or that govern athletic participation for transgender students. In doing so, they aim to improve school climates and experiences for LGBTQ+ students by challenging discriminatory policies or petitioning for affirming policies.

This systems-level focus is an important counterpart to other GSA initiatives focused on individual attitude and behavior change. These efforts can be challenging and often require sustained approaches extending beyond a single school year. As an example, one of our partner GSAs petitioned for a gender-neutral bathroom in their school. Their efforts involved a long series of meetings and extensive conversations with administrators, both individually and at district meetings. Although some administrators, school personnel, and peers supported their efforts, the GSA also faced hostility, counterarguments, and claims that drew upon fears based in bias or prejudice. Although the GSA did succeed in securing a gender-neutral bathroom, they nonetheless have experienced ongoing concern that their efforts could be overturned. This example and other efforts like it highlight the need for more work to identify best practices for pursuing, achieving, and then maintaining systems-level changes in schools.

Actions to Build Community Coalitions

Finally, GSAs pursue advocacy to enact change at a more expansive level through their focus on salient sociopolitical issues. They often do so by forming coalitions with other social justice-oriented groups in order to have a broader impact (Fetner et al., 2012; St. John et al., 2014). For example, as the US Supreme Court debated marriage equality, GSAs elevated the issue in their communities to raise awareness of its importance for LGBTQ+ people (Fetner et al., 2012), with some GSAs attending rallies in support (Mayo, 2015; Toomey & Russell, 2013) and meeting with government officials (Mayo, 2015).

A number of GSAs have built coalitions with other groups in their schools and local communities or with national organizations to engage in advocacy around current sociopolitical issues. Some GSAs partner with other LGBTQ+ organizations in the process. These coalitions aim to have a larger collective impact by sharing resources, providing trainings, and supporting the organizing potential of GSAs (Fetner et al., 2012; GLSEN, n.d.; GSA Network, n.d.; St. John et al., 2014). For example, the GSA Network, a national organization, offers leadership trainings, camps, and summits for youth, helping them to learn strategies and skills to organize and advocate for changes within their schools and communities. They also provide digital platforms for youth to come together across the country, giving GSA members the tools needed to organize events, create petitions, and make change in their communities.

Gender–sexuality alliances also partner with and aim to amplify the work of groups and organizations centered on promoting social justice in related areas, such as racial justice. For example, GSAs have worked with racial justice organizations to fight White supremacy and to lobby against school pushout that disproportionately affects students of color (Advancement Project et al., n.d.). Gender–sexuality alliances have also partnered with community organizations to host GSA Days for Racial Justice, advocacy events that aim to fight for the rights of LGBTQ+ youth and youth of color in schools and their larger communities (Shaw, 2018). These collective actions aim to address the intersectional oppression that LGBTQ+ youth of color experience and to highlight the experiences of oppression that cisgender, heterosexual people of color, and White LGBTQ+ people face (Advancement Project et al., n.d.). In a similar way, GSAs have formed coalitions with immigrant youth organizations to fight for immigrant rights (GSA Network, 2014; Liberty Hill, 2015). These intersectional coalitions are examples of ways in which GSAs build and leverage community power to push for systemic changes to tackle multiple forms of discrimination and marginalization.

Youth Empowerment in GSAs

In turning to ways in which youth may experience empowerment through their GSA involvement, it is first helpful to illustrate how GSAs operate in ways that are consistent with positive youth development models. These models contend that all youth have strengths and that positive development and thriving occur when youth have access to resources in their environments that foster these strengths and promote their well-being (Damon, 2004). This view is further situated in the developmental systems paradigm, which underscores the need to examine youth within their social contexts and the bidirectional influence that each has on the other (Lerner et al., 2015). Youth's social environments, such as schools or extracurricular settings, can shape their experiences and development. At the same time, youth also influence these settings and enact change within them. In this respect, youth are agentic in their development and in their communities and society at large. Although youth's social settings may be sources of stress, they also have potential to promote thriving and resilience in the face of adversity. Gender–sexuality alliances play an important role in providing an environment that supports LGBTQ+ youth's development and provide youth with opportunities to contribute and to enact change.

Positive youth development models emphasize that settings must provide youth with safe environments, opportunities for peer connection and leadership, sufficient structure for the group to operate, and adults who can scaffold and support youth's decision-making and serve as mentors (Lerner et al., 2015). Each of these elements is evident within the context of GSAs. A principal aim of GSAs is to offer a safe, LGBTQ+-affirming setting for youth to socialize, build a sense of community, and support one another (Griffin et al., 2004). Youth members' perceived support from their GSA is associated with a sense of purpose, mastery, and self-esteem (Poteat et al., 2015). In addition, GSAs provide opportunities for youth leadership. Adult advisors in GSAs often take on complementary responsibilities and supportive roles to help sustain and scaffold youth's work in planning larger events, ensuring that the group follows applicable administrative policies (e.g., to set up school displays or to attend outside events), or to liaison between GSA youth members and other school personnel (Graybill et al., 2009).

As GSAs aim to facilitate LGBTQ+ youth's positive development, one potential mechanism for this may be through a process of empowerment. Youth have shared that their GSA is an empowering space (Mayberry, 2013; Russell et al., 2009). Youth settings are considered empowering when they promote members' self-efficacy, peer connection, and sense of agency (Zimmerman et al., 2018). These qualities are reflective of psychological empowerment, defined as a person's gained sense of confidence, agency, and control over factors affecting them and an increased ability to identify and achieve their personal goals (Christens et al., 2016; Zimmerman, 2000).

Psychological empowerment can include emotional, cognitive, behavioral, and relational empowerment (Christens et al., 2016; Russell et al., 2009; Zimmerman, 2000). Emotional empowerment can reflect a person's sense that they can enact changes in their environment and counteract stressors (e.g.,

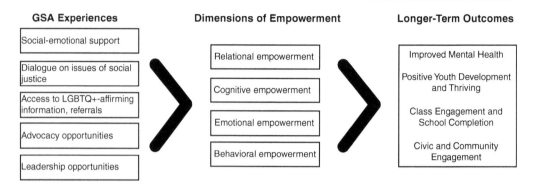

Figure 21.1 *Conceptual model of how GSA experiences may facilitate empowerment processes among youth and yield longer-term benefits.*

discrimination). Cognitive empowerment can reflect a person's knowledge of available resources (e.g., LGBTQ+-affirming health-care providers) and ways to challenge systems of oppression. Behavioral empowerment can reflect a person's actions toward achieving their goals and counteracting systems of oppression. Finally, relational empowerment can reflect a person's sense of connection, mutual encouragement, and solidarity with their peers. Youth consider relational empowerment as core to their experience of empowerment (Christens, 2012; Russell et al., 2009).

Gender–sexuality alliances likely facilitate the process of youth empowerment along each of these dimensions (see Figure 21.1 for a conceptual depiction). For instance, dialogue around discrimination and learning ways to counteract it are fundamental to the empowerment process for youth facing oppression (Ginwright & James, 2002; Kirshner & Ginwright, 2012). Notably, GSA meeting time is allotted for youth to discuss discrimination and other stressors in order to solicit and provide social-emotional support, learn about specific LGBTQ+ issues, identify problem-solving and self-care strategies, or engage in advocacy against discrimination (Griffin et al., 2004). These foci align with relational, cognitive, emotional, and behavioral empowerment, respectively. Finally, by placing youth in positions to lead, take on responsibilities, and make decisions, GSAs could further cultivate youth's self-efficacy, confidence, and sense of control in achieving their goals (Wong et al., 2010; Zimmerman et al., 2018).

In our recent work, we found that youth's more active engagement in their GSA over the school year predicted relative increases along several indicators of empowerment (Poteat et al., 2020a). Specifically, we considered perceived peer validation (an indicator of relational empowerment) as well as self-efficacy to promote social justice and hope (indicators of both cognitive and emotional empowerment). We considered youth's level of GSA engagement in terms of their consistency in attending meetings, contributing to conversations, taking on group responsibilities, and helping with events. Youth who reported greater active engagement over a six-month period of the school year also reported significant relative increases in their perceived peer validation, self-efficacy to promote social justice, and hope at the school year's end after adjusting for their respective levels at the beginning of the year.

These findings offer encouraging evidence of a developmental process whereby youth's involvement in their GSA could foster their sense of psychological empowerment. Through their active engagement in GSAs, youth may have been able to access needed social-emotional support, reassurance, and affirmation from peers and advisors. LGBTQ+-affirming support may have been important in building LGBTQ+ youth members' sense of validation, given their experiences of societal stigma and marginalization. For heterosexual cisgender allies such support may have been critical as well, as they too can experience bullying and harassment due to their perceived or implied sexual orientation and gender expression (Rivers, 2011). Furthermore, opportunities to discuss current LGBTQ+ social issues, learn about LGBTQ+ community resources, and engage in advocacy may have elevated youth's confidence and self-efficacy to promote social justice.

We call particular attention to our findings on hope. Scholars have argued that cultivating hope is a powerful way to heal from discrimination (Duncan-Andrade, 2009; Ginwright, 2015). In the context of GSAs, the LGBTQ+ affirmation and support that youth receive as well as the opportunities for collective action against discrimination may have bolstered their sense of hope over the school year. Furthermore, we found that hope went on to predict decreases in youth's depressive and anxiety symptoms at the school year's end. This latter finding aligns with other studies showing associations between empowerment and well-being among youth (Christens & Peterson, 2012; Lardier et al., 2018; Zimmerman et al., 2018).

Ultimately, through increased hope, greater GSA engagement predicted decreases in these mental health concerns (Poteat et al., 2020a). Cultivating hope could be an important way in which GSAs promote mental health. In this respect, it may help to unpack how hope has been defined in the psychology literature. Hope has been defined as a belief in one's ability to pursue and achieve one's goals, with the knowledge of ways in which to do so (Snyder et al., 1996). This definition reflects two key dimensions of hope: a sense of agency and illuminated pathways. These dimensions suggest what GSA advisors or youth leaders might seek to target in order to engender hope among members. For example, GSA members might identify immediate or long-term goals that are important to individual members or to the group collectively. Members then can identify possible courses of action that they (as individuals or as a group) could take toward reaching those goals. They may also identify resources that they would need if they were to take each course of action. Finally, GSA members can provide one another with social-emotional support, identify resources and other supportive individuals or groups, and build one another's confidence and abilities as they proceed toward their individual or collective goals.

Additionally, it is important to consider the extent to which benefits from GSAs may apply differentially to members from different backgrounds. Gender–sexuality alliances aspire to be inclusive of youth from diverse socio-cultural backgrounds and to address other systems of oppression as they intersect with sexual orientation and gender. Yet, there is limited knowledge of how well GSAs meet these aims, and extant findings are mixed. We did not find significant differences in the extent to which youth's GSA engagement predicted their sense of empowerment on account of sexual orientation, gender identity, or race (Poteat et al., 2020a). However, some of our other findings and those of other scholars suggest that youth of color feel less supported in their GSA than White youth (McCready, 2004; Poteat et al., 2015). Research needs to give careful attention to potential variability in the experiences of GSA members based on their sociocultural backgrounds and to potential variability in the benefits youth may derive through membership.

Gender–sexuality alliances face a formidable challenge in meeting a range of needs and interests among members who experience different constellations of privilege and marginalization. Ongoing research is needed to identify practices and approaches that GSAs can use to ensure that they are welcoming and inclusive to youth who may be among the most marginalized or invisible in their school and GSA. In sum, research is needed on how GSAs can be most responsive to their members' interests, needs, and strengths, with a focus on youth who are underrepresented in the GSA and who face multiple forms of marginalization.

Group Structure, Youth Leadership, and Advisor Roles

Up to this point, we have discussed interpersonal experiences within GSAs that could foster community power and psychological empowerment. In addition, there are factors at the organizational level that are essential in order for social justice-oriented groups to support members' empowerment but are less often considered (Christens, 2019). Among these are adequate organizational structure, opportunities for youth leadership, and the presence of an adult to support and mentor youth (Christens, 2019; Lerner et al., 2015). Emerging findings show how these elements are featured in GSAs and how they may benefit members.

Organizational Structure of the GSA

Gender–sexuality alliances tend to share some features in how their meetings are organized and structured, albeit with some variability across GSAs. As one example, GSA meetings may include a brief check-in with members at the beginning of the meeting to ask about any needs or concerns, accomplishments, interests, or updates that members wish to share or discuss during

Conceptualizing the Potential Curvilinear Effects of Group Structure

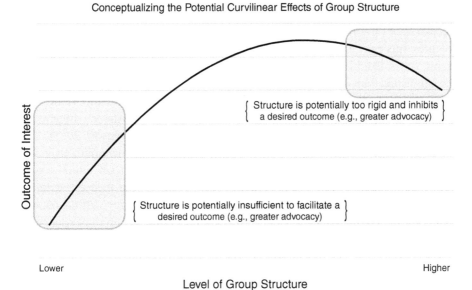

Figure 21.2 *Conceptual representation of the potential curvilinear effect of greater group structure within GSAs on a desired outcome for individual members or the group.*

the meeting. Gender–sexuality alliance youth leaders or advisors also may follow-up on discussions or efforts from prior meetings or events. To varying degrees, GSAs may follow a meeting agenda, which may be prepared, facilitated, or cofacilitated by youth leaders or adult advisors.

Organizational structure within GSAs may be important in the process of cultivating and exercising community power. At one end of the continuum, too little organizational structure could prove detrimental and dissuade youth from becoming involved in the GSA. Youth have reported not joining their school's GSA due to their perception of its disorganization (Heck et al., 2013). Other findings suggest that some degree of structure could be beneficial. In one study, youth's perceived support and reported advocacy in the GSA were more strongly associated with a greater sense of agency when they were in GSAs characterized as having more organizational structure (Poteat et al., 2016). At the other end of the continuum, however, too rigid a structure could also prove detrimental. It could inhibit organic conversations that arise during meetings or prevent flexibility in GSAs' responses to unanticipated events or issues raised by members during meetings. We depict this potential curvilinear process in Figure 21.2. Indeed, several studies have shown a curvilinear association between the amount of structure to GSA meetings and youth's level of advocacy and overall engagement in them (Poteat et al., 2016, 2022). Greater organizational structure in the GSA was associated with youth's greater advocacy and overall engagement up to a point, after which it was associated with slightly less advocacy and engagement.

Youth Leadership in GSAs

Youth take on formal and informal leadership roles in GSAs. As one indicator of how this may benefit members, youth in GSAs characterized as having a more youth-led orientation later reported a greater sense of efficacy to promote social justice than youth in more advisor-led GSAs (Poteat et al., 2020b). This finding adds further weight to calls of scholars underscoring the importance of a youth-led approach in building youth's efficacy to counteract systems of oppression (Ginwright & James, 2002; Watts & Hipolito-Delgado, 2015).

Youth leaders can change within a GSA, as is the case in other youth programs (Akiva & Petrokubi, 2016). Formal positions may carry term limits (e.g., a yearlong position), some charismatic leaders may age out of their GSA due to graduation, and others may discontinue their membership for various reasons (e.g., competing responsibilities or new interests). These group dynamics highlight the need for GSAs to plan for potential discontinuity, disruptions, or transitions in leadership among members. Such challenges and how GSAs approach them have not been studied. Anecdotally, we know that some GSAs elect officers for the next school year at the end of their current school year in order to ensure a level of leadership continuity and to facilitate the transition. Some GSAs also designate shared leadership roles (e.g., copresidents) to distribute responsibilities and buffer any disruptions in the event that a leader cannot attend a meeting or remain involved. In addition, some GSAs host alumni panels for graduates to share their postgraduate experiences and how they remain engaged in advocacy in their communities. Apart from these practices, we know less about what other steps GSAs take to cultivate leadership skills among members and how they provide opportunities for leadership pipelines wherein members can take on more leadership responsibilities during their time in GSAs or facilitate youth's active engagement in their communities after graduation.

In some states, statewide GSA networks and leadership councils provide youth leadership development opportunities through summits and regular regional meetings within a local area (Massachusetts Department of Elementary and Secondary Education, 2021; Russell et al., 2009). In addition, these networks and councils provide an infrastructure, resources, and support for youth leaders and other members of multiple GSAs to collaborate and engage in larger collective action on certain issues (e.g., to address homelessness among LGBTQ+ youth or violence against trans people of color). These larger networks and connections across GSAs can cultivate community power for youth in GSAs located in schools with fewer resources and in areas with fewer LGBTQ+-affirming spaces or with fewer members that may limit the ability to engage in efforts requiring a larger number of people to complete.

The Roles of Adult Advisors

Whereas growing attention has been directed toward youth members of GSAs, limited work has explored the role of adult advisors. Adults play influential roles in youth settings and do much to support their success (Grossman & Bulle, 2006; Zeldin et al., 2013). Several studies have described the roles of adult advisors in GSAs. These roles include cofacilitating meetings, providing emotional support, serving as a liaison between students and school administrators, and offering guidance as youth pursue certain initiatives (Graybill et al., 2009; Poteat et al., 2015).

Many advisors have served in their role for multiple years and hold the historical memory of past GSA efforts, challenges, and successes. Similarly, they offer a consistent presence at GSA meetings during the year and can provide a level of continuity as GSAs work on longer-term efforts. These roles can be important because, in our own work with GSAs, advisors anecdotally have shared that their GSA can vary from year to year in its level of activity and membership. In some years, their GSA may be large, active, and led by charismatic youth leaders. In other years, advisors characterize their GSAs as being in a "rebuilding year." Often this has followed the graduation of key members or leaders or other strains that arose within or outside of the group.

Advisors can support their GSAs uniquely because of their professional role in the school. Advisors have knowledge of policies that could come to bear on how their GSA operates (e.g., whether it be on rules for holding bake sales or for attending off-campus events). Also, they may have a unique perspective on the internal politics of their school or school district and how to navigate them. Advisors may know of allies in key administrative positions who will support their GSA's endeavors. In addition, advisors may be uniquely positioned to facilitate communication between GSA members and other school or district personnel.

These points suggest that advisors can hold important complementary or shared responsibilities with youth in the GSA. The youth–adult partnership literature could serve as a key source to inform future research to identify how advisors can partner with youth members to empower them and build the collective social power of the GSA to address pressing issues in their school and community.

Implications for Application

Collectively, the findings from GSA research carry implications for schools and school administrators, adult allies, and youth leaders. Each group has an important role to play in supporting GSAs and GSA efforts to support member empowerment and to promote justice in their schools. Here we raise several points on applying current GSA research findings.

School and District Administrators

Gender–sexuality alliance research generally has not directly involved school or district administrators, but feedback from GSA advisors and members

highlights several supportive actions that they could take in their administrative role. The number of schools with GSAs continues to increase, yet
GSAs still encounter barriers to formation. Notwithstanding continued
instances of overt hostility to GSA formation (Graybill et al., 2015; Mayo,
2008), we give focus here to how administrators might address additional
challenges that GSAs face. For instance, administrators with influence over
scheduling could include an elective period during the school day for students
to attend clubs such as GSAs. After-school meetings prevent some youth from
attending due to competing responsibilities (e.g., employment), forced choices
between interests (e.g., sports), or limited transportation options. Though
some GSAs meet during lunch periods, this significantly limits their meeting
time.

Also, administrators should review school and district policies for club
activities to ensure that they are responsive to unique concerns faced by
LGBTQ+ youth. For instance, some GSAs grapple with permission slip
requirements for their members to attend events outside of school (e.g.,
regional LGBTQ+ conferences or events). In some schools, their required
level of detail deters LGBTQ+ members who are not out to a parent or legal
guardian from attending events that could be beneficial. Furthermore, administrators can support GSAs by facilitating youth's involvement in these types
of events (e.g., treating them as excused absences) and approving other
common GSA-sponsored school events (e.g., movie screenings or dances).

Administrators also can support GSA advisors in several ways. Some
advisors hesitate to serve in this role, fearing repercussions from other school
personnel, students, and parents (Graybill et al., 2015; Watson et al., 2010).
This fear is salient for teachers who have not yet earned tenure or "professional status" in their position (Watson et al., 2010). Administrators can be
deliberate in conveying to advisors that they value their service in this role,
that they recognize the time advisors give in doing so, and that they will stand
in support of advisors in the event of any hostility that the advisor or GSA
experiences. In addition, administrators can serve as an important model to
others by voicing public support for the GSA, its members, and their work.

Finally, administrators can amplify the efforts and showcase the accomplishments of GSAs. Although GSAs play crucial roles in schools, they cannot
be treated as a panacea. Administrators can amplify the work of GSAs by also
implementing policies and practices in the district or school that recognize and
affirm LGBTQ+ people. These mutual partnerships between GSAs and
administrators could go far to create more inclusive schools and to support
LGBTQ+ youth empowerment.

GSA Adult Advisors

A number of findings in the GSA literature are relevant for GSA advisors and
their roles within these groups. One clear priority pertains to professional

development opportunities for advisors. As noted, GSAs bring together youth from diverse backgrounds and experiences who thus experience different constellations of privilege and marginalization. Scholars have underscored the importance of advisor self-efficacy to address issues related to specific forms of diversity and marginalization (Herdt et al., 2006; McCready, 2004). Yet, corresponding professional development for advisors remains limited. Professional development could ensure that advisors feel equipped to provide culturally informed and responsive support to members, raise intersectional perspectives in GSA discussions and activities, and foster inclusive climates in their GSA.

Similarly, given the mental health concerns reported by GSA members, it may be important to assist advisors in their own efforts to support these students. Advisors vary in their professional background. Some advisors have backgrounds in health-related fields (e.g., as school counselors, nurses, or social workers), while others may value additional professional development focused on ways in which to identify and best respond to GSA members' mental health needs. This may include covering ways in which to assess for mental health concerns, with attention to how symptoms may manifest differently for some youth based on their sociocultural backgrounds. Also, professional development could aid advisors in determining the scope of support that their GSA can provide and when they should refer a member to an LGBTQ+-affirming mental health professional.

Advisors may also benefit from exploring ways in which to navigate their role in the GSA. At the beginning of the school year, advisors may wish to discuss with youth leaders and members the supportive roles and responsibilities that they each may adopt. In years when a GSA has a strong and established youth leadership team and active members, advisors may provide general guidance or liaison with school administrators as needed. In years when a GSA is composed primarily of new members or is facing various challenges, advisors may need to provide more scaffolded support for their group's decision-making and efforts and play a greater co-leadership role. These discussions between advisors and youth members may help to ensure an optimal distribution of responsibilities among them and to ensure that advisors are responsive to their members' needs and interests during a given year.

GSA Youth Leaders

Several findings in the GSA literature also are relevant to GSA youth leaders. One consistent finding is that GSAs have the potential to benefit those within and those outside of the GSA. Youth leaders may play a pivotal role in providing social-emotional support for their peers in the GSA and cultivating a safe environment that is conducive to their own and their peers' well-being. They may also take charge of identifying and relaying resources and information of interest to members and of maintaining the overall youth-led nature of the GSA. Youth may collaborate with advisors in facilitating conversations and modeling behavior for their peers to encourage support-seeking and provision.

Youth leaders stand to play a role in their GSA's efforts to shape their school and broader community. They may serve as role models in the school with the aim of reducing bias-based harassment and fostering affirming school climates. They may also work to raise the visibility of the GSA and its advocacy and awareness-raising efforts that could benefit not only the immediate members of the GSA but also members of the school in general. Beyond the immediate school setting, youth leaders can be instrumental in forging coalitions with other school and community groups oriented around social justice in order to pursue broader initiatives in their communities that address multiple and intersecting forms of oppression.

Avenues for Future Research

There is an expanding knowledge base on youth's experiences in GSAs and how they may gain a greater sense of empowerment through their GSA involvement. With this comes a number of avenues for future research that could further aid GSAs in their aspirations to promote thriving among their members and social justice in their schools. We point to several prospects in this section.

The extant GSA literature suggests both clear mental health needs among GSA members and the potential for GSAs to meet those needs. Nevertheless, there has been a paucity of interventions developed for delivery within GSAs. Only a few programs have been piloted to address relational and mental health issues (Heck, 2015; Lapointe & Crooks, 2018). Youth's feedback suggests interest for such programming if they are tailored appropriately to the GSA context. Future research on GSAs could focus on program development for GSAs tailored to align with their aims, structure, and current approaches to promoting their members' health.

More research is also needed on the community-oriented efforts of GSAs. In addition to the benefits of GSAs for their members, how and to what extent does GSA advocacy shape the larger school environment and improve conditions for youth in the school who are not GSA members? An understanding of the mechanisms by which GSAs exert an outward influence on others in the school could inform various advocacy efforts undertaken by GSAs. Research might consider which efforts exert the broadest influence within the school, which efforts have the greatest impact on specific groups of students, and which efforts have the most influence on changing specific attitudes and behaviors at an individual level or policies and practices at an institutional level.

Gender–sexuality alliances aspire to address multiple interlocking systems of oppression experienced by their members. Members come with experiences shaped by their many other intersecting sociocultural identities, underscoring the need for GSAs to adopt a holistic approach in their work. Still, there remains limited research on how GSAs discuss and act on issues related to race, immigration, ability, and economic injustice, among others, as they intersect with the group's focal orientation around sexual orientation and gender identity. Similarly, there is limited research on how GSAs foster inclusivity in their space for members who face multiple forms of marginalization or the extent to which GSAs are responsive to their unique experiences. Further, it is unclear how the experiences of youth in GSAs with certain marginalized identities may vary according to the representation of other youth who also share these identities in their GSA. Future GSA research should elevate the voices of youth who contend with multiple forms of marginalization in an effort to capture the rich diversity of their experiences. Their provision of more detail on their reasons for joining their GSA, their experiences within their GSA, as well as their reasons for discontinuing their involvement in their GSA could illuminate how GSAs can be most responsive to their needs, interests, and strengths.

In addition to their inward-facing efforts to address multiple systems of oppression among members, research is needed on how GSAs build coalitions with other social justice-oriented groups in their schools or communities. Although there is evidence of GSAs engaging in some types of intersectional advocacy, there is less research on how GSAs collaborate with each other or with other groups across schools or through statewide or national organizations to engage in this type of advocacy at a larger scale. Scholars might use case studies or participatory research to examine what such coalition efforts might look like. Research on these efforts could do much to ensure that GSAs uphold their aspirations to address interlocking systems of oppression not only within their own groups but also within their larger school and community settings.

Finally, as we raised at the outset of this chapter, limited research has been conducted to showcase the experiences of LGBTQ+ and ally youth in groups similar to GSAs in schools and communities outside of the US context. A far more globally oriented research agenda is needed not only in this area but also within the larger field of research among LGBTQ+ youth. There is a pressing need for more global attention to school- or community-based groups for LGBTQ+ youth and allies, to the common and unique barriers they may face in their formation, to the similarities and differences in their aims, how they function, and the issues they address, and to how they support youth empowerment.

Conclusions

Demonstrable progress has been made in promoting the safety and well-being of LGBTQ+ youth in schools, yet LGBTQ+ youth also continue to face numerous adversities and overt hostility in this setting. Gender–sexuality alliances initially formed and have since expanded within this social and historical context. They have come to serve as a crucial space wherein LGBTQ+ youth and their allies harness their community power and gain a sense of empowerment. As GSAs continue to address a range of needs among their members that stem from multiple contemporary challenges and socio-political crises, it is imperative that their members and advisors receive the support they need in the face of these events and in their efforts. The promise of equipping GSAs to address these needs is clear, as GSAs stand to benefit their immediate members and the larger student population. We have sought to highlight how GSAs are structured and function, the ways in which they seek to facilitate youth's empowerment, and the practices that may help GSAs to be responsive to the needs, experiences, and strengths of their diverse membership. We anticipate that ongoing advances in GSA research and in the organizing and work of GSAs themselves will go far in further promoting justice for LGBTQ+ youth in their schools and their communities.

References

Advancement Project, Equality Federation Institute, & GSA Network. (n.d.). *Power in partnerships: Building connections at the intersections of racial justice and LGBTQ movements to end the school-to-prison pipeline.* Advancement Project, Equality Federation Institute, and GSA Network. https://advancementproject.org/wp-content/uploads/1970/01/899c2f19d719059027_h3cm6wplt.pdf

Akiva, T., & Petrokubi, J. (2016). Growing with youth: A lifewide and lifelong perspective on youth–adult partnership in youth programs. *Children and Youth Services Review, 69*, 248–258.

Baams, L., & Russell, S. T. (2021). Gay–straight alliances, school functioning, and mental health: Associations for students of color and LGBTQ students. *Youth & Society, 53*, 211–229.

Bohnert, A., Fredricks, J., & Randall, E. (2010). Capturing unique dimensions of youth organized activity involvement: Theoretical and methodological considerations. *Review of Educational Research, 80*, 576–610.

Busseri, M. A., & Rose-Krasnor, L. (2009). Breadth and intensity: Salient, separable, and developmentally significant dimensions of structured youth activity involvement. *British Journal of Developmental Psychology, 27*, 907–933.

Calzo, J. P., Poteat, V. P., Yoshikawa, H., Russell, S. T., & Bogart, L. M. (2020). Person–environment fit and positive youth development in the context of high school gay–straight alliances. *Journal of Research on Adolescence, 30*, 158–176.

Centers for Disease Control and Prevention. (2015). *Results from the School Health Policies and Practices Study 2014.* Centers for Disease Control and Prevention.

Centers for Disease Control and Prevention. (2019). *School health profiles 2018: Characteristics of health programs among secondary schools.* Centers for Disease Control and Prevention.

Christens, B. D. (2012). Toward relational empowerment. *American Journal of Community Psychology, 50*, 114–128.

Christens, B. D. (2019). *Community power and empowerment.* Oxford University Press.

Christens, B. D., & Peterson, N. A. (2012). The role of empowerment in youth development: A study of sociopolitical control as mediator of ecological systems' influence on developmental outcomes. *Journal of Youth and Adolescence, 41*, 623–635.

Christens, B. D., Winn, L. T., & Duke, A. M. (2016). Empowerment and critical consciousness: A conceptual cross-fertilization. *Adolescent Research Review, 1*, 15–27.

Damon, W. (2004). What is positive youth development? *The Annals of the American Academy of Political and Social Science, 591*, 13–24.

Davis, B., Stafford, M. B. R., & Pullig, C. (2014). How gay–straight alliance groups mitigate the relationship between gay-bias victimization and adolescent suicide attempts. *Journal of the American Academy of Child and Adolescent Psychiatry, 53*, 1271–1278.

Day, J. K., Fish, J. N., Grossman, A. H., & Russell, S. T. (2020). Gay–straight alliances, inclusive policy, and school climate: LGBTQ youths' experiences of social support and bullying. *Journal of Research on Adolescence, 30*, 418–430.

Duncan-Andrade, J. (2009). Note to educators: Hope required when growing roses in concrete. *Harvard Educational Review, 79*, 181–194.

Fetner, T., Elafros, A., Bortolin, S., & Drechsler, C. (2012). Safe spaces: Gay–straight alliances in high schools. *Canadian Review of Sociology/Revue canadienne de sociologie, 49*, 188–207.

Ginwright, S. (2015). *Hope and healing in urban education: How urban activists and teachers are reclaiming matters of the heart.* Routledge

Ginwright, S., & James, T. (2002). From assets to agents of change: Social justice, organizing, and youth development. *New Directions for Youth Development, 96*, 27–46.

GLSEN. (n.d.). *Support student GSAs.* GLSEN. www.glsen.org/support-student-gsas

Goodenow, C., Watson, R. J., Adjei, J., Homma, Y., & Saewyc, E. (2016). Sexual orientation trends and disparities in school bullying and violence-related experiences, 1999–2013. *Psychology of Sexual Orientation and Gender Diversity, 3*, 386–396.

Graybill, E. C., Varjas, K., Meyers, J., Dever, B. V., Greenberg, D., Roach, A. T., & Morillas, C. (2015). Demographic trends and advocacy experiences of gay–straight alliance advisors. *Journal of LGBT Youth, 12*, 436–461.

Graybill, E. C., Varjas, K., Meyers, J., & Watson, L. B. (2009). Content-specific strategies to advocate for lesbian, gay, bisexual, and transgender youth: An exploratory study. *School Psychology Review, 38*, 570–584.

Griffin, P., Lee, C., Waugh, J., & Beyer, C. (2004). Describing roles that gay–straight alliances play in schools: From individual support to school change. *Journal of Gay & Lesbian Issues in Education, 1*, 7–22.

Grossman, J. B., & Bulle, M. J. (2006). Review of what youth programs do to increase the connectedness of youth with adults. *Journal of Adolescent Health, 39*, 788–799.

GSA Network. (2014, April 22). *LGBT and immigrant youth unite for White House action*. GSA Network. https://gsanetwork.org/press-releases/lgbt-and-immigrant-youth-unite-for-white-house-action/

GSA Network. (n.d.). *Build the GSA movement*. GSA Network. https://gsanetwork.org/build-the-gsa-movement/

Hamby, R. L. (2007). Gay–straight alliances help bring education to all students. *Journal of Curriculum and Pedagogy, 4*, 116–119.

Heck, N. C. (2015). The potential to promote resilience: Piloting a minority stress-informed, GSA-based, mental health promotion program for LGBTQ youth. *Psychology of Sexual Orientation and Gender Diversity, 2*, 225–231.

Heck, N. C., Lindquist, L., Stewart, B., Brennan, C., & Cochran, B. N. (2013). To join or not to join: Gay–straight student alliances and the high school experiences of lesbian, gay, bisexual and transgender youths. *Journal of Gay and Lesbian Social Services, 25*, 77–101.

Herdt, G., Russell, S. T., Sweat, J., & Marzullo, M. (2006). Sexual inequality, youth empowerment, and the GSA: A community study in California. In N. Teunis & G. H. Herdt (Eds.), *Sexual inequalities and social justice* (pp. 233–252). University of California Press.

Kirshner, B., & Ginwright, S. (2012). Youth organizing as a developmental context for African American and Latino adolescents. *Child Development Perspectives, 6*, 288–294.

Kosciw, J. G., & Pizmony-Levy, O. (2013). *Fostering a global dialogue about LGBT youth and schools: Proceedings from a meeting of the Global Network Combating Homophobic and Transphobic Prejudice and Violence in Schools Sponsored by GLSEN & UNESCO*. GLSEN.

Kosciw, J. G., Clark, C. M., Truong, N. L., & Zongrone, A. D. (2020). *The 2019 National School Climate Survey: The experiences of lesbian, gay, bisexual, transgender, and queer youth in our nation's schools*. GLSEN.

Kull, R. M., Greytak, E. A., Kosciw, J. G., & Villenas, C. (2016). Effectiveness of school district antibullying policies in improving LGBT youths' school climate. *Psychology of Sexual Orientation and Gender Diversity, 3*, 407–415.

Lapointe, A. A. (2017). "It's not pans, it's people": Student and teacher perspectives on bisexuality and pansexuality. *Journal of Bisexuality, 17*, 88–107.

Lapointe, A. A., & Crooks, C. (2018). GSA members' experiences with a structured program to promote well-being. *Journal of LGBT Youth, 15*, 300–318.

Lardier, D. T., Jr., Garcia-Reid, P., & Reid, R. J. (2018). The interacting effects of psychological empowerment and ethnic identity on indicators of well-being among youth of color. *Journal of Community Psychology, 46*, 489–501.

Lee, C. (2002). The impact of belonging to a high school gay/straight alliance. *The High School Journal, 85*, 13–26.

Lerner, R. M., Lerner, J. V., Bowers, E. P., & Geldhof, G. J. (2015). Positive youth development and relational-development-systems. In R. M. Lerner, W. F. Overton, & P. C. M. Molenaar (Eds.), *Handbook of child psychology and developmental science. Volume 1, theory and method* (7th ed., pp. 607–651). Wiley.

Liberty Hill. (2015, January 30). *Immigrant Youth Coalition*. Liberty Hill Foundation. www.libertyhill.org/tags/immigrant-youth-coalition

Macgillivray, I. K. (2005). Shaping democratic identities and building citizenship skills through student activism: México's first gay–straight alliance. *Equity & Excellence in Education, 38*, 320–330.

Marx, R. A., & Kettrey, H. H. (2016). Gay–straight alliances are associated with lower levels of school-based victimization of LGBTQ+ youth: A systematic review and meta-analysis. *Journal of Youth and Adolescence, 45*, 1269–1282.

Massachusetts Department of Elementary and Secondary Education. (2021, March 19). *Massachusetts gender and sexuality alliance (GSA) leadership council.* Massachusetts Department of Elementary and Secondary Education. www.doe.mass.edu/sfs/lgbtq/GSALcouncil.html

Mayberry, M. (2013). Gay–straight alliances: Youth empowerment and working toward reducing stigma of LGBT youth. *Humanity & Society, 37*, 35–54.

Mayberry, M., Chenneville, T., & Currie, S. (2013). Challenging the sounds of silence: A qualitative study of gay–straight alliances and school reform efforts. *Education and Urban Society, 45*, 307–339.

Mayo, C. (2008). Obscene associations: Gay–straight alliances, the Equal Access Act, and abstinence-only policy. *Sexuality Research and Social Policy, 5*, 45–55.

Mayo, J. B. (2015). Youth work in gay straight alliances: Curriculum, pedagogy, and activist development. *Child & Youth Services, 36*, 79–93.

McCready, L. T. (2004). Some challenges facing queer youth programs in urban high schools: Racial segregation and de-normalizing Whiteness. *Journal of Gay and Lesbian Issues in Education, 1*, 37–51.

Miceli, M. (2005). *Standing out, standing together: The social and political impact of gay–straight alliances.* Taylor & Francis.

Poteat, V. P., Calzo, J. P., Yoshikawa, H., Lipkin, A., Ceccolini, C. J., Rosenbach, S. B., O'Brien, M. D., Marx, R. A., Murchison, G. R., & Burson, E. (2020a). Greater engagement in gender–sexuality alliances and GSA characteristics predict youth empowerment and reduced mental health concerns. *Child Development, 91*, 1509–1528.

Poteat, V. P., Godfrey, E. B., Brion-Meisels, G., & Calzo, J. P. (2020b). Development of youth advocacy and sociopolitical efficacy as dimensions of critical consciousness within Gender-Sexuality Alliances. *Developmental Psychology, 56*, 1207–1219.

Poteat, V. P., Heck, N. C., Yoshikawa, H., & Calzo, J. P. (2016). Greater engagement among members of gay–straight alliances: Individual and structural contributors. *American Educational Research Journal, 53*, 1732–1758.

Poteat, V. P., O'Brien, M. D., Yang, M. K., Rosenbach, S. B., & Lipkin, A. (2022). Youth advocacy varies in relation to adult advisor characteristics and practices in gender–sexuality alliances. *Applied Developmental Science, 26*(3), 460–470.

Poteat, V. P., Yoshikawa, H., Calzo, J. P., Gray, M. L., DiGiovanni, C. D., Lipkin, A., Mundy-Shephard, A., Perrotti, J., Scheer, J. R., & Shaw, M. P. (2015). Contextualizing gay–straight alliances: Student, advisor, and structural factors related to positive youth development among members. *Child Development, 86*, 176–193.

Rivers, I. (2011). *Homophobic bullying: Research and theoretical perspectives.* Oxford University Press.

Russell, S. T., & Fish, J. N. (2019). Sexual minority youth, social change, and health: A developmental collision. *Research in Human Development*, *16*, 5–20.

Russell, S. T., Muraco, A., Subramaniam, A., & Laub, C. (2009). Youth empowerment and high school gay–straight alliances. *Journal of Youth and Adolescence*, *38*, 891–903.

Seelman, K. L., & Walker, M. B. (2018). Do anti-bullying laws reduce in-school victimization, fear-based absenteeism, and suicidality for lesbian, gay, bisexual, and questioning youth? *Journal of Youth and Adolescence*, *47*, 2301–2319.

Shaw, C. (2018, February 27). *Queer youth leaders mobilize for GSA Day of Racial Justice*. Liberty Hill Foundation. www.libertyhill.org/2018/02/27/queer-youth-leaders-mobilize-for-gsa-day-of-racial-justice

Snapp, S. D., Burdge, H., Licona, A. C., Moody, R. L., & Russell, S. T. (2015). Students' perspectives on LGBTQ-inclusive curriculum. *Equity & Excellence in Education*, *48*, 249–265.

Snyder, C. R., Sympson, S. C., Ybasco, F. C., Borders, T. F., Babyak, M. A., & Higgins, R. L. (1996). Development and validation of the State Hope Scale. *Journal of Personality and Social Psychology*, *70*, 321–335.

St. John, A., Travers, R., Munro, L., Liboro, R., Schneider, M., & Greig, C. L. (2014). The success of gay–straight alliances in Waterloo Region, Ontario: A confluence of political and social factors. *Journal of LGBT Youth*, *11*, 150–170.

Stonefish, T., & Lafreniere, K. D. (2015). Embracing diversity: The dual role of gay–straight alliances. *Canadian Journal of Education/Revue Canadienne de l'éducation*, *38*, 1–27.

Toomey, R. B., & Russell, S. T. (2013). Gay–straight alliances, social justice involvement, and school victimization of lesbian, gay, bisexual, and queer youth: Implications for school well-being and plans to vote. *Youth & Society*, *45*, 500–522.

Uribe, V., & Harbeck, K. M. (1992). Addressing the needs of lesbian, gay, and bisexual youth: The origins of PROJECT 10 and school-based intervention. *Journal of Homosexuality*, *22*, 9–28.

Vella, D. R., Nowottnick, L., Selun, B., & Van Roozendaal, B. (2009). Empowering LGBTQ youth in Europe: The work of IGLYO. *Journal of LGBT Youth*, *6*, 101–105.

Walls, N. E., Kane, S. B., & Wisneski, H. (2010). Gay–straight alliances and school experiences of sexual minority youth. *Youth & Society*, *41*, 307–332.

Watson, L. B., Varjas, K., Meyers, J., & Graybill, E. C. (2010). Gay–straight alliance advisors: Negotiating multiple ecological systems when advocating for LGBTQ youth. *Journal of LGBT Youth*, *7*, 100–128.

Watts, R. J., & Hipolito-Delgado, C. P. (2015). Thinking ourselves to liberation? Advancing sociopolitical action in critical consciousness. *The Urban Review*, *47*, 847–867.

Wong, A. (2019, July 9). *How schools reinvigorated the Stonewall revolution*. The Atlantic. www.theatlantic.com/education/archive/2019/07/role-school-gsas-lgbt-rights-movement/593491/

Wong, N. T., Zimmerman, M. A., & Parker, E. A. (2010). A typology of youth participation and empowerment for child and adolescent health promotion. *American Journal of Community Psychology*, *46*, 100–114.

Zeldin, S., Christens, B. D., & Powers, J. L. (2013). The psychology and practice of youth–adult partnership: Bridging generations for youth development and community change. *American Journal of Community Psychology*, *51*, 385–397.

Zimmerman, M. A. (2000). Empowerment theory. In J. Rappaport & E. Seidman (Eds.), *Handbook of community psychology* (pp. 43–63). Springer.

Zimmerman, M. A., Eisman, A. B., Reischl, T. M., Morrel-Samuels, S., Stoddard, S., Miller, A. L., Hutchison, P., Franzen, S., & Rupp, L. (2018). Youth empowerment solutions: Evaluation of an after-school program to engage middle school students in community change. *Health Education & Behavior*, *45*, 20–31.

22 Youth Participatory Action Research in School Settings

Kimalee Dickerson, Mariah Kornbluh, and Adrienne M. Duke

Introduction

The function and goals of education have long been debated. From transmitting culture and enhancing citizenship to spurring innovation and economic growth, schools have been lauded by some as the "great equalizer" and critiqued by others as mechanisms for social control and the reproduction of social inequalities (Goslin, 1965; Irizarry & Brown, 2014; Lightfoot, 1986; Ozer et al., 2013; Unicef, 2022). Despite the debate, schools have been and continue to be important community settings. Access to primary education is a basic right of every child, with clear implications for poverty as well as social change. On an international scale, approximately 90 percent of children attend primary school (Unicef, 2022).

The dominant education system situates young people as receivers of knowledge and adult educators as experts who share information. Freire (1970) describes this as "banking education," a model in which adults "make deposits" of knowledge that students passively "receive, memorize, and repeat" (pp. 71–72). This traditional model ignores students' preexisting knowledge and their ability to share their expertise and actively participate in knowledge creation. Freire proposed that when teachers and students engage together in critical dialogue, reflection, and action, the traditional power structures dissolve, producing "teacher-students" and "student-teachers" (p. 80). International efforts have stressed youth participation in their everyday settings as a moral right (United Nations, 1989). Youth participatory action research (YPAR) is one way for youth and adult educators to engage in this critical dialogue together. In YPAR, youth engage in systematic inquiry with adult researchers to identify problems that they want to improve, conduct research to understand these problems, and advocate for changes based on research evidence (Frasquilho et al., 2018; Ozer & Wright, 2012; Prati et al., 2020). Youth participatory action research inherently challenges traditional power structures by calling into question whose knowledge is considered credible, as well as the roles that participatory research can play in social change.

Brief History of YPAR

Participatory action research (PAR) is rooted in numerous intellectual and critical traditions, including the practices of Indigenous communities of various continents. German-American psychologist Kurt Lewin coined the phrase "action research" in the 1940s, and Brazilian educator Paulo Freire described the process of "conscientization" to reflect the interchangeable role of critical inquiry into systems of power and social political action (Caraballo et al., 2017; Mirra & Rogers, 2016; Mirra et al., 2015). From its inception, PAR has articulated an explicit goal of social justice and societal transformation (Caraballo et al., 2017). In PAR, people who are directly affected by a problem and therefore possess expert knowledge engage as coresearchers in the research process (Rodriguez & Brown, 2009).

While PAR has a long history of practice, conducting PAR with youth developed more recently (Caraballo et al., 2017). Youth participatory action research as a field of scholarly inquiry and practice has grown markedly since the early 2000s (Mirra & Rogers, 2016; Ozer, 2016; Prati et al., 2020). Although youth have historically been the objects rather than subjects of research, YPAR positions youth as having expertise in the issues – and potential research topics – that affect their lives (Ozer, 2016). Youth participatory action research engages youth in systematic processes of identifying problems, choosing research designs and methods, collecting, analyzing, and interpreting data, and presenting findings to relevant stakeholders to advocate for change (Ozer et al., 2020).

Core Principles and Process of YPAR

Scholars have identified three key principles of YPAR. First, YPAR is inquiry-based, meaning that topics of investigation are grounded in youth's lived experiences and concerns. Second, it is participatory, such that youth are collaborators in the methodological and pedagogical process. Finally, YPAR is transformative because the purpose is to change knowledge and practices to improve the lives of youth and their communities (Anyon et al., 2018; Rodriguez & Brown, 2009). Consistent with these principles and mindful that YPAR projects require flexibility, researchers have also identified core YPAR processes including: (1) iterative integration of research and action, (2) training and practice of research skills, (3) engagement in strategic thinking and strategies for influencing change; and (4) adults' sharing of power with students in the research and action process (Ozer & Douglas, 2015). Other youth development processes that typically occur during YPAR projects but are not unique to YPAR include the development of skills to communicate with other youth and adult stakeholders, opportunities and guidance for working in groups to achieve goals, and expansion of the social networks of youth (Ozer & Douglas, 2015).

Power-sharing is a central dimension of YPAR that requires intentionality and preparation given the inherent inequality of adult–youth relationships (Kohfeldt et al., 2011; Ozer et al., 2013; Zeldin et al., 2013). Sharing of power over key aspects of the research and action processes does not mean that all ideas or interpretations generated by youth researchers should be supported without critique. Rather, it means that youth's ideas are respected and seriously considered by the group for their strengths and limitations rather than being vetoed by adults (Ozer, 2016).

YPAR in Schools: Challenges and Trends

Although adult–youth power-sharing can be challenging to achieve when conducting YPAR in any setting, it is a particular challenge in structured hierarchical settings like schools (Ozer, 2016). Tensions and challenges identified in school-based settings include time constraints, competing demands, centralized control over policies affecting the school, student and staff turnover, and increasing student agency within constrained educational settings (Brion-Meisels & Alter, 2018; Buttimer, 2018; Kohfeldt et al., 2011; Ozer et al., 2013). In part because of these challenges, YPAR has often been conducted outside of school settings (Buckley-Marudas & Soltis, 2020; Irizarry & Brown, 2014). Within schools, YPAR projects most often occur during elective blocks or special classes or through student clubs/organizations (Brion-Meisels & Alter, 2018; Buttimer, 2018; Prati et al., 2020).

In recent years, however, scholars and educators have called for increased implementation of YPAR in schools (Anderson, 2020; Ozer et al., 2020; Prati et al., 2020). In addition to promoting the positive youth outcomes associated with YPAR, it is a good fit for youth developmentally. Particularly during adolescence, youth are responsive to autonomy-enhancing messages and experiences (Anderson, 2020) and are seeking experiences that clarify their sense of self and amplify their feelings of autonomy (Suleiman et al., 2021). Furthermore, youth in this age group are also beginning to have an increase sensitivity to rejection, unfairness, discrimination, and inequality related to themselves and others (Umaña-Taylor, 2016). Such programming has also been found to enhance sentiments of well-being and citizenship (Prati et al., 2020). Therefore, engaging youth in a YPAR project that encourages autonomy, promotes equity, and supports positive social connection in a school setting can have positive results.

In the context of school, scholars have advocated for YPAR as a strategy for increasing student academic and civic competence, particularly among marginalized students (Duncan-Andrade & Morrell, 2008; Kornbluh et al., 2015; Prati et al., 2020). Conducting YPAR projects in after-school settings offers many of the same benefits, including creating valuable opportunities for youth to build relationships with peers, engage in meaningful work, and develop important skills (Bulanda & McCrea, 2013). Additionally, implementing YPAR in school settings allows for the inclusion of more and diverse youth not served by community programs, builds upon a preexisting network of teachers, students, and district stakeholders, and has potential for youth to exercise community power by influencing the school setting (Ozer & Wright,

2012). Youth participatory action research is a critical pedagogy used to help youth develop critical consciousness for civic action in schools and communities (Cammarota & Romero, 2011). Youth who participate in YPAR have also gained the socioemotional skills, academic skills, and cognitive skills needed to succeed in school and in their careers (Kohfeldt et al., 2011). Other important benefits are helping youth develop confidence, learn critical thinking skills, and become more effective decision-makers (Rodriguez & Brown, 2009; Zimmerman, 2000). Within the empirical literature, YPAR projects situated in school and after-school settings have been predominantly focused within the US (Branquinho et al., 2020; see an exception in Prati et al., 2020). Such omissions may be less due to the prevalence of YPAR in educational settings internationally and more due to inequities in publication requirements and processes.

In the next section, we provide three examples of YPAR projects situated in different contexts within schools (a leadership class, a school club, and an after-school program) located in the US. In the US, around 49.4 million students attended public schools in prekindergarten to grade 12 (National Center for Education Statistics, 2020). Moreover, 7.8 million children attended after-school programs in 2020, 76 percent of which were in a public school building (Afterschool Alliance, 2020). Thus, these case examples have important implications both internationally and within a national context. Each case involves youth coresearchers, school administrators, and school staff in ways that support the YPAR process. We discuss the context of our projects as well as the stages of problem identification, data collection, data analysis, and social action. We also weave in a discussion of how our YPAR projects are impacted by power dynamics occurring in the school or community.

Case Examples of YPAR in Schools

Leadership Class

Mariah Kornbluh (White cisgendered woman) is a university-based researcher who partnered with a nonprofit organization that was running yearlong leadership elective classes led by public school teachers focused on empowering high school students to promote a positive school climate (see Bell & Kornbluh, 2022; Kornbluh, 2019; Kornbluh et al., 2015, 2016). For forty-two years, the organization has operated under the guiding values of enhancing young people's sense of self-worth, leadership development, and voice in their everyday settings. For this particular study, Kornbluh collaborated with one high school classroom focused on improving their school health curriculum. The high school teacher (who identified as a Persian cisgendered woman) was beginning her first year as a teacher at the school and was new to the district. She had just begun incorporating YPAR into her class leadership curriculum (an elective course). Sixteen students ranging from freshmen to seniors were active coresearchers in the YPAR project. In regards to major ethnic and demographic groups, almost half of the students identified as Latinx (45 percent), 30 percent as Asian, 7 percent as White, and 16 percent as Black. Notably, as a young woman of color and a new educator, several power dynamics impacted how the teacher approached the YPAR project. She felt pressure from the organization to deliver a "high-impact YPAR project." In turn, she placed pressure on the student-researchers to focus on areas that she deemed important. Furthermore, her colleagues often scrutinized the pedagogy of YPAR involving student-led discussions and participatory learning. For example, colleagues who observed students' engaging in data collection described it as "running around the school" during class hours. Additionally, the school was identified as an "underperforming school within the district." Thus, school leaders, teachers, and staff felt pressure to paint the school in a positive light, which included focusing time on instruction tied directly to standardized test preparation and performance.

Problem Identification

Initially, Kornbluh worked in partnership with the teacher to build student self-interest in action research and demonstrate that the adult researchers valued elevating the students' voices. To initiate this process, they used a modified version of photovoice (an arts-based research methodology rooted in action research) utilizing facilitation strategies from the SHOWED technique.[1] Touring the school with students, Kornbluh asked them to take photographs on their phones regarding issues that they thought were important to discuss and explore as a group. When students returned to the classroom, they engaged in a period of self-reflection and disclosure, documenting the stories behind their photographs through guided reflection. Written reflection prompts included: (1) What inspired you to take this photograph? (2) What is the story behind the photograph? (3) What would you hope others would take away from this photograph? Students posted the photographs and reflections on a secure private online platform allowing them to respond to and engage in discourse with one another. Photographs taken for photovoice projects are often symbolic of larger issues (e.g., showing an outdated textbook related to a sexual health curriculum with a student sleeping next to it to depict the need for updated resources; see Figure 22.1). The research team discussed key issues and areas of interest that emerged from the photographs. Based on these discussions, a major theme and area of interest converged regarding the school health curriculum. Yet, this was not the only topic that

[1] The SHOWED technique consists of five guiding questions: (1) What do you See here? (2) What is really Happening here? (3) How does this relate to Our lives? (4) Why does this condition Exist? (5) What can we Do about it? (Shaffer, 1983).

Figure 22.1 *Photograph taken for a photovoice project.*

students were interested in. Several students indicated interest in structural challenges and the maintenance of the school grounds. Notably, the teacher had a vested interest in the topic of the school health curriculum and thus steered the project in that direction. The inherent power differences between the teacher and students had implications surrounding the ultimate direction of the project. While Kornbluh was heavily invested in elevating student voices, she had to navigate the blurry boundaries between her own positionality in both empowering a new teacher and the class.

Data Collection

To further understand potential gaps or challenges in their school health curriculum, students developed a qualitative interview protocol to elicit perspectives from the student body as well as assess their knowledge about key health competencies (e.g., safe sex practices, hygiene). Students conducted research online and, as a group, identified key content areas surrounding health and wellness to explore with their peers. They then piloted the protocol on their peers (i.e., making edits, testing the phrasing of the questions, etc.), discussed concerns surrounding research ethics (i.e., protecting the anonymity of their peers, not judging or ridiculing participant responses), and then set out to recruit the larger student body to participate in the study. Not all student-researchers were able to participate equitably in data collection. For example, students who did not have work or familial obligations after class were often able to engage in more data collection activities. This showed that even within the research team there were potential power differentials among youth who had the resources (time) to engage in the YPAR project.

Data Analysis

Students reviewed their interviews to identify emerging themes and key gaps in knowledge within the student body. To increase student interest and comfort in qualitative data analysis, they employed two games from the ReACT (Research Actualizing Critical Thought) data analysis method developed by Foster-Fishman et al. (2010). ReACT consists of a series of games to facilitate young people's skill set in qualitative coding. The first game (*candy sorting*) consisted of introducing students to thematic analysis by sorting different types of candy into piles based on similarities (first-order analysis) and then resorting that same candy into fewer piles (second-order analysis). This game increased student comfort with the concept of qualitative data and key steps in the analysis. In the second game (*identifying key messages*), students noted key messages from the interview through memoing (Birks et al., 2008; see Foster-Fishman et al., 2010 for full descriptions of the games). Memoing includes listening to the interviews, describing key findings, and documenting personal reactions (Birks et al., 2008). In their qualitative data analysis of peer interviews, students noted their peers' lack of understanding or awareness surrounding safe sexual health practices. Findings were shared with the larger YPAR classroom in group reporting sessions.

Social Action

Students decided to create a comical informational video to promote information about safe sexual practices and raised money through a bake sale to recruit a nonprofit to help deliver an updated sexual health curriculum to the larger student body. Students disseminated their informational video through online peer social networks. The school also elected to play the video one day during daily class announcements. The youth researchers also worked with the nonprofit to offer teach-ins during lunchtime and for all of the lead teacher's classes. However, these informational events were limited to one school year, and major modifications to the overall school curriculum did not come to fruition, as further resources (time, budgetary constraints) and school buy-in (staff and school board support) were needed in the school to invest in such curricular revisions. Here, support from school leaders and the availability of resources in the school dictated the length, impact, and ability for sustained social change.

School Club

Kimalee Dickerson (Black cisgendered woman), a university-based researcher, partnered with a relatively new high school club focused on supporting Black students. At the time, Dickerson was leading a new youth action research initiative at a university that aimed to train and support youth, particularly those from historically marginalized communities, to use research to improve their lives and communities. Dickerson and the university team partnered with Black Student Union (BSU), a student club at a high school that is open to all and focused on sharing and supporting the culture and experiences of Black students. Black Student Union is led by elected student officers (president, vice president, secretary, and treasurer) and a faculty sponsor who teaches at the high school (a White, cisgendered man with several years of teaching experience). Approximately eight to ten students contributed to the YPAR project over the course of the school year, with the four BSU officers serving as the most consistent active student-researchers. All active student-researchers identified as Black or biracial Black. Several other teachers attended club meetings throughout the year, including a Black cisgendered man in his twenties who attended regularly. Dickerson and an undergraduate student team (two White and one Black cisgendered women) met with BSU biweekly to deliver a YPAR curriculum in virtual meetings throughout the 2020–2021 school year.

Problem Identification

During initial meetings, BSU students engaged in a series of activities designed to build community and explore social identities, such as community asset mapping (Lightfoot et al., 2014) and the social identities wheel (Adams et al., 2007). As BSU youth identified and discussed the assets and issues in their school community, many shared feelings of being excluded, ignored, or hypervisible as the only or one of few Black students in higher-level courses at their high school. Through these discussions, the youth decided to examine the lack of racial/ethnic diversity in dual enrollment (DE) and advanced placement (AP) classes. The youth researchers were interested in better understanding the underlying factors contributing to a lack of diversity and developing potential solutions for this issue. In particular, the youth researchers were interested in exploring the disproportionately low enrollment of Black students in higher-level classes (Black students account for about 16 percent of the student body but 7 percent of AP classes and 11 percent of DE classes).

Data Collection and Analysis

The youth researchers decided to conduct a mixed-method study that engaged multiple stakeholders in their school community, including students, families, teachers, and counselors. Before starting the study, the research team met with the school administration, including the school principal, who expressed enthusiasm and support for the project. The university researchers collaborated with youth researchers to develop a survey for each stakeholder group using Google Forms that included multiple-choice and open-response questions about the course selection process, factors that influence enrollment or recommendations to enroll in different courses, experiences of/support in different course levels, and recommendations for the course selection process. The school principal sent emails to each stakeholder group inviting them to participate in the BSU survey. Additionally, BSU students tapped into their social networks, including using social media, to encourage their peers and teachers to participate. Approximately 150 students, 40 teachers, and 75 families completed surveys. Notably, none of the school counselors (about eight to ten counselors) participated in the surveys.

After initial analysis and group discussion of the survey data, students developed interview protocols and conducted focus-group interviews with a small sample of students, teachers, and counselors. Students recruited interview participants from people who indicated an interest in follow-up interviews on the survey, and they utilized purposeful sampling to recruit populations that were underrepresented in the survey data (e.g., no school counselors completed the survey, so students actively recruited them to participate in interviews). The BSU officers conducted the majority of the focus groups in pairs, with one person taking notes to create a record of the interview. The youth and adult research team worked together to analyze qualitative data from surveys and interviews using thematic analysis (Braun & Clarke, 2006). After introducing the steps of thematic analysis and collectively coding a sample of the data, the research team (university team and youth researchers) coded data individually then discussed and identified themes collectively.

Findings and Social Action

Across participant groups, findings indicated several barriers to racial/ethnic diversity in higher-level courses, including: (1) (mis)communication about courses in terms of available options, expectations, and differences between DE and AP classes; (2) a lack of understanding about the course selection process and progression of courses over time, including prerequisites; (3) finances, including AP exam expenses and textbooks; and (4) perceptions of experiences in DE and AP courses.

With the goal of stimulating institutional changes, youth researchers presented their findings to administrators and staff in two meetings. First, the youth presented to a small group of school administrators who were interested in taking action to address some of the barriers identified in the findings and requested a list of specific recommendations. Subsequently, the youth team presented to over 125 school staff at a regularly scheduled staff meeting. Staff were engaged in the research findings and had numerous questions for the students about the findings and how certain recommendations could be implemented. During and after both meetings, administrators expressed support for and interest in enacting changes that could be implemented at the school level, such as developing a program for older students to donate AP books to younger students to reduce the cost barrier. However, administrators and school staff expressed more hesitancy about taking action on recommendations beyond the school level, such as district-level changes to the course catalog, which is provided to all high schoolers in the district, including those at other high schools. Accordingly, perceived feasibility and the school's sphere of influence were important factors in determining whether school leaders were interested in moving forward with the initiatives suggested by the student-researchers.

After-School Project

Adrienne M. Duke is a university-based researcher who partnered with a middle school principal who wanted to implement an after-school program that focused on promoting leadership development. After discussing YPAR as an option, the principal was very excited about the skills and potential outcomes of PAR. He was mainly interested in understanding how to foster a more positive school climate. Eight sixth grade girls who identified as Black were recruited through open recruitment methods as active coresearchers on the YPAR project (see Figure 22.2). As a Black, cisgendered woman, Duke particularly wanted to hear the perspectives of students who identified as Black girls. In this school, Black girls were disproportionately suspended

Figure 22.2 *Meeting of participants in the after-school project.*

and expelled and were often missing from school leadership roles. Duke intentionally used an open recruitment method via flyers around the school instead of asking for counselor or teacher recommendations. Teacher and counselor sponsorship might have left out girls who might have wanted to participate but were not recommended by school staff.

Problem Identification

The principal was interested in school climate issues, but that was a very broad topic. Accordingly, Duke sought to understand what the youth researchers viewed as issues that impacted their everyday lives at school. Duke engaged the youth team in a series of conversations and used a collage-based methodology to facilitate the problem identification process. Collage can be used as an art-based methodological approach to convey knowledge through images and text. Studies indicate that the ability to use images instead of vocalizing ideas opens an avenue for research participants to explore the subtleties of their experiences in creative, nonlinear, and nonverbal ways (Black, 2002; Leitch, 2006; Roberts & Woods, 2018). This approach also allowed girls who may not have been as verbal as others to more equitably participate and communicate their concerns about the school environment.

For the collage, Duke brought a diverse set of magazines to a meeting and offered the prompt: "Using images from these magazines, what are the most pressing issues that affect your time at school?" The youth researchers cut out pictures and put them on their individual posters. After they completed their collages, there were two written reflection prompts: (1) What inspired you to use these images or words? (2) How does this image relate to an issue that you believe is important to address in your school? The research team discussed key issues and areas of interest that emerged from the collages. Based on these discussions, a major theme and area of interest was relational aggression and physical aggression (fighting) among girls.

Data Collection

To further understand fighting and relational aggression in school among girls, the youth went to the library computer lab to research and take notes on gender differences in relational aggression and fighting. During the next meeting, the team discussed how the literature compared to the youth's lived experiences to identify key questions to explore with their peers. The researcher, with help from the youth research team, developed an interview protocol. After designing the questionnaire, they piloted the protocol on each other (i.e., making edits, testing the phrasing of the questions, etc.), discussed protecting the anonymity of their peers, and created a recruitment list so that they could each ask two people to participate in the study. There were a few youth on the participant list who declined to be interviewed. Therefore, the people who were supposed to conduct these interviews became responsible for finding others to interview. The youth researchers conducted interviews during different elective periods over the course of the school day and recorded them with small audio recorders.

Duke and the youth listened to the interviews and transcribed them into a Word document without names. After the sixteen interviews were transcribed, Duke combined the transcripts, and the research team reviewed them to identify the emerging themes.

Findings and Social Action

Across all participants, findings suggest that girls did not feel like they had effective alternative ways to handle conflict. When asked about help-seeking behavior, adults were seen as unhelpful when conflicts happen. We also found that youth had particular trouble regulating their emotions when dealing with betrayal related to breaches of trust.

Students decided to create a girls-only, in-school assembly to discuss their findings related to girl fighting and relational aggression. During the process of preparing for the assembly, one of the girls on the research team was in a fight and was suspended. The research team held a meeting to decide whether she would stay on the team or have to be dismissed. The discussion was important because this team member engaged in actions that were not in line with the message we wanted to convey during our assembly. The team decided she should stay on the team and, during the assembly, discuss how hard it is to regulate your emotions. She agreed that she could help write a script to talk through those issues.

Since the team had administrative buy-in, the assembly was conducted during the last period of the day and all 6th grade girls were allowed to leave class to attend. The youth researchers decided to discuss their findings during an assembly because they wanted to show the other girls how conflict arises between them and have space to talk about conflict in a productive way. The assembly included poetry, two skits about productive and nonproductive ways of handling conflict, and a presentation on situational strategies for avoiding conflict. While the action did not yield any specific institutional changes, the girls were pleased that they had brought greater awareness to the issues.

Community Power (School-Based Power)

Having presented these three examples of YPAR in school and after-school settings, we now turn to an examination of key elements of power in relation to YPAR. Specifically, we explore the intersections of community and individual power. We also bring in details from our case examples to illuminate how concepts of power played out in diverse YPAR scenarios within school settings.

Christens (2019) proposes three different types of community power: situational, institutional, and systemic. The *situational dimension* focuses on who "wins" and "loses" in publicly visible conflicts over particular community or social issues. In the context of YPAR, such power may encompass student engagement in social action surrounding a particular action research project (e.g., pushing for a change in policy, a new program, or resources). Oftentimes, these projects consist of an action component in which YPAR findings and solutions are shared with key decision-makers. Youth participatory action research projects are most likely to be successful and "win" in terms of changing power structures when adult allies are present and continually working to activate networks of allies to support youth voice and decision-making. Next, the *institutional dimension* expands the analysis to examine what issues are and are not brought into the larger public discourse. Youth participatory action research projects can also foster social action and public dialogue by sharing findings and recommendations in multiple public venues and formats (e.g., social media, school board presentations, mayoral offices). Lastly, the *systemic dimension* stresses how the status quo, dominant ideology, and public opinions are cultivated. Youth participatory action research can also begin to dismantle or challenge the status quo by intentionally pushing to include youth knowledge, ideas, and experiences in everyday social life, fostering a long-term ripple effect.

Situational

Youth participatory action research projects can lead to changes in school and community environments. In a recent meta-review, Shamrova and Cummings (2017) found that YPAR projects tended to promote the integration and inclusion of child-friendly practices into the everyday settings of children and adolescents (i.e., schools, organizations, community centers). Similarly, Kennedy et al. (2019) found in a meta-review that YPAR projects promoted growth in practitioner (i.e., teachers, volunteers, researchers) mindsets and behaviors. In particular, they found that adults learned to value youth's lived experiences, viewed them as valuable stakeholders, were more open to discussing issues of equity, and were more reflective on existing power dynamics. They also noted changes in peer norms embodying increased knowledge surrounding YPAR content, closer peer relationships, and stronger linkages between home, school, and their community.

In the context of our three case examples, the YPAR teams pushed for social change through traditional decision-making channels (i.e., getting permission from the school principal, buy-in from the administrative team) and spurred excitement from school stakeholders. Yet, to our knowledge, none of the projects were successful in changing school practices over the long term. However, they were successful in disseminating knowledge to youth peers and school staff via informational videos, meetings, and assemblies and in creating opportunities for students and staff to better understand social issues and barriers. We noted that all three projects were tied to the school year; thus, momentum for such projects was impacted by the summer break. In the two case examples in which YPAR was conducted during school hours and in partnership with teachers, the teachers recounted how engaging in intergenerational knowledge construction and development shaped their own pedagogical practices (i.e., incorporating and valuing student-led inquiry into teaching) and how they valued their relationships with students. In Duke's project, the YPAR project was focused on peers (mitigating fighting or aggression), and the outcomes were tied to a deeper understanding of aggression from a gendered analysis. The youth researchers put together an assembly to address their peers directly and challenge the status quo of being highly reactional in emotionally tense situations. In reflecting upon our projects, we note that the focus of each social action project was dependent on the target audience and whose perceptions were changed.

Institutional

In their meta-review, Shamrova and Cummings (2017) also found that YPAR projects created opportunities for formal organizational and institutional structures and platforms to elevate child and adolescent perspectives. These activities included involving children and adolescents in early program development, evaluation, advocacy campaigns, and future funding mechanisms. Kennedy et al. (2019) found institutional policy development or improvement to be achieved as a result of YPAR. Projects included redistributing funding to support youth-related services, involving students as cotrainers in teacher training programs, and formalizing opportunities for youth voice in school and community settings. Across all three projects, the uniqueness of the data collection process involving students as coresearchers stimulated critical conversations and spurred public discourse within the school community. Additionally, all three projects used purposeful sampling to engage members of the school community who may not typically participate in research studies. For example, in Duke's project, students who were interviewed about fighting may not have traditionally volunteered to participate in research. The fact that other female students were serving as the interviewers made a difference in who was in conversation about this critical school issue. The role of youth as presenters disrupted how knowledge was traditionally disseminated and potentially increased curiosity and engagement with the findings. Youth also used creative means to share their findings, making them accessible to multiple audiences.

Systemic

In the context of systemic power, YPAR projects have been successful in shaping larger public opinions. Shamrova and Cummings (2017) noted several

YPAR projects in their meta-review that raised community awareness through targeted social media outreach and infrastructure change within the larger community. Kennedy et al. (2019) found similar results, with three studies yielding city-level policy changes (e.g., a prohibition on drive-through restaurants, restrictions on tobacco and alcohol advertisements on storefronts, and the addition of two bus routes).

Across all three of our examples, the projects were focused within the school community, restricting who had access to information from the YPAR projects. Thus, while the projects shaped public opinion within the schools, they did not attempt to shift broader narratives or resource allocation beyond the school communities. By comparison, some YPAR projects addressing issues at a school district level have been more successful in changing the status quo and wider public opinion (Cohen et al., 2020).

Psychological Empowerment: Four Dimensions

The most common outcome identified in YPAR projects is the development of sentiments of psychological empowerment in youths. Christens (2019) identifies these gains as (1) affective, (2) behavioral, (3) cognitive, and (4) relational domains.

Affective

Researchers stress that YPAR participation often yields social-emotional learning developmental outcomes such as positive ethnic identity development, self-awareness, and relational skills (i.e., self-management; Jagers et al., 2019; Ozer et al., 2010). Youth participatory action research creates opportunities for young people to tap into their personal voice and document their lived experiences, engage in collective dialogue with their peers and adults, and gather data that allow them to expand their understanding of others' perspectives. Interestingly, social emotional development outcomes have not been widely assessed or documented as outcomes within YPAR projects (see Anyon et al., 2018; Jagers et al., 2019). However, Levy et al. (2018) recently employed YPAR with hip-hop therapy and provide anecdotal examples that such programming may foster opportunities for young people to exercise self-expression and a collective gathering of emotions through music that can be leveraged to promote social change. Furthermore, Voight (2015) found preliminary evidence of a rise in prosocial behaviors as well as positive peer norms among young people engaged in a YPAR project focused on addressing bullying.

In our projects discussed earlier in this chapter, students reported that YPAR helped foster their ability to understand, be empathetic toward, and learn from the perspectives, differing backgrounds, and diverse lived experiences of their peers. In our YPAR projects in which youth researchers shared similar racial identities, specifically Black identity, the youth reported positive impacts on their racial/ethnic identities. In particular, Duke's project focused on intersecting identities (gender and race), thus creating a space for both identities to be explored and affirmed.

Behavioral

The action research cycle embedded within YPAR fosters an environment and opportunity structure that facilitates civic action (Kornbluh et al., 2015). Solórzano and Delgado-Bernal (2001) note that transformational resistance can be facilitated through YPAR, consisting of student behavior that entails both a critical analysis of oppressive structures and a desire for social justice. Cammarota and Romero (2011) described students' growth in understanding and documenting the political inequalities forced upon Latinx students. Data gathered from personal reflections and peer interviews yielded social action strategies involving leveraging student voices to share their findings and recommendations for structural change with family members, the school leadership team, and state officials. All three projects provided opportunities for students to engage in social action. The topics explored across these cases required a critical analysis lens to honor and recognize students' lived experiences and the processes that impact them on a daily basis.

Cognitive

Youth participatory action research is a pedagogical process that intentionally creates opportunity structures, defined by Watts and Guessous (2006) as transformative experiences to practice behaviors that enhance or facilitate a critical analysis of one's environment and recognition of oppression. These behaviors may encompass critical thinking, a richer understanding of institutional inequity, and promoting young peoples' collective agency. Notably, many YPAR projects have reported critical consciousness as an outcome for young people. Critical consciousness refers to an individual's awareness of systems of oppression and power inequities within society (*critical reflection*), a sense of agency to work against oppression (*critical motivation*), and engagement in individual or collective action to challenge social inequities (*critical action*; Freire, 1970; Watts et al., 2011). For instance, Anyon et al. (2018) found in a recent meta-review of sixty-three studies that 30.8 percent of studies reported critical consciousness outcomes. The same meta-review also found that 75 percent of the YPAR studies indicated other dimensions of cognitive empowerment, including increased self-determination, self-efficacy, and confidence to be able to change and influence everyday environments.

Among our projects, we noted that the process of data collection, specifically capturing diverse stakeholders within the schools' voices, and analyzing such themes fostered an awareness of how school systems and structures operate. The YPAR process fostered collective feelings of agency and youth became more aware of the power of their group to do more to address issues they experienced individually. In particular, Dickerson's and Kornbluh's projects helped the youth researchers to locate their individual experiences of exclusion in a larger system that perpetuated inequities.

Relational

Youth participatory action research is a collective process. Through critical discussions, sharing of personal experiences, capturing information, and exploring diverse narratives, students form social-emotional bonds and support networks with one another (Kornbluh et al., 2016). Furthermore, young people are often supported by one or more adults (teachers, mentors, volunteers, researchers) and other decision-makers, yielding intergenerational knowledge-sharing and opportunities to foster social capital. Notably, 36.5 percent of the YPAR studies included in Anyon et al.'s (2018) meta-review reported young people indicating enhanced sentiments of connectedness, social support, community attachment, and belonging.

The theme of building relationships came up across all three case examples yet diverged in terms of creating new relationships versus deepening established relationships. Kornbluh used social network analysis to examine peer support networks over time and found more diverse and robust connections among peers as the project progressed (Kornbluh, 2019). In Dickerson's project, many of the youth researchers were friends before participating in the YPAR project, and thus youth reported deeper connections with each other and the adult researchers after working together on the research project. In Duke's project, the youth coresearchers shared similar racial and gender identities, which created a strong relational component to our research time. Research time was also a time to be social and commensurate around other school issues that they were experiencing.

Features of YPAR Settings

While YPAR presentations can be empowering experiences for students, limited research has explored the potential for such discourse to compel action and institutional change (Bertrand & Lozenski, 2023). Bertrand and Lozenski (2023) warn of fetishizing youth voice and "conflating it with actual policy change" (p. 2). Furthermore, political climate influences the approaches/theories permitted in a school curriculum. For example, a Mexican American studies program in Tucson, Arizona, which included a social justice-oriented YPAR program, was halted by Arizona's Commissioner of Education due to supposed misalignment with American values (Orozco, 2012).

Kennedy et al. (2019) found several key features associated with community and social change as a result of a YPAR project. First, YPAR projects that utilized action strategies focused on advocacy and organizing were more likely to report social change outcomes as compared to general awareness or education-oriented strategies. Furthermore, having a clear target (representatives of schools/organizations or policymakers) for social action were associated with greater community outcomes and power as compared to the general public, peer social networks, or researchers within the academy. Lastly, the duration of the YPAR project was also strongly associated with greater environmental outcomes.

In the context of YPAR in school settings, Anderson (2020) found that the researcher's positionality in relation to the school setting was a critical bridge to supporting the incorporation of YPAR into the everyday school curriculum. However, she also found that YPAR projects within schools but outside of class instructional time (i.e., after-school programs, clubs) may provide more pedagogical freedom in content and activities. Anderson also noted that many YPAR projects were aligned with the school calendar, and yet more successful projects advocating for change and transformation required a thoughtful postcontingency plan. Her review highlighted several other features that can help build community power within school settings, including compensating students for their time with academic credit or monetary stipends. Notably, academic credit was found to further hierarchical relationships between teachers, researchers, and students (i.e., teachers or researchers imposing a grade associated with a student's YPAR project), whereas financial compensation tended to equalize relationships and foster more reciprocal knowledge-sharing. Furthermore, many YPAR projects in school settings rely on outside networks (university researchers or community-based organizations) to provide technical support (professional development opportunities, training, facilitators), resources (data collection instruments, analysis software), and unique connections (university staff, policymakers). In addition, school administrators have been identified as being powerful allies in promoting YPAR and disseminating study findings. Administrators can also create roadblocks, censure, or attempt to direct the YPAR project. Similarly, policymakers and district staff can play a role in supporting or blocking the implementation of YPAR within school settings. Overall, Anderson (2020) found that strategic alignment of YPAR projects with diverse stakeholders (specifically creating power maps to identify allies) may be a particularly important strategy and process for facilitating social change.

In reflecting across our case examples described earlier, we noted that the extent to which YPAR was embedded within the institution may have been connected with the opportunity to observe civic engagement beyond the YPAR project. In Dickerson's and Duke's projects, they were the initial creators, designers, and evaluators of the YPAR process. The researchers therefore had less time and opportunity to observe or track civic engagement over time. In contrast, Kornbluh worked with an established YPAR program allowing her to track participation over time. As such, she found that YPAR engagement increased youth's civic activities. Across the three cases, administrators served as allies and supporters of the YPAR projects. For example, in Dickerson's project, administrators encouraged staff and students to participate in the research project and provided a platform for youth researchers to share findings and recommendations with the staff at a meeting. Despite being supportive of the YPAR projects, administrators seemed to view YPAR as an educational and leadership development opportunity for students rather than a mechanism to systematically transform schools. For administrators, this perspective placed the focus of change on the students rather than on the school system.

Application and Future Research

This chapter has highlighted implications for multiple stakeholders involved in YPAR: youth, adult educators and researchers, and schools and communities.

For youth, the literature provides evidence of a host of benefits to be gained from participating in YPAR. In particular, given the continued segregation of students within schools (Dalane & Marcotte, 2022; Francis & Darity, 2021), school-based YPAR provides an opportunity for students to build relationships within and across identity groups. Moreover, in the context of a hierarchical education system, school-based YPAR offers a space for students and adults to share power in a way that centers the lived experiences and concerns of youth. In some cases, YPAR may therefore serve as a context for learning, for social-emotional development, and for involvement in transformations to school and community contexts.

Adult educators should consider the benefits and challenges of YPAR in different school settings. For example, while students may be more likely to regularly participate in a YPAR project included in a leadership program or upper-level course, students from historically marginalized groups may have limited access to these opportunities. In addition to considering which students are participating, adult educators should explore potential partnerships with local colleges and universities or nonprofit programs that offer a YPAR curriculum, personnel to support YPAR projects, or evaluation services. Additionally, teacher preparation programs should offer training to teachers in conducting YPAR and similar project-based learning opportunities that center on youth voice and in which youth and adults share power.

Like many school-based YPAR projects, our case examples focused on action and change at the school level. School-based YPAR teams are drawn to school-level issues and actions for several reasons, including that the school provides a basis for shared community for student researchers and adult educators. Moreover, adult educators often feel empowered (or pressured) to focus on the school level. Lastly, partnerships with school administrators and decision-makers frequently occur at the school level, thereby making the school a more feasible target for change in comparison to the broader community. Although there are many reasons for school-based YPAR projects to target issues that exist primarily within the school, school-level change is not the only possibility. School-based YPAR project teams should consider the benefits and drawbacks of selecting a school-level issue and should not assume that they cannot address issues beyond the school community.

The field would benefit from empirical evidence that examines the shared educational system features surrounding YPAR projects that have been successful in pushing for transformative sustainable change and community power. Critical questions include: Why are key power brokers/decision-makers interested in conducting a youth participatory project? What forms of youth action are currently supported by the system? What system-level infrastructures (policies, mechanisms, access to technical support) are in place to sustain YPAR processes after the research team leaves? Gaining insights into contextual questions such as these could allow researchers to better understand current power dynamics within the educational system and how YPAR can serve as a sustainable and long-term disruptor in elevating student voices.

References

Adams, M., & Bell, L. A. (Eds.). (2016). *Teaching for diversity and social justice* (3rd ed.). Routledge.

Adams, M., Bell, L. A., & Griffin, P. (2007). *Teaching for diversity and social justice* (2nd ed.). Routledge.

Afterschool Alliance (2020, December). *America after 3pm: Demand grows, opportunity shrinks*. Afterschool Alliance. http://afterschoolalliance.org/documents/AA3PM-2020/National-AA3PM-2020-Fact-Sheet.pdf

Anderson, A. J. (2020). A qualitative systematic review of youth participatory action research implementation in US high schools. *American Journal of Community Psychology*, 65(1–2), 242–257.

Anyon, Y., Bender, K., Kennedy, H., & Dechants, J. (2018). A systematic review of youth participatory action research (YPAR) in the United States: Methodologies, youth outcomes, and future directions. *Health Education & Behavior*, 45(6), 865–878.

Bell, S., & Kornbluh, M. (2022). Networking in the digital age: Identifying factors that influence adolescents' online communication and relationship building. *Applied Developmental Sciences*, 26, 109–126.

Bertrand, M., & Lozenski, B. D. (2023). YPAR dreams deferred? Examining power bases for YPAR to impact policy and practice. *Educational Policy*, 37(2), 437–462.

Birks, M., Chapman, Y., & Francis, K. (2008). Memoing in qualitative research: Probing data and processes. *Journal of Research in Nursing*, *13*(1), 68–75.

Black, A. (2002) Making sense of what it means to teach: Artful representations as meaning-making tools, *Teacher Development*, *6*(1), 75–88.

Branquinho, C., Tomé, G., Grothausen, T., & Gaspar de Matos, M. (2020). Community-based youth participatory action research studies with a focus on youth health and well-being: A systematic review. *Journal of Community Psychology*, *48*(5), 1301–1315.

Braun, V., & Clarke, V. (2006). Using thematic analysis in psychology. *Qualitative Research in Psychology*, *3*(2), 77–101.

Brion-Meisels, G., & Alter, Z. (2018). The quandary of youth participatory action research in school settings: A framework for reflecting on the factors that influence purpose and process. *Harvard Educational Review*, *88*(4), 429–454.

Buckley-Marudas, M. F., & Soltis, S. (2020). What youth care about: Exploring topic identification for youth-led research in school. *The Urban Review*, *52*(2), 331–350.

Bulanda, J. J., & McCrea, K. T. (2013). The promise of an accumulation of care: Disadvantaged African-American youths' perspectives about what makes an after school program meaningful. *Child and Adolescent Social Work Journal*, *30*(2), 95–118.

Buttimer, C. J. (2018). The challenges and possibilities of youth participatory action research for teachers and students in public school classrooms. *Berkeley Review of Education*, *8*(1), 39–81.

Cammarota, J., & Romero, A. (2011). Participatory action research for high school students: Transforming policy, practice, and the personal with social justice education. *Educational Policy*, *25*(3), 488–506.

Caraballo, L., Lozenski, B. D., Lyiscott, J. J., & Morrell, E. (2017). YPAR and critical epistemologies: Rethinking education research. *Review of Research in Education*, *41*(1), 311–336.

Christens, B. D. (2019). *Community power and empowerment*. Oxford University Press.

Cohen, A. K., Ozer, E. J., Abraczinskas, M., Voight, A., Kirshner, B., & Devinney, M. (2020). Opportunities for youth participatory action research to inform school district decisions. *Evidence & Policy*, *16*(2), 317–329.

Dalane, K., & Marcotte, D. E. (2022). The segregation of students by income in public schools. *Educational Researcher*, *51*(4), 245–254.

Duncan-Andrade, J. M., & Morrell, E. (2008). Youth participatory action research as critical pedagogy. *Counterpoints*, *285*, 105–131.

Foster-Fishman, P. G., Law, K. M., Lichty, L. F., & Aoun, C. (2010). Youth ReACT for social change: A method for youth participatory action research. *American Journal of Community Psychology*, *46*(1–2), 67–83.

Francis, D. V., & Darity, W. A. (2021). Separate and unequal under one roof: How the legacy of racialized tracking perpetuates within-school segregation. *RSF: The Russell Sage Foundation Journal of the Social Sciences*, *7*(1), 187–202.

Frasquilho, D., Ozer, E. J., Ozer, E. M., Branquinho, C., Camacho, I., Reis, M., Tomé, G., Santos, T., Gomes, P., Cruz, J., Ramiro, L., Gaspar, T., Simões, C., Piatt, A. A., Holsen, I., & de Matos, M. G. (2018). Dream teens: Adolescents-led participatory project in Portugal in the context of the economic recession. *Health Promotion Practice*, *19*(1), 51–59.

Freire, P. (1970). *Pedagogy of the oppressed*. Continuum

Goslin, D. A. (1965). *The school in contemporary society*. Scott, Foresman.

Irizarry, J. G., & Brown, T. M. (2014). Humanizing research in dehumanizing spaces: The challenges and opportunities of conducting participatory action research with youth in schools. In D. Paris & M. T. Winn (Eds.), *Humanizing research: Decolonizing qualitative inquiry with youth and communities* (pp. 63–80). Sage.

Jagers, R. J., Rivas-Drake, D., & Williams, B. (2019). Transformative social and emotional learning (SEL): Toward SEL in service of educational equity and excellence. *Educational Psychologist*, *54*(3), 162–184.

Kennedy, H., DeChants, J., Bender, K., & Anyon, Y. (2019). More than data collectors: A systematic review of the environmental outcomes of youth inquiry approaches in the United States. *American Journal of Community Psychology*, *63*(1–2), 208–226.

Kohfeldt, D., Chhun, L., Grace, S., & Langhout, R. D. (2011). Youth empowerment in context: Exploring tensions in school-based YPAR. *American Journal of Community Psychology*, *47*(1), 28–45.

Kornbluh, M. (2019). Building bridges: Exploring the communication trends and perceived sociopolitical benefits of adolescents engaging in online social justice efforts. *Youth & Society*, *51*(8), 1104–1126.

Kornbluh, M., Neal, J. W., & Ozer, E. J. (2016). Scaling-up youth-led social justice efforts through an online school-based social network. *American Journal of Community Psychology*, *57*(3–4), 266–279.

Kornbluh, M., Ozer, E. J., Allen, C. D., & Kirshner, B. (2015). Youth participatory action research as an approach to sociopolitical development and the new academic standards: Considerations for educators. *The Urban Review*, *47*(5), 868–892.

Leitch, R. (2006) Limitations of language: Developing arts-based creative narrative in stories of teachers' identities. *Teachers and Teaching: Theory and Practice*, *12*(5), 549–569.

Levy, I. P., Cook, A. L., & Emdin, C. (2018). Remixing the school counselor's tool kit: Hip-hop spoken word therapy and YPAR. *Professional School Counseling*, *22*(1), 1–11.

Lightfoot, E., McCleary, J. S., & Lum, T. (2014). Asset mapping as a research tool for community-based participatory research in social work. *Social Work Research*, *38*(1), 59–64.

Lightfoot, S. L. (1986). On goodness in schools: Themes of empowerment. *Peabody Journal of Education*, *63*(3), 9–28.

Mirra, N., & Rogers, J. (2016). Institutional participation and social transformation: Considering the goals and tensions of university-initiated YPAR projects with K–12 youth. *International Journal of Qualitative Studies in Education*, *29*(10), 1255–1268.

Mirra, N., Garcia, A., & Morrell, E. (2015). *Doing youth participatory action research: Transforming inquiry with researchers, educators, and students*. Routledge.

National Center for Education Statistics. (2020). *Fast facts: Back-to-school statistics*. National Center for Education Statistics. https://nces.ed.gov/fastfacts/display .asp?id=372#PK12-enrollment

Orozco, R. A. (2012). Racism and power Arizona politicians' use of the discourse of anti-Americanism against Mexican American studies. *Hispanic Journal of Behavioral Sciences, 34*(1), 43–60.

Ozer, E. J. (2016). Youth-led participatory action research: Developmental and equity perspectives. *Advances in Child Development and Behavior, 50*, 189–207.

Ozer, E. J., & Douglas, L. (2015). Assessing the key processes of youth-led participatory research: Psychometric analysis and application of an observational rating scale. *Youth & Society, 47*(1), 29–50.

Ozer, E. J., & Wright, D. (2012). Beyond school spirit: The effects of youth-led participatory action research in two urban high schools. *Journal of Research on Adolescence, 22*(2), 267–283.

Ozer, E. J., Abraczinskas, M., Voight, A., Kirshner, B., Cohen, A. K., Zion, S., Glende, J. R., Stickney, D., Gauna, R., Lopez, S. E., & Freiburger, K. (2020). Use of research evidence generated by youth: Conceptualization and applications in diverse US K–12 educational settings. *American Journal of Community Psychology, 66*(1–2), 81–93.

Ozer, E. J., Newlan, S., Douglas, L., & Hubbard, E. (2013). "Bounded" empowerment: Analyzing tensions in the practice of youth-led participatory research in urban public schools. *American Journal of Community Psychology, 52*(1), 13–26.

Ozer, E. J., Ritterman, M. L., & Wanis, M. G. (2010). Participatory action research (PAR) in middle school: Opportunities, constraints, and key processes. *American Journal of Community Psychology, 46*(1–2), 152–166.

Prati, G., Mazzoni, D., Guarino, A., Albanesi, C., & Cicognani, E. (2020). Evaluation of an active citizenship intervention based on youth-led participatory action research. *Health Education & Behavior, 47*(6), 894–904.

Roberts, A., & Woods, P. A. (2018). Theorising the value of collage in exploring educational leadership. *British Educational Research Journal, 44*(4), 626–642.

Rodríguez, L. F., & Brown, T. M. (2009). From voice to agency: Guiding principles for participatory action research with youth. *New Directions for Youth Development, 123*, 19–34.

Shaffer, R. (1983). *Beyond the dispensary*. African Medical and Research Foundation.

Shamrova, D. P., & Cummings, C. E. (2017). Participatory action research (PAR) with children and youth: An integrative review of methodology and PAR outcomes for participants, organizations, and communities. *Children and Youth Services Review, 81*, 400–412.

Solórzano, D. G., & Delgado- Bernal, D. (2001). Examining transformational resistance through a critical race and Latcrit theory framework: Chicana and Chicano students in an urban context. *Urban Education, 36*(3), 308–342.

Suleiman, B. A., Ballard, P. J., Hoyt, L. T., & Ozer, E. J. (2021). Applying a developmental lens to youth-led participatory action research: A critical examination and integration of existing evidence. *Youth & Society, 53*(1), 26–53.

Umaña-Taylor, A. J. (2016). A post-racial society in which ethnic-racial discrimination still exists and has significant consequences for youths' adjustment. *Current Directions in Psychological Science, 25*(2), 111–118.

Unicef. (2022, June). *Primary education*. Unicef. https://data.unicef.org/topic/education/primary-education/

United Nations. (1989, November 20). *United Nations Convention on the Rights of the Child*. United Nations. www.ohchr.org/Documents/ProfessionalInterest/crc.pdf

Voight, A. (2015). Student voice for school-climate improvement: A case study of an urban middle school. *Journal of Community & Applied Social Psychology, 25*(4), 310–326.

Watts, R. J., & Guessous, O. (2006). Sociopolitical development: The missing link in research and policy on adolescents. In S. Ginwright, P. Noguera, & J. Cammarota (Eds.), *Beyond resistance! Youth activism and community change: new democratic possibilities for practice and policy for America's youth* (pp. 59–80). Routledge.

Watts, R. J., Diemer, M. A., & Voight, A. M. (2011). Critical consciousness: Current status and future directions. *New Directions for Child and Adolescent Development, 134*, 43–57.

Zeldin, S., Christens, B. D., & Powers, J. L. (2013). The psychology and practice of youth–adult partnership: Bridging generations for youth development and community change. *American Journal of Community Psychology, 51*(3), 385–397.

Zimmerman, M. A. (2000). Empowerment theory. In J. Rappaport & E. Seidman (Eds.), *Handbook of community psychology* (pp. 43–63). Kluwer Academic/Plenum Publishers.

23 Community-Based Education

Moisés G. Contreras, Virginia Downing, Carl D. Greer, and Bianca J. Baldridge

Introduction

Community-based educational spaces (CBESs) have always played a pivotal role in marginalized communities as sites of empowerment for youth. Community-based educational spaces afford communities room to build young people's civic capacity, to organize for social change, and to create learning environments that foster a political – and, in certain respects, a more meaningful – education. Community-based educational spaces can have transformative impacts on youth and community members writ large by allowing them to dictate their organizations' curriculum, initiatives, and overall structure. Certainly, CBESs can have powerful implications for social change within communities and their potential impacts on larger systems.

Although in educational discourse "after-school programs," "community-based organizations," and "community centers" have been used interchangeably, we deploy Baldridge's (2018) use of "community-based educational spaces" to guide our discussion on power-building and empowerment in community settings. As a term, CBESs "provide a broader understanding of the full range of pedagogical practices employed within such settings ... [and elucidate] the strength and agency of community" (Baldridge, 2018, p. 4). Further, CBESs and their efforts can be situated as a part of one or many of the following nine sectors (Baldridge et al., in press): (1) district and county-based providers, (2) national youth programs, (3) independent and grassroots programs, (4) university–community-based partnerships, (5) faith-based programs and religious spaces, (6) outreach and basic needs-driven programming, (7) cultural enrichment programs, (8) private enrichment programs, and (9) capacity-building programs.

In addition to being sites where people can build power, CBESs also meet the specific needs of communities such as providing access to food and opportunities for learning, identity exploration, and the development of skill sets and talents (Baldridge, 2019). Youth engage with youth workers within these spaces to create supportive and encouraging relationships that stand in contrast to their experiences in schools (Lardier et al., 2020a). Indeed, CBESs are crucial in their communities for the important role they play in activating and sustaining the co-construction of rich social networks (Dill & Ozer, 2019).

As Nancy Erbstein (2013) notes, young people can turn to youth workers for support with challenges: legal issues associated with immigration status, abuse, trouble with graduating high school, inadequate access to health care, and police harassment, for example. In the same vein, youth workers facing personal challenges can also activate their relationships with young people to access their knowledge and rich social networks. Without a doubt, CBESs are indispensable for many communities, especially for the ways they intimately understand and respond to their respective local contexts.

Historically, participation in CBESs has steadily increased; however, participation has uncharacteristically decreased amid the COVID-19 global health pandemic. Currently, in the US, 7.8 million young people are enrolled in a community-based education program compared to 10.2 million in 2014 (Afterschool Alliance, 2020b). In addition, CBES leaders have expressed their concerns about the sustainability of their programming amid COVID-19, citing their worries of having to permanently close their spaces and having long-term funding plans dictating their programs' futures (Afterschool Alliance, 2020a). Nevertheless, in the face of uncertainty, there are many young people still willing to participate in community-based programming, which reached 24.6 million youth participants in 2020 (Afterschool Alliance, 2020b). There is an unmet need in the investment of CBESs, especially along the lines of race and ethnicity, where more than half of Black and Latinx youth would participate in CBESs if given the opportunity and access (Afterschool Alliance, 2020b). Of the 25 million young people unable to access such programs, roughly 59 percent are low-income Black families and 52 percent are Latinx (Afterschool Alliance, 2020b).

In their rich history, CBESs have demonstrated their importance as centerpieces in their communities and their power to bring about social change and spur transformative change for those they serve. Namely, through centering racial identity development and sociopolitical awareness, CBESs provide spaces for racially minoritized young people to engage in critical literacy development and culturally responsive and sustaining pedagogies (Gay, 2000; Paris, 2012; Watson, 2013), embrace the arts to create counter-discourses challenging deficit narratives (Hess, 2018; Ngo et al., 2017), and leverage activism to increase self-, social-, and global awareness (Carey et al., 2021; Kirshner, 2015). In many ways, these spaces respond to local, state, and federal disinvestment by "mobilizing for civil rights, cleaning up the environment, rehabilitating houses for homeless families, and organizing against violence in the schools" (Checkoway, 2011, p. 391).

In this chapter, we offer the history of Urban Underground (UU) to further exemplify the liberatory education, youth empowerment, and power-building possibilities within CBESs. Urban Underground highlights the potential of community-based education to build power in community settings and nurture the humanity of Black and Latinx youth served. In our collaboration with UU, we have witnessed the organization's ability to respond to community needs, namely by training and bolstering youth to lead social change efforts. Community-based educational spaces succeed at creating humanizing spaces and at fostering youth leadership to varying degrees, as we will discuss in this chapter. Therefore, we aim to provide a description of UU's work as a representation of the power-building and youth empowerment that are possible in CBESs. The following section provides a brief review of the scholarship about the power-building features of CBESs as an entrée to UU's story.

Power-Building Features of CBESs

Community-based educational spaces like UU are often sites that facilitate the building and exercising of social power. Not only can they take on the role of intermediaries between institutional powers and those who are pushing for change within those institutions (McLaughlin et al., 2009), but they can also elevate individual community voices as a collective (Cohen et al., 2018). In considering features that facilitate community power-building, the literature on youth power makes clear that it begins with the basics: relationships (Christens, 2012). While considered essential to CBESs and their work, relationship-building and relational organizing are not aspects of organizations that are measured or valued in the nonprofit sector (especially when it comes to recognition and funding; Colvin et al., 2020). Relationship-building is a continuous and constantly shifting process shaped by the community and context in which it is situated.

Further, the sociopolitical dynamics of neighborhoods are important for CBESs to understand as these dynamics are foundational to how relationships are built (Erbstein & Fabionar, 2019; Sampson et al., 2019; Warren & Mapp, 2011). For example, Sampson et al. (2019) highlighted the organization We Will Rise, located in Nevada's Las Vegas metropolitan area, to show that CBESs can build trust and engage more deeply with their communities by considering their context – including the families and youth involved – and being more flexible and responsive to community needs. The organization responded to its community by encouraging youth and volunteers involved to engage in efforts that shed light on systemic inequities and to host events or meetings within the neighborhood "as a way of highlighting the positive community attributes for those inside and outside the community" (Sampson et al., 2019, p. 219). Within a school context, when community members deemed the school districts as negligent of meeting young people's academic needs, We Will Rise looked at how it could address what the schools could not or were unwilling to provide (such as preparing their youth for postsecondary education when the school instead guided their youth toward the service and tourism industry). Scholars have also named organizational detachment from community needs as a barrier to engaging communities; for example, youth may not engage with an organization if it is not embedded within their community or if it asks youth to travel long distances to attend

(Ginwright & Cammarota, 2009). Organizations need to consider how they are engaging with the community they aim to serve as this is foundational for relationship-building and community power-building.

When considering group dynamics and their connection to relationship-building, scholars have spoken to the utility of CBESs engaging in intergenerational youth–adult partnerships that acknowledge shared power in theory and practice (Lopez, 2021; Sampson et al., 2019). Discussions of power-sharing in community settings must acknowledge that power and agency already exist within communities. Community-based educational spaces that believe in the capacity of youth and communities can build strong relationships and exercise that power through organizing and addressing community needs (Sampson et al., 2019). This is practiced through structures and roles that facilitate power-sharing between youth and adults. In Nicholas and Eastman-Mueller's (2020) study, the authors highlighted how a youth-driven CBES in St. Louis, Missouri, established power-sharing norms that were revisited in every meeting to acknowledge how youth and adults would communicate and organize together. Additionally, adults within these spaces have taken advantage of opportunities to share vulnerabilities and open communication to build relationships that highlight the development process as a collective effort (Bonfiglio, 2017; Ginwright, 2010; Wu et al., 2016).

Once power and communication norms are established, scholarship speaks to the ways adults can center youth agency and develop organizational structures that allow for adults to step back and for young people to lead. Larson and Hansen (2005) highlight how adults within a youth activism program help to create an agenda but allow the youth to establish what needs to be discussed. Additionally, Flores (n.d.) implores adults to create opportunities for youth leadership development that allow them to gain skills in a supportive environment and, within this structure, create "rehearsal" spaces for youth to prepare for organizing engagements such as public comments at school boards or leading in political education. Building these processes and developing an organizational culture around them show the possibilities to effectively build community power in CBESs.

The literature is expansive on recognizing the power that comes from developing a critical consciousness to exercise community power, especially for youth development (Christens et al., 2016; Ginwright & Cammarota, 2009; Johnson, 2017; Lardier et al., 2020b; Murray & Milner, 2015; Watts & Hipolito-Delgado, 2015). In particular, the settings and features that facilitate the development of critical consciousness merit explication. Existing scholarship speaks to how CBESs curate opportunities for youth to travel not only within their city but also out of the state and country to make sense of the world and make sociopolitical connections (Sampson et al., 2019). Research also highlights the importance of carving out space in programming for young people to reflect on the development of their critical consciousness through political education workshops (Ginwright, 2010; Ginwright & Cammarota, 2009).

Youth, specifically those who identified as Black and LGBTQ+, can engage in critical reflection through "writing self" programming (Johnson, 2017), in which they write about themselves and their identities in an uninfluenced manner without having to consider societal perceptions and expectations.

Community-based educational spaces become conducive sites for power-building when they leverage relationships and foster a political education for their members and communities. Sustaining the involvement of young people, and community members writ large, requires their trust in the organization and the people therein. Youth and adults in CBESs can strengthen trust by entering into partnerships and sharing power within their organizations. In fact, entering in authentic youth–adult partnerships can serve as a window to complicate interpersonal power dynamics and encourage further critical consciousness development (Brion-Meisels et al., 2020). In the next section, we examine UU as an exemplary organization that embodies the promise of power-building within CBESs, especially in the way it embraces youth leadership.

Urban Underground

Background

Founded in 2000 in Milwaukee, Wisconsin, UU aims to "[provide] support and opportunity for young people to address the most pressing issues of our time" by authentically uplifting their narratives and talents (Little Black Book, 2020). Urban Underground draws its namesake inspiration from Harriet Tubman and her steadfast fight for freedom, her courageous efforts, and her labor throughout her time organizing the Underground Railroad. As UU seeks to replicate the fierce fight against bondage and oppression present in Harriet's legacy, they added "Urban" to their name to denote the context and population that the organization aims to serve.

Urban Underground's program structure reflects its belief that youth voice and power must be centered to address all social issues facing young people. Urban Underground has a commitment to the spirit of racial justice, advocacy, and centering youth voice; in doing so, the organization regularly hosts numerous events and programming reaching Black and Latinx youth throughout the Milwaukee area (see Figure 23.1). Milestone moments include UU hosting a youth-led forum to address the blatant racial profiling of youth in the Sherman Park community; developing a Youth Empowerment Program piloted with twenty-five young people (resulting in a 100 percent completion rate) assisting young people in their successful campaign against having armed police officers placed in every Milwaukee Public Schools high school; and partnering with the National Black Youth Vote alliance in efforts to enhance voter registration and turnout among young adults in the greater Milwaukee area (Urban Underground, n.d.).

Figure 23.1 *Youth participating in an Urban Underground event.*
Source: *"Gallery," by Urban Underground, 2022 (www.urbanunderground.org/untitled-cu1w). Reprinted with permission.*

Neighborhood Context(s)

Milwaukee presents young people with a variety of regional contexts to navigate. For example, the historical racial segregation in the city has created racial and ethnic enclaves with rigid boundaries (e.g., Latinx communities primarily located in Milwaukee's southern area). Racial segregation in Milwaukee has also resulted in vast disparities along the lines of race and class. Among the US's largest cities, Milwaukee has the second-lowest Black homeownership rate (Levine, 2020). Certainly, the extremely low Black home-ownership rate in Milwaukee is not incidental. As Anne Bonds (2019) contends, housing is an essential race-making institution tied intimately to the carceral state. (Sub)urban White mobilization to exclude racially minoritized communities from residential property markets, law-and-order policing, and White vigilantism have all played important roles in maintaining racial segregation in Milwaukee (Bonds, 2019). On a larger level, housing policies and practices, such as redlining, have also barred racially minoritized communities in Milwaukee from accessing loans and housing opportunities (Foltman et al., 2019).[1] This segregation creates potential barriers for many organizations to engage with youth around the city. As a result, leaders at UU have responded to Milwaukee's segregation by meeting youth and their families where they are located.

---

[1] For depictions of racist housing practices in Milwaukee, Foltman et al. (2019) provide useful visuals, such as maps depicting the Federal Housing Association and the Home Owners' Loan Administration's rating of neighborhoods juxtaposed to a map of Milwaukee's racial demographics. Dismally, both the redlining map and racial demographic map are very similar.

Urban Underground has foregrounded the geographical accessibility of their physical space when determining the location of its organization over the past two decades. For example, the organization has called several downtown-oriented spaces home in its earlier years. Downtown Milwaukee provides numerous public transportation services for young people. However, as the need for additional space became apparent, UU transitioned into a space more accessible to the historically Black neighborhoods on the North Side of Milwaukee. Currently housed out of the Center for Youth Engagement (CYE), UU positions itself along a popular bus line in Milwaukee while also being in a centralized location. In many instances, UU leaders drove young people to their homes when needed as well. These characteristics mitigate some of the accessibility barriers young people desiring engagement with community-based spaces face (Afterschool Alliance, 2020b). Additionally, holding space within the CYE encourages cross-organizational activities for UU, as several other youth-serving entities call the CYE home too.

Youth and Youth Worker Demographics

Urban Underground's staff consists of four adult-led positions within the organization, including the Executive Director, Assistant Director, Assistant Executive Director, and the Project Coordinator affiliated with Public Allies, an AmeriCorps program. Furthermore, UU's predominantly Black organizational leadership intentionally reflects the demographics of the youth and community the organization reaches. Historically, UU has served young Black and Latinx people who reside within Milwaukee.

Program Attributes

Urban Underground creates programming that centers both organizing and professional development to guide youth to be young leaders in their community. During the academic year, UU focuses on offering academic support sessions for youth during the week while also organizing and keeping a pulse on what is going on in the community. In doing so, UU values building relationships and supporting work on local issues like racial profiling, the removal of police officers in schools, promoting healthy food access, and more. A component of organizing is political education through discussion and action, which UU creates via youth workshops, community service, and youth-led town halls. Workshop examples have included sessions on organizing for justice and accountability and navigating police interactions. Youth-led town halls speak to how political education topics impact the daily lives of youth. Most recently, UU hosted a town hall amid the COVID-19 pandemic addressing virtual learning as the primary mode for schooling and its impact on youth.

Figure 23.2 *Youth participating in an Urban Underground retreat.*
Source: *"Gallery," by Urban Underground, 2022 (www.urbanunderground.org/untitled-cu1w). Reprinted with permission.*

Organizing is a key feature of UU that leads to sustained empowerment among youth participants. Urban Underground constantly stays deeply engaged with the community to address and move to action on any issues or concerns. Community action often occurs through conversations among community members that lead to collective problem-solving and action. Urban Underground can adapt quickly as young people share their desires and concerns about the social and political problems they face in Milwaukee. Youth voice is not simply a slogan to UU but is integral to the organization's mission and is a driver of social action. During the summer, UU hosts a paid opportunity for youth to engage deeply in the organization's mission and "learn how to use their voice to change their community" (Urban Underground, n.d.). During the six-week program, youth attend field trips and engage in hands-on reflective activities on sharpening their passion for enacting change in their community (see Figure 23.2). In a conversation with the Executive Director, we learned that within the program youth are asked to be their authentic selves and are provided space to understand change based on their reflection on their lived experiences. Young people are allowed to be vulnerable and are given space and time in a retreat hosted outside of the city. During this retreat, youth can build relationships with their peers and youth workers at UU and learn about the systemic forces of oppression that shape the world. Toward the end of the retreat, UU provides a space for youth to share what is on their minds around a campfire. While often beginning in silence, occasionally broken by brief stories by youth and thoughts on their experiences, the campfire talk eventually leads youth to a stronger sense of themselves, their social worlds, and what these mean for them as change-makers in their community.

While organizing is a large part of UU's programming, the organization's programs also aim to center the needs of its members and foster a sense of community. Urban Underground exemplifies how CBESs are not always an extension of schools – although they may host "back-to-school" social events or academic tutoring – by being an educative space of its own for youth and families (Baldridge, 2018). For example, UU has hosted forums for parents and community members that address educational issues, public safety concerns, training on "knowing your rights" during encounters with police, and more. The CBES also creates platforms for community members to voice their opinions and concerns through "community listening" sessions accompanied by dinners. Additionally, UU's educational sessions and workshops are largely led by youth, which powerfully topples deficit-based views of young people as incapable of leadership or knowledge production. Workshops have encompassed relevant educational topics to youth (which may not be adequately discussed in schooling spaces), such as sessions on sexuality, defining community, interrogating schooling conditions, sex education (delivered alongside contraceptive distributions), and the like. Urban Underground also responds to community needs by organizing events such as neighborhood cleanups, hosting social gatherings like game or movie nights, and even featuring local artists through gallery nights. As these initiatives show, fostering a sense of belonging and centering the knowledge, perspectives, and imperatives of community members are of utmost importance to UU. What is more, flexibility, autonomy, and the community-centered mission of UU is indicative of the power of CBESs. The nature of the CBES as its own autonomous space provides youth with opportunities for civic engagement, organizing, and sociopolitical development that they may not otherwise find in other spaces throughout the city – especially schools.

Current Work

Urban Underground fosters strong ties in the community, and it extends its initiatives to the statewide level as well. Two of UU's current projects with Wisconsin's Department of Public Instruction (DPI) and the University of Wisconsin–Madison (UW) elucidate approaches to include young people's perspectives in institutional settings and provide evaluation training for youth. With DPI, youth and youth workers from UU are part of a group spearheading a statewide initiative to better engage youth as education decision-makers. Through this project, UU is advancing its mission of promoting youth leaders given youth's integral role in defining youth engagement and how to allow youth to shape educational policy. This process also entails youth from UU leading workshops for DPI staff on shared decision-making with youth and on rejecting tokenism by sharing power, allowing youth to lead initiatives, and building authentic partnerships. Additionally, in further advocating for youth power, UU collaborates with the Wisconsin Evaluation Collaborative at UW. As youth engage in "communities of practice" about culturally responsive evaluation, they obtain tools to evaluate programs in their community and consider ways to improve them together.

Youth Empowerment and Community Power

Urban Underground operates under a theory of youth empowerment that troubles transactional conceptions of "giving" power or empowerment to youth. Instead, youth workers at UU leverage youth's existing talents and skills to address issues in their community together. For example, in providing space for youth to identify an area of improvement in their city, UU launched the Fresh PLAITS campaign (People Learning Agriculture in Today's Society). Through Fresh PLAITS, youth and youth workers collaborated to address food deserts in their community by introducing community gardening, calling for environmental justice, and pushing for sustainability efforts in Milwaukee. This initiative was also successful due to community partnerships with the Urban Ecology Center (a nonprofit organization in Milwaukee) and undergraduate students from UW. Certainly, UU's theory of youth empowerment necessitates structural inclusion of youth voice, decision-making capabilities, and leadership, as well as intentionally fostering networks and connections with community members and organizations.

Furthermore, UU builds power by organizing community members, building coalitions, and cultivating civic engagement among its members (see Figure 23.3). For example, the student walkouts on the fiftieth anniversary of *Brown vs. The Board of Education* hosted by UU demonstrate the organization's strength in mobilizing its community members, especially around racial disparities in schools. True to their mission, UU ensured that the rally and teach-in were youth-led, which ultimately garnered the support of over 700 young people in Milwaukee. Given youth's political engagement, it is not surprising that 92 percent of the organization's alumni who were surveyed reported being civically engaged, either by signing a petition, volunteering, or voting (Urban Underground, n.d.). Urban Underground demonstrates that community power can be cultivated through mobilizing around issues identified by the community, prioritizing youth leadership in finding solutions, and developing critical consciousness among its members.

Antibureaucratic, Anti-Order of Business

Urban Underground moves beyond the "order of business" and prioritizes its work based on the interests, passions, and needs of the youth involved. As mentioned in their program attributes, UU dedicates the academic year to organizing, determined by conversations with youth and what they hear in

Figure 23.3 *Young person speaking through a bullhorn at a protest.*
Source: *"Gallery," by Urban Underground, 2022 (www.urbanunderground.org/untitled-cu1w). Reprinted with permission.*

their communities (see Figure 23.4). Urban Underground staff recognize that this often requires adaptability in terms of organizing and the ability to push the bureaucratic needs of the organization aside. Often, the meetings, emails, and tasks that staff planned for the day may completely change due to pressing issues in the community. For example, one of the young people of UU published a Facebook post about the conditions of their high school and its lack of air-conditioning while wearing masks in August. This frustration prompted other youth members and staff to discuss what could be done to organize around the conditions of high schools amid the return to in-person instruction during the pandemic. The Facebook post led to conversations in the community, organizing with both community and school leaders, and pressuring schools to meet the needs of their students. This form of organizing power did not result from a planned campaign; instead, UU contributed to generating community power by letting go of previous plans and leaving the order of business aside for youth needs in the community.

Urban Underground remains mindful of existing power structures and seeks change within bureaucratic spaces that limit youth voice. The organization complicates decision-making protocols that do not allow for youth involvement or nonresponsive practices that limit youth participation, like holding meetings during school hours. Further, UU differs from bureaucratic spaces that value dominant notions of professionalism since the organization understands youth's authenticity and diverse forms of expression as essential when discussing community needs and generating ideas for change. Urban Underground strives to continue chipping away at bureaucratic spaces and

Figure 23.4 *Protest in Milwaukee, Wisconsin.*
Source: *"Gallery," by Urban Underground, 2022 (www.urbanunderground.org/
untitled-cu1w). Reprinted with permission.*

processes while challenging why youth are not included therein and asking
what is needed to include authentic youth voice.

"Relational Organizing"

At its core, UU roots its work in relational organizing. Building relationships
with the youth involved and the communities that they are a part of is the
foundation of its organizational structure and can be felt through multiple
spaces. Urban Underground staff stress the importance of knowing the entir-
ety of the youth they work with as well as understanding their community and
family backgrounds. Additionally, UU focuses on building relationships with
youth's families and creating a familial space within the organization. In doing
so, families know and trust the UU staff who may pick up their young person
from school or events and know that they are safe. Certainly, familial trust
benefits all of the relationships fostered within UU and facilitates the organization's initiatives. These relationships lead to an understanding of how
members and their community show up for one another, not just when they
are directly involved with UU but also throughout their lives. For example,
when one alumnus ran for public office in Milwaukee, he received full support
from UU members and alumni, who showed up for him as if they were family,
asked what he needed, shared his platform, and got involved in his campaign.
Relational organizing at UU not only encompasses familial trust but also a

Figure 23.5 *Young people from Urban Underground participating in a rally, featuring now-representative David Bowen.*
Source: *"Gallery," by Urban Underground, 2022 (www.urbanunderground.org/ untitled-cu1w). Reprinted with permission.*

sustained group membership through which alumni who have moved into their careers remain active within the organization to care for and support fellow UU members.

Urban Underground provides meaningful engagement within coordinated programming and is less concerned about narrow measures of success dictated by external grant-makers. Urban Underground staff have noted the importance of making space to build relationships with youth and each other, whether in transit to an event or through conversations in the hallway. These meaningful moments of engagement matter to youth and staff members. Even in the moments when UU staff provide rides home to youth after programming, many young people want to be dropped off last to not miss out on conversations occurring during the drive. As a component of relational organizing, meaningful engagement and connection create shared vulnerability and reciprocal relationships between youth and adults (Christens, 2012). These relationships are essential to the collective organizing and fostering of community power at UU (see Figure 23.5).

A Commitment to Youth and Communities

Urban Underground acknowledges the current landscape for youth-serving organizations shaped by neoliberal beliefs that promote competition over collaboration (Baldridge, 2019; Kwon, 2013), and the organization actively resists these pressures. Instead, UU intentionally positions itself alongside its peers (by training individuals for other organizations or roles), values staff agency (by not pressuring youth workers to stay if they desire a different path), leverages youth authenticity (by shaping programming around youth), pushes back against opportunity-hoarding (through sharing resources with other youth-serving organizations), and rejects the pressure to alter its mission to meet funders' interests. This unique approach becomes more evident in the ways UU treats its members. Routinely, UU elevates youth workers and youth by aligning their needs with the organization's direction.

Urban Underground exemplifies an organization not only staying true to its mission but also having a larger understanding of the purpose of CBESs and community-based youth work. Instead of further entrenching silos among organizations, UU situates its work in a larger community effort to nurture youth holistically, from their passions and talents to their livelihoods. Local grassroots organizations embedded within communities warrant focus especially from funders and foundations who sometimes favor large, national youth development organizations. Urban Underground demonstrates that efforts toward community power and youth empowerment begin with strengthening local ties – among youth and their families, other local organizations, institutions, and beyond – and creating a space that is truly responsive to the needs and desires of youth. Indeed, power-building in CBESs thrives when their physical space is geographically accessible, when their members have a say in the organization's direction, and when they foster space for those most impacted by systemic inequities (such as racially minoritized young people) to address challenges in their communities together.

Community-Based Educational Spaces and Power-Building: A Brief Scan of the Field

Community Power

Essential to power-building in communities is an ability to name social issues and collectively decide through which channels to take action. It is through rich social networks fostered in CBESs that Black and Latinx youth, in partnership with youth workers, can critically examine societal structures and make meaning of the world. Youth can offer forceful critiques of structural inequities; to do so, they may simply need the adequate frames to articulate their valuable perspectives (Lardier et al., 2019). Therefore, youth and youth workers in CBESs can collaborate to challenge deficit narratives about themselves and their communities, build a collective racial and cultural identity, and understand problems within their schools and communities as social and political issues they can challenge (Ginwright, 2007).

Developing young peoples' sociopolitical awareness strengthens their political efficacy, or their belief that they can affect social change, and fuels their critical motivation, or their commitment to addressing social issues in their communities (Shiller, 2013; Sulé et al., 2021; Watts et al., 2003). David C. Turner III (2021) offers a rendition of this process called Black Transformative Agency, "which is cultivated in young people who seek to combat the unique dispossession that Black boys and young men experience by adopting individual and collective means to challenge social isolation, institutional power, and hegemony" (pp. 424–425). In his framework, Turner (2021) provides nuance to youth agency by delineating four types – navigational, relational, movement-building, and structurally transformative – and he underscores that each type of agency is developed through participation in CBESs. Through their action, youth lead voter engagement campaigns, intervene in the creation or dissolution of policies affecting them, and spearhead initiatives to meet specific community needs (Turner, 2021; Valladares et al., 2021).

As a result, CBESs have always been and continue to be integral in leveraging community power toward addressing local problems and systemic structures. For example, in affording community members space to convene and deliberate on collective action, CBESs have played important roles in stymieing the gentrification of Latinx neighborhoods in the city of Chicago (Sanchez, 2019). Michael P. Evan (2019) also notes the power of CBESs in addressing teacher turnover in schools in Chicago, Illinois, collaborating with policymakers to create legislation curtailing the suspensions of youth in Denver, Colorado, and holding school districts accountable by monitoring their implementation of policies (also in Denver). Furthermore, community members in CBESs can intimately address issues of food justice, stemming from governmental disinvestments in marginalized communities, by creating community gardens, distributing produce from gardens in local markets, incorporating training on sustainable food production in high school curricula, and collaborating with local business owners to further their cause (Kelley & Dombrowski, 2018). The power-building capabilities of and within CBESs are truly immense; however, it is equally as important to consider the implications of decontextualizing community-based power.

Power-building and empowerment processes can inadvertently reinforce neoliberal ideology and market-based reforms in CBESs. Soo Ah Kwon (2013) forcefully troubles empowerment, especially in community settings, and describes it as a strategy of self-governance that does not unsettle existing power relations. Kwon (2013) asserts that "empowerment" serves as a

> relationship of government [that] operates through affirming and empowering traditionally marginalized populations, such as "at-risk" youth of color, allowing them to govern and improve themselves through their voluntary and active participation in community programs set up to help them. Specifically, this management of youth has involved – and continues to involve – intimate

>cooperation, not separation, among state representatives, private philanthropic foundations, and youth experts through community programs.   (p. 11)

To be clear, cautious insights like Kwon's do not discredit the resistance in CBESs; instead, they provide context and complexity to discussions of power and empowerment in community settings. Indeed, the ability to simultaneously oppose and entrench unequal power dynamics elucidates CBESs as sites of contestation rife with paradoxes and contradictions (Baldridge, 2020b; Kwon, 2013; Nygreen, 2017; Roy, 2011). Community members in CBESs still resist and refuse intricate systems of power and domination, remain influential players in politics and policymaking, and reorient public understandings of political participation from an individual to social practice.

Tensions and Hindrances to Power-Building in CBESs

Indeed, building power or fostering egalitarian, transformative, and meaningful relationships in CBESs are not simple feats. In fact, youth–youth worker relationships and programming can be simultaneously encouraging as well as place blame on racially minoritized youth for structural inequality (Lardier et al., 2020b). Shawn Ginwright (2007) offers the concept of critical social capital to combat the blame placed on young people and their communities. Ginwright's (2007) work requires youth, youth workers, and leaders in CBESs to acknowledge the personal challenges of low-income Black and Latinx communities as products of structural, historical, and political legacies. Otherwise, community-based youth work practices can easily reproduce the deficit-based view of youth as being "at risk" or in need of fixing (Baldridge, 2014; Kwon, 2013). In this light, "at-risk" youth are encouraged to "beat the odds," embrace meritocracy, and simply work harder (Clay, 2019; Dumas, 2016). Deficit-based views of low-income Black and Latinx youth frame the solution to racial inequality as a matter of individual choices and cultural defects (Dumas, 2016). Moreover, interrogating tensions in CBESs intimately implicates funders, evaluators, and policymakers by questioning what resources are valued in CBESs. Refusing deficit-oriented views of Black and Latinx youth necessitates a refusal of paternalism and other pathological narratives of communities of color. More importantly, it requires an acknowledgment of the ways low-income Black and Latinx youth contribute to their communities.

Funders', evaluators', and policymakers' actions can shape the capacity of CBESs and youth work practices since they decide which programs merit funding and in turn define what constitutes "good" community-based youth work. It is also the case that these three groups of actors often hold paternalistic and deficit-oriented views of low-income Black and Latinx youth (Baldridge, 2019). Consequently, a program's effectiveness is understood through restricting criteria, such as the number of youth served, test scores, or tracking the number of minutes youth workers intervene in the lives of young people (Baldridge, 2019; Carpenter, 2017; de St Croix, 2018). Thus, framing the effectiveness of youth work through limiting, quantifiable measures reduces the transformative impact that CBESs can have on both youth and youth workers. As Baldridge (2019) asserts, "increasing attention to solely improving test scores or basing success on the number of students who enter community-based after-school programs only … causes young people to become objects whose abilities and values can only be measured quantitatively, misappropriated, or dismissed" (p. 208). Reducing youth interaction to a game of numbers begs the question: What are the implications of such an approach for youth workers?

Youth workers in CBESs often find themselves dealing with daily paperwork, recordkeeping, accountability measures, and administrative reporting instead of spending time building trust with youth and having the freedom to produce knowledge together. In London, Tania de St Croix (2018) describes such an approach to accountability as neoliberal managerialism, since managerialism "[relies] on surveillance, comparison, and routine administrative practices, which are likely to restrict and undermine the potential contribution of youth work in young people's lives" (p. 4). As a result, a tightly monitored daily regimen produces a slew of numbers – or quantifiable measures – that serve as proof of the effectiveness of youth workers' intervention, which then get used to secure funding with the federal government or private donors (Carpenter, 2017; de St Croix, 2018).

Moreover, on an individual level, surveillance and administrative practices can profoundly affect a youth worker. From her institutional ethnography of the AmeriCorps program in the US, Carpenter (2017) contends that accountability measures and administrative reporting fit within an input–output logic model in which youth worker interventions or activities are understood as inputs and the quantifiable evidence of having performed activities is understood as the output. Logic models deserve critical attention since accountability measures can serve as powerful tools that organize a youth worker's labor, shape how they learn from their labor, and, in turn, shape how they learn to think about the youth with whom they work (Carpenter, 2017). Following this reasoning, youth workers who are required to abide by market-based logic models inadvertently fall short of asset-based, egalitarian, and humanizing approaches. Instead, their interventions focus on altering individual youth behavior rather than focusing on broader structural, institutional, or societal issues. Consequently, youth workers engage in praxis where deficit-based, individualistic, and pathological notions of marginalized communities intimately influence the youth worker's inductive processes of thinking and acting (Carpenter, 2017). Funders, evaluators, and policymakers have the responsibility to rethink their assumptions, practices, and approaches to their work. In doing so, they will be able to collaborate with youth and youth workers to create equitable learning environments in CBESs that foster rich social networks and leverage the power-building capabilities of these spaces.

Psychological Empowerment Processes

Community-based educational spaces such as UU can offer unique developmental opportunities for minoritized young people through centering their experiences, offering a space that they can shape, and fostering partnerships with youth workers who recognize them holistically. These youth-centric spaces circumvent the stringent regulations and result-driven ideologies that are commonplace in school settings. As mentioned earlier, all too often minoritized youth are chastised by a cynical system that frames who they are as "problems" and "burdens" (Ginwright & Cammarota, 2002; Nicholson et al., 2004). Historically, schools have been sites that uphold this deficit framing by providing positive reinforcement for White young people, while racially minoritized youth receive comparatively fewer resources and affirmations around exploring their numerous identities (race, sociopolitical, gender, sexuality, etc.; Lewis & Diamond, 2015; Patel, 2016; Valencia, 1997). For instance, in a research project engaging young people in participatory action research, Hope et al. (2015) highlighted the lack of in-school engagement with race and culture. McCarty-Caplan (2013) adds to this discussion by emphasizing the potential hostile influence that school climate and classroom teachers have in covering issues of gender and sexuality for racially minoritized youth. Many CBESs reject deficit-based and dehumanizing standards by intentionally cultivating "sanctuaries" for the exploration of young people's lives through practices such as providing reflection activities and counternarratives against deficit-based tropes (Akiva et al., 2017; Baldridge, 2014; Dill & Ozer, 2019; Johnson, 2017; Ngo et al., 2017; Watson, 2012). Bax and Ferrada's (2018) reflections as educators navigating a youth-centered CBES also illuminate the philosophical tensions present for "formal" educators in authentically engaging young people. Community-based educational spaces present fertile ground to embrace the assets that minoritized youth bring with them to community-based spaces (Nicholson et al., 2004).

Community-based educational spaces can promote youth empowerment that is responsive to sociopolitical context, race, gender, sexuality, and other social factors and can reject mainstream Eurocentric youth paradigms (Erbstein & Fabionar, 2019). Namely, affirming identity practices, such as affinity groups, are associated with positive psychosocial outcomes for minoritized youth (Tatum, 2017). Furthermore, sociopolitical development is associated with positive academic trajectories as youth acquire knowledge of social and political systems (Anyiwo et al., 2020; Kirshner & Ginwright, 2012; Watts & Flanagan, 2007; Watts et al., 2003). Previous scholarship has also attributed CBES participation as an ideal avenue for positive youth development (Afterschool Alliance, 2014; McCombs et al., 2017; Morrissey & Werner-Wilson, 2005; Ngo et al., 2017). The youth-centric programming found in CBESs intentionally cultivates a space for aligning young people's diverse identities with topics they find interesting (Baldridge, 2018; Gonsalves et al.,

2013). Ettekal and Agans (2020) build on this argument by highlighting the increased importance that CBESs have for young people in the context of the COVID-19 pandemic. Leveraging community-based and out-of-school time (OST) spaces for the development of minoritized youth is critical in our current social and political climate (Baldridge, 2020a; Brown et al., 2018). For instance, Detzler et al.'s (2007) discussion of the Facilitating Leadership in Youth OST program (based out of Washington, DC) features a young person vocalizing how the program fostered "encouragement" and "dream-chasing" of her talents through persistent leadership capacity-building. Lardier et al. (2020b) build on this by suggesting that CBESs assist youth in "unpacking" their perceptions of the world and "healing" from social ills.

Like UU, the literature surrounding CBESs encompasses the numerous benefits fostered through the empowerment-focused programming present within these spaces (Afterschool Alliance, 2014; Erbstein & Fabionar, 2019; McCombs et al., 2017; Ngo et al., 2017). Additionally, the nuanced richness of community-based, youth-centric programming provides opportunities for minoritized youth to explore who they are and who they can become through encouraging youth agency (Detzler et al., 2007). Community-based educational spaces serve as powerful spaces that allow marginalized young people to navigate systems of oppression and create counternarratives against deficit-based views, which illuminate the value of these spaces to communities (Akiva et al., 2017; Dill & Ozer, 2019; Johnson, 2017; Ngo et al., 2017).

Application and Future Research

The literature on CBESs, community power, and empowerment provides routes of possibility for social change in community settings while also acknowledging the sociopolitical context and power imbalances in which they are situated. Urban Underground serves as an excellent example of the ways CBESs can act as conduits in their communities toward strengthening relationships and spurring change across various levels, from the individual to the systemic. Furthermore, acts of resistance by community members occur within a complex political terrain (Ginwright & James, 2002), one that Kysa Nygreen (2017) understands as "a field of power relations constituted by vast material inequalities along with regimes of knowledge and discourses that naturalize and legitimize those inequalities" (p. 56). Therefore, to fully support the liberatory struggle that communities are engaged in, namely in CBESs, we offer the following considerations:

> *Embrace and get into good trouble.* Racially minoritized young people are far too often framed as "problems to be fixed" within educational discourse and youth development spaces. Regarded as "troublemakers," racially minoritized youth are often pathologized for their resistance to and refusal

of oppression within their schools and communities. In a viral tweet from 2018 by the late Congressman John Lewis, he implored us to "never, ever be afraid to make some noise and get in good trouble, necessary trouble." Following Turner's (2021) and Lewis's call to embrace and get into good trouble, we encourage community-based leaders and youth workers to create spaces for young people to express their authentic selves, develop critical consciousness, and achieve sociopolitical development that leads toward social action and community power and change.

Evaluation needs to center the voices and experiences of community members: youth, youth workers, parents, and the like. Communities understand their needs. As such, evaluation should center the voices and priorities of all community stakeholders, including youth, youth workers, and parents. As Tania de St Croix (2018) aptly notes, "there is a need to develop youth-centered and qualitative evaluation methodologies that are congruent with youth work itself ... not necessarily to identify young people's 'outcomes' (although this may be relevant for some services) but to find out from their own perspectives how and why they value the services they take part in" (p. 18). Youth's perspectives and inclusion in evaluation processes are essential avenues to building youth power and increasing young people's attachment to youth programs. Further, youth participatory action research (YPAR) opportunities are important avenues to center young people's voices and experiences. However, they are still subject to an imbalance of power with adult allies and may not always lead to the outcomes we anticipate. In any case, authentically engaging youth in YPAR and community-engaged research that values youth as researchers and agents of change is essential to shifting the hegemonic paradigms of the research process that perpetuate research "on communities" instead of "with communities."

Funders and policymakers need to similarly consider how funding policies and restrictions limit the transformative work of CBESs. Funding entities that reward programs for narrow measures of success – including the number of students served or test scores – ultimately overshadow other powerful dimensions of youth programming like sociocultural, identity, and political development (Baldridge, 2014). These narrow approaches to measuring success counter the shared mission of creating spaces for young people to learn and grow in CBESs. Further, funding opportunities typically come with strings attached that can restrict the flexibility of CBESs, strain the capacity of staff members, and sometimes move programs further away from their missions (Baldridge, 2019; Kwon, 2013). Funders and other stakeholders should work in collaboration with CBESs to lift restrictions that limit the ways in which youth workers and CBESs can utilize funding.

Complicate discourses of empowerment and center youth and community desires. There is a long history of young people becoming emboldened to resist the layers of oppression they encounter within their schools and communities through CBESs and youth programs that center organizing (Akiva et al., 2017; Christens, 2011; Kirshner, 2015). However, discourses of empowerment are sometimes rooted in the paternalistic foundations of youth work (Kwon, 2013). Community-based leaders and youth work practitioners must be mindful that no one person can "give" empowerment to others; rather, being intentional about pedagogical practices, creating a humanizing and flexible culture within programs, and valuing and centering young people's needs are imperative for this process.

Conclusion

Community-based educational spaces simultaneously brim with potential for transformative change while also being constrained by larger political economic forces and pervasive deficit orientations of marginalized communities. However, when CBESs practice humanizing and asset-based approaches, youth embrace them as "free" spaces: "free to challenge the parameters of [the space], free to decide whether they [want] to participate at all, and even free to challenge [educators therein] as individuals" (Bax & Ferrada, 2018, p. 73). At a time when youth are increasingly demanding community-based programming (Afterschool Alliance, 2020b), we continue calling for educational researchers to give critical care and attention to community-based youth work. Through recognizing the sociopolitical context(s) in which CBESs are situated, educational research can continue to elucidate their complexity and unravel their contradictions (Baldridge, 2020b). Inquiry alone, however, will not lead us toward liberation. We urge youth, youth workers, and other community members to continue entering into partnerships to realize an education that speaks to our shared struggle for humanity and self-actualization. In doing so, we envision educational spaces and futures handcrafted by young people and the wisdom ubiquitous in their communities.

References

Afterschool Alliance. (2014). *Taking a deeper dive into afterschool: Positive outcomes and promising practices*. ERIC Clearinghouse.

Afterschool Alliance. (2020a, July). *Afterschool in the time of COVID-19*. Afterschool Alliance. http://afterschoolalliance.org/documents/Afterschool-COVID-19-Wave-1-Fact-Sheet.pdf

Afterschool Alliance. (2020b, December). *America after 3pm: Demand grows, opportunity shrinks. Executive summary*. Afterschool Alliance. http://afterschoolalliance .org/documents/AA3PM-2020/AA3PM-Executive-Summary.pdf

Akiva, T., Carey, R. L., Cross, A. B., Delale-O'Connor, L., & Brown, M. R. (2017). Reasons youth engage in activism programs: Social justice or sanctuary? *Journal of Applied Developmental Psychology, 53*, 20–30.

Anyiwo, N., Palmer, G. J., Garrett, J. M., Starck, J. G., & Hope, E. C. (2020). Racial and political resistance: An examination of the sociopolitical action of racially marginalized youth. *Current Opinion in Psychology, 35*, 86–91.

Baldridge, B. J. (2014). Relocating the deficit: Reimagining Black youth in neoliberal times. *American Educational Research Journal, 51*(3), 440–472.

Baldridge, B. J. (2018). On educational advocacy and cultural work: Situating community-based youth work[ers] in broader educational discourse. *Teachers College Record, 120*(2), 1-28.

Baldridge, B. J. (2019). *Reclaiming community: Race and the uncertain future of youth work*. Stanford University Press.

Baldridge, B. J. (2020a). Negotiating anti-Black racism in "liberal" contexts: The experiences of Black youth workers in community-based educational spaces. *Race, Ethnicity, and Education, 23*(6), 747–766.

Baldridge, B. J. (2020b). The youthwork paradox: A case for studying the complexity of community-based youth work in educational research. *Educational Researcher, 49*(8), 618–625.

Baldridge, B. J., DiGiacomo, D., Kirshner, B., Mejias, S., & Vasudevan, S. R. (in press). Out-of-school time programs in the United States in an era of racial reckoning: Insights on equity from practitioners, scholars, policy influencers, and young people. *Educational Researcher*.

Bax, A., & Ferrada, J. S. (2018). Sounding White and boring: Race, identity, and youth freedom in an after-school program. In M. Bucholtz, D. I. Casillas, & J. S. Lee (Eds.), *Feeling it: Language, race, and affect in Latinx youth learning* (pp. 72–88). Routledge.

Bonds, A. (2019). Race and ethnicity I: Property, race, and the carceral state. *Progress in Human Geography, 43*(3), 574–583.

Bonfiglio, A. M. (2017). On being disrupted: Youth work and Black Lives Matter. *Journal of Youth Development, 12*(1), 108–125.

Brion-Meisels, G., Fei, J. T., & Vasudevan, D. S. (Eds.). (2020). *At our best: Building youth–adult partnerships in out-of-school time settings*. Information Age Publishing.

Brown, A. A., Outley, C. W., & Pinckney, H. P. (2018). Examining the use of leisure for the sociopolitical development of Black youth in out-of-school time programs. *Leisure Sciences, 40*(7), 686–696.

Carey, R. L., Akiva, T., Abdellatif, H., & Daughtry, K. A. (2021). "And school won't teach me that!" Urban youth activism programs as transformative sites for critical adolescent learning. *Journal of Youth Studies, 24*, 941–960.

Carpenter, S. (2017). "Modeling" youth work: Logic models, neoliberalism, and community praxis. *International Studies in Sociology of Education, 29*(2), 105–120.

Checkoway, B. (2011). Education for democracy by young people in community-based organizations. *Youth & Society, 45*(3), 389–403.

Christens, B. D. (2011). Adapt to youth while working for social change. *The Prevention Researcher, 18*(Suppl.), 10–11.

Christens, B. D. (2012). Toward relational empowerment. *American Journal of Community Psychology*, *50*, 114–128.

Christens, B. D., & Inzeo, P. T. (2015). Widening the view: Situating collective impact among frameworks for community-led change. *Community Development*, *46* (4), 420–435.

Christens, B. D., Winn, L. T., & Duke, A. M. (2016). Empowerment and critical consciousness: A conceptual cross-fertilization. *Adolescent Research Review*, *1*, 15–27.

Clay, K. L. (2019). "Despite the odds": Unpacking the politics of Black resilience neoliberalism. *American Educational Research Journal*, *56*(1), 75–110.

Cohen, J., Golden, M. M., Quinn, R., & Simon, E. (2018). Democracy thwarted or democracy at work? Local public engagement and the new education policy landscape. *American Journal of Education*, *124*(4), 411–443.

Colvin, S., White, A. M., Akiva, T., & Wardrip, P. S. (2020). What do you think youth workers do? A comparative case study of library and afterschool workers. *Children and Youth Review*, *119*, 1–14.

de St Croix, T. (2018). Youth work, performativity, and the new youth impact agenda: Getting paid for numbers? *Journal of Education Policy*, *33*, 414–438.

Detzler, M. L., Van Liew, C., Dorward, L. G., Jenkins, R., & Teslicko, D. (2007). Youth voices thrive in facilitating leadership in youth. *New Directions for Youth Development*, *2007*(116), 109–116.

Dill, L. J., & Ozer, E. J. (2019). "The hook-up": How youth-serving organizations facilitate network-based social capital for urban youth of color. *Journal of Community Psychology*, *47*(7), 1614–1628.

Dumas, M. J. (2016). Against the dark: Antiblackness in education policy and discourse. *Theory Into Practice*, *55*, 11–19.

Erbstein, N. (2013). Engaging underrepresented youth populations in community youth development: Tapping social capital as a critical resource. *New Directions for Youth Development*, *2013*(138), 109–124.

Erbstein, N., & Fabionar, J. O. (2019). Supporting Latinx youth participation in out-of-school time programs: A research synthesis. *Afterschool Matters*, *29*, 17–27.

Ettekal, A. V., & Agans, J. P. (2020). Positive youth development through leisure: Confronting the COVID-19 pandemic. *Journal of Youth Development*, *15*(2), 1–20.

Evans, M. P. (2019). Power and authenticity in education focused community-based organizations. In S. B. Sheldon & T. A. Turner-Vorbeck (Eds.), *The Wiley handbook of family, school, and community relationships in education* (pp. 379–397). John Wiley & Sons.

Flores, K. S. (n.d.). *Transforming positive youth development: A case for youth organizing*. Funders Collaborative on Youth Organizing. https://fcyo.org/resources/transforming-positive-youth-development-a-case-for-youth-organizing

Foltman, L., Jones, M., & Bourdeau, C. (2019, February 28). *How redlining continues to shape racial segregation in Milwaukee: 1930s lending map reveals the policy roots of housing discrimination*. WisCONTEXT. www.wiscontext.org/how-redlining-continues-shape-racial-segregation-milwaukee

Gay, G. (2000). *Culturally responsive teaching: Theory, research, and practice.* Teachers College Press.

Ginwright, S. (2007). Black youth activism and the role of critical social capital in Black community organizations. *American Behavioral Scientist, 51*(3), 403–418.

Ginwright, S. (2010). *Black youth rising: Activism and radical healing in urban America.* Teachers College Press.

Ginwright, S., & Cammarota, J. (2002). New terrain in youth development: The promise of a social justice approach. *Social Justice, 4*(90), 82–95.

Ginwright, S., & Cammarota, J. (2009). Youth activism in the urban community: Learning critical civic praxis within community organizations. *International Journal of Qualitative Studies in Education, 20,* 693–710.

Ginwright, S., & James, T. (2002). From assets to agents of change: Social justice, organizing, and youth development. In B. Kirshner, J. L. O'Donoghue, & M. McLaughlin (Eds.), *Youth participation: Improving institutions and communities* (pp. 27–46). Jossey-Bass.

Gonsalves, A., Rahm, J., & Carvalho, A. (2013). "We could think of things that could be science": Girls' re-figuring of science in an out-of-school-time club. *Journal of Research in Science Teaching, 50*(9), 1068–1097.

Hess, J. (2018). Detroit youth speak back: Rewriting deficit perspectives through song-writing. *Bulletin of the Council for Research in Music Education, 216,* 7–30.

Hope, E. C., Skoog, A. B., & Jagers, R. J. (2015). "It'll never be the White kids, it'll always be us": Black high school students' evolving critical analysis of racial discrimination and inequity in schools. *Journal of Adolescent Research, 30*(1), 83–112.

Johnson, L. P. (2017). Writing the self: Black queer youth challenge heteronormative ways of being in an afterschool writing club. *Research in the Teaching of English, 52*(1), 13–33.

Kelley, M. A., & Dombrowski, R. D. (2018). Community-based action for food justice. In R. A. Cnaan & C. Milofsky (Eds.), *Handbook of community movements and local organizations in the 21st century* (pp. 405–422). Springer International Publishing.

Kirshner, B. (2015). *Youth activism in an era of education inequality.* New York University Press.

Kirshner, B., & Ginwright, S. (2012). Youth organizing as a developmental context for African American and Latino adolescents. *Child Development Perspectives, 6* (3), 288–294.

Kwon, S. A. (2013). *Uncivil youth: Race, activism, and affirmative governmentality.* Duke University Press.

Lardier, D. T., Herr, K. G., Barrios, V. R., Garcia-Reid, P., & Reid, R. J. (2019). Merit in meritocracy: Uncovering the myth of exceptionality and self-reliance through the voices of urban youth of color. *Education and Urban Society, 51* (4), 474–500.

Lardier, D. T., Herr, K. G., Bergeson, C., Garcia-Reid, P., & Reid, R. J. (2020a). Locating disconnected minoritized youth within urban community-based educational programs in an era of neoliberalism. *International Journal of Qualitative Studies in Education, 33*(4), 404–420.

Lardier, D. T., Suazo, C. M., Barrios, V. R., Forenza, B., Herr, K. G., Bergeson, C., Garcia-Reid, P., & Reid, R. J. (2020b). Contextualizing negative sense of community and disconnection among urban youth of color: "Community ... we ain't got that." *Journal of Community Psychology, 48*(3), 834–848.

Larson R., & Hansen, D. (2005). The development of strategic thinking: Learning to impact human systems in a youth activism program. *Human Development, 48* (6), 327–349.

Levine, M. V. (2020). *The state of Black Milwaukee in national perspective: Racial inequality in the nation's 50 largest metropolitan areas in 65 charts and tables.* Center for Economic Development Publications, 56. https://dc.uwm.edu/ced_pubs/56

Lewis, A. E., & Diamond, J. B. (2015). *Despite the best intentions: How racial inequality thrives in good schools.* Oxford University Press.

Little Black Book. (2020, August 19). *Urban Underground installation invites people to "March with us. Invest in us."* Little Black Book. www.lbbonline.com/news/urban-underground-installation-invites-people-to-march-with-us-invest-in-us

Lopez, J. (2021). *Commentary: Youth organizing in the US.* The Forge. https://forgeorganizing.org/article/commentary-youth-organizing-us?emci=69b73419–1e04-ec11-b563–501ac57b8fa7&emdi=017cf498-e304-ec11-b563–501ac57b8fa7&ceid=826624

McCarty-Caplan, D. M. (2013). Schools, sex education, and support for sexual minorities: Exploring historic marginalization and future potential. *American Journal of Sexuality Education, 8*(4), 246–273.

McCombs, J. S., Whitaker, A., & Yoo, P. (2017). *The value of out-of-school time programs.* Rand Corporation.

McLaughlin, M., Scott, W. R., Deschenes, S., Hopkins, K., & Newman, A. (2009). *Between movement and establishment: Organizations advocating for youth.* Stanford University Press.

Morrissey, K. M., & Werner-Wilson, R. J. (2005). The relationship between out-of-school activities and positive youth development: An investigation of the influences of communities and family. *Adolescence, 40*(157), 67–85.

Murray, I. E., & Milner, H. R. (2015). Toward a pedagogy of sociopolitical consciousness in outside of school programs. *Urban Review, 47*, 893–913.

Ngo, B., Lewis, C., & Maloney Leaf, B. (2017). Fostering sociopolitical consciousness with minoritized youth: Insights from community-based arts programs. *Review of Research in Education, 41*(1), 358–380.

Nicholas, C., & Eastman-Mueller, H. (2020). Supporting critical social analysis: Empowerment processes in youth organizing. *Urban Review, 52*, 708–729.

Nicholson, H. J., Collins, C., & Holmer, H. (2004). Youth as people: The protective aspects of youth development in afterschool settings. *The Annals of the American Academy of Political and Social Science, 591*(1), 55–71.

Nygreen, K. (2017). Negotiating tensions: Grassroots organizing, school reform, and the paradox of neoliberal democracy. *Anthropology & Education Quarterly, 48*(1), 42–60.

Paris, D. (2012). Culturally sustaining pedagogy: A needed change in stance, terminology, and practice. *Educational Researcher, 41*(3), 93–97.

Patel, L. (2016). Pedagogies of resistance and survivance: Learning as marronage. *Equity & Excellence in Education, 49*(4), 397–401.

Roy, P. (2011). Nonprofit and community-based green space production in Milwaukee: Maintaining a counter-weight within neo-liberal urban environmental governance. *Space and Polity, 15*, 87–105.

Sampson, C., Overholser, A., & Schafer, J. G. (2019). A critical paradox: The politics of an urban community-based nonprofit in expanding educational opportunities to underserved youth. *Leadership and Policy in Schools, 18*(2), 210–225.

Sanchez, G. (2019). *Unidad en comunidad: The role of community-based organizations in dealing with gentrification in Chicago's Pilsen and Logan Square neighborhoods* [Unpublished master's thesis]. University of Chicago.

Shiller, J. T. (2013). Preparing for democracy: How community-based organizations build civic engagement among urban youth. *Urban Education, 48*(1), 69–91.

Sulé, V. T., Nelson, M., & Williams, T. (2021). They #woke: How Black students in an after-school community-based program manifest critical consciousness. *Teacher College Record, 123*, 1–38.

Tatum, B. D. (2017). *Why are all the Black kids sitting together in the cafeteria? And other conversations about race.* Hachette UK.

Turner, D. C., III (2021): The (good) trouble with Black boys: Organizing with Black boys and young men in George Floyd's America. *Theory Into Practice, 60*(4), 422–433.

Urban Underground. (n.d.). *Impact.* Urban Underground. www.urbanunderground.org/untitled-cc16

Valencia, R. R. (Ed.). (1997). *The evolution of deficit thinking: Educational thought and practice.* The Falmer Press/Taylor & Francis.

Valladares, S., Valladares, M. R., Garcia, M., Baca, K., Kirshner, B., Terriquez, T., Sanchez, J., & Kroehle, K. (2021). *20 years of youth power.* Funders Collaborative on Youth Organizing.

Warren, M. R., & Mapp, K. L. (2011). *A match on dry grass: Community organizing as a catalyst for school reform.* Oxford University Press.

Watson, V. M. (2012). *Learning to liberate: Community-based solutions to the crisis in urban education.* Routledge.

Watson, V. M. (2013). Censoring freedom: Community-based professional development and the politics of profanity. *Equity & Excellence in Education, 46*(3), 387–410.

Watts, R. J., & Flanagan, C. (2007). Pushing the envelope on youth civic engagement: A developmental and liberation psychology perspective. *Journal of Community Psychology, 35*(6), 779–792.

Watts, R. J., & Hipolito-Delgado, C. P. (2015). Thinking ourselves to liberation?: Advancing sociopolitical action in critical consciousness. *The Urban Review, 47*(5), 847–867.

Watts, R. J., Williams, N. C., & Jagers, R. J. (2003). Sociopolitical development. *American Journal of Community Psychology, 31*(1–2), 185–194.

Wu, H.-C. J., Kornbluh, M., Weiss, J., & Roddy, L. (2016). Measuring and understanding authentic youth engagement: The youth–adult partnership rubric. *Afterschool Matters, 23*, 8–17.

24 Community-Engaged Research

Krista A. Haapanen, Nina Wallerstein, and Shannon T. Sanchez-Youngman

Introduction

Community-engaged research (CEnR) within academic and research institutions has gained considerable traction in recent decades, with goals of social, racial, and health equity. This trend reflects an evolving understanding of how higher education can and should serve society, aligning with calls for universities to embrace social accountability as anchor institutions and recognize their place in local economies and communities. It further seeks to counter generations of ivory tower elitism, including historic abuses such as researchers invading communities for their data and considering neither community decision-making nor community benefit.

Transforming inequitable social structures requires fundamental shifts in the ways that research and academic institutions engage with the public. Recognizing the critical roles of communities in identifying their own priorities, CEnR approaches build from community partners' strengths and seek their equal voice in the knowledge creation process. An authentic participatory approach demands that traditional investigator-driven research give way to shared decision-making or community-driven research. It reconsiders, moreover, the nature of institutional and knowledge power structures that maintain the status quo in favor of dominant members of society. If CEnR is to reach its potential for benefiting communities that have faced long-standing unjust conditions, those involved must be cognizant of power dynamics in the context of research endeavors and seek to diminish the influence of imbalances within the partnership between academic and community partners as well as to promote outcomes that confront societal inequities.

The construct of empowerment can be used to understand how CEnR may contribute to advances in equity. Empowerment takes place when the people most affected by inequity participate in relational processes that build their collective ability to exert influence over systems that affect them (Kleba et al., 2022). The social power built through ongoing empowerment processes enables those communities to act together through democratic structures to set agendas, shift public discourse, influence who makes decisions, and cultivate ongoing relationships of mutual accountability with decision-makers that change inequitable systems (Speer et al., 2020b, p. 4). Empowerment can thus tip the balance of power in communities toward residents and organizations, creating more balanced power structures and reducing oligarchic domination (Christens, 2019).

In this chapter, we will consider how CEnR both contributes to and gains from processes of community empowerment. Although CEnR or participatory action research (PAR) approaches have been used in multiple disciplines, in this chapter we use a health and health equity lens based on our own experiences in public health and community psychology. Much of this work aligns with the rich tradition of community-based participatory research (CBPR), with ties to the Global South. At the same time, we acknowledge the many typologies of CEnR have emerged that align with particular contexts, available resources, and partner goals (Haapanen & Christens, 2021; London et al., 2020). We first look briefly at the development of academic community engagement and its underlying philosophical traditions. We then consider empowerment within CEnR and provide distinct ways of viewing power within individuals, partnerships, organizations, and communities. Here we introduce and describe a conceptual model for empowerment in CEnR that synthesizes ideas and empirical advances from community psychology and public health. We end with an examination of the processes by which social power can be built and exercised through CEnR at multiple levels of analysis. We suggest that the power that comes from community-based organizations and interorganizational advocacy and social movements has the greatest significance for equity-based CEnR and ultimately for goals of equity and justice-focused social change.

The Engaged University

Toward the end of the twentieth century, universities were challenged to "be more energetically engaged in the pressing issues of our time" (Boyer, 1990, p. 77) and to develop new academic approaches that would better align university resources and purpose with the needs and interests of the public. Instead of merely generating and disseminating expert knowledge, the notion of an engaged campus framed academic institutions as "participants in a highly complex learning society where discovery, learning, and engagement are integrated activities that involve many sources of knowledge, generated in diverse settings by a variety of contributors" (Holland, 2005, para. 3). This approach called upon universities to be responsive to community needs, make university knowledge accessible to multiple audiences, treat nonacademic partners with respect and dignity, and coordinate academic and nonacademic assets to address social issues (Fitzgerald et al., 2012).

Growing emphasis on academic community engagement elevated the importance of various forms of public and participatory research that emerged in the 1960s. The origins of these approaches are often traced back to Kurt Lewin's "action research" (Lewin, 1946). Lewin, a German-American social scientist, focused on the effects of democratic decision-making in organizational settings, an approach that has now been called the "Northern tradition" of participatory research. His Harwood Factory study, for example, revealed that involving workers in organizational change processes yielded more effective interventions while also improving employees' productivity and morale (Wilmsen et al., 2008). Through his commitment to linking theory with action, Lewin – as well as other philosophical pragmatists such as John Dewey – laid a foundation for research to build fundamental knowledge while solving practical problems (Christens et al., 2016).

Lewin's ideas about democratic participation in research did not, however, extend to broader critiques of the social, economic, and political forces shaping labor (Adelman, 1993), and they have been critiqued for upholding oppressive and exploitative structural conditions (Wallerstein & Duran, 2018). The "Southern tradition" of participatory research was developed by radical academics in the 1960s and 1970s in Latin America, Asia, and Africa who left the ivory tower to join with social movements seeking to disrupt systems of oppression (Brandão, 1981; Fals-Borda, 1980). Brazilian educator Paulo Freire (1970) provided a political-philosophical grounding for education to facilitate "conscientization," or the knowledge of oneself as a subject within one's sociohistorical conditions. Conscientization, he suggested, enabled participants to identify hegemonic ideologies of colonial domination and take action to change inequitable conditions. The Freirian methodology of praxis, or continuous cycles of listening, dialogue, and action, supports participants to engage with others to claim both personal and political power (Minkler & Wakimoto, 2021).

These traditions have since coalesced and proliferated into a rich and dynamic set of models, principles, and frameworks for integrating nonacademic perspectives into scholarly research. Scholars now emphasize both the practical and the ideological benefits of involving nonacademic communities in research (Cornwall & Jewkes, 1995), including: the generation of socially relevant research questions (Balazs & Morello-Frosch, 2013); opportunities to ensure that underserved communities are not manipulated or exploited (Brenner & Manice, 2011); research methods and instruments that are culture-centered (Dutta, 2007) and thus more rigorous; pathways for translating research into action and policies (Cacari-Stone et al., 2014; Kline, 2022); and opportunities for marginalized populations to become agents of social change (Kirshner et al., 2021). Early calls for tribal participatory research grounded research in sovereign nation ownership (Fisher & Ball, 2003) and led to greater recognition of Indigenous knowledge contributions (Walters et al., 2020), with parallel calls for decolonizing, feminist, and antiracist methodologies to create new epistemologies (Drame & Irby, 2016; Lykes et al., 2018; Smith, 2012). More recently, calls for knowledge democracy and cognitive justice have promoted equal recognition of community knowledges for authentic engagement in research (de Sousa Santos, 2015; Hall et al., 2015).

Variations on these participatory approaches can be found in such fields as community psychology (e.g., Speer & Christens, 2013), education (e.g., Anderson et al., 2007), community development (e.g., Cornwall, 2008), public health (e.g., Israel et al., 2013; Wallerstein et al., 2018), Indigenous and decolonial research (Smith, 2012), and natural resource management (e.g., Wilmsen et al., 2008). Numerous terms are used, including PAR, youth PAR, CBPR, action research, citizen science, practitioner research, participatory health research, and community–academic partnerships.

For the purposes of this discussion, we use "community-engaged research" as an umbrella term to describe the array of participatory approaches to research. Community-engaged research has been characterized as forming a continuum of approaches, from outreach to shared leadership (McCloskey et al., 2011). To best capture this diversity, we define CEnR as (1) involving community members (directly or through indirect representation) who have knowledge of the phenomenon being studied, as well as academic researchers, (2) having research that is primarily relevant to the community, and (3) aiming to produce new knowledge that can help communities generate change (Drahota et al., 2016; Wilmsen et al., 2008). As one of the most established forms of CEnR, CBPR arose out of community-based public health with principles of power-sharing and goals of health equity (Israel et al., 2013). Drawing from the Southern tradition, CBPR extends the continuum of CEnR beyond shared leadership to community-driven research. While we focus on CEnR in this chapter, representing multiple disciplines and philosophies, we also highlight the specific contributions from CBPR that support an empowerment approach.

Empowerment and Power in Community-Engaged Research

The idea that involvement in research is empowering for participants has been growing as a justification for CEnR approaches (Roura, 2021). Community psychologists were among the early adopters of empowerment as a value orientation and topic of study. They defined it as participation by marginalized people to gain control over processes that affected them, framing them as agents of change rather than passive recipients of services (Rappaport, 1987). Empowerment was later integrated into public health by Wallerstein (1992) as a multilevel social action process of people, organizations, and communities toward goals of social justice. By creating opportunities for nonacademics to create and use new knowledge, CEnR is understood to enhance individuals' or groups' capacities to make purposive choices toward desired outcomes (Roura, 2021).

Prevailing theories of empowerment define the process as involving people and groups and underscore the interconnectedness of psychological, organizational, and community empowerment (Rappaport, 1987). Psychological empowerment is the sense of personal power tied to the ability to advocate for change (Speer & Hughey, 1995; Zimmerman, 2000) – different from feelings of individual mastery and self-determination that are disconnected from efforts to build and exercise social power. Organizational empowerment includes organizations' internal capacity to cultivate members' psychological empowerment and their external power to advocate for and produce change in systems and structures. Community empowerment involves the power of organizations, with their constituents and other community members, to transform policies, systems, and resources to change social conditions (Kleba et al., 2022; Wallerstein, 2006).

Each of these levels calls for grounding in an understanding of social power. Power is central to processes that cultivate communities' participation in decision-making and other systems that affect them. Participation alone, however, does not imply having power to influence or make policy decisions to improve health and social equity. The concept of empowerment builds on power, not as a transitive verb (e.g., "I empower you") but as a process, with people and community groups claiming their power to demand changes in their lives. Definitions of power are therefore important. Power "over" repre-sents oppressive structures, often constructed through racialized and gendered hierarchies that enforce histories of social exclusion (i.e., through autocratic regimes, neoliberal policies that favor corporations, institutional discrimination, and ideological dominance that makes these socioeconomic structures appear fair and normal; Gaventa & Cornwall, 2015; Stoeffler, 2018). These systems can be exercised covertly (Muhammad et al., 2018) or become internalized, creating greater perceptions of powerlessness.

Foucault (1980), however, claims that these powers are not monolithic but are practices and policies within unstable webs that can be resisted. Power as an emancipatory force recognizes histories of community resistance and organizing, with alliances engaging community strengths and benefiting from power "with" others and having power "to" act (Stoeffler, 2018). A complementary perspective on power emphasizes the importance of micro (individual characteristics), meso (organizations and partnerships), and macro (societal) spheres for understanding how and where power can be exercised (Roura, 2021). Community participation under macro conditions of auto-cratic nations, for example, is highly constrained compared to opportunities for community participation under more democratic regimes.

We propose an approach to power and empowerment in CEnR that pro-vides opportunities for research teams and communities to challenge oppres-sive practices and policies by engaging in critical reflection about their contexts, building power through cocreation of knowledge, exercising power through – and in collaboration with – organizations to increase their propor-tion of valued resources in relation to whole populations, and seeking to disrupt the "regimes of truth" that maintain inequitable social, political, and economic structures. Empowerment, therefore, can be seen as dynamic processes of building social power within and between organizational settings. While these processes can and should increase the psychological sense of empowerment among individuals, it is through organizational and community power that social changes of consequence are made.

Power and Empowerment in CBPR

Drawing from the Southern tradition, CBPR, more than some other forms of CEnR, aims to build power for social justice. While CBPR uses the language of community, this approach embraces a wide variety of stakeholders (i.e., community members, organizational/agency staff, practitioners, clinicians, and even policymakers) who are collaborating with academics and other researchers. In seeking equity, many within this tradition have identified both structural and relational processes to promote community voice and influence within a partnership. In addition to structural agreements for community ownership and use of data, for example, these have included privileging community knowledge during research design and promoting deliberative democratic dialogue and joint decision-making (Pratt, 2019; Sanchez-Youngman et al., 2021).

In 2006, the University of New Mexico Center for Participatory Research started a multiphase National Institutes of Health (NIH)-funded research inquiry, Engage for Equity, with national partners, including a think tank of academic and community CBPR experts, to strengthen the science of engagement, including understanding the role of power for achieving social, health, and racial equity outcomes (Wallerstein et al., 2020). In the first phase of funding, a CBPR conceptual model was created with four domains: (1) *contexts* (including micro, meso, and macro levels), which influence (2) *partnering processes* of who is collaborating and the quality of their interactions, which then impact the (3) *intervention and research* actions and outputs, which then contribute to (4) intermediate- and long-term *health and equity outcomes* (Kastelic et al., 2018). The next two phases of NIH funding sought to identify best partnering practices and pathways that contribute to outcomes and to test tools to strengthen partnerships. Questionnaires of measures based on the four domains of the CBPR conceptual model were created, with the first validation of instruments based on Internet surveys of 200 federally funded partnerships (Oetzel et al., 2015) and the second refinement and validation based on another 215 (Boursaw et al., 2021). Multiple analyses have identified promising CBPR participatory practices, including relationships and pathways of trust (Lucero et al., 2020), shared governance and structural power-sharing (Sanchez-Youngman et al., 2021), collective empowerment (Oetzel et al., 2022), and the importance of collective reflection tools and workshops based on the philosophy and dialogical methodology of Paulo Freire (Freire, 1970; Parker et al., 2020; see https://engageforequity.org). Particularly important for this chapter, seven case studies by Engage for Equity investigators enabled a deeper dive into dimensions of power, examining how partnerships can challenge oppressive structures, build on emancipatory contexts, and generate knowledge that reflects the experiences and realities of nonelites (Wallerstein et al., 2019).

Empowerment Model for Community-Engaged Research

Starting with existing models of empowerment (Christens, 2019), we developed a new model for empowerment and CEnR that centers power and integrates social-ecological levels (micro, meso, and macro) into the four domains and pathways of the CBPR conceptual model described earlier. The intention of this "Empowerment CEnR" model is to specifically elucidate how, through CEnR, power can be built and exercised within interconnected processes of individual, organizational, community, and epistemic (or *knowledge*) empowerment. The model starts with a *context* domain, which identifies micro, meso, and macro contexts that shape the processes by which social power is cultivated within and outside of CEnR partnerships. Development of power through *partnership and power-building processes* influences *empowering actions and outputs* of CEnR, such as enhancing participants' skills and sense of power and the development and strengthening of organizations and social movements that can act collectively to change community conditions. These *actions and outputs* ultimately contribute to *empowerment and community health outcomes* at multiple social-ecological levels.

Partnership and Power-Building Processes

The next sections deconstruct Figure 24.1, providing a deeper conceptualization of empowerment and CEnR pathways at four levels of analysis: psychological, organizational (or settings), community, and knowledge (epistemic). We first consider how CEnR can contribute to building power at each level of analysis, before focusing explicitly upon the ways that power can be exercised. Although inextricably linked in the process of empowerment, a distinction is made between building and exercising power for heuristic purposes.

Micro Pathways (Psychological Empowerment)

Personal or psychological empowerment refers to people's perceived control of their lives as they develop a critical awareness of their socially and historically determined socioeconomic and political contexts while becoming aware of and acting upon their power to transform the reality in which they live (Kleba et al., 2022; Zimmerman, 2000). Psychological empowerment involves gains in sociopolitical control (or belief that one can act for change), collective efficacy (or belief that working together as a group can make a difference), critical

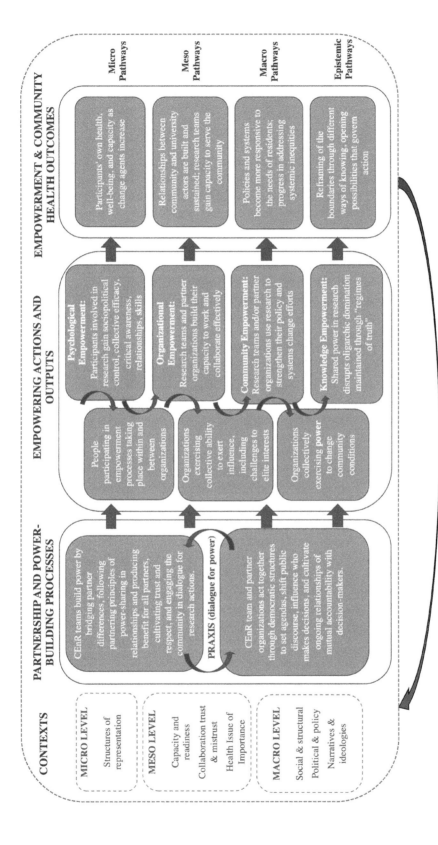

Figure 24.1 *Empowerment community-engaged research (CEnR) model (with adaptations from the CBPR Conceptual Model (Wallerstein et al., 2020), empowerment pathways (Christens, 2019), and Roura (2021) levels of power).*

awareness of one's role in society, understanding of the sources and mechanisms of social power (Speer & Hughey, 1995), and the development of relationships within an organization (Zimmerman, 2000). By recognizing both personal and collective resources and opportunities for change, people develop skills to face adverse situations and uncertainties in their daily lives (Kleba et al., 2022).

Community-engaged research processes can provide the context through which participants make these psychological gains. Participation in research can provide opportunities for participants to build relationships with researchers and other stakeholders, take on new social and leadership roles, acquire research and advocacy skills, and gain a better understanding of sociopolitical systems (Woods-Jaeger et al., 2021), including personal gains outside of the partnership (Rodríguez Espinosa et al., 2020). These processes, however, require that participants develop relationships of mutual respect and accountability. Sociopolitical understanding and leadership competence grow through research, action, and reflection with other members of the organization as participants improve their critical analysis skills, broaden their civic involvement, and gain confidence in their leadership abilities with the organization's mentorship and support (Christens et al., 2011).

For CEnR, this view of psychological and sociopolitical development underscores the dynamic nature of leadership development not as an "end point" but rather as a complex interplay of social and behavioral processes and cognitive, emotional, and relational outcomes. Emotional connectedness and trust are central to developing leadership competence and sociopolitical understanding, with trust seen throughout the CEnR literature as key (Lucero et al., 2020). Differences in language, culture, and self-interests and legacies of mistrust between institutions and communities can therefore pose obstacles to effective CEnR (London et al., 2018). Sociopolitical development also takes time, an investment that cannot take place without personal commitment to the issue of concern. This is why community organizing often emphasizes mutual self-interest (i.e., recognizing how one's interests are connected to the self-interests of the community; Beck & Eichler, 2000). Community organizing also emphasizes the importance of small wins to build power (Minkler & Wakimoto, 2021), as people share commitment and gain confidence in their collective ability to effect change (Speer & Hughey, 1995). This mirrors the CEnR principle of starting with community priorities and needs (Israel et al., 2013).

Though involving changes at the level of the individual, psychological empowerment is therefore inextricably linked to social processes within organized groups. It is through these social processes that individuals experience improvements in their own health and well-being, with civic engagement associated with enhanced social belonging and social support as well as reductions in stress (Thoits, 2012). Gains in members' collective efficacy and cohesion are also central to the development of powerful organizations that are capable of exerting influence over larger systems and processes.

Meso Pathways (Organizational Empowerment)

Empowerment is not something that can be given to people by others – rather, organizational settings create environments that facilitate psychological empowerment by building bonds of belonging and collective ability to exercise power (Speer & Hughey, 1995). Viewing power in this way contradicts the dominant cultural value of individualism in America in which individual sources of power, such as financial resources or intelligence, are considered most important (Speer et al., 2020b). Individual sources of power can be most effective when combined in organizations, and organizational power can be built and sustained within socially marginalized communities (Galbraith & Bartel, 1983; Speer, 2008).

Organizational empowerment incorporates both internal and external elements: internal capacity to promote transparency, power-sharing, and collaborative decision-making among its members and effectiveness in exerting sociopolitical influence on larger, external societal conditions (Christens, 2019). Groups and organizations mediate individuals' connections to their communities, offering their members emotional, material, cognitive, and informational support (Peterson et al., 2008). Organizations that provide empowering settings for their members can then exercise their collective power to set agendas, shift public discourse, and cultivate ongoing relationships of mutual accountability with decision-makers (Speer & Hughey, 1995; Speer et al., 2020b). Organizations therefore also connect members to interorganizational networks and social movements that exert influence to change systems (Kleba et al., 2022).

It is typically assumed that when CEnR contributes to empowerment, the CEnR partnership serves as a setting for participants' development and primarily leverages the power of academic research to affect social systems. However, research teams may not be equipped to facilitate the cognitive and relational development that have the greatest impacts on communities. Moreover, public (e.g., federal) funding may prohibit academics from taking political or policy actions, necessitating that community members of the CEnR team take on advocacy roles. We therefore discuss not only the opportunity for the CEnR partnership to contain empowering settings but also CEnR's potential impacts on partner organization(s).

Community-Engaged Research Partnership Settings

Empowerment within CEnR partnerships has been shown to be capable of producing gains in community power related to research leadership and decision-making, as well as in capacities to improve health outcomes related to the research (Boursaw et al., 2021; Stack & McDonald, 2018). For a CEnR partnership to be an empowering setting, it must create spaces for participants to share commitment to the partnership, take on leadership roles, learn from peers and mentors, and receive support as they grow and learn (Christens, 2019).

Inequities in social, economic, and political power between university and community members, however, can be considerable, particularly when community members come from marginalized and underserved communities (London et al., 2018). Communities have historically been "used" by researchers (Brenner & Manice, 2011), with "drive-by" or "helicopter" research often extracting data without returning findings to communities (Balazs & Morello-Frosch, 2013). Well-publicized instances of research abuse (e.g., the Tuskegee Institute study of syphilis in Black men or the more recent Havasupai diabetes study) have also generated deep mistrust of research and medical establishments. Even in the absence of large disparities in power between team members, CEnR projects may lack alignment between team members' objectives, capacities, and larger contexts (Egid et al., 2021; London et al., 2020). Academic knowledge may be privileged rather than seen as equal to community knowledge, or partners may simply employ different jargon, leading them to "speak past" or unwittingly offend one another. Partners in community-engaged research collaborations must be cognizant of these dynamics if empowerment is the goal.

Community-engaged research – and CBPR scholarship in particular – has been attentive to power dynamics within research partnerships (Andress et al., 2020; Muhammad et al., 2015; Wallerstein et al., 2019). Informed by the social ecological model, Roura (2021) provides a useful approach to understanding how power asymmetries can be disrupted or reinforced at the micro, meso, and macro levels. Disrupting power at the micro level requires self-reflexivity of one's position within intersecting systems of power and oppression. The meso level (e.g., the research team) focuses on creating project reward and governance structures that "are unambiguously and proactively committed to an equitable distribution of power and where participants feel genuinely free to express themselves without fear of reprisals nor any type of coercion" (Roura, 2021, p. 782). At the macro level, supportive sociopolitical environments (e.g., governments with consistent rule of law and robust democratic practices and norms) may facilitate more dramatic improvements to social conditions.

In the University of New Mexico Engage for Equity study of 215 federally funded partnerships, cogovernance of formal agreements, shared resources and participatory decision-making (Sanchez-Youngman et al., 2021), and "collective empowerment" were identified at the meso level as key drivers of relationships and structures that matter for health outcomes. "Collective empowerment" includes four practices: (1) Partners share participatory principles; (2) partners perceive that their opinions are influential in decisions; (3) partners integrate community history and knowledge to create culture-centered research, and (4) partners engage in collective reflection on their processes and achievements toward equity (Oetzel et al., 2022). Two of these components especially matter for power-sharing: partners having influence in decisions and partners engaging in collective reflection on their practices toward equity. Relationships and cogovernance structures form the basis of partnerships' power, enabling the group to navigate challenges, flexibly adapt to changing conditions, and pursue improvements to community conditions (London et al., 2018).

Partner Organization Settings

Recognizing the history of power inequities within CEnR suggests a forward-thinking strategy of aligning academic resources with the empowering processes already occurring in community organizations. Community-based organizations, for instance, build and exercise power by organizing civic and democratic participation around issues of concern with those directly affected. Instead of building power to support a predetermined research agenda, CEnR can align academic interests and resources with groups that are already responding to community-identified issues.

Drawing from their experience working with community organizing groups, Speer and Christens (2013) suggest that researchers can maximize their social impact by identifying powerful grassroots organizations that can guide and make use of academic research. They emphasize communicating openly about the skills and resources that they (researchers) can offer and developing a research approach that aligns academic interests and capacities with the needs and strengths of the partner(s). This approach recognizes the unique abilities that certain community organizations possess, including skills, resources, and organizational infrastructure.

Researchers interested in partnering with grassroots organizations should be aware that grassroots organizations may be at varying stages of power-building, and their interests and capacities should not be assumed. Clear communication about organizations' interests, capacities, and structural constraints should be part of forming a partnership, with goals also to enhance capacity. Flexibility and methodologic pluralism (i.e., willingness to employ a variety of research methods) become critical and showcase the benefits of interdisciplinary teams and teams with diverse stakeholders.

Macro Pathways (Community Empowerment)

Community empowerment takes place when communities most impacted by structural inequities develop, sustain, and grow an organized base of people who act together through democratic structures to change systems (Speer et al., 2020a). Community empowerment builds upon processes of psychological, organizational, and partnered empowerment, involving the development of connections between institutions and their constituencies, interorganizational linkages, and individuals and organizations coalescing into social movements (Speer & Hughey, 1995; Zimmerman, 2000). Building community power, Speer et al. (2020a) explain, "requires developing both an organizational infrastructure capable of exercising power to alter local policies and conditions and developing active and open mechanisms for bringing new residents and constituents into an organization or a base in ways that stimulate a political analysis and a sense of agency to affect change" (p. 4). To build community power, structures are needed that favor and mobilize greater interaction and dialogue between different social actors. This implies ensuring greater access to information and the adoption of democratic practices. It also requires a greater sense of community, openness and respect for differences, and willingness to share and articulate existing resources (Kleba et al., 2022).

In a set of three articles, Popay et al. (2021) expand on the concept of community power by highlighting the dimensions of emancipatory power. Their ten-year study of citizen-led development in the UK identified two main kinds of participatory spaces that shape the development of community power and community transformation. It is not just about creating governance spaces in which residents make formal decisions on actions, allocate resources, manage accountability, and create alliances. It is equally about supporting sense-making spaces where residents meet informally, make sense of local issues, and gain the ability to inform and influence local issues (Powell et al., 2021). This builds on the role of reflection in collective empowerment within partnerships (Oetzel et al., 2022) and adds to our understanding of the importance of deliberative dialogue for community organizing.

Universities can play an institutional role in either constraining or enabling community empowerment. Universities have made strides in developing infrastructure to support engagement with local coalitions and networks. With federal funders such as the NIH increasingly supporting CEnR and community engagement "cores" in transdisciplinary centers, dedicated engagement staff have become more commonplace in research universities. Although these cores and other community engagement centers have supported the development of CEnR partnerships (London et al., 2020), institutional barriers are prevalent, such as a lack of engagement of community stakeholders in ethics reviews, financial processes, and insufficient compensation, among others (Carter-Edwards et al., 2021). Community-based organizations have also made it clear that government and foundation funders often provide substantial benefits to universities without providing similar compensation to these community-based organizations (Cohen & Mascarenhas, 2022). Nevertheless, institutional practices and policies represent fertile ground for future research for supporting community empowerment within mutually beneficial CEnR projects (Petteway et al., 2019).

Community-engaged research has shown its promise for advancing equity-focused policy change, with partnerships among communities and academics bridging what can otherwise be a considerable gap between research evidence and policy (Cacari-Stone et al., 2014; Minkler et al., 2012). Although academics might aspire to produce research that translates readily into policies and practices, scholars and practitioners increasingly emphasize that "political pressures from below, and structures of government from above, shape, define and direct policy choices" (Labonte et al., 2005, p. 12). Community-based organization advocacy and power therefore often provide the critical political leverage for the desired policy change that academics may be restricted from exerting.

Epistemic Pathways (Knowledge Empowerment)

In the study of CEnR, scholars have shown critical interest in the relationship between power and knowledge. Building from Gaventa's (1980) work on the mechanisms of power, Gaventa and Cornwall (2015) outlined key ways in which knowledge operates in the exercise of social power. In the first dimension, knowledge can be seen as a resource to be mobilized to influence public debates. Brown and Zavestoski (2004) explain, for instance, how the "scientization of decision-making" has framed political and moral questions in scientific terms, "ensuring that it becomes the purview of 'experts'" (p. 681). Under the guise of fairness, this process enables powerful interests to deploy scientific experts in policy debates, prevailing over those without access to "valid" science and limiting public participation in decision-making.

Where the first dimension of power described by Gaventa assumes an open conflict over clearly defined issues, the second dimension is about keeping issues and actors from getting to the table where decisions are made (Bachrach & Baratz, 1962; Gaventa & Cornwall, 2015). Drawing from Brown and Zavestoski's (2004) concept of scientization, we can see how repeated failures to provide "valid" evidence would eventually exclude less powerful groups from public debates altogether. Nondominant groups have historically been underrepresented in the creation of new research, both as investigators and as research participants. This has effectively excluded these groups from contributing to academic discourse and, consequently, the construction of prevailing theories of human experience.

Lukes (1974) offered a third dimension of power: the ability to influence consciousness. For Lukes, "the most effective and insidious use of power is to prevent such conflict from arising in the first place" (Lukes, 1974, p. 24). This form of power serves to subjugate through internalized oppressions, creating rules and values that make inequity and injustice appear normal, routine, and inevitable. Black feminist scholar Patricia Hill Collins (2000) illustrated how such images as "mammies" – Black maternal figures as obedient domestic servants – taught Black women their assigned place in White power structures, maintaining economic subordination and gender oppression. Her work shows how female Black intellectuals resist this ideology by defining African American women as "complex individuals who show tremendous strength under adverse conditions, even under incessant demands of providing for families" (Collins, 2000, p. 83). Antiracist scholars have named complementary oppressive dimensions of racism, from structural shaping of conditions, to personally mediated expressions of discriminatory bias, to internalized racism (Jones, 2000). Muhammad et al. (2018) more directly uncover the linguistic impacts of covert racism (often as coded language that becomes microaggressions or microinvalidations) and linguistic racial accommodation of dominant groups shaping language to deny realities (i.e., statements that we are a postracial society).

Countering power inequities along the third consciousness-influencing dimension involves the production of knowledge that elucidates the power relations that affect the powerless (Gaventa & Cornwall, 2015). For Rappaport (1995), this means amplifying the value of community members through having people "discover their own stories, create new ones, and develop settings that make such activities possible" (p. 796). Participatory researcher Michelle Fine (1994) extends this further by critiquing researchers who speak for community members by presenting their quotes and challenges scholars to seek community meaning-making. For Gupta (2021), constrained political subjectivities – or understandings of oneself as lacking political power and agency – are a central mechanism in maintaining existing power asymmetries. She describes the work of Faith in Action, a faith-based community organizing network, to produce political subjects who see themselves "as a member of a political community [who] can engage in struggle, cultivate an awareness and critique of power, experience individual and collective agency, voice, and recognition by authorities as an equal" (p. 3143). Producing political selves, she argues, is critical for achieving progress toward equity.

Portuguese sociologist Boaventura de Sousa Santos (2015) has named the sociopolitical processes that canonized academic disciplines within universities as *epistemide*, or the killing of community knowledge systems. To combat these academic regimes of truth, he calls for knowledge democracy within CEnR that promotes multiple ways of knowing (i.e., through narrative, poetry, or theater) and that uses knowledge as a tool for social action and democracy (Hall et al., 2015). Knowledge democracy requires unpacking processes of racism and other discriminations that prevent community knowledge and experiences from being seen as valid. For CEnR practitioners, it also involves reflexive practice about our own positionalities of power and how to best co-construct knowledge for community change. From a Freirean perspective, knowledge democracy involves dialogical strategies toward critical consciousness, overcoming internalized oppressions, and developing Indigenous or popular knowledge as key resources in the change process (Gaventa & Cornwall, 2015).

Empowering Actions and Outputs (Exercising Power)

Now that we have discussed the opportunities for CEnR to contribute to building social power, we wish to take a step back and think about what it really means to exercise power. As stated in previous sections, transforming inequitable social conditions requires not only the development of power but also the exercise of power. These two processes do not occur sequentially but are inextricably linked; in order for organizations to build power *internally*, they must take action to exercise power *externally* (Speer, 2008). By accounting for the ways in which people build and exercise social power at the organizational and community levels, we aim to delineate the processes through which CEnR teams can disrupt inequitable systems and structures.

Central to this framework are two interrelated ideas: that power must be exercised in order to produce social change and that conflict is inevitable in efforts to transform oppressive social structures (Speer, 2008). Although the CEnR policy literature recognizes the critical role of political pressure and advocacy for transformational social change, much of the CEnR literature overrepresents conflict-free power dynamics as an approach to achieving health and health equity outcomes (Speer & Christens, 2013). The prevailing view of power in CEnR emphasizes the opportunities for power to act in concert with others, at times ignoring the fact that efforts that successfully challenge injustice in the status quo will meet strong resistance (Christens & Inzeo, 2015). Speer (2008) argues that "successful efforts to create social change by those who are relatively powerless will certainly lead to conflict. Strategically, cooperation and collaboration are critically important, but they will not circumvent the inevitability of conflict" (p. 205). How CEnR teams can make space for both collaboration with and political action by powerful organizations is an underdiscussed and yet critically important question. By supporting the sociopolitical development of participants to build power through organizing, CEnR can align academic resources with organizations as they build and exercise power and join broader networks of community actors aiming to achieve equity-focused change.

Empowerment processes that pay inadequate attention to power can create opportunities for change that only superficially impact community conditions. While CEnR participation may promote greater motivation for advocacy, psychological empowerment is insufficient for genuine community benefit (Seidman, 1988). Speer (2008) contends that such efforts need to materially increase community knowledge or resources. From this perspective, empowerment must involve sustained changes to a community's access to power, the ability to exercise that power, and systems and policies that shape the distribution of valued resources to that community.

Conflict should be seen as a natural and constructive feature of these processes. Changes that benefit communities – improvements to physical infrastructure or health-enhancing policies, for example – typically require that administrators do something that they might not ordinarily do (Couto, 1998). Ensuring that decision-makers are accountable to community interests may require consequences when community requests are ignored (Speer, 2008). However, once an organization's influence is established, the relationship between the organization and decision-makers may become amiable or even collaborative.

The following sections describe two different case examples of building and exercising power for health equity. The first describes how a collaboration between researchers and environmental justice advocates navigated conflict as their efforts to reduce pollution threatened the self-interests of powerful industrial polluters. The second demonstrates a Freirean empowerment arts-based process with youth as they gained power to define and advocate for their own narrative with local policymakers.

Policy Action for Environmental Justice in California

Through participatory policy-focused coalitions, CEnR and CBPR teams have deployed research evidence as well as strategic political analyses and actions to achieve policy goals (Freudenberg & Tsui, 2013; Minkler et al., 2012). Petersen et al. (2006) describe a collaborative effort by a community-based nonprofit organization, a progressive local philanthropy, and an interdisciplinary academic team to renegotiate the risk levels for toxic air emissions set by air quality management districts in Southern California (Rule 1402). The partnership described their strategy as "three-pronged," with each partner playing a distinct role to generate credible research on the harms associated with Rule 1402, deploy "people power," and utilize policy tools and actions to help effect a policy change. To produce research that would be maximally defensible, the multidisciplinary research team made a strategic decision to use government data when conducting their analyses. As one of their academic members remarked, "they [government officials] are hard pressed to tell you your data sucks because it's *their* data" (Petersen et al., 2006, p. 344, emphasis in original).

The community partners took steps to raise public awareness of Rule 1402 and its disproportionate burdens on communities of color, including conducting door-to-door outreach, giving presentations in local schools, organizing "Toxic Tours" for policymakers, and publicizing research results in the mass media. The research team made use of publicly available and secondary data to demonstrate that the communities most impacted by toxic waste facilities in Los Angeles County were working-class communities of color working in predominantly industrial areas. The collaborative ultimately played a substantial role in tightening toxic emissions standards from stationary facilities and was widely credited with helping to achieve a 75 percent reduction in the allowable cancer risk levels. They were, moreover, "seen as preparing local community organizations for advocacy work and participation in decision-making ... contributing to the sustainability of the regional and statewide environmental justice movement by leaving behind a trained cadre of community people who could continue the work" (Petersen et al., 2006, p. 350). Thus, through strategic collaboration and the application of academic research, the collaborative both bolstered and exercised community power to advance health equity.

Youth Engagement and Action through Art in New Mexico

Motivated by the murder of George Floyd and other inequities produced by COVID-19, a group of youth between the ages of ten and nineteen partnered with diverse, multisectoral stakeholders in thinking about and taking action for racial and social justice using a mural-painting project in early 2021. Hand-painted murals covering anti-Black racism, anti-immigrant policies, and climate change served as a catalyst for increasing skills and capacity for youth advocacy and created a platform to foment political transformation. First, youth participants worked with a local community artist to paint large mobile murals expressing their perspectives on injustices. Youth then participated in a cultural mobilization training with an academic and two student researchers from the University of New Mexico. Using Freirean methodology, following the SHOWED model,[1] the research team leveraged the visual story of each mural to engage youth in critical dialogue (partly represented in this section) regarding their lived experiences and to lead onto subsequent action steps.

> *Descriptive* responses to what they *Saw Happening*: Reflecting on the mural of protestors for Black Lives Matter, the majority of youth stated that the image showed resistance against racism. However, one younger participant felt that the image reflected violence by protestors.
>
> *Personalizing* responses to how issues related to *Our* lives: Several youth described their own personal experiences of discrimination based on the color of their skin, their sexual identity, and their immigration status.
>
> *Analysis* of *Why* they as youth face these issues: Dialogue was provoked about media portrayals of protest as violent versus the progressive intentions of peaceful protest. Youth discussed how the media tend to sensationalize these events.
>
> *Action* responses on how they can be *Empowered* to *Do* advocacy: Youth suggested that they launch a campaign to dispel myths about criminalizing peaceful protest.

Through this process, youth engaged in productive dialogue about protest politics, how the arts can mobilize communities of color, and how to sustain collective action.

That summer, the University of New Mexico Community Health Workers Initiative coordinated a multisectoral convening for youth to engage in dialogue about policy change with representatives of the Albuquerque Mayor's Office, city councilors, neighborhood coalitions, health councils, and other leaders. Youth shared their murals with adult stakeholders and advocates for

---

[1] SHOWED stands for: S = What did you **S**ee? H = What **H**appened? O = Was this **O**ur experience? W = **W**hy does this happen? E = **E**valuate the process. D = What can we **D**o about it?

policy reforms, and a prominent community center permanently installed them in a major media event. Another organization hired the two student researchers to continue training youth in collective mobilization. Individual participants have continued their advocacy via their own youth networks.

Looking Forward: An Agenda for Power, Empowerment, and Community-Engaged Research

Power and empowerment warrant more intentional integration into academic discourses around translating research into action (e.g., Freudenberg & Tsui, 2013; Labonte et al., 2005; Speer et al., 2020a). Community-engaged research, with its emphasis on multidirectional communication and learning, interest in epistemological and methodological pluralism, and commitment to action, has emerged as a promising strategy for navigating power hierarchies that hinder efforts to produce sustained and transformative social change. This chapter draws from the authors' experiences in the fields of public health and community psychology to outline key perspectives on power, empowerment, and CEnR for health. We emphasize, in particular, the importance of organizations and interorganizational mobilization as sources of power, the roles that CEnR can play in building and exercising power, and the importance of interrelated processes at the psychological, organizational, partnership, and community levels for producing transformative changes to social conditions. We elevate both material and epistemic perspectives on power as crucial to understanding the processes through which CEnR can disrupt existing hierarchies, build power among communities most affected by social inequities, and ultimately contribute to transforming systems and processes that perpetuate those inequities.

Looking forward, we highlight several burgeoning areas of study that hold promise for advancing our understanding of power, empowerment, and CEnR. First, projects such as Engage for Equity have made considerable advances in identifying constructs for the measurement and analysis of promising CEnR practices contributing to health and health equity outcomes (Wallerstein et al., 2020). Evaluation of CEnR processes is highly consequential, as evaluation metrics inevitably impose external measures of success to which organizations will adapt. There is great need, therefore, for nuanced and deeply validated criteria to guide future evaluation efforts for CEnR.

Second, the collaborative development of this chapter between scholars of community psychology and public health reflects the complementarity of perspectives from these scholarly traditions. One of the key opportunities presented by CEnR is its epistemological plurality; as Barnes et al. (2016) observe, "social problems are not the provenance of any one discipline" (p. 1). Surveying the wide array of disciplinary contributions to our current understanding of power, empowerment, and CEnR, we wish to emphasize the value of cross-fertilization between disciplines, particularly for advancing understanding of CEnR for health.

Third, although this chapter has broadly focused on CEnR rather than any particular typology, we also highlight the contributions made by CBPR. With its particular attention to power and social justice, CBPR has paved the way for transformative research practices across the CEnR spectrum. However, acceptance of academic incentives for community engagement, such as tenure and the promotion criteria of grants received, has led to the concern that researchers may still be appropriating community–academic collaborative strategies to extract knowledge from communities, which is fundamentally at odds with CBPR goals (Trickett, 2011). In light of this concern, there is a need for more rigorous attention to the communication and teaching of CEnR principles, evaluation of CEnR projects, and role of academic structures and funding mechanisms in shaping CEnR projects. (Haapanen et al., 2023). Finally, Speer (2008) and Speer et al. (2020a) note the potential for "empowerment" to be coopted by adapting individuals to inequitable conditions rather than changing structures and resources to better meet their needs. It is critical that, as power and empowerment occupy a more prominent place in CEnR discourses, scholars develop approaches to support communities that are building and exercising power for sustained changes in material and social conditions.

References

Adelman, C. (1993). Kurt Lewin and the origins of action research. *Educational Action Research*, *1*(1), 7–24.

Anderson, G., Herr, K., & Nihlen, A. (2007). *Studying your own school: An educator's guide to practitioner action research* (2nd ed.). Corwin Press.

Andress, L., Hall, T., Davis, S., Levine, J., Cripps, K., & Guinn, D. (2020). Addressing power dynamics in community-engaged research partnerships. *Journal of Patient-Reported Outcomes*, *4*(1), 24.

Bachrach, P., & Baratz, M. S. (1962). Two faces of power. *The American Political Science Review*, *56*(4), 947–952.

Balazs, C. L., & Morello-Frosch, R. (2013). The three Rs: How community-based participatory research strengthens the rigor, relevance, and reach of science. *Environmental Justice*, *6*(1), 9–16.

Barnes, S. L., Brinkley-Rubinstein, L., Doykos, B., Martin, N. C., & McGuire, A. (2016). Introduction. In S. L. Barnes, L. Brinkley-Rubinstein, B. Doykos, N. C. Martin, & A. McGuire (Eds.), *Academics in action! A model for community-engaged research, teaching, and service* (pp. 1–22). Fordham University Press.

Beck, E. L., & Eichler, M. (2000). Consensus organizing. *Journal of Community Practice*, *8*(1), 87–102.

Boursaw, B., Oetzel, J. G., Dickson, E., Thein, T. S., Sanchez-Youngman, S., Peña, J., Parker, M., Magarati, M., Littledeer, L., Duran, B., & Wallerstein, N.

(2021). Scales of practices and outcomes for community-engaged research. *American Journal of Community Psychology*, *67*(3–4), 256–270.

Boyer, E. L. (1990). *Scholarship reconsidered: Priorities of the professoriate*. Carnegie Foundation for the Advancement of Teaching.

Brandão, C. R. (1981). *Pesquisa participante* (1st ed.). Brasiliense.

Brenner, B. L., & Manice, M. P. (2011). Community engagement in children's environmental health research. *Mount Sinai Journal of Medicine: A Journal of Translational and Personalized Medicine*, *78*(1), 85–97.

Brown, P., & Zavestoski, S. (2004). Social movements in health: An introduction. *Sociology of Health and Illness*, *26*(6), 679–694.

Cacari-Stone, L., Wallerstein, N., Garcia, A. P., & Minkler, M. (2014). The promise of community-based participatory research for health equity: A conceptual model for bridging evidence with policy. *American Journal of Public Health*, *104*(9), 1615–1623.

Carter-Edwards, L., Grewe, M. E., Fair, A. M., Jenkins, C., Ray, N. J., Bilheimer, A., Dave, G., Nunez-Smith, M., Richmond, A., & Wilkins, C. H. (2021). Recognizing cross-institutional fiscal and administrative barriers and facilitators to conducting community-engaged clinical and translational research. *Academic Medicine: Journal of the Association of American Medical Colleges*, *96*(4), 558–567.

Christens, B. D. (2019). *Community power and empowerment*. Oxford University Press.

Christens, B. D., & Inzeo, P. T. (2015). Widening the view: Situating collective impact among frameworks for community-led change. *Community Development*, *46*(4), 420–435.

Christens, B. D., Faust, V., Gaddis, J., Inzeo, P. T., Sarmiento, C. S., & Sparks, S. M. (2016). Action research. In L. Jason & D. Glenwick (Eds.), *Handbook of methodological approaches to community-based research: Qualitative, quantitative, and mixed methods* (pp. 243–251). Oxford University Press.

Christens, B. D., Peterson, N. A., & Speer, P. W. (2011). Community participation and psychological empowerment: Testing reciprocal causality using a cross-lagged panel design and latent constructs. *Health Education*, *38*(4), 339–347.

Cohen, E., & Mascarenhas, L. (2022, November 28). *Community health groups that played crucial role during Covid-19 pandemic say they're being left out of government funding*. CNN. www.cnn.com/2022/11/28/health/public-health-funding-community-groups/index.html

Collins, P. H. (2000). *The politics of Black feminist thought*. Routledge.

Cornwall, A. (2008). Unpacking "participation": Models, meanings and practices. *Community Development Journal*, *43*(3), 269–283.

Cornwall, A., & Jewkes, R. (1995). What is participatory research? *Social Science & Medicine*, *41*(12), 1667–1676.

Couto, R. A. (1998). Community coalitions and grassroots policies of empowerment. *Administration & Society*, *30*(5), 569–594.

de Sousa Santos, B. (2015). *Epistemologies of the south: Justice against epistemicide*. Routledge.

Drahota, A., Meza, R. D., Brikho, B., Naaf, M., Estabillo, J. A., Gomez, E. D., Vejnoska, S. F., Dufek, S., Stahmer, A. C., & Aarons, G. A. (2016). Community-academic partnerships: A systematic review of the state of the literature and recommendations for future research. *The Milbank Quarterly*, *94*(1), 163–214.

Drame, E. R., & Irby, D. J. (Eds.). (2016). *Black participatory research: Power, identity, and the struggle for justice in education.* Palgrave Macmillan.

Dutta, M. J. (2007). Communicating about culture and health: Theorizing culture-centered and cultural sensitivity approaches. *Communication Theory, 17*(3), 304–328.

Egid, B., Roura, M., Aktar, B., Quach, J.A., Chumo, I., Dias, S., Hegel, G., Jones, L., Karuga, R., Lar, L., Lopez, Y., Pandya, A., Norton, T., Sheikhattari, P., Tancred, T., Wallerstein, N., Zimmerman, E., & Ozano, K., (2021). "You want to deal with power while riding on power": Global perspectives on power in participatory health research and co-production approaches. *BMJ Global Health, 6*, e006978.

Fals-Borda, O. (1980). The negation of sociology and its promise: Perspectives of social science in Latin America today. *Latin American Research Review, 15* (1), 161–166.

Fine, M. (1994). Working the hyphens. In N. K. Denzin & Y. S. Lincoln (Eds.), *Handbook of qualitative research* (pp. 70–82). SAGE Publications.

Fisher, P. A., & Ball, T. J. (2003). Tribal participatory research: Mechanisms of a collaborative model. *American Journal of Community Psychology, 32*(3–4), 207–216.

Fitzgerald, H. E., Bruns, K., Sonka, S. T., Furco, A., & Swanson, L. (2012). The centrality of engagement in higher education. *Journal of Higher Education Outreach and Engagement, 16*(3), 7–27.

Foucault, M. (1980). *Power/knowledge: Selected interviews and other writings, 1972–1977* (C. Gordon, Ed.; 1st American ed.). Pantheon Books.

Freire, P. (1970). *Pedagogy of the oppressed.* Continuum.

Freudenberg, N., & Tsui, E. (2013). Evidence, power, and policy change in community-based participatory research. *American Journal of Public Health, 104*(1), 11–14.

Galbraith, J. K., & Bartel, R. D. (1983). The anatomy of power. *Challenge, 26*(3), 26–33.

Gaventa, J. (1980). *Power and powerlessness: Quiescence and rebellion in an Appalachian Valley.* University of Illinois Press.

Gaventa, J., & Cornwall, A. (2015). Power and knowledge. In H. Bradbury (Ed.), *The SAGE handbook of action research* (3rd ed., pp. 465–471). SAGE Publications.

Gupta, J. (2021). Resistance, race, and subjectivity in congregation-based community organizing. *Journal of Community Psychology, 49*(8), 3141–3161.

Haapanen, K. A., & Christens, B. D. (2021). Community-engaged research approaches: Multiple pathways to health equity. *American Journal of Community Psychology, 67*(3–4), 331–337.

Haapanen, K. A., London, J. K., & Andrade, K. (2023). Creating the current and riding the wave: Persistence and change in community-engaged health sciences research. *Social Sciences, 12*(5), Article 5.

Hall, B., Tandon, R., & Tremblay, C. (2015). *Strengthening community university research partnerships: Global perspectives.* University of Victoria Libraries.

Holland, B. (2005). *Scholarship and mission in the 21st century university: The role of engagement*. Paper presented at the Australian Universities Quality Forum, Sydney.

Israel, B. A., Eng, E., Schulz, A. J., & Parker, E. A. (Eds.). (2013). *Methods for community-based participatory research for health* (2nd ed.). Jossey-Bass.

Jones, C. P. (2000). Levels of racism: A theoretic framework and a gardener's tale. *American Journal of Public Health, 90*(8), 1212–1215.

Kastelic, S., Wallerstein, N., Duran, B., & Oetzel, J. (2018). Socio-ecologic framework for CBPR: Development and testing of a model. In N. Wallerstein, B. Duran, J. Oetzel, & M. Minkler (Eds.), *Community-based participatory research for health: Advancing social and health equity* (3rd ed., pp. 77–93). Jossey-Bass.

Kirshner, B., Zion, S., Lopez, S., & Hipolito-Delgado, C. (2021). A theory of change for scaling critical civic inquiry. *Peabody Journal of Education, 96*(3), 294–306.

Kleba, M. E., Wallerstein, N., van der Donk, C., Wright, M., Belon, A. P., Gastaldo, D., Avery, H., & Shier, H. (2022). *Position paper 4 (empowerment and participatory health research)*. International Collaborative of Participatory Health Research.

Kline, N. (2022, November 8). *Merging science and political action: The call for activist research approaches in public health* [Oral presentation]. APHA 2022 Annual Meeting and Expo, Boston, MA.

Labonte, R., Polanyi, M., Muhajarine, N., Mcintosh, T., & Williams, A. (2005). Beyond the divides: Towards critical population health research. *Critical Public Health, 15*(1), 5–17.

Lewin, K. (1946). Action research and minority problems. *Journal of Social Issues, 2* (4), 34–46.

London, J. K., Haapanen, K. A., Backus, A., Mack, S. M., Lindsey, M., & Andrade, K. (2020). Aligning community-engaged research to context. *International Journal of Environmental Research and Public Health, 17*(4), 1187.

London, J. K., Schwarz, K., Cadenasso, M. L., Cutts, B. B., Mason, C., Lim, J., Valenzuela-Garcia, K., & Smith, H. (2018). Weaving community–university research and action partnerships for environmental justice. *Action Research, 16*(2), 173–189.

Lucero, J. E., Boursaw, B., Eder, M., Greene-Moton, E., Wallerstein, N., & Oetzel, J. G. (2020). Engage for Equity: The role of trust and synergy in community-based participatory research. *Health Education & Behavior, 47*(3), 372–379.

Lukes, S. (1974). *Power: A radical view* (2nd ed.). Macmillan.

Lykes, M. B., Lloyd, C. R., & Nicholson, K. M. (2018). Participatory and action research within and beyond the academy: Contesting racism through decolonial praxis and teaching "against the grain." *American Journal of Community Psychology, 62*(3–4), 406–418.

Maton, K. I. (2008). Empowering community settings: Agents of individual development, community betterment, and positive social change. *American Journal of Community Psychology, 41*(1–2), 4–21.

McCloskey, D. J., Akintobi, T. H., Bonham, A., Cook, J., & Coyne-Beasley, T. (2011, June). *Principles of community engagement* (2nd ed.). National Institutes of

Health. www.atsdr.cdc.gov/communityengagement/pdf/PCE_Report_508_FINAL.pdf

Minkler, M., & Wakimoto, P. (Eds.). (2021). *Community organizing and community building for health and social equity* (4th ed.). Rutgers University Press.

Minkler, M., Rubin, V., & Wallerstein, N. (2012). *Community-based participatory research: A strategy for building healthy communities and promoting health through policy change*. PolicyLink. www.policylink.org/sites/default/files/CBPR.pdf

Muhammad, M., Garzón, C., & Reyes, A. (2018). Understanding contemporary racism, power, and privilege and their impacts on CBPR. In N. Wallerstein, B. Duran, J. G. Oetzel, & M. Minkler (Eds.), *Community-based participatory research for health: Advancing social and health equity* (pp. 47–59). Jossey-Bass.

Muhammad, M., Wallerstein, N., Sussman, A. L., Avila, M., Belone, L., & Duran, B. (2015). Reflections on researcher identity and power: The impact of positionality on community based participatory research (CBPR) processes and outcomes. *Critical Sociology*, *41*(7–8), 1045–1063.

Oetzel, J. G., Boursaw, B., Magarati, M., Dickson, E., Sanchez-Youngman, S., Morales, L., Kastelic, S., Eder, M., & Wallerstein, N. (2022). Exploring theoretical mechanisms of community-engaged research: A multilevel cross-sectional national study of structural and relational practices in community–academic partnerships. *International Journal for Equity in Health*, *21*(1), 59.

Oetzel, J. G., Zhou, C., Duran, B., Pearson, C., Magarati, M., Lucero, J., Wallerstein, N., & Villegas, M. (2015). Establishing the psychometric properties of constructs in a community-based participatory research conceptual model. *American Journal of Health Promotion*, *29*(5), e188–e202.

Parker, M., Wallerstein, N., Duran, B., Magarati, M., Burgess, E., Sanchez-Youngman, S., Boursaw, B., Heffernan, A., Garoutte, J., & Koegel, P. (2020). Engage for equity: Development of community-based participatory research tools. *Health Education & Behavior*, *47*(3), 359–371.

Petersen, D., Minkler, M., Vásquez, V. B., & Baden, A. C. (2006). Community-based participatory research as a tool for policy change: A case study of the Southern California environmental justice collaborative. *Review of Policy Research*, *23*(2), 339–354.

Peterson, N. A., Speer, P. W., Hughey, J., Armstead, T. L., Schneider, J. E., & Sheffer, M. A. (2008). Community organizations and sense of community: Further development in theory and measurement. *Journal of Community Psychology*, *36*(6), 798–813.

Petteway, R., Mujahid, M., Allen, A., & Morello-Frosch, R. (2019). Towards a people's social epidemiology: Envisioning a more inclusive and equitable future for social epi research and practice in the 21st century. *International Journal of Environmental Research and Public Health*, *16*(20), 3983.

Popay, J., Whitehead, M., Ponsford, R., Egan, M., & Mead, R. (2021). Power, control, communities and health inequalities I: Theories, concepts and analytical frameworks. *Health Promotion International*, *36*(5), 1253–1263.

Powell, K., Barnes, A., Anderson de Cuevas, R., Bambra, C., Halliday, E., Lewis, S., McGill, R., Orton, L., Ponsford, R., Salway, S., Townsend, A., Whitehead, M., & Popay, J. (2021). Power, control, communities and health inequalities

III: Participatory spaces – An English case. *Health Promotion International*, *36*(5), 1264–1274.

Pratt, B. (2019). Constructing citizen engagement in health research priority-setting to attend to dynamics of power and difference. *Developing World Bioethics*, *19*(1), 45–60.

Rappaport, J. (1987). Terms of empowerment/exemplars of prevention: Toward a theory for community psychology. *American Journal of Community Psychology*, *15*(2), 121–148.

Rappaport, J. (1995). Empowerment meets narrative: Listening to stories and creating settings. *American Journal of Community Psychology*, *23*(5), 795–807.

Rodríguez Espinosa, P., Sussman, A., Pearson, C. R., Oetzel, J. G., & Wallerstein, N. (2020). Personal outcomes in community-based participatory research partnerships: A cross-site mixed methods study. *American Journal of Community Psychology*, *66*(3–4), 439–449.

Roura, M. (2021). The social ecology of power in participatory health research. *Qualitative Health Research*, *31*(4), 778–788.

Sanchez-Youngman, S., Boursaw, B., Oetzel, J., Kastellic, S., Devia, C., Scarpetta, M., Belone, L., & Wallerstein, N. (2021). Structural community governance: Importance for community–academic research partnerships. *American Journal of Community Psychology*, *67*(3–4), 271–283.

Seidman, E. (1988). Back to the future, community psychology: Unfolding a theory of social intervention. *American Journal of Community Psychology*, *16*(1), 3–24.

Smith, L. T. (2012). Decolonizing methodologies: Research and indigenous peoples (2nd Ed.). Zed Books.

Speer, P. W. (2008). Social power and forms of change: Implications for psychopolitical validity. *Journal of Community Psychology*, *36*(2), 199–213.

Speer, P. W., & Christens, B. D. (2013). An approach to scholarly impact through strategic engagement in community-based research. *Journal of Social Issues*, *69*(4), 734–753.

Speer, P. W., & Hughey, J. (1995). Community organizing: An ecological route to empowerment and power. *American Journal of Community Psychology*, *23*, 729–748.

Speer, P. W., Gupta, J., & Haapanen, K. A. (2020a, September). *A research agenda for developing and measuring community power for health equity*. Robert Wood Johnson Foundation. https://static1.squarespace.com/static/5ee2c6c3c085f746bd33f80e/t/5f89f10f74988d6050aea648/1602875664986/Forward+Looking+Research+Agenda+%281%29.pdf

Speer, P. W., Gupta, J., & Haapanen, K. A. (2020b, September). *Developing community power for health equity: A landscape analysis of current research and theory*. Robert Wood Johnson Foundation. https://static1.squarespace.com/static/5ee2c6c3c085f746bd33f80e/t/5f89f1325e27a51436c97b74/1602875699695/Landscape+-+Developing+Community+Power+for+Health+Equity+%281%29.pdf

Stack, E. E., & McDonald, K. (2018). We are "both in charge, the academics and self-advocates": Empowerment in community-based participatory research. *Journal of Policy and Practice in Intellectual Disabilities*, *15*(1), 80–89.

Stoeffler, S. W. (2018). Community empowerment. In R. A. Cnaan & C. Milofsky (Eds.), *Handbook of community movements and local organizations in the 21st century* (pp. 265–280). Springer International Publishing.

Thoits, P. A. (2012). Role-identity salience, purpose and meaning in life, and well-being among volunteers. *Social Psychology Quarterly*, *75*(4), 360–384.

Trickett, E. J. (2011). Community-based participatory research as worldview or instrumental strategy: Is it lost in translation(al) research? *American Journal of Public Health*, *101*(8), 1353–1355.

Wallerstein, N. (1992). Powerlessness, empowerment, and health: Implications for health promotion programs. *American Journal of Health Promotion*, *6*(3), 197–205.

Wallerstein, N. (2006). *Evidence of effectiveness of empowerment interventions to reduce health disparities and social exclusion* (Health Evidence Network, p. 37). WHO Press.

Wallerstein, N., & Duran, B. (2018). The theoretical, historical, and practice roots of CBPR. In N. Wallerstein, B. Duran, J. Oetzel, & M. Minkler (Eds.), *Community-based participatory research for health: Advancing social and health equity* (3rd ed., pp. 17–30). Jossey-Bass.

Wallerstein, N., Duran, B., Oetzel, J., & Minkler, M. (Eds.). (2018). *Community-based participatory research for health: Advancing social and health equity* (3rd ed.). Jossey-Bass.

Wallerstein, N., Muhammad, M., Sanchez-Youngman, S., Rodriguez Espinosa, P., Avila, M., Baker, E. A., Barnett, S., Belone, L., Golub, M., Lucero, J., Mahdi, I., Noyes, E., Nguyen, T., Roubideaux, Y., Sigo, R., & Duran, B. (2019). Power dynamics in community-based participatory research: A multiple-case study analysis of partnering contexts, histories, and practices. *Health Education & Behavior*, *46*(1 Suppl.), 19S–32S.

Wallerstein, N., Oetzel, J. G., Sanchez-Youngman, S., Boursaw, B., Dickson, E., Kastelic, S., Koegel, P., Lucero, J. E., Magarati, M., Ortiz, K., Parker, M., Peña, J., Richmond, A., & Duran, B. (2020). Engage for Equity: A long-term study of community-based participatory research and community-engaged research practices and outcomes. *Health Education & Behavior*, *47*(3), 380–390.

Walters, K. L., Johnson-Jennings, M., Stroud, S., Rasmus, S., Charles, B., John, S., Allen, J., Kaholokula, J. K., Look, M. A., de Silva, M., Lowe, J., Baldwin, J. A., Lawrence, G., Brooks, J., Noonan, C. W., Belcourt, A., Quintana, E., Semmens, E. O., & Boulafentis, J. (2020). Growing from our roots: Strategies for developing culturally grounded health promotion interventions in American Indian, Alaska native, and native Hawaiian communities. *Prevention Science*, 21(Suppl. 1), 54–64.

Wilmsen, C., Elmendorf, W., Fisher, L., Ross, J., Sarathy, B., & Wells, G. (Eds.). (2008). *Partnerships for empowerment: Participatory research for community-based natural resource management*. Earthscan.

Woods-Jaeger, B., Daniel-Ulloa, J., Kleven, L., Bucklin, R., Maldonado, A., Gilbert, P. A., Parker, E. A., & Baquero, B. (2021). Building leadership, capacity, and power to advance health equity and justice through community-engaged research in the Midwest. *American Journal of Community Psychology*, *67*(1–2), 195–204.

Zimmerman, M. A. (2000). Empowerment theory. In J. Rappaport & E. Seidman (Eds.), *Handbook of community psychology* (pp. 43–63). Springer US.

Concluding Thoughts on Building Community Power

Brian D. Christens

Introduction

The chapters in this book have each examined different approaches to building community power through organizations and participatory processes. Some of these approaches represent long-standing and widespread forms of practice (e.g., community organizing, neighborhood associations, participatory urban planning) that are continuously evolving. Other approaches are more emergent or are currently spreading to more localities (e.g., action civics, participatory budgeting) and are exerting influences on existing organizations and forms of practice. Research into each of these approaches varies accordingly, with some approaches having a robust foundation of research-based insights and others that have only recently become the focus of empirical studies. The contributors to this book are at the forefront of advancing research on each of these types of community empowerment processes. Many of them are doing so from an action research orientation, in collaboration with the organizations, initiatives, and networks that are establishing and supporting these efforts.

One elemental way that this book can be useful is for developing an understanding of discrete approaches – their history, purposes, defining features, challenges, and what practitioners and researchers currently understand and are learning about dynamics of power, empowerment, and related impacts on participants and broader communities. Yet, reading any one chapter can also provide insights and raise questions that are relevant across other approaches. Empowerment theory provides a useful set of conceptual distinctions for bridging what is being learned in one context, domain, or type of approach to others. As one way to illustrate this potential, I begin this concluding chapter[1] by reflecting on a single chapter – Chapter 21 on gender–sexuality alliances (GSAs) by Poteat, Marx, O'Brien, and Yang. I examine research on GSAs from the perspective of empowerment theory and consider ways that it can inform practice and engaged research across other approaches. After this, I will bring the discussion back out to the broader range of approaches.

---

[1] Thank you to Kathryn Y. Morgan (first author of Chapter 20 on action civics) for helpful feedback on an earlier draft of this concluding chapter.

Empowerment Processes in Gender–Sexuality Alliances

Gender–sexuality alliances create affirming spaces within schools for LGBTQ+ youth and their allies to access resources, to give and receive support, and to exert influence on their schools and communities through advocacy and collective actions. Gender–sexuality alliances have been instrumental in establishing antidiscriminatory school and district policies, for instance, and have countered attempts to prevent discussion of LGBTQ+ identities within schools. Many GSAs also collaborate on advocacy and build coalitions with other types of organizations, such as with groups advocating for racial justice and immigrant rights. Despite backlash and attempts to restrict young people from participating in GSAs, there has been a rapid expansion from their origins just over three decades ago, such that a slight majority of high schools in large urban districts in the US now have a GSA (albeit with large variation across states and regions in the US).

As Poteat, Marx, O'Brien, and Yang explain in Chapter 21, as GSAs have been established in more schools, research has progressed from more general to more fine-grained designs. Some early research, for instance, compared schools with GSAs to those without them, finding that students in schools with GSAs were more likely to report feelings of safety and a positive school climate. Other early research compared students who were members of GSAs to those in the same schools who were not participating. This second line of inquiry identified fewer consistent differences between these two groups (members and nonmembers). In their chapter, Poteat and colleagues speculate that this is because: (1) GSAs are having effects on school environments that are benefiting students regardless of whether they themselves are participating in the GSA's activities and (2) this member/nonmember dichotomy masks the wide variability in GSAs and the many different ways that youth are participating in and experiencing these alliances.

These complexities are emblematic of the challenges facing researchers seeking to disentangle the influences of many other approaches to community empowerment on participants, institutions, and broader environments. One way to think about these multiple influences is as interrelated "pathways" through which empowerment processes are contributing to health and well-being: (1) participant pathways, (2) ecological pathways, and (3) pluralist pathways. Participant pathways refer to the beneficial influences of empowering community settings for those who participate directly. Ecological pathways refer to the influences that empowerment processes can have on broader populations (i.e., including nonparticipants) through the changes that they bring about in policies, systems, and environments. Pluralist pathways refer to the broader beneficial effects of more egalitarian power structures, which empowerment processes can bring about through their efforts to reduce power imbalances. Although these pathways are interrelated and can all take place simultaneously, distinguishing between them can help to disentangle the complexity of empowerment processes and their effects.[2]

Gender–Sexuality Alliance Participant Pathways

Scholars studying GSAs are meeting the challenges that this complexity presents with sophisticated research designs that are yielding insights into numerous dynamics at play within GSAs and between GSAs and their broader school and community environments. For example, their research has examined how participants' perceptions of support from their GSA is associated with positive developmental outcomes (Poteat et al., 2015) and how greater consistency and higher levels of active participation in GSAs are generating youth psychological empowerment processes and, in turn, reducing mental health concerns (Poteat et al., 2020). These studies help to explain how the empowerment processes taking place through GSAs are influencing the health and well-being of the people who are themselves directly participating (i.e., participant pathways).

Gender–sexuality alliances organize their activities in a variety of ways, however, creating unique opportunities and experiences for participants. For instance, GSAs tend to have some activities that provide opportunities for youth leadership and other activities that are led by adult advisors. Poteat et al. (2020) found greater evidence of psychological empowerment processes taking place within GSAs that were characterized by greater relative levels of youth leadership; however, adult advisors also play many important roles in GSA functioning. Furthermore, GSAs vary in terms of how formally structured their meetings and activities are. Poteat et al. (2016, 2022) have found that more organizational structure is valuable for cultivating youth's sense of agency and engagement in advocacy, at least up to a point. Beyond a certain threshold, though, additional structure may inhibit youth agency, potentially because the settings within the GSA become too formalized and rigid. Findings on both of these organizational features point to a need for balance between youth and adult leadership and between structure and flexibility.

Of course, organizational characteristics and the features of settings do not affect all participants in the same ways. Research on GSAs has also begun to develop insights into the fit between certain types of organizational settings and participatory opportunities and youth with different backgrounds, identities, and reasons for being involved. For instance, Calzo et al. (2020) identified different profiles of participants in GSAs based on what they desired from their involvement and the types of opportunities that they were provided through participation. Civic developmental outcomes (such as civic engagement and self-perceptions of agency) were higher among those who were

---

[2] A more detailed discussion of these pathways and how empowerment processes relate to health and well-being is presented in chapter 7 of Christens (2019).

participating in GSAs that offered opportunities equivalent to or exceeding what they desired. Research on these topics is advancing quickly, yielding greater understanding of how the features of GSAs and meetings affect positive sociopolitical development among participants (e.g., Poteat et al., 2023a).

Gender–Sexuality Alliance Ecological Pathways

Research on GSAs is also providing insights into ecological pathways, or the ways that these alliances can influence the well-being of students who are not directly involved. For instance, GSAs can influence schools' climates and cultural norms. Through advocacy efforts, they can also exert influences on schools' policies and practices. As mentioned previously, some research has compared students' outcomes in schools with and without GSAs, finding greater levels of self-reported well-being and perceived safety among students attending schools that have GSAs (e.g., Davis et al., 2014; Marx & Kettrey, 2016). Building on this work, a recent study found that the extent to which GSAs reported engaging in advocacy was independently associated with disparities in depression between LGBQ+ and heterosexual students in the broader populations of schools (Poteat et al., 2023b). Greater levels of advocacy in the GSA appear to reduce these disparities within schools. This research into how GSAs are influencing their schools is thus becoming ever more specific. It is increasingly scrutinizing the relative emphases and features of GSAs in different schools and how this variance may be producing differential types and degrees of influence on broader school environments.

Gender–Sexuality Alliance Pluralist Pathways

Although less research has investigated pluralist pathways (or GSAs' influences on power relations),[3] GSAs can reduce power imbalances in the school contexts in which they operate, and, on aggregate, they are contributing to equity and egalitarianism in broader sociopolitical systems (Miceli, 2005). In their chapter, Poteat and colleagues describe the efforts by a particular GSA (one that they have partnered with to conduct research) to establish a gender-neutral bathroom in the GSA's school. Although these efforts were successful, the GSA faced resistance, criticism, and hostility from some in the school and the district. Consequently, participants in the alliance are concerned that their efforts could be overturned. As with changes to policies and systems across many other contexts, conflict with defenders of the status quo is inevitable. Groups must continuously strategize about how to hold decision-makers accountable to their

---

[3] This relative lack of research into pluralist pathways is not unique to the study of GSAs. There has been less research into this set of pathways across most of the approaches discussed in this book.

constituents' concerns. Gender–sexuality alliances can make their school envir-onments more pluralistic and egalitarian simply by demonstrating the possibil-ities for student collective action to change systems and practices. It is likely that there are ripple effects from these alterations in power relations in the schools where GSAs are active, and beyond.

Relevance to Other Approaches

Part of my intent in spotlighting the chapter on GSAs by Poteat and colleagues and discussing it through the lens of these three pathways (participant, ecological, and pluralist) has been to demonstrate the potential for insights that transcend the focal approach of each chapter. A deep dive into any chapter can provide ideas that relate to many others. For instance, the evidence of a likely influence (along an ecological pathway) of the relative levels of advocacy by GSAs on reduced disparities in students' mental health at the school level (Poteat et al., 2023b) should be of interest to practitioners and researchers involved with many approaches to community empowerment. Are there parallels in the influences of greater levels of advocacy within youth participatory action research (YPAR) projects, for example, or in action civics initiatives? Might there be similarly beneficial influences on mental health across other contexts and settings in which community organizing and activism are taking place?

Likewise, the findings that suggest a curvilinear relationship between the level of structure in GSAs and the sense of agency that participants in these settings tend to develop are relevant to empowerment theory and practice across other contexts. These findings call to mind Freeman's (1972) piece on *the tyranny of structurelessness*, which argued for more formalized structures within the organ-izational settings taking shape within the women's liberation movement. This critique of structurelessness has been influential in practice and scholarship, primarily within community organizing, activist, and social movement organ-izations. Note that Freeman's argument was not that groups should swing all the way to the opposite extreme and embrace maximally formalized structures. Instead, she advocated for something akin to what scholarship on GSAs is finding to be most effective at cultivating a sense of agency among participants: principled experimentation with different forms of "democratic structuring" (Freeman, 1972, p. 163) that can allow participants to balance the need for formalized structures with the need for flexibility, adaptability, and openness.

Research into participant pathways for GSAs is advancing rapidly, moving past questions like whether involvement tends to be beneficial for participants on average toward more complex questions that account for variance across GSAs and diversity in the interests, needs, identities, and forms of engagement among participants. By utilizing a person–environment fit framework (Calzo et al., 2020), scholars in this area are advancing what is understood about ecological commonality and specificity – concepts described in the introduc-tory chapter to this book. Moreover, research on GSAs is now going beyond considering the features of GSAs in general toward an understanding of the influences of specific meetings on participants' outcomes over time (Poteat et al., 2023a).[4] Those engaged in research and reflective practice with other types of community empowerment processes would be remiss not to consider these insights from studies of GSAs and their relevance to practical strategies and action-oriented research designs in other approaches and contexts.

Examining Different Organizational Approaches to Community Empowerment

The chapters in this book provide many such opportunities for cross-currents of ideas, strategies, research designs, and findings across approaches. Because each chapter describes what is known about psychological, organizational, and community-level dynamics, we can consider transactional[5] dynamics between micro-, meso-, and macro-level processes and outcomes across different approaches and contexts. A perhaps simpler but no less important objective involves comparisons and distinctions between different approaches. Examining approaches side by side enables their differences to be clarified, as well as their relative strengths and emphases. This can yield useful insights for practitioners and grassroots leaders seeking to implement or draw from these approaches in their work. Once they are clearly delineated, however, it is then necessary to again muddy things by looking into how these approaches can influence, feed into, complement, or even compete in local communities. Here I highlight some examples of each of these types of opportunities.

Clarifying Distinctions and Decision-Making

Many of the approaches in this book are described using similar terminology (e.g., "collective action," "community-engaged," "community-based," "participatory") and can involve some of the same types of organizations (e.g., schools, nonprofits, community centers, neighborhood groups). For this reason, it is understandably common for observers and even participants in these efforts to fail to make key distinctions between them. This was apparent recently when colleagues and I edited a themed issue of a journal on community organizing. In response to an open call for papers, we received numerous proposals for articles that were not really addressing community organizing but were instead focused on other approaches discussed in this book (e.g.,

---

[4] This is analogous to studies in other contexts that have empirically differentiated between *setting genotypes* (broader structures such as GSAs) and *setting phenotypes* (settings within these broader structures such as different types of meetings; e.g., Christens & Speer, 2011; Luke et al., 1991).

[5] "Transactional" here refers to the study of changing relations and dynamics from a holistic perspective (see Altman & Rogoff, 1987).

community-based research, community coalitions). In the article introducing the themed issue (Christens et al., 2021), we differentiated these approaches from community organizing while also acknowledging some of their common features and potential points of intersection.

Although they may seem subtle or even trivial, understanding the differences between these approaches can be very consequential. Community coalitions, for instance, have strengths that may make them a preferred approach for addressing certain types of problems, whereas an approach that centers on community-engaged research may make more sense in other situations. Citizens' governance spaces, as described in Chapter 7 by Dzur and Hendriks, involve participants directly in efforts to address social issues. This contrasts with many other approaches that seek, for instance, to change public policies so that institutions will better address issues.

Deciding how to configure collective efforts often requires extensive deliberations among potential participants. The greater the collective understanding of the variety of possibilities, the higher the likelihood that groups will be able to select and pursue approaches that are well suited to their situation and goals. As another example, employment social enterprises (ESEs) are a promising approach for reducing unemployment, for skill-building, and for increasing economic resilience, and as Byrd and Weaver emphasize in Chapter 17, they can be particularly valuable for specific populations such as opportunity youth, formerly incarcerated people, people in recovery, and people experiencing mental health issues. Understanding the relative strengths of ESEs can help those considering approaches of this sort to determine the potential fit with their context and objectives.

Identifying a suitable approach is only the beginning in terms of consequential decisions. Across all these approaches, there are many subtle differences in how efforts can be configured that often profoundly influence whether they are capable of building and sustainably exercising community power to achieve their goals. In Kegler and Bigger's chapter on community coalitions (Chapter 12), for example, they note that "the extent to which these empowerment outcomes are realized, and for whom, depends on who initiates the coalition, who is invited to join the coalition, how the coalition is structured to accommodate diverse voices and life experiences, removal of barriers to participation for those who cannot participate as part of their work responsibilities, and the intentional creation of opportunities for skill development and leadership opportunities" (p. 330). There are parallel complexities in the structure and functioning of each of the approaches described in this book.

Comparisons and Crosscurrents

Paradoxically, clearly distinguishing between approaches only enables one to see the extent to which they are often interrelated, intersecting, or even comingled in practice. Some organizations, for instance, have a broad enough scope that they are simultaneously pursuing multiple approaches (e.g., the United Teen Equality Center described by Byrd and Weaver in Chapter 17). Some approaches tend to be most effective when they adopt features from others. For example, YPAR, as described in chapter by Dickerson, Kornbluh, and Duke (Chapter 22), tends to be most effective when it adopts features of youth organizing approaches, as described in chapters by Conner (Chapter 1) and Tivaringe and Kirshner (Chapter 2). Furthermore, all three of the examples of YPAR projects that Dickerson and colleagues describe in their chapter involve collaborations with university-based researchers and can thus also be viewed from the perspective of community-engaged research as described in Chapter 24 by Haapanen, Wallerstein, and Sanchez-Youngman. However, the ability to intentionally borrow from, mix, or merge elements of various approaches depends on awareness of their (sometimes subtle but crucial) distinctions.

Many approaches can lead directly into or prompt the initiation of others. For example, the municipal youth council described in Chapter 10 by Augsberger and Collins engaged in a participatory budgeting process of the type described in Chapter 8 by Peabody, and the United Teen Equality Center, highlighted by Byrd and Weaver in Chapter 17 for its ESE work, was founded in response to youth organizing. The neighborhood associations described in Chapter 14 by Anderson and Christens are often participants in the community coalitions described in Chapter 12 by Kegler and Bigger.

In other cases, some of these approaches can provide pipelines of participants and community leaders for others (Ginwright, 2010). For instance, in Chapter 23, Contreras, Downing, Greer, and Baldridge describe how community-based education spaces can create the building blocks for organizing (as exemplified in the case of Urban Underground in Milwaukee, Wisconsin). The Design Your Neighborhood action civics curriculum in Nashville, Tennessee – described in Chapter 20 by Morgan and Ballard – has also built a foundation that enabled the creation of a local youth organizing initiative (see Morgan et al., 2022b, 2024). Moreover, creating pipelines for community leadership is explicitly the primary goal of the approach described by Majee, Massengale, Rippel, and Adams in Chapter 11.

As participants and leaders flow between different types of efforts, this can create vectors for the broader adoption of innovative strategies, tactics, models, and methodologies. Many of the chapters in this book describe innovative forms of practice that other types of organizations and efforts could emulate. Here is just a small sample of these: Brazzell (Chapter 6) describes ways that racial justice advocacy organizations are blurring the lines between digital and in-person forms of participation and engagement, and prioritizing culture, community-building, and care in ways that enable participants to find and maintain "political and social homes" (p. 181); Hennessy, Gold-Watts, Pietrzak, Lapoint, and Bell (Chapter 18) describe the potential for participatory arts-based approaches to exert powerful influences not only on those involved in creating art but also through their interactions with broader audiences[6]; Cooper (Chapter 9) describes the increasing use of health impact assessments and racial equity impact assessments to evaluate the potential effects of decisions made in urban planning processes; and Sonn, Agung-Igusti, Jayawardana, Quayle, and Keast (Chapter 19) describe the use of a youth-led digital radio station to resist dominant narratives and shape new public narratives about youth and their community. These all provide potentially promising strategies for other types of efforts to consider incorporating into their work. Chapters by Tivaringe and Kirshner (Chapter 2) and Sonn and colleagues (Chapter 19), furthermore, provide models for decolonial praxis that clearly situate contemporary struggles within their historical and geographic contexts, both addressing immediate concerns and opening possibilities for broader transformative work.

Some approaches can be natural allies to others, particularly those with complementary strengths. The approaches to grassroots organizing and activism described in chapters by Menon and Allen (Chapter 3), Speer (Chapter 4), and Escudero (Chapter 5), for instance, have capabilities that approaches rooted in (or even involving) public institutions typically lack. For example, participants in the planning processes described in Chapter 9 by Cooper and the youth councils described in Chapter 10 by Augsberger and Collins often gain useful insights into how consequential decisions are made and who is exerting influence on decision-makers, but they are often limited in terms of how much power and influence they can build or exercise through these prescribed participatory and/or consultative roles. Community organizing groups can exert outside pressure on institutions to hold them accountable to residents' concerns that are identified through participatory deliberative processes (e.g., Haapanen et al., 2024). When there is alignment between participatory processes and more autonomous grassroots organizing, this can be a particularly potent combination.

Although there are many examples of this type of complementarity, however, there can also be trade-offs or ways in which some approaches may detract from or limit the possibilities of others. For example, in Chapter 12, Kegler and Bigger note that for some organizations participating in coalitions there can be a loss of autonomy and control. Local groups often compete for resources and participants and sometimes even jockey for turf, visibility, or credit for collective accomplishments. Some approaches, furthermore, can accentuate the weaknesses of others. For example, note that many of the organizations involved in creating, funding, and studying the types of empowering community settings described in this book lack any semblance of workplace democracy or egalitarianism in the workplace (they are most

---

[6] Many of the other approaches described in the book do incorporate participatory arts, such as the Asian/Pacific Islander Youth Promoting Advocacy and Leadership (AYPAL) youth organizing initiative described by Conner in Chapter 1.

often nonprofits governed by boards of directors) that is being pursued by the worker cooperatives described in Chapter 16 by Meyers, Pinto, Schlachter, and Prushinskaya. Can those working toward egalitarianism and participatory democracy in communities and society also build more of it into the organizational settings and institutional structures where they work?

Furthermore, many of the challenges faced by those seeking to build community power can be similar or parallel to those encountered by others taking different approaches. For example, many organizations and approaches have been segregated by age (e.g., adult-centric organizations that exclude young people) and could benefit from insights into how to become more intergenerational (see Chapter 13 by Collura, Raffle, Joseph, and Stevens). Most participatory efforts, moreover, experienced existential threats to their work and organizational sustainability during the quarantine periods of the COVID-19 pandemic (Cohen et al., 2022; Fatima & Josephson, 2023). In contrast, some efforts face unique challenges due to their contexts but can nevertheless help to inform efforts elsewhere. For example, Hu, Wang, and Lian, in their chapter entitled "State-Led Community (Dis)empowerment in China" (Chapter 15), describe how gains in the first dimension of power (situational) can be achieved simultaneously with setbacks in the second (institutional) and third (systemic) dimensions.[7] This is an incisive point with applicability across a range of approaches and contexts. What might appear to be progress toward more democratic and participatory forms of engagement may in fact only be reinforcing power imbalances.

A multidimensional perspective on power can help to determine how and when participatory processes are truly building community power. Broadly speaking, claims around empowerment should be scrutinized from this perspective. Some of the chapters in this book provide examples of this critical orientation, and some contest abuses of the term "empowerment" within the approaches that they describe. For example, Contreras, Downing, Greer, and Baldridge (Chapter 23) note the potential for some of what gets described as youth empowerment practices in community-based educational spaces to reinforce unequal power dynamics (such as those between youth/community organizations and governmental funders) rather than challenging them.

Thinking Holistically

Each of these approaches can create crucial niches in broader community empowerment processes. Many people who are active in their communities become involved and/or interface with many of the types of efforts described in this book. When any of these approaches are operating effectively, they also have the potential to generate what Meyers and colleagues (in Chapter 16) describe as *civic spillover* effects, when what is learned and what is experienced

---

[7] These three dimensions of power, described briefly in the introductory chapter and in several other chapters of this book, drawn on work by Lukes (1974) and Gaventa (1980).

in one issue domain or form of collective action influence and build momentum across others. These sorts of ripple effects remain generally poorly understood, however, because studies either tend to focus on specific approaches, ignoring ways they are influencing and are influenced by other processes taking place in communities, or tend to study people's sociopolitical capacities without sufficient differentiation of the types of settings in which they have been civically active. To what extent do the skills, knowledge, perspectives, and propensities that people develop through participation in any one of these efforts enable them to be more effective in others as well? In which cases are they highly specific and applicable only within certain types of organizations or collective efforts? Are there common inflection points in civic trajectories from certain experiences and types of involvement (e.g., Morgan et al., 2022a; Terriquez, 2015)?

Similar questions persist about the local landscapes of these types of approaches. For example, how many of these various sorts of efforts should be operating in a given city or region to provide residents there with the best chances of achieving their goals? What should the scope or scale of each individual effort be? Among those who grasp the potential of these approaches, there tends to be a simplistic notion that *more* will be better, both in quantity of organizations/efforts and in their size or ability to engage participants. For instance, organizations that are leading successful initiatives of various sorts will often seek to operate at larger scales and/or to increase the scope of their work (e.g., the Center for Economic Opportunities as described in Chapter 17 by Byrd and Weaver). Scaling up can enable broader impacts, but growth can also create tensions regarding the depth and/or autonomy of local efforts. Those pursuing scale and aiming to increase the quantity of civic opportunities need to take these tensions and contradictions seriously and consider not only breadth but also depth, quality, culture, leadership development, connections between local efforts, and sustainability (e.g., Kirshner et al., 2021). This is especially true when larger organizations or networks become enmeshed with philanthropic foundations, which will often promote market-based models, metrics, and mentalities that valorize growth (Eikenberry, 2009; McGoey, 2015).

External supports and resources for local efforts can be vital in some cases, but there are trade-offs and potential tensions that must be kept in mind. Kegler and Bigger (Chapter 12), for instance, note that external resources and technical assistance are key to the effectiveness of many community coalitions. They also describe the possibility for coalitions to develop a dependency on external funding and how this can limit autonomy and stifle the potential for empowerment processes to take place through coalitions. Policies that seek to cultivate local civic/community engagement can be similarly thorny, as exemplified by the Minneapolis Neighborhood Revitalization Program discussed in Chapter 14 by Anderson and Christens. When resources flow from government agencies to community groups, moreover, there is the possibility that this represents a neoliberalization process, in which functions and services that were once the responsibility of the public sector are pushed onto nonprofit and voluntary groups, which must then compete to retain their contracts and become less likely to challenge actors in the public sector.[8] In some contexts, there may be more direct or overt forms of state control, as discussed in Chapter 15 by Hu, Wang, and Lian.

Advancing Understanding

Clearly there is much still to be learned about community empowerment processes. Within and across each of these types of participatory approaches, there is a great deal of variance in organizational structures, processes, and norms in the settings in which people come together to try to bring about changes and improve their communities. These differences are sometimes codified into explicit models that can guide practices (e.g., the models for congregation-based organizing discussed in Chapter 4 by Speer). Models of this sort can be invaluable for summarizing and transmitting a theory of how to create change. Even among those approaches that have prominent guiding models, however, much of the everyday decision-making remains improvisational as people adapt practices and processes to the particularities of their contexts and concerns. Most approaches, though, do not have well-established guiding frameworks or models, so practices and processes tend to be even more varied and idiosyncratic.

This variety is reflected in the many different types of organizations that seek to cultivate empowerment processes. Collectively, these organizations are often referred to as "mediating institutions" (e.g., Flanagan et al., 2011; Mendel, 2003; Todd & Allen, 2011) since they function as bridges between residents and the larger institutions, systems, structures, and environments that affect their lives. Acting alone, residents' ability to influence or change these macro-level entities (e.g., local governmental agencies, corporations) is of course very limited. The approaches discussed in this book work to convene people for collective endeavors intending to exert systemic influences. Variance in these collective participatory processes across different organizational types therefore shapes (1) the experiences, skills, knowledge/perspectives, and relationships among residents (micro-level dynamics), (2) power relations and dynamics at a community level (macro-level dynamics), and (3) the ways that residents can collectively interface with systems in their communities (transactions between micro- and macro-level dynamics mediated through meso-level dynamics). Learning more about these mediating institutions and the various approaches that they can take is therefore crucial

---

[8] See Elwood (2002), a study discussed in the chapter on neighborhood associations (Chapter 14) by Anderson and Christens.

for sociopolitical change efforts, but there are noteworthy challenges for those seeking to build on what is known.

One challenge is the prevailing program evaluation mindset that institutional decision-makers (e.g., funders, policymakers) will often bring to their work with community groups. This mindset identifies a specific problem (e.g., violence, substance misuse), then seeks efficacious and efficient ways of making progress on measurable indicators of the magnitude of that problem. Groups that are funded to work toward progress on the problem are often held accountable to externally determined metrics that tend to miss the complexities of both community empowerment processes and the issues and problems that they are working to address. For instance, evaluation designs often ignore the interconnectedness of the issues facing communities and the need for grassroots groups to remain flexible as they continuously adapt their work to the most pressing concerns of residents (see Haapanen et al., in press).

In their chapter on community-based educational spaces (Chapter 23), Contreras, Downing, Greer, and Baldridge point out that policymakers, funders, and researchers/evaluators have often established metrics that reinforce deficit-based notions of low-income Black and Latinx youth and/or impose a narrow view of the contributions of youth workers. Metrics such as the number of young people served, they point out, can turn administrative reporting into a numbers game and can play a role in reinforcing neoliberal managerialism (parallel concerns are noted in other contexts – for example, in Chapter 6 by Brazzell on racial justice advocacy). Consider this quote from Chapter 23 by Contreras and colleagues (p. 595):

> ... youth workers who are required to abide by market-based logic models inadvertently fall short of asset-based, egalitarian, and humanizing approaches. Instead, their interventions focus on altering individual youth behavior rather than focusing on broader structural, institutional, or societal issues. Consequently, youth workers engage in praxis where deficit-based, individualistic, and pathological notions of marginalized communities intimately influence the youth worker's inductive processes of thinking and acting (Carpenter, 2017). Funders, evaluators, and policymakers have the responsibility to rethink their assumptions, practices, and approaches to their work. In doing so, they will be able to collaborate with youth and youth workers to create equitable learning environments in community-based educational spaces that foster rich social networks and leverage the power-building capabilities of these spaces.

Many contributors to this book would echo this call by Contreras and colleagues for external actors and entities (e.g., funders, evaluators, researchers, and policymakers) to collaborate with community-based and resident-led groups on knowledge generation. The chapters on YPAR (Chapter 22 by Dickerson, Kornbluh, and Duke) and community-engaged research (Chapter 24 by Haapanen, Wallerstein, and Sanchez-Youngman) provide the most detail on this perspective and the various ways it can be implemented. However, collaborative and community-engaged research approaches are not a panacea. In Chapter 24, for instance, Haapanen and colleagues stress that a risk of community-engaged research is an imposition of academic and/or disciplinary lenses onto community organizations. They call instead for engaged research that centers the perspectives of participants and residents.

Designing research in collaboration with community groups is a complex endeavor that is the focus of a growing body of literature. Much of this literature, however, remains narrowly focused on the interactions between researchers and community collaborators and is less attentive to the community power dynamics in which these collaborations are taking place.[9] Haapanen and colleagues (Chapter 24) urge engaged researchers to consider not only power dynamics within community–academic partnerships but also the ways that power is operating outside of them and how these partnerships can be strategically positioned within local ecologies to reduce power imbalances. They identify epistemological aspects of power relations and the ways that community-engaged research can intervene to create greater knowledge democracy, yet they acknowledge many barriers, including the ways that universities and university-based researchers tend to organize and privilege certain types of knowledge.

This last point is an enduring challenge for those seeking to deepen understanding of the types of processes described in this book. The diverse set of disciplines that study community empowerment processes bring their own orientations, emphases, conceptual frameworks, and terminologies. There are some commonalities across the relevant social science disciplines, but many things must be translated or bridged. For example, Kegler and Bigger note in their chapter on coalitions (Chapter 12) that the interdisciplinary nature of scholarship on that topic has led to inconsistencies in research approaches and terminology. Their chapter contrasts an emphasis on community capacity, which has tended to be more common in studies of coalitions, with an emphasis on community empowerment, which, "while occasionally used interchangeably with community capacity, typically has a more explicit focus on the process through which communities gain control and self-agency" (p. 321). Comparable complexity exists in the research literature on most of the approaches described in this book, and, like Kegler and Bigger, many of the contributors are engaged in inter- and trans-disciplinary work that seeks to bridge – or at least map and navigate – these disjunctures.

Zooming Out

To some, the types of locally focused and community-based efforts described in this book may seem paltry or piecemeal in comparison with the

---

[9] Stoecker and Falcón's (2022) edited volume is oriented toward addressing this deficiency in the literature.

magnitude of the interrelated societal and global crises we are facing, including growing economic inequality, environmental destruction, climate change, erosion of democracy, and continuation of long-standing forms of oppression and marginalization. Critics from this viewpoint might advocate for greater emphasis on attempts to achieve wider-scale changes (e.g., national and international policy and politics). However, attempts to engage people in large-scale political and policy change efforts are often individualistic, transactional, and short-lived and therefore ultimately disempowering (Boyte, 2004; Speer & Han, 2018).

Like many of the contributors to this book, I believe it is crucial to find ways that more people can be meaningfully engaged in change and community-building efforts at every scale, but we must not overlook the local organizations that create settings that engage people deeply in efforts to change systems that directly affect their lives. These organizations and processes are indispensable generators of social power. We should be working to understand and amplify the potential for these efforts to reciprocally influence larger-scale change processes, including through the interplay between various types of efforts and multiscalar networks of locally based groups.

Some defenders of unjust systems do seem attentive to the connections between community-building, grassroots leadership development, and efforts to bring about social change on larger scales. For instance, years after serving a prison sentence for his role as a coconspirator in the Watergate scandal, John Ehrlichman was interviewed about US drug policies. Ehrlichman had been a top aide to US President Richard Nixon, who had coined the term "War on Drugs" as he launched what would become a notorious set of harsh policies and law enforcement practices. "You want to know what this was really all about?" Ehrlichman asked his interviewer (Baum, 2016, p. 24), and he then went on to explain:

> The Nixon campaign in 1968, and the Nixon White House after that, had two enemies: the antiwar left and Black people. You understand what I'm saying? We knew we couldn't make it illegal to be either against the war or Black, but by getting the public to associate the hippies with marijuana and Blacks with heroin, and then criminalizing both heavily, we could disrupt those communities. We could arrest their leaders, raid their homes, break up their meetings, and vilify them night after night on the evening news. Did we know we were lying about the drugs? Of course we did.

In this sinister and corrupt admission, note the emphasis on disrupting communities, arresting leaders, and breaking up meetings. According to Ehrlichman, Nixon and his collaborators understood that these were ways to suppress potential challenges to status quo power relations at a national scale. There are many other examples of dominant groups entrenching their power by preventing those who are oppressed from meeting, organizing, and building community leadership at the local level (e.g., Gaventa, 1980; King, 2004).

Although many community empowerment efforts start (or even remain) small, they provide venues for engagement that develop relationships, trust, and shared commitments to collective goals (Flanagan et al., 2011; Medellin et al., 2021). In aggregate, the types of efforts described in this book are capable of increasing "the weight of social power" (Wright, 2013, p. 22) in societies (relative to economic and state power). They can act as "meso-mobilization structures" (Clemens & Minkoff, 2004, p. 156), engaging people and groups in activities that can have "radiating impacts" (Rappaport, 1987, p. 132) on both micro- and macro-level dynamics (Morris, 1984).

This potential can be glimpsed in many of the contributions to this book. For instance, in Chapter 2, Tivaringe and Kirshner describe the evolution of youth organizing and activist campaigns in South Africa over several decades. There have been reciprocal influences from the local to the national, with actions at each level feeding into and generating actions at the other. In some cases, single initiatives are operating and having impacts at multiple levels, such as the multilevel intervention against domestic violence in India described in Chapter 3 by Menon and Allen. Likewise, in Chapter 4, Speer describes how local community organizing around public transit in Minnesota resulted in improvements in local transportation infrastructure and alterations to US federal transportation policy.

These types of reverberations between meso- and macro-level dynamics, however, remain only hazily understood. There does seem to be movement in this direction, however, from multiple vantage points. For instance, Han et al. (2022) recently called for political scientists to examine various strategies that civic organizations employ and their relative ability to influence public policy. Scholars and leaders focused on public health are increasingly viewing local community power-building as key to addressing health inequities through policy and systems changes (e.g., Heller et al., 2023; Iton et al., 2022; Speer et al., 2020). Scholars and practitioners in education and youth development are experimenting with ways of linking, scaling, and sustaining what can often be fragmented or isolated efforts to engage young people in civic inquiry and action (e.g., Flanagan et al., 2022; Kirshner et al., 2021) Psychologists, social work researchers, and others, meanwhile, are building on traditions of empowerment-focused research and practice in their fields (e.g., Hoffman, 1978; Rappaport, 1981), but in many cases they are now doing so with a clearer emphasis on community power and policy change (e.g., Evans & Fernandez-Burgos, 2023; Fernandes-Jesus et al., 2020).

This book draws these complementary lines of work from different disciplines and fields of practice together to build shared understanding and shared purposes across them. Regardless of your point of entry and path that have brought you here as a reader, I hope that this book generates new ideas about how to build community power, how to develop new insights into community empowerment processes, and how to contribute those insights to conversations across disciplines, domains of practice, and different geographic and sociopolitical contexts. Our collective ability to make progress on both long-standing and emerging societal crises will depend in no small part on how effective these types of efforts can be at accomplishing their goals.

References

Altman, I., & Rogoff, B. (1987). World views in psychology: Trait, interactional, organismic, and transactional perspectives. In D. Stokols & I. Altman (Eds.), *Handbook of environmental psychology* (pp. 7–40). Wiley.

Baum, D. (2016, April). *Legalize it all: How to win the war on drugs.* Harper's Magazine. https://harpers.org/archive/2016/04/legalize-it-all/

Boyte, H. C. (2004). *Everyday politics: Reconnecting citizens and public life.* University of Pennsylvania Press.

Calzo, J. P., Poteat, V. P., Yoshikawa, H., Russell, S. T., & Bogart, L. M. (2020). Person–environment fit and positive youth development in the context of high school gay–straight alliances. *Journal of Research on Adolescence, 30*(S1), 158–176.

Carpenter, S. (2017). "Modeling" youth work: Logic models, neoliberalism, and community praxis. *International Studies in Sociology of Education, 29*(2), 105–120.

Christens, B. D. (2019). *Community power and empowerment.* Oxford University Press.

Christens, B. D., & Speer, P. W. (2011). Contextual influences on participation in community organizing: A multilevel longitudinal study. *American Journal of Community Psychology, 47*(3–4), 253–263.

Christens, B. D., Gupta, J., & Speer, P. W. (2021). Community organizing: Studying the development and exercise of grassroots power. *Journal of Community Psychology, 49*(8), 3001–3016.

Clemens, E. S., & Minkoff, D. C. (2004). Beyond the iron law: Rethinking the place of organizations in social movement research. In D. A. Snow, S. A. Soule, & H Kriesi (Eds.), *The Blackwell companion to social movements* (pp. 155–170). Blackwell Publishing.

Cohen, A. K., Brahinsky, R., Coll, K. M., & Dotson, M. P. (2022). "We keep each other safe": San Francisco Bay area community-based organizations respond to enduring crises in the Covid-19 era. *RSF: The Russell Sage Foundation Journal of the Social Sciences, 8*(8), 70–87.

Davis, B., Stafford, M. B. R., & Pullig, C. (2014). How gay–straight alliance groups mitigate the relationship between gay-bias victimization and adolescent suicide attempts. *Journal of the American Academy of Child and Adolescent Psychiatry, 53*, 1271–1278.

Eikenberry, A. M. (2009). Refusing the market: A democratic discourse for voluntary and nonprofit organizations. *Nonprofit and Voluntary Sector Quarterly, 38*(4), 582–596.

Elwood, S. (2002). Neighborhood revitalization through "collaboration": Assessing the implications of neoliberal urban policy at the grassroots. *GeoJournal, 58* (2/3), 121–130.

Evans, S. D., & Fernandez-Burgos, M. (2023). From empowerment to community power in participatory budgeting. *American Behavioral Scientist, 67*(4), 578–592.

Fatima, N., & Josephson, J. (2023). Pandemic-era organizing. *Urban Affairs Review.* https://doi.org/10.1177/10780874231189669

Fernandes-Jesus, M., Barnes, B., & Diniz, R. F. (2020). Communities reclaiming power and social justice in the face of climate change. *Community Psychology in Global Perspective, 6*(2), 1–21.

Flanagan, C. A., Gallay, E., & Pykett, A. (2022). Urban youth and the environmental commons: Rejuvenating civic engagement through civic science. *Journal of Youth Studies, 25*(6), 692–708.

Flanagan, C. A., Martínez, M. L., Cumsille, P., & Ngomane, T. (2011). Youth civic development: Theorizing a domain with evidence from different cultural contexts. *New Directions for Child and Adolescent Development, 134,* 95–109.

Freeman, J. (1972). The tyranny of structurelessness. *Berkeley Journal of Sociology, 17,* 151–164.

Gaventa, J. (1980). *Power and powerlessness: Quiescence and rebellion in an Appalachian valley.* University of Illinois Press.

Ginwright, S. (2010). *Building a pipeline for justice: Understanding youth organizing and the leadership pipeline.* Funders' Collaborative for Youth Organizing. https://fcyo.org/resources/ops-10-building-a-pipeline-for-justice-understanding-youth-organizing-and-the-leadership-pipeline

Haapanen, K. A., Christens, B. D., Cooper, D. G., & Jurinsky, J. (2024). Alliance-building for equity and justice: An inter-organizational perspective. *Evaluation and Program Planning, 102,* 102382.

Haapanen, K. A., Christens, B. D., Speer, P. W., & Freeman, H. E. (in press). Narrative change in grassroots community organizing: A study of initiatives in Michigan and Ohio. *American Journal of Community Psychology.* https://doi.org/10.1002/ajcp.12708

Han, H., Campbell, A. L., & McKenna, E. (2022). Civic feedbacks: Linking collective action, organizational strategy, and influence over public policy. *Perspectives on Politics.* https://doi.org/10.1017/S1537592722000986

Heller, J. C., Little, O. M., Faust, V., Tran, P., Givens, M. L., Ayers, J., & Farhang, L. (2023). Theory in action: Public health and community power building for health equity. *Journal of Public Health Management and Practice, 29*(1), 33–38.

Hoffman, C. (1978). Empowerment movements and mental health: Locus of control and commitment to the United Farm Workers. *Journal of Community Psychology, 6*(3), 216–221.

Iton, A., Ross, R. K., & Tamber, P. S. (2022). Building community power to dismantle policy-based structural inequity in population health. *Health Affairs, 41*(12), 1763–1771.

King, P. (2004). Ida B. Wells and the management of violence. *Critical Review of International Social and Political Philosophy, 7*(4), 111–146.

Kirshner, B., Zion, S., Lopez, S., & Hipolito-Delgado, C. (2021). A theory of change for scaling critical civic inquiry. *Peabody Journal of Education, 96*(3), 294–306.

Luke, D. A., Rappaport, J., & Seidman, E. (1991). Setting phenotypes in a mutual help organization: Expanding behavior setting theory. *American Journal of Community Psychology, 19*(1), 147–167.

Lukes, S. (1974). *Power: A radical view*. MacMillan.

Marx, R. A., & Kettrey, H. H. (2016). Gay–straight alliances are associated with lower levels of school-based victimization of LGBTQ+ youth: A systematic review and meta-analysis. *Journal of Youth and Adolescence, 45*, 1269–1282.

McGoey, L. (2015). *No such thing as a free gift: The Gates Foundation and the price of philanthropy*. Verso.

Medellin, P. J., Speer, P. W., Christens, B. D., & Gupta, J. (2021). Transformation to leadership: Learning about self, the community, the organization, and the system. *Journal of Community Psychology, 49*(8), 3122–3140.

Mendel, S. C. (2003). The ecology of games between public policy and private action: Nonprofit community organizations as bridging and mediating institutions. *Nonprofit Management & Leadership, 13*(3), 229–236.

Miceli, M. (2005). *Standing out, standing together: The social and political impact of gay–straight alliances*. Routledge.

Morgan, K. Y., Anderson, K. M., & Christens, B. D. (2022a). Pathways to community leadership: Transitions, turning points, and generational continuity. *Applied Developmental Science*. https://doi.org/10.1080/10888691.2022.2154211

Morgan, K. Y., Anderson, K. M., KaiKai, J., Shaltaf, L., & Christens, B. D. (2024). "Real change takes time": Building multi-dimensional youth community power in a participatory design collective. In J. Conner (Ed.), *Handbook on youth activism* (pp. 320–336). Edward Elgar Publishing.

Morgan, K. Y., Christens, B. D., & Gibson, M. (2022b). Design Your Neighborhood: The evolution of a city-wide urban design learning initiative in Nashville, Tennessee. In R. Stoecker & A. Falcón (Eds.), *Handbook on participatory action research and community development* (pp. 281–300). Edward Elgar Publishing.

Morris, A. D. (1984). *The origins of the civil rights movement*. Free Press.

Poteat, V. P., Calzo, J. P., Sherwood, S. H., Marx, R. A., O'Brien, M. D., Dangora, A., Salgin, L., & Lipkin, A. (2023a). Gender–sexuality alliance meeting experiences predict weekly variation in hope among LGBTQ+ youth. *Child Development, 94*(4), e215–e230.

Poteat, V. P., Calzo, J. P., & Yoshikawa, H. (2016). Promoting youth agency through dimensions of gay–straight alliance involvement and conditions that maximize associations. *Journal of Youth and Adolescence, 45*(7), 1438–1451.

Poteat, V. P., Godfrey, E. B., Brion-Meisels, G., & Calzo, J. P. (2020). Development of youth advocacy and sociopolitical efficacy as dimensions of critical consciousness within gender–sexuality alliances. *Developmental Psychology, 56*(6), 1207–1219.

Poteat, V. P., Gray, M. L., Digiovanni, C. D., Lipkin, A., Mundy-shephard, A., Perrotti, J., Scheer, J. R., & Shaw, M. P. (2015). Contextualizing gay–straight alliances: Student, advisor, and structural factors related to positive youth development among members. *Child Development, 86*(1), 176–193.

Poteat, V. P., O'Brien, M. D., Yang, M. K., Rosenbach, S. B., & Lipkin, A. (2022). Youth advocacy varies in relation to adult advisor characteristics and practices in gender–sexuality alliances. *Applied Developmental Science, 26*(3), 460–470.

Poteat, V. P., Yoshikawa, H., Rosenbach, S. B., Sherwood, S. H., Finch, E. K., & Calzo, J. P. (2023b). GSA advocacy predicts reduced depression disparities between LGBQ+ and heterosexual youth in schools. *Journal of Clinical Child & Adolescent Psychology*. https://doi.org/10.1080/15374416.2023.2169924

Rappaport, J. (1981). In praise of paradox: A social policy of empowerment over prevention. *American Journal of Community Psychology, 9*(1), 1–25.

Rappaport, J. (1987). Terms of empowerment/exemplars of prevention: Toward a theory for community psychology. *American Journal of Community Psychology, 15*(2), 121–148.

Speer, P. W., & Han, H. (2018). Re-engaging social relationships and collective dimensions of organizing to revive democratic practice. *Journal of Social and Political Psychology, 6*(2), 745–758.

Speer, P. W., Gupta, J., & Haapanen, K. A. (2020). *Developing community power for health equity: A landscape analysis of current research and theory.* Robert Wood Johnson Foundation.

Stoecker, R., & Falcón, A. (Eds.). (2022). *Handbook on participatory action research and community development.* Edward Elgar.

Terriquez, V. (2015). Training young activists: Grassroots organizing and youths' civic and political trajectories. *Sociological Perspectives, 58*(2), 223–242.

Todd, N. R., & Allen, N. E. (2011). Religious congregations as mediating structures for social justice: A multilevel examination. *American Journal of Community Psychology, 48*(3), 222–237.

Wright, E. O. (2013). Transforming capitalism through real utopias. *American Sociological Review, 78*(1), 1–25.

Contributor Details

JOHANNA REED ADAMS, PhD, MPA, is an associate Professor Emerita in the Department of Social Sciences in the College of Food and Natural Resources with the University of Missouri System. Her early work focused on rural and suburban communities in northeast Missouri brokering resources of University of Missouri Extension by providing skills and knowledge created through Land Grant University research. She primarily works in the field of community leadership development in curriculum development and research. She codesigned, led, and coached the Leadership Online for Today program targeted at millennials, which provided the opportunity to build social and human capital through an online platform, along with the Step Up to Leadership curricula for underserved audiences across the US and Canada. She has a PhD in Educational Leadership and Policy Analysis, an MPA, and a BA in Political Science – all from University of Missouri–Columbia.

RAMA P. AGUNG-IGUSTI, PhD, is a research Associate in the School of Indigenous Studies at the University of Western Australia. Before this, he completed his doctoral research in community psychology at the Institute of Health and Sport at Victoria University, located on the lands of the Woi Wurrung and Boon Wurrung people of the Kulin Nation. His research interest has been the ways racially marginalized communities respond to structural and cultural violence. A primary focus has been the creation of self-determined alternative settings and the mobilization of community arts and creative practice as public pedagogy and a mechanism for transformative social change.

NICOLE E. ALLEN, PhD, is Professor and Chair of the Department of Human and Organizational Development at Vanderbilt University. Her research examines systems change processes in the community response to social issues (especially intimate partner violence and sexual assault) and the role of collaborative settings in facilitating such change; individuals' experiences as they navigate complex systems (such as criminal justice, human service, and health care, as well as informal systems); and the effectiveness of social interventions that aim to alter the contexts of individuals' lives to promote health and well-being. Dr Allen conducts primarily field-based research and often works in collaboration with community partners responding to gender-based violence in the community, including the campus community. She is the Editor-in-Chief of the *American Journal of Community Psychology*. Dr Allen also provides support to the implementation of the Community Advocacy Project (CAP) model, an empirically supported approach to work with intimate partner violence survivors.

KAYLA M. ANDERSON, MEd, is a PhD student in Community Research and Action at Vanderbilt University. Her research examines how individuals collectively respond to local issues within the built and natural environments and how engagement in these efforts can lead to the development of collective power and empowerment. She specifically utilizes action research and community-based methods to study the impacts of environmental degradation on community health and well-being and the ways in which the built environment impacts young people's ability to thrive in urban environments.

ASTRAEA AUGSBERGER, PhD, is an associate professor at Boston University School of Social Work. Her research examines youth and family engagement in program and policy decision-making in multiple systems including municipal government, child welfare, health care, and education. Her research has been shaped by over fifteen years of clinical social work practice experience working with children, youth, and families involved in various systems. Dr Augsberger has published multiple peer-reviewed articles (in journals including *Children and Youth Services Review*, *Journal of Adolescent Research*, and *National Civic Review*), presented at national and international conferences, and served as an expert advisor on youth engagement strategies and best practices to federal, state, and local agencies.

BIANCA J. BALDRIDGE, PhD, is an associate professor of Education with expertise in community-based education and critical youth work practice at the Harvard Graduate School of Education. Baldridge's research explores the sociopolitical context of community-based youth work and critically examines the confluence of race, class, and gender and their impacts on educational reforms that shape community-based spaces engaging Black youth in the US. In addition, she explores the organizational and pedagogical practices employed by youth workers amid educational reforms and restructuring.

PARISSA JAHROMI BALLARD, PhD, is an associate professor of Family and Community Medicine at the Wake Forest University School of Medicine. Her research focuses on understanding how young people engage with their communities, increasing equitable and meaningful opportunities for youth voice in communities, and understanding how community engagement is related to healthy youth development.

ANA BESS MOYER BELL, MA, RDT, is a drama therapist, applied theater artist, and commissioned playwright. She is the Executive Director of 2nd Act, a national nonprofit with the mission to change the ways people and communities respond to the impacts of substance use through theatre and drama therapy. She specializes in treating trauma, grief, and addiction. She has practiced and taught drama therapy nationally and internationally. Mrs Moyer Bell is on the advisory board at the Rhode Island Department of Health that created the medical regulations for the nation's first legal harm reduction centers. She is a senior advisor to Rhode Island Governor Daniel J. McKee on substance use, harm reduction, and recovery. She is proud to be a member of the recovery community.

LAUREN M. BIGGER, MPH, is a doctoral student in the Department of Behavioral, Social and Health Education Sciences in the Rollins School of Public Health at Emory University. Her primary research interests are in implementation science and community-based approaches to understanding health inequities, including what contextual factors contribute to community capacity. She currently employs mixed methods to evaluate a community-based rural health equity initiative. Ms Bigger holds a master's degree in Public Health from Northeastern University and a Bachelor of Arts in Communication of Science and Technology from Vanderbilt University.

MELANIE BRAZZELL, MA, is a social movement researcher, a predoctoral fellow at the P3 Lab (Johns Hopkins University) and a graduate student and Chancellor's fellow at the University of California–Santa Barbara. Melanie recently authored the *Building Structure Shapes* report based on a collaboration with the Realizing Democracy Project and movement partners including Color Of Change. Melanie's other strand of research builds off of their experience over the past fifteen years organizing for transformative justice alternatives to prison and policing for gendered harm under the umbrella of the What Really Makes Us Safe? Project.

KYMBERLY L. BYRD, PhD, is Director of Impact Services at ResultsLab, a social enterprise that propels organizations, communities, and networks to the next level of impact by providing strategic design and capacity-building for data-informed decision-making. Her research examines social enterprise as a pathway to economic opportunity. Her research interests include: (1) social enterprise and entrepreneurship combating postincarceration unemployment and underemployment; (2) social enterprises providing wraparound services to their employees; and (3) not-for-profit social enterprises that utilize market-based strategies to support the financial sustainability of their organizations.

BRIAN D. CHRISTENS, PhD, is Professor of Human and Organizational Development at Vanderbilt University, where he directs the PhD program in

Community Research and Action. His research is focused on how different organizational approaches to collective action – and different interorganizational network dynamics – can lead to changes in systems that benefit communities. His research also seeks to understand sociopolitical development processes among participants in these types of change efforts. He is the author of *Community Power and Empowerment* (Oxford University Press, 2019).

MARY ELIZABETH COLLINS, PhD, is a professor at the Boston University School of Social Work. Her research focuses on vulnerable young people, the systemic inequities they face, and the policy and program support that can facilitate a positive life trajectory. Currently, she is researching the employment and training systems available to youth in foster care, including the opportunities for young people to have voice in policy decisions. Dr Collins is the author of *Macro Perspectives on Youth Aging Out of Foster Care* (NASW Press, 2015) and over ninety published articles and book chapters. In 2011–2012 she was a Fulbright Scholar in Vietnam.

JESSICA J. COLLURA, PhD, is a senior research associate at the Ohio Education Research Center in the John Glenn College of Public Affairs at The Ohio State University. She received her doctorate in Civil Society and Community Research from the University of Wisconsin–Madison. Jessica's work focuses on engaging young people in local settings to promote the healthy development of youth and communities. Prior to attending graduate school, Jessica was a high school English teacher in Camden, New Jersey.

JERUSHA CONNER, PhD, is Professor of Education at Villanova University, where she directs the graduate program in Education. Her research focuses on youth activism and organizing, student engagement, and student voice. She authored *The New Student Activists* (Johns Hopkins University Press, 2020) and edited the *Handbook on Youth Activism* (Edward Elgar Publishing, 2024).

MOISÉS G. CONTRERAS is a PhD student in Education at Harvard University. He earned his MA in Educational Policy Studies from the University of Wisconsin–Madison. Contreras is interested in the promise and potential of liberatory and humanizing education occurring within community-based educational spaces. He particularly aims to examine the relationships between marginalized youth and youth workers and the window they provide to reimagining education and educational spaces.

DANIEL G. COOPER, PhD, is Senior Director of Research at the Metropolitan Planning Council (MPC) in Chicago. His applied research examines various aspects of urban inequality and public policy. He has worked with numerous organizations, policy change collaboratives, and organizing efforts on issues including housing and community development, violence prevention, youth development, justice system reform, environmental justice, and health equity. He is coauthor of the book *The War on Neighborhoods: Policing, Prison, and Punishment in a Divided City* (Beacon Press, 2018) – a narrative-driven exploration of the impacts of urban blight and incarceration in Chicago and a new vision for repairing urban neighborhoods. He has a PhD in Community Research and Action from Vanderbilt University and a master's degree in Urban Planning and Policy from the University of Illinois Chicago.

KIMALEE DICKERSON, PhD, JD, is an Assistant Professor in the School of Government at the University of North Carolina at Chapel Hill. She earned her PhD from the University of Virginia School of Education and Development and her JD from the University of North Carolina at Chapel Hill. As an applied researcher, Dr Dickerson uses qualitative and participatory approaches to explore how public-sector leaders and organizations can build more equitable organizations and communities.

VIRGINIA DOWNING is a PhD candidate in Educational Policy Studies in the social sciences concentration at the University of Wisconsin–Madison. Virginia's research interest surrounds community involvement within and around schools and the relationship between community-based and educational spaces.

ADRIENNE M. DUKE, PhD, is an Associate Professor and Extension Specialist in the Human Development and Family Sciences Department at Auburn University. Dr Duke is an applied researcher who incorporates a participatory and positive youth development approach to program design and program evaluation. Her research broadly focuses on adolescent health and well-being and ways that programs that occur within and outside of school settings can better serve the youth they seek to support.

ALBERT W. DZUR, PhD, is Distinguished Research Professor in Political Science and Philosophy at Bowling Green State University. His research focuses on citizen participation and power-sharing innovations in criminal justice, public administration, and education. He is the author of *Democracy Inside: Participatory Innovation in Unlikely Places* (Oxford University Press, 2019), *Rebuilding Public Institutions Together: Professionals and Citizens in a Participatory Democracy* (Cornell University Press, 2017), *Punishment, Participatory Democracy, and the Jury* (Oxford University Press, 2012), and *Democratic Professionalism: Citizen Participation and the Reconstruction of Professional Ethics, Identity, and Practice* (Penn State University Press, 2008) and a coeditor, with Ian Loader and Richard Sparks, of *Democratic Theory and Mass Incarceration* (Oxford University Press, 2016). His interviews with democratic innovators appear in *Boston Review*, *The Good Society*,

International Journal of Restorative Justice (where he is an Associate Editor), and *National Civic Review* (where he is a Contributing Editor).

KEVIN ESCUDERO, PhD, is an assistant professor of American Studies and Ethnic Studies at Brown University. His research and teaching interests include comparative studies of race, ethnicity, and Indigeneity; US empire and settler colonialism; immigration and citizenship; social movements; and law. His book *Organizing while Undocumented* (New York University Press, 2020) examines undocumented Asian, Latinx, and queer and formerly undocumented activists' strategic use of an intersectional movement identity. He is currently working on a book on immigrant and Indigenous activists' participation in Guam's decolonization movement and leading a research project focused on immigrant students' experiences along the educational pipeline and into the US workforce, paying particular attention to the role of legal status. This project is also training students in the use of mixed-methods research approaches to community-engaged research.

ANISE GOLD-WATTS, PhD, joined KPMG's International Development Advisory Services (IDAS) in 2020 as a researcher/consultant specializing in creative and innovative approaches to global health intervention programming, evaluation, and research within low- and middle-income country contexts. Anise has a master's degree in public health focusing on health behavior from the Gillings School of Global Public Health at the University of North Carolina at Chapel Hill (USA) and a PhD in public health science from the Norwegian University of Life Sciences (Norway). Her dissertation utilized empowering and nonstigmatizing approaches to improve health outcomes, including arts-based approaches to research, with a distinct focus on contextual influences and discourses that pertain to gender and power. Her research interests involve global health, health behavior, health equity, community-based participatory research, arts-based approaches to health promotion, and the interrelationships between culture and health.

CARL D. GREER is a doctoral candidate in the Department of Educational Leadership and Policy Analysis at the University of Wisconsin–Madison. Leveraging critical qualitative approaches, Greer's research explores three areas: (1) the relationship between community-based educational spaces and PreK-12 schooling institutions, (2) how youth display leadership and activism in and outside the classroom, and (3) Critical Race Theory in education.

KRISTA A. HAAPANEN, MS, is a PhD candidate in Community Research and Action at Vanderbilt University. She earned her MS in Community Development from the University of California, Davis. She studies organizations' efforts to change systems and structures that influence health. Her research examines the possibilities and pitfalls of interorganizational collaboration and the mechanisms linking community-led collaborative processes to advances in health equity.

CAROLYN M. HENDRIKS, PhD, is a Professor of Public Policy and Governance in the Crawford School of Public Policy at the Australian National University. She is an international scholar of contemporary democratic governance and has published widely on citizen participation, community engagement, public deliberation, representation, and listening. Carolyn undertakes engaged interpretive social research that brings democratic practice into dialogue with political theory. She has published three books, including *Mending Democracy: Democratic Repair in Disconnected Times* (with S. A. Ercan and J. Boswell, Oxford University Press, 2020), *The Politics of Public Deliberation* (Palgrave, 2011), and *Environmental Decision-Making: Exploring Complexity and Context* (with R. Harding and M. Faruqi, Federation Press, 2009). She has also authored over sixty other scholarly publications, a number of which have won international prizes.

EMILY A. HENNESSY, MPhil., PhD, is Assistant Professor of Harvard Medical School and Associate Director of Biostatistics at the Recovery Research Institute and the National Center for Youth Prevention, Treatment, and Recovery. Dr Hennessy completed her PhD in Community Research and Action at Vanderbilt University and her postdoctoral fellowship at the University of Connecticut in the Systematic Health Action Research Program (SHARP) Lab. Dr Hennessy's research examines factors associated with health behavior change among adolescents. Her primary area of research – adolescent addiction recovery – is currently funded by a K01 career development award from the National Institute on Alcohol Abuse and Alcoholism. A secondary area of her research is in conducting evidence syntheses and in improving methods for evidence synthesis. She is Co-Chair and Editor for the Substance Use Treatment and Recovery (SUTR) Coordinating Group of the Campbell Collaboration and is on the editorial boards of *Psychological Bulletin* and *Addiction Research & Theory*.

MING HU, PhD, is an assistant professor in Macau University of Science and Technology's School of Business Nonprofit Management program. Prior to this he was an Assistant Professor of Social Work and Social Policy at Nanjing University in China. His research interests include nonprofit management, volunteering and charitable giving, and community development. His recent articles on these themes have been published in *Administration & Society* and *Voluntas: International Journal of Voluntary and Nonprofit Organizations*.

ROSHANI J. JAYAWARDANA is a PhD candidate from the Institute for Health and Sport at Victoria University in Melbourne, Australia. Having obtained her honors degree in psychology, her background and current work sit within the community psychology realm. Roshani's research interests focus on youth empowerment, navigating ethnic identity, and responding to displacement and exclusion. She has experience doing community-engaged research and utilizing creative vehicles within her research, particularly drawing upon radio and podcasting processes. Her current research focuses on doing research with young people who are placed on the margins due to their race, gender, and class and exploring how using digital and expressive methods can liberate and propel their voices and experiences, which are often diminished.

MEAGAN R. JOSEPH, MPA, OCPC, works for Impact Prevention in Ironton, Ohio, where she serves as program manager and an Ohio Certified Prevention Consultant. She earned her bachelor's degrees in Elementary Education and Japanese from Marshall University and holds a Master of Public Administration from Ohio University. While she began her career as a high school Japanese language teacher, her heart led her to the field of prevention in early 2020. In her role at Impact Prevention, Meagan provides suicide prevention training and programming in schools, works with youth-led prevention teams, and coordinates the community coalition, the River Hills Prevention Connection.

SAMUEL P. KEAST, PhD, is a Research Officer in the Institute of Health and Sport and a Sessional Lecturer in the College of Health and Biomedicine, Victoria University. Sam's work and research are focused on critical community psychology, cultural psychology, and qualitative methodologies. He is also a member of the Community, Identity, Displacement Research Network (CIDRN), and his research interests include epistemic justice, historical thinking, antiracism, Whiteness, and critical policy analysis.

MICHELLE C. KEGLER, DrPH, is a professor of Behavioral, Social and Health Education Sciences in the Rollins School of Public Health at Emory University. She directs the Emory Prevention Research Center, which focuses on community-engaged chronic disease prevention. Dr Kegler received her Doctor of Public Health degree in Health Behavior and Health Education from the University of North Carolina–Chapel Hill and her Master of Public Health from the University of Michigan. She evaluates coalition-driven community improvement initiatives. She recently led a team to evaluate a health equity initiative in rural Georgia and co-led a community randomized trial in Armenia and Georgia to examine whether and how community coalitions can support smoke-free environments outside of the US. Past evaluations of coalition-based initiatives include California Healthy Cities and Communities and mayor-initiated community coalitions in the Mississippi Delta. Dr Kegler codeveloped the Community Coalition Action Theory, which often informs her evaluations of community coalitions.

BEN KIRSHNER, PhD, is a professor of Education at the University of Colorado Boulder. In his work with the Research Hub for Youth Organizing he codesigns educational tools and research studies with youth organizing groups and networks that build capacity for young people to claim power in the public sphere. Ben's book, *Youth Activism in an Era of Education Inequality* (NYU Press, 2015), received the social policy award for best authored book from the Society of Research on Adolescence.

MARIAH KORNBLUH, PhD, is Assistant Professor in the Psychology Department at the University of Oregon. Dr Kornbluh employs a community-based approach (youth-led participatory action research) in her research by exploring not only how systems of power impact development but also how children and youth can be their own agents of change in reimagining and transforming institutions that have systematically disadvantaged our most vulnerable communities. Her research also explores how youth-guided approaches to research can help inform policy and practice as well as promote accountability to young people among adult leaders and decision-makers.

SAM LAPOINT is a senior clinical research coordinator at the Recovery Research Institute at Massachusetts General Hospital, currently studying pathways for recovery from substance use disorders. He has also completed work on the impacts of harm reduction policy, conducted evaluations of human service programs, and published research on adjustment to the college environment for first-generation students.

YULONG LIAN is a postgraduate student at the School of Social and Behavioral Science at Nanjing University. He has experience working with urban neighborhoods to foster grassroots nonprofit organizations and improve community participation. His research interests include community development and nonprofit management.

WILSON MAJEE, PhD, MPH, MBA, is an associate professor with the University of Missouri Departments of Health Sciences and Public Health. His research interests are in exploring, identifying, and implementing place-based approaches to health and well-being among those living in resource-limited communities. The interdisciplinary nexus of community leadership development, community engagement, and health promotion is the center of his work. His work closes knowledge and practice gaps using a socioecological approach regarding the multilevel individual, family, and place-based factors affecting health and well-being. Dr Majee is also an Extraordinary Professor at the University of the Western Cape in South Africa. Prior to joining the University of Missouri, he worked as University of Missouri Extension's Regional Community Development Specialist in rural Missouri, where he partnered with county commissioners, church leaders, school administrators, health departments, and community action agencies in developing and implementing programs to improve the health and well-being of community members.

ROBERT A. MARX, PhD, is an Assistant Professor of Child and Adolescent Development at San José State University. Their research focuses on the family, school, and community supports that help queer and trans adolescents live rich, meaningful lives.

SARAH HULTINE MASSENGALE, PhD, is a State Specialist in Community Development with University of Missouri Extension and an Assistant Extension Professor in Political Science at University of Missouri – St. Louis. Sarah works with communities to strengthen collaborative leadership and act on community priorities for more resilient economic and social well-being. Her research interests focus on rural communities and exploring how social and cultural capitals influence individual and community decision-making. She has a doctoral degree in Rural Sociology from University of Missouri–Columbia, a Master of Urban Planning degree from the University of Illinois Urbana-Champaign, and a bachelor's degree in biology and environmental studies from Knox College.

SUVARNA V. MENON, PhD, is a research associate at the Center for the Study of Family Violence and Sexual Assault at Northern Illinois University. She received her PhD in Clinical and Community Psychology from the University of Illinois Urbana-Champaign. Her research focuses on gender-based violence (GBV) and early childhood adversities. Specifically, using an ecological lens and multimethod approaches with domestic and international samples, her research examines the consequences of trauma and systems responses to GBV by focusing on the mental health consequences of exposure to trauma; survivors' help-seeking and systems-change efforts in their responses to GBV; examining how empowerment-based approaches can be effectively utilized with survivors of GBV in a survivor-centered and culturally competent manner; and understanding how community organizing and community empowerment approaches can be used to promote social change in response to GBV.

JOAN S. M. MEYERS, PhD, is an associate professor of Sociology in the Department of Social Sciences and teaching faculty in the department of Women's, Gender, and Queer Studies at California Polytechnic State University, San Luis Obispo. An organizational sociologist, her ethnographic and mixed-method research on intersectional workplace inequality and workplace democracy has been published as award-winning academic journal articles, book chapters, and an academic monograph, *Working Democracies: Managing Inequality in Worker Cooperatives* (Cornell University Press, 2022).

Her scholarship has been supported with grants from the W. K. Kellogg Foundation, the Rutgers University Institute for the Study of Employee Ownership and Profit Sharing, and the University of California Institute for Labor and Employment. Joan received her MA and PhD in sociology from the University of California, Davis, her MA in gender studies from San Francisco State University, and her BA in English from Cornell University.

KATHRYN Y. MORGAN, PhD, is an assistant professor of Psychology at Sewanee: The University of the South. She completed her PhD in Community Research and Action at Vanderbilt University. Her research explores civic and sociopolitical identity development among young people as they take part in efforts to build collective power and promote community well-being. As a community-based researcher, she partners with schools and other youth-serving organizations to understand, promote, and sustain empowering community contexts in which young people can engage in social change efforts.

MICHAEL D. O'BRIEN, MA, is a doctoral candidate in Counseling Psychology at Boston College in the Carolyn A. and Peter S. Lynch School of Education and Human Development. His research focuses on how marginalized youth, such as sexual and gender minority youth, perceive, respond to, and are impacted by sociopolitical events.

LOREN PEABODY is a doctoral candidate in sociology at the University of Wisconsin–Madison. His current research agenda centers on the politics of residential development in Chicago by examining the impacts of adopting participatory democratic processes for zoning change decisions in several wards. He has worked as a research fellow at the Participatory Budgeting Project and has taught courses on introductory sociology, urban sociology, American society, and the sociology of international development and sustainability.

AGATA Z. PIETRZAK is a PhD student in clinical psychology at the University of South Florida. Before this, she was a Clinical Research Coordinator at the Recovery Research Institute at Massachusetts General Hospital. At the Recovery Research Institute, Agata worked on a variety of projects examining recovery pathways among adolescents and adults.

SANJAY PINTO, PhD, is a research fellow at The Worker Institute at Cornell University's Institute for Labor Relations and a Fellow at the Roosevelt Institute. He is a sociologist working at the intersection of academic and applied research. His recent work has included projects looking at survivor-led approaches for confronting gender-based violence, the use of digital tools to build worker voice and power, models that advance greater equity and inclusion within the care economy, and strategies for confronting racial capitalism through the advancement of economic democracy. Sanjay has also taught courses on labor, political economy, and public policy at Columbia, Princeton, and Rutgers. He currently codirects the program on unions and worker ownership at the Rutgers School of Management and Labor Relations and serves on the advisory committees of the Real Utopias project and Citizen Share Brooklyn. Previously, Sanjay was a writer tracking White supremacist movements at the Southern Poverty Law Center and a union researcher with the American Federation of Labor and Congress of Industrial Organizations (AFL-CIO) and the Service Employees International Union (SEIU). He has an MSc in Development Studies from the London School of Economics and a PhD in Sociology and Social Policy from Harvard.

V. PAUL POTEAT, PhD, is a Professor at Boston College in the Carolyn A. and Peter S. Lynch School of Education and Human Development. His research focuses on the school-based experiences of LGBTQ+ youth. His work on gender–sexuality alliances has identified individual- and group-level mechanisms by which these school-based clubs foster empowerment and resilience among youth from diverse sexual orientations and gender identities. His research also examines bias-based harassment using an ecological framework to identify individual and peer factors that contribute to such behavior or that buffer against its effects.

OLGA PRUSHINSKAYA, MPH, is the Metrics and Impact Analyst at the Democracy at Work Institute (DAWI). In this role, Olga works to understand and communicate impact in the growing field of worker ownership. Olga's background in health equity has resulted in work that spanned a variety of fields in addition to worker ownership, including youth housing services, pulmonary medicine, chronic disease management, and maternal and infant health. Olga has an MPH in Health Behavior and Health Education from the University of Michigan and a BS in Microbiology from Michigan State University. Olga is a 2021/2022 Executive Fellow at Rutgers University's Institute for the Study of Employee Ownership and Profit Sharing at the School of Management and Labor Relations.

AMY F. QUAYLE, PhD, is a lecturer in Psychology, College of Health and Biomedicine and a Research Fellow in the Institute of Health and Sport, Victoria University in Melbourne on the lands of the Wurundjeri people of the Kulin Nation. Amy's training is in community psychology, and her research has focused on understanding the psychosocial impacts of ongoing histories of colonization and racism, including the implications for individual subjectivities, communities, and intergroup relations as well as the ways individuals and communities respond, resist, and heal. A further focus of her work has been how community arts and cultural practice and creative, participatory methodologies can be mobilized to create spaces and opportunities to amplify stories and counter-stories, create community and connection, and democratize processes of knowledge production.

HOLLY RAFFLE, PhD, MCHES, is a Professor at Ohio University's Voinovich School of Leadership and Public Service. As an engaged scholar, she is responsible for a portfolio of work in the areas of community health, promotion, and prevention. Holly is the Faculty Director of Ohio's Center of Excellence of Behavioral Health Prevention and Promotion and has worked on a wide variety of alcohol and other drug (AOD) prevention and mental health promotion initiatives across Ohio. She is a Master Certified Health Education Specialist and received her doctorate in Educational Research and Evaluation at Ohio University.

CLAIRE RIPPEL, MSW, is the Community Development Education Director and the Director of Creating Whole Communities for the University of Missouri–St. Louis (UMSL). Her work focuses on building civic capacity for thriving places by cultivating belonging, engagement, collective leadership, and vitality. Claire is deeply dedicated to bolstering social capital and championing lived experience to solve critical community challenges. Prior to her work at UMSL, Claire was the Director of Community Development at Grace Hill Settlement House. She received her BA and MSW from Washington University in St. Louis.

SHANNON T. SANCHEZ-YOUNGMAN, PhD, is an assistant professor, College of Population Health, University of New Mexico, with expertise in Latino mental health disparities intervention research, organizational empowerment, and health equity policy development. She has over twenty years of experience in developing community-based health interventions aimed at reducing social and health disparities among economically marginalized groups and racial and ethnic groups in the US. Dr Sanchez-Youngman seeks to bridge the gap between social science theories and methods with community-based, multilevel health intervention research.

LAURA HANSON SCHLACHTER, PhD, is a research analyst in the AmeriCorps Office of Research and Evaluation and an Honorary Associate at the University of Wisconsin Center for Cooperatives with expertise in mixed-methods research, survey design, and community economic development policy. Her research and teaching are at the intersection of environmental, economic, and political sociology. Laura earned her PhD in Sociology and Community and Environmental Sociology at the University of Wisconsin–Madison in 2020 and has published peer-reviewed articles, policy reports, and an undergraduate textbook in addition to directing the Democracy at Work

Institute's 2017 Individual Worker Co-op Census. Her scholarship has received generous support from the National Science Foundation, AmeriCorps, and the Rutgers University Institute for the Study of Employee Ownership and Profit Sharing. She also holds a master's degree in Public Affairs from Princeton University and a BA from Whitman College.

CHRISTOPHER C. SONN, PhD, is a professor at Victoria University, Melbourne, Australia, where he lives and works on the land of the Wurundjeri people of the Kulin Nation. He is a fellow of the Institute of Health and Sport and Deputy Director, Research and Research Training. His research is concerned with understanding and changing dynamics of oppression, examining structural violence such as racism and its effects on social identities, intergroup relations, and belonging. A core focus is on the cocreation of settings and approaches within and outside the university that can support resistance, healing, and liberation-oriented actions. He holds a Visiting Professorship at the University of the Witwatersrand, South Africa. Christopher is coeditor of *Creating Inclusive Knowledges* (Routledge, 2018), *Psychology of Liberation* (Springer, 2009), and *Decoloniality and Epistemic Justice in Contemporary Community Psychology* (Springer, 2021), coauthor of *Social Psychology and Everyday Life* (2nd edition, Red Globe Press, 2020), and Associate Editor of the *American Journal of Community Psychology* and *Community Psychology in Global Perspective*.

PAUL W. SPEER, PhD, is Seven Turns Professor of Human and Organizational Development at Vanderbilt University. His research is focused on community organizing, social power, and community change. He studies the processes and mechanisms of community organizations as these groups work to alter social conditions in their communities. Additionally, he is interested in linking these organizational processes to their associated impacts on the broader community as well as the impacts on individual participants.

MOLLIE F. STEVENS, OCPS, is an Ohio Certified Prevention Specialist and the founder and CEO of Impact Prevention in South Point, Ohio. Much of her work throughout her more than thirty-year career has focused on improving the health and wellness of the people of Appalachia through evidence-based prevention strategies. Mollie has a special place in her heart for helping young people find their voice and become community change agents. In her spare time, she enjoys camping, painting, and spending time with her grandchildren.

TAFADZWA TIVARINGE, PhD, is a research and evaluation officer at the Susan Thompson Buffett Foundation and a Research Associate at the Research Hub for Youth Organizing. He was previously an Associate Program Officer at The Spencer Foundation. An interdisciplinary scholar, Tafadzwa's work seeks to understand ways of advancing equity in education systems, with an emphasis on young people's role in shaping transformation efforts. Having worked with youth in South Africa and the US, Tafadzwa's research employs international and comparative lenses.

NINA WALLERSTEIN, DrPH, is Distinguished Professor, College of Population Health, University of New Mexico (UNM). For over forty years, she has integrated the liberatory education of Paulo Freire in her work. Her research, funded by the US Centers for Disease Control and Prevention, the National Institutes of Health, and the Patient-Centered Outcomes Research Institute, focuses on empowerment and culture-centered interventions with Native and other underserved communities and on identifying and strengthening best practices of community-based participatory research (CBPR), contributing to health equity outcomes. She facilitates CBPR and Empowerment Institutes in Spanish in Latin America, in Portuguese in Brazil, and at UNM.

XIAOYUN WANG, PhD, is an assistant professor of the School of Public Administration and Policy at Renmin University of China. She received her PhD in philanthropic studies from the Indiana University Lilly Family School of Philanthropy. Her research interests are community philanthropy and community foundations. She has also published research on philanthropic giving and grassroots nonprofits' responses to COVID-19 in China.

RASHEDA L. WEAVER, PhD, is one of the world's leading experts on social and commercial entrepreneurship. She conducted the first large-scale empirical study on the social, economic, and legal activities of social enterprises in the US and is the Founder of Weaver's Social Enterprise Directory, Inc. As a professor, she has taught entrepreneurship to over 1,000 students globally. She served as the first Assistant Professor for the Hynes Institute for Entrepreneurship and Innovation that was established with a $15 million donation to Iona College in 2017, helping to build its teaching, research, and service foundation. Dr Weaver's book *Social Entrepreneurship: A Practical Approach* (Routledge, 2022) is considered a seminal work in the field of social entrepreneurship.

MEGAN K. YANG, MA, is a counseling psychology doctoral student at Boston College in the Carolyn A. and Peter S. Lynch School of Education and Human Development. Their research interests include the intersection between multiple marginalized identities, trauma, and mental health outcomes. Specifically, they focus on sexual orientation and gender identity diversity, cultural and racial identity, physical and psychological trauma, discrimination, resilience, and empowerment.

Index

For EU product safety concerns, contact us at Calle de José Abascal, 56–1°, 28003 Madrid, Spain or eugpsr@cambridge.org.